EVERYMAN'S TALMUD

A PAGE OF THE BABYLONIAN TALMUD

EVERYMAN'S TALMUD

BY

The Rev. Dr. A. COHEN

M.A. (Cantab.), Ph.D. (Lond.)

WITH AN INTRODUCTION TO THE NEW AMERICAN EDITION

BY

PROF. BOAZ COHEN

NEW YORK
E. P. DUTTON & CO., INC.

TO THE MEMORY

OF THE LATE

CHIEF RABBI

VERY REV. DR. J. H. HERTZ

IN ESTEEM AND GRATITUDE

talmud
Judaism
Ethics, kwish
lews - social life &
customs

INTRODUCTION TO THE NEW AMERICAN EDITION

By Dr. Boaz Cohen

Associate Professor of Rabbinics
at the Jewish Theological Seminary of America

WHAT is this book which has stimulated the mind and the emotions of the Jews, and to a lesser extent has aroused the attention of Christians and Mohammedans throughout the ages? The Talmud is a work wherein is deposited the bulk of the literary labors of numerous Jewish scholars over a period of some 700 years, roughly speaking, between 200 B.C.E. and 500 C.E. The Talmud is extant in two recensions. What is known as the Palestinian Talmud was composed shortly after 400 C.E., whereas the Babylonian Talmud, always referred to as the Talmud, was put into shape about 500 C.E.

From the point of view of literary form and structure, the Talmud may be described as a commentary upon the Mishnah of R. Judah, the Patriarch, composed about 220 C.E. The Mishnah is an epitome of the religious and civil law of the Jews, as it was interpreted, formulated and developed in Palestine up to the beginning of the third century. The Mishnah, which compares favorably with the *Digesta* of Julian or the *Institutes* of Gaius, became established very soon after its compilation as a book of authority in Palestine and Babylonia. In the celebrated academies of these two countries, it became the official textbook for instruction and was debated, commented upon, and interpreted for three centuries.

Since the prime purpose of the redactors of the Talmud was to preserve the ancient discussions of the Mishnah, the body of the Talmud assumed the form of a dialogue of the Amoraim, the official expositors of the law who flourished between 200–

500 C.E. Interspersed in the commentary are numerous digressions, large and small—ostensibly justified by the principle of the association of ideas—containing copious fragments from a genre of literature known as the Haggada, in contradistinction to the Halakah. The latter embraces two areas of prescribed conduct, one relating to the rules of ritual and religion, the other pertaining to the rights and obligations of men in civil society. The norms known as Halakah were, under normal conditions, enforceable with appropriate sanctions. That portion of the Halakah which corresponds to what is generally known as civil law bears many resemblances in form and content to the *Digest* of Justinian.

As for the Haggada, it embraces whatever is excluded from the Halakah. The contents of Haggada appeal primarily to the conscience, the mind, and the imagination. The Haggada prescribes countless norms of conduct, unenforceable in the courts of law but required by a society possessing a sensitive and refined conscience. The Haggada contains much that will satisfy the intellectual curiosity of man, such as reflections on the cosmos and its Prime Mover, impressions of the character and manners of the rabbis of the Talmud, views on the economy of nature, observations of a scientific caliber, passages illuminating the religious experience and social life of the Jews and their association with non-Jews.

While there is a goodly amount of historical fact in the Haggada, it is in its appeal to fancy that it is most alluring. The significance of the Biblical characters, and the hold they were able to obtain upon the imagination of the Jews for more than a thousand years, is due primarily to the Jewish preachers of the Talmudic era, who looked upon the Biblical times as the golden age. They made bold to depict the lives of the Biblical heroes as immaculate, scriptural narrative notwithstanding, and idealized the celebrated incidents in Israel's history and invested them with a romantic charm that stirred the heart and mind of the Jews for countless generations.

In the ancient world, where notions of natural law were still unknown, it was perfectly natural that miraculous events of every description were considered as indubitable phenomena. This faith, of course, the rabbis shared with the masses of the people. What is curious is that the rabbis entertained certain folk beliefs that were inconsistent with more rationalistic views of their own. In any event, the Haggada is a veritable store-house of folklore, custom, superstition and legend current in the Babylonia and the Palestine of their day.

As for the literary forms in which the Haggada is clothed, it is important to recall that we possess only fragments and quotations from lost haggadic writings. The Haggada has preserved biographical and historical pieces, short stories and tall tales, proverbs and parables, sermons and conversations, maxims and reflections *à la Rochefoucauld.*

In fine, Halakah is to the Jews what religion, ceremonies and civil law (to use Cicero's phrase, *De Oratore,* I.10,39) were to the Romans. Haggada represents the imaginative, artistic and scientific literature of the Jews. The Haggada, which embraces one third of the Talmud, is for the Jews what Latin literature was to the Romans. It would not be difficult to cull from the vast stretches of the Haggada an immense number of pieces that are parallel to, or in the vein of, Cicero's *On the Nature of the Gods,* Seneca's *Moral Essays,* the *Scriptores Historiae Augustae,* Varro's *Latin Language,* Gellius' *Attic Nights,* Pliny's *Natural History,* Celsus' *On Medicine,* and Ovid's *The Art of Love,* just to mention a few.

This is, of course, due to the fact that the rabbis did not live in an intellectual ghetto, but were highly susceptible to the deas current in the Greco-Roman world. The numerous discussions between the Jewish and Roman sages recorded in the Talmud, are evidence of a great deal of intellectual relations between learned Jews and pagans, which must have had a stimulating effect upon their thinking in a great many ways.

The Talmud, for the Jew, is not merely a great literary pro-

duction, which it is. It is not merely a great repository of law
and ritual, which it is. The Talmud is a great fund of Jewish
religious experience and wisdom accumulated throughout the
course of the ages. The Talmud ranks next to the Sacred Scriptures in significance as a source for religious insight, inspiration
and practice, and will instruct the last generations of mankind.
Great stress has often been laid upon the rabbis as schoolmen
and scholastics, as adepts in casuistry and dialectics, which they
certainly were. However, little note has been taken of them as
sages and moralists, exerting all their precious energy and intelligence to preserve the notions of justice and spirituality first
propagated by Moses, and subsequently preached by Isaih,
Amos, Micah, Jeremiah and the other Hebrew Prophets.

John Morley in his *Notes on Politics and History* remarked
as follows: "A learned American judge found three great in-
struments in human history—The Ten Commandments, The
Sermon on the Mount, and the Declaration of American Independence." According to Philo, the Decalogue contains the
essence of the entire law.

It is a truism accepted by enlightened scholars, for the long-
est time, that a knowledge of the Talmud is indispensable to a
true understanding of the origin and background of the teachings of the New Testament and the Koran. Many a Christian
or Muslim doctrine is well-nigh unintelligible apart from the
original context in the Talmud.

The author informs us in the preface to this volume that his
aim is merely "to provide a summary of the teachings of the
Talmud on Religion, Ethics, Folk-lore, and Jurisprudence," and
it must be admitted that he has executed his task admirably.
The author, by fitting into his narrative copious citations from
the Talmud, enables the reader to obtain a great deal of the
flavor of the original. It is not too much to hope that this book
will find its way into the home of every scholar and intelligent
layman who would be reliably informed concerning the main
teachings of the Talmud.

PREFACE

WHILE there is now no lack of books which regale the English reader with selections from the Talmud, tales from the Talmud, and wise sayings of the Rabbis, there is no work which attempts a comprehensive survey of the doctrine of this important branch of Jewish literature. To supply that want is the task undertaken in the present volume. Its aim is to provide a summary of the teachings of the Talmud on Religion, Ethics, Folk-lore, and Jurisprudence.

The need for such a work will hardly be gainsaid. There is a growing interest being taken at the present time in the Talmud. It is frequently referred to and even quoted by modern writers, the majority of whom are evidently not equipped with the specialized knowledge which can alone unfasten its seven-sealed tomes. In the Middle Ages we hear of a friar who displayed the little learning which is proverbially dangerous, by introducing a quotation with the words, *ut narrat rabbinus Talmud* (as *Rabbi* Talmud relates). Less excusable, however, was the ignorance of a nineteenth-century theologian who poured ridicule on the Talmud because a whole tractate, as he alleged, was concerned with the subject of eggs! Being unaware of the elementary fact that the Jews had the practice of naming a book, or section of it, after its opening word, he was obviously incompetent to pass judgment upon the literature of the Rabbis; and there are still too many scholars whose impression of the Talmud has been derived from works which have the object of vilifying rather than interpreting. This book, it is hoped presents material which will help to a better understanding o the thoughts and aims of the great teachers in Israel after the Biblical age.

The extreme difficulty of the task which is here essayed will be appreciated by all who have any acquaintance with the original text. Not only is the Talmudic literature vast in extent; but, to the modern mind at least, it is without system and order. Rarely is a subject treated fully in any one passage. A tenet has to be gleaned and pieced together from the entire field. Moreover, the opinions which are expressed in its folios emanate from many hundreds of teachers who range over a period of more than six centuries. It is scarcely to be expected, therefore, that they should speak with one voice on any theme. Usually we are faced with a variety of views which are often contradictory, and it is by no means easy to achieve a coherent presentation of a doctrine.

Occasionally I have found it necessary to exhibit this divergence of thought; but wherever possible I have indicated what appears to be the representative opinion of the Rabbis. In this labour of selection I have endeavoured to be impartial and not restrict myself to citations which read well and show the Talmud in a favourable light. The harsh utterances, which traducers of the Rabbis are fond of quoting, are also included to sketch a true picture, but the circumstances which called them forth are explained.

There is no claim to completeness in the treatment of any subject. So extensive is the material that an exhaustive collection and discussion could easily expand each chapter into a separate treatise. All that is offered is a sufficient number of extracts to give the reader a general idea of the Talmudic doctrine. The bibliography which is provided will act as a guide to further study, if it is desired.

An important question which had to be decided at the outset was the interpretation of the term 'Talmud.' In its narrower connotation, as will be explained in the Introduction, it comprises the Mishnah and Gemara; but if that source is exclusively drawn upon, it is impossible to furnish anything like an accurate account of Rabbinic teaching. The Talmud is only part of the Talmudic literature. Speaking generally, it introduces us into the academies of Palestine and Babylon where the Torah was expounded and discussed. But there was another place where expositions were regularly given for the instruction of the masses, viz. the Synagogue. In particular, the ethical and religious tenets of Judaism were imparted to the assemblies in the house of worship, and the subject-matter of these addresses has been preserved in a series of compilations known as Midrashim. To ignore this supplementary source must inevitably result in an imperfect account of Rabbinic lore.

Judicious care must, however, be exercised in the use of the Midrashim, because some of them are late in the time of their composition and reflect modes of thought which are a subsequent

PREFACE ix

development of those that were current in the Talmudic era. I
have consequently, as far as possible, confined myself to extracts
of those works which are in the name of Rabbis who are cited in
the Talmud, or, if anonymous, appear to synchronize with its
period.

References to the Bible are quoted according to the chapter and
verse as they are found in the English version when these do not
coincide with the system of the Hebrew text. This will be more
convenient for the general reader although a hardship to the
student of the original. The Revised Version is usually followed
except where the Rabbinic interpretation deviates from it.

All the passages from the Talmud and Midrash have been rendered
anew sor this work, apart from quotations from Tractate *Berachoth*
which I have taken from the translation I published in 1921, and
the extracts from Tractate *Aboth*, where I have used the version by
the Rev. S. Singer in his edition of the *Authorised Daily Prayer
Book* as well as his numbering of the paragraphs.

The earnest hope of the author is that this volume will be a
reliable aid to those who wish to acquaint themselves with the
contents of the Talmud and form an unbiased conception of what
the religious guides of the Jews believed and taught in the critical
period which preceded and followed the fall of Temple and State.
It has been truly said: 'In the light of subsequent history, the great
achievement of these centuries was the creation of a normative
type of Judaism and its establishment in undisputed supremacy
throughout the wide Jewish world' (Moore, *Judaism*, i, p. 3). The
influence which the Rabbis exerted upon the Judaism of the past
two thousand years has been decisive. Countless millions of men
and women, during more than forty generations, found in them
inspiring guides whose teachings proved intellectually illuminating
and spiritually refreshing. They do not, therefore, deserve to be
lightly dismissed or contemptuously ignored. A note of warning
must, however, be sounded. The wrong way to judge them is by
the criterion of modern standards. They must be fitted into the
age in which they lived. Their fundamental theses must be understood and their aims appreciated before their system of thought
can be rightly appraised. If this book assists the student or general
reader who ventures on such a quest, the labour of its preparation
will be deemed well rewarded.

It is my duty and pleasure, in conclusion, to express my indebted-ness to friends who have given me their assistance. The chapter on Jurisprudence was read in MS. by Rabbi Z. Hodes of Birming-ham and Mr. G. J. Webber, LL.B., Lecturer in Law at the Univer-sity of Manchester, who made helpful suggestions, although I am alone responsible for the collection and arrangement of the material. My colleague, the Rev. S. I. Solomons, B.A., undertook the laborious task of proof-reading, for which act of kindness I tender to him my appreciative thanks.

A. C.

BIRMINGHAM,
December 1931.

NOTE TO REVISED EDITION

THE reception given to this book is most gratifying. It has been reprinted several times as well as translated into French and Italian. Many communications have reached me from Christian scholars and laymen acknowledging the help it has been to them as an intro-duction to the literature of the Rabbis. In this revised edition a number of corrections have been made which, I trust, may render the volume still more serviceable.

BIRMINGHAM,   A. C.
July 1948.

TABLE OF CONTENTS

xi

CONTENTS

CHAPTER VII. THE MORAL LIFE

CHAPTER VIII. THE PHYSICAL LIFE

CHAPTER IX. FOLK-LORE

CHAPTER X. JURISPRUDENCE

(a) CRIMINAL LAW: CIVIL AND CRIMINAL PROCEDURE

CHAPTER X. JURISPRUDENCE (*continued*)

(*b*) CIVIL LAW

CHAPTER XI. THE HEREAFTER

INTRODUCTION

§ I. Historical Antecedents

In the year 586 B.C. the Kingdom of Judea, which then represented all that was left of the people of Israel in Canaan, underwent a devastating experience. The Temple was laid in ruins, its ritual brought to an end, the best part of the nation led as captives to Babylon, and 'the captain of the guard left of the poorest of the land to be vinedressers and husbandmen' (2 Kings xxv. 12). There was bitter justification for the despairing cry: 'How doth the city sit solitary, that was full of people! How is she become as a widow! She that was great among the nations and princess among the provinces, how is she become tributary!' (Lament. i. 1).

The crisis, from the national standpoint, was intensified by the circumstance that a century and a half earlier, in 722, the Northern Kingdom, comprising the ten tribes, had been overrun by the army of Assyria and the inhabitants driven into exile where they had, for the most part, become absorbed. If the disaster to Judea met with a like ending, the entire nation would be obliterated and the name of Israel blotted out of existence.

This grave thought must have given the leaders of the Jews in Babylon the deepest concern and induced them to concentrate on the problem of survival. How could the fate of extinction be averted? Recognizing that the distinctiveness of the Israelite people had always rested on its religion, which had centred around the Temple, they were forced to ask themselves by what means that distinctiveness could be maintained now that the Sanctuary had fallen and the people, resident in a foreign land, were exposed to powerful alien influences.

The Biblical sources, which deal with that period, do not provide detailed information, but certain references help to an understanding of the course of events. The outstanding personality in the captive community was the prophet Ezekiel, and he took the lead in the quest for the solution of the problem upon which, humanly speaking, the preservation of Israel depended. In his prophecies he tells of three occasions when 'the elders of Judah' assembled at his house,[1] and we may fairly surmise that at these gatherings the question which was uppermost in their minds was discussed.

The solution which they evolved may be summarized in a single word, Torah. This Hebrew word, incorrectly translated 'law,' means 'teaching, direction.' For the exiles it denoted the body of doctrine, written and oral, which had come down from past ages. Without entering upon the vexed question of the origin and date of the Pentateuch, we may assume that the Jews in Babylon had in their possession the Mosaic revelation in one form or another. They also had some of the prophetical writings and Psalms. These relics of their former national life constituted the only rock upon which the exiled Jews could stand securely in a gentile environment until the time God restored them to their homeland. These Scriptures must consequently be forced upon their attention and impressed upon their hearts; then they would remember that though in Babylon they were not of Babylon, and the sacred obligation rested upon them to remain a people apart.

There is general agreement among scholars that the institution of the Synagogue originated in the time and place of the captivity. Its Hebrew designation, *Beth Hakenéseth* (House of Assembly), accurately indicates its initial purpose. It was the rallying centre of a homeless nation, and at the gatherings the Scriptures were read and expounded. In course of time prayers were included and so the Synagogue developed into a place of worship. The effect of these assemblies was the awakening of interest in the study of the Hebrew writings. The desire for knowledge among the masses necessarily created a demand for men who were equipped with the learning to qualify them to act as teachers. These instructors are known as *Sopherim* (scribes), not in the sense of writers, but 'men of letters.' Some of them are no doubt referred to in the list of men who are described as 'teachers' in Ezra viii. 16, and as men who 'caused the people to understand the Torah' in Nehem. viii. 7.

Foremost among this class of teachers was Ezra, who is characterized as 'a ready scribe in the Torah of Moses' (Ezra vii. 6), i.e. an expert *Sopher*. He it was who worked out the solution of his predecessors to its practical conclusions. The Talmud, with justification, compares the work he did for his people with what had been accomplished by Moses. As the great lawgiver created a nation out of the released slaves by bringing them the Torah, so did Ezra renew the vitality of a moribund community, both in

---

[1] Ezek. viii. 1; xiv. 1; xx. 1.

Babylon and Judea, by restoring the Torah as its guide of living. In admiration of his achievement the Rabbis declared: 'Ezra was worthy that the Torah should be given to Israel by his hand, were it not that Moses had forestalled him' (Sanh. 21b), and 'When the Torah had been forgotten by Israel, Ezra came up from Babylon and re-established it' (Suk. 20a).

The policy of Ezra has been elsewhere described by the present writer in these terms: 'Zangwill once said, "History, which is largely a record of the melting of minorities in majorities, records no instance of the survival of a group not segregated in space or not protected by a burning faith as by a frontier of fire." This lesson of history had evidently been discerned by Ezra. He understood that the Jews could not be utterly segregated in space. Not only were there branches of the national tree in Egypt, Babylon, and Persia to be taken into consideration; but contact between the Jews in Judea and their neighbours could not be avoided. If, then, the Jewish nation was to be preserved, it must be ringed round "by a burning faith as by a frontier of fire"—a most apposite metaphor, since the Bible itself speaks of "a fiery law." The Jew must have a religion which would not only continually distinguish him from the heathen, but would likewise be a constant reminder to him that he was a member of the Jewish race and faith. The Jew was to be demarcated from his neighbours not merely by a creed, but by a mode of living. His manner of worship would be different; his home would be different; even in the common acts of daily life there would be distinguishing features which would constantly recall his Jewishness. His life, in every detail, was to be controlled by Torah—by the written enactments of the Mosaic code and their development in the corporate life of the people, as the altered conditions demanded change.'[1]

Unless this viewpoint is thoroughly grasped, there can be no possibility of understanding the mentality of the Rabbis, the trend of their activities and their method of Bible-exegesis. It is the seed out of which the Talmud grew. We have it mentioned very distinctly in the account of Ezra's work: 'He had set his heart to seek the Torah of the Lord, and to do it, and to teach in Israel statutes and judgments' (Ezra vii. 10). The Hebrew verb used in this sentence for 'to seek,' *darash*, is of the utmost importance for our theme. Its true sense is 'to deduce, interpret' the ideas which profound study of the text could elucidate. This process of deduction is called *Midrash*[2] and is the system of interpretation

[1] See Introductory Lecture in *The Jews at the Close of the Bible Age*, pp. 37 f.
[2] The word occurs in 2 Chron. xxiv. 27, where it is translated 'commentary.'

employed throughout the Rabbinic literature. By its aid a Scriptural passage yielded far more than could be discerned on the surface. The sacred words became an inexhaustible mine which, when quarried, produced rich treasures of religious and ethical teaching.

Starting from the axiom that the divine will is revealed in the Torah, Ezra taught that the daily existence of the Jew must be regulated in every phase by its precepts; and since the Torah has to be the *complete* guide of living, it must be made capable of yielding helpful guidance for every circumstance of human life. A prerequisite to the achievement of this aim was knowledge of the Torah. Before they could be expected to perform the commandments the people had to be educated in them. He therefore introduced into Judea the public reading of the Pentateuch in order to make the masses familiar with its contents. 'They read in the book, in the Torah of God, with an interpretation; and they gave the sense, so that they understood the reading' (Nehem. viii. 8).

According to Jewish tradition, Ezra founded the *Kenéseth Hagedolah* (the Great Assembly), a synod of teachers who received the corpus of doctrine which had been preserved to their day, adapted and developed it to suit the new conditions of their age, and then transmitted it to the pioneers of the Talmudic Rabbis. The chain of authority is thus described: 'Moses received the Torah on Sinai, and handed it down to Joshua; Joshua to the Elders; the Elders to the Prophets; and the Prophets handed it down to the men of the Great Assembly' (Aboth i. i).

The existence of such a synod has been questioned by modern scholars. While it must be admitted that the two and a half centuries which followed the career of Ezra are wrapped in obscurity and practically no historical data are available, yet there seems no sound reason to doubt that an official body of teachers must have functioned during that period. A far-seeing reformer like Ezra could not have failed to realize that his work would inevitably fall to pieces soon after his death unless he was succeeded by men who, imbued with his own zeal, would continue his policy. To create an authoritative council to which people could turn for instruction appears the most obvious course for him to have adopted.

Furthermore, when the veil of ignorance lifts, we find ourselves in the early part of the second century B.C. witnessing a heroic struggle on the part of a small band of Jews to resist an attempt to destroy their religion. The Hasmoneans pitted themselves against the armies of Syria because Antiochus Epiphanes dared to order them to violate the precepts of Judaism, 'to the end they might forget the Torah and change all the ordinances' (1 Macc. i. 49). Mattathias, on raising the standard of revolt, proclaimed: 'Whoever is zealous of the Torah, and maintaineth the covenant, let him follow me' (ibid. ii. 27); and before his death he exhorted his sons: 'Be valiant and shew yourselves men in the behalf of the Torah' (ibid. 64).

Hence we see beyond all doubt that early in the second century the Torah had become firmly rooted among at least a section of the Jews. How can the deathless attachment to it which distinguished the Hasmoneans be explained if there had been no channel through which the knowledge of Torah passed to them from the fifth century when Ezra lived? The known facts of history postulate a body of teachers such as that which is named 'the Great Assembly.' If that be so, the probability is that its members would be drawn mainly, if not entirely, from the *Sopherim*, since they were the best qualified to discharge the duties which would fall to it.[1]

Three leading maxims are attributed to this Assembly: 'Be deliberate in judgment, raise up many disciples, and make a fence around the Torah' (Aboth I. 1). These represent the three principles which motived their activities. Judgment was to be deliberate in the sense that questions, which had to be determined by the rule of Torah, must be minutely studied and the closest investigation made as to the decision it suggested. That was one reason for the exact scrutiny of the Scriptural text which distinguished the Rabbis of the Talmud. A superficial reading could only result in a hasty judgment. An exhaustive inquiry was essential if the judgment was to be deliberate. The raising of many disciples had obviously to be the unceasing concern of the teachers if knowledge of the Torah was to be handed down to future generations. This ideal of spreading scholarship, and the consequent deference which was paid to the instructor and student of the Torah, provided a powerful urge towards the kind of learning which culminated in the compilation of the Talmud. To 'make a fence around the Torah' was a corollary of the desire to live by its precepts. If a person kept too close to its letter, he might inadvertently be led to transgress it. As a cultivated field had to

---

[1] The *Keneseth Hagedolah* and the *Sopherim* are actually identified in Tanchuma Beshallach § 16. A tradition tells that the Assembly consisted of a hundred and twenty members (Meg. 17b), and the number may have been suggested by the fact that 'it pleased Darius to set over the kingdom an hundred and twenty satraps' (Dan. vi. 1).

be hedged round to prevent even innocent trespass, so the sacred domain of the Torah must be enclosed by additional precautionary measures for the purpose of avoiding unintentional encroachment. Accordingly, the purposes which actuated the members of the Great Assembly created the type of study to which the teachers of later generations conformed. Theirs was the sowing which ultimately produced the extensive harvest of the Talmud.

An important piece of historical information is contained in the statement: 'Simon the Just was one of the last survivors of the Great Assembly' (Aboth I. 2). Unfortunately its value is minimized by the uncertainty as to which man of that name is meant. Josephus mentions a High Priest, 'Simon who was called the Just, both because of his piety towards God and his kind disposition to those of his own nation' (Antiq. XII. ii. 5). He died about the year 270 B.C. Another High Priest, Simon, the grandson of the former, is also referred to by the historian (ibid. XII. iv. 10), and he died about 199. In favour of identifying the grandfather with the last survivor of the Great Assembly is the fact that he is actually called by Josephus 'the Just'; but against it is the circumstance that if the Assembly came to an end about 270 a chronological difficulty is created. The Tractate *Aboth* informs us that Antigonos of Socho was the disciple of Simon the Just and 'José b. Joezer,[1] and José b. Jochanan received the Torah from them' (I. 4). These scholars died about the year 160, which seems to give too long a period of time if the sense of the passage is that they were disciples of Simon and Antigonos. To fill in the gap it has been suggested that 'from them' means from a succession of teachers whose names have not been recorded.[2]

However this may be, the Great Assembly ceased to exist either towards the middle of the third century or at its end. It was followed by another organization, known as a Sanhedrin,[3] which took charge of the affairs of the community in Judea. In a letter from Antiochus III to Ptolemy, preserved by Josephus, it is called a 'senate' (Antiq. XII. iii. 3). Jewish tradition relates that there were five *Zugoth*, or 'pairs' of Rabbis in succession, ending with Hillel and Shammai (died about A.D. 10), one of whom was *Nasi*

---

[1] b. is an abbreviation of the Hebrew *ben* or the Aramaic *bar*, 'son of.'

[2] Another theory has been put forward to the effect that Simon the Hasmonean is intended, in connection with whom we hear of 'the Great Assembly of the priests, and people, and rulers of the nation and elders of the country' (1 Macc. xiv. 28). But since he died in 136–5, he lived much later than the authorities who received the Torah from Simon the Just! On the whole question, see Moore, *Judaism*, III, pp. 8 ff. The 'Great Assembly' alluded to may have been the Great Sanhedrin which succeeded the *Kenéseth Hagedolah*.

[3] This is a Hebraized form of the Greek word *sunhedrion*.

or 'Prince,' i.e. President, and the other *Ab Beth Din* or 'Father of the Court of Law,' i.e. Vice-President (Chag. II. 2).

Modern historical study has come to a different conclusion. The Sanhedrin was a composite body of priests and laymen, presided over by the High Priest. In the deliberations which took place at its sessions a cleavage soon occurred, resulting in the formation of two distinct parties. The priests favoured a policy of compromise with Hellenistic thought, even at the expense of complete loyalty to the Torah. Ranged against them were the laymen who were the direct heirs of Ezra and the *Sopherim*,[1] and they took a firm stand in demanding whole-hearted adherence to the rule of Torah.[2] Their leaders were the Rabbis known as the *Zugoth*.

The rift between the two parties was closed during the Maccabean struggle, but manifested itself in a more pronounced form when John Hyrcanus (135–105 B.C.) came to the throne. It gradually widened until two sects appeared, called Sadducees and Pharisees. Among the differences which divided them was one of the utmost importance in the development of Judaism. Josephus refers to it in these terms: 'The Pharisees have delivered to the people a great many observances by succession from their fathers which are not written in the law of Moses; and for that reason it is that the Sadducees reject them, and say that we are to esteem those observances to be obligatory which are in the written word, but are not to observe what are derived from the tradition of our forefathers; and concerning these things it is that great disputes and differences have arisen among them' (Antiq. XIII. x. 6).

This controversy over the validity of the Oral Torah stimulated its defenders to a fresh study of the Scriptural text. They set out to demonstrate that the Oral Torah was an integral part of the Written Torah, that they were warp and woof of the one fabric; and they further developed methods of exegesis previously employed by which the traditions rejected by the Sadducees could be shown to be contained in the wording of the Pentateuch. Exposition of Torah now entered upon a new phase and led directly to the creation of the Talmud.

§ II. THE MISHNAH

With the invention of new methods of interpretation the Torah

[1] The New Testament constantly brackets the Scribes and Pharisees together.
[2] Josephus says of them: 'The Pharisees are esteemed most skilful in the exact interpretation of their laws' (War II. viii. 14).

became a science, and only men who were duly qualified to expound the text spoke with authority. They received the designation of *Tannaïm* (Teachers). It is the name given to the Rabbis during the period which closed with the codification of the law in the Mishnah. A pioneer who left a profound influence on their work was Hillel. He was a Babylonian by birth and, so tradition related, a descendant of David through his mother. He migrated to Judea and for about forty years was one of the acknowledged guides of his community.

Hillel exemplified the Pharisaic standpoint at its best. He recognized that life, with its ever-changing conditions, was incapable of compression within a fixed and immutable written code; and he perceived in the freedom of interpretation allowed by the Oral Law an invaluable instrument for making the Torah adaptable to varying circumstances.

A good illustration of his method is afforded by the enactment of Deut. xv. 1 ff.: 'At the end of every seven years thou shalt make a release. And this is the manner of the release: every creditor shall release that which he hath lent unto his neighbour.' That is to say, if a loan had not been repaid by the Sabbatical year, it could no longer be claimed. The Scriptural ordinance really deals with an act of charity performed by an Israelite towards a member of his nation in distress and not with a loan contracted in the ordinary course of business. The sociological background of the law is a nation of smallholders, each living on the produce of his allotment. When conditions altered and a large section of the population derived a livelihood from commerce, the Biblical regulation became a serious impediment. Men must have been afraid to give credit when they were precluded from claiming what was due to them after the incidence of the year of release, and the attendant hardship was undoubtedly very great.

From the Sadducean standpoint there was no redress. Such was the law and it must be obeyed. Hillel disagreed, and contended that a close study of the text would disclose a way out of the difficulty. Starting from the hypothesis that the Torah did not include a superfluous word, he pointed to the phrase 'whatsoever is thine with thy brother thine hand shall release' (ibid. 3). At first sight this appears to be an unnecessary repetition of the statement in the preceding verse: 'He shall not exact it of his neighbour and brother.' That, however, could not be, since there is nothing redundant in the Torah. Therefore the words, 'what soever is thine *with thy brother*,' must have been added to exclude a certain contingency, viz. the case where 'whatsoever is thine' is not with the debtor. By such reasoning Hillel deduced that if the creditor handed to a Court of Law a signed document which made over the indebtedness to its members, it was within his right to claim the debt through the Court even after the expiration of the Sabbatical year.

We may, if we so choose, criticize the argument as casuistry; but it served a vital purpose, which was to make the Torah a practical guide of life of everlasting validity. The Torah could never grow antiquated so long as it was capable of re-interpretation to comply with new contingencies.

Hillel was the creator of a School of *Tannaïm*. His contemporary, Shammai, also founded a School; and during the first seven decades of the first century, the two teachers and their disciples dominated the thought which was current in Pharisaic circles. On the whole the Hillelites favoured a more lenient interpretation of the law, while the other School took the stricter view. The Talmud records over three hundred points of divergence between them, and in the end the teaching of Hillel prevailed. The establishment of a School demanded a systematic presentation of the subject-matter of study. It must be borne in mind that in the Orient, even to-day, memory is more highly developed than in the West. A mass of learning is acquired not from books but from the lips of teachers. Hillel would therefore find it necessary to examine the rules of exegesis which had come down from previous generations, and recommend to his disciples those which he considered logically valid. He adopted seven such principles of interpretation which became generally accepted, though others were added at a later stage. In his instruction he would also have to arrange the large volume of traditional lore for the convenience of the learners. His arrangement was preserved orally and may be regarded as the first edition of the Mishnah.

The next personality to claim attention is Jochanan b. Zakkai, the youngest and most distinguished of Hillel's disciples, characterized by the master shortly before his death as 'the father of wisdom and father of (future) generations (of scholars)' (p. Ned. 39b). He was the outstanding authority at the time of the destruction of the Temple by Titus. Foreseeing the defeat of the Jews in their struggle with Rome, he urged peace because the preservation of Judaism meant more to him than national independence. When his advice was rejected, he planned measures to prevent the extermination of the community when the Temple and State would come to an end. A story tells that, in order to leave the besieged city whose gates were closely guarded by the Jewish zealots, he

circulated news of his illness and then of his death. With the con-
nivance of trusted adherents, he was carried out of Jerusalem in
a coffin for burial; and only the respect in which he was held saved
him from having a spear thrust through his body by the guards
who adopted this method of assuring themselves that nobody
passed through the gates alive. He thereupon made his way to
the Roman camp, gained admission to the presence of Vespasian
and petitioned him: 'Give me Jabneh [1] and its Sages' (Git. 56b).
The emperor kept his word and Jabneh was spared. At the end
of the war Jochanan removed there, with the result that its School,
previously of small importance, became the centre of Jewish life
and thought. Jabneh replaced the Holy City as the seat of the
Sanhedrin and virtually became the new capital. By his fore-
sight, he preserved the Torah from probable annihilation in the
national disaster, and thereby assured the survival of the defeated
people.

Before the occurrence of the catastrophe, Jochanan had been
the foremost antagonist of the Sadducean attitude towards the
Torah. On rational grounds he proved it to be inadequate; but
events were to provide an even more convincing demonstration
of the weakness of the Sadducean position and the strength of the
Pharisaic. With the Sadducees Judaism was a hidebound system,
fixed for all time by the written code of the Pentateuch; it was also
inseparably bound up with the ritual of the Temple. Consequently,
when the Sanctuary ceased to exist, the Sadducees very soon afterwards disappeared. The Pharisaic theory of the Oral Torah
received remarkable vindication in that time of crisis. It un-
questionably kept the religion of the people alive by adapting
it to the new conditions which had arisen; and nobody more than
Jochanan b. Zakkai achieved that result. In his School at Jabneh
he transmitted to his pupils the learning he had received from his
master, and they in turn became the teachers of the next generation.
He thus forged another link in the chain of Jewish traditional
lore.

Passing over one generation we come to the beginning of the
second century, when two names stand out prominently. The first
is Ishmael b. Elisha, a martyr in the Hadrianic persecution, who
was the founder of a School. He specialized in the scientific study
of Jewish law, and elaborated the seven rules of Hillel into thirteen,
which became the recognized principles of interpretation. His
main work was the endeavour to co-ordinate the large number of

[1] Jabneh is mentioned as a Philistine city in 2 Chron. xxvi. 6, and its Greek
name was Jamnia. It is located near the coast in southern Palestine.

decisions by attaching them to the Biblical texts from which they were deduced. He composed a commentary on the legalistic passages of the last four Books of the Pentateuch; but only that on Exodus, commencing at chap. xii, has been preserved, although in a later redaction. It is known as *Mechilta* (Measure).[1] His work on the other books formed the basis of similar commentaries which were compiled subsequently to the Mishnah, but may be conveniently mentioned here. They are the *Sifra*[2] on Leviticus which was edited by Chiyya b. Abba, who flourished in the earlier part of the third century, and the *Sifré*[3] on Numbers and Deuteronomy, which doubtless had a separate editor for each book although issued together. The commentary on Numbers seems to date from the same period as the *Sifra* and that on Deuteronomy belongs to a somewhat later time.

Both the *Sifra* and *Sifré* display traces of the influence of another eminent teacher, Akiba b. Joseph, who suffered martyrdom under the Romans in 132. He developed the science of *Midrash* to its extreme limits. Not a letter of the Scriptural text was held to be without significance, and he gave proof of extraordinary acumen in his interpretations. By the application of his exegetical method, a traditional practice no longer remained detached from the written code. By some means or other it was provided with an authoritative basis in the text.

In addition to his work as expositor and teacher, he also did much as a systematizer. It was said of him that he made the Torah into 'a series of rings' (ARN xviii), by which is to be understood that he collated the multitude of legal dicta which had accumulated down to his time and reduced them to order. He may be described as the architect of the plan of the Mishnah which was brought into existence a century later. Without his pioneer labours the Talmud may never have been ultimately produced. His disciples continued along the lines marked out by him and became the dominating influence in Torah-study during the generations that followed. The most important of them was Meïr, for the reason that he was responsible for the edition of a Mishnah which was accepted by Judah the Prince as the groundwork of his codification.

The Talmud remarks that 'when Akiba died Judah was born'

[1] The edition of M. Friedmann (1870) is the one quoted in this work.
[2] 'The Book,' abbreviated from *Sifra d'Bé Rab*, 'The book of the House of the Master,' i.e. the Book of the School. No critical edition has yet been published.
[3] 'The Books,' probably an abbreviation similar to the former. The critical edition by M. Friedmann (1864) is the one used in this volume.

(Kid. 72*b*). As a statement of chronology this is not quite correct, because the date of Judah's birth was 135. The intention was probably to link together these two pre-eminent figures in the history of Jewish literature. What Akiba started Judah completed. The former was, as stated, the architect and the other was the master-builder.

Judah was the son of a famous teacher, Simeon b. Gamaliel II, and so belonged to a wealthy and influential family. He was given a liberal education, which included Greek, and he enjoyed the friendship of Roman nobles.[1] His learning and social status combined to give him a position of unquestioned authority among the Jews of Palestine, and for over fifty years until his death in 219 or the following year he occupied the office of *Nasi* (Prince, Patriarch), i.e. he was the officially recognized leader of his community.

The great achievement of his life was the compilation of the corpus of Jewish law, called the Mishnah. The name is derived from a root *shanah*, 'to repeat,' and indicates oral teaching, what is learnt by repetition. The noun is the opposite of *Mikra*, 'the text (of Scripture) for reading.' It therefore signifies the codification of the Oral Torah in contradistinction to the Written Torah of the Pentateuch. He succeeded in preparing a code which was adopted throughout the Schools of Palestine and Babylon, and it resulted in the disuse of all other collections of laws made by individual Rabbis for their own academies. He established the uniform textbook for future study and discussion.

The language in which it is composed is a vernacular form of Hebrew, distinguished from Biblical Hebrew by a less strict conformity to grammatical rules and the infiltration of Latin and Greek words. It is characterized by extreme terseness of expression and the absence of literary flourishes. The language admirably suits the subject-matter.

Since the Middle Ages the question has been debated whether Judah committed his Mishnah to writing or whether it remained for some time a verbal arrangement. Scholars are still in disagreement, but the weight of opinion is gradually accumulating in favour of the view that it was issued in the form of a written code. It is arranged in six sections called *Sedarim* (Orders); each Order consists of a number of *Massichtoth* (Tractates), the total being sixty-three; and each tractate is divided into chapters and subdivided into paragraphs. There are 523 chapters in all.[2]

---

[1] See pp. 77, 89, 157. Cf. also p. 152.
[2] Or 524 if the sixth chapter of *Aboth*, which is a later addition, is included. The Misnah is cited by tractate, chapter, and paragraph, e.g. Ber. III, 2.

The following is a summary of the arrangement and contents of the Mishnah:

I. Order *Zeraïm*, 'Seeds'

1. *Berachoth*, 'Benedictions' (Ber. 9 PB).[1] Regulations dealing with the liturgy.

2. *Peah*, 'Corner' (8 P). Questions arising out of the law concerning 'the corners of the field' (Lev. xix. 9).

3. *Dammai*, 'Doubtful' (7 P). Treatment of corn, etc., purchased from a person suspected of not having given the tithe to the priest.

4. *Kilayim*, 'Mixtures' (9 P). On mixture of seeds, cross-breeding, etc., prohibited by Lev. xix. 19.

5. *Shebiïth*, 'Seventh' (10 P). Law of the Sabbatical year (Exod. xxiii. 11; Lev. xxv. 2 ff.; Deut. xv. 1 ff.).

6. *Terumoth*, 'Heave-offerings' (11 P). Law of the heave-offering (Num. xviii. 8 ff.).

7. *Maaseroth*, 'Tithes' (5 P). Law of the tithe of the Levite (Num. xviii. 21 ff.).

8. *Maaser Shéni*, 'Second Tithe' (5 P). Regulations based on Deut. xiv. 22 ff.

9. *Challah*, 'Dough' (4 P). The portion of dough to be given to the priests according to Num. xv. 21.

10. *Orlah*, 'Uncircumcision' (3 P). Law of fruits of trees during the first four years of planting (Lev. xix. 23 ff.).

11. *Bikkurim*, 'First-fruits' (3 P). The first-fruits brought to the Temple (Deut. xxvi. 1/ff.).

II. Order *Moéd*, 'Season'

1. *Shabbath*, 'Sabbath' (Shab. 24 PB). Prohibited labour during the Sabbath.

2. *Erubin*, 'Amalgamations' (Erub. 10 PB). Treats of a technical point which arises out of a Sabbatical law, viz. the boundary which may not be overstepped on the Sabbath and how it may be extended.

3. *Pesachim*, 'Passovers' (Pes. 10 PB). Observance of the Passover-Festival.

4. *Shekalim*, 'Shekels' (Shek. 8 P). The annual tax to the Temple treasury (Exod. xxx. 12 ff.).

5. *Joma*, 'The Day' (8 PB). The ritual of the Day of Atonement (Lev. xvi).

6. *Sukkah*, 'Booth' (Suk. 5 PB). Observance of the Feast of Tabernacles (Lev. xxiii. 34 ff.).

7. *Bétzah*, 'Egg' also called *Jom Tob*, 'Festival' (Betz. 5 PB). On prohibited and permitted labour on a festival.

---

[1] Within brackets are given the abbreviated name of the tractate employed in citations in the present work and the number of chapters it contains. The letters P and B denote that there is a Gemara to the tractate in the Palestinian and Babylonian Talmud respectively.

8. *Rosh Hashanah*, 'New Year' (R.H. 4 PB).   Observance of the feast which marks the New Year.

9. *Taanith*, 'Fast' (Taan. 4 PB).   On the public fasts.

10. *Megillah*, 'Scroll' (Meg. 4 PB).   Concerning the public recital of the Book of Esther on the Feast of Purim (Esth. ix. 28).

11. *Moéd Katan*, 'Minor Feast' (M.K. 3 PB).   Concerning the intermediate days of Passover and Tabernacles.

12. *Chagigah*, 'Festival Offering' (Chag. 3 PB).   On the sacrifices offered on the three Pilgrimage-Festivals (Deut. xvi. 16 f.).

III. Order *Nashim*, 'Women'

1. *Jebamoth*, 'Levirate Marriage' (Jeb. 16 PB).   Deals with the law of marriage with a childless sister-in-law (Deut. xxv. 5 ff.) and forbidden degrees of relationship in connection with marriage (Lev. xviii).

2. *Kethuboth*, 'Marriage Documents' (Keth. 13 PB).   Treats of the dowry and marriage-settlement.

3. *Nedarim*, 'Vows' (Ned. 11 PB).   On the making and annulment of vows particularly with regard to women (Num. xxx. 3 ff.).

4. *Nazir*, 'Nazirite' (Naz. 9 PB).   Concerning the vow of the Nazirite (Num. vi).

5. *Sotah*, 'Suspected Adultress' (Sot. 9 PB).   Relating to the wife suspected of infidelity (Num. v. 12 ff.).

6. *Gittin*, 'Divorces' (Git. 9 PB).   Laws relating to the annulment of marriage (Deut. xxiv. 1 ff.).

7. *Kiddushin*, 'Sanctification' (Kid. 4 PB).   On the marriage status.

IV. Order *Nezikin*, 'Torts'

1. *Baba Kamma*, 'The First Gate' (B.K. 10 PB).   On damages to property and injury to the person.

2. *Baba Metzia*, 'The Middle Gate' (B.M. 10 PB).   On found property, bailment, sales, and hiring.

3. *Baba Bathra*, 'The Last Gate' (B.B. 10 PB).   On real estate and hereditary succession.

4. *Sanhedrin*, 'Courts' (Sanh. 11 PB).   Deals with courts of law and their procedure and capital crimes.

5. *Makkoth*, 'Stripes' (Mak. 3 PB).   On the punishment of perjurers, cities of refuge (Num. xxxv. 10 ff.) and crimes punished by lashes.

6. *Shebuoth*, 'Oaths' (8 PB).   On the oaths made privately or administered in a court.

7. *Eduyyoth*, 'Testimonies' (Eduy. 8).   A collection of testimonies of Rabbis concerning the decisions of earlier authorities.

8. *Abodah Zarah*, 'Idolatry' (A.Z. 5 PB).   On heathenish rites and worship.

9. *Pirké Aboth*, 'Chapters of the Fathers' (Aboth 5).   An ethical treatise collecting the favourite maxims of the *Tannaïm*.   There is

INTRODUCTION xxix

also an Appendix called 'the Chapter of R. Meïr on the Acquisition of the Torah.'

10. *Horayoth*, 'Decisions' (Hor. 3 PB). On inadvertent sin through the misdirection of religious authorities.

V. Order *Kodashim*, 'Sanctities'

1. *Zebachim*, 'Sacrifices' (Zeb. 14 B). On the sacrificial system of the Temple.

2. *Menachoth*, 'Meal-offerings' (Men. 13 B). Deals with the meal and drink offerings (Lev. ii).

3. *Chullin*, 'Profane Things' (Chul. 12 B). On the slaughter of animals and the dietary laws.

4. *Bechoroth*, 'Firstborns' (Bech. 9 B). Concerning the firstborn of man and animals (Exod. xiii. 12 ff.; Num. xviii. 15 ff.).

5. *Arachin*, 'Estimations' (Arach. 9 B). On the value-equivalent of persons and objects vowed to the Temple (Lev. xxvii).

6. *Temurah*, 'Substitution' (Tem. 7B). Treats of the exchange of animals dedicated as a sacrifice (Lev. xxvii. 10, 33).

7. *Kerithoth*, 'Excisions' (Ker. 6 B). On the sins punishable by 'cutting off' (cf. Exod. xii. 15).

8. *Meilah*, 'Trespass' (6 B). On the sacrilegious treatment of Temple property.

9. *Tamid*, 'Continual Offering' (7 B). Describes the daily ritual in the Temple.

10. *Middoth*, 'Dimensions' (5). On the architecture of the Temple.

11. *Kinnim*, 'Birds' Nests' (3). On the offerings of birds (Lev. i. 14; v. 7; xii. 8).

VI. Order *Teharoth*, 'Purities'

1. *Kélim*, 'Vessels' (30). Deals with the ritualistic defilement of utensils (Lev. xi. 33 ff.).

2. *Ohaloth*, 'Tents' (18). On the defilement caused by a corpse (Num. xix. 14 ff.).

3. *Negaïm*, 'Plagues' (14). Laws relating to leprosy (Lev. xiii f.).

4. *Parah*, 'Cow' (12). Regulations concerning the Red Heifer (Num. xix).

5. *Teharoth*, 'Purities' (10). A euphemism for the defilements which last until sunset (Lev. xi. 24 ff.).

6. *Mikwaoth*, 'Baths' (10). On the requirements of cisterns to be used for ritualistic purification (Lev. xv. 11 f.).

7. *Niddah*, 'Uncleanness of Menstruation' (Nid. 10 PB). Deals with the laws of Lev. xii; xv. 19 ff.

8. *Machshirin*, 'Preparations' (6). On liquids as a conductor of defilement (Lev. xi. 34, 37 f.).

9. *Zabim*, 'Persons Suffering from a Running Issue' (5). Treats of uncleanness caused by physical issues (Lev. xv. 2 ff.).

10. *Tebul Jom*, 'Immersed during a Day' (4). On the status of a person who has undergone immersion but whose purification is not complete until sunset.

11. *Jadayim* 'Hands' (Jad. 4). On the defilement of the hands and their purification.

12. *Uktzin*, 'Stalks' (Uktz. 3). Treats of fruit-stalks as a conductor of defilement.

APOCRYPHAL TRACTATES OF POST-MISHNAIC DATE

Aboth d'Rabbi Nathan (ARN 41). An elaboration of *Pirké Aboth*.

Sopherim, 'Scribes' (Soph. 21). Deals with the rules for the writing of scrolls of the Torah for use in the Synagogue and other liturgical matters.

Ebel Rabbathi, 'The Great Mourning,' more usually called euphemistically *Semachoth*, 'Joys' (Sem. 14). Regulations concerning burial and mourning customs.

Kallah, 'Bride.' A short tractate in one chapter on Chastity.

Dérech Eretz Rabbah, 'Large Treatise on Behaviour' (11). On prohibited marriages and ethical conduct.

Dérech Eretz Zuta, 'Small Treatise on Behaviour' (10). Collection of rules of good conduct.

Pérek Shalom, 'A Chapter on Peace.'

Gérim, 'Proselytes' (4). Rules concerning conversion to Judaism.

Kuthim, 'Samaritans' (2). On practices of Samaritans in relation to Jewish law.

Abadim, 'Slaves' (3). Concerning Hebrew slaves.

To these must be added four small tractates published, together with the last three enumerated above, by R. Kirchheim in 1851.

Sépher Torah, 'Scroll of the Law'; *Mezuzah*, 'Sign on the Door-post' (Deut. vi. 9); *Tephillin*, 'Phylacteries'; and *Tzitzith*, 'Fringes' (Num. xv. 38).

There has come down to us another work, analogous to the Mishnah, called *Tosifta* (Supplement). It is also a collection of laws in systematic arrangement, in many respects running parallel to the Mishnah, but containing additional matter. The style is more diffuse than that employed by Judah, and it frequently adds the proof-texts which are normally omitted in the Mishnah. Its exact relationship to the official codification has not yet been determined, and many problems connected with its authorship still remain in doubt. The nucleus of the work is now usually attributed to two Rabbis of the third century, Rabbah and Oshaya, although in its present form it probably dates from the fifth century.[1]

[1] The authoritative edition is by M. S. Zuckermande](1881).

§ III. GEMARA AND MIDRASH

The purpose which Judah had in view in editing the Mishnah was not to fix the law. That would have been contrary to the spirit which animated the Rabbis and militated against the fundamental principle of the Oral Torah. His object was to facilitate its study. For that reason he records the opposing views of different authorities, but where an accepted decision had been arrived at he indicates what it is. His codification stimulated further research rather than checked it.

The Mishnah provided the schools with a much needed textbook, and its use rapidly advanced Torah-study both in extent and depth. Every clause was carefully examined and discussed for the purpose of testing its validity, definition, and scope. The editor had by no means exhausted the whole of the available material in his compilation, and teachers had handed down by word of mouth or in writing many legal opinions which had not been incorporated in the Mishnah. Such an excluded dictum is called *Baraita*, 'that which is external.' A debate on a paragraph of the Mishnah often opens with the quotation of a *Baraita* which appears to take a different side on the law in question, and much ingenuity is expended in the harmonization of the two opinions.

For several centuries to come, scholarship among the Jews consisted mainly, if not entirely, in the acquisition of knowledge of the Mishnah and the commentary which gradually accumulated around it. This commentary is designated *Gemara* (Completion), because it completes the Mishnah. Its exponents, in contrast to the pre-Mishnaic Rabbis or *Tannaim*, were named *Amoraïm* (Speakers, Expounders).[1] The principal Schools where this study was prosecuted were Caesarea, Sepphoris, Tiberias, and Usha in Palestine, and Nehardea, Sura, and Pombeditha in Babylon.

The Palestinian and Babylonian Academies carried on their researches independently, although Rabbis passed to and fro between the countries and in this way created an interchange of views. In Palestine the most distinguished teacher was Jochanan b. Nappacha (199–279), the head of the Academy of Tiberias. He began the collection of the reports of the discussions which were taking place on the Mishnah in the Palestinian Schools. He cannot

---

[1] An ordained scholar, like a graduate of a modern university, received a title of honour. The *Tannaim* and Palestinian *Amoraïm* had 'Rabbi' prefixed to their name, the Babylonian *Amoraïm* 'Rab'; while the special title of respect, 'Rabban,' was assigned to Gamaliel I and II, Simeon b. Gamaliel, and Jochanan b. Zakkai. In the present work they are all alike designated by R.

be accredited, as used to be supposed, with the composition of the
Palestinian Talmud, since authorities belonging to three generations after his death are cited in it. He may well have laid the
foundation of the work which others added to until towards the
end of the fourth century it reached its final form. The Mishnah,
with its commentary the Gemara, are together denoted the *Talmud*
(Study), an abbreviation of Talmud Torah.

The Palestinian Talmud, accordingly, consists of the text of
the Mishnah and the glosses upon it which emanated from the
Academies of that country. Simultaneously the same process was
at work in Babylon. The Jewish community there was more
numerous and better circumstanced than their co-religionists in
Palestine, and they produced or attracted men of superior intellectual powers. At any rate, the teaching in its Schools was deeper
and more thorough, and this distinction is clearly evident in the
compilation of the Gemara which was made there. R. Ashé
(352–427) began the task of its composition, to which he devoted
thirty years, leaving it unfinished at his death. Rabina brought
it to a close in 499.

Neither Talmud consists of a complete Gemara, although there
is evidence that it existed on certain tractates where it is no longer
extant. In the Palestinian Talmud it covers thirty-nine tractates
and in the Babylonian thirty-seven; but the Babylonian Gemara
is seven to eight times the size of the other.

The first complete edition of both Talmuds, as we now have
them, was issued by Daniel Bomberg in Venice, the Babylonian in
1520–3 and the Palestinian in 1523–4. His pagination has been
followed in nearly all subsequent issues. He printed the Palestinian
Talmud without any commentary, two columns on each side of
the folio; but the Babylonian Talmud he printed with a portion
of the Gemara in the centre of each side surrounded by the commentary of Solomon b. Isaac (better known as Rashi, 1040–1105),
and notes of later glossators called Tosafists.[1]

The language of the two Talmuds also varies and represents two
different dialects of Aramaic. The Palestinian Gemara is composed in Western Aramaic and closely resembles the Biblical
Aramaic of parts of Ezra and Daniel. The Babylonian Gemara
is in Eastern Aramaic, which is more akin to Mandaitic.

---

[1] For that reason references to the Palestinian Talmud (denoted in this
volume by p. before the name of the tractate) may be, e.g. 6*a*, *b*, *c*, or *d*,
representing folio 6, column 1 and 2 of the verso and 1 and 2 of the
recto respectively, Hebrew print running from right to left and a folio consisting of the two sides of the page. In the Babylonian Talmud we only
have *a* and *b*.

From the sketch which has been given of the history of the Talmud, it at once becomes evident that it cannot be regarded, in the strict sense of the term, as a literary work. The ordinary canons of literature do not apply to it. Although, in so far as it follows the text of the Mishnah, it is founded on a system, if taken as a whole it presents the appearance of a disorderly mass of the most heterogeneous material. As a record of the proceedings of the Schools, it faithfully reflects all that was discussed within their walls. Teachers and pupils allowed themselves to digress from the point under examination and wander off at will into every conceivable kind of topic. They relieved the tedium of a keen debate on an abstruse legal theme by taking up a lighter subject. They poured forth for mutual edification the treasures stored in their memories relating to history, legend, folk-lore, medicine, astronomy, botany, zoology, and a host of other matters. Not only the sharp battle of wits but likewise the ordinary conversation which passed within the Academies—all are vividly portrayed in the Talmud.

Furthermore, Torah, as understood by the Rabbis, touched life at every point. It dealt with the whole existence of the human being. Religion, ethics, the physical life—even his superstitions —in fact, nothing that pertained to man fell outside its purview. Therefore, instructors and disciples could not restrict their discussions to questions of law. They were in the closest touch with the mass of the people, and what the ordinary man and woman were thinking and saying penetrated into the Schools and found a place on the Talmudic folios.

The miscellaneous material which constitutes the subject-matter of the Talmud is divisible into two main categories known as *Halachah* and *Haggadah*. The former term denotes 'walking,' and indicates the way of life to tread in conformity with the precepts of the Torah. It therefore comprises the Mishnah and that section of the Gemara which treats of law. The *Halachah* is the logical working out by many generations of devoted scholars of the theory devised by Ezra for the salvation of the people of Israel. It provided the community as a whole and its individual members with a distinctive code of action which fulfilled the purpose of keeping the Jewish consciousness alive. The *Halachah* moulded the existence of the Jew. It directed his steps so that he walked humbly with his God. It also created a breakwater, behind which he found security from the alien influences that tended to sweep him from his racial moorings. Its efficacy as a preservative force has been thoroughly tested and proved by centuries of experience down to the present day. The *Halachah* is the regime under which the Jew lived *qua* Jew in past generations and still lives; and it supplies the answer to the question why a minority has for such a length of time maintained its identity and not been absorbed in the surrounding majority.

Even if it were possible to isolate the *Halachah* from the other elements in the Talmud, it would still be a mistake to envisage it as a system of dry legalism devoid of all spiritual content, as its critics invariably allege. A modern student of Rabbinic literature has truly said: 'The Pharisees and the Rabbis were, before anything else, teachers; and what they set out to teach was practical religion, the doing of right actions for the service of God and man. They sought to strengthen the factors which make for unity and peace amongst men—the sense of justice, truth, probity, brotherly love, sympathy, mercy, forbearance, and the rest—in a word, to raise the moral standard amongst their people from age to age. They had this purpose mainly in view when they developed the *Halachah* and kept it from becoming a rigid system. They made it a means of ethical training by defining right conduct in terms of a progressive morality, a standard which was raised and not lowered in course of time.' [1]

But it is impossible to separate the *Halachah* from the other main constituent, the *Haggadah*, without creating a distorted picture of Rabbinic teaching. The *Haggadah* was the concern of the same teachers who pondered over the technicalities of the *Halachah*. The two were imparted side by side in the same Schools to the same pupils, and together they form the interwoven strands from which the Talmud was constructed.

Haggadah (Narration), therefore, signifies the non-legal sections of Rabbinic literature, and is equally important as the other for a correct understanding of the world of thought which generations of teachers lovingly evolved. Striking though the contrast be between *Halachah* and *Haggadah*, they complement each other, spring from the same root, and aim at the same goal. If the *Halachah* pointed out the way of the godly life, so did the *Haggadah*. 'Is it your desire to know Him Who spake and the world came into being? Learn the *Haggadah*; for from it you will come to know the Holy One, blessed be He, and cleave to His ways' (Sifré Deut. § 49; 85*a*). They both grew from the same soil. Exactly as the Rabbi strove to derive sanction for a legal decision from the text of the Torah, he likewise endeavoured to corroborate an ethical or moral lesson by a quotation from that source. 'As it is said,' or 'as it is written,' followed by a Scriptural reference, is the

[1] R. T. Herford, *The Pharisees*, p. 111.

ordinary way of presenting a piece of *Haggadah*. One important point of difference must, however, be noted. Whereas the *Halachah* remained the law to be observed in practice until it was abrogated by a competent authority, *Haggadah* was always held to be nothing more than the personal opinion of the teacher. It possessed no binding force upon the community as a whole or any part of it.

A Jewish scholar has happily defined the relationship of these two elements in the following terms: '*Halachah* is law incarnate; *Haggadah* liberty regulated by law bearing the impress of morality. *Halachah* stands for the rigid [1] authority of the law, for the absolute importance of theory—the law and theory which the *Haggadah* illustrates by public opinion and the dicta of common-sense morality. The *Halachah* embraces the statutes enjoined by oral tradition, which was the unwritten commentary of the ages on the Written Law, along with the discussions of the Academies of Palestine and Babylonia, resulting in the final formulating of the Halachic ordinances. The *Haggadah*, while also starting from the word of the Bible, only plays with it, explaining it by sagas and legends, by tales and poems, allegories, ethical reflections, and historical reminiscences. For it, the Bible was not only the supreme law, from whose behests there was no appeal, but also "a golden nail upon which" the *Haggadah* "hung its gorgeous tapestries," so that the Bible word was the introduction, refrain, text, and subject of the poetical glosses of the Talmud. It was the province of the *Halachah* to build, upon the foundation of Biblical law, a legal superstructure capable of resisting the ravages of time, and, unmindful of contemporaneous distress and hardship, to trace out, for future generations, the extreme logical consequences of the Law in its application. To the *Haggadah* belonged the high, ethical mission of consoling, edifying, exhorting, and teaching a nation suffering the pangs, and threatened with the spiritual stagnation, of exile; of proclaiming that the glories of the past prefigured a future of equal brilliancy, and that the very wretchedness of the present was part of the divine plan outlined in the Bible. If the simile is accurate that likens the *Halachah* to the ramparts about Israel's Sanctuary, which every Jew was ready to defend with his last drop of blood, then the *Haggadah* must seem "flowery mazes, of exotic colours and bewildering fragrance," within the shelter of the Temple walls.' [2]

We have seen that from the time of the Babylonian exile the practice grew of Jews gathering together for the purpose of hearing

---

[1] The adjective is questionable, because the *Halachah* was essentially plastic.
[2] G. Karpeles, *Jewish Literature and Other Essays*, pp. 54 f.

the Pentateuch read and expounded, and from this kind of assembly the Synagogue originated. Right through the Talmudic period, not to speak of later ages, the Synagogue was the school of the public as well as the place of prayer. The mass of the people who had no time or inclination or ability for Halachic dialectics had their need of religious learning catered for within its precincts. In particular, the Sabbath afternoons were spent in listening to discourses which were intended to satisfy the eager audience intellectually, spiritually, and morally. Homilies corrective of prevalent faults, addresses to instil hope and courage into a harassed community and preserve its will to live, lectures on the relation of God and His Universe or of man and his Maker, skilful elucidations of Scriptural texts which revealed them in a new light or opened up fresh avenues of thought—such was the fare provided in the Synagogues for the instruction and delectation of the people.

With such a comprehensive goal in view, it will be readily appreciated that the preacher would not be satisfied with imparting to his hearers merely the superficial interpretation of the Bible. More than the desire to understand and teach the meaning of a verse was the eagerness to see what the verse could be made to mean. Four methods of exegesis were employed, and they are indicated by the consonants of the word for 'garden, Paradise' (*Pardes*). They were, respectively: *Peshat* (simple), i.e. literal interpretation; *Remez* (allusion), i.e. allegorical explanation; *Derash* (exposition), i.e. homiletical commentary; and *Sod* (mystery), i.e. esoteric teaching. By these methods the teachers garnered rich stores of ideas which contributed to the material of the *Haggadah*.

It follows, therefore, that apart from the Schools, a fertile source of Haggadic teaching was found in the Synagogues. In course of time a desire was felt to have this material collected for private reading and study. This need created the branch of Rabbinic literature called *Midrashim*. The most important of them is the *Midrash Rabbah* (Great Midrash), which has the form of a kind of Haggadic Gemara on the Pentateuch and the five *Megilloth* or Scrolls—Song of Songs, Ruth, Lamentations, Ecclesiastes, and Esther—which were read during the Synagogue services in the course of a year. These were compiled at various dates between the fifth and twelfth centuries, but the material belongs in the main to the period of the Talmud. Other notable Haggadic works are the *Midrash Tanchuma* on the Pentateuch,[1] which emanated from

---

[1] It exists in two recensions, one of them edited by S. Buber in 1885. In the present volume the other and fuller version is adopted.

a Palestinian Rabbi named Tanchuma who lived in the latter part of the fourth century, but in its extant form is of much later date; the *Pesikta d'Rab Kahana* on the lessons read on festivals and special Sabbaths, which belongs to the sixth century; [1] and a Midrash on the Psalms.[2]

These are the sources which are drawn upon in the pages that follow to illustrate the doctrines of the Talmud. They faithfully mirror the world of ideas in which the Jews lived during the great formative period, extending from the third century B.C. to the end of the fifth century A.D., the period which witnessed the development of the Mosaic and prophetical dispensations into the Judaism which has survived to the present day.

---

[1] Edited by S. Buber (1868); another edition (published by Romm) 1925.
[2] Of uncertain date. Buber, who edited it in 1891, holds that, apart from interpolations of a later date, it is an old Palestinian work.

SELECTED BIBLIOGRAPHY

THE literature on the Talmud in its various aspects is immense and only a selection is here attempted for the guidance of the reader. The list is limited to works in English. A more comprehensive bibliography will be found in H. L. Strack, *Einleitung in den Talmud* (5th ed.). This extremely valuable work is now available in English translation: *Introduction to the Talmud and Midrash*, 1931.

INTRODUCTORY

Articles in *Jewish Encyclopaedia, Encyclopaedia Britannica, Encyclopaedia of Religion and Ethics,* and *Dictionary of the Bible* (extra volume).

Darmesteter, A. *The Talmud* (a valuable essay translated from the French).

Deutsch, E. Essay on the Talmud in *Literary Remains*, 1874.

Mielziner, M. *Introduction to the Talmud* (3rd ed., 1925). Helpful to the student of the original text.

Oesterley, W. O. E., and Box, G. H. *A Short Survey of the Literature of Rabbinical and Medieval Judaism.* 1920.

Waxman M. *A History of Jewish Literature,* I. 1930.

Wright, D. *The Talmud,* 1932.

TRANSLATIONS

An authoritative and complete translation of the Babylonian Talmud is being issued by the Soncino Press, under the editorship of Rabbi Dr I. Epstein, 1935, etc.

Rodkinson, M. L. *The Babylonian Talmud,* 10 vols. 1902. (Moore says of it: 'R.'s so-called English translation is in every respect impossible'—*Judaism*, I, p. 173 n.). Suitable for the general reader but inadequate for the serious student.

English translations of the following tractates have been published:

Cohen, A. *Berachoth.* 1921.

Malter, H. *Taanith.* 1928.

Streane, A. W. *Chagigah.* 1891.

A translation of the entire Mishnah was made by H. Danby, 1933.

The following tractates are available separately in translation:

Danby, H. *Sanhedrin,* 1919.

Elmslie, W. A. L. *Abodah Zarah.* 1911.

Goldin, H. *Baba Metzia.* 1913.

Greenup, A. W. *Taanith.* 1918.
Sukkah. 1921.

Herford, R. T. *Pirke Aboth.* 1925.

Oesterley, W. O. E. *Shabbath.* 1927.

Rabbinowitz, J. *Megillah.* 1931.

Taylor, C. *Sayings of the Jewish Fathers, Pirke Aboth* (2nd ed.). 1897.

Williams, A. L. *Berachoth.* 1921.

There are also D. A. de Sola and M. J. Raphall, *Eighteen Tractates from the Mishnah* (1845), and J. Barclay, *The Talmud* (1878), which likewise consists of a translation of eighteen tractates of the Mishnah.

A complete translation of the Midrash Rabbah was published by the Soncino Press in 1939, in 10 volumes, edited by Rabbi Dr. H. Freedman and M. Simon.

RELIGION AND ETHICS

Abelson, J. *The Immanence of God in Rabbinical Literature.* 1912.

Abrahams, I. *Studies in Pharisaism and the Gospels.* 1st series, 1917; 2nd series, 1924.
Akiba: Scholar, Saint, and Martyr. 1936.

Büchler, A. *Types of Jewish-Palestinian Piety.* 1922.
Studies in Sin and Atonement. 1928.

Finkelstein, L. *The Pharisees: the Sociological Background of their Faith,* 2 vols. 1938.

Herford, R. T. *Pharisaism, its Aim and Method.* 1912.
The Pharisees. 1924.
Judaism in the New Testament Period. 1928.
Talmud and Apocrypha. 1933.

Lazarus, M. *The Ethics of Judaism.* 2 vols. 1901.

Marmorstein, A. *The Doctrine of Merits in Old Rabbinical Literature.* 1920.
The Old Rabbinic Doctrine of God. I. The Names and Attributes of God. 1927.

Montefiore, C. G. *The Old Testament and After.* 1923. Chapter III.
Rabbinic Literature and Gospel Teachings. 1930.

Montefiore, C. G., and H. Loewe. *A Rabbinic Anthology.* 1938.

Moore, G. F. *Judaism in the First Centuries of the Christian Era.* 2 vols., 1927, and a volume of notes, 1930. (A reliable and impartial presentation, fully documented.)

Porter, F. C. *The Yetser Hara, A Study in the Jewish Doctrine of Sin.* 1902.

Schechter, S. *Some Aspects of Rabbinic Theology.* 1909. A masterly work.

LAW

Amram, D. W. *The Jewish Law of Divorce.* 1897.

Benny, P. B. *The Criminal Code of the Jews.* 1880.

Mendelsohn, S. *The Criminal Jurisprudence of the Talmud.* 1891.

Mielziner, M. *The Jewish Law of Marriage and Divorce,* 1884. *The Rabbinical Law of Hereditary Succession.* 1901.

MISCELLANEOUS

Abelson, J. *Jewish Mysticism.* 1913.

Cohen, A. *Ancient Jewish Proverbs.* 1911.

Delitzsch, F. *Jewish Artisan Life.* 1906.

Feldman, A. *The Parables and Similes of the Rabbis.* 2nd ed. 1927.

Feldman, W. M. *Rabbinical Mathematics and Astronomy.* 1931.

Ginzberg, L. *The Legends of the Jews.* 4 vols., 1913; 2 vols. of notes, 1925–8; and Index Volume, 1938.

Gollancz, H. *Pedagogics of the Talmud.* 1924.

Rappoport, A. S. *Myth and Legend of Ancient Israel.* 3 vols. 1928.

Schechter, S. *Studies in Judaism.* 1st series, 1896; 2nd series, 1908; 3rd series, 1924.

CHAPTER I

THE DOCTRINE OF GOD

§ I. Existence

As in the Bible, so throughout the literature of the Rabbis, the existence of God is regarded as an axiomatic truth. No proofs are offered to convince the Jew that there must be a God. To avoid the profane use of the sacred Name, in accordance with the Third Commandment, various designations were devised, common among them being 'the Creator' and 'He Who spake and the world came into being.' They indicate the view that the existence of God follows inevitably from the existence of the Universe.

This thought is well expressed in the Midrashic account of the first interview which took place between Pharaoh and Moses and Aaron. When the Egyptian king asked them, 'Who is your God that I should hearken unto His voice?' they replied, 'The Universe is filled with the might and power of our God. He existed ere the world was created, and He will continue in being when the world comes to a final end. He formed you and infused into you the breath of life. He stretched forth the heavens and laid the foundations of the earth. His voice hews out flames of fire, rends mountains asunder and shatters rocks. His bow is fire and His arrows flames. His spear is a torch, His shield the clouds and His sword the lightning. He fashioned mountains and hills and covered them with grass. He makes the rains and dew to descend, and causes the herbage to sprout. He also forms the embryo in the mother's womb and enables it to issue forth as a living being' (Exod. R. v. 14).

That Nature reveals God is illustrated by the tradition that Abraham discovered His existence by reasoning back to a First Cause. Two different versions of his discovery are given. According to one story, when he revolted against idolatry, his father took him before King Nimrod, who demanded that since he would not worship images he should worship fire. The following argument ensued. 'Abraham replied to him: "We should rather worship water which extinguishes fire." Nimrod said to him: "Then worship water." Abraham retorted: "If so, we should worship the cloud which carries water!" Nimrod said: "Then worship the cloud." Abraham retorted: "If so, we should worship the wind which disperses the cloud!" Nimrod said: "Then worship the wind." Abraham retorted: "Rather should we worship the human being who carries the wind!"'[1] (Gen. R. XXXVIII. 13).   Such a line of reasoning leads to the hypothesis of an ultimate Creator.

The other legend tells that Abraham had to be hidden away soon after his birth because astrologers had warned King Nimrod that a child was about to be born who would overthrow his kingdom, and advised that he be killed while still a babe. The child lived with a nurse in a cave for three years. The story continues: 'When he left the cave, his heart kept reflecting upon the creation of the Universe, and he determined to worship all the luminaries until he discovered which of them was God. He saw the moon whose light illumined the darkness of night from one end of the world to the other and noticed the vast retinue of stars. "This is God," he exclaimed, and worshipped it throughout the night. In the morning when he beheld the dawn of the sun before which the moon darkened and its power waned, he exclaimed: "The light of the moon must be derived from the light of the sun, and the Universe only exists through the sun's rays." So he worshipped the sun throughout the day. In the evening, the sun sank below the horizon, its power waned, and the moon reappeared with the stars and the planets. He thereupon exclaimed: "Surely these all have a Master and God!"'[2]

Another Rabbinic passage teaches that it is possible to arrive at a realization of God out of one's spiritual consciousness, and by this method Abraham and others discovered His existence. 'Abraham perceived the Holy One, blessed be He, by himself and nobody taught him this knowledge. He is one of four human beings who accomplished this. Job perceived the Holy One, blessed be He, by himself, as it is said "I have treasured up the words of His mouth from my bosom"[3] (Job xxiii. 12). Hezekiah, King of Judah, likewise perceived the Holy One, blessed be He, by himself, since it is written concerning him: "Butter and honey shall he eat, when he knoweth to refuse the evil and choose the good" (Is. vii. 15). The King Messiah also perceived the Holy One, blessed be He, by himself' (Num. R. XIV. 2).

[1] In the breath of the body.
[2] This passage is quoted from the *Midrash Hagadol*, ed. Schechter, l. 189 f. This is a late collection of Midrashic material; but the story, although not found in the Talmud or standard Midrashim, occurs in the *Apocalypse of Abraham*, which belongs to the middle of the first century of the present era, and so falls within the Talmudic period.
[3] The Midrash reads *mecheki* (from my bosom) instead of *mechukki*, as in the received text, which is translated 'more than my necessary food.' It is noteworthy that the Septuagint and Vulgate also read the text in the sense of 'in my bosom.'

THE DOCTRINE OF GOD

Not only is God the Creator of the Universe, but the cosmic order is ever dependent upon His will. Creation is not an act in the past which continues automatically. The processes of Nature represent the unceasing functioning of the divine creative power.[1] 'Every hour He makes provision for all who come into the world according to their need. In His Grace He satisfies all creatures, not the good and righteous alone, but also the wicked and idolaters' (Mech. to xviii. 12; 59a). 'During a third of the day He is occupied with sustaining the whole world from the mightiest to the most insignificant of living beings' (A.Z. 3b).

In their intercourse with Gentiles, the Rabbis were sometimes challenged to demonstrate that the God they worshipped, an invisible Deity, was actual. It is recorded that the Emperor Hadrian said to R. Joshua b. Chananya: 'I desire to behold your God.' 'That is an impossibility,' he replied. The emperor persisted; so the Rabbi bade him face the sun, it being the time of the summer solstice, and said: 'Gaze at that.' 'I cannot,' he answered. Whereupon the Rabbi exclaimed: 'You admit that you are unable to look at the sun, which is only one of the attendants upon the Holy One, blessed be He; how much more beyond your power must it be to look at God Himself!' (Chul. 59b et seq.).

Whether atheism, in the sense of the dogmatic denial of God's existence, was accepted by anybody in Biblical and Rabbinic times is doubtful; but both in Bible and Talmud the concern was with the practical atheist who conducted his life as though he would never be held to account for his deeds. In Biblical literature the statement 'There is no God' is made by the *Nabal*, i.e. the morally corrupt person who, while acknowledging the existence of a Creator, refused to believe that He was at all interested in the actions of His creatures.[2] His counterpart in the Talmud is the *Apikoros*, or Epicurean, who likewise 'denies the fundamental principle of religion' (B.B. 16b) by his abominable conduct. The Rabbis defined the atheist as one who affirmed 'There is no judgment and no Judge' (Gen. R. xxvi. 6) in the Universe, irrespective of his disbelief in the existence of God.[3]

On one occasion, it is related, R. Reuben stayed in Tiberias, and

[1] In the Hebrew Prayer Book, God is mentioned as 'renewing the creation every day continually' (ed. Singer, p. 128).
[2] Ps. xiv. 1, and liii. 1. See also x. 13, and Jer. v. 12.
[3] The use of the term 'Epicurean' in this sense is already found in Josephus, who refers to this type as men 'who cast providence out of human life, and who do not believe that God takes care of the affairs of the world, nor that the Universe is governed and continued in being by that blessed and immortal nature, but say that the world is carried along of its own accord, without a ruler and guardian' (Antiq. x. xi. 7).

a philosopher asked him: 'Who is the most hateful person in the world?' 'The person who denies his Creator,' was the reply. 'How is that?' the philosopher asked; and the Rabbi answered: 'Honour thy father and thy mother; thou shalt not murder; thou shalt not commit adultery; thou shalt not steal; thou shalt not bear false witness against thy neighbour; thou shalt not covet— behold, a person does not repudiate any of these laws until he repudiates the root of them (viz. God Who ordained them); and nobody proceeds to commit a transgression without first having denied Him Who prohibited it' (Tosifta Shebuoth III. 6).

According to Talmudic teaching, therefore, the existence of God was more than an intellectual affirmation; it included moral obligation. The recital of the declaration: 'Hear, O Israel, the Lord our God, the Lord is one' (Deut. vi. 4), which forms part of the morning and evening prayers of the Jew, is defined as 'the acceptance of the yoke of the Kingdom of Heaven' (Ber. II. 2), which means submission to the Divine discipline.

§ II. UNITY

The conception of God held by the Rabbis is monotheistic in the strictest degree. 'He created in the beginning one man only, so that heretics should not say that there are several Powers in heaven' (Sanh. 38a); since, had there been more human beings created at first, it might be argued that some had been formed by God and the remainder by other deities. 'All agree,' it is stated, 'that nothing was created on the first day, so that people should not say that the archangel Michael stretched the south end of the firmament and Gabriel the north end; for "I am the Lord that stretched forth the heavens alone" (Is. xliv. 24)' (Gen. R. I. 3).

On the verse, 'Hear, O Israel, the Lord our God, the Lord is one,' the comment is made: The Holy One, blessed be He, said to Israel, 'My children, everything that I created in the Universe is in pairs—e.g. heaven and earth, the sun and moon, Adam and Eve, this world and the World to Come; but I am one and alone in the Universe' (Deut. R. II. 31).

Stress was laid upon the Unity of God in defence against two currents of thought. The first was idolatry, which was identified by the Rabbis with immoral living, doubtless under the impression caused by Roman and Greek polytheism. The idolater 'breaks the yoke of God's law from off him' (Sifré Num. § 111; 31b), it was said; i.e. he lives without moral restraint. 'He who professes idolatry repudiates the Ten Commandments' (ibid.) expresses the same thought still more explicitly. The rejection of the first half of the Decalogue results in the infraction of the second half. The same idea underlies such statements as 'The prohibition of idolatry is equal in weight to all the other commandments of the Torah' (Hor. 8a); 'So important is the matter of idolatry, that whoever rejects it is as though he acknowledges the whole Torah' (Chul. 5a).

The moral implications of the concept may be seen from the Rabbinic decision, 'If a person is required to transgress all the ordinances of the Torah under threat of being put to death, he may do so with the exception of those relating to idolatry, immorality, and bloodshed' (Sanh. 74a).

The Rabbis also had occasion to defend the monotheistic view of God against attack from the early Christians who sought a foundation for their trinitarian doctrine in the text of the Hebrew Bible. The principal passage bearing on the subject reads: 'The *Minim* [1] asked R. Simlai, "How many gods created the Universe?" He answered: "Let us consult the former days; for it is written, 'Ask now of the former days which were before thee, since the day that God [2] created man upon the earth' (Deut. iv. 32). It is not written here 'created' as a verb in the plural, but in the singular, denoting therefore a singular subject. The same answer applies to Genesis i. 1."

'R. Simlai said: "In every place where you find a text which is used by the *Minim* in support of their opinions, you will find the refutation by its side." They returned and asked him: "What of that which is written, 'Let *us* make man in *our* image, after *our* likeness' (Gen. i. 26)?" He answered: "Read what follows: it is not said, 'And gods created man in their image,' but 'And God created man in His own image.'" When they had departed, his disciples said to him: "You have thrust them aside with a reed; what answer will you give us?" He said to them: "In the past Adam was created from the dust of the ground and Eve was created from Adam. Henceforward it is to be 'in our image, after our likeness'—meaning, man will not be able to come into existence without woman, nor woman without man, nor both without the *Shechinah*."' [3]

[1] The word denotes 'sectaries' and usually refers to Christians. On the whole subject see R. T. Herford, *Christianity in Talmud and Midrash*, and on the passage quoted above, pp. 255 ff. of that scholarly work.
[2] The Hebrew word for 'God,' *Elohim*, has a plural form.
[3] On the *Shechinah*, see pp. 42 ff. The Rabbi explained 'our' to mean God in addition to man and woman; i.e. each human being is formed by three parents. For this doctrine of the human being's threefold parentage, see p. 22.

'They returned and asked him: "What is that which is written, 'The Lord, the God of gods, the Lord, the God of gods,[1] He knoweth' (Josh. xxii. 22)?" He answered: "It is not written 'they know' but 'He knoweth.'" His disciples (after their departure) said to him: "You have thrust them aside with a reed; what answer will you give us?" He said to them: "The three of them are a Divine name; just as a person refers to a king as Basileus, Caesar, and Augustus"' (Gen. R. viii. 9).

Religious polemic also underlies this piece of commentary: 'The Holy One, blessed be He, said, "I am the first" (Is. xliv. 6) for I have no father; "and I am the last" for I have no brother; "and beside me there is no God" for I have no son' (Exod. R. xxix. 5).

Since monotheism was the important characteristic dogma of Judaism which distinguished it from the other religions of that age, we have the declaration: 'Whoever repudiates idolatry is accounted a Jew' (Meg. 13a).

§ III. INCORPOREALITY

Closely bound up with the doctrine of God's Unity was the teaching that He has no bodily form. To account for the numerous passages in the Bible where physical organs are attributed to Him, the Rabbis remarked: 'We borrow terms from His creatures to apply to Him in order to assist the understanding' (Mech. to xix. 18; 65a).[2]

To assist the comprehension of the place of the incorporeal God in the Universe, an analogy is drawn from the incorporeal part of the human being—the soul. 'As the Holy One, blessed be He, fills the whole world, so also the soul fills the whole body. As the Holy One, blessed be He, sees but cannot be seen, so also the soul sees but cannot be seen. As the Holy One, blessed be He, nourishes the whole world, so also the soul nourishes the whole body. As the Holy One, blessed be He, is pure, so also the soul is pure. As the Holy One, blessed be He, dwells in the inmost part of the Universe, so also the soul dwells in the inmost part of the body' (Ber. 10a).

'In the same manner that nobody knows the place of the soul, so does nobody know the place of the Holy One, blessed be He.

---

[1] In the Hebrew text there are three designations of God: *El, Elohim,* and *JHVH,* which were understood by the early Christians as pointing to a trinity.

[2] There is another Talmudic maxim to the effect, 'The Torah speaks according to the language of the sons of man' (Ber. 31b); and it is frequently quoted to explain the Biblical anthropomorphisms. This is incorrect, since the words apply always to the idiomatic structure of a Scriptural phrase.

Even the holy *Chayyoth* [1] which bear the Throne of Glory do not know where is His place and therefore exclaim: "Blessed be the glory of the Lord from His place" (Ezek. iii. 12).[2] It happened that somebody asked R. Gamaliel where the Holy One, blessed be He, was located. He replied: "I do not know." The other said to him: "This is your wisdom that you daily offer prayer to Him without knowing where He is!" R. Gamaliel answered him: "You have questioned me concerning One Who is remote from me a distance corresponding to a journey of three thousand five hundred years.[3] Let me question you about something which is with you day and night and tell me where it is—I refer to your soul!" The man said: "I do not know." Then the Rabbi retorted: "May you perish! You cannot tell me the place of something which is actually with you; and you ask me about One Who is remote from me a distance corresponding to a journey of three thousand five hundred years!" The man thereupon said: "We act well, because we worship the works of our hands which we can always see." "Yes," was the reply, "you can see the works of your hands but they cannot see you. The Holy One, blessed be He, sees the works of His hands but they cannot see Him!"' (Midrash to Ps. ciii. 1; 217a).

Despite the insistence on the incorporeality of God, Rabbinic literature contains numerous passages which rather startle the reader by reason of their strong anthropomorphic ascriptions. He is said to wear the phylacteries (Ber. 6a) and wrap Himself in the *Tallit* or praying-shawl (R.H. 17b); He offers prayer to Himself and studies the Torah during three hours of the day (A.Z. 3b); He weeps over the failings of His creatures (Chag. 5b), and much more of a similar character. He is likewise depicted as performing certain deeds which would be considered meritorious in a human being. He interested Himself in the marriage of Adam and Eve, acting as groomsman to the former and plaiting the bride's hair to adorn her for her husband (Ber. 61a). He visits the sick, sympathizes with the mourner and buries the dead (Gen. R. VIII. 13).

However these passages be explained, it is impossible to maintain that their authors believed in a corporeal God Who actually performed the actions ascribed to Him. One scholar accounts for

---

[1] The celestial 'creatures' referred to in Ezekiel's vision (chaps. i and x). See below, pp. 31, 40.

[2] They use the vague term 'from His place,' because they are ignorant of His exact location.

[3] God was thought of as dwelling in the highest, i.e. the seventh, heaven, and the distance between each heaven would take five hundred years to traverse. See pp. 40 f.

them as 'the humanizing of the Deity and endowing Him with all the qualities and attributes which tend towards making God accessible to man.'[1] More probably the thought behind them is the doctrine of imitation. As will be shown later,[2] the Imitation of God is a cardinal principle of human conduct in Rabbinic ethics, and it applies to the whole of life—to religious observances as well as to moral conduct. God is accordingly represented as Himself obeying the precepts which He desires Israel to observe.

This theory is supported by the statement: 'The attributes of the Holy One, blessed be He, are unlike those of a human being. The latter instructs others what they are to do but may not practise it himself. Not so is the Holy One, blessed be He; whatever He does He commands Israel to perform' (Exod. R. xxx. 9).

§ IV. Omnipresence

A corollary of God's incorporeality is His omnipresence. A finite body must be located in space, but to the infinite Spirit space is meaningless. 'With an earthly king, when he is in the bed-chamber he cannot be in the reception-hall; but the Holy One, blessed be He, fills the upper regions and the lower. As it is said, "His glory is over the earth and heaven" (Ps. cxlviii. 13)—simul-taneously; and it is written, "Do not I fill the heaven and the earth?" (Jer. xxiii. 24)' (Midrash to Ps. xxiv. 5; 103a).

A common term for the Deity in Rabbinic literature is 'the Place,' which originates in the doctrine: 'The Holy One, blessed be He, is the place of His Universe, but His Universe is not His place' (Gen. R. lxviii. 9), i.e. He encompasses space but space does not encompass Him.

The omnipresence of God is finely taught in the following anec-dote: 'A ship, belonging to a heathen owner, was once sailing over the sea, one of the passengers being a Jewish boy. A great storm arose, and all the Gentiles aboard took hold of their idols and prayed to them, but to no avail. Seeing that their prayers had been in vain, they said to the lad: "Call upon your God, for we have heard that He answers your petitions when you cry to Him and that He is all-powerful." The boy immediately stood up and called with all his heart upon God, Who hearkened to his prayer, and the sea became calm. On reaching land, they disembarked to purchase their requirements and said to him: "Do you not wish to buy anything?" He answered: "What do you want of a poor

[1] Schechter, *Aspects of Rabbinic Theology*, pp. 36 ff.
[2] See pp. 210 ff.

alien like me?" They exclaimed: "You a poor alien! We are
the poor aliens; for some of us are here and have our gods in
Babylon; others have them in Rome; others have their gods with
them but they are of no benefit to us. As for you, however,
wherever you go your God is with you!"' (p. Ber. 13*b*).

There is also an anecdote about a Gentile who asked a Rabbi:
'What purpose did your God have in speaking with Moses from
the midst of a bush?' He answered: 'To teach that there is no
place void of the Divine Presence, not even so lowly a thing as a
bush' (Exod. R. II. 5). The saying is attributed to God: 'In
every place where you find the imprint of men's feet there am I'
(Mech. to xvii. 6; 52*b*).

The Talmud offers this demonstration of divine omnipresence:
'The messengers of God are unlike those of men. The messengers
of men are obliged to return to those who sent them with the
object of their mission; but God's messengers return at the place
whither they had been dispatched. It is written: "Canst thou
send forth lightnings, that they may go and say unto thee, Here
we are?" (Job xxxviii. 35). It is not stated "they return" but
"they go and say," i.e. wherever they go they are in the presence
of God. Hence it is to be deduced that the *Shechinah* is in every
place' (Mech. to xii. 1; 2*a*; B.B. 25*a*).

The question how God could be everywhere at the same time
received various answers. The problem was elucidated by this
analogy: 'It may be likened to a cave situated by the seashore.
The sea rages and the cave is filled with water, but the waters of
the sea are not diminished. Similarly the Tent of Meeting was
filled with the lustre of the *Shechinah*, which was not diminished
in the Universe' (Num. R. XII. 4).

Other solutions that were suggested find illustration in such
stories as these. 'A Samaritan asked R. Meïr: "How is it possible
to accept the statement of Scripture, 'Do not I fill heaven and
earth?' (Jer. xxiii. 24)? Did He not speak with Moses between
the two staves of the Ark?" He told him to bring large mirrors
and said: "Look at your reflection in them." He saw it magnified.
He next asked him to bring small mirrors and look into them, and
he saw his reflection diminished in size. R. Meïr then said: "If
you, a mere mortal, can change your appearance at will, how much
more so can He Who spake and the world came into being!"'
(Gen. R. IV. 4). Another Rabbi declared: 'At times the Universe
and its fullness are insufficient to contain the glory of God's
Divinity; at other times He speaks with man between the hairs
of his head' (ibid.).

'A heretic said to R. Gamaliel: "You Rabbis declare that where-ever ten people assemble for worship [1] the *Shechinah* abides amongst them; how many *Shechinahs* are there then?' He called the heretic's servant and struck him with a ladle. "Why did you strike him?" he was asked, and he replied, "Because the sun is in the house of an infidel." "But the sun shines all over the world!" exclaimed the heretic; and the Rabbi retorted: "If the sun, which is only one out of a million myriads of God's servants, can be in every part of the world, how much more so can the *Shechinah* radiate throughout the entire Universe!"' (Sanh. 39*a*).

A reason why such emphasis was laid upon the idea of Divine omnipresence was to impress the human being with the conscious-ness that he was always under the supervision of God. 'Reflect upon three things,' taught R. Judah, the redactor of the Mishnah, 'and you will never fall into the power of sin: Know what is above you—a seeing eye, and a hearing ear, and all your deeds are recorded' (Aboth II. 1).

The doctrine is impressively enunciated in the exhortation which R. Jochanan b. Zakkai addressed to his disciples on his death-bed. He said to them: 'May it be His will that the fear of Heaven be upon you as great as the fear of flesh and blood.' They exclaimed: 'Only as great!' He replied: 'Would that it be as great; for know ye, when a man intends to commit a transgression, he says, "I hope nobody will see me"' (Ber. 28*b*). The thought, then, that man is always under observation by God should be a powerful deterrent against sinning.

That it is impossible to escape the Divine Presence is illustrated by a conversation between R. José and a Roman matron who said to him: 'My god is greater than yours, because when your God revealed Himself to Moses in the burning bush, he hid his face; but when he saw the serpent, which is my god, he fled from before it!' (Exod. iv. 3). The Rabbi replied: 'At the time that our God revealed Himself to Moses in the bush, there was no place to which he could flee, since He is everywhere; but as for the serpent, which is your god, a man has only to step back two or three paces in order to escape it!' (Exod. R. III. 12).

§ V. Omnipotence

God was naturally thought of as the all-mighty Power and He is frequently denominated 'the Might.' The Rabbis ordained that 'on beholding shooting-stars, earthquakes, thunders, storms, and

[1] The quorum required for a congregational service.

lightnings, the benediction to be uttered is, Blessed art thou, O Lord our God, King of the Universe, Whose strength and might fill the world' (Ber. IX. 2).

Generally speaking, no limit was set upon the Divine power. 'The attribute of human beings is unlike that of God. A human being cannot say two things at the same time; but the Holy One, blessed be He, uttered the Ten Commandments simultaneously. A human being cannot listen to the cries of two men at the same time, but the Holy One, blessed be He, hearkens even to the cries of all who enter the world' (Mech. to XV. 11; 41b).

An oft-quoted Rabbinic principle is, 'Everything is in the power of Heaven except the fear of Heaven' (Ber. 33b), which indicates that God determines the fortunes of the individual, but not whether he will be God-fearing or not. That is left to his own choice.

That He performed miracles was never questioned, their purpose being 'to sanctify His great name in the world' (Sifré Deut. § 306; 132b). But there was a desire to avoid interpreting miraculous occurrences as departures from the natural order of the Universe, since they might otherwise be taken as evidence that the Creation was imperfect. It was therefore taught that the miracles recorded by Scripture were preordained from the beginning of the world. 'At the Creation God made a condition with the sea that it should be divided for the passage of the children of Israel, with the sun and moon to stand still at the bidding of Joshua, with the ravens to feed Elijah, with fire not to injure Hananiah, Mishael, and Azariah, with the lions not to harm Daniel, and with the fish to spew out Jonah' (Gen. R. v. 5).

The same thought underlies the statement: 'Ten things were created on the eve of the (first) Sabbath in the twilight:[1] the mouth of the earth (Num. xvi. 32); the mouth of the well (ibid. xxi. 16); the mouth of the ass (ibid. xxii. 28); the rainbow; the manna; the rod (Exod. iv. 17); the Shamir;[2] the shape of the written characters; the writing, and the tables of stone' (Aboth v. 9).

After the destruction of the Temple and State by the Romans, the calamities which had befallen the Jews aroused doubts in the minds of some of them regarding Divine omnipotence. Such a feeling appears to motive the saying: 'If He is Master of all works

---

[1] 'All phenomena that seemed to partake at once of the natural and supernatural were conceived as having had their origin in the interval between the close of the work of Creation and commencement of the Sabbath' (Singer's note, *Authorised Daily Prayer Book*, p. 200).

[2] Since no iron tool was to be used in the construction of the Temple, tradition relates that Solomon made use of a worm, called Shamir, which split any stone over which it crawled.

as He is Master over us, we will serve Him; if not, we will not serve Him. If He can supply our needs we will serve Him, otherwise we will not serve Him' (Mech. to xvii. 7; 52b).

An apologetic purpose obviously prompted the following extracts, which offer a defence of the dogma of God's omnipotence. 'It is related that when Trajan put Julian and his brother Pappos to death in Laodicea, he said to them: "If you are of the people of Hananiah, Mishael, and Azariah, let your God come and rescue you from my hand in the same way that He rescued them from the hand of Nebuchadnezzar." They replied: "Those men were perfectly righteous and worthy that a miracle should be wrought for them; and Nebuchadnezzar was likewise an honourable king and worthy that a miracle should be wrought through him. You, however, are ignoble and unworthy of being made the medium of a miracle. As for us, we have been condemned to death by God; and if you are not our executioner, God has many others to slay us. He has many bears, leopards, or lions to attack and kill us; but He has only delivered us into your hand so as to avenge our blood upon you"' (Taan. 18b).

'Have you ever heard of the sun being ill and unable to dawn and function? To God's servants we cannot ascribe ailments which induce weakness, so how can we ascribe such to Him? The matter may be likened to a warrior who resided in a city and the inhabitants relied upon him, saying: "So long as he is with us, no troops will attack us." Occasionaly troops did march against the city; but as soon as he showed his face they fled. Once, however, there was an assault, but he said: "My right hand is afflicted with weakness!" With the Holy One, blessed be He, it is not so: "Behold, the Lord's hand is not shortened that it cannot save" (Is. lix. 1)' (Lament. R. I. 2. § 23).

'The Jewish Elders in Rome were asked: "If your God takes no pleasure in idolatry, why does He not make an end of it?" They answered: "If people worshipped things of which the world was not in need, He would do so; but they worship the sun, the moon, and stars. Should He destroy His Universe for the sake of fools?" They said to them: "If that is so, let Him destroy that which is useless to the world and leave whatever is essential." They replied: "In that event we should but strengthen the hands of those who worship these latter objects, because they would be able to assert that these must be deities inasmuch as they had not been brought to an end"' (A.Z. IV. 7).

§ VI. OMNISCIENCE

As with God's might, so His knowledge was declared to be limitless. The Biblical doctrine that He is all-knowing is developed to its utmost extent in the teachings of the Rabbis.

'Who beholds a crowd of people should utter the benediction, Blessed is He Who is wise in secrets. Just as faces differ one from another, so are minds also different, but God knows them all' (p. Ber. 13c). 'All is revealed and known before Him, as it is said: "He knoweth what is in the darkness, and the light dwelleth with Him" (Dan. ii. 22)' (Mech. to xii. 23; 12a).

The conception that nothing is hidden from His ken is abundantly illustrated. 'It is like an architect who built a city with its inner chambers, underground channels, and caves. After a time he was appointed the collector of taxes. When the citizens hid their wealth in these secret places, he said to them: "It was I who constructed these secret places, so how can you conceal your possessions from me?" Similarly: "Woe unto them that seek deep to hide their counsel from the Lord, and their works are in the dark, and they say, Who seeth us? and who knoweth us?" (Is. xxix. 15)' (Gen. R. XXIV. 1).

'Although God is in the heavens, His eyes behold and search the sons of man. Parable of a king who had an orchard. He built in it a high tower, and commanded that workmen should be appointed to work in the orchard. They who work faithfully shall receive full payment, and they who are slack shall be penalized' (Exod. R. II. 2). From the high tower the king could supervise the men who worked for him and judge the quality of their labour. Similarly from the heights of Heaven He oversees the actions of His creatures.

The supernatural character of the Divine knowledge is vividly taught in such dicta as these: 'Before even a creature is formed in his mother's womb his thought is already revealed to God' (Gen. R. IX. 3); 'Before even a thought is created in man's heart it is already revealed to God' (ibid.); 'Before even a man speaks, He knows what is in his heart' (Exod. R. XXI. 3).

Inextricably connected with the attribute of omniscience is foreknowledge. God knows all that will be in addition to all that is and has been. 'Everything is foreseen' (Aboth III. 19), was the dictum of R. Akiba, and it is part of the Talmudic doctrine. 'All is foreseen before the Holy One, blessed be He' (Tanchuma Shelach § 9); 'God knows what is to be in the future' (Sanh. 90b).

In numerous passages He is described as foreseeing that an event would happen long before it actually transpired. Some instances are: 'If the Holy One, blessed be He, had not foreseen (at the Creation) that after the passing of twenty-six generations Israel would accept the Torah, he would not have written in it [1] such phrases as "Command the children of Israel," or "Speak unto the children of Israel"' (Gen. R. i. 4). 'Only the sun was created for the purpose of giving light to the world. If so, why was the moon created? It teaches that the Holy One, blessed be He, foresaw that idolaters would make them as deities; He therefore said: "Since when there are two of them, one denying the other, idolaters make them as deities, how much more would they do so if there were only one!"' (ibid. vi. 1). 'Why is the narrative of the twelve spies immediately preceded by the account of the slander of Moses by Miriam (Num. xii. f.)? It was foreseen before the Holy One, blessed be He, that the spies would utter a slanderous report concerning the land; so to avoid their being able to plead that they were unaware of the penalty of slander, He attached the one incident to the other for the purpose of letting everybody know what is its punishment' (Tanchuma Shelach § 5).

From the theory of miracles referred to in the preceding section it follows that the Rabbis believed that God foresaw the history of the world even at the time it was created. This teaching is explicitly enunciated. 'From the beginning of Creation, the Holy One, blessed be He, foresaw the deeds of the righteous and the wicked' (Gen. R. ii. 5). How this dogma bears on the idea of Free Will a later section of this work will show.[2]

The Rabbis had sometimes to defend this belief against hostile critics, as the following dialogue between a heretic and a Rabbi demonstrates. 'Do you assert that God foresees what is to happen?' 'Certainly.' 'How, then, is it written in the Scriptures, "It repented the Lord that He had made man on the earth, and it grieved Him at His heart" (Gen. vi. 6)?' 'Has there ever been a son born to you?' 'Yes.' 'What did you do at his birth?' 'I rejoiced and made it an occasion of rejoicing for others.' 'But did you not know that a time would come when he would have to die?' 'That is so; but in a time of joy let there be joy, and in a time of mourning let there be mourning.' 'So did it happen with the Holy One, blessed be He. God mourned for seven days [3] over the fate of His Universe before bringing the flood' (Gen. R. xxvii. 4).

---

[1] This is based on the theory that the Torah existed before the world was created. See p. 132.

[2] See p. 94.

[3] This is the period of time prescribed by Judaism for mourning a bereavement.

§ VII. ETERNITY

Time has no meaning in relationship to God. In His capacity as Creator of the Universe He must necessarily have been the first, and He will also be the last in time, continuing in existence when all else has passed away. 'Everything decays but Thou dost not decay' (Lev. R. XIX. 2), declared a Rabbi of the Deity. By a play on the word (*en*) *biltéka*, 'there is none beside Thee' (1 Sam. ii. 2), the consonants of which can be read as (*en*) *balloteka*, the sense was derived, 'There is none to outlast Thee,' and the comment was added, 'Not like the attribute of man is the attribute of God. With man his works outlive him; but the Holy One, blessed be He, outlives His works' (Meg. 14*a*).

'God's seal is truth,' runs a Rabbinic maxim; and it was pointed out that as the consonants of the word for 'truth,' viz. AMT, are respectively the first, middle, and final letters of the Hebrew alphabet, they indicated that He is the first, middle, and last in time (Gen. R. LXXXI. 2).

The contrast is also frequently drawn between 'a human king who to-day is here and to-morrow in the grave' and 'the King of kings Who lives and endures for all eternity' (Ber. 28*b*). The addition of the words 'before Me' in the Second Commandment was explained thus: 'The purpose is to teach that as I live and endure for all eternity, so you and your offspring until the end of all generations are forbidden to worship idols' (Mech. to xx. 3; 67*b*).

A parable relates: 'A human king once entered a city and all the inhabitants came out to applaud him. Their acclamation pleased him so much that he said to them: "To-morrow I will erect various kinds of baths for you. To-morrow I will provide you with a water-conduit." He went away to sleep, but never rose again. Where is he or his promise? But with the Holy One, blessed be He, it is otherwise; because He is a God Who lives and reigns for ever' (Lev. R. XXVI. 1).

Another parable concerns 'a person who lost his son and went to inquire for him in a cemetery. A wise man saw him and asked, "Is the son you have lost alive or dead?" He answered, "He is alive." Then said the other, "You fool! Is it the way to inquire for the dead among the living or the living among the dead? Surely it is always the practice of the living to attend to the needs of the dead, not vice versa!" So is it with our God Who lives and endures for all eternity; as it is said, "The Lord is the true God; He is the living God and an everlasting king" (Jer. x. 10); but the gods of the idolaters are lifeless things. Shall we, then forsake Him Who lives for ever and worship dead objects?' (Lev. R. VI. 6).

Noteworthy in this connection is the comment on 'The enemy are come to an end, they are desolate for ever' (Ps. ix. 6), which is explained as follows: 'The enemy are come to an end, their structures [1] are for ever. For instance, Constantine built Constantinople, Apulus built Apulia,[2] Romulus built Rome, Alexander built Alexandria, Seleucus built Seleucia. The founders have come to an end, but the cities they established endure. As for Thee, if one may say so, "The cities which Thou hast overthrown, their very memorial is perished" (ibid.). This refers to Jerusalem and Zion, as it is written, "Thy holy cities are become a wilderness, Zion is become a wilderness, Jerusalem a desolation" (Is. lxiv. 10). "But the Lord sitteth enthroned for ever" (Ps. ix. 7)—the Holy One, blessed be He, will restore them. (The builders of the cities) were only human and they come to an end and are cut off; likewise the cities which they founded will be destroyed for ever. The Lord, however, Who exists and endures for all eternity, "sitteth enthroned for ever, and hath prepared His throne for judgment." He will rebuild Jerusalem, Zion, and the cities of Judah; as it is said, "At that time they shall call Jerusalem the throne of the Lord" (Jer. iii. 17)' (Midrash to Ps. ix. 6 (Heb. 7); 43a, b).

§ VIII. JUSTICE AND MERCY

The first Hebrew patriarch addressed the Deity as 'the Judge of the whole earth' (Gen. xviii. 25), and the Talmud regards Him in the same light. As the Creator of the world and of the human race, He holds His creatures to account for the manner of their living.

His judgments are always just. 'With Him there is no unrighteousness, nor forgetfulness, nor respect of persons, nor taking of bribes' (Aboth IV. 29). R. Jochanan b. Zakkai, on his deathbed, told his disciples that he was about to be judged by One 'Whom I cannot appease with (flattering) words nor bribe with money' (Ber. 28b).

Nor is there anything arbitrary about His decisions. A Roman matron said to a Rabbi: 'Your God draws near to Himself whomever He likes, without regard to justice!' He set before her a

---

[1] This is evidently the sense in which the Midrash understood the word rendered 'desolate.' Daiches has shown that there are several passages in the Old Testament where choraboth must mean 'cities, palaces,' and not 'ruins.' See the *Jewish Quarterly Review* (old series) xx, pp. 637 ff.

[2] The correct reading is probably: Philip (of Macedon) built Philippi.

basket of figs, from which she kept picking and eating the choicest. He said to her: 'You know how to make a wise selection, and would you assert that the Holy One, blessed be He, does not? He chooses and draws near unto Himself the person whose acts are good' (Num. R. III. 2).

In the Rabbinic literature an eternal conflict is represented as being waged between God's justice and mercy. There is scarcely a passage which refers to His capacity as Judge which does not also allude to His attribute of compassion.

The divine appellation *Elohim*, translated 'God,' was understood to denote His aspect of judgment and JHVH, translated 'Lord,' His aspect of mercy (Gen. R. XXXIII. 3), and the combination of the two names in the verse, 'These are the generations of the heaven and earth when they were created, in the day that the Lord God (JHVH *Elohim*) made earth and heaven' (Gen. ii. 4) is explained as follows: 'It may be likened to a king who had empty vessels. The king said, "If I put hot water into them they will crack; if I put icy cold water into them they will contract." What did the king do? He mixed the hot with the cold and poured the mixture into the vessels, and they endured. Similarly said the Holy One, blessed be He, "If I create the world only with the attribute of mercy, sins will multiply beyond all bounds; if I create it only with the attribute of justice, how can the world last? Behold, I will create it with both attributes; would that it might endure!"' (Gen. R. XII. 15).

Indeed, it was only because the quality of mercy prevailed at Creation that the human race was allowed to come into being. 'When the Holy One, blessed be He, came to create the first man, He foresaw that both righteous and wicked would issue from him. He said, "If I create him, wicked men will issue from him; if I do not create him, how can righteous men spring from him?' What did He do? He removed the way of the wicked from before Him, allied the attribute of mercy with Himself and created him' (Gen. R. VIII. 4).

If compassion was the deciding cause of Creation, its victory over stern justice is the reason of the world's continuance in the face of wickedness. 'There were ten generations from Adam to Noah, to make known how long-suffering God is, seeing that all those generations continued to provoke Him before He brought upon them the waters of the flood' (Aboth v. 2).

When Abraham addressed his plea to God, 'Shall not the Judge of all the earth do justly?' the meaning of his words was: 'If You desire the world to continue there cannot be strict justice;

if You insist on strict justice, the world cannot endure' (Gen. R. xxxix. 6).

The Hebrew expression for divine forbearance is not *erech af* but *erech apayim*, the second word having a dual form. This was explained as denoting that God is not long-suffering with the righteous only but equally with the wicked (B.K. 50*b*). The Bible relates that when God revealed His attributes to Moses, he 'made haste and bowed his head toward the earth and worshipped' (Exod. xxxiv. 8). To the question, What overwhelmed him so much? the answer is given, 'The recognition of the Divine forbearance' (Sanh. 111*a*).

The apparent victory of evil over good in the world was understood as the manifestation of His mercy. 'Moses described God as "great, mighty, and terrible" (Deut. x. 17). Jeremiah referred to Him only as "the great and mighty God" (xxxii. 18), because, said he, where are His terrible acts, seeing that heathens dance in His Temple? Daniel referred to Him only as "the great and terrible God" (ix. 4), because, said he, where are His mighty acts, seeing that heathens enslave His children? Then came the men of the Great Assembly [1] and restored all the attributes (see Nehem. ix. 32); for they said: "On the contrary, this is the greatest manifestation of His might that He subdues His anger and shows long-suffering with the wicked; and it is likewise the manifestation of His terrible acts, without which how could a single nation be allowed to continue in existence?"' (Joma 69*b*).

'The attribute of grace,' it was taught, 'exceeds that of punishment (i.e. justice) by five-hundredfold.' This conclusion was deduced from the fact that in connection with punishment God described Himself as 'visiting the iniquity of the fathers upon the children unto the third and fourth generation' (Exod. xx. 5); but in connection with grace it is said: 'And showing mercy unto the thousandth generation' (ibid. 6). The last phrase is, in the Hebrew, *alafim*, which is literally 'thousands' and must indicate at least two thousand. Retribution, therefore, extends at most to four generations, whereas mercy extends to at least two thousand generations (Tosifta Sot. iv. 1).

'Even in the time of His anger He remembers mercy,' declares the Talmud (Pes. 87*b*); and He is actually depicted as praying to Himself that His compassion should overcome His wrath. This thought gave rise to the bold flight of imagination contained in the following passage: 'R. Jochanan said in the name of R. José: Whence is it known that the Holy One, blessed be He, prays?

[1] See Introduction, pp. xviii f.

As it is said, "Even them will I bring to My holy mountain, and make them joyful in My house of prayer"[1] (Is. lvi. 7). It is not said, "their prayer" but "My prayer"; hence we infer that the Holy One, blessed be He, prays. What does He pray? R. Zotra b. Tobiah said in the name of Rab: "May it be My will that My mercy may subdue My wrath; and may My mercy prevail over My attribute of justice, so that I may deal with My children in the quality of mercy and enter on their behalf within the line of strict justice."

'There is a teaching: R. Ishmael b. Elisha said, Once I entered the Holy of Holies to offer incense in the innermost part of the Sanctuary, and I saw Okteriël,[2] Jah, the Lord of Hosts, seated upon a high and exalted throne. He said to me, "Ishmael, My son, bless Me." I replied, "May it be Thy will that Thy mercy may subdue Thy wrath; and may Thy mercy prevail over Thy attribute of justice, so that Thou mayest deal with Thy children in the quality of mercy and enter on their behalf within the line of strict justice' (Ber. 7a).

In the same strain it is declared: 'During three hours of each day He sits and judges the whole world. When He sees that the world is deserving of being destroyed because of the prevalent evil, He arises from the throne of justice and sits upon the throne of mercy' (A.Z. 3b).

Much use is made of the prophetic doctrine, 'I have no pleasure in the death of the wicked, but that the wicked turn from his way and live' (Ezek xxxiii. 11). Upon it is based the theory of Repentance which occupies so prominent a place in Rabbinic thought.[3] The idea is beautifully expressed in the statement, 'Not like the attribute of the Holy One, blessed be He, is the attribute of man. When a man is conquered he grieves; when the Holy One, blessed be He, is conquered, so that He averts His wrath and can display mercy, He rejoices' (Pes. 119a).

The divine compassion is evidenced by extreme eagerness to save man from condemnation. 'Though nine hundred and ninety-nine angels attest for a man's conviction and only one angel attests for his defence, the Holy One, blessed be He, inclines the scales in his favour' (p. Kid. 61d). When, however, He is compelled by justice to exact punishment from evil-doers, He does so with regret and

---

[1] The Hebrew is literally 'the house of My prayer.'
[2] A Divine Name usually explained as a combination of kéter 'throne' and el 'God.' Ishmael b. Elisha, according to tradition, was identical with Ishmael b. Phabi, one of the last of the High Priests before the destruction of the Second Temple.
[3] See pp. 104 ff.

pain. Noble expression is given to this thought in the legend that at the overthrow of the Egyptians by the Red Sea, the ministering angels wished to offer a song of triumph to God; but He checked them, saying: 'The work of My hands is drowned in the sea, and you would offer Me a song!' (Sanh. 39b).

While believing, therefore, that He is the Judge of the Universe, the Rabbis delighted in calling Him *Rachmana* (the Merciful), and taught that 'the world is judged by grace' (Aboth III. 19).

§ IX. FATHERHOOD

Throughout the utterances of the Talmudic Sages, the relationship which exists between the Creator and His creatures is conceived under the image of Father and children. God is constantly addressed, or referred to, as 'Father Who is in heaven.' One Rabbinic maxim, for example, exhorts: 'Be strong as a leopard, light as an eagle, fleet as a hart, and strong as a lion, to do the will of your Father Who is in heaven' (Aboth v. 23). And it was considered a mark of exceptional grace on His part that this intimate relationship exists and was revealed to man. 'Beloved are Israel, for they were called children of the All-present; but it was by special love that it was made known to them that they were called children of the All-present; as it is said, "Ye are children of the Lord your God" (Deut. xiv. 1)' (Aboth III. 18). Although this dictum specifies Israel, it being based on a Biblical passage, the doctrine of Fatherhood was not restricted to one people and was extended to all human beings.[1]

Difference of opinion existed as to whether this precious boon is bestowed upon man conditionally or unconditionally. On the text 'Ye are children of the Lord your God,' R. Judah commented: 'At the time that you conduct yourselves as dutiful children, you are called God's children; but when you do not so conduct yourselves, you are not called God's children. R. Meïr, on the other hand, declared that in either case the name of "God's children" applied; and he urged in favour of his contention that in the Scriptures there occur such phrases as "they are sottish children" (Jer. iv. 22) and "children in whom is no faith" (Deut. xxxii. 20), thus proving that although they were unworthy they were still called "children"' (Kid. 36a).

In addressing the people of Israel, God is accredited with these words: 'All the miracles and mighty acts which I performed for you were not with the object that you should give Me a reward,

[1] See pp. 22 and 67.

but that you should honour Me like dutiful children and call Me your Father' (Exod. R. XXXII. 5).

Especially when in the act of prayer, the individual was exhorted to think of himself as addressing his petitions to One Who stood to him in the relationship of Father. It is recorded that 'the pious men of old used to wait an hour in silent meditation and then offer their prayer, in order to direct their heart to their Father in heaven' (Ber. v. 1).

One of the earliest prayers in the Hebrew liturgy [1] opens with the words: 'With great love hast Thou loved us, O Lord our God, with great and exceeding pity hast Thou pitied us. Our Father, our King, for our fathers' sake, who trusted in Thee, and whom Thou didst teach the statutes of life, be also gracious unto us and teach us.' A prayer, offered by R. Akiba in a time of drought, has been preserved and reads: 'Our Father, our King, we have sinned before Thee. Our Father, our King, we have no king beside Thee. Our Father, our King, have compassion upon us' (Taan. 25b).

The familiarity of the conception of the divine Fatherhood is particularly evidenced by its frequency in Rabbinic parables and similes. To account for the difference of phraseology between the words addressed to Abraham, 'Walk *before* Me' (Gen. xvii. 1) and the description of Noah who 'walked *with* God' (ibid. vi. 9), we have the parable of a prince who had two children, one grown up and the other young. To the little child he says: 'Walk with me'; but to the big one he says: 'Walk before me' (Gen. R. xxx. 10).

On the text, 'And the angel of God, which went before the camp of Israel, removed and went behind them' (Exod. xiv. 19), there is the parable of a man who was walking by the way, having with him his child whom he allowed to proceed in front. Brigands came to kidnap the child; so the father took him from in front and placed him behind. A wolf appeared in the rear; so he took the child from behind and again placed him in front. Afterwards brigands came in front and wolves behind; so he took the child up and carried him in his arms. The child began to be troubled by the glare of the sun, and the father spread his own garment over him. The child hungered and the father fed him; he thirsted and the father gave him to drink. So did God act toward Israel when he was delivered from Egypt (Mech. ad loc.; 30a).

Another parable, pointing the same moral, tells: 'A king's son fell into evil ways. The king sent his tutor to him with the message, "Return, O my son." But the son sent to his father the

[1] Referred to by name, i.e. its opening words, in Ber. 11b.

reply: "With what can I return? I am ashamed to come before
you." Then the father sent to him, saying: "Can a son be ashamed
to return to his father? If you return, do you not return to your
father?"' (Deut. R. II. 24).

The doctrine of Fatherhood reaches its culminating point in the
teaching that God participates in the formation of the human
being. 'There are three partners in the production of the human
being: the Holy One, blessed be He, the father and the mother.
The father provides the white matter from which are formed the
bones, sinews, nails, brain, and the white part of the eye; the
mother provides the red matter from which are formed the skin,
flesh, hair, and pupil of the eye; and the Holy One, blessed be He,
infuses into him breath, soul, features, vision, hearing, speech,
power of motion, understanding, and intelligence' (Nid. 31a). This
means that the parents create only the physical part of the human
being; but all the faculties and that which constitutes personality
are an endowment from the heavenly Father.

The Fatherhood of God is synonymous with His love for the
human family. Every creature is living proof that the Father of
all is a God of love. The best expression of this idea is found in
the aphorism of R. Akiba: 'Beloved is man, for he was created in
the image of God; but it was by a special love that it was made
known to him that he was created in the image of God; as it is
said, "For in the image of God made He man"' (Aboth III. 18).

§ X. HOLINESS AND PERFECTION

To the Rabbis the idea of God was not a metaphysical abstrac-
tion but the very foundation of right human living. As already
mentioned, idolatry was synonymous with immorality and a
degraded standard of life. Conversely, belief in God was the
inspiration of a lofty plane of thought and action. It will be
shown later that the doctrine of *imitatio Dei*,[1] the Imitation of
God, lies at the root of Talmudic ethics.

The characteristic term which distinguishes the Deity from this
point of view is 'holiness.' It implies apartness from everything
that defiles as well as actual perfection. The Rabbinic Jew always
thought of God as 'the Holy One, blessed be He,' that being the
commonest of all the names ascribed to Him.

Both the divine holiness and its meaning for human beings are
emphasized in this passage: 'The Holy One, blessed be He, says to
man, "Behold, I am pure, My abode is pure, My ministers are

[1] See pp. 210 ff.

pure, and the soul I give you is pure. If you return it to Me in the same state of purity that I give it to you, well and good; if not, I will destroy it before you"' (Lev. R. xviii. 1).

But the term 'holiness' has a special connotation when applied to God. It has a perfection which is beyond the attainment of any human being. In the text, 'For he is a holy God' (Josh. xxiv. 19), the adjective has a plural form, which is explained to mean, 'He is holy with all kinds of holiness,' i.e. He is the perfection of holiness (p. Ber. 13a). On the words 'Ye shall be holy' (Lev. xix. 2) the comment is made: 'It is possible to imagine that man can be as holy as God; therefore Scripture adds, " for I am holy"— My holiness is higher than any degree of holiness you can reach' (Lev. R. xxiv. 9).

Not only did the Rabbis believe in this perfect holiness of God, but they insisted that it was the paramount duty of the Jew to guard it from profanation by discreditable conduct on his part. The House of Israel, as the chosen people of God, were the guardians of His reputation in the world. By worthy actions they brought credit upon Him and 'sanctified His name.' Base conduct, on the other hand, had the effect of causing *Chillul Hashem* (profanation of the Name).

This tenet concerning the interrelationship between God and Israel is of Biblical origin and finds its fullest expression in the prophecies of Ezekiel.[1] It was seized upon and elaborated by the Rabbis until it became for them a fundamental motive of behaviour. A bad action more than involved the Jew in personal guilt; it was treachery to his God and people. Therefore a distinction was drawn between a wrong done to a Gentile and to a co-religionist on that ground. 'More serious is the defrauding of a non-Jew than the defrauding of a brother Israelite on account of the profanation of the Name' (Tosifta B.K. x. 15).

To profane the Name was regarded as one of the most heinous of sins. How serious was the view taken of such an offence may be gathered from the statement, 'He who is guilty of profaning the Name cannot rely on repentance, nor upon the power of the Day of Atonement to gain him expiation, nor upon sufferings to wipe it out; death alone can wipe it out' (Joma 86a). In other places we find an even stricter attitude taken up, and the profaner of the Name is classed among the five types of sinner for whom there is no forgiveness (ARN xxxix).

In most matters Jewish law draws a distinction between a wrong done wilfully or inadvertently, but no such allowance is made

[1] See especially xxxvi. 22-33.

in connection with this offence. 'Whosoever profanes the Name of Heaven in secret will suffer the penalty for it in public; and this, whether the heavenly Name be profaned unintentionally or in wilfulness' (Aboth IV. 5).

Although it was so firmly held that human conduct reflects upon the divine Name, yet God's holiness is independent of the actions of His creatures. Hence we find this comment on the verse: '"Ye shall be holy, for I the Lord your God am Holy." That is to say, if you make yourselves holy, I ascribe it to you as though you had sanctified Me; but if you do not make yourselves holy, I ascribe it to you as though you have not sanctified Me. Perhaps, however, the intention of the verse is—if you sanctify Me, I am rendered holy; but if you do not sanctify Me, I am not rendered holy! The text states, "For I am holy"—I am in a condition of holiness whether you sanctify Me or not' (Sifra to xix. 2).

§ XI. The Ineffable Name

To the Oriental, a name is not merely a label as with us. It was thought of as indicating the nature of the person or object by whom it was borne. For that reason special reverence attached to 'the distinctive Name' (*Shem Hamephorash*) of the Deity which He had revealed to the people of Israel, viz. the tetragrammaton, JHVH.

In the Biblical period there seems to have been no scruple against its use in daily speech. The addition of *Jah* or *Jahu* to personal names, which persisted among the Jews even after the Babylonian exile, is an indication that there was no prohibition against the employment of the four-lettered Name. But in the early Rabbinic period the pronunciation of the Name was restricted to the Temple service. The rule was laid down: 'In the Sanctuary the Name was pronounced as written; but beyond its confines a substituted Name was employed' (Sot. VII. 6).

The tetragrammaton was included in the priestly benediction which was daily pronounced in the Temple (Sifré Num. § 39; 12a). It was also used by the High Priest on the Day of Atonement, when he made the threefold confession of sins on behalf of himself, the priests, and the community. The third occasion is described in this manner: 'Thus did he say: O JHVH, Thy people, the House of Israel, have committed iniquity, have transgressed, have sinned before Thee. I beseech Thee by the Name JHVH,[1] make Thou atonement for the iniquities and for the transgressions and for the

[1] i.e. the name indicative of mercy; see above, p. 17.

sins wherein Thy people, the House of Israel, have committed iniquity, have transgressed and sinned before Thee; as it is written in the Torah of Thy servant Moses, saying: "For on this day shall atonement be made for you, to cleanse you; from all your sins shall ye be clean before JHVH" (Lev. xvi. 30). And when the priests and the people that stood in the Court heard the glorious and revered Name pronounced freely out of the mouth of the High Priest, in holiness and purity, they knelt and prostrated themselves, falling on their faces, and exclaiming: Blessed be His glorious, sovereign Name for ever and ever' (Joma VI. 2).

In the last stage of the Temple's existence, there was reluctance to give a clear enunciation of the tetragrammaton. This practice is attested by R. Tarphon, who belonged to a priestly family. He records that in his boyhood, before he was old enough to officiate, 'On one occasion I followed my uncles on to the dais, and I inclined my ear to catch what the High Priest said. I heard him cause the Name to be drowned by the singing of his brother-priests' (Kid. 71a).[1]

Behind the care not to give explicit utterance to the Name may be detected a lowering in the moral standard of the priests. The Talmud declares: 'At first the High Priest used to proclaim the Name in a loud voice; but when dissolute men multiplied, he proclaimed it in a low tone' (p. Joma 40d).

On the other hand, there was a time when the free and open use of the Name even by the layman was advocated. The Mishnah teaches: 'It was ordained that a man should greet his friends by mentioning the Name' (Ber. IX. 5). It has been suggested that the recommendation was based on the desire to distinguish the Israelite from the Samaritan, who referred to God as 'the Name' and not as JHVH, or the Rabbinite Jew from the Jewish-Christian.

This custom, however, was soon discontinued, and among those who are excluded from a share in the World to Come is 'he who pronounces the Name according to its letters' (Sanh. X. 1). A third-century Rabbi taught: 'Whoever explicitly pronounces the Name is guilty of a capital offence' (Pesikta 148a).

Instead of JHVH the Name was pronounced *Adonai* (my Lord) in the Synagogue service; but there is a tradition that the original pronunciation was transmitted by the Sages to their disciples periodically—once or twice every seven years (Kid. 71a). Even

---

[1] Josephus, who also belonged to a family of priests, likewise displays hesitation to mention the tetragrammaton in explicit terms. He wrote: 'Whereupon God declared to him (viz. to Moses) His name, which had never been discovered to men before, concerning which it is not lawful for me to speak' (Antiq. II. xii. 4).

that practice ceased after a while, and the method of pronouncing the Name is no longer known with certainty.

The conception of the Deity, as outlined above, shows that the Jews in the Talmudic period, like their forebears in the Biblical Age, worshipped no mere abstract First Cause. Theirs was essentially a 'personal' God in the sense that He was a reality to those who acknowledged Him. The accessibility and nearness of God will be discussed in the next chapter; but enough has been cited to demonstrate that the thought of Him was intended to be an inspiration to holy and righteous living.

Certain doctrines in connection with the Deity were forced into general prominence and received special emphasis at the hands of the Rabbis because of contemporaneous circumstances. The attribute of Unity had to be underlined when a trinitarian dogma began to be preached by the new sect of Christians. The incorporeality and holiness of God were constantly stressed as a protest against the immoral and degrading actions which neighbouring peoples associated with their gods.

The Rabbis strove to keep their doctrine of God pure and undefiled, so that it might become a refining and elevating force in the lives of those who acclaimed Him. He was an approachable God with Whom the human being could commune, the merciful and gracious Father Who loved His earthly family and desired their happiness. Though He was necessarily apart from His creatures by reason of His infinite majesty and absolute perfection, there was a firm and secure connecting link between them, because man had been created in His image. This supremely important tenet separated the human race from the rest of the animal kingdom and raised humanity towards divinity, although the dividing line between the two can never be bridged.[1]

[1] See p. 67 and p. 386 n. 1.

CHAPTER II

GOD AND THE UNIVERSE

§ I. COSMOLOGY

THE interest in metaphysical speculation which characterized the thinkers of Greece and Rome was not shared by the teachers of Israel to any great extent. The theories of Aristotle and Plato about the constitution of the Universe were probably not unknown to some of the Rabbis and were not without influence upon them; but natural science as a subject of study was not cultivated in the Schools of Palestine and Babylon.

On the contrary, it was strongly discouraged, as may be seen from this warning: 'Whoever reflects on four things, it were a mercy if he had never come into the world, viz. what is above, what is beneath, what is before and what is after' (Chag. II. 1). The verse of Ben Sira (i.e. Ecclesiasticus) is quoted in the Talmud with approval: 'Seek not out the things that are too hard for thee, and into the things that are hidden from thee inquire thou not. In what is permitted to thee instruct thyself; thou hast no business with secret things' (iii. 21 f.; Chag. 13a). That is typical of the Rabbinic attitude. To the question, Why does the story of Creation begin with the letter *beth*? [1] the answer is given: 'In the same manner that the letter *beth* is closed on all sides and only open in front, similarly you are not permitted to inquire into what is before or what was behind, but only from the actual time of Creation' (p. Chag. 77c).

Two reasons prompted the antagonism to such lines of inquiry. In the first place, it was a menace to religious faith,[2] and even eminent Jewish scholars had suffered from it. There is a striking passage which relates: 'Four men ascended into Paradise, Ben Azzai, Ben Zoma, Acher, and R. Akiba. R. Akiba said to them, When you arrive at the stones of pure marble do not exclaim, "Water, water." Ben Azzai gazed and died; Ben Zoma gazed

---

[1] i.e. the second letter of the Hebrew alphabet and not the first. The shape of the *beth* is a square on the left side. Hebrew writing runs from right to left.

[2] On the whole, it may be truly said that the Rabbis were not averse to rational inquiry, and advocated that faith should be based on reason. Compare Hillel's saying, 'An ignorant person cannot be pious' (Aboth II. 6)

and became demented; Acher [1] cut the plants; R. Akiba departed in peace' (Chag. 14b).

The interpretation of this cryptic passage is uncertain, but the mention of water perhaps offers the clue. The Greeks, and later the Gnostics, taught that water was the original element out of which the Universe was created, and that belief is actually mentioned in the Talmud.[2] It is, therefore, possible that Akiba's words meant that when, in their investigation, they approached 'the stones of pure marble,' i.e. the Throne of God representing ultimate reality, they must avoid the theory that water supplies the explanation of the origin of the Universe.

Another reason why this kind of research was deprecated is to be looked for in the fact that the Rabbis felt that the problems of this world were more than sufficient to occupy their minds, and the consideration of transcendental theories would divert attention from matters of more practical importance. 'Not inquiry but action is the chief thing' (Aboth I. 17) was their guiding principle.

Nevertheless, there were branches of study, called *Maaseh Bereshith* (The Work of Creation), based on Genesis i, and *Maaseh Merkabah* (The Work of the Chariot), based on Ezekiel i, which were cultivated by some Rabbis. The tenets were only expounded in private to selected disciples singly. No record exists of the nature of this esoteric doctrine unless parts of it are embodied in the cosmological references in the Talmud and Midrash. These references are fairly numerous, but they have no scientific value. They are not the result of rational inquiry into the phenomena presented by the Universe, but rather an attempt to deduce from the text of Scripture what it teaches on the origin and constitution of the world.

That the Rabbis should have turned there for a source of enlightenment on such a matter is easy to understand. A passage in the Bible declares: 'The Lord made me (i.e. wisdom) as the beginning of His way, the first of His works of old. I was set up from everlasting, from the beginning, or ever the earth was' (Prov. viii. 22 f.). Wisdom, which is here said to have come into being even before the creation of the world, was naturally identified with Torah; and since God created it first, He must have done so for a purpose. That purpose was to draft the plan according to which the Universe was to be constructed. 'The Torah said, I was

---

[1] Acher means 'another.' His real name was Elisha b. Abuyah. He became a sceptic and abandoned Judaism. Thereupon his former colleagues referred to him under that opprobrious title. 'Cut the plants' seems to be a metaphorical allusion to his apostasy.

[2] See pp. 35 f.

the architectural instrument of the Holy One, blessed be He. It is customary when a human king erects a palace that he does not build it according to his own ideas but according to the ideas of an architect. The architect likewise does not depend upon the thoughts of his mind, but has parchments and tablets to know how he is to plan the rooms and entrances. So did the Holy One, blessed be He, look into the Torah and created the Universe accordingly' (Gen. R. 1; 1).

This is a Platonic idea which was adopted by Philo, who wrote: 'God having determined to found a mighty state, first of all conceived its form in His mind, according to which form He made a world perceptible only by the intellect, and then completed one visible to the external senses, using the first one as a model.'[1] The Torah reflected the 'mind' of God; and therefore the Rabbis searched its words for knowledge about the process of Creation and the structure of the Universe. This hypothesis accounts for most of the cosmic theories which are found in Rabbinic literature.

That God pre-existed all things was, as we have seen, one of His attributes. It follows, then, that everything in the Universe must have been created and could not have existed like Him without beginning. Aristotle taught the eternity of matter, and his theory was resisted by the Rabbis. This question formed the subject of a discussion between a philosopher and R. Gamaliel. The philosopher said: 'Your God is a great Craftsman, but He found good materials which were of assistance to Him in the work of Creation, viz. Tohu, Bohu, darkness, spirit, water, and the deeps.'[2] The Rabbi answered, 'A curse alight upon you! In connection with all of them, Scripture mentions that they were created. With Tohu and Bohu it is said, "I make peace and create evil" (Is. xlv. 7); with darkness it is said, "I form the light and create darkness" (ibid.); with water it is said, "Praise Him, ye heavens of heavens, and ye waters that are above the heavens" (Ps. cxlviii. 4). Why are they to praise Him? "Because He commanded and they were created" (ibid. 5). With wind it is said, "He formeth the mountains and createth the wind" (Amos iv. 13); with the deeps it is said, "When there were no depths I (wisdom) was brought forth" (Prov. viii. 24)' (Gen. R. 1. 9).

The same emphasis on *creatio ex nihilo* is to be discerned in the declaration, 'Ten things were created on the first day, viz. heaven

---

[1] *On the Creation of the World*, IV.
[2] All these terms occur in the opening verses of Genesis. Tohu and Bohu are the words translated 'waste and void.' The meaning attached to them by the Rabbis will be given below.

and earth, Tohu and Bohu, light and darkness, wind and water, the duration of day and the duration of night' (Chag. 12a). In this enumeration are the primal elements from which the Universe was constituted, and the ideas concerning them in the Talmud must be given.

HEAVEN. The Hebrew term for heaven, *Shamayim*, was explained as the combination of *sham* and *mayim* (the place where there is water), or *esh* and *mayim* (fire and water), and from these two elements the celestial region was made (Chag. 12a).

The Bible has seven different designations for heaven; therefore there must be seven heavens. 'There are seven heavens, named respectively *Vilon, Rakia, Shechakim, Zebul, Maon, Machon,* and *Araboth*. *Vilon* performs no other function than that it retires in the morning and issues forth in the evening, and renews the work of Creation daily; as it is said, "That stretcheth out the heavens as a curtain [1] and spreadeth them out as a tent to dwell in" (Is. xl. 22). *Rakia* is that in which the sun, moon, stars, and planets are fixed; as it is said, "And God set them in the firmament (*Rakia*) of the heaven" (Gen. i. 17). *Shechakim* is that in which the millstones are located and grind manna for the righteous; as it is said, "He commanded the skies (*Shechakim*) above and opened the doors of heaven; and He rained down manna upon them to eat" (Ps. lxxviii. 23 f.). *Zebul* is that where the celestial Jerusalem is and the Temple in which the altar is erected, and Michael, the great Prince, stands and offers a sacrifice upon it; as it is said, "I have surely built thee an house of habitation (*Zebul*), a place for thee to dwell in for ever" (1 Kings viii. 13). Whence do we know that it is called heaven? Because it is written, "Look down from heaven and behold from the habitation (*Zebul*) of Thy holiness and of Thy glory" (Is. lxiii. 15). *Maon* is that in which are bands of ministering angels, who utter a song in the night but are silent during the day for the sake of the honour of Israel; [2] as it is said, "The Lord will command His lovingkindness [3] in the daytime and in the night his song shall be with Me" (Ps. xlii. 8). Whence do we know that it is called heaven? Because it is written, "Look down from Thy holy habitation (*Maon*) from heaven" (Deut. xxvi. 15). *Machon* is that in which are the treasuries of snow and the treasuries of

---

[1] *Vilon* is the Latin *velum*, 'a curtain.' Its purpose is to cover up the light of the sun during the night and for that reason it is withdrawn at daybreak.

[2] To enable the song of praise uttered by the people of Israel during the day to be heard.

[3] The command issued to the angels to be silent is a sign of mercy to Israel by giving them an opportunity to sing. The text is given the meaning, 'Israel's song will be with God,' not His song with the Psalmist.

hail, the loft containing harmful dews, the lofts of the round drops (which injure plants), the chamber of the whirlwind and storm, and the cavern of noxious smoke, the doors of which are made of fire; as it is said, "The Lord shall open unto thee His good treasure" [1] (ibid. xxviii. 12). Whence do we know that it is called heaven? Because it is written, "Hear Thou in heaven, the habitation (*Machon*) of Thy dwelling" (1 Kings viii. 39). *Araboth* is that in which are righteousness, judgment, and charity, the storehouses of life, of peace and of blessing, the souls of the righteous, the spirits and souls which are still to be created, and the dew with which the Holy One, blessed be He, will hereafter revive the dead. There are the *Ophannim, Seraphim*, holy *Chayyoth*,[2] the ministering angels, the Throne of Glory, and the King, the living God, high and exalted, abiding above them in the clouds; as it is said, "Cast up a highway for Him that rideth upon the clouds (*Araboth*); His name is Jah" (Ps. lxviii. 4)' (Chag. 12b).

As to the material out of which the heaven was constructed, one Rabbi declared: 'At the time when the Holy One, blessed be He, said, "Let there be a firmament in the midst of the waters," the central drop of water became congealed and both the lower and upper heavens were made' (Gen. R. iv. 2). Another opinion was: Fire issued from above and licked the surface of the firmament' (ibid.), i.e. the fire dried the surface of the water and hardened it. A third view, playing on the etymology of the word *shamayim*, is: 'The Holy One, blessed be He, took fire and water, mingled them together, and so the heaven was formed' (ibid. 7).

EARTH. Corresponding to the seven heavens, the earth was also pictured as consisting of seven strata, since there are seven different words for it in the Bible (Esth. R. i. 12).

Both heaven and earth were fashioned out of the same materials, although there was difference of opinion about the number of them. How did the Holy One, blessed be He, create His Universe? R. Jochanan said, He took two coils, one of fire and the other of snow, wove them into each other, and from them the Universe was created. R. Channina said, There are four elements, corresponding to the four winds of heaven. R. Chama b. Channina said, There were six, corresponding to the four winds of heaven

---

[1] Since 'good' treasure is specified, the deduction is drawn that there must also exist a treasury of bad things.

[2] *Ophannim* means 'wheels' and *Chayyoth* 'living creatures.' They have their origin in Ezekiel's mystic vision (chaps. i and x) and play a prominent part in the celestial region as conceived by the Rabbis. The *Seraphim* are described in Is. vi. 2 as angelic beings, possessing wings and in form partly human and partly animal.

and in addition one from above and one from below' (Gen. R. x. 3).

Opposite sides were also taken on the question whether heaven and earth originated independently of each other. 'R. Eliezer said, All that is in heaven had its origin from heaven; all that is on earth had its origin from earth. He deduced it from the verses, "Praise ye the Lord from the heavens, etc. . . . Praise the Lord from the earth, etc." (Ps. cxlviii. 1 ff., 7 ff.). R. Joshua said, All that is in heaven and earth had its origin from heaven. He deduced it from the verse, "For He saith to the snow, Fall thou on the earth" (Job xxxvii. 6). As with snow which exists on earth but has its origin in heaven, so everything that is in heaven and earth originates in heaven. R. Huna declared in the name of R. Joseph, All that is in heaven and earth had its origin in the earth; as it is said, "As the rain cometh down and the snow from heaven" (Is. lv. 10). Although the rain descends from heaven, it originates in the earth; similarly all that is in heaven and earth has its origin in the earth' (Gen. R. XII. 11).

Tradition related that in the Temple there was *Eben Shetiyyah* (a foundation stone), which was so named because upon it the world was founded, and from this as a centre the earth was created (Joma 54*b*). This legend reflects the view that since the Holy Land was God's chosen country it must have been first in creation; and because the site of the Temple was the most sacred of all places, the process of creation must have begun there. The legendary stone also points to another widespread belief in ancient times which is explicitly mentioned in Rabbinic literature, viz.: 'The Holy One, blessed be He, cast a stone into the primeval sea from which the world was formed' (ibid.)

The Rabbis shared the general belief that the earth was flat and supported upon pillars, although there was disagreement about the number. 'Upon what does the earth stand? Upon pillars, as it is said, "Which shaketh the earth out of her place, and the pillars thereof tremble" (Job ix. 6). The pillars stand upon the waters, as it is said, "That spreadeth forth the earth upon (*sic*) the waters" (Ps. cxxxvi. 6). The waters stand upon the mountains, as it is said, "The waters stood upon (*sic*) the mountains" (ibid. civ. 6). The mountains stand upon the wind, as it is said, "He that formeth the mountains and createth the wind" (Amos iv. 13). The wind stands upon the storm, as it is said, "Stormy wind fulfilling His word" (Ps. cxlviii. 8); and the storm is suspended upon the arm of the Holy One, blessed be He, as it is said, "Underneath are the everlasting arms" (Deut.

xxxiii. 27). The Sages declare, It rests upon twelve pillars, as it is said, "He set the bounds of the peoples according to the number (of the tribes) of the children of Israel" (ibid. xxxii. 8). Others maintain there are seven, as it is said, "Wisdom hath hewn out her seven pillars" (Prov. ix. 1). R. Eleazar b. Shammua said, Upon one pillar whose name is "the Righteous," as it is said, "The Righteous One is the foundation of the world" (sic ibid. x. 25)' (Chag. 12b).

As for the dimensions of the earth, we are informed: 'Egypt extends over four hundred parasangs square; Egypt is one-sixtieth the size of Ethiopia; and Ethiopia is one-sixtieth the size of the world' (Taan. 10a). This yields an area of 576 million square parasangs, and the parasang of the Rabbis is two and four-fifths English miles; but the term 'a sixtieth' is employed very loosely in the Talmud and does not denote an exact proportion. The thickness of the earth was said to be a thousand cubits (Suk. 53b).

TOHU and BOHU. These are defined as follows: 'Tohu is a green line which encompasses the whole world from which darkness issued; as it is said, "He made darkness His hiding-place round about Him" (Ps. xviii. 11). Bohu denotes the slime-covered stones sunk in the depths from which water issued; as it is said, "He shall stretch upon it the line of chaos (Tohu) and the stones of emptiness (Bohu)" (Is. xxxiv. 11)' (Chag. 12a). They are, accordingly, the two primeval substances out of which the Universe came into being—darkness, which was considered a created thing and not merely the absence of light, and water.

LIGHT. The question was discussed whether the creation of light preceded the creation of the world. 'R. Isaac said, Light was created first of all. Parable of a king who wished to erect a palace and the locality was in darkness. What did he do? He lit torches and lanterns to know where he had to fix the foundations. Similarly was light created first.. R. Nehemiah said, The world was created first. Parable of a king who built a palace and then adorned it with torches and lanterns' (Gen. R. III. 1).

Since the sun was not created until the fourth day, whence did light have its origin? Two answers were given to the question. One Rabbi affirmed: 'The Holy One, blessed be He, enwrapped Himself in light like a garment, and the brilliance of His splendour shone forth from one end of the Universe to the other' (Gen. R. III. 4). The second Rabbi maintained that light emanated from the site of the Temple which, as mentioned above, was the centre of the earth's creation (ibid.). Both utterances express the same thought, viz., that only through the medium of the spiritual light which radiates from God could chaos be reduced to order.

DARKNESS. It has already been mentioned that darkness was not thought of as the absence of light but a created substance. One of the questions which, according to the legend, Alexander of Macedon set 'the elders of the South,' was: Which was created first—light or darkness? The majority decided in favour of darkness (Tamid 32a). Darkness issues to the world from the north (Num. R. II. 10).

WIND. The Hebrew word *ruach* in Gen. i. 2 can be translated either 'spirit' or 'wind.' It was understood by the Talmud in the latter sense and explained as one of the necessities of the world which had been created in the beginning. There was a teaching: 'Four winds blow every day, and the north wind blows with them all; were it not so, the world could not exist for even a single hour' (B.B. 25a). The north wind, as the commentator Rashi remarks, being neither excessively hot nor cold, tempers the others and makes them endurable.

The effect of the different winds is described in this piece of folk-lore: 'At the termination of the last day of the Feast of Tabernacles,[1] all the people gazed at the smoke which ascended from the altar. If it inclined towards the north, [2] the poor were happy and landowners grieved, because the rain would be abundant and the fruits rot.[3] If it inclined towards the south, the poor grieved and the landowners rejoiced, because the rains would be meagre and the fruits could be stored. If it inclined towards the east, all were happy;[4] if towards the west, all grieved'[5] (Joma 21b).

This opinion is not consistent with other statements on the subject. The east wind is elsewhere described as a bringer of rain: 'The east wind stirs up the whole world like a demon' (B.B. 25a), and 'The east wind makes the firmament black like a goat' (Sifré Deut. § 306; 132a). The north wind, on the other hand, resulted in a shortage of rain. 'The north wind makes gold cheap' (B.B. loc. cit.); and 'The north wind makes the firmament pure like gold' (Sifré, loc. cit.). This wind clears the heavens of clouds so that a drought ensues. The harvest is meagre and money decreases in value.

The south wind also was a bringer of rain. It 'brought the

---

[1] This occurs in October.
[2] i.e. a south wind blew.
[3] The owners could not keep them in store and therefore would sell at a cheap price.
[4] The rains would be just right for a bountiful harvest.
[5] Because the east wind threatened a drought.

showers and made the herbage grow' (B.B. 25*a*); and there is a statement that 'R. Zira never walked among palm-trees on a day when the south wind blew' (Shab. 32*a*), because it was so violent that there was danger of the trees being uprooted.

Another characterization of the winds reads: 'The north wind is beneficial in summer and harmful in winter. The south wind is harmful in summer and beneficial in winter. The east wind is always beneficial. The west wind is always harmful' (Sifré, loc. cit.).

WATER. There was a conflict of opinion between the two principal academies of the first century—the School of Hillel and the School of Shammai—on many questions, including the subject of cosmogony. Their difference as to whether heaven or earth was created first will be cited below. Out of this disagreement arose the question whether water was to be included among the original elements.

'R. Nehemiah of Kefar Sihon expounded the verse, "For in six days the Lord made heaven and earth, the sea and all that in them is" (Exod. xx. 11). These three things (viz. heaven, earth, and water) are the three primal elements in the creation of the Universe; and they waited three days and each brought forth three species. Earth was created on the first day in accord with the view of the School of Hillel. It waited three days—the first, second, and third—and produced three species, viz. trees, herbage, and the Garden of Eden. Heaven was created on the second day and waited three days—the second, third, and fourth—and produced three species, viz. the sun, moon, and planets. Water was created on the third day and waited three days—the third, fourth, and fifth—and produced three species, viz. birds, fish, and leviathan.[1] R. Azariah disagreed and based his argument on the text, "In the day that the Lord God made earth and heaven" (Gen. ii. 4). Two things are the primal elements (viz. earth and heaven), and they each waited three days and their work was completed on the fourth. Heaven was created first in accord with the view of the School of Shammai. It waited three days—the first, second, and third—and its work was completed on the fourth day. What was its completion? The heavenly luminaries. Earth was created on the third day and brought forth its rudimentary products. It waited three days—the third, fourth, and fifth—and its work was completed on the sixth. What was its completion? Man' (Gen. R. XII. 5).

An extreme view is that water was the ultimate origin of the

[1] See p. 385.

elements from which the others were formed. 'In the beginning
the Universe consisted of water within water; as it is written,
"The spirit of God moved upon the face of the waters" (Gen. i. 2).
He then turned it into ice, as it is written, "He casteth forth
His ice like crumbs" (Ps. cxlvii. 17). He then turned it into earth,
as it is written, "For He saith to the snow, Be thou (*sic*) earth"
(Job xxxvii. 6)' (p. Chag. 77*a*).

'The whole world is surrounded by the ocean' (Erub. 22*b*).
This is corroborated by the legend that Alexander of Macedon
once ascended high above the earth until 'the world appeared like
a ball and the sea like a dish' (in which it was set) (p. A.Z. 42*c*).
The primeval waters were divided by God into two portions,
one being placed in the firmament and the other half forming the
ocean (Gen. R. IV. 4).

The origin of rain was debated. 'R. Eliezer declared, The whole
Universe drinks from the ocean; as it is said, "There went up a
mist from the earth, and watered the whole face of the ground"
(Gen. ii. 6). R. Joshua said to R. Eliezer, "But is not the water
of the ocean salty?" He answered, "It becomes sweetened in the
clouds." R. Joshua declared, The whole Universe drinks from the
water above the firmament; as it is said, "A land that drinketh
water as the rain of heaven cometh down" (Deut. xi. 11). How
then is the verse, "There went up a mist from the earth," to be
explained? It teaches that the clouds swell and ascend to the
firmament, where they open their mouths like a bottle and receive
the rain water, as it is said, "They distil rain from His vapour"
(Job xxxvi. 27). The clouds are perforated like a sieve and distil
water to the earth. Between each drop of rain there is no more
space than the breadth of a hair, which is to teach us that a day
of rain is as great before the Holy One, blessed be He, as the day
on which heaven and earth were created' (Taan. 9*b*).

The cloud was therefore conceived as only a hollow vessel, the
water being poured into it from heaven. On this theory, thunder
was explained as 'the clouds in a whirl,' or 'the clouds pouring
water one into the other.' Alternative explanations are: 'A mighty
lightning-flash strikes against a cloud and the latter is shattered
into hailstones'; 'The clouds are not full of water, and a blast of
wind comes and blows across their mouths, it being like the blast
across the mouth of a jar'; 'The most probable view is that the
lightning strikes, the clouds are made to rumble and rain descends'
(Ber. 59*a*).

DURATION OF DAY AND NIGHT. Since the Bible tells that day and
night existed before the sun and moon were made, the conclusion

is that time was created separately. God fixed the duration of the day and night and then arranged for the appearance of the sun and moon to conform therewith. Behind this belief we are perhaps to discern the thought that time is meaningless so far as God is concerned and did not exist until He created the world.

One Rabbinic passage reduces all things to three elements only: 'Three created things preceded the formation of the Universe: water, wind, and fire. Water conceived and bore darkness; fire conceived and bore light; wind conceived and bore wisdom. By these six principles is the Universe regulated: wind, wisdom, fire, light, darkness, and water' (Exod. R. xv. 22).

An interesting theory is that all things were created simultaneously on the first day and only made their appearance at different stages. 'R. Judah and R. Nehemiah discussed the process of creation. R. Judah said, "The heaven and the earth were finished" (Gen. ii. 1) in their time; "And all the host of them" were finished in their time; i.e. at different times. R. Nehemiah said to him, "But it is written, 'These are the generations of the heaven and the earth when they were created, *in the day* that the Lord God made earth and heaven' (ibid. 4), which teaches that they were all created on the same day. On the same day they brought forth their generations." The other retorted, "But the Scriptures mention the first, second, third, fourth, fifth, and sixth days!' R. Nehemiah said to him, "The matter is like the gatherers of figs. The figs are all together in the basket, but each one is selected in its time"' (Gen. R. xii. 4).

Which was produced first, heaven or earth? 'The School of Shammai said that heaven was created first and then the earth. The School of Hillel said that the earth was created first and then the heaven. Each of them gives a reason for its opinion. The School of Shammai likened the matter to a king who made a throne for himself and afterwards a footstool. Thus said the Holy One, blessed be He, "The heaven is My throne and the earth My footstool" (Is. lxvi. 1). The School of Hillel likened the matter to a king who erected a palace. He first built the lower stories and then the upper. R. Simeon b. Jochai said, "I am astonished how these fathers of the world, the Schools of Shammai and Hillel, can differ on this point. I declare that both were only constructed like a pot and its lid;[1] as it is said, 'When I call unto them (viz. earth and heaven) they arise together' (ibid. xlviii. 13)." He was asked, "In that case, why at times does Scripture mention earth before heaven and at other times heaven before earth?" He

---

[1] They are parts of the one thing and were constructed at the same time.

answered, "It is to teach that they are of equal importance"' (Gen. R. I. 15).

R. Jochanan, using the same simile as the School of Hillel, reached a different conclusion: 'A human king, when erecting a palace, builds the lower stories and then the upper; but the Holy One, blessed be He, built the upper and lower stories simultaneously' (ibid. XII. 12).

With reference to the stars the following utterance is attributed to God: 'Twelve constellations have I created in the firmament, and for each constellation I have created thirty hosts, and for each host I have created thirty legions, and for each legion I have created thirty files, and for each file I have created thirty cohorts, and for each cohort I have created thirty camps,[1] and in each camp I have suspended three hundred and sixty-five thousand myriads of stars, in accordance with the days of the solar year' (Ber. 32b).

This total exceeds even the computation of modern astronomers and is not to be taken literally. The passage demonstrates that the Rabbis appreciated the immensity of the heavenly host. One of them classified the stars into three categories: 'The big stars which are visible by day, small stars visible by night, and medium stars (visible in the twilight)' (Shab. 35b).[2]

On this point there was unanimity, viz. that the world being the production of God Who is perfect must itself be perfect in every respect. Even in the time of its appearance perfection was manifested. On the text, 'He hath made every thing beautiful in its time' (Eccles. iii. 11), the remark is made: 'In its proper time was the Universe created, and it was not meet for the Universe to have been created before then. Hence one may deduce that the Holy One, blessed be He, created several worlds and destroyed them until He created the present world and said, This one pleases Me, whereas the others did not' (Gen. R. IX. 2). 'Parable of a king who built a palace. He inspected it and it gave him delight. He said, "O palace, may you always be to me a source of pleasure even as at this moment." Similarly spake the Holy One, blessed be He, "O My Universe, would that you will always give Me pleasure as at this moment"' (ibid. 4).

On this theory, everything that God has created must of necessity serve a beneficent purpose. The insertion of the adverb

[1] The words employed are taken from the Roman military terminology, and the stellar system is imaged as organized on the same plan as the Roman army.

[2] An enumeration of the planets, with their supposed influence over human life, is given on pp. 281 f.

'very' in the judgment, 'God saw everything that He had made, and, behold, it was very good' (Gen. i. 31), was explained as including death, the evil impulse in man, sufferings and Gehinnom, as each of them contributed in the end to the welfare of the human race (Gen. R. ix. 5–9).

'Even such things as you deem superfluous in the world, e.g. flies, fleas, and gnats, are necessary parts of the cosmic order and were created by the Holy One, blessed be He, for His purpose— yea, even serpents and frogs' (ibid. x. 7). This thought is elaborated in the Talmud as follows: 'Among all the things that the Holy One, blessed be He, created in His Universe, He created nothing that is useless. He created the snail as a cure for scab, the fly as a cure for the sting of the wasp, the gnat as a cure for the bite of the serpent, the serpent as a cure for a sore, and the spider as a cure for the sting of a scorpion' (Shab. 77b).

'Why does the story of Creation begin with the letter *beth* and not *aleph*, which is the first letter of the alphabet? Because *beth* is the initial of *berachah* (blessing) and *aleph* is the initial of *arirah* (curse). The Holy One, blessed be He, said, I will only create My Universe with *beth*, that they who come into the world shall not say, "How can the world endure since it was created with a letter of ill-omen?" Behold, I will create it with a letter of good omen, peradventure it will endure' (p. Chag. 77c).

Indeed the Universe is above all criticism. 'When a human king builds a palace, people enter it and criticize. If the pillars were taller, they say, it would be better; if the walls were higher, it would be better; if the roof were higher, it would be better! But has a man ever come and said, "If I had three eyes or three hands or three legs, if I walked on my head or my head were turned backward, I should have preferred it?" If we may so express ourselves, the supreme King of kings, the Holy One, blessed be He, and His court (of angels) decided upon every limb which you have and set it in its proper place' (Gen. R. xii. 1; Sifré Deut. § 307; 132b).

The Universe was created as the habitation of man and all that it contains was provided for his benefit. 'God created man with a purpose, because He first created the necessities for his sustenance and afterwards created him. The ministering angels spoke before the Holy One, blessed be He, "O Sovereign of the Universe, 'What is man that Thou art mindful of him, and the son of man that Thou visitest him?' (Ps. viii. 4). For what purpose is this source of trouble to be created?" He replied to them, "In that case, for what purpose were 'all sheep and oxen, yea, and the beasts of

the field' (ibid. 7) created? For what purpose were 'the fowl of
the air and the fish of the sea' (ibid. 8) created? Parable of a king
who had a tower stocked with all good things. If he had no
guests, what pleasure has the king that he so stocked it?" The
angels replied, "'O Lord, our Lord, how excellent is Thy name in
all the earth!' (ibid. 9). Do as it seemeth Thee best"' (Gen. R.
VIII. 6).

With what object, then, did God form man and the world?
The ultimate aim of His design is indicated in the aphorism:
'Whatsoever the Holy One, blessed be He, created in His Universe,
He created but for His glory' (Aboth VI. 11). We shall find this
thought developed in the Rabbinic doctrine of man.[1]

§ II. TRANSCENDENCE AND IMMANENCE

What, in Rabbinic teaching, is God's relation to the world?
Is He thought of as transcendent and far removed from His
creatures, or is He considered as being near to, and in contact
with, them? The true answer is to be found in a combination
of both ideas. The Rabbis did not look upon the two conceptions as contradictory or mutually exclusive, but rather as
complementary.

When they reflected upon the ineffable Majesty of the Creator,
His absolute perfection and boundless might, they reverentially
spoke of Him as a Being immeasurably removed from the limita-
tions of the finite world. But they, at the same time, realized
that such a transcendent God was of little use to the human being
who was grappling with the problems of life and yearned for communion with a Helper and Comforter and Guide amidst his per-
plexities and struggles. They, accordingly, stressed the doctrine
that God was immanent in the world, and was very near to all
who called upon Him in sincerity.

We have seen that in the cosmology of the Talmud, the Deity
is located in the seventh heaven. His habitation was therefore
infinitely remote from earth. The imagination of that age could
not have ventured on a bolder flight than to depict the immense
distance which separates God from the world in this manner:
'The thickness of each firmament is equal to a journey of five
hundred years, and so are the spaces between the seven firma-
ments. Above them are the holy *Chayyoth*. Their feet measure
a distance equal to all of these put together; their ankles are of
similar dimension, their legs of similar dimension, their knees of

[1] See p. 68.

similar dimension, their thighs of similar dimension, their bodies of similar dimension, their necks of similar dimension, their heads of similar dimension, their horns of similar dimension. Above them is the Throne of Glory. The feet of the Throne are of similar dimension and the Throne itself is of similar dimension. The King, the living and eternal God, high and exalted, abides above them' (Chag. 13*a*).

The words of the Song of Moses, 'I will sing unto the Lord, for He is highly exalted' (Exod. xv. 1), receive this explanation: 'It implies a song to Him Who is exalted high above those who are lofty; as a teacher declared: The king among the beasts is the lion, the king among the domestic animals is the ox, the king among the birds is the eagle, man is exalted above them, and the Holy One, blessed be He, is exalted above them all as well as above the entire Universe' (Chag. 13*b*). The purpose of such teaching was to stress the Divine Majesty, but also to avoid the error of Pantheism which would identify the Creator with His Creation.

Much more prominent, however, in the Talmudic literature is the conception of God's immanence in the world and His nearness to man. It follows as a corollary from the doctrine of His omnipresence. How happily the Rabbis synthetized the two aspects of Deity is illustrated by this extract: 'An idol appears to be near at hand but is in reality afar off. Why? "It is borne upon the shoulder, it is carried and set in its place; but though one cry to it, it cannot answer, nor save him out of his trouble" (Is. xlvi. 7). The end of the matter is, he has his god with him in his house, but he may cry unto it until he dies without its hearing or rescuing him from his plight. On the other hand, the Holy One, blessed be He, appears to be afar off, but in reality there is nothing closer than He.' There follows a reference to the immeasurable distance of His dwelling-place from the earth, as cited above, and then the moral is drawn: 'However high He be above His world, let a man but enter a Synagogue, stand behind a pillar [1] and pray in a whisper, and the Holy One, blessed be He, hearkens to his prayer. Can there be a God nearer than this, Who is close to His creatures as the mouth is to the ear?' (p. Ber. 13*a*).

In Deut. iv. 7, 'For what great nation is there that hath God so nigh unto them as the Lord our God,' the adjective 'nigh' is in the plural. This is explained as implying 'every kind of nearness,' which means nearness in the closest degree (ibid.).

The outstanding effect of Abraham's mission was to proclaim God's sovereignty over earth as well as over heaven. 'Until our

[1] i.e. in an obscure place.

father Abraham came, the Holy One, blessed be He, was, as it
were, only King over heaven; as it is said, "The Lord, the God of
heaven, took me from my father's house" (Gen. xxiv. 7). But
since the time that our father Abraham entered the world, he
made Him King over the earth also; as it is said, "I make thee
swear by the Lord, the God of heaven and the God of the earth"
(ibid. 3)' (Sifré Deut. § 313; 134b).

The common appellation of 'King' as applied to God contains no
suggestion of remoteness. It is a mistaken idea that underlying
the word is the imagery of an Oriental potentate who holds himself
severely aloof from his subjects. Kingship with reference to the
Deity indicates nothing more than the aspect of Majesty; and any
thought of autocratic seclusion is removed by the frequent addition
of 'our Father' to 'our King.'

With the object of utilizing the doctrine of the immanence of
God in the world, while avoiding the suggestion that He could be
located in any spot, the Rabbis invented certain terms to express
the Divine Presence without giving support to a belief in His
corporeality. The most frequent of these terms is *Shechinah*,
which literally means 'dwelling.' It denotes the manifestation of
God upon the stage of the world, although He abides in the far-
away heaven. In the same way that the sun in the sky illumines
with its rays every corner of the earth, so the *Shechinah*, the
effulgence of God, may make its presence felt everywhere (Sanh.
39a).[1]

Accordingly, the *Shechinah* is often depicted under the figure of
light. The Scriptural phrase, 'The earth did shine with His glory'
(Ezek. xliii. 2), receives the comment, 'This is the face of the
Shechinah' (ARN 11); and the priestly benediction, 'The Lord make
His face to shine upon thee' (Num. vi. 25), is interpreted, 'May
He give thee the light of the *Shechinah*' (Num. R. xi. 5).

This Divine Presence brings God, as it were, into the most
intimate contact with human beings so that He even shares their
sorrows. 'During the time that a man is in trouble, what language
does the *Shechinah* employ? "I have a heaviness in My head;
I have a heaviness in My arms." If the Holy One, blessed be He,
is so grieved when the blood of wicked men is shed, how much
more so when the blood of righteous men is shed' (Chag. 15b).

Although the *Shechinah* is omnipresent, its reality is more deeply
felt in places and circumstances which, by their sacred character,
tend to attune the person spiritually to God. Especially in view
of the command, 'Let them make for Me a sanctuary, that I may

[1] See p. 10.

dwell among them' (Exod. xxv. 8), the Tent of Meeting was regarded as a place where the *Shechinah* was manifest most vividly.
The candelabrum of the Tabernacle burnt 'without the veil of the
testimony' (Lev. xxiv. 3), to act as 'a witness to all who come into
the world, that the *Shechinah* abides in the midst of Israel'
(Shab. 22*b*). The purpose of the construction of the Sanctuary
was to form a medium whereby God could dwell among His
creatures. This thought is finely expounded as follows: 'From
the first day that the Holy One, blessed be He, created the
Universe, He longed to abide among His creatures in the lower
regions, but He did not do so. When, however, the Tabernacle
was set up and the Holy One, blessed be He, caused the *Shechinah*
to rest within it, He said, "Let it be written that on this day the
world was created"' (Num. R. XIII. 6). The implication seems to
be that until the *Shechinah* took up its abode among men through
the erection of the Sanctuary, the world could not really be said
to exist in the full sense of the term.

The question how God, Who fills all space, could choose an earthly
dwelling-place for Himself, receives this answer: 'When the Holy
One, blessed be He, said to Moses, "Make a Tabernacle for Me,"
he began to wonder and exclaimed, "The glory of the Holy One,
blessed be He, fills the upper and lower worlds, and He commands
me to make a Tabernacle for Him!" Furthermore, he foresaw
that Solomon would erect a Temple greater than the Tabernacle
and declare before the Holy One, blessed be He, "But will God in
very truth dwell on the earth? Behold, heaven and the heaven of
heavens cannot contain Thee; how much less this house that I
have builded!" (1 Kings viii. 27). Then said Moses, "If Solomon,
whose Temple is very much larger than the Tabernacle, speaks
thus, how much more must I!" Thereupon he uttered the words,
"He dwelleth in the secret place of the Most High" (Ps. xci. 1).
But the Holy One, blessed be He, said to him, "Not as you think
do I think. If I so desire, I make My abode between twenty boards
on the north and south and eight boards on the west.[1] More
even than that—I can descend and restrict My *Shechinah* within
a square cubit"' (Exod. R. XXXIV. 1).

What was true of the Temple held good likewise of places of
prayer and study which similarly turned man's mind Godward.
'Whence is it that the Holy One, blessed be He, is found in the
Synagogue? As it is said, "God standeth in the godly congregation" (Ps. lxxxii. 1). And whence is it that when ten assemble

---

[1] This is the number of boards used in the construction of the Tabernacle
(Exod. xxvi. 18 ff.).

for prayer the *Shechinah* is in their midst? As it is said, "God standeth in the godly congregation." [1] And whence is it that when three sit and judge, the *Shechinah* is in their midst? As it is said, "In the midst of the judges [2] He judgeth" (ibid.). And whence is it that when two sit and occupy themselves with the study of the Torah, the *Shechinah* is in their midst? As it is said, "Then they that feared the Lord spoke one with another,[3] and the Lord hearkened and heard" (Mal. iii. 16). And whence is it that even if an individual sits and occupies himself with the study of the Torah the *Shechinah* is with him? As it is said, "In every place where I cause My name to be remembered I will come unto thee and will bless thee" (Exod. xx. 24)' (Ber. 6a). There is also the statement of R. Simeon b. Jochai: 'Wherever the righteous go, the *Shechinah* goes with them' (Gen. R. LXXXVI. 6).

Just as prayer and sacred study make a person more sensitive to the *Shechinah*, sin has the reverse effect of driving it away so that the Presence is not felt and, for all practical purposes, is non-existent there. The Rabbis taught: 'Whoever sins in secret presses against the feet of the *Shechinah*' (Kid. 31a); 'A man may not walk even four cubits with a haughty demeanour, because the whole earth is full of God's glory' (ibid.); 'When a man gives pain to his father or mother, the Holy One, blessed be He, says: "Well have I done in not dwelling amongst them, for had I dwelt amongst them I too would have felt pained"' (ibid.).

'Originally the place of the *Shechinah* was in the lower regions. When Adam sinned it ascended to the first heaven; when Cain sinned it ascended to the second; in the generation of Enoch [4] it ascended to the third; in the generation of the Flood to the fourth; in the generation of the Tower of Babel to the fifth; the men of Sodom caused it to depart to the sixth; and the Egyptians in the time of Abraham to the seventh. In contradistinction, seven righteous men arose and made it descend. Abraham brought it down to the sixth, Isaac to the fifth, Jacob to the fourth, Levi to the third, Kohath to the second, Amram to the first, and Moses caused it to come down from above to below on earth' (Gen. R. XIX. 7). This is a way of teaching that, as the wicked drive the

---

[1] For the number ten as constituting a congregation, see p. 302. A minimum of ten adult males is required to form a quorum for the service in Synagogue.

[2] *Elohim* means 'God or gods' and also 'judges.' According to Jewish law a case was tried by at least three judges; see p. 304.

[3] 'One with another' denotes a minimum of two; and since they are 'fearers of the Lord' it is presumed that their conversation would be regarding Torah.

[4] Gen. iv. 26, is interpreted as, 'Then was there profanation in calling upon the name of the Lord,' i.e. idolatry was begun to be practised.

Shechinah away from the abode of men, so the righteous restore its blessing to the human race.

Another Rabbinic concept to indicate the nearness of God and His direct influence on man is that of *Ruach Hakodesh* (the Holy Spirit). Sometimes it seems to be identical with the *Shechinah* as expressing the divine immanence in the world as affected by what transpires there. For instance, it is related that after the destruction of the Temple, the Emperor Vespasian dispatched three ship-loads of young Jews and Jewesses to brothels in Rome, but during the voyage they all threw themselves into the sea and were drowned, rather than accept so degraded a fate. The story ends with the statement that on beholding the harrowing sight: 'The Holy Spirit wept and said, "For these do I weep" (Lament. i. 16)' (Lament. R. I. 45).

More often it is employed to describe the endowment of a person with special gifts. Prophecy, in the sense of the ability to interpret the will of God, is the effect of which the Holy Spirit is the cause.[1] Its possession also endows one with foreknowledge. Thus we are told: 'The men of prehistoric times,[2] being able to use the Holy Spirit, gave names to their children which indicated events that were to happen to them later in their lives; we, on the other hand, who cannot employ the Holy Spirit, name our children after our ancestors' (Gen. R. XXXVII. 7).

Isaac gave Jacob a second blessing, 'because he saw by the Holy Spirit that his descendants would be exiled among the nations of the world' (Gen. R. LXXV. 8). The question why Jacob wept when he kissed Rachel (Gen. xxix. 11) is answered: 'He saw by the Holy Spirit that he would not be buried by her side' (Gen. R. LXX. 12). 'By the aid of the Holy Spirit, Moses foresaw that Israel would be oppressed by heathen powers' (p. Hor. 48c).

Just as human effort can attract or drive away the *Shechinah*, it may have the same effect on the Holy Spirit. 'He who studies Torah with the aim of fulfilling its precepts is worthy to receive the Holy Spirit' (Lev. R. XXXV. 7). 'When the sons of Samuel amended their conduct they became worthy of the Holy Spirit' (Num. R. x. 5). Conversely, 'Esau by his wickedness caused the Holy Spirit to depart from his father' (Gen. R. LXV. 4).

Another manifestation of Divine immanence is the *Bath Kol*, literally 'daughter of a voice.' It refers to the supernatural method of communicating God's will to men, especially when the Hebrew prophets had come to an end. 'After the death of Haggai, Zechariah, and Malachi, the last of the prophets, the

---

[1] See pp. 121 ff.　　　　[2] Those who are enumerated in Gen. x.

Holy Spirit ceased from Israel; nevertheless they received communications from God through the medium of the *Bath Kol*' (Tosifta Sot. XIII. 2). Examples are: 'Jochanan, the High Priest,[1] heard a *Bath Kol* from the Holy of Holies, announcing that the young men (viz. his sons) who had gone to wage war against Antioch had been victorious' (Sot. 33a).[2] 'When Solomon had to decide who was the mother of the disputed child, a *Bath Kol* announced, "She is the mother thereof" (1 Kings iii. 27)' (Gen. R. LXXXV. 12).

The *Bath Kol* likewise made known to man the feelings and intentions of God. A Rabbi once went among some ruins to pray and there he heard 'A *Bath Kol* moaning like a dove, crying, "Alas for My children, for whose iniquities I destroyed My house, burnt My Temple, and exiled them among the nations!"' (Ber. 3a). When R. Akiba suffered martyrdom, dying with the words 'The Lord is one' on his lips, 'A *Bath Kol* issued forth and announced, "Happy art thou, R. Akiba, that thy soul went out with that word *one*!"' (ibid. 61b).

The *Bath Kol* was said to have been the means of ending the long conflict between the two great Rabbinic Schools. 'Three years did the Schools of Shammai and Hillel debate, each declaring that the laws were to be decided in its favour. A *Bath Kol* issued forth and proclaimed: "Both of them speak the words of the living God, but the decision in law is in accord with the School of Hillel"' (Erub. 13b).

But in a matter of this kind the *Bath Kol* was not always accepted as final. On one occasion a fierce discussion arose between R. Eliezer and his colleagues on a point of law. 'R. Eliezer adduced every possible argument, but his colleagues remained unconvinced. He said to them: "If the law is according to my view, may this carob-tree prove it." The carob-tree moved a hundred cubits from its place, or, as some declare, four hundred cubits. They replied to him: "No proof can be brought from a carob-tree." He thereupon said to them: "If the law is according to my view, may this water-channel prove it"; and the water flowed backward. They replied to him: "No proof can be brought from a water-channel." He thereupon said to them: "If the law is according to my view, let the walls of this House of Study prove it." The walls then caved in and were on the point of falling. R. Joshua rebuked them, saying: "If students of the Torah contend with one another on a point of law, what has it to do with you?" Out of respect for R. Joshua they did not fall, and out of respect for

<hr>

[1] i.e. John Hyrcanus, King of Judea, 135–105 B.C.
[2] The same story is told by Josephus (Antiq. XIII. x. 3).

R. Eliezer they did not become erect, but still remain aslant. He finally said to them: "If the law is according to my view, let it be proved from heaven." A *Bath Kol* issued forth and declared: "What have you against R. Eliezer? The legal decision is always according to his view." R. Joshua rose to his feet and exclaimed: "It is not in heaven" (Deut. xxx. 12). What does this intend? R. Jeremiah said: "The Torah having been once delivered on Mount Sinai, we pay no attention to a *Bath Kol*'" (B.M. 59*b*). In this quaint manner the point is made that reason alone must decide the correct interpretation of the Torah.

Sufficient has been quoted to demonstrate how untenable is the view that the Talmudic conception of God is wholly transcendental. However reluctant the teachers of Israel were to identify God with His Universe and insisted on His being exalted high above the abode of men, yet they thought of the world as permeated through and through with the omnipresent *Shechinah*. God is at once above the Universe and the very soul of the Universe.

§ III. Angelology

The Universe, as envisaged in the Talmud, is inhabited by two classes of beings—the *Elyonim* (those above), the angels, and the *Tachtonim* (those below), the human race. If there is a great deal about angels in the teachings of the Rabbis, angelology did not originate with them. The picture of a celestial court, with God as King and a host of ministers surrounding Him, is to be found in the Bible,[1] and angels, as servants of the Most High, are frequently mentioned in its narratives.

The Oriental, with his love for the picturesque and gorgeous colouring, elaborated the heavenly scene until it grew very full and crowded. We may see the process at work in the post-Biblical literature—the Apocrypha and Pseudepigrapha—and its culmination in the Talmud and Midrash.

The underlying motive of Rabbinic angelology was certainly not to invent intermediaries between God and the world, as is sometimes alleged. What has been said on the subject of divine immanence proves that there was neither need of, nor place for, such go-betweens. The true purpose was the glorification of God. In their daily experience the people saw the sovereign of their country accorded the highest honours and held in the profoundest reverence. The more magnificent the surroundings of the monarch and the larger his retinue, the greater was the admiration extended to him.

[1] See 1 Kings xxii. 19; Is. vi. 1 ff.; Job i. 6.

Although the Jew was commanded by his religion to honour the king—on beholding a gentile ruler he should pronounce the benediction, 'Blessed art Thou, O Lord our God, King of the Universe, Who hast imparted of Thy glory to Thy creatures,' and he had to bestir himself to go out to greet the king on his passing by (Ber. 58a)—for all that he looked upon an earthly monarch as only flesh and blood, a mortal being like himself. God was the King of kings, the Sovereign of the whole Universe; and in his imagination he pictured 'earthly kingship as being like the Kingship of heaven' (ibid.), only on an infinitely reduced scale. As the ruler of so vast a kingdom, God provided Himself with an enormous host of ministers to carry out His behests.

The angels, as beings worthy to stand in proximity to the Throne of Glory, necessarily were more perfect creatures than man. Nevertheless, they too were created and could never attain the perfection of God. 'When were the angels created? R. Jochanan said, On the second day, since it is written, "Who layest the beams of Thine upper chambers in the waters.[1] . . . Who makest winds Thy messengers, the flaming fire Thy ministers" (Ps. civ. 3 f.). R. Channina said, On the fifth day, since it is written, "winged things flying above the earth" (Gen. i. 20), and "with two wings he (i.e. the seraph) flew" (Is. vi. 2). All agree they were not created on the first day, so that people should not say that Michael stretched the south end of the firmament and Gabriel the north end' (Gen. R. i. 3).

Another opinion about the creation of angels is to be found in the conversation between the Emperor Hadrian and R. Joshua b. Chananyah, the former asking: 'Do you maintain that a band of ministering angels do not offer praise to God more than once, and He daily creates a fresh band who sing before Him and then perish?' 'That is so.' 'Where do they go?' 'To the place where they were created.' 'Whence are they created?' 'From the river of fire.'[2] 'What is the nature of the river of fire?' 'It is like the Jordan, which does not cease its flow day or night.' 'Whence does it originate?' 'From the perspiration of the *Chayyoth* which they exude while carrying the Throne of the Holy One, blessed be He' (Gen. R. LXXVIII. 1).

This theory of the origin of the angels was disputed and others put forward. 'From every utterance that issues from the mouth

---

[1] Since the separation of the waters occurred on the second day (Gen. i. 6 ff.) and the Psalmist associates the 'upper chambers' with the angels, no doubt as their habitation, these latter must also have been created on the second day.

[2] See Dan. vii. 10.

of the Holy One, blessed be He, an angel is created; as it is said, "By the word of the Lord were the heavens made; and all the host [1] of them by the breath of his mouth" (Ps. xxxiii. 6)' (Chag. 14*a*). According to another view, angels were constituted of the same elements as heaven itself: 'An angel consists half of water and half of fire, and possesses five wings' (p. R.H. 58*a*).

The general belief was that angels were immortal and did not propagate their species (Gen. R. VIII. 11). On occasion, however, God may destroy numbers of them when they withstand His will (Sanh. 38*b*). They require no physical nourishment (Gen. R. XLVIII. 14), being sustained by the lustre of the *Shechinah* (Exod. R. XXXII. 4). They are not troubled by the *Jetzer Hara*, the evil impulse, which means that they are not subject to normal human passions (Gen. R. XLVIII. 11).

Human beings are akin to the angels in three respects: 'They have knowledge like the ministering angels; they have an erect stature like the ministering angels; they converse in the Holy Tongue (i.e. Hebrew) like the ministering angels' (Chag. 16*a*). On the point of language, with the exception of Gabriel, who was acquainted with every mode of speech, the angels were said to be ignorant of Aramaic; and for that reason one should not offer petitions for his needs in that language, since it was an angelic duty to carry the prayers which were uttered to the Throne of God (Sot. 33*a*). It has been suggested that there was a practical purpose behind that assertion, viz. the desire to preserve Hebrew as at least the language of prayer, although it had been displaced by Aramaic as the vernacular of the Jews.

As will be pointed out, angels are delegated special duties, and one of them is appointed to function in connection with prayer. It was said: 'After all the places of worship have completed their services, the angel who is appointed over prayer gathers up all the devotions which had been offered in all the places of worship, forms them into crowns and sets them upon the head of the Holy One, blessed be He' (Exod. R. XXI. 4). Since this is a homily on the verse, 'O Thou that hearest prayer, unto Thee shall all flesh come' (Ps. LXV. 2), the intention could not possibly be to describe the angel as an intermediary between the worshipper and God. Such an idea would be in direct contradiction with the general teaching that He is near to all who call upon Him in truth. We have to see in the passage nothing more than a play on the word *adécha* (unto Thee), the consonants of which are capable of being read as *édyecha* (Thy adornment); and the prayers alluded to are

---

[1] 'Host' is interpreted as bands of angels, not the sun, moon, and stars.

doubtless the expressions of praise of God which are prominent in the Hebrew service.

It is possible, on the other hand, that a practice grew up among the people of invoking angels.[1] That it was deprecated by the Rabbis is evident from the words they put into the mouth of God: 'If trouble befall a man, let him not cry to Michael or Gabriel; but let him cry to Me and I will answer him at once' (p. Ber. 13a).

In the Bible we do not find any angels named until we reach the Book of Daniel, where occur the names of Gabriel (viii. 16; ix. 21) and Michael, who is described as 'one of the chief princes' (x. 13) and 'the great prince' (xii. 1). This fact led the Rabbis to assert: 'The names of the angels came up in the possession of Israel from Babylon' (p. R.H. 56d); and the reference to 'one of the chief princes' created the belief in different ranks in the angelic host. At the head are four archangels, corresponding to the four divisions of the army of Israel as described in Num. ii. 'As the Holy One, blessed be He, created four winds (i.e. directions) and four banners (for Israel's army), so also did He make four angels to surround His Throne—Michael, Gabriel, Uriel, and Raphael. Michael is on its right, corresponding to the tribe of Reuben; Uriel on its left, corresponding to the tribe of Dan, which was located in the north; Gabriel in front, corresponding to the tribe of Judah as well as Moses and Aaron who were in the east; and Raphael in the rear, corresponding to the tribe of Ephraim which was in the west' (Num. R. II. 10).

Michael and Gabriel are the most prominent of all the angels and are often mentioned together as co-operating in a task. They were the two groomsmen at Adam's marriage at which God Himself officiated (Gen. R. VIII. 13), and they assisted at the burial of Moses (Deut. R. XI. 10). Michael is even superior to Gabriel in rank (Ber. 4b), and wherever he appears the glory of the *Shechinah* is also bound to be found (Exod. R. II. 5). Each nation has its guardian angel, Michael being the guardian angel of Israel. He acts as the counsel for Israel's defence when the wicked angel Samael brings charges against them before God (ibid. XVIII. 5). He brought the news to Sarah that she would give birth to a son (B.M. 86b). He was the instructor of Moses (Deut. R. XI. 10). In the history of the nation he often proved himself a reliable

[1] A trace still remains in the Hebrew prayer book. In the prayers to be recited before retiring at night occurs: 'In the name of the Lord, the God of Israel, may Michael be at my right hand, Gabriel at my left, before me Uriel, behind me Raphael, and above my head the divine presence of God' (ed. Singer, p. 297).

protector. He smote the army of Sennacherib (Exod. R. XVIII. 5).
He endeavoured to prevent the exile by offering up the plea to
God, 'Save them for the sake of the good men who are in their
midst' (Joma 77a), but the sins of the people were too grievous.
When Haman plotted to destroy the Jews of Persia, Michael
defended them in heaven (Esth. R. VII. 12).

Gabriel was the messenger of God on numerous missions. He
was one of the three angels who visited Abraham, his task being
the overthrow of Sodom (B.M. 86b). He wished to rescue Abraham
from the furnace into which he had been flung by order of King
Nimrod, but God said: 'I am One in the Universe and he is likewise unique; so it is proper that I Who am One should rescue
him who is unique' (Pes. 118a). He saved Tamar from the fate
of being burnt as a punishment for her unchastity (Sot. 10b). He
was the protector of Joseph against the evil designs of Potiphar
(ibid. 13b) and taught him the seventy languages of the world
(ibid. 33a). He smote the handmaidens of Pharaoh's daughter
who tried to dissuade her from rescuing Moses (ibid. 12b). He
also struck the infant Moses to make him weep so that the princess
should feel compassionate towards him (Exod. R. I. 24). He again
saved Moses' life when, according to the legend, Pharaoh, on the
advice of his counseller Jethro, submitted him to the test to ascertain whether he was the person destined to overthrow his rule.
The king set before him coals of fire and a crown; and had the
child grasped the latter he would have been killed. The child
wished to snatch the crown, but Gabriel pushed his hand on to
the coal (ibid. 26).

A curious legend in connection with Gabriel reads: 'At the time
that Solomon married Pharaoh's daughter, Gabriel descended and
stuck a reed in the sea around which there gathered a mud-bank,
and upon it was the great city of Rome built' (Sanh. 21b). The
meaning appears to be that through Solomon's folly, a new empire
was brought into existence which was destined to overthrow the
kingdom of Israel.

Gabriel was the angel spoken of by Ezekiel (ix. 3 f.) who, equipped
with the writer's ink-horn, set a mark on the foreheads of the
people of Jerusalem who were to be spared (Shab. 55a). He
rescued Hananiah, Mishael, and Azariah from death by burning
(Pes. 118a, b). He helped to secure the salvation of Israel in the
days of Ahasuerus by preventing Vashti from obeying the king's
command to appear at his banquet (Meg. 12b), thus securing the
election of Esther as queen in her stead; and he rewrote in the
king's Chronicles the service that Mordecai had rendered in

exposing the plot against his life, the record having been expunged by Shimshai (ibid. 16a).

Little is told concerning the other two archangels. Raphael, as his name implies, was the prince of healing; and he joined Michael and Gabriel in their visit to Abraham, his mission being to cure the patriarch of the indisposition which followed his circumcision (B.M. 86b). Uriel, meaning 'light of God,' was the medium by which the knowledge of God came to men. 'Why was his name called Uriel? Because of the Torah, the Prophets and the Hagiographa by means of which the Holy One, blessed be He, atones for sins and gives light to Israel' (Num. R. II. 10).

An angel was designated as 'prince' over each of the elements. Gabriel was the prince of fire (Pes. 118a); Jurkemi, prince of hail (ibid.); Ridya, prince of rain (Taan. 25b); Rahab, prince of the sea (B.B. 74b); Lailah, prince of night (Sanh. 96a) and also of conception (Nid. 16b); Dumah, the angel of death (Ber. 18b). Other princes are mentioned without names being attached to them; e.g. prince of the world (Jeb. 16b) and prince of Gehinnom (Arach. 15b).

The 'prince of the world' was identified by later writers with the angel Metatron. The name is probably borrowed from the Latin *Metator*, which signifies 'a precursor,' and he was regarded as the angel who 'went before' the Israelites in the wilderness (Exod xxiii. 20). He must have been held at one time in 'very high reverence, since special mention is made of the fact that prayers must not be offered to him. 'A Sadducee said to R. Idith, "It is written, 'And unto Moses He said, Come up unto the Lord' (ibid. xxiv. 1). It ought to have stated, "Come up unto Me"!' He replied, "The speaker was Metatron, whose name is the same as his Master's, for it is written, 'My name is in him (viz. the angel)' (ibid. xxiii. 21)." "In that case," said the Sadducee, "we ought to pray to him!" "No," was the Rabbi's answer, "for the context declares, 'Do not exchange (Me) for him,'"[1] "If that is so, why does the verse continue, 'For He will not pardon your transgression'?" "I assure you," the Rabbi answered, "we did not accept him even as a forerunner; for it is written, 'If Thy (God's) presence go not with me, carry us up not hence' (ibid. xxxiii. 15)'" (Sanh. 38b).

This heretical identification of Metatron with God is hinted at elsewhere. Of the apostate Acher[2] it is related that when he ascended to Paradise, 'He saw Metatron, to whom permission was

---

[1] This is how the Hebrew phrase is understood instead of its literal rendering: 'Be not rebellious against him.'
[2] See p. 28 n. 1.

given to remain seated while he recorded the merits of Israel. Acher said, "It has been taught that in heaven there is no sitting, contention, back,[1] or weariness. Are there then *two* Powers?"' (Chag. 15a).

Metatron co-operates with God in the teaching of the young. While God devotes the last three hours of the day to this work, Metatron is in charge during the remainder of the day (A.Z. 3b).

Coupled with Metatron is another angel named Sandalphon, a word from the Greek meaning 'co-brother.' He is the tallest of the angels. 'He stands upon earth and his head reaches to the level of the *Chayyoth*. He is taller than his fellow-angels by a space equal to a journey of five hundred years. He stands behind the celestial chariot (Ezek. i. 15 ff.) and weaves crowns (out of the prayers which are offered) for his Maker' (Chag. 13b).

The angels constitute God's *familia* amongst whom strife occasionally breaks out, which is disturbing to peace upon earth. A Rabbi, accordingly, used to add this petition to his daily prayers: 'May it be Thy will, O Lord our God, to grant peace in the household above and the household below' (Ber. 16b). They form a celestial court, and God does nothing in this world without consulting them. The final decision, however, rests with Him alone (p. Sanh. 18a). Thus He consulted them about the creation of man and overruled their objections (Gen. R. VIII. 4).

The angelic host as a body is a force which makes for righteousness in the world, although, as will be seen, there are wicked angels among that body. Consider two striking sayings such as these: 'At the time that the Israelites first said "We will do" and then "We will hear" (Exod. xxiv. 7),[2] sixty myriads of ministering angels came, one for each of the people, and bound two crowns upon him, one for "We will do" and the other for "We will hear." When, however, they sinned with the golden calf, a hundred and twenty myriads of destroying angels came and snatched the crowns away' (Shab. 88a). 'Two ministering angels accompany a man on the Sabbath-eve from the Synagogue to his house—one good and the other evil. On entering the house and finding the Sabbath-light burning, the table prepared and the couch arranged, the good angel exclaims, "May it be His will that it might be like this next

[1] Angels are supposed to have no back but four faces, so as always to be able to behold God (cf. Ezek. i. 6). Seeing Metatron seated while all the other angels had to stand in the presence of God, Acher concluded that Metatron may also have been a divine power.
[2] The verb *shama* means both 'to hear' and 'to obey.' Taking it in the first sense, the Rabbis make much of the promise of Israel to 'do' the Divine will even before they had heard it.

Sabbath," and the wicked angel is compelled to answer Amen. But if the house is not properly prepared in honour of the Sabbath, the wicked angel exclaims, "May it be His will that it might be like this next Sabbath," and the good angel is compelled to answer Amen' (ibid. 119*b*). Here the angel is the radiation of divine grace encouraging the human being to persevere in his endeavour to be faithful to his religious duties. Indeed, it was sometimes taught that two ministering angels always accompanied the human being to testify concerning his daily conduct (Chag. 16*a*), which merely emphasized the thought that whatever man did, even in secret, was recorded against him.

The story of the fallen angels, which figures in the Apocalyptic literature, is not found in Talmud or Midrash. In the writings of the Rabbinic period the evil angels are nothing more than an invention to express the divine wrath, and their function is to carry out the decree when God has to punish men for their wickedness. This is clearly stated in several places. For instance: 'What is the meaning of "slow to anger" as ascribed to God? It signifies keeping anger afar off. The matter may be likened to a king who had two legions consisting of cruel soldiers. If, he said, they dwell in the same city with me, should the inhabitants provoke me, my men will stand against them and act cruelly towards them. I will therefore send them on a long journey, so that if the citizens provoke me, before I send to bring my soldiers back, they will seek to appease me and I will accept it of them. Similarly said the Holy One, blessed be He, *Aph* and *Chémah* [1] are the angels of destruction. I will send them a long way off, so that if the children of Israel provoke Me, before I can fetch them back, they will repent and I will accept it of them' (p. Taan. 65*b*). 'When the Holy One, blessed be He, said to Moses, "Arise, get thee down quickly from hence" (Deut. ix. 12), five angels of destruction heard it and wished to do him harm. They are *Aph*, *Chémah*, *Kétzeph*,[2] *Mashchith* (destroyer), and *Mechalleh* (consumer)' (Deut. R. III. 11).

'The wicked angel Samael, the chief of all the Satans' (Deut. R. XI. 10)—in this way is the army of the evil angels and their captain designated. 'Satan' is the personification of wickedness. A significant remark is: 'Satan, the *Jetzer Hara* [3] and the Angel of Death are all one' (B.B. 16*a*). It indicates that the prompting to evil is rather a force within the individual than an influence from without. It also explains why God permits Satan to be active and does not destroy him. The reason is that, as will be

---

[1] Words meaning 'anger.'   [2] Three words for 'anger.'
[3] See pp. 88 ff.

explained, the *Jetzer Hara* is an essential constituent in human nature, without which the race would soon become extinct.

One should always be alert to escape the power of Satan; and a Rabbi suggested as a suitable blessing for a guest to pronounce over his host: 'May he prosper in all his possessions; may not Satan have power over the works of his hands nor over ours; and may there not leap before him or us any thought of sin, transgression or iniquity from now and for evermore' (Ber. 46a).

It is recommended: 'Let not a man open his mouth to Satan' (ibid. 19a), i.e. he should not say anything unpropitious which might recoil upon him. As an illustration we have the quaint story about a certain man named Pelimo. 'He used to exclaim every day, "An arrow in the eyes of Satan." [1] Once, on the eve of the Day of Atonement, Satan appeared to him in the guise of a beggar, and went and called upon him at his door. Pelimo handed him a loaf of bread. Satan said to him, "On such a day as this all people are within their houses; am I to stand outside?" He brought him in and placed bread before him. Satan said, "On such a day as this all people are seated at table (preparatory to the fast); am I to be by myself?" A seat was given to him at the table and he sat down. Now his body was covered with boils and ulcers, and his behaviour with them was most objectionable. Pelimo said to him, "Sit properly (and behave yourself)!" Satan said, "Give me a cup." A cup was handed to him. He coughed and spat the phlegm into the cup. He was rebuked for his conduct, and sank down (pretending to be) dead. The host heard voices crying out, "Pelimo has killed a man! Pelimo has killed a man!" He fled and hid himself in a closet. Satan followed and prostrated himself before him. Seeing that Pelimo was so upset, he disclosed his identity to him, and asked, "Why do you use that expression?" [2] "How, then, should I say?" he was asked, and the answer was, "You should say, May the All-merciful rebuke Satan"' (Kid. 81a, b).

Since he is only able to be in one place at a time, he must necessarily have many emissaries to do his bidding. As pointed out above, good angels accompany the righteous and evil angels the wicked. Therefore the advice was given: 'If you see a righteous man setting out on a journey and you have to travel the same road, start out three days earlier or three days later than you originally intended on his account, so that you may be in his society; because the ministering angels accompany such a one; as it is said, "For He will give His angels charge over thee to keep

[1] i.e. I defy Satan.   [2] viz. 'an arrow in the eyes of Satan.'

thee in all thy ways" (Ps. xci. 11). But if you see a wicked man
setting out on a journey and you have to travel the same road,
start out three days earlier or three days later than you originally
intended on his account, so that you may not be in his society;
because the angels of Satan accompany him, as it is said, "Set
thou a wicked man over him, and let an adversary (*Heb*. Satan)
stand at his right hand" (ibid. cix. 6)' (Tosifta Shab. XVII. 2).

Satan performs three functions: he seduces men, he accuses
them before God, he inflicts the punishment of death (B.B. 16*a*).
He is the seducer *par excellence*, and his methods are well exemplified
in his conduct towards the first patriarch. The Scriptures relate,
'Abraham made a great feast on the day that Isaac was weaned'
(Gen. xxi. 8). On this verse the Talmud tells: 'Satan said before
the Holy One, blessed be He, "Sovereign of the Universe! Thou
didst graciously bestow offspring upon this old man at the age of
a hundred years; and of all the feast he made, he did not think of
offering a single dove or pigeon unto Thee!" He replied to him,
"Did he not do it all only for the sake of his son? If I were to tell
him to sacrifice his son unto Me, he would immediately obey"'
(Sanh. 89*b*).

Having in this way been responsible for the test, Satan proceeds to make it fail in its purpose. 'Samael came to see our father
Abraham and said to him, "Old man, old man, have you lost
your senses? Are you going to slay a son who was granted to you
when you were a hundred years old?" "Certainly," said Abraham.
"And should God impose still severer tests upon you, will you be
able to endure them?" "I will," he answered, "even stronger
than this one." "But to-morrow he will say to you, Shedder of
blood! you are guilty of having shed the blood of your son!"
"Even so," said Abraham, "I must obey." Seeing that he could
not succeed with him, he went to Isaac and said, "Son of an unhappy mother, your father is going to slay you." Isaac replied,
"Nevertheless, I must submit." Then Satan said, "And all the
beautiful garments which your mother made for you will pass
into the possession of Ishmael, the enemy of your house; do you
pay no attention to that?" Although the whole of it did not
enter (Isaac's mind), part of it did; so it is written, "And Isaac
spoke unto Abraham his father and said, My father" (Gen. xxii. 7).
"Father" is mentioned twice, indicating Isaac's wish that Abraham
should be filled with compassion towards him' (Gen. R. LVI. 4).

Satan was similarly responsible for the making of the Golden
Calf. The text has: 'When the people saw that Moses delayed
(*boshesh*) to come down from the mount' (Exod. xxxii. 1). The

Talmud comments: 'Read not *boshesh* but *baü shesh*, "the sixth (hour) had come." When Moses ascended on high, he said to Israel, "At the end of forty days, at the beginning of the sixth hour, I will return." At the end of forty days Satan came and confused the world, saying, "Where is your master, Moses?" They answered, "He has ascended on high." "But the sixth hour has gone," he told them. They paid no attention. "He is dead," he said to them; but still they took no notice. He thereupon caused them to behold a vision of his bier. Then it was they said to Aaron, "As for this man Moses, we know not what is become of him"' (Shab. 89*a*).

In addition to his mischief-making on earth he is the accuser of men before God; and it is said, 'Satan accuses only in a time of danger' (p. Shab. 5*b*). Thus: 'At the time of childbirth, the angel of death (i.e. Satan) becomes the accuser of the mother. In three circumstances of danger Satan is found as accuser: when a person stays in an unsafe house which might collapse, when he walks along a road alone, and when he undertakes a voyage on the ocean' (Eccles. R. III. 2).

It is related that 'when Israel left Egypt, the angel Samael stood up to accuse them. He spake before the Holy One, blessed be He, "Sovereign of the Universe! Up to now they have been worshippers of idols, and wouldst Thou divide the sea for them?"' (Exod. R. XXI. 7).

He wished to be especially active in this respect during the ten days of penitence between the New Year and Day of Atonement, when Israelites seek forgiveness for their sins; but in God's mercy he is then rendered impotent against them. 'The sounding of the ram's horn (*Shofar*) on the New Year confounds Satan' (R.H. 16*b*); and 'On the Day of Atonement Satan is powerless to oppose (Israel's plea for forgiveness). The letters of *Ha-Satan* (the Satan) have the numerical value of three hundred and sixty-four, indicating that on three hundred and sixty-four days of the year he has power to oppose, but on the Day of Atonement he has not that power' (Joma 20*a*).

Lastly, he is the instrument whereby people are killed and, in that capacity, is known as the 'angel of death.' Much is told of him in that character.[1] For example: 'When Korah rebelled against Moses, the angel of death came to proceed against Israel and do them harm. If he had proceeded against them, he would have destroyed the whole nation' (Num. R. v. 7). He was prevented from doing this by the action of Moses.

[1] For the part he plays in the death of the individual, see p. 74.

Among the advice given by R. Judah the Prince to his sons was: 'Do not stand in front of an ox when it comes up from the pool, because Satan dances between its horns' (Pes. 112b), i.e. it is more liable to gore and kill a person. A recommendation of another Rabbi was: 'If there is a plague in a city, let not a person walk in the middle of the road, because the angel of death walks in the middle of roads. Since permission has been granted him (to kill) he walks about openly. If there is a condition of well-being in a city, a person should not proceed along the sidewalks, because the angel of death, having no permission granted him, slinks about in secret' (B.K. 60b).

The principal antidote to the allurements of Satan and the danger of the angel of death is the Torah. That is the idea which motived the statement, 'When Israel stood by Mount Sinai and exclaimed, "All that the Lord hath spoken will we do and hear" (Exod. xxiv. 7), the Holy One, blessed be He, summoned the angel of death and said to him, "Although I have appointed you a world-ruler over human beings, you have no concern with this people because they are My children"' (Lev. R. xviii. 3).

In spite of the fact, as the foregoing amply proves, that the belief in angels was deep-rooted among the Jews of the Talmudic period, there is evidence that attempts were made to weaken faith in them and belittle their importance. In particular it was urged that man, when he is God-fearing, is superior to the angels. That is the point of the declaration, 'When Adam was in the Garden of Eden (and sinless), he used to recline while the ministering angels roasted flesh and filtered wine for him' (Sanh. 59b). It was like-wise taught, 'Greater are the righteous than the ministering angels' (ibid. 93a); and 'If a man abstain from practising magic, he is introduced into a division of heaven which even the ministering angels cannot penetrate' (Ned. 32a). This teaching reaches its climax in the declaration, 'The Holy One, blessed be He, will in the Hereafter make the division of heaven in which the righteous dwell within that of the ministering angels' (p. Shab. 8d). They will consequently stand nearer the Throne.

§ IV. ISRAEL AND THE NATIONS

Having considered the *Elyonim*, the creatures whose dwelling-place is in the heavens, we come now to the *Tachtonim*, the creatures who inhabit earth. Basing themselves upon the genealogical table in Gen. x, the Rabbis asserted that the world was peopled by seventy nations and the languages spoken were that number also.

In a literature written by Jews for Jews it is but natural to find exceptional prominence given to the people of Israel. Indeed, the classification of the world's inhabitants may there be said to be Israel and the other nations. It was a cardinal dogma that Israel was the chosen people. This is, of course, a Biblical doctrine; but it receives the richest amplification in the treatment of the Rabbis. Over and over again in the Talmud stress is laid upon the intimate and unique relationship which exists between God and His people.

As typical of this standpoint the following may be cited: 'The Holy One, blessed be He, said to Israel, I am God over all who come into the world, but I have only associated My name with you. I am not called the God of idolaters but the God of Israel' (Exod. R. xxix. 4). 'The Holy One, blessed be He, attached His great name to Israel. It may be likened to a king who had a key to a small chest. Said the king, "If I leave it as it is, it will be lost. Behold, I will make a chain for it, so that if it should go astray the chain will indicate where it is." Similarly said the Holy One, blessed be He, "If I leave the Israelites as they are, they will be swallowed up among the heathen nations. I will therefore attach My great name to them, so that they shall live"' (p. Taan. 65d).

This last quotation suggests the reason why the doctrine holds so prominent a place in Rabbinic teaching. It dates from a period when the people had gone through an overwhelming crisis. The Temple had been destroyed, the State broken up, and the population dispersed in alien lands. In their depression many must have felt that their God had discarded them. Consequently, in the Schools and Synagogues the comforting message was preached that Israel was still God's people and His guardianship over them had not ceased.

As an example of such a heartening message we have: 'Come and see how beloved are the Israelites before the Holy One, blessed be He; for wherever they were exiled the *Shechinah* was with them. They were exiled to Egypt and the *Shechinah* was with them; as it is said, "Did I indeed exile [1] Myself to the house of thy father when they were in Egypt?" (1 Sam. ii. 27). They were exiled to Babylon and the *Shechinah* was with them; as it is said, "For your sake I was sent (*sic*) to Babylon" (Is. xliii. 14). Also when in the future they will be redeemed, the *Shechinah* will be with them; as it is said, "The Lord will return [2] with thy captivity" (Deut. xxx. 3).

---

[1] The Hebrew verb *galah* means both 'to reveal' and 'to be exiled.'
[2] Since the Hebrew verb is intransitive, the particle *eth* is construed as the preposition 'with' and not as the sign of the objective case.

It is not stated "the Lord will restore," but "will return with,'' which teaches that the Holy One, blessed be He, will come back with them' (Meg. 29a).

The same tendency may be detected in the explanation that when Israel sang at the Red Sea, 'The Lord is my strength and song' (Exod. xv. 2), what they meant was—and the lesson applied to later ages also—'Thou art the helper and supporter of all who come into the world, but more so of me. All the peoples of the world proclaim the praise of the Holy One, blessed be He, but mine is more acceptable to Him than theirs. Israel declares, "Hear, O Israel, the Lord our God, the Lord is one" (Deut. vi. 4), and the Holy Spirit cries, "Who is like Thy people Israel, a nation one in the earth?" (1 Chron. xvii. 21). Israel says, "Who is like unto Thee among the mighty, O Lord?" (Exod. xv. 11), and the Holy Spirit cries, "Happy art thou, O Israel, who is like unto thee?'' (Deut. xxxiii. 29). Israel says, "Who is like the Lord our God, whensoever we call upon Him?" (ibid. iv. 7), and the Holy Spirit cries, "What great nation is there that hath God so nigh unto them?" (ibid.). Israel says, "For Thou art the glory of their strength" (Ps. lxxxix. 17), and the Holy Spirit cries, "Israel, in whom I will be glorified" (Is. xlix. 3)' (Mech. to xv. 2; 36b).

So close is the relationship between them that the treatment accorded to Israel on earth is reflected upon God in heaven. 'Whoever rises up against Israel is as though he rose against the Holy One, blessed be He' (Mech. to xv. 7; 39a); 'Whoever helps Israel is as though he helped the Holy One, blessed be He' (ibid. 39b); 'Whoever hates Israel is like one who hates Him' (Sifré Num. § 84; 22b).

If, however, Israel is the chosen people, it is not for the purpose of receiving special marks of favouritism from God. Far from being in a better position than the other nations from the material point of view as the result of this choice, Israel bears a heavier responsibility and his liability to punishment is greater. 'Israel is the retinue of the King and his duty is to imitate the King' (Sifra to xix. 2). 'Because God loved Israel He multiplied sufferings for him' (Exod. R. i. 1). 'Three precious gifts did the Holy One, blessed be He, bestow upon Israel, and all of them He gave only through the medium of suffering: they are Torah, the land of Israel, and the World to Come' (Ber. 5a).

The main responsibility of Israel is the guardianship of the Torah, the Divine Revelation. Since the purpose of the world's creation was the glorification of God's name through the medium of the Torah, and Israel was to be its recipient, it follows that

'Israel was in the thought of God before the creation of the Universe' (Gen. R. I. 4), that 'Heaven and earth were only created through the merit of Israel' (Lev. R. XXXVI. 4), and 'As the world could not exist without the winds, so is it impossible for the world to exist without Israel' (Taan. 3b). No self-glorification is here meant, since the sayings refer only to Israel as the guardian of the Torah and therefore state a spiritual fact.

The selection of Israel was no arbitrary choice, and to avoid the imputation of favouritism to God, a tradition related that the Torah was offered to all the nations, but Israel alone agreed to accept it. 'Why did the Holy One, blessed be He, choose Israel? Because all the peoples repudiated the Torah and refused to receive it; but Israel agreed and chose the Holy One, blessed be He, and His Torah' (Num. R. XIV. 10).

This idea is fully elaborated in the legend: 'When the All-present revealed Himself to give the Torah to Israel, not to them alone did He manifest Himself but to all the nations. He first went to the sons of Esau, and said to them, "Will you accept the Torah?" They asked what was written in it. God told them, "Thou shalt not murder"; and they replied, "Sovereign of the Universe! The very nature of our ancestor was bloodshed; as it is said, 'The hands are the hands of Esau' (Gen. xxvii. 22), and for that reason his father promised him, 'By thy sword shalt thou live' (ibid. 40)." He then went to the sons of Ammon and Moab and said to them, "Will you accept the Torah?" They asked what was written in it. He replied, "Thou shalt not commit adultery." They said to Him, 'Sovereign of the Universe! The very existence of this people springs from an act of unchastity." [1] He went and found the children of Ishmael and said to them, "Will you accept the Torah?" They asked what was written in it. He replied, "Thou shalt not steal." They said to Him, "Sovereign of the Universe! The very life of our ancestor depended upon robbery; as it is said, 'He shall be as a wild ass among men; his hand shall be against every man' (ibid. xvi. 12)." There was not a single nation to whom He did not go and offer the Torah; for thus it is said, "All the kings of the earth shall give Thee thanks, O Lord, for they have heard the words of Thy mouth" (Ps. cxxxviii. 4). Even the seven commandments which the sons of Noah had accepted [2] they were unable to preserve, but rejected and gave them to Israel' (Sifré Deut. § 343; 142b).

If there had been no nation to accept the Revelation, the purpose of Creation would have failed and the entire population of the world been blotted out, since the Torah is its *raison d'être*. 'Parable

[1] See Gen. xix. 36 f.   [2] See p. 65

of a king who possessed an orchard planted with rows of figs, vines, pomegranates, and apples. He delivered it into the charge of a keeper and went away. After a while, the king came to inspect the orchard and ascertain what the keeper had done. He found it full of thorns and thistles; so he brought hewers to cut them down. He perceived, however, among the thorns, one beautiful rose which he plucked and smelt, and its fragrance delighted him. Said the king, "For the sake of this rose, the whole orchard shall be spared." Similarly, the whole Universe was only created for the sake of the Torah. After twenty-six generations the Holy One, blessed be He, inspected His world to see what had become of it, and found it full of water, by means of which the wicked generations had perished. He brought hewers to destroy the world; as it is said, "The Lord sat at the Flood" (Ps. xxix. 10). But He perceived in it one rose, viz. Israel, which He took and smelt at the time when He delivered the Decalogue to them, and it delighted Him. When Israel exclaimed, "We will do and hear" (Exod. xxiv. 7), the Holy One, blessed be He, said, "For the sake of this rose shall the orchard be spared, and by the merit of the Torah and Israel shall the world be saved"' (Lev. R. XXIII. 3).

Israel, too, would have perished in the wilderness after the exodus from Egypt if they had rejected the Revelation. 'The Holy One, blessed be He, inverted Mount Sinai over them like a huge vessel and declared, "If you accept the Torah, well and good; if not, here shall be your sepulchre"' (Shab. 88a).

It is therefore evident that, in the opinion of the Rabbis, their people possessed no exceptional inherent superiority for which they merited the distinction conferred upon them by God, and the special status would come to an end immediately on the abandonment of the Torah. Furthermore, they did not look upon the Torah as their exclusive possession. On the contrary, it was destined for all mankind, and happy the day when all nations accepted it.

From this hope emanate such sayings as: 'Every phrase which issued from the mouth of the All-powerful divided itself into seventy languages' (Shab. 88b), and 'Moses expounded the Torah in seventy languages' (Gen. R. XLIX. 2). The finest expression of this thought is found in the exposition of the verse, 'Ye shall therefore keep My statutes and Mine ordinances, which if a man do, he shall live by them' (Lev. xviii. 5): 'Whence is it deduced that even a Gentile who obeys the Torah is the equal of the High Priest? From the words, "which if *a man* do he shall live by them." Similarly it is said, "This is the law of mankind, Lord

God" (2 Sam. vii. 19). It is not stated, "This is the law of the priests, or the Levites, or of Israel," but "the law of mankind." In like manner it is not stated, "Open the gates, that priests or Levites or Israel may enter," but, "Open the gates that a righteous Gentile [1] keeping faithfulness may enter" (Is. xxvi. 2). Furthermore, it is not stated, "This is the gate of the Lord, priests or Levites or Israel shall enter into it," but "the righteous shall enter into it" (Ps. cxviii. 20). In the same way it is not stated, "Rejoice in the Lord, O ye priests or Levites or Israel," but "Rejoice in the Lord, O ye righteous" (ibid. xxxiii. 1); and it is not stated, "Do good, O Lord, to the priests or Levites or Israel," but "unto the good" (ibid. cxxv. 4). Hence even a Gentile who obeys the Torah is the equal of the High Priest' (Sifra to xviii. 5).

The universalistic scope of this doctrine is most impressive and contradicts the belief which prevails that the outlook of Rabbinic Judaism is essentially narrow and racial. Even the sacrifices in the Temple were intended for the whole of humanity. 'On the eighth day of the Feast of Tabernacles, seventy bullocks were offered on behalf of the seventy nations. Woe to the peoples of the world who have lost but know not what they have lost; because while the Temple stood the altar atoned for them, but now who atones for them?' (Suk. 55b).

On the other hand, it must be admitted that we do occasionally meet with dicta which breathe a very different spirit. Typical examples are: 'A Gentile who occupies himself with the study of Torah is deserving of death; as it is said, "Moses commanded us a Torah, an inheritance for the assembly of Israel" (Deut. xxxiii. 4) —the inheritance is for us, not for them' (Sanh. 59a). 'Moses sought that the *Shechinah* should rest upon Israel, and He granted it; as it is said, "Is it not in that Thou goest with us?" (Exod. xxxiii. 16). He sought that the *Shechinah* should not rest upon the other peoples of the world, and He granted it; as it is said, "So that we are distinguished, I and Thy people" (ibid.)' (Ber. 7a). In all probability such declarations as these were called forth by the rise of the Christian Church whose members also studied the Scriptures and claimed that the Divine Grace rested upon them.

The ideal of the religion of the Rabbis was the extension of God's Kingship over all the peoples of the world, and the Jews had a constant reminder of it in the regulation, 'A benediction which contains no reference to the Divine Kingship is no benediction' (Ber. 40b). That means that the benediction had to be introduced by the formula, 'Blessed art Thou, O Lord our God, *King of the*

[1] The Hebrew word *goi* denotes 'Gentile' as well as 'nation.'

Universe.' It followed from this that the doors could not be bolted against any Gentile who desired admittance from pure motives.

Genuine converts were welcomed and highly esteemed. 'Proselytes are dear (to God), for they are described in the same terms as Israelites. The children of Israel are called "servants," as it is said, "For unto Me the children of Israel are servants" (Lev. xxv. 55), and proselytes are called "servants," as it is said, "To love the name of the Lord to be His servants" (Is. lvi. 6). Israelites are called "ministers," as it is said, "Ye shall be named the priests of the Lord, men shall call you ministers of our God" (ibid. lxi. 6), and proselytes are called "ministers," as it is said, "The strangers that join themselves to the Lord to minister unto Him" (ibid. lvi. 6). The children of Israel are called "friends," as it is said, "The seed of Abraham, My friend" (ibid. xli. 8), and proselytes are called "friends," as it is said, "(God is) the friend of the proselyte" (Deut. x. 18). The word "covenant" is used in connection with Israel, as it is said, "My covenant shall be in your flesh" (Gen. xvii. 13)," and similarly with proselytes, as it is said, "Who hold fast by My covenant" (Is. lvi. 6). The word "acceptance" is used in connection with Israel, as it is said, "That they may be accepted before the Lord" (Exod. xxviii. 38), and with proselytes it is said, "Their burnt-offerings and their sacrifices shall be accepted upon Mine altar" (Is. lvi. 7)' (Mech. to xxii. 20; 95a). There is more to the same effect, which goes to demonstrate that the Israelite and the convert were placed on exactly the same level.

On the verse, 'And the souls that they had gotten [1] in Haran' (Gen. xii. 5), we are told, 'Abraham made proselytes among the men and Sarah among the women. Whoever brings a heathen near (to God) and converts him is as though he had created him' (Gen. R. xxxix. 14). One Rabbi even declared: 'The Holy One, blessed be He, did not exile Israel among the nations for any other reason than that proselytes should be added to them' (Pes. 87b).

In one passage we find a a contrary opinion expressed, viz., 'Proselytes are as troublesome to Israel as a sore' (Jeb. 47b), but it originated from the experience of a time when they proved themselves a source of trouble and danger to the community. Great care was then exercised in the examination of would-be converts and their motives closely scrutinized. The ceremony of reception is described as follows: 'When a proselyte comes in these times to be accepted as a convert, he is asked, "What is your purpose in coming to be converted? Do you not know that Israel is now

[1] The Hebrew is literally 'made.'

afflicted, persecuted, humbled, distracted, and suffering chastisements?" If he replies, "I know and am unworthy (to share their hardships)," he is accepted forthwith and instructed in some of the minor and more important precepts, as well as in the penalties which are attached to them. He is told, "You must know that before taking this step you partook of forbidden fat and profaned the Sabbath without incurring punishment; but henceforward if you do these things dire penalties will befall you." In the same way that he is informed of the punishments attached to the precepts, he is likewise informed of the rewards. He is told, "You must know that the World to Come is reserved for the righteous, and Israel at the present time is unable to accept abundance of good or abundance of punishment." They must not, however, repel him excessively. If he accepts, he is circumcised forthwith. After he is healed, he undergoes immersion [1] without delay, and two disciples of the Sages stand by him and instruct him in some of the minor and more important precepts. When he has immersed himself and ascended from the water he is an Israelite in every respect' (Jeb. 47a, b).

The most prominent of the advocates on behalf of proselytes was Hillel, whose maxim was: 'Be of the disciples of Aaron, loving peace and pursuing peace, loving your fellow-creatures and drawing them near to the Torah' (Aboth I. 12). The story is told that a heathen came to Shammai with the request to be accepted as a convert on condition that he was taught the whole of the Torah while he stood on one foot. The Rabbi drove him away with the yard-stick which he was holding. He then went to Hillel with the same request; and he said to him: 'What is hateful to yourself, do not to your fellow-man. That is the whole of the Torah and the remainder is but commentary. Go, learn it' (Shab. 31a).

To the Gentiles who were not preparaed to enter the fold of Judaism, a moral code, known as the seven commandments of the sons of Noah, was offered. It consisted of the precepts: 'The practice of equity, prohibitions against blaspheming the Name, idolatry, immorality, bloodshed, robbery, and devouring a limb torn from a live animal' (Sanh. 56a). By righteous conduct, based upon these fundamental laws, they would earn the divine approval. The text, 'Righteousness exalteth a nation, but sin is a reproach to the peoples' (Prov. xiv. 34), was applied to Israel as regards the first clause and to Gentiles as regards the second. Since the word for 'reproach' (chésed) also denotes 'piety,' the words were given the meaning that even the pious actions of the Gentiles are a sin

[1] In a tank specially arranged for ritual purposes.

to them because their motives were impure. This interpretation was rejected by R. Jochanan b. Zakkai, who declared: 'Just as the sin-offering atones for Israel, so righteousness atones for the peoples of the world' (B.B. 10b). And so righteous is God in His judgment that 'He judges the Gentiles by the best among them' (p. R.H. 57a).

The harsh sayings which are occasionally found in the Talmud with respect to non-Jews often spring from the conviction that 'Gentiles are addicted to licentiousness' (Jeb. 98a). The Rabbis were revolted by the low standards of conduct they saw practised around them and were thankful for the finer ideals which their religion offered them. A prayer, composed to be said on leaving the House of Study, reads: 'I give thanks before Thee, O Lord my God and God of my fathers, that Thou has set my lot among those who sit in the House of Study and the Synagogue, and hast not set my lot with those who frequent the theatres and circuses; for while I labour to inherit Paradise, they labour for the pit of destruction' (p. Ber. 7d).

Some of the bitter sayings were wrung from anguished lips under extreme provocation. The most criticized utterance of this type is: 'Kill the best of the Gentiles! Crush the head of the best of snakes!' (Mech. to xiv. 7; 27a). But it should be remembered that the author was R. Simeon b. Jochai, who had lived through the terrible Hadrianic persecutions, seen his beloved teacher, R. Akiba, subjected to fiendish cruelties at the hands of the Romans, and been compelled to hide with his son in a cave for thirteen years to escape the oppressors of his people. His words expressed his personal feelings; but to quote them as illustrative of Talmudic ethics is grossly unjust.

That the objection to the Gentile was ethical and not racial becomes quite evident from this extract: 'R. Eliezer declared, "No Gentiles will have a share in the World to Come; as it is said, 'The wicked shall return to the nether-world, even all the nations that forget God' (Ps. ix. 17); 'the wicked' refers to the evil among Israel." R. Joshua said to him, "If the verse had stated 'The wicked shall return to the nether-world and all the nations,' and had stopped there, I should have agreed with you. Since, however, the text adds, 'that forget God,' behold, there must be righteous men among the nations who will have a share in the World to Come"' (Tosifta Sanh. XIII. 2). That the righteous of all peoples will inherit the bliss of the Hereafter is the accepted doctrine of Rabbinic Judaism.[1]

[1] See p. 369.

CHAPTER III

THE DOCTRINE OF MAN

§ I. The Human Being

THAT the human being was created in the image of God lies at the root of the Rabbinic teaching concerning man. In that respect he is pre-eminent above all other creatures and represents the culminating point in the work of Creation. 'Beloved is man, for he was created in the image of God; but it was by a special love that it was made known to him that he was created in the image of God; as it is said, "For in the image of God made He man" (Gen. ix. 6)' (Aboth III. 18).

This fact gives the human being his supreme importance in the economy of the Universe. 'One man is equal to the whole of Creation' (ARN XXXI). 'Man was first created a single individual to teach the lesson that whoever destroys one life,[1] Scripture ascribes it to him as though he had destroyed a whole world; and whoever saves one life, Scripture ascribes it to him as though he had saved a whole world' (Sanh. IV. 5).

Moreover, since men are formed in the divine semblance, they must keep that knowledge always in mind in their relationship with one another. An affront to man is *ipso facto* an affront to God. R. Akiba declared the text, 'Thou shalt love thy neighbour as thyself' (Lev. xix. 18), to be an important basic principle of the Torah, and deduced from it the doctrine: 'You should not say that inasmuch as I am despised let my fellow-man be despised with me; inasmuch as I am cursed, let my fellow-man be cursed with me. R. Tanchuma said, If you act in this manner, know Who it is you despise, for "in the image of God made He man"' (Gen. R. XXIV. 7).

While stressing the idea of man's kinship with God, the Rabbis were equally insistent upon the gulf which divides them. If part of him was divine, another part was earthly. 'All creatures which are formed from heaven, both their soul and body are from heaven; and all creatures which are formed from earth, both their soul and body are from earth, with the exception of man whose soul is from heaven and his body from earth. Therefore, if a man obeys the

---

[1] This is the original wording. There is a later interpolation, 'one soul of Israel,' which destroys the universal character of the teaching.

Torah and does the will of his Father in heaven, behold he is like the creatures above; as it is written, "I said, Ye are gods, and all of you sons of the Most High" (Ps. lxxxii. 6). But if he obey not the Torah and perform not the will of his Father in heaven, he is like the creatures below; as it is said, "Nevertheless ye shall die like men" (ibid. 7)' (Sifré Deut. § 306; 132a).

This dual nature of the human being is described in another way: 'In four respects man resembles the creatures above, and in four respects the creatures below. Like the animals he eats and drinks, propagates his species, relieves himself and dies. Like the ministering angels he stands erect, speaks, possesses intellect, and sees [1]' (Gen. VIII. 11).

The purpose of his creation was to afford him an opportunity of glorifying the Maker of the Universe. 'From the beginning of the world's formation, praise ascended to the Holy One, blessed be He, only from the waters; as it is said, "Above the voices of many waters, the mighty breakers of the sea" (Ps. xciii. 4). What did they proclaim? "The Lord on high is mighty." The Holy One, blessed be He, declared: "If these, which have no mouth or speech, offer Me such praise, how much more will I be extolled when I create man!"' (Gen. R. v. 1).

Life must therefore be interpreted and conducted in that light. The phrase, 'The dead praise not the Lord' (Ps. cxv. 17), was explained as pointing that moral. 'Always should a man occupy himself with Torah and the commandments before he dies; because at his death he is exempt from Torah and the commandments, and the Holy One, blessed be He, can derive no praise from him' (Shab. 30a).

To spend one's existence in toiling for material possessions is senseless, since wealth of that kind has only a transitory value. This truth is illustrated by a parable which also occurs in Æsop's collection: 'It may be likened to a fox which found a vineyard fenced around on all sides; but there was just one hole. He wished to enter through it, but was unable to do so. What did he do? He fasted three days, until he became very thin, and then went through the aperture. He feasted there and, of course, grew fat again. When he wanted to go out, he was unable to pass through the hole. So he fasted another three days until he had grown thin and then went out. When he was outside, he turned back and, gazing upon it, cried, "O vineyard! What use have you been to me and what use are your fruits? All that is inside is beautiful and praiseworthy, but what benefit has one from you?

[1] The meaning is he has eyes in front and not on the side like an animal.

As one enters so he comes out." Such, too, is the world. When a person enters it his hands are clenched as though to say, "Everything is mine; I will inherit it all." When he departs from the world, his hands are open, as though to say, "I have acquired nothing from the world"' (Eccles. R. v. 14).

What he is able to gain and should strive to accumulate during his lifetime is a store of worthy actions. Such a treasure preserves its value even after death. 'In the hour of man's departure neither silver nor gold nor precious stones nor pearls accompany him, but only Torah and good works; as it is said, "When thou walkest it shall lead thee, when thou liest down it shall watch over thee, and when thou awakest it shall talk with thee" (Prov. vi. 22)— "when thou walkest it shall lead thee"—in this world; "when thou liest down it shall watch over thee"—in the grave; "and when thou awakest it shall talk with thee"—in the World to Come' (Aboth vi. 9).

It is related of Monobazus, King of Adiabene, who lived in the first century of the present era and became a convert to Judaism, that during a period of famine he gave away all his wealth to the poor. When his relatives upbraided him for squandering his riches in this manner, he replied to them, 'My ancestors stored up treasures for below, but I have stored up treasures for above; they stored treasures in a place over which force can prevail, but I in a place where force is powerless. They stored up treasures which yield no fruit, but mine will be productive. They stored up treasures of money, but I of souls. They stored up treasures for others, I for my own good. They stored up treasures in this world, but I for the World to Come' (Tosifta Peah iv. 18).

The thought that 'man is here to-day and gone to-morrow' (p. Sanh. 23d) is often mentioned to urge man to action and not to waste the fleeting years. The text, 'Our days on the earth are as a shadow, and there is no abiding' (1 Chron. xxix. 15), suggested the moralization: 'Would that life were like the shadow cast by a wall or a tree; but it is like the shadow of a bird in flight' (Gen. R. xcvi. 2). The same idea is also expressed in this way: 'The day s short, and the work is great, and the labourers are sluggish, and the reward is much, and the Master of the house is urgent' (Aboth ii. 20).

If life is made full and rich by occupation with the precepts of the Torah and good deeds, the reverse is also true, that certain faults rob life of its sweetness and even shorten it. 'The evil eye (i.e. envy), the evil inclination (i.e. over-indulgence), and hatred of his fellow-creatures put a man out of the world' (ibid. 16). Another form of the same doctrine is: 'Envy, cupidity, and ambition take a man from the world' (ibid. iv. 28).

Although the Rabbis dwelt much upon the spiritual nature of man in their discourses, they did not belittle the value and importance of the body. It was God's masterpiece and proved His infinite goodness as well as His boundless wisdom. The fact that each man was a different individuality exercised their wonder. 'It declares the greatness of the Supreme King of kings, the Holy One, blessed be He; because a man strikes many coins from one die and they are all alike. But the Holy One, blessed be He, strikes every person from the die of the first man, but not one resembles another. And why do not faces look alike? That a man shall not see a beautiful dwelling or a beautiful woman and claim them as his. In three respects is a man distinguished from his fellows—in voice, appearance, and mind; in voice and appearance as a safeguard to morality, and in mind because of robbers and men of violence' (Sanh. 38a).[1]

In one passage man is described as a microcosm. 'All that the Holy One, blessed be He, created in the world He created in man' (ARN xxxi). This idea is worked out with much detail; e.g. the hair corresponds to forests, lips to walls, teeth to doors, necks to towers, fingers to nails, and so on.

The views of the Rabbis on the pre-natal stage and that of birth are contained in this extract: 'To what is the child like in its mother's womb? To a book which is folded up and laid aside. Its hands are upon its two temples; the two arm-joints upon the two knees; the two heels upon the buttocks; and the head is set between the knees. The mouth is closed and the navel open. It is nourished from what the mother eats and drinks from what she drinks; but it does not perform evacuation lest it kill the mother. When it emerges into the air of the world, what was closed (viz. the mouth) opens and what was open (viz. the navel) closes; for were it not so, the child could not survive even a single hour. A light is kindled for it upon its head, so that it can see from one end of the world to the other; as it is said, "When His lamp shined upon my head, and by His light I walked through darkness" (Job xxix. 3). Be not astonished at this; for behold, a man may sleep in this spot and see a dream in Spain. The human being experiences no happier days than these. It is then taught the whole of the Torah; but when it enters the atmosphere of the world, an angel comes and smites it upon the mouth and makes

---

[1] If all had the same mind, robbers would know where innocent people hid their valuables and plunder them.

it forget all. It does not emerge from the womb until an oath is imposed, viz., Be righteous and not wicked; even if everybody tells you that you are righteous, be in your own eyes a wicked person; and know that the Holy One, blessed be He, is pure and His ministers are pure, and the soul which He has implanted in you is pure. If you will preserve it in its purity, well and good; but if not, behold I will take it from you' (Nid. 30b).

The anatomy of the human being is explained as follows: 'There are two hundred and forty-eight limbs (including parts of limbs) in the human body: thirty in the sole of the foot, viz. six in each toe; ten in the ankle; two in the foreleg; five in the knee-joint; one in the thigh; three in the hip-joint; eleven ribs; thirty in the palm of the hand, viz. six in each finger; two in the forearm; two in the elbow; one in the arm and four in the shoulder. There are one hundred and one on each side. In addition, there are eighteen vertebrae in the spinal column; nine in the head; eight in the neck; six in the thorax and five in the genitals' (Ohaloth I. 8).

The marvellous construction of the body excited the wonder of the Rabbis and called forth from them exclamations of praise. 'If a bladder is pricked by only a needle all the air in it comes out; but man is made with numerous orifices, and yet the breath in him does not come out' (Gen. R. I. 3). 'The face which the Holy One, blessed be He, created in the human being is in measure equal to the space between the outstretched fingers, yet it contains several sources of water which do not intermingle. The water of the eyes is salty, of the ears greasy, of the nose evil-smelling, and of the mouth sweet. Why is the water of the eyes salty? Because when a person weeps for the dead constantly he becomes blind; but since tears are salty (and make the eyes smart) he stops weeping. Why is the water of the ears greasy? Because when a person hears bad news, were he to seize it with his ears, it would entwine his heart and he would die; but because the water is greasy, he lets the news into one ear and out of the other. Why is the water of the nose evil-smelling? Because when a person inhales a bad odour, were it not that the water of the nose was evil-smelling and preserved him, he would die on the spot. And why is the water of the mouth sweet? At times when man eats something which is repugnant and spews it out, were it not that his spittle was sweet, his soul would not return to him' (Num. R. XVIII. 22). 'Come and see how many miracles the Holy One, blessed be He, performed with man and he is unaware of it. Were he to eat a piece of bread which is hard, it would descend into the intestines and scratch them; but the Holy One, blessed be He, created a fountain in the middle of the throat, which allows the bread to descend in safety (by moistening it)' (Exod. R. xxiv. 1).

With the limited physiological knowledge at their command the Rabbis were evidently anxious to demonstrate how every function of every organ had been designed by God for the well-being of the individual and the prolongation of life. They also believed that different parts of the body were responsible for certain emotions and effects. 'The reins prompt thought, the heart exercises intelligence, the tongue pronounces, the mouth completes the enunciation of the words. The gullet lets in and brings out all kinds of food, the windpipe produces voice, the lungs absorb all kinds of liquids, the liver arouses anger, the gall lets a drop fall upon it and stills it, the milt produces laughter, the large intestine grinds the food, the maw induces sleep, and the nose awakens from sleep. Should the organ which induces sleep arouse from sleep, or should the organ which arouses from sleep induce sleep, the person pines away. Should both of them induce sleep or arouse from sleep simultaneously, one immediately dies' (Ber. 61a, b).

From the point of view of moral conduct the parts of the body are thus classified: 'Six organs serve the human being: three are under his control and three are not. The latter are the eye, ear, and nose. He sees what he does not wish to see, hears what he does not wish to hear, and smells what he does not wish to smell. Under his control are the mouth, hand, and foot. If he so desire he reads in the Torah, or uses bad language or blasphemes. As for the hand, if he so desire, it performs good deeds or steals or murders. As for the foot, if he so desire, it walks to theatres and circuses, or to places of worship and study' (Gen. R. LXVII. 3).

Shakespeare's seven stages of life have been anticipated in the Midrash: 'The seven vanities which Ecclesiastes [1] mentioned correspond to the seven worlds which a man experiences. At one year old he is like a king, placed in a covered litter, and all embrace and kiss him. At two or three he is like a pig which pokes about the sewers. At ten he jumps about like a kid. At twenty he is like a neighing horse; he adorns his person and seeks a wife. Having married, he is like an ass (bearing a heavy burden). Then having become the father of children, he grows bold like a dog to procure sustenance for them. When finally he has grown old, he is (bent) like a monkey' (Eccles. R. i. 2).

[1] The word for 'vanity' occurs five times in Eccles. i. 2, but twice it is in the plural, denoting at least two, hence the total of seven.

Another classification from a different standpoint is given in the ethical treatise *Aboth*: 'At five years the age is reached for the study of Scripture; at ten for the study of Mishnah; at thirteen for the fulfilment of the Commandments;[1] at fifteen for the study of Talmud; at eighteen for marriage; at twenty for seeking a livelihood;[2] at thirty for entering into one's full strength; at forty for understanding; at fifty for counsel; at sixty a man attains old age; at seventy the hoary head; at eighty the gift of special strength;[3] at ninety he bends beneath the weight of his years; at a hundred he is as if he were already dead and had passed away from the world' (v. 24).

Death was held to be the consequence of sin and a sinless person would necessarily be immortal. 'There is no death without sin' (Shab. 55a). 'The ministering angels spake before the Holy One, blessed be He, "Why didst Thou inflict the penalty of death upon Adam?" He replied, "I imposed a light precept upon him but he transgressed it"' (Shab. 55b). 'If a man tells you that had Adam not sinned and eaten of the forbidden tree, he would have lived for ever, answer him that actually happened with Elijah' (Lev. R. XXVII. 4).

Death is the strongest thing which God made in the Universe, and as such cannot be overcome. 'Ten strong things have been created in the world: a mountain is strong but iron can break it; iron is strong but fire can melt it; fire is strong but water can extinguish it; water is strong but clouds can bear it; clouds are strong but the wind can scatter them; wind is strong but the body can carry it (as breath); the body is strong but terror can break it; terror is strong but wine can drive it out; wine is strong but sleep can counteract it; death, however, is stronger than them all' (B.B. 10a).

Many guises are assumed by death and it comes in diverse forms. 'Nine hundred and three varieties of death have been created in the world; as it is said, "The issues[4] of death"' (Ps. lxviii. 20). The severest of them all is croup, and the lightest is the kiss of death. Croup is like a thorn in a ball of clipped wool which tears backwards.[5] Others say it is like the whirling waters at

---

[1] At this age he becomes *Bar Mitzvah*, 'a son of the Commandment,' and is received into membership of the community.
[2] The meaning is uncertain; some translate 'for pursuit (of righteousness).'
[3] See Ps. xc. 10.
[4] The Hebrew for 'issues' is *totzaoth*, the letters of which have the numerical value of nine hundred and three.
[5] viz. when one tries to pull the thorn out; similarly croup tears the membranes of the throat.

the entrance of a canal. The kiss of death is like taking a hair out of milk'[1] (Ber. 8a).

The actual process of dying is described in this manner: 'When a person's end comes to depart from the world, the angel of death appears to take away his soul (Neshamah). The Neshamah is like a vein full of blood, and it has small veins which are dispersed throughout the body. The angel of death grasps the top of this vein and extracts it. From the body of a righteous person he extracts it gently, as though drawing a hair out of milk; but from the body of a wicked person it is like whirling waters at the entrance of a canal or, as others say, like taking thorns out of a ball of wool which tear backwards. As soon as this is extracted the person dies, and the spirit issues forth and settles on his nose until the body decays. When this happens, it cries and weeps before the Holy One, blessed be He, saying, "Lord of the Universe! Whither am I being led?" Immediately (the angel) Dumah takes and conducts him to the court of death among the spirits. If he had been righteous, it is proclaimed before him, "Clear a place for such and such a righteous man"; and he proceeds, stage by stage, until he beholds the presence of the Shechinah' (Midrash to Ps. xi. 7; 51b, 52a).

Another account of the death-process reads: 'They say concerning the angel of death that he is full of eyes all over; and at the time of the decease of an invalid, he stands above his pillow with a drawn sword in his hand, upon which a drop of gall is suspended. When the invalid beholds him, he takes fright and opens his mouth into which the angel lets the drop fall. On account of this the person dies, and on account of it the corpse gives forth an evil odour and the face turns ghastly pale' (A.Z. 20b).

The people of that time looked for omens in the circumstances which accompanied the demise of a person. 'Who dies in the midst of laughter it is a good omen for him, but amidst weeping it is a bad omen for him. If his face is turned upward the omen is good, if downward the omen is bad. If his face is turned towards the people the omen is good, if towards the wall it is bad. If his face is pale the omen is bad; if ruddy it is good. Who dies on the eve of the Sabbath it is a good omen for him; if at the termination of the Sabbath, it is a bad omen for him. Who dies on the eve of the Day of Atonement it is a bad omen for him; at its termination the omen is good. If he die of abdominal disease it

---

[1] A metaphor to describe an easy process. Aaron (Num. xxxiii. 38) and Moses (Deut. xxxiv. 5) are said to have died 'at the command (lit. mouth) of the Lord,' which is explained as meaning by the divine kiss (B.B. 17a).

is a good omen, because most of the righteous die from this cause'[1] (Keth. 103b).

The Rabbis sought to minimize the dread with which the end of life was normally contemplated. They stressed the thought that it was a perfectly natural process. On the words, 'There is a time to be born and a time to die' (Eccles. iii. 2), the Midrash (ad loc.) makes the remark, 'From the moment of birth there is always the possibility of death'; and they exhorted, 'Repent one day before your death' (Shab. 153a), which means immediately, since the actual day is unknown. As we have seen, death was even classed among the 'very good' things made by the Creator.

The time of death is determined by God, and none dare anticipate His decree. Suicide was regarded with the utmost abhorrence and denounced as a heinous sin. The Rabbis explained the verse, 'And surely your blood, the blood of your lives, will I require' (Gen. ix. 5), as follows: 'The word "surely" includes one who strangles himself' (Gen. R. xxxiv. 13), i.e. a death which does not involve the actual shedding of blood. We find this discussion on the subject: 'A person may not do injury to himself; some authorities declare that he may. But in view of the text, "Surely your blood, the blood of your lives (lit. souls), will I require," which was interpreted to mean self-destruction, it is different' (B.K. 91b). The meaning is that where self-harm ends in suicide, all teachers agree that it is forbidden.

More impressive than theory is the practice as disclosed in the story of the martyrdom of Channina b. Teradyon, who was burnt alive by the Romans. They had enwrapped his body in a Scroll of the Torah and placed balls of wool, soaked in water, around him to prolong the agony. His disciples cried to him: 'Open your mouth and let the fire into you (to hasten the end).' He replied: 'It is better that He should take (the soul) Who gave it, and let nobody do violence to it himself' (A.Z. 18a).[2]

A sane and wholesome view of life and death is to be found in the treatment of the text, 'Better is the day of death than the day of one's birth' (Eccles. vii. 1): 'When a person is born, all rejoice; when he dies, all weep. But it should not be so. On the

---

[1] This malady, being of a most distressing character, was thought of as suffering which atoned for sin; but also the physical purgation which was a symptom affected likewise the moral constitution and rendered the person purified. See p. 106.

[2] Josephus takes the same view: 'The souls of those whose hands have acted madly against themselves are received in the darkest place in Hades, and God, Who is their Father, punishes them that offend against either soul or body in their posterity. So God hates suicide, and it is punished by our most wise legislator' (War iii. viii. 5).

contrary, when a person is born, there should not be rejoicing because nobody knows what will be his lot and career, whether righteous or wicked, good or bad. When, on the other hand, he dies, it is an occasion for rejoicing if he departed with a good name and left the world peacefully. Parable of two ships making their way through the ocean, one leaving the harbour and the other entering it. People rejoiced over the ship on its departure, but not over the one which was arriving. A clever man stood there and said to them: "My opinion is the opposite of yours. You should not rejoice over the ship which has set out as nobody knows what lies in store for it, what rough seas and storms it may encounter; but when a ship reaches its harbour, all should rejoice that it arrived in safety"' (Eccles. R. ad loc.).

§ II. The Soul

Man is akin to God in having been endowed with a soul. The possession of this Godlike feature is the cause of his affinity to his Maker and his superiority over the other creatures. The Rabbis, as already pointed out, credited the human being with a dual nature. 'Man's soul is from heaven and his body from earth' (Sifré Deut. § 306; 132a). The body is described by them as 'the scabbard of the soul' (Sanh. 108a); and they taught that the soul holds the same relationship to the body that God does to the Universe.[1]

The character of a life depends upon the care which the individual devotes to keeping his soul pure and unstained. A beautiful homily is preached on the verse, 'And the spirit returneth unto God Who gave it' (Eccles. xii. 7): 'Give it back to Him; as He gave it to you in purity, so return it in purity. Parable of a king who distributed regal garments among his slaves. The wise among them folded and stored them in a box. The foolish among them did their work in them. After a time the king demanded the garments back. The wise returned them in a clean condition; the foolish returned them in a filthy condition. The king was pleased with the wise slaves and angry with the foolish. Concerning the former, he ordered that they restore the garments to the treasury and go to their homes in peace. As for the foolish slaves, he ordered that they give the garments to the washer and they be imprisoned. So the Holy One, blessed be He, says with regard to the body of the righteous, "He entereth into peace; they rest in

[1] See p. 6.

their beds, each one that walketh in his uprightness" (Is. lvii. 2), and with regard to the soul, "The soul of my Lord shall be bound in the bundle of life with the Lord thy God" (1 Sam. xxv. 29). Concerning the body of the wicked He says, "There is no peace for the wicked" (Is. xlviii. 22), and concerning the soul, "The souls of thine enemies, them shall He sling out, as from the hollow of a sling" (1 Sam. loc. cit.)' (Shab. 152b).

'The soul,' we are informed, 'is called by five names: *Néphesh, Ruach, Neshamah, Jechidah,* and *Chayyah. Néphesh* is the blood; as it is said, "For the blood is the life (*néphesh*)" (Deut. xii. 23). *Ruach* is that which ascends and descends; as it is said, "Who knoweth the spirit (*ruach*) of man whether it goeth upward?" (Eccles. iii. 21). *Neshamah* is the disposition.[1] *Chayyah* is so called[2] because all the limbs die but it survives. *Jechidah,* "the only one," indicates that all the limbs are in pairs, while the soul alone is unique in the body' (Gen. R. xiv. 9).

Of these terms the first three are in common use in Rabbinic literature, but it is difficult exactly to define their difference. Since the *Néphesh* is identified with the blood, it denotes vitality and is applicable to animals as well as human beings. There is, for example, a saying: 'Every *néphesh* restores the *néphesh,* and everything near to the *néphesh* restores the *néphesh*' (Ber. 44b). This means that any creature, animal or fish, which itself possessed vitality adds to the vitality of a person who eats it, and this is specially true of the part of the creature which is close to the vital organ. Accordingly the *Néphesh* ceases at death.

Ruach and *Neshamah* appear to be used interchangeably, to denote the *psyche* of the human being, which is his exclusively. It is the immortal part of his composition, the 'breath'[3] infused into him by God.

The question as to the point of time in which the human embryo becomes endowed with soul is said to have been discussed by R. Judah, the editor of the Mishnah, and his Roman friend Antoninus.[4] 'Antoninus asked R. Judah, "When is the soul implanted in the human being, at the moment of conception or at the time of the embryo's formation?" He answered, "At the time of formation." The other said, "Is it possible for a piece of meat to

---

[1] For another explanation of the term, see p. 74.
[2] It signifies 'endowed with life.'
[3] This is the literal signification.
[4] They are frequently mentioned together in the Talmud as being intimate friends. Antoninus has usually been identified with Marcus Aurelius; but Professor S. Krauss disputes this and thinks Avidius Cassius, a famous general of Marcus Aurelius and a procurator of Judea, is meant.

remain unsalted without going bad?[1] Surely it must be at the moment of conception." R. Judah exclaimed, "Antoninus has taught me something, and a text supports his view, viz., 'Thy visitation[2] hath preserved my spirit' (Job x. 12)'" (Sanh. 91b).

The Talmud teaches the pre-existence of souls. 'In the seventh heaven, *Araboth*, are stored the spirits and souls which have still to be created' (Chag. 12b), i.e. the unborn souls which have yet to be united to bodies. There was a common belief that the Messianic era will not dawn until all these unborn souls have had their term of existence on earth. 'The son of David (i.e. the Messiah) will not come until all the souls in the *Guph* come to an end' (Jeb. 62a), the *Guph* being the celestial store-house where these souls await their time to inhabit a human body.

The soul is the spiritual force within man which raises him above an animal existence, inspires him with ideals, and prompts him to choose the good and reject the evil. Since the Sabbath also is a spiritualizing force in human life, we find the Rabbinic teaching: 'An additional soul is given to man on the eve of the Sabbath, which is taken from him at the termination of the Sabbath' (Taan. 27b). That means that the due observance of the holy day heightens the power of the soul and increases its dynamic force in human life.

Only when man is mindful of this precious endowment can his life be influenced by the divine will. It was therefore ordained that his first prayer on waking up every morning should be: 'O my God, the soul which Thou hast given me is pure. Thou didst create it within me, and Thou wilt take it from me, but wilt restore it unto me hereafter. So long as the soul is within me, I will give thanks unto Thee, O Lord my God and God of my fathers, Sovereign of all worlds, Lord of all souls. Blessed art Thou, O Lord, Who restorest souls unto dead bodies' (Ber. 60b).

§ III. FAITH AND PRAYER

The kinship between God and man, which results from his spiritual equipment, places upon him the responsibility of proving himself worthy of this heavenly gift. If honour has been conferred upon man by his having been created in the divine likeness, a corresponding obligation rests upon him of living his life so as to win the approval of his Maker.

---

[1] How, then, can the embryo exist and not become putrid unless it is endowed with soul?

[2] The same Hebrew word as for conception.

What, then, is expected of him? The answer is given in this sentence: 'Seven qualities avail before the Throne of Glory: faith, righteousness, justice, lovingkindness, mercy, truth, and peace' (ARN xxxvii). These represent the crowning virtues, and first place is assigned to faith which, indeed, is declared to be the principle upon which the whole relationship of man with God ultimately rests. 'Six hundred and thirteen commandments were addressed to Moses—three hundred and sixty-five prohibitions corresponding to the number of days in the solar year, and two hundred and forty-eight positive commands corresponding to the number of limbs in the human body. David came and reduced them to eleven principles, which are enumerated in Ps. xv. Isaiah came and reduced them to six; as it is said, "He that walketh righteously, and speaketh uprightly; he that despiseth the gain of oppressions, that shaketh his hands from holding of bribes, that stoppeth his ears from hearing of blood, and shutteth his eyes from looking upon evil" (Is. xxxiii. 15). Micah came and reduced them to three; as it is written, "What doth the Lord require of thee, but to do justly, and to love mercy, and to walk humbly with thy God?" (Micah vi. 8). Isaiah subsequently reduced them to two; as it is said, "Thus saith the Lord, Keep ye justice and do righteousness" (Is. lvi. 1). Lastly came Habakkuk and reduced them to one; as it is said, "The righteous shall live by his faith" (Hab. ii. 4)' (Mak. 24a).

The Sages pointed out that faith was the distinguishing feature in the lives of the heroes of the Bible and also of Israel by which they merited the special favour of God. 'Great is the faith with which Israel believed in Him Who spake and the world came into being. In reward for this faith the Holy Spirit [1] rested upon them and they uttered a song; as it is said, "They believed in the Lord and in Moses His servant" (Exod. xiv. 31), which is immediately followed by, "Then sang Moses and the children of Israel this song unto the Lord." Similarly you find that our father Abraham only inherited this world and the World to Come by virtue of faith; as it is said, "He believed in the Lord, and He counted it to him for righteousness" (Gen. xv. 6).' Other examples are cited in the context, and it concludes with the statement: 'Whoever receives upon himself a single precept in faith is worthy of the reception of the Holy Spirit' (Mech. to xiv. 31; 33b).

Many of the commands which God gave to Moses for Israel had for their object the instilling of faith into the people. Two striking instances are furnished with such an interpretation. In Exod.

[1] In the sense of inspiration; see pp. 121 ff.

xvii. 11, it is related that Moses held his hands aloft during the fight with the Amalekites; and the question is asked: 'Could the hands of Moses give victory to Israel or break the might of Amalek? But all the time he held his hands up toward the heaven, the Israelites kept gazing at him and believing in Him Who commanded Moses to act thus, and the Holy One, blessed be He, performed miracles on their behalf. Similarly with the making of the brazen serpent (Num. xxi. 8). Could the image of the serpent kill or save life? But the Israelites kept looking at it and believing in Him Who commanded Moses to act thus, and the Holy One, blessed be He, performed a cure for them' (Mech. to xvii. 11; 54a).

We are informed that 'men of faith' were highly esteemed in Israel. They were men who placed implicit trust in God at all times and in all circumstances. The fact was deplored that 'since the Temple was destroyed, men of faith have ceased' (Sot. IX. 12). What was understood by such faith may be gathered from the remark: 'Whoever has a morsel of bread in his basket and says, "What shall I eat to-morrow?" belongs only to those who are small of faith' (Sot. 48b).

The Talmud has preserved anecdotes concerning two men who were specially distinguished for their unshakable trust in God. The first is known as Nahum of Gamzo [1] and this story explains how he came to be so named: 'Why was he called Nahum, the man of Gamzo? Because whatever happened to him, he used to exclaim, "This also (gam zo) is for good." Once the Rabbis wished to send a gift to the emperor and discussed by whom they should send it. They decided, "Let us send it through Nahum, the man of Gamzo, because he is used to miracles happening to him." So they dispatched the present through him. In the course of the journey he slept at an inn; and the other occupants arose during the night, extracted the contents of his bag and filled it with dust. When he reached his destination, the bag was untied and found to be filled with dust. The emperor cried, "The Jews are making a laughing-stock of me!" and ordered Nahum to be put to death; and still he said, "This also is for good." Elijah [2] thereupon appeared in the guise of one of the emperor's attendants and said, "Perhaps this dust is part of the dust of their patriarch Abraham. Whenever he threw some of it at his enemies it turned into swords, and when he threw stubble it turned into arrows." There

---

[1] A town Gimzo is mentioned in 2 Chron. xxviii. 18, and possibly Nahum was really named after this place.

[2] Elijah, of whom the Bible relates that he did not die, is often introduced into Talmudic stories, usually appearing as the *deus ex machina* in a time of emergency.

happened to be at that time a province which they were unable to conquer. They tried some of the dust against it and subdued it. The emperor then took Nahum to his treasury, filled his bag with precious stones and pearls, and dismissed him with great honour. When he arrived at the same inn, the occupants said to him: "What did you take to the emperor that such great respect has been shown to you?" He answered: "I only took what I carried away from here." So they, too, conveyed some of that dust to the emperor; but when it was tested and did not change into swords and arrows, the men were executed' (Taan. 21a).

The other instance is R. Akiba, of whom this is related: 'A man should always accustom himself to say, "Whatever the All-merciful does, He does for the best." As when R. Akiba was journeying by the way, he came to a certain town and asked for hospitality, but it was refused him; so he exclaimed, "Whatever the All-merciful does is for the best." He went and spent the night in the field, having with him a cock, an ass, and a lamp.[1] A gust of wind came and extinguished the lamp, a cat came and ate the cock, and a lion came and devoured the ass; but he exclaimed, "Whatever the All-merciful does is for the best." That same night a band of robbers came and plundered the town. He thereupon said to the inhabitants, "Did I not tell you that whatever the Holy One, blessed be He, does is all for the best?"' (Ber. 60b).

The Mishnah lays down the rule: 'A man is in duty bound to utter a benediction for the bad, even as he utters one for the good' (Ber. ix. 5).

Faith finds its truest expression in the act of prayer, because only one who sincerely believes in God and His willingness to befriend His creatures addresses petitions to Him. Not that prayer signifies only asking for one's needs. In its highest sense it is the intimate communion between the creature and his Creator, deep speaking to deep. As such, it is gratifying to Him as well as helpful to man. It is even said that 'the Holy One, blessed be He, longs for the prayer of the righteous. Why is the prayer of the righteous likened to a shovel?[2] In the same way that a shovel removes produce from one place to another, so the prayer of the righteous turns His attribute of anger to one of compassion' (Jeb. 64a).

For a prayer to be heard by God not only must it be sincere,

[1] The cock to waken him at dawn, the ass to ride upon, and the lamp by which to study during the night.
[2] The Hebrew word is *éter*, and the same letters give a root with the meaning 'to pray.'

but the person who offers it must be worthy of his petition being answered. 'Whoever performs the will of the All-present and directs his heart to Him in prayer is heard' (Exod. R. XXI. 3); 'Every man in whom is the fear of God, his words are heard' (Ber. 6b). But no person should refrain from praying because he feels himself undeserving of a response; he should persevere with his prayer. 'If a man sees that he prays and is not answered, he should repeat his prayer' (ibid. 32b); and it is further advised, 'Even if a sharp sword be laid upon a man's neck, let him not despair of the divine mercy' (ibid. 10a)—he should not give up hope to the last moment of his life.

One must not only think of himself when praying; he should also be mindful of the needs of his fellows. 'Whoever has it in his power to pray on behalf of his neighbour and fails to do so, is called a sinner; as it is said, "Moreover, as for me, far be it from me that I should sin against the Lord in ceasing to pray for you" (1 Sam. xii. 23)' (Ber. 12b). 'Whoever prays on behalf of a fellow-man, while himself being in need of the same thing, will be answered first' (B.K. 92a).

A certain Rabbi composed the following prayer to be said when starting out on a journey, which was a perilous undertaking in those days: 'May it be Thy will, O Lord my God, to conduct me in peace, to direct my steps in peace, to uphold me in peace, and to deliver me from every enemy and ambush by the way. Send a blessing upon the work of my hands, and let me obtain grace, lovingkindness and mercy in Thine eyes and in the eyes of all who behold me. Blessed art Thou, O Lord, Who hearkenest unto prayer.' But a colleague objected to the wording and commented: 'Always should a man associate himself with the community when praying. How should he pray? "May it be Thy will, O Lord *our* God, to conduct *us* in peace," etc.' (Ber. 29b et seq.). This was the adopted view of prayer, with the consequence that in the Synagogue liturgy the use of the first person singular is very rare.

The importance of prayer is emphasized in such an observation as: 'Greater is prayer than sacrifices. Greater is prayer than good deeds; for you have no one greater in good deeds than our teacher, Moses; nevertheless he was only answered through prayer, as it is said, "Speak no more unto Me of this matter" (Deut. iii. 26), which is followed by "Get thee up into the top of Pisgah" (ibid. 27)' (Ber. 32b). The inference which is drawn is that Moses' prayer secured for him permission to view the land of promise before his death.

True prayer is more than the utterance of the lips; it must come from the heart. 'A person's prayer is not heard unless he places his heart in his hands; as it is said, "Let us lift up our heart with our hands unto God in the heavens" (Lament. iii. 41)' (Taan. 8*a*)—i.e. we must not merely raise our hands in prayer, but our heart also. The Talmud offers this terse and pointed definition of prayer: '"To love the Lord your God and to serve Him with all your heart" (Deut. xi. 13)—which is the service in the heart? Prayer' (Taan. 2*b*).

That the act of prayer must be performed in a reverent manner is strongly urged. 'He who prays must direct his heart to heaven' (Ber. 31*a*). 'When one prays, he must turn his eyes downward and his heart upward' (Jeb. 105*b*). 'Who prays must imagine that the *Shechinah* is over against him; as it is said, "I have set the Lord always before me" (Ps. xvi. 8)' (Sanh. 22*a*). 'When you pray, know before Whom you stand' (Ber. 28*b*). 'He who makes his voice heard during prayer is of the small of faith; he who raises his voice when praying is of the prophets of falsehood' (ibid. 24*b*), because they resemble the prophets of Baal who 'cried aloud' (1 Kings xviii. 28).

The Talmud tells an anecdote which vividly illustrates these exhortations: 'It happened that a pious man was saying his prayers by the roadside. A nobleman passed and greeted him, but he did not respond. The nobleman waited until he had concluded his devotions; and after he had concluded them, he said to him, "Good-for-nothing! When I greeted you, why did you not return my salutation? If I had cut your head off with a sword, who would have demanded your blood at my hands?" He replied, "Wait until I shall have conciliated you with words." And he continued, "If you had been standing before a human king, and your friend had greeted you, would you have responded to him?" "No," he replied. "And if you had responded to him, what would they have done to you?" He answered, "They would have cut off my head with a sword." He said to him, "May we not use the argument from the small to the great: If you, standing before a human king, who is here to-day and to-morrow in the grave, act thus, how much more so I who was standing before the supreme King of kings, the Holy One, blessed be He, Who lives and endures for all eternity?" The nobleman was at once appeased, and the pious man departed for his house in peace' (Ber. 32*b et seq.*).

In addition to private devotions which give utterance to one's personal requirements, there is the congregational act of worship in which the individual should join. The importance of this kind of service is stressed in such declarations as: 'A man's prayer is only heard by God when offered in a Synagogue' (Ber. 6*a*). 'If one is accustomed to attend the Synagogue regularly and absents himself one day, the Holy One, blessed be He, makes inquiry about him; as it is said, "Who is among you that feareth the Lord, that obeyeth the voice of His servant, that walketh in darkness and hath no light?" (Is. l. 10). If his absence is because he went to perform a religious duty, he will have light; but if he went to attend to some secular business he will have no light. "Let him trust in the name of the Lord" (ibid.). For what reason is the light denied him? Because he should have trusted in the name of the Lord, but did not. When the Holy One, blessed be He, enters a Synagogue, and does not find there ten to constitute a quorum, He is immediately filled with wrath; as it is said, "Wherefore, when I came, was there no man? when I called, was there none to answer?" (ibid. 2)'[1] (Ber. 6*b*). So important is this matter of a quorum that, on one occasion, ' R. Eliezer went into a Synagogue and did not find ten there, so he freed his slave and with him completed the requisite number' (ibid. 47*b*).[2]

Further on the subject of the Synagogue service it was taught: 'Whoever has a Synagogue in his town, and does not enter it to pray, is called "an evil neighbour"; as it is said, "Thus saith the Lord, As for all Mine evil neighbours, that touch the inheritance which I have caused My people Israel to inherit" (Jer. xii. 14). More than that, he causes exile to come upon himself and his sons; as it is said, "Behold, I will pluck them up from off their land, and will pluck up the house of Judah from among them" (ibid.). It was told to R. Jochanan, who was a Palestinian, "There are old men to be found in Babylon." He was astonished and exclaimed, "It is written, 'That your days may be multiplied, and the days of your children, upon the land' (Deut. xi. 21)—upon the land of Israel, but not outside it!" When they told him that the old men are in the Synagogue early and late, he said, "It is this which helps them to live long." This is like what R. Joshua b. Levi said to his sons, "Rise early and stay up late to enter the Synagogue, so that you may prolong your life"' (Ber. 8*a*).

While, on the one hand, we have a Rabbi who believed that 'whoever prays much will be answered' (p. Ber. 7*b*), the general opinion was that the length of a prayer bore no relation to its efficacy. 'It happened that a disciple who descended before the

---

[1] When there is not a quorum in the Synagogue, certain parts of the liturgy, including important responses (hence 'none to *answer*') for the congregation, are omitted.

[2] See p. 201.

Ark [1] in the presence of R. Eliezer unduly prolonged the prayers. His disciples said to him, "Our master, what a prolonger he is!" He replied, "Did he prolong more than Moses, our teacher, of whom it is written that he prayed forty days and nights?" (Deut. ix. 25). It again happened that a disciple who descended before the Ark in the presence of R. Eliezer unduly shortened the prayers. His disciples said to him, "What a shortener he is!" He replied, "Did he shorten more than Moses, our teacher; for it is written, 'Heal her now, O God, I beseech Thee'?" (Num. xii. 13)' (Ber. 34a).

The folly of using exaggerated praise of God when praying is likewise impressed upon us. 'A certain man descended before the Ark in the presence of R. Channina. He said, "O God, the great, the mighty, the revered, the gracious, the powerful, the feared, the strong, the courageous, the certain, the honoured." R. Channina waited until he had finished, and then said to him, "What is the use of all those adjectives? The three which we do say, 'The great, mighty, and revered,' if Moses our teacher had not used them in the Torah (see Deut. x. 17) and the men of the Great Assembly instituted them in the liturgy,[2] we should not have been able to say; and you go on saying all those!" A parable: it may be likened to a human king who possessed a million gold pieces, and people praise him as the possessor of a million silver pieces; is it not an insult to him?' (Ber. 33b). Prolonging one's prayer deliberately, for the purpose of 'calculating' upon it, i.e. hoping that its very length will yield an answer, is denounced as folly since such a hope is bound to be falsified (ibid. 32b).

Although the Rabbis commended the act of participating in the three daily statutory services,[3] they were careful to demand that such devotions must not be allowed to degenerate into a mechanical and perfunctory performance. The guiding rule was advocated: 'When you pray, regard not your prayer as a fixed task (kéba), but as an appeal for mercy and grace before the All-present' (Aboth II. 18). The meaning of the word kéba is discussed in the Talmud and variously defined: 'It includes any one whose prayer seems to him a burden; any one who does not recite it in language

[1] The Ark was a chest in the east wall of the Synagogue where the Scrolls of the Torah were deposited. In the older form of the Synagogue the reader's desk was placed in front of the Ark and not, as is now customary, in the centre of the building. 'To descend before the Ark' means to act as the precentor who leads the congregation in prayer.'

[2] This body was accredited with the authorship of parts of the Synagogue liturgy (Meg. 17b).

[3] Tradition ascribed their origin to the three patriarchs respectively (Ber. 26b).

of supplication; any one who is not able to add something new thereto' (Ber. 29b). It was also advised: 'Any one whose mind is not at rest should not pray' (Erub. 65a); 'A man should always examine himself (before offering prayer); if he can direct his heart (to God), let him pray, otherwise he should not pray' (Ber. 30b).

Among the Rabbis of the Talmud are the authors of many prayers which have become part of the Ritual of the Synagogue. Some specimens will be given. 'May it be Thy will, O Lord our God, to grant us long life, a life of peace, a life of good, a life of blessing, a life of sustenance, a life of bodily vigour, a life marked by the fear of sin, a life free from shame and reproach, a life of prosperity and honour, a life in which the love of Torah and the fear of Heaven shall cleave to us, a life wherein Thou fulfillest all the desires of our heart for good' (Ber. 16b).

'O my God, before I was formed I was nothing worth, and now that I have been formed I am but as though I had not been formed. Dust am I in my life; how much more so in my death. Behold, I am before Thee, like a vessel filled with shame and confusion. O may it be Thy will, O Lord my God, that I may sin no more; and as to the sins I have committed, purge them away in Thine abounding compassion though not by means of affliction and sore diseases' (Ber. 17a). This has become part of the confession of sins to be said on the Day of Atonement.

'O my God! Guard my tongue from evil and my lips from speaking guile; and to such as curse me let my soul be dumb, yea, let my soul be unto all as the dust. Open my heart to Thy Torah, and let my soul pursue Thy commandments. And do Thou deliver me from mishap, from the evil impulse, and from an evil woman and all evil which breaks forth to come upon the world. If any design evil against me, speedily make their counsel of none effect, and frustrate their designs. Let the words of my mouth and the meditation of my heart be acceptable before Thee, O Lord, my Rock and Redeemer' (ibid.).

A short prayer to be offered in time of danger reads: 'Do Thy will in heaven above; grant tranquillity of spirit to those who fear Thee below, and do that which is good in Thy sight. Blessed art Thou, O Lord, Who hearkenest unto prayer' (ibid. 29b).

At the conclusion of the statutory service a Rabbi used to pray: 'May it be acceptable before Thee, O Lord my God and God of my fathers, that no hatred against us may enter the heart of any man nor hatred of any man enter our heart, that no envy of us enter the heart of any man nor envy of any man enter our heart;

may Thy Torah be our occupation all the days of our life; and may our words be supplication before Thee.' To this another Rabbi added: 'Do Thou unite our hearts in the fear of Thy Name, keep us far from whatever is hateful to Thee, bring us near to all that Thou lovest, and do justly with us for the sake of Thy Name' (p. Ber. 7d).

A prayer to be said on waking in the morning is: 'Blessed art Thou, O Lord, Who revivest the dead.[1] My Lord, I have sinned before Thee. May it be acceptable before Thee, O Lord my God, that Thou grant me a good heart, a happy lot, a good inclination, a good friend, a good name, a generous eye, a liberal soul and a humble spirit. May not Thy Name ever be profaned through us and let us not become a byword among our fellow-creatures. May our fate not be to be cut off by Thee (through sinfulness), nor our hope turn to despair. Let us not be in want of the help of others and let not our sustenance be dependent upon them, for their gift is small but the shame they inflict is great. Set our portion in Thy Torah with those who perform Thy will. Rebuild Thy Temple and Thy city speedily in our days' (ibid.).

As a last illustration may be cited: 'May it be acceptable before Thee, O Lord my God and God of my fathers, that Thou break and cause to cease the yoke of the evil impulse from our hearts, for Thou hast created us to perform Thy will and so we are bound to do. Such is Thy desire and such is our desire, too; but what impedes us? The leaven in the dough.[2] It is revealed and known before Thee that we have not the strength to resist it; may it therefore be acceptable before Thee, O Lord my God and God of my fathers, that Thou cause it to cease from upon us and subdue it so that we may do Thy will as our will with a perfect heart' (ibid.).

These selections must make it clear that the Rabbis considered prayer to be something greater than the mere petitioning for material needs. While not overlooking the claims of the physical life, they used prayer as the medium for enjoying fellowship with God and the development of what was purest and highest in human nature. The act of praying was their spiritual exercise for increasing the power of their soul to the end that it may become the dominant force in their life, the master of the flesh.

[1] Sleep was said to be a sixtieth part of death (Ber. 57b).
[2] i.e. the evil impulse, which will be explained in the next section.

§ IV. The Two Impulses

In some of the prayers quoted above, mention is made of the 'evil impulse' as a force which drives to wickedness and as an endowment of man which proves a formidable obstacle in the way to a righteous life. It is described as 'the leaven in the dough'—the fermenting ingredient that stirs up evil elements in man's nature which, unless suppressed, overrule the finer instincts and result in wicked actions.

The belief that in every human being there are two urges— one to evil and the other to goodness—figures prominently in Rabbinic ethics. Having to find a basis for the doctrine in the text of the Bible, the Rabbis deduced it in this way: 'What means that which is written, "Then the Lord God formed man" (Gen. ii. 7), the word *wajjitzer* (and He formed) being spelt with two letters *j*? The Holy One, blessed be He, created two impulses,[1] one good and the other evil' (Ber. 61*a*).

The character of a person is determined by which of the two impulses is dominant within him. 'The good impulse controls the righteous; as it is said, "My heart is wounded[2] within me" (Ps. cix. 22). The evil impulse controls the wicked; as it is said, "Transgression speaketh to the wicked, in the midst of the heart, There is no fear of God before his eyes" (ibid. xxxvi. 1). Both impulses control average people' (Ber. 61*b*).

An allegorical interpretation of Eccles. ix. 14 f. reads into the verses the idea of the two impulses: '"There was a little city," i.e. the body; "and few men within it," those are the limbs; "there came a great king against it," i.e. the evil impulse; "and built great bulwarks against it," viz. sins; "now there was found in it a man, poor and wise," i.e. the good impulse; "and by his wisdom delivered the city," that means repentance and good deeds; "yet no man remembered that same poor man," because at the time the evil impulse holds sway the good impulse is forgotten' (Ned. 32*b*).

A similar interpretation is placed on Eccles. iv. 13: '"Better is a poor and wise child than an old and foolish king." The first clause refers to the good impulse. Why is it called a child? Because it does not attach itself to a person until the age of thirteen and upward. Why is it called poor? Because all do not hearken to it. Why is it called wise? Because it teaches creatures

---

[1] The Hebrew word for 'impulse' is *Jetzer*; hence the two *j*'s were taken to indicate two—the *Jetzer Tob*, 'good impulse' and *Jetzer Hara*, 'evil impulse.'
[2] In gaining the victory over the evil impulse.

the right path. The second clause refers to the evil impulse. Why does he call it a king? Because all hearken to it. Why does he call it old? Because it attaches itself to a person from youth to old age. Why does he call it a fool? Because it teaches man the wrong path' (Eccles. R. ad loc.).

While the evil impulse, according to this extract, is born with the individual, the good impulse only manifests itself at the age of thirteen, when a boy is held to be responsible for his actions.[1] The good impulse is accordingly identified with the moral consciousness. This idea is more clearly expressed in the following passage: 'The evil impulse is thirteen years older than the good impulse. It exists from the time of a person's emergence from his mother's womb; it grows with him and accompanies him through life. It begins to desecrate the Sabbath, to kill and act immorally, but there is nothing (within him) to prevent it. After thirteen years the good impulse is born. When he desecrates the Sabbath it warns him, "Good-for-nothing! behold it is said, 'Every one that profaneth it shall surely be put to death' (Exod. xxxi. 14)." If he thinks of committing a murder it warns him, "Good-for-nothing! behold it is said, 'Whoso sheddeth man's blood, by man shall his blood be shed' (Gen. ix. 6)." If he proposes to act immorally it warns him, "Good-for-nothing! behold it is said, 'Both the adulterer and the adulteress shall surely be put to death' (Lev. xx. 10)." When a man excites his passions and sets out to indulge in immorality, all his limbs obey him, because the evil impulse is king over the two hundred and forty-eight organs. When he sets out to perform a meritorious act, all his limbs begin to suffer through him, because the evil impulse within him is king over them all and the good impulse is only like a prisoner in a jail; as it is said, "For out of prison he came forth to be a king" (Eccles. iv. 14)—that refers to the good impulse' (ARN xvi).

The exact moment when the human being becomes endowed with the evil impulse was discussed by Antoninus and R. Judah the Prince, and the decision was as stated above, viz. the urge comes into existence at the time of birth. 'Antoninus asked R. Judah, "From what time does the evil impulse exercise its power in the human being—from the time of the embryo's formation or its emergence from the body?" He answered, "From the time of its formation." The other retorted, "In that case it ought to kick about in the womb and come out of its own accord! Surely it is from the time of its emergence!" R. Judah said, "Antoninus has taught me something which is corroborated by

[1] See p. 73 n. 1.

a Scriptural text, viz. 'Sin coucheth at the door' (Gen. iv. 7)—i.e. the opening of the mother's body"' (San. 91b).

According to one opinion, the evil impulse has a physiological location in one of the body's organs. 'The evil impulse is like a fly that dwells between the two entrances of the heart. There are two reins in man, one prompting him to goodness, the other to evil. It is probable that the good is on the right side and the bad on the left; for it is written, "A wise man's understanding is at his right side, but a fool's understanding at his left" (Eccles. x. 2)' (Ber. 61a).

Another view is that it is a force external to the person which takes possession of him, if allowed the opportunity. The teaching has already been quoted which identifies Satan and the evil impulse.[1] Its working is thus described: 'The evil impulse does not proceed along the sidewalks but in the middle of the highway. When it sees a man ogling with his eyes, straightening his hair and walking with a swaggering gait,[2] it says, "This person belongs to me"' (Gen. R. XXII. 6).

But the common opinion was that the evil impulse is just the disposition of the human being which results from natural instincts, especially sexual desire. Consequently it is not something that is essentially bad, since God creates only what is good. It is evil only in so far as it is liable to be misused. We see this aspect very clearly in the interpretation of the words 'very good' in the verse, 'And God saw everything that He had made and, behold, it was very good' (Gen. i. 31). They were explained as indicating the good impulse and the evil impulse. 'But,' it is asked, 'is the evil impulse very good?' and the answer is given, 'Were it not for that impulse, a man would not build a house, marry a wife, beget children or conduct business affairs' (Gen. R. IX. 7).

So the urge, although it eventuates in wrongdoing, is an essential equipment of man and, indeed, grants him the opportunity of becoming a moral being; because without it there would be no possibility of his doing evil and, as a consequence, goodness also would be meaningless. The logical deduction was drawn, 'There is no evil impulse in animals' (ARN XVI), since they have no moral sense. The same idea underlies the declaration, 'Come, let us ascribe merit to our ancestors; for if they had not sinned we should not have come into the world' (A.Z. 5a). By 'sinned' must be understood their having been under the influence of the evil impulse; and its effect is described as a merit since it preserved the race. Similarly the words, 'Thou shalt love the Lord thy God

[1] See p. 54.   [2] To attract the attention of women.

with all thy heart' (Deut. vi. 5), received the comment: 'With two impulses—the good and the evil' (Sifré Deut. § 32; 73*a*). Even the evil impulse can be employed in the service of God and become a means of demonstrating love of Him.

Why it is called evil and man has to be constantly warned against its allurement is because it seduces him to bad conduct. 'The evil impulse leads a man astray in this world and testifies against him in the World to Come' (Suk. 52*b*). 'Often a man makes his heart to do a charitable act, but the evil impulse within him says: "Why practise charity and reduce your possessions? Rather than give to strangers, give to your children." But the good impulse prompts him to do charity' (Exod. R. xxxvi. 3). 'Strong is the evil impulse, since even its Creator calls it evil; as it is said, "For the imagination[1] of man's heart is evil from his youth" (Gen. viii. 21)' (Kid. 30*b*). '"There shall be no strange god in thee" (Ps. lxxxi. 9). Which is the strange god that is inside a man's body? It is the evil impulse' (Shab. 105*b*).

The great danger to be apprehended from this urge is that it is liable to grow ever stronger unless it is controlled in the early stage. This thought is expressed in several striking aphorisms. 'The evil impulse is at first like a spider's web, but in the end it is like cart-ropes' (Suk. 52*a*). 'The evil impulse is at first like a passer-by, then like a lodger, and finally like the master of the house' (ibid. 52*b*). 'The evil impulse is at first sweet; in the end it is bitter' (p. Shab. 14*c*). 'Such is the device of the evil impulse, to-day it tells a man to do something trivial; to-morrow it tells him to do something more serious; finally it tells him to go and serve idols, and he will go and serve them' (Shab. 105*b*)—that means, it will eventually lead him to abandon all the restraints imposed by the service of God.

The difference between the righteous and wicked is defined in this way: 'The wicked are under the control of their heart (i.e. their evil impulse), but the righteous have their heart under their control' (Gen. R. xxxiv. 10); and to the question, Who is mighty? the answer is given, 'He who conquers his impulse' (Aboth iv. 1).

The Rabbis were under no delusion about the tyrannical power of this deep-rooted instinct. They declare, 'The evil impulse may cause a man to fall at seventy or even eighty' (Gen. R. liv. 1); and they ask, 'How can a man keep himself far from the evil impulse which is within him, since his very birth is the effect of its working?' (ARN xvi). It must, however, be fought and overcome; and the means to overcome it is by meeting it with a mind

[1] The Hebrew word is *Jetzer*, the same as for impulse.

sobered by serious thoughts. 'A man should always oppose the good impulse to the evil impulse. If he conquer it, well and good; but if not, let him occupy himself with Torah. Should this gain him the victory, well and good; but if not, let him recite the night prayer. If he conquer it, well and good; but if not, let him reflect upon the day of death' (Ber. 5a). Statements to the same effect are: 'The Holy One, blessed be He, said to Israel, My children, I have created the evil impulse, and I have created the Torah as an antidote to it; if you occupy yourselves with Torah you will not be delivered into its power' (Kid. 30b). 'If this despicable thing meets you, drag it along to the House of Study' (ibid.). 'Happy are the Israelites! At the time they are engaged with Torah and beneficent acts, their evil impulse is delivered into their power and they are not delivered into the power of their impulse' (A.Z. 5b).

The Talmud is not satisfied to give a mere counsel of perfection; it recognizes the facts of life as they are. What is a person to do who struggles earnestly but unsuccessfully against the evil urge? The answer given is this: 'If a man sees that his evil impulse is gaining the mastery over him, let him go to a place where he is unknown, put on black clothes [1] and do what his heart desires; but let him not profane the Name publicly' (Chag. 16a). The idea here cannot possibly be that he is allowed to sin in secret because it will not be known to God. Any such interpretation is ruled out by the fact that in the same context there is the solemn warning, 'Who commits a transgression in private is as though he pushed the feet of the *Shechinah*.' This is the common Rabbinic doctrine that God's Presence is everywhere and to do wrong secretly is to deny in a practical way that He is omnipresent. The true motive is that if a man succumbs to his evil nature, let him not add to his sin the personal disgrace which will also involve a profanation of the Name. The distinction between public and secret sinning will be further discussed.[2]

Since the evil impulse was created by God for a definite purpose, viz. the preservation of the human race, it follows that in the future state, when that purpose will no longer hold good,[3] there will be no further need for it. Hence the teaching: 'In the Here-after, the Holy One, blessed be He, will bring the evil impulse and slay it in the presence of the righteous and wicked. To the righteous it will appear like a high mountain, to the wicked like a single hair. Both will weep. The righteous will weep and

[1] As a sign of mourning; it might achieve the purpose of sobering him.
[2] See pp. 102 f.   [3] See p. 365.

exclaim, "How were we able to subdue such a lofty mountain as this?" The wicked will weep and exclaim, "How were we unable to subdue a single hair like this?"' (Suk. 52a).

§ V. Free Will

Inasmuch as the evil impulse is an inherent and indispensable part of man's constitution, is he not bound to sin? To this question the Rabbis gave an emphatic negative answer. That element in man's nature, which is essential to the preservation of the race, is under his control. 'If your impulse seeks to incite you to frivolous conduct, banish it with words of Torah. Should you say that it is not under your control, I (God) have declared unto you in the Scriptures, "Unto thee is its desire, but thou mayest rule over it" (Gen. iv. 7)' (Gen. R. xxii. 6).

Josephus has recorded that the doctrine of free will distinguished the Pharisees. 'When they say that all things happen by fate, they do not take away from men the freedom of acting as they think fit; since their notion is that it has pleased God to mix up the decrees of fate and man's will, so that man can act virtuously or viciously' (Antiq. xviii. i. 3).

This claim is fully substantiated in the Talmud, as the following passages demonstrate: 'The angel appointed over conception is named Lailah. He takes a seminal drop, sets it before the Holy One, blessed be He, and asks, "Sovereign of the Universe! what is to become of this drop? Is it to develop into a person strong or weak, wise or foolish, rich or poor?" But no mention is made of its becoming wicked or righteous' (Nid. 16b). An oft-quoted maxim reads: 'All is in the hands of Heaven except the fear of Heaven' (Ber. 33b), which means that although God decides the fate of the individual, a reservation is made with respect to the moral character of his life.

The idea of choice being left to the individual is well brought out in the commentary on the text, 'Behold, I set before you this day a blessing and a curse' (Deut. xi. 26). 'Why is this stated, since it has likewise been said, "See, I have set before thee this day life and good, and death and evil" (ibid. xxx. 15)? Perhaps the Israelites will say, "Since God has set before us two ways, the way of life and the way of death, we can walk in whichever of them we like." Therefore it is taught, "Choose life that thou mayest live, thou and thy seed" (ibid. 19). Parable of a person who was sitting at the cross-roads, before whom two paths branched out. The beginning of one was plain and its end full of thorns;

the beginning of the other was thorny and its latter part plain. He used to warn the passers-by and say to them, "You see this path that its beginning is plain and for two or three steps you walk in comfort, but at its end you meet with thorns. You also see the other path the beginning of which is thorny; for two or three steps you walk through thorns, but in the end you come to a straight road." Similarly said Moses to Israel, "You see the wicked prospering; for two or three days they prosper in this world, but in the end they will be thrust out. You also see the righteous in trouble; for two or three days they suffer in this world, but in the end they will have occasion for rejoicing"' (Sifré Deut. § 53; 86a). Similarly on the words, 'Behold, man is become as one of us to know good and evil' (Gen. iii. 22), it is said, 'The All-present has set before him two ways, the way of life and the way of death; but he chose for himself the latter path' (Gen. R. XXI. 5).

A curious explanation is given why the whole human race originated from one man: 'Because of the righteous and the wicked, that the rightous should not say, "We are the descendants of a righteous ancestor," and the wicked say, "We are the descendants of a wicked ancestor"' (Sanh. 38a). The moral is that neither can plead hereditary influence as the deciding factor in their character.

The philosophical problem connected with free will was appreciated by the Rabbis, but they would not allow it to restrict in any way the belief in man's power to control his actions. They made no attempt to solve the relationship between God's foreknowledge and freedom of will, but offered as a practical rule of life, 'Everything is foreseen (by God), yet freedom of choice is given' (Aboth III. 19).

God does, however, intervene to this extent, that after man has made his choice, whether good or bad, opportunity is granted to him to persevere in the course he has taken. The good man is encouraged to be good, and the bad to remain bad. 'In the way in which a man wishes to walk he is guided' (Mak. 10b). 'If one goes to defile himself, openings are made for him; and he who goes to purify himself, help is afforded him' (Shab. 104a). 'If a man defiles himself a little, they (i.e. God) defile him much; if he defiles himself here below, they defile him from above; if he defiles himself in this world, they defile him for the World to Come. Should a man hallow himself a little, they hallow him much; if he hallows himself here below, they hallow him from above; if he hallows himself in this world, they hallow him for the World to Come' (Joma 39a). 'If a man hearkens to one commandment, they cause him to hearken to many commandments; but if he forgets one commandment, they make him forgetful of many' (Mech. to xv. 26; 46a).

The conviction that man's will is unfettered is therefore seen to be the foundation of Rabbinic ethics. The nature of his life is moulded by his desires. He *can* misuse life's opportunities if he so wish; but in no circumstance would it be agreed that he *must* misuse them. The evil impulse constantly tempts him; but if he fall, the responsibility is his and his alone.

§ VI. SIN

The Talmud records that 'two and a half years the School of Shammai and the School of Hillel were divided on the following point: The latter maintained that it had been better if man had never been created; while the former maintained that it is better that he was created. The count was taken and the majority decided that it would have been better if he had not been created; but since he has been created, let him investigate his (past) actions. Another version is: Let him examine his (present) actions' (Erub. 13b).

At the root of the discussion was the agreed opinion that man is essentially a sinful creature who is bound during his lifetime to do many deeds which earn for him the condemnation of God. We have already seen that part of human nature is the evil impulse which can be mastered, but all too often takes control and demoralizes.

On the question whether it is possible for any person to be perfectly sinless, the Rabbinic literature gives contradictory answers. On the one hand it is declared, 'The first patriarchs were without trace of iniquity or sin' (Mech. to xvi. 10; 48a); but another Rabbi stated, 'If the Holy One, blessed be He, had entered into judgment with Abraham, Isaac, and Jacob, they would not have been able to stand against the reproof' (Arach. 17a). Similarly we find it said, 'Four died only on account of the advice of the serpent (which tempted Eve). They are: Benjamin the son of Jacob, Amram the father of Moses, Jesse the father of David, and Kileab the son of David' (Shab. 55b). This means that they were without sin and should therefore never have suffered death. As against this view we find a Rabbi citing the text, 'There is not a righteous man upon earth that doeth good, and sinneth not' (Eccles. vii. 20), when assured by his disciples that his life had been spent free of sin (Sanh. 101a).

This difference of opinion has a bearing on the question whether the Talmud teaches the doctrine of original sin, viz. whether the human being has inherited the guilt incurred by the first parents and in consequence is essentially corrupt in nature. That the Rabbis subscribed to the view that the sin in the Garden of Eden had repercussions on all subsequent generations has already been shown. It was the direct cause of death which is the fate of every creature. In the same way they believed that the sin of the Golden Calf left its taint and affected the destinies of mankind ever since. 'There is no generation in which there is not an ounce from the sin of the Golden Calf' (p. Taan. 68c).

Such a thought, however, is far removed from the doctrine that man inherits sin. He may be burdened by the consequences of the wrongdoings of his forefathers; but no Rabbi of the Talmudic age would admit that any human being committed a wrong for which he or she was not personally responsible. Such an admission would have been at variance with the dogma of free will.

Many utterances can be adduced from the Talmud to prove that man is sinless by nature. There is, e.g. such a statement as, 'A child aged one year who has not tasted sin' (Joma 22b). Upon the words of Ecclesiastes, 'There is a time to be born and a time to die' (Eccles. iii. 2), was based the aspiration, 'Happy the man whose hour of death is like the hour of his birth; as at his birth he is free of sin, so at his death may he be free of sin' (p. Ber. 4d). Here the possibility of an unstained life is not only admitted, but actually held forth as an ideal to which man should strive. A similar exhortation was derived from the verse, 'Then shall the dust return to the earth as it was; and the spirit shall return unto God Who gave it' (Eccles. xii. 7)—'Give it back to Him as He gave it to you, in a condition of purity' (Shab. 152b).

From the Rabbinic standpoint, sin is nothing more nor less than rebellion against God. He has revealed His will in the Torah and to run counter to any of its ordinances is transgression. Virtue is conformity to the Torah; sin is its disregard. This attitude is very clearly expressed in this extract: 'A man should not say, It is impossible for me to eat swine's flesh; it is impossible for me to enter into an incestuous alliance. (He should rather say), It is possible for me to perform such acts; but what am I to do, seeing that my Father in Heaven has so decreed for me?' (Sifra to xx. 26). The merit does not lie in withholding oneself from what is forbidden because there is no desire for it. The desire should exist, but be withstood because it is forbidden.

In theory, therefore, there is no difference in the seriousness of a sin, every offence being an act of revolt against the divine will;

but in practice a distinction was drawn. Three cardinal sins were recognized, the commission of which involved special heinousness. It is related that during the Hadrianic persecutions in the early part of the second century, when Roman tyranny restricted the freedom of religious observance under penalty of death, a Synod of Rabbis was convened to consider what was the duty of the Jew towards his religion under duress. The decision arrived at was: 'In connection with all the prohibitions mentioned in the Torah, if a man is told, "Transgress and be not killed," he may transgress and save his life, with the exception of idolatry, unchastity, and bloodshed' (Sanh. 74a). Rather than be guilty of these sins he must forfeit his life.

To the three sins named, a fourth is added as an evil of exceptional gravity, viz. slander. 'There are four offences for the commission of which punishment is exacted in this world and the capital (of the sin) remains for the World to Come. They are: idolatry, unchastity, bloodshed, and slander. Idolatry is equal to them all together in point of seriousness. Whence is this derived? From the text, "That soul shall utterly be cut off; its iniquity shall be in it" (Num. xv. 31). What is the purpose of the words "its iniquity shall be in it"? They teach that the soul will be cut off (from this world) and still its iniquity will be in it. Whence is it derived in connection with unchastity? From the text, "How then can I do this great wickedness and sin against God?" (Gen. xxxix. 9). Whence is it derived in connection with bloodshed? From the text, "Cain said unto the Lord, My sin is too great for forgiveness" (sic, ibid. iv. 13). And what is said in connection with slander? "May the Lord cut off all flattering lips, the tongue that speaketh proud things" (Ps. xii. 3)' (p. Peah 15d).

The seriousness of these sins is frequently touched upon in the Talmud. Idolatry was accorded precedence because it entailed the denial of Revelation and consequently the shattering of the basis of the whole system of religion and ethics. 'Whoever acknowledges idolatry denies the Ten Commandments as well as the precepts given to Moses, to the prophets and the patriarchs; and whoever repudiates idolatry acknowledges the whole of the Torah' (Sifré Num. § 111; 32a). 'In whatever a prophet commands you to do which involves a transgression of the Torah hearken to him, with the exception of idolatry; for even if he cause the sun to stand still in the middle of the sky, do not hearken to him' (Sanh. 90a).

The strictest standard of sexual morality is demanded by the Talmud. That the adulterer is a practical atheist was deduced from the verse, 'The eye also of the adulterer waiteth for the twilight, saying, No eye shall see me' (Job xxiv. 15): 'He does not say, "No man will see me," but, "No eye shall see me," neither the eye of one below nor the eye of Him above' (Num. R. IX. 1). Even to lust with the eye was considered an unchaste act. 'Not merely one who sins with his body is called an adulterer, but he who sins with his eye is also so named' (Lev. R. XXIII. 12).

As a safeguard to morality a man was strictly enjoined to avoid doing anything which might excite his passion. It gave rise to the recommendation, 'Engage not in much gossip with women. This applies even to one's own wife; how much more so then to the wife of one's neighbour. Hence the Sages say, Whoso engages in much gossip with women brings evil upon himself, neglects the study of the Torah, and will in the end inherit Gehinnom' (Aboth I. 5). 'A man should never walk behind a woman along the road, even his own wife. Should a woman meet him on a bridge, he should let her pass by on the side; and whoever crosses a stream behind a woman will have no portion in the World to Come. He who pays money to a woman, counting it from his hand into hers for the sake of gazing at her, even if he possess Torah and good deeds like Moses our teacher, he will not escape the punishment of Gehinnom. A man should walk behind a lion rather than behind a woman' (Ber. 61a). 'Jesting and levity lead a man on to lewdness' (Aboth III. 17).

Immodesty of speech was likewise severely condemned. 'Whoever uses obscene language, even if a favourable decree of seventy years' standing be to his credit, it will be altered to an unfavourable one. For him who uses obscene language Gehinnom is deepened; and this applies even to one who listens to such talk without protesting' (Shab. 33a). 'Why are the fingers tapered like pegs? So that if one hears anything improper he can insert them in his ears' (Keth. 5b).

The third cardinal sin, bloodshed, is condemned as an offence against God, since it entails the destruction of one created in His image. 'How were the Ten Commandments given? There were five on one tablet and five on the other. On the one was inscribed, "I am the Lord thy God," and over against it, "Thou shalt not murder." The inference to be drawn is that if one sheds blood, Scripture imputes it to him as though he had diminished the likeness of the King' (Mech. to XX. 17; 70b). 'A man once came before Raba and said to him: "The ruler of my city has ordered me to kill a certain person, and if I refuse he will kill me." Raba told him, "Be killed and do not kill; do you think that your

blood is redder than his? Perhaps his is redder than yours"'
(Pes. 25*b*).

In the following circumstances homicide was considered justifiable: 'If one comes to kill you, be first and kill him' (Sanh. 72*a*).
'If there is a company of men (i.e. Israelites), and Gentiles say to
them, "Hand over one of you that we may kill him, and if not,
we will kill all of you," they must all suffer death rather than surrender one of them. Should they, on the other hand, specify an
individual in their demand, they must deliver him up; for since
both he and they would be killed, they must surrender him and not
all incur death' (Tosifta Terumoth VII. 20).

Hatred is also severely denounced because it may lead to murder.
'Wanton hatred is equal to the three transgressions of idolatry,
unchastity, and bloodshed, and was the cause of the destruction
of the Second Temple' (Joma 9*b*). The command, 'Thou shalt not
hate thy brother in thy heart' (Lev. xix. 17), was expounded in this
manner: 'It is possible to think that it is sufficient not to smite
or smack or curse him; therefore the text adds "in thy heart"
to indicate that hatred in the heart is meant' (Arach. 16*b*). How
God abominate hatred is illustrated by the observation, 'Since
the builders of the Tower of Babel loved one another, the Holy
One, blessed be He, was not willing to destroy them from the
world but scattered them in all directions; with the men of Sodom,
however, since they hated one another, the Holy One, blessed be
He, blotted them out from this world and the World to Come'
(ARN XII).

The fourth cardinal sin is slander. A curious phrase is employed
to denote this vice, viz. *lishan telitaë* (the third tongue), and it was
so called because 'it slays three persons: the speaker, the spoken
to, and the spoken of' (Arach. 15*b*). The strongest language is
used in denunciation of anybody guilty of this offence. 'Whoever
speaks slander is as though he denied the fundamental principle
(i.e. the existence of God)'; 'Whoever speaks slander is deserving
of being stoned to death'; 'The Holy One, blessed be He, says of
such a person, I and he cannot dwell together in the world';
'Whoever speaks slander magnifies iniquities equal to the three
sins of idolatry, unchastity, and bloodshed' (ibid.); 'The retailer of
slander, the receiver of it, and who gives false evidence against his
fellow, deserve to be cast to the dogs' (Pes. 118*a*). The aphorism
of R. Eliezer, 'Let the honour of your neighbour be as dear to you
as your own' (Aboth II. 15), received this amplified explanation:
'Just as a man esteems his own honour, so let him esteem the
honour of his neighbour. Just as nobody wishes his own reputation

slandered, so let him never desire to slander his neighbour's reputation' (ARN xv).

The misuse of the gift of speech is often the subject of warning. The Rabbis appreciated how unruly a member the tongue is, and for that reason, they declared, God provided it with exceptional controls. 'The Holy One, blessed be He, said to the tongue, All the limbs of man are erect but you are horizontal; they are all outside the body but you are inside. More than that, I have surrounded you with two walls, one of bone and the other of flesh' (Arach. 15b).

Overmuch talking is deprecated. The proverb, 'Speech is silver, silence golden,' has its counterpart in the Talmud: 'A word for a *sela*,[1] silence for two' (Meg. 18a); 'Silence is a healing for all ailments' (ibid.); 'Silence is good for the wise; how much more so for the foolish' (Pes. 99a); 'All my days I have grown up amongst the wise, and I have found nought of better service than silence' (Aboth 1. 17).

Lying is the equivalent of theft and its worst form. 'There are seven classes of thieves, and first among them all is he who steals the mind of his fellow-creatures (by lying words)' (Tosifta B.K. VII. 8). It is also said, 'The band of liars cannot receive the presence of the *Shechinah*' (Sot. 42a), and in this respect they are associated with scoffers, hypocrites, and slanderers. 'Whoever equivocates in his speech is as though he worshipped idols' (Sanh. 92a). 'The Holy One, blessed be He, hates the person who speaks one thing with his mouth and another in his heart' (Pes. 113b). 'The penalty of the liar is that he is not believed even when he speaks the truth' (Sanh. 89b). 'A person should not even promise a child to give him something and not keep his word, because he thereby teaches him falsehood' (Suk. 46b).

Connected with the misuse of speech is the sin of hypocrisy. 'Every person in whom is hypocrisy brings wrath upon the world, his prayer remains unheard, is cursed even by the embryos in their mothers' womb, and will fall into Gehinnom. A community addicted to hypocrisy is loathsome like an unclean thing, and will be driven into exile' (Sot. 41b et seq.).

The Talmud divides Pharisees into seven classes, and satirizes those who display hypocritical tendencies: 'There is the *shichmi* Pharisee who acts like Shechem;[2] the *nikpi* Pharisee who knocks

---

[1] The name of a coin.

[2] Who submitted to circumcision from an unworthy motive (Gen. xxxiv). The Palestinian Talmud explains differently: 'who carries his religious duties upon his shoulder (*shechem*)' (p. Ber. 14b).

his feet together;[1] the *kizai* Pharisee who makes his blood flow against walls;[2] the "pestle" Pharisee who walks with bowed head like a pestle in the mortar; the Pharisee who is always exclaiming, "What is my duty that I may perform it?"; the Pharisee from love (of God) and the Pharisee from fear' (Sot. 22*b*).

Another sin against which harsh things are said is dishonesty. A bold teaching on this subject is to the effect that when the human being presents himself before the heavenly tribunal to give an account of his life, the first question addressed to him is, 'Hast thou been honest in thy business transactions?' (Shab. 31*a*). 'Whoever robs his fellow-man of even what is worth a farthing is as though he had taken his life from him' (B.K. 119*a*). 'Come and see how grievous is the power of robbery; for the generation of the Flood committed every kind of offence but their fate was not sealed until they put forth their hands to robbery; as it is said, "The earth is filled with violence through them, I will destroy them with the earth" (Gen. vi. 13)' (Sanh. 108*a*). 'Whoever has his hands stained by robbery may call upon the Holy One, blessed be He, but He will not answer him' (Exod. R. xxii. 3). 'Suppose a person stole a measure of wheat, ground it, kneaded it, baked it, and separated the dough,[3] what benediction should he utter? Such a person cannot utter a benediction at all, he blasphemes' (B.K. 94*a*). 'The associate of a thief is like a thief' (p. Sanh. 19*b*) and 'Steal from a thief and you also have a taste of it' (Ber. 5*b*), —that also is theft. The saying that the receiver is worse than the thief is quaintly expressed in a proverb: 'Not the mouse is the thief, but the hole is the thief; for if there is no mouse, of what use is the hole?' (Arach. 30*a*).

Many other sins are denounced in the Talmud, but what has been quoted suffices to illustrate the point of view that a wrong done to a fellow-man was an offence against God. It was more serious than the breach of a precept which affected only the relationship between man and his Maker, and entailed stricter conditions before forgiveness could be obtained. 'The Day of Atonement brings expiation for transgressions between man and the All-present;

[1] He walks in such a way as to display exaggerated meekness. The Palestinian Talmud explains: 'The Pharisee who says, "Spare me a moment that I may perform a religious duty."'
[2] In his anxiety to avoid looking at a woman he dashes his face against a wall. The Palestinian Talmud explains the term as 'calculating Pharisee,' i.e. he performs a good deed and then a bad deed, setting one off against the other.
[3] In accordance with Num. xv. 21, the custom survived, even after the fall of the Temple, of separating a portion of the dough, burning it, and then uttering a benediction.

but as for transgressions between man and his fellow, the Day of Atonement brings no expiation until he give his fellow satisfaction' (Joma VIII. 9). Remorse and penitence are insufficient; reparation also must be made.

The greatest of all sins is to be the cause of others sinning. 'To make another to sin is worse than to kill him; because to murder a person is only to remove him from this world, but to cause him to sin is to exclude him from the World to Come as well' (Sifré Deut. § 252; 120a). 'If in connection with trees, which cannot eat or drink or smell, the Torah commands that they shall be burnt when used for idolatrous worship (Deut. xii. 3), since through them men come to stumble, how much more deserving of extermination is a person who causes his fellow to wander from the ways of life to the ways of death!' (Sanh. 55a). And conversely, 'Whoever causes his fellow to perform a precept has it ascribed to him as though he had made him' (ibid. 99b).

A rather important distinction is drawn between sinning in private and sinning in public. From one point of view the former is more serious because it virtually involves a denial of God's existence and omnipresence. 'Such is the way of those who commit transgressions; they think that the Holy One, blessed be He, does not see their actions' (Num. R. IX. 1); and the warning was uttered, 'If a man commit a transgression in secret, God will proclaim it publicly' (Sot. 3a). From another point of view, sinning in public is the more heinous offence; and an illustration may be supplied by the treatment of the text, 'Ye shall therefore keep My statutes and Mine ordinances, which if a man do, he shall live by them' (Lev. xviii. 5)—'"Shall live by them," and not die by them. R. Ishmael used to say, Whence can you maintain that if a person is ordered to worship idols privately and save his life that he may do so? From the words "He shall live by them." Perhaps, then, he may yield and practise idolatry publicly (to save his life)! Therefore Scripture declares, "Ye shall not profane My holy name" (ibid. xxii. 32)' (Sifra ad loc.).

The reason why, in such a circumstance, open transgression is treated more seriously is that it may lead to others following his example, particularly if he is a man of standing in his community. He is allowed to do wrong privately, since God understands that he is acting under compulsion and is not motived by the thought that He is unaware of what he is doing. But to do wrong in public involves 'profanation of the Name,' and renders him guilty of the worst offence, viz. causing others to sin.

As with the evil impulse, sin must be checked in its early stage or it grows into a confirmed habit. There is sound psychology in the saying, 'If a man commit an offence and repeat it, it becomes to him something permitted' (Joma 86b). And one sin leads to another. 'Run to do even a slight precept and flee from transgression; for precept draws precept in its train, and transgression draws transgression; for the recompense of a precept is a precept, and the recompense of a transgression is a transgression' (Aboth IV. 2). The thought is given fuller expression: 'If one transgress a slight precept, he will end by transgressing a serious precept. If he transgress "Thou shalt love thy neighbour as thyself" (Lev. xix. 18), he will in the sequel transgress "Thou shalt not hate thy brother in thy heart" (ibid. 17); then "Thou shalt not take vengeance nor bear any grudge" (ibid. 18); then "That thy brother may live with thee" (ibid. xxv. 36), until he will eventually come to shed blood' (Sifré Deut. § 187; 108b). 'Who performs a single precept for its own sake,[1] let him not rejoice over it, for it will in the sequel lead to the performance of many precepts; and who commits a single transgression, let him not worry over it, since it will lead to the performance of many transgressions' (Sifré Num. § 112; 33a). The reverse is also true: 'If a transgression comes to a man a first and second time without his sinning, he is immune from the sin' (Joma 38b).

Wrongdoing can only result from the loss of self-control. Hence it was taught: 'A man does not commit a transgression unless a spirit of madness has entered into him' (Sot. 3a). Whatever, therefore, leads to a weakening of control must be shunned. Two of the causes are indicated in the advice which Elijah was alleged to have given a Rabbi: 'Be not wrathful and you will not sin; be not intoxicated and you will not sin' (Ber. 29b).

Important safeguards against sinning were suggested by R. Judah the Prince and his son Gamaliel. The first said: 'Reflect upon three things and you will not come within the power of sin: Know what is above you—a seeing eye, and a hearing ear, and all your deeds are written in a book.' The second said: 'An excellent thing is the study of the Torah combined with some worldly occupation, for the labour demanded by them both makes sin to be forgotten. All study of the Torah without work must in the end be futile and become the cause of sin' (Aboth II. 1 f.).

That is the Rabbinic philosophy of right living. Keep the mind occupied with wholesome thoughts and the hands engaged in honest toil. There will be neither time nor inclination for sinful actions.

---

[1] *Lishmah*, i.e. without thought of reward. See p. 139.

§ VII. Repentance and Atonement

Inasmuch as God created man with the evil impulse, by reason
of which he is prone to sin, justice demanded that an antidote
should likewise be provided for his salvation. If wickedness is
a disease to which the human being is susceptible, it was necessary
for him to have a medium of healing. Such is to be found in
repentance.

Quite logically, therefore, the Rabbis declared that repentance
was one of the things which were designed by God even before
the world itself was formed. 'Seven things were created before
the Universe came into being. They are: Torah, repentance,
Paradise, Gehinnom, the Throne of Glory, the Sanctuary, and the
name of the Messiah' (Pes. 54a). The world, having been created
as the abode of man, had to be equipped for his reception. In
the Torah was the scheme of right living which he was to follow.
But allowance had also to be made for his lapses from the paths of
perfection, and this was done by the other things enumerated.

First place is assigned to repentance, because without it mankind could not endure and would be overwhelmed by a flood of
wickedness. Not only has it the power of stemming the tide of
evil; it is capable of neutralizing it and making life wholesome
after it has been tainted by wrongdoing. 'Great is repentance,
for it reaches to the Throne of Glory. Great is repentance, for
it makes the Redemption (by the Messiah) to come near. Great
is repentance, for it lengthens the years of a man's life' (Joma 86a
et seq.). 'The place which the penitent occupy the perfectly
righteous are unable to occupy' (Ber. 34b). 'There is nothing
greater than repentance' (Deut. R. II. 24). 'Better is one hour
of repentance and good deeds in this world than the whole life of
the World to Come' (Aboth IV. 22).

Since, as the Bible declares, God delights not in the death of
the wicked but that he turn from his evil way and live (Ezek.
xxxiii. 11), it follows that He is anxious for man to repent and
facilitates his endeavour to do so. 'Not like the attribute of the
Holy One, blessed be He, is the attribute of man. When a human
being is conquered he grieves; but when He is conquered [1] He
rejoices. The words of Ezekiel, "They had the hands of a man
under their wings" (i. 8), refer to the hand of God which is extended
beneath the wings of the Chayyoth to receive penitents from the
power of judgment' (Pes. 119a). 'The Holy One, blessed be He,

[1] By having His anger overcome by means of repentance and turned to
mercy.

said to Israel, My sons, open for Me an aperture of repentance as narrow as the eye of a needle, and I will open for you gates through which wagons and coaches can pass' (Cant. R. v. 2). 'The gates of prayer are sometimes open and sometimes closed, but the gates of repentance are ever open. As the sea is always accessible, so is the hand of the Holy One, blessed be He, always open to receive penitents' (Deut. R. II. 12).

Although, as one naturally expects, the Talmud is concerned chiefly with Israel, there is nothing exclusive about its doctrine of repentance. It is available to all who would use it. It is said that 'the Holy One, blessed be He, looks to the peoples of the world, hoping that they will repent and so bring them near beneath His wings' (Num. R. x. 1); and 'the Holy One, blessed be He, bids the peoples of the world repent so that He may bring them near beneath His wings' (Cant. R. vi. 1).

With the fall of the Temple and the cessation of the atonement offerings, the importance of repentance as a means of expiation became inevitably enhanced. This is also true of the efficacy of the Day of Atonement. Even when the sacrificial system was in operation, the Rabbis assert, contrition was essential before an offering could prove acceptable to God. There is the explicit teaching: 'Neither sin-offering nor trespass-offering nor death nor the Day of Atonement can bring expiation without repentance' (Tosifta Joma v. 9). When the sacrifices could no longer be offered, the people needed to be reminded that their hope for atonement was not in the least affected; and so they were told: 'Whence is it derived that if one repents, it is imputed to him as if he had gone up to Jerusalem, built the Temple, erected an altar and offered upon it all the sacrifices enumerated in the Torah? From the text, "The sacrifices of God are a broken spirit" (Ps. li. 17)' (Lev. R. vii. 2). 'I do not want of you sacrifices and offerings, but words (of contrition); as it is said, "Take with you words and turn to the Lord" (Hos. xiv. 2)' (Exod. R. xxxviii. 4).

An important passage on the subject reads: 'Wisdom (i.e. the Hagiographa) was asked, What is the penalty of a sinner? and the reply was, "Evil pursueth sinners" (Prov. xiii. 21). When Prophecy was asked the question it answered, "The soul that sinneth, it shall die" (Ezek. xviii. 4). When the Torah [1] was asked the question it answered, Let him bring a trespass-offering and he will be forgiven; as it is said, "And it shall be accepted of him to make atonement for him" (Lev. i. 4). When the question was asked of

---

[1] The Hagiographa, the Prophets, and the Torah (i.e. the Pentateuch) are the three divisions of the Hebrew Scriptures.

the Holy One, blessed be He, He replied, Let him repent and he will be forgiven; as it is written, "Good and upright is the Lord, therefore will He teach sinners in the way" (Ps. xxv. 8)' (p. Mak. 31*d*).

We must not see here a contradiction between the answer given by God and the answers given in the three sections of the Scriptures. Such a lack of harmony would have been unthinkable to the Rabbis, for whom the Sacred Writings were the revealed expression of the divine mind. What we have in this extract is an enumeration of various media by which the sinner atones for his wrongdoing, chief of all being repentance. It depicts the scheme of atonement as drawn up in the Jewish religion, and each item calls for consideration.

According to the 'Wisdom' literature of the Bible atonement is secured through 'evil,' by which suffering is to be understood. Illustrative of this idea are such statements as: 'There are chastenings which purge all the iniquities of man' (Ber. 5*a*); 'Whoever manifests the symptoms of plague is to regard them as nothing but an altar of atonement' (ibid. 5*b*); 'Let a man rejoice in sufferings more than in happiness; for if a man has lived all his life in happiness, any sin which he may have committed has not been pardoned; but what is pardoned through suffering is forgiven him. Beloved are sufferings, because just as the sacrifices secured acceptance, so do sufferings secure acceptance. Nay, sufferings bring even greater acceptance, since sacrifices entail money only, while sufferings affect his body' (Sifré Deut. § 32; 73*b*).

A curious extension of the thought is the belief that intestinal trouble may lead to a moral as well as physical purgation. 'The pious men of old used to be afflicted with illness of the bowels about twenty days before their death, to purge them completely, so that they may come in a pure state into the Hereafter' (Semachoth III. 10). 'Three classes of persons will not behold the face of Gehinnom: they who have suffered the afflictions of poverty, disease of the bowels, and the tyranny of Roman rule' (Erub. 41*b*). The privations they endured were punishment for their evil deeds, and having tasted their bitterness they become purified.

The answer of Prophecy mentioned death. That, too, is a medium of atonement and is effective in the most serious types of sin. 'If one transgress a positive commandment and repent, he does not move from his place without being forgiven. If one transgress a prohibition and repent, his repentance remains in suspense and the Day of Atonement brings expiation. If one commit an offence which incurs the penalty of excision (by the hand of God) or capital punishment by a Court of Law and repent, both his repentance and the Day of Atonement remain in suspense and sufferings purge him. But he who has been guilty of profaning the Name, repentance has no power of being in suspense, the Day of Atonement has no power of bringing expiation, and sufferings have not the power to purge; but they all remain in suspense and death purges him' (Joma 86a).

Even death cannot bring atonement unless it is preceded by penitence. 'Death and the Day of Atonement expiate together with repentance' (Joma VIII. 8). On Num. xv. 31, 'Because he hath despised the word of the Lord, and hath broken His commandment, that soul shall utterly be cut off; his iniquity shall remain in him,' there is the comment, 'All who die receive atonement in their dying; but as for this person, "his iniquity shall remain in him." Is this so even if he repent? Therefore the text states, "his iniquity shall remain in him," i.e. not when he has repented' (Sifré Num. § 112; 33a), the deduction being that penitence removes the sin. A criminal, on the way to execution, was exhorted to utter the confession, 'May my death be an expiation for all my iniquities' (Sanh. VI. 2).

The answer of the Torah referred to the atonement-sacrifices which, except in the earliest part of the Talmudic period, were a thing of the past. In their place the Synagogue Ritual of the Day of Atonement became in the popular mind the supreme path to purification from sin. Its power to effect this is a tenet of Rabbinic Judaism. 'For light transgressions, whether of commission or omission, repentance atones; for the serious transgressions repentance holds the matter in suspense until the Day of Atonement comes and brings expiation' (Joma VIII. 8). 'In the case of a sin of commission the Day of Atonement brings expiation even if he has not repented, but with a sin of omission only if he has repented' (p. Joma 45b). The view that the Day of Atonement, as it were, acts automatically with certain classes of offences and forgiveness can be obtained without repentance is quite exceptional. Indeed, the warning to the contrary is sounded very clearly: 'Who says, "I will sin and the Day of Atonement will bring expiation," the Day of Atonement does not expiate for him' (Joma VIII. 9).

A conspicuous feature of the Day of Atonement was the rigorous fast in which it was spent. Even the religious leaders attached importance to the fast as an act of penance. It is reported that a certain Rabbi used to say this prayer on a fast-day: 'Lord of the Universe! it is revealed before Thee that when the Sanctuary was in existence, a man sinned and brought an offering, of which they sacrificed only the fat and the blood, and atonement was made for him. But now, I observe a fast, and my fat and blood are diminished. May it be Thy will, that my fat and blood which have been diminished may be accounted as though I had offered them before Thee upon the altar, and do thou favour me' (Ber. 17a). A much higher view may be seen in the practice which was adopted on fast-days. 'The Elder of the congregation addressed the worshippers with words of admonition: "Brethren, it is not said of the men of Nineveh, 'And God saw their sackcloth and their fasting,' but, 'God saw their works, that they turned from their evil way' (Jonah iii. 10)"' (Taan. II. 1).

That no amount of prayer or confession of sins can secure atonement, unless accompanied by a change of conduct, is explicit Talmudic doctrine. 'If a man is guilty of a transgression, makes a confession of it but does not amend his behaviour, to what is he like? To a man who holds a defiling reptile in his hand. Even if he immerse his body in all the waters of the world, his immersion is of no avail to him. Let him, however, cast the reptile aside, and should he immerse in forty *seah* of water,[1] it immediately avails him; as it is said, "Whoso confesseth (his sins) and *forsaketh* them shall obtain mercy" (Prov. xxviii. 13)' (Taan. 16a).

And so we arrive at the divine answer, viz. repentance, as the ultimate means of cleansing man from sin; but the repentance must be proved sincere. 'Who says, "I will sin and repent and again sin and repent," will be denied the power of repenting' (Joma VIII. 9). Conscience is a delicate instrument which becomes deranged by misuse. Repentance must result from heartfelt remorse. 'Whoever commits a transgression and is filled with shame thereby, all his sins are forgiven him' (Ber. 12b); 'One chastisement in the heart of man (i.e. self-reproach) is better than many lashes' (ibid. 7a) as a means of securing atonement. As evidence of sincerity, words of repentance must be accompanied by acts of benevolence. 'Repentance and good deeds are man's advocates' (Shab. 32a); 'Repentance and good deeds are a shield against punishment' (Aboth IV. 13); 'Three things can annul evil decrees: prayer, charity, and repentance' (Gen. R. XLIV. 12). The criterion of a true penitent is: 'That temptation to transgress should come to him a first and second time and he resist it' (Joma 86b).

The thought that it is never too late to mend is conveyed by

---

[1] *Seah* is a measure; and forty *seah* is the minimum capacity of the special type of bath required for the purpose of ritual cleanliness.

the words: 'If one has been utterly wicked throughout his life and repents in the end, his wickedness is never again remembered (by God) against him' (Kid. 40b); but, as we shall see, the act of penitence should not be deferred, lest death intervene.

Is it possible to repent after death? Divergent answers are given to the question. One teaching is that a sinner who has descended to Gehinnom is, as the effect of repentance, 'shot out of it like an arrow from a bow' (Tanchuma to Deut. xxxii. 1). On the other side is the passage in the Midrash to Eccles. i. 15, 'That which is crooked cannot be made straight, and that which is wanting cannot be numbered': 'In this world he who is crooked (morally) can be made straight and he who is wanting (in virtuous deeds) can be numbered; but in the Hereafter he who is crooked cannot be made straight, and he who is wanting cannot be numbered. Imagine two wicked men who were associates in this world. One of them did penance early in his lifetime, before he died, and the other failed to do so. The former, by merit of his act of repentance, takes his place in the company of the righteous. The latter, standing in the company of the wicked, beholds his companion and cries, "Woe is me, there is partiality shown here! The two of us lived alike, we stole and robbed alike, and committed all sorts of villainies alike. Why, then, is he among the righteous and I among the wicked?" They (the angels) reply to him, "You fool! you were despicable two or three days after your death, when people did not give you honourable burial in a coffin, but dragged your corpse to the grave with ropes. Your associate saw your vileness and swore to turn from his evil way. He repented like a righteous man, and the effect of his penitence is that he here receives life and honour, and a portion with the righteous. You similarly had the opportunity of repenting; and if you had done so, it would have been well with you." Then says he to them, "Permit me to go and repent"; and they answer, "You fool! do you not know that this world is like a Sabbath and the world from which you have come like a Sabbath-eve? If a man does not prepare his meal on the Sabbath-eve, what has he to eat on the Sabbath? Do you not know that the world from which you have come is like dry land and this world like a sea? If a man does not prepare his food on dry land, what has he to eat on the sea? Do you not know that this world is like a desert, and the world from which you have come like cultivated land? If a man does not prepare his food on cultivated land, what has he to eat in the desert?" He gnashes his teeth and gnaws his flesh; then he says, "Allow me to look upon the glory of my companion." To this they reply, "You fool! we have been commanded by the Almighty that the righteous must not stand with the wicked or the wicked with the righteous, the pure with the unclean or the unclean with the pure." He thereupon rends his garments in despair and plucks his hair.'

However true it be that repentance is possible up to the moment of death, it is considered unwise to postpone it. 'R. Eliezer said, "Repent one day before your death." His disciples asked him, "Does, then, anybody know on which day he will die?" He replied to them, "How much more reason is there for him to repent to-day, lest he be dead to-morrow; and as a consequence all his days will be spent in repentance"' (Shab. 153a).

§ VIII. Reward and Punishment

Justice being an attribute of God, it follows that He deals justly with His creatures. That the righteous should be rewarded for their faithfulness to the divine will and the wicked punished for their rebelliousness is what one naturally expects in a Universe governed by a just Judge. If the facts of life seem to be in conflict with this conclusion, there must be an explanation which reconciles the apparent absence of the reign of justice with the certainty that God is upright in all His decrees.

When a Rabbi ventured to interpret a Biblical verse in the sense that God is not bound by rules of equity and can act as He pleases, he received a sharp rebuke. 'R. Pappos expounded the words, "But He is one, and who can gainsay Him? What He desireth, even that He doeth" (Job xxiii. 13), in this manner: He judgeth alone all who come into the world and nobody can question His decisions. R. Akiba said to him, "Enough, Pappos!" "How, then, do you explain the verse?" he was asked; and he answered, "We may not question the decisions of Him Who spake and the world came into being; but He judges all in truth and everything is in accordance with strict justice"' (Mech. to xiv. 29; 33a).

This insistence on God's just dealings with man is a conspicuous feature of R. Akiba's teaching. An aphorism of his bears on the subject and employs the language of everyday business life to drive home the thought with greater force: 'Everything is given on pledge, and a net is spread for all the living; the shop is open, the dealer gives credit, the ledger lies open, the hand writes, and whosoever wishes to borrow may come and borrow. But the

collectors regularly make their daily round and exact payment
from man, whether he be content or not; and they have that
whereon they can rely in their demand. The judgment is a judgment of truth, and everything is prepared for the feast' (Aboth
III. 20). The final clause means that after retribution has been
exacted from the sinner he is admitted to the feast of good things
in store for the righteous in the Hereafter.[1]

He upheld the same point of view in a discussion upon Psalm
xxxvi. 6, 'Thy righteousness is like the great mountains; Thy
judgments are a great deep': 'R. Ishmael said, By the merit of the
righteous who accepted the Torah which was given from "the great
mountains" (i.e. Sinai), Thou doest with them righteousness until
it is like the great mountains; but as for the wicked who rejected
the Torah which was given from the great mountains, Thou wilt
be exacting with them down to the "great deep" (i.e. Gehinnom).
R. Akiba said, With both classes God is exacting down to the great
deep. He is exacting with the righteous and penalizes them for
the few evil actions which they committed in this world, so as to
grant them tranquillity and a good reward in the World to Come;
and He grants tranquillity to the wicked and gives them the reward
of the few meritorious deeds they may have performed in this
world, in order to penalize them (for their wrongdoings) in the
World to Come' (Gen. R. xxxIII. 1).

On the theory that justice must rule in the divine government
of human beings, one is obliged to believe that God rewards the
good according to their merits and punishes the wicked according
to their deserts. That is, indeed, the general doctrine found in the
Talmud. 'There is no suffering without iniquity' (Shab. 55a)
was a widely held belief which is given expression in various forms.
'He who does one precept has gotten himself one advocate, and he
who commits one transgression has gotten himself one accuser'
(Aboth IV. 13); 'All the judgments of the Holy One, blessed be
He, are on the basis of measure for measure' (Sanh. 90a).

The Rabbis discovered corroboration in the narratives of the
Bible, both as regards punishment and reward. Illustrative of
the former are these instances: 'By the plan which the Egyptians
devised to destroy Israel I judge them. They planned to destroy
Israel by water, and I will punish them with nothing else than
water' (Mech. to xiv. 26; 32b). 'Samson went after his eyes,
therefore the Philistines plucked out his eyes. Absalom gloried
in his hair, therefore he was caught by his hair' (Sot. I. 8).

Two Rabbinic examples may be quoted: 'Hillel saw a skull

[1] See pp. 385 f.

floating on the surface of the water; [1] he said to it, "Because you drowned others, they have drowned you, and in the end they that drowned you shall themselves be drowned."' (Aboth II. 7). An extreme case is that of the saintly Nahum of Gamzo [2] which, if authentic, vividly reveals how firm was the belief in the principle of measure for measure.

'It was related of Nahum of Gamzo that he was blind in both eyes, that both hands were amputated, both legs cut off, and his body entirely covered with boils, so that (the feet of) his couch rested in basins of water to prevent the ants from climbing up to him. On one occasion his couch was resting in a ruined house and his disciples wished to remove him. He said to them, "First clear out the furniture and lastly my couch, because so long as my couch is in the house you may be assured that the house will not collapse." They removed the furniture and then the couch; immediately afterwards the house fell in. [3] His disciples said to him, "Since you are a perfectly righteous man, why has all this suffering come upon you?" He answered, "I am myself responsible for it. Once I was going to my father-in-law's house, and I had with me a load borne by three asses: one of food, the second of drink, and the third of various kinds of dainties. A man chanced to meet me and cried, 'Rabbi, give me something to eat.' I said to him, 'Wait until I alight from my ass.' When I had alighted and turned round I discovered that he had died. I fell upon him and said, 'May my eyes that had no pity on your eyes become blind; may my hands which had no pity on your hands be amputated; may my legs which had no pity on your legs be cut off.' Nor was my mind at rest until I said, 'May all my body be full of boils.'" They said to him, "Woe to us that we see you thus!" He replied to them, "Woe would it have been to me if you did *not* see me thus!"' (Taan. 21a).

As for reward following on the basis of measure for measure, we are told that 'Joseph buried his father in Canaan and was therefore worthy that his bones should be interred there' (Sot. I. 9). On the verse, 'The Lord went before them by day in a pillar of cloud' (Exod. xiii. 21), the remark is made: 'This is to teach that by the measure with which a man measures is it meted out to him. Abraham accompanied the ministering angels on their way (Gen. xviii. 16), so the All-present accompanied his descendants in the

---

[1] Presumably he knew to whom the skull had belonged.
[2] See p. 80.
[3] This is told to show what a saint he was and throw into bolder relief what follows.

wilderness forty years. With our father Abraham it is said, "I will
fetch a morsel of bread" (ibid. 5), so the Holy One, blessed be He,
caused manna to descend forty years. With Abraham it is said,
"Let a little water be fetched" (ibid. 4), and the Holy One, blessed
be He, caused a well to ascend for his offspring in the wilderness
(Num. xxi. 17 f.). With Abraham it is said, "He ran to the
herd" (Gen. xviii. 7), and the Holy One, blessed be He, drove
along quails for his descendants (Num. xi. 31). With Abraham
it is said, "Rest yourselves under a tree" (Gen. xviii. 4), and the
Holy One, blessed be He, spread seven clouds of glory for his
descendants; as it is said, "He spread a cloud for a covering, and
fire to give light in the night" (Ps. cv. 39). With Abraham it is
written, "He stood by (*lit.* over) them" (Gen. xviii. 8), and the
Holy One, blessed be He, protected his descendants in Egypt
that they should not be smitten by the plagues' (Mech. ad loc.;
25*a*).

So fixed did the law of measure for measure appear, that many
Rabbis taught that certain sins were inevitably followed by certain
penalties. 'Seven kinds of punishment come into the world for
seven important transgressions. If some give their tithes and
others do not, a dearth ensues from drought, and some suffer
hunger while others are full. If they all determine to give no
tithes, a dearth ensues from tumult and drought. If they further
resolve not to give the dough-cake,[1] an exterminating dearth
ensues. Pestilence comes into the world to fulfil those death
penalties threatened in the Torah, the execution of which, however, is not within the function of a human tribunal, and for the
violation of the law regarding the fruits of the seventh year (Lev.
xxv. 1 ff.). The sword comes into the world for the delay of
justice, and for the perversion of justice, and on account of the
offence of those who interpret the Torah not according to its true
sense. Noxious beasts come into the world for vain swearing, and
for the profanation of the Name. Captivity comes into the world
on account of idolatry, immorality, bloodshed, and the neglect of
the year of rest for the soil (ibid.)' (Aboth v. 11).

The same idea is found in such passages as these: 'For three
transgressions (Israelite) women die in childbirth: because they
have been negligent in regard to their periods of separation, in
respect to the consecration of the dough and in the lighting of the
Sabbath lamp' (Shab. 11. 6). 'For seven causes plagues occur:
slander, bloodshed, vain swearing, unchastity, pride, robbery, and
envy' (Arach. 16*a*). 'For the sin of vain swearing and false

[1] See p. 101 n. 3.

swearing, of profaning the Name and desecrating the Sabbath wild beasts multiply so that cattle are destroyed, the population diminishes and the roads are deserted' (Shab. 33a).

But however implicit their faith in God's justice, the Rabbis could not escape the problem created by the experiences of life. It was only too evident that the righteous were not rewarded by happiness and prosperity; very often they seemed to be marked out for exceptional adversity. The wicked, similarly, were not seen to be conspicuously frowned upon by God and His displeasure with them proved by hardships and sufferings. On the contrary, fortune seemed to smile upon them and they prospered. Such phenomena could not possibly be overlooked and had to be fitted into the divine scheme of government. Attempts at an answer are found scattered throughout Rabbinic literature, but no agreed solution is offered. As we shall see, the problem is treated in various ways.

Particularly in the critical periods which preceded and followed the destruction of Temple and State, the justification of God's ways pressed itself upon the attention of the religious leaders. The people were perplexed over the triumph of the godless Romans. Not without good cause did a Rabbi utter the exhortation: 'Abandon not belief in retribution' (Aboth I. 7). The unsettled state of mind at the time is reflected in this legend: 'When Moses ascended to heaven and there beheld R. Akiba (still unborn) expounding the Torah in a wondrous manner, he said to God, "Thou hast shown me his learning, now show me his reward." He was told to turn round, and, on so doing, beheld Akiba's flesh being sold in the market-places.[1] He spake before Him, "Sovereign of the Universe! such is his scholarship and such is his reward!" God replied to him, "Keep silent; so has it come up in thought before Me"' (Men. 29b). The legend seems to indicate that the problem is beyond human understanding. Events, inexplicable to man, were so determined by God and he must submit resignedly. One Rabbi boldly declared—if that is the correct interpretation of his words [2]—'It is not in our power to explain either the prosperity of the wicked or the afflictions of the righteous' (Aboth IV. 19).

A notable passage which treats the problem is the discussion of the meaning of the request which Moses made of God, 'Show me Thy ways' (Exod. xxxiii. 13): 'Moses spake before Him,

---

[1] He suffered martyrdom under the Romans.
[2] The Hebrew is literally: 'It is not in our hands, neither the prosperity,' etc. Many scholars prefer to translate: 'We (average people) enjoy neither the prosperity,' or, 'It is not in our power to allot the fate of the wicked or the righteous,' that being only in the power of God.

"Sovereign of the Universe! why is there a righteous man enjoying prosperity and a righteous man afflicted with adversity? Why is there a wicked man enjoying prosperity and a wicked man afflicted with adversity?" He answered him, "Moses, the righteous man who enjoys prosperity is the son of a righteous father; the righteous man who is afflicted with adversity is the son of a wicked father; the wicked man who enjoys prosperity is the son of a righteous father; the wicked man who is afflicted with adversity is the son of a wicked father."

'But it is not so; for lo, it is written, "Visiting the iniquity of the fathers upon the children" (ibid. xxxiv. 7), and it is also written, "The children shall not be put to death for their fathers" (Deut. xxiv. 16)! We set these verses one against the other and conclude there is no contradiction; because the former passage refers to those children who continue in their fathers' ways, and the latter to those who do not continue in their fathers' ways. But we may suppose that God answered Moses in this manner, "The righteous man who enjoys prosperity is perfectly righteous; the righteous man who is afflicted with adversity is not perfectly righteous; the wicked man who enjoys prosperity is not perfectly wicked; the wicked man who is afflicted with adversity is perfectly wicked." R. Meïr declared: "When God said, 'I will be gracious to whom I will be gracious' (Exod. xxxiii. 19), He meant, although he may not be deserving; 'and I will show mercy on whom I will show mercy' likewise means, although he may not be deserving"' (Ber. 7a).

Here we see different methods of facing the problem. R. Meïr holds that the elucidation is beyond the grasp of the human intellect. God acts in His wisdom which may not be understandable by man. In the first-mentioned solution we have the theory that *Zachuth Aboth*, 'the merit of ancestors,' may to a degree mitigate the punishment which is due to sinful descendants. This conception took a firm grip of the Jewish mind and often appears in the liturgy of the Synagogue. Only one Talmudic citation need be given. 'Abraham spake before the Holy One, blessed be He: Sovereign of the Universe! it is revealed and known before Thee that when Thou didst order me to offer up Isaac, it was possible for me to have answered Thee by saying that yesterday Thou didst assure me, "In Isaac shall thy seed be called" (Gen. xxi. 12), and now Thou commandest, "Offer him for a burnt-offering" (ibid. xxii. 2); but far be it from me to do so. I subdued my feeling and carried out Thy command. So may it be acceptable before Thee, O Lord my God, that when the descendants of my son Isaac are afflicted by trouble and there is nobody to speak in their defence, do Thou defend them' (p. Taan. 65d).

Although the plea of ancestral merit may be used by the suppliant in his prayers to God, it was not adopted as a help to the solution of the problem of evil, principally because it rather militated against the idea of individual responsibility. We detect this objection in the remark: 'Moses said, "Visiting the sins of the fathers upon the children"; but Ezekiel came and annulled it, saying, "The soul that sinneth, it shall die" (xviii. 4)' (Mak. 24a). Every person is answerable for his deeds.

More acceptable was the alternative suggestion that when a good man suffered it was because he was not completely good, and when a wicked man prospered it was because he was not wholly bad. The Rabbis did not view life on earth as something complete in itself. Death did not mean the end of human existence. There was a life beyond the grave; and only by combining the experiences of the two stages of life, here and in the Hereafter, can God's providence be understood.

A good example of this viewpoint is the treatment of Deut. xxxii. 4, 'A God of truth and without iniquity, just and right is He': '"A God of truth"—as the Holy One, blessed be He, bestows a reward of good in the World to Come upon the righteous for each light precept which they performed in this world, so He bestows in this world a reward upon the wicked for each light precept which they performed in this world. "Without iniquity"—as the Holy One, blessed be He, exacts a penalty in the World to Come of the wicked for each light transgression of which they have been guilty in this world, so He exacts a penalty in this world of the righteous for each light transgression of which they have been guilty in this world. "Just and right is He"—it is said that on a man's death, all his deeds are enumerated before him and he is told, "So-and-so have you done in such a place on such a day." He admits his guilt and is ordered to sign the record, which he does; as it is stated, "He sealeth up the hand of every man" (Job xxxvii. 7). Not only that, but he admits the verdict passed upon him to be equitable and says, "Thou hast judged me aright"; as it is written, "That Thou mayest be justified when Thou speakest, and be clear when Thou judgest" (Ps. li. 4)' (Taan. 11a).

'To what are the righteous like in this world? To a tree, the whole of which stands in a clean place but its branches extend into an unclean place. When the branches are lopped, the whole of it is in a clean place. Similarly the Holy One, blessed be He, brings sufferings upon the righteous in this world so that they may inherit the World to Come; as it is said, "Though thy beginning was small, yet thy latter end shall greatly increase" (Job viii. 7). And to what are the wicked like in this world? To a tree, the whole of which stands in an unclean place but its branches extend into a clean place. When the branches are lopped, the whole of it is in an unclean place. Similarly the Holy One, blessed be He, grants happiness to the wicked in this world in order to banish and drive them to the lowest degree (of Gehinnom); as it is said, "There is a way which seemeth right unto man, but the end thereof are the ways of death" (Prov. xiv. 12)' (Kid. 40b).

'There is no commandment recorded in the Torah where the reward is mentioned in the context which is not dependent for its fulfilment upon the future life. In connection with honouring parents it is written, "That thy days may be prolonged and that it may go well with thee" (Deut. v. 16); and in connection with the release of the mother-bird it is written, "That it may be well with thee, and that thou mayest prolong thy days' (ibid. xxii. 7). Behold a person whom his father told to climb to the top of a tower and fetch him the pigeons that were there. He went up, set the mother free and took the young; but on his return he fell and was killed.[1] Where was the well-being or the prolongation of days of this person? But the meaning of "that it may be well with thee" is, in the world where all is good; and the meaning of "that thou mayest prolong thy days" is, in the world of endless days' (Kid. 39b).

A very quaint illustration of this doctrine is found in this anecdote: 'The wife of R. Channina said to her husband, "Pray that there may be given to you now some of the good which is reserved for the righteous in the World to Come." He prayed, and there was thrown to him a leg of a golden table. He subsequently dreamt that (in the next world) everybody was eating at a golden table with three legs while his table had only two. (On hearing this) his wife asked him to pray that it be taken back. He prayed and it was taken back' (Taan. 25a). Evidently, in the opinion of the Rabbis, one cannot have the best of both worlds, or, as they put it, 'eat at two tables.'

A rather curious development of the doctrine that the righteous are deliberately made to suffer in this world, is the suggestion that when God sends punishment for the sins of the wicked, it falls first upon the righteous. It signifies that when the effects of wrong-doing are felt, not only must the innocent be also involved in the consequences, but they experience the attendant suffering even

---

[1] This incident is said to have shattered the faith of Elisha b. Abuyah and turned him into an unbeliever (p. Chag. 77b).

more than the guilty. 'Punishment does not come upon the world unless there are wicked persons in existence, and it only makes a beginning with the righteous; as it is said, "If fire break out and catch in thorns, so that the stacks of corn have been consumed" (Exod. xxii. 6). When does fire (i.e. punishment) break out? When there are thorns (i.e. wicked) found about. And it only makes a beginning with the righteous (represented by corn stacks); as it is said, "So that the stacks of corn have been consumed." The text does not state, "will be consumed" (after the thorns), but "have been consumed." They were burnt first. What is the intention of the verse, "And none of you shall go out of the door of his house until the morning, for the Lord will pass through to smite the Egyptians" (ibid. xii. 22 f.)? Since permission had been granted to the angel of death to destroy, he does not discriminate between the righteous and the wicked. More than that, he begins with the righteous; as it is said, "I will cut off from thee the righteous and the wicked" (Ezek. xxi. 3)' (B.K. 60a). The righteous are mentioned first.

Occasionally we find it stated that the good suffer on behalf of the bad; e.g. 'When there are righteous in a generation, the righteous are punished for the sins of that generation. If there are no righteous, then the schoolchildren [1] suffer for the evil of the time' (Shab. 33b). Even the thought of vicarious atonement occurs, as in the question why the account of Miriam's death (Num. xx. 1) immediately follows the law of the red heifer (ibid. xix. 1). The answer given is, 'As the red heifer brought atonement for sins, similarly does the death of the righteous bring atonement for sins' (M.K. 28a). Other extracts which point in the same direction are: 'Moses spake before the Holy One, blessed be He, "Will not a time come when Israel will have neither Tabernacle nor Temple? What will happen to them (as regards atonement)?" He replied, "I will take a righteous man from amongst them and make him a pledge on their account, and I will atone for their iniquities"' (Exod. R. xxxv. 4). When Moses said to God, in connection with the incident of the Golden Calf, 'Blot me, I pray Thee, out of Thy book' (Exod. xxxii. 32), he offered his life as an atonement for the sin of his people (Sot. 14a).

The problem of evil was attacked from another angle, by the denial that sufferings endured in this life were intended by God as punishment, or that they were evidence of His disapproval. On the contrary, they were indicative of His love and served a beneficent purpose. The declaration, 'Behold it was very good'

---

[1] Who are, of course, innocent.

(Gen. i. 31), was referred to suffering. 'Is, then, suffering good? Yes, because through its means human beings attain to the World to Come' (Gen. R. IX. 8). 'Which is the way that leads a man to the World to Come? The answer is, the way of suffering' (Mech. to XX. 23; 73a). 'Whoever rejoices in the sufferings that come upon him in this life brings salvation to the world' (Taan. 8a).

The idea of suffering being a manifestation of divine love is conveyed in this manner: 'Should a man see sufferings come upon him, let him scrutinize his actions; as it is said, "Let us search and try our ways, and return unto the Lord" (Lament. iii. 40). If he has scrutinized his actions without discovering the cause, let him attribute them to neglect of Torah; as it is said, "Happy is the man whom Thou chastenest, and teachest out of Thy Law" (Ps. xciv. 12). If he attributed them to neglect of Torah without finding any justification, it is certain that his chastenings are chastenings of love; as it is said, "For whom the Lord loveth He correcteth" (Prov. iii. 12)' (Ber. 5a).

Why, then, should sufferings be inflicted upon the righteous? The answer suggested is: 'The potter does not test cracked vessels, for he need only knock upon them once and they break; but if he test sound vessels, he can knock upon them many times without their breaking. Similarly the Holy One, blessed be He, does not try the wicked but the righteous; as it is said, "The Lord trieth the righteous" (Ps. xi. 5), and it is written, "God did test Abraham" (Gen. xxii. 1). Parable of a householder who had two cows, one strong and the other weak. Upon which of them does he place the yoke? Surely upon the strong. In the same manner God tests the righteous' (Gen. R. XXXII. 3).

In the light of this higher conception of suffering a beautiful lesson is read into the text, 'Ye shall not make with me gods of silver' (Exod. xx. 23): 'Do not behave towards Me as heathens behave towards their gods. When happiness comes to them, they sing praises to their gods, but when retribution comes upon them they curse their gods. If I bring happiness upon you give thanks, and when I bring sufferings give thanks also' (Mech. ad loc.; 72b). That is the standpoint of Rabbinic law: 'A man is in duty bound to utter a benediction for the bad even as he utters one for the good; as it is said, "And thou shalt love the Lord thy God with all thy heart, and with all thy soul, and with all thy might" (Deut. vi. 5)—"with all thy heart," i.e. with thy two impulses, with the good and the evil impulse; "with all thy soul," i.e. even if He take thy soul; "with all thy might," i.e. with all thy wealth. Another explanation of "with all thy might" is, with whatever measure He metes out to thee, do Thou return Him thanks'[1] (Ber. IX. 5).

Although, as we have seen, the doctrine of reward and punishment figures prominently in Talmudic teaching, nevertheless it is exhorted again and again that the service of God must be disinterested and His commandments observed from pure motives. The subject will be given fuller treatment later;[2] for the present, two extracts may be quoted: '"Blessed is the man that delighteth greatly in His commandments" (Ps. cxii. 1)—in His commandments, not in the reward of His commandments' (A.Z. 19a). 'Be not like servants who minister to their master upon the condition of receiving a reward; but be like servants who minister to their master without the condition of receiving a reward; and let the fear of Heaven be upon you' (Aboth I. 3).

[1] There is a play of words here: 'might' is *meod*, 'measure' is *middah*, and 'thank' is *modeh*.

[2] See pp. 149 ff.

CHAPTER IV

REVELATION

§ I. Prophecy

For a body of religious and ethical doctrine like that contained in the Talmud, which is rooted in the Hebrew Scriptures, the reality of prophecy must be axiomatic. The very foundation of the Rabbinic creed is that God made His will known through certain spokesmen who are called prophets.

A theory which found favour with later Jewish philosophers, that prophecy was not a gift conferred by God arbitrarily upon a number of persons but was the crowning point of exceptional mental and spiritual equipment, is also found in the Talmud. The stages which culminate in the qualification for the prophetic endowment are even enumerated in detail: 'Zeal leads to cleanliness, cleanliness to ritual purity, ritual purity to self-control, self-control to holiness, holiness to humility, humility to fear of sin, fear of sin to saintliness, and saintliness to the Holy Spirit' (Sot. IX. 15).

Besides these moral qualities other conditions were essential. 'The Holy One, blessed be He, does not cause His *Shechinah* to alight except on one who is rich, wise and humble' (Ned. 38*a*). 'The Holy One, blessed be He, does not cause His *Shechinah* to alight except on one who is wise, strong, rich, and of tall stature' (Shab. 92*a*).[1] Moreover, a lapse from ethical perfection has the effect of destroying, either permanently or temporarily, the prophetic endowment. 'If a prophet is proud, his prophecy departs from him; and if he is angry, it likewise leaves him' (Pes. 66*b*).

Since Israel was the depositary of the Revelation, men from that nation were naturally chosen as the divine messengers, but not exclusively. 'Seven prophets prophesied for the Gentiles: Balaam and his father, and Job and his four friends' (B.B. 15*b*). God's justice demanded that He should raise up spokesmen among the

---

[1] The Jewish philosopher, Moses Maimonides (twelfth century), interpreted the words in their special Rabbinic sense. 'Rich' means to be contented, and 'strong' to be master of oneself (Aboth IV. 1). See his treatise, *The Eight Chapters*, ed. Gorfinkle, p. 80. More probably the intention is that even the physical appearance must be such as to command respect, and he was required to be rich because it would give him a feeling of independence.

heathen peoples also. Commenting on the verse, 'The Rock, His work is perfect, for all His ways are judgment' (Deut. xxxii. 4), the Midrash remarks: 'The Holy One, blessed be He, did not leave the peoples of the world a plea for the Hereafter to the effect, "Thou didst keep us at a distance." What did He do? Just as He set up kings, wise men and prophets for Israel, He set them up similarly for the other nations. As He raised up Moses for Israel, so He raised up Balaam for the heathens' (Num. R. xx. 1).

It was never supposed, however, that gentile prophets and Hebrew prophets were inspired to the same degree. The higher level on which the latter stood resulted in a corresponding elevation in prophetic gift. Since it is narrated that 'God came to Abimelech in a dream of the night' (Gen. xx. 3), the inference is drawn that 'the Holy One, blessed be He, only revealed Himself to gentile prophets at a time when it is customary for people to take leave of each other. What is the difference between the prophets of Israel and the prophets of the Gentiles? Parable of a king and a friend who were together in a room and a curtain hung between them. When the king wished to converse with his friend he rolled it up. (In this way He spoke with the prophets of Israel); but when He spoke with the prophets of the Gentiles, He did not roll up the curtain, but addressed them from behind it. Parable of a king who had a wife and a concubine. The former he visits openly, the latter in secret. Similarly the Holy One, blessed be He, communicated with gentile prophets only in half-speech; but with the prophets of Israel He communicated in full speech, in language of love, in language of holiness, in the language wherewith the ministering angels praise Him' (Gen. R. LII. 5).

A reason why so few prophets arose among the heathen peoples and why they ceased is also suggested. 'See the difference between the prophets of Israel and the prophets of the Gentiles. The Israelite prophets warned their hearers against transgressions; as it is said, "Son of man, I have made thee a watchman" (Ezek. iii. 17); but the prophet who arose from the peoples (i.e. Balaam) initiated licentiousness to destroy his fellow-men from the world. Not only that, but the prophets of Israel were moved with compassion for their own people and also for Gentiles; as Jeremiah said, "My heart doth sound for Moab like pipes" (xlviii. 36), and Ezekiel was told, "Son of man, take up a lamentation for Tyre" (xxvii. 2). This cruel one, on the other hand, aimed at uprooting an entire nation (viz. Israel) without cause. For that reason the section about Balaam is included in the Scriptures, to inform us why the Holy One, blessed be He, removed the Holy Spirit from the heathen peoples, since this one arose from among them and He saw what he did' (Num. R. xx. 1).

Of the Hebrew prophets, Moses was pre-eminent and stands in a class by himself. 'What was the distinction between Moses and the other prophets? The latter looked through nine *specularia*, whereas Moses looked only through one. They looked through a cloudy *specularia*, but Moses through one that was clear' (Lev. R. 1. 14).[1] His apprehension of the divine message was therefore more intimate than theirs. The Revelation granted to him was the source from which all the later prophets drew. 'What the prophets were destined to prophesy in subsequent generations they received from Mount Sinai' (Exod. R. xxviii. 6). 'Moses gave utterance to all the words of the other prophets as well as his own, and whoever prophesied only gave expression to the essence of Moses' prophecy' (ibid. xlii. 8).

It followed from this that nothing spoken by a later prophet could in any way be in conflict with, and add to or detract from, the writings of Moses. 'Forty-eight prophets and seven prophetesses spoke prophecies for Israel, and they neither deducted from nor added to what was written in the Torah, with the exception of the law to read the Book of Esther on the Feast of Purim' (Meg. 14a).[2] The number forty-eight included the patriarchs and other outstanding personalities of the Bible. The seven prophetesses are Sarah, Miriam, Deborah, Hannah, Abigail, Huldah, and Esther.

Another dictum increases very considerably the number of inspired persons in the ranks of Israel. 'Many prophets arose from Israel, double the number of those who left Egypt.[3] Only the prophecy which was required for subsequent generations was written down, and what was not so required was not committed to writing' (Meg. 14a).

Even with the canonical prophets, apart from Moses, different grades of inspiration were recognized. 'The Holy Spirit which alights on the prophets only does so by measure. Some prophesied to the extent of one book, others of two books. Beeri only prophesied two verses, which, being insufficient for a separate book, were incorporated in Isaiah (viii. 19 f.)' (Lev. R. xv. 2). According

---

[1] There must always be something which intervenes between man and God. This intervening medium exists for prophets and is denoted *specularia* ('window-pane'). In the case of Moses it was reduced to an absolute minimum.

[2] The feast which commemorates the escape of the Jews of Persia from the plot of Haman. All the laws of Judaism are traced to the Mosaic legislation, but obviously the regulation that the Book of Esther should be recited annually must be a later addition.

[3] That number was six hundred thousand.

to one opinion, Hosea was the greatest of his age. 'At one period four prophets prophesied, Hosea, Isaiah, Amos, and Micah, of whom Hosea was pre-eminent' (Pes. 87a). Another view awards the palm to Isaiah. 'All the other prophets received their prophecies one from another, but Isaiah received it direct from the Holy One, blessed be He' (Lev. R. x. 2). His superiority over Ezekiel was characterized in this manner: 'All that Ezekiel beheld Israel beheld; but to what is Ezekiel like? A rustic who gazed at the king. To what is Isaiah like? A townsman who gazed at the king' (Chag. 13b).[1]

There was general agreement that prophecy, in its special connotation, ceased with the overthrow of the first Temple, although it lingered with a few men during the exile. 'When the latter prophets, Haggai, Zechariah, and Malachi, died, the Holy Spirit departed from Israel' (Sanh. 11a). Another Rabbi remarked: 'From the day the Temple was destroyed the prophetic gift was taken away from the prophets and given to the Sages' (B.B. 12a). This saying indicates the links in the chain of tradition whereby the Torah passed through the generations from Moses down to the period of the Talmud.[2]

A less complimentary statement is: 'From the day the Temple was destroyed, prophecy was taken away from the prophets and given to fools and children' (B.B. 12b). There may be a religious polemic behind the words, since, as we know from Josephus,[3] every now and then a person arose, claiming to be a prophet or the promised deliverer of Israel.

The supreme message of Hebrew prophecy was the call to erring men and women to retrace their steps to God. 'Every prophet only prophesied for the days of the Messiah and the penitent' (Ber. 34b). In this sense must the rather strange dictum be understood: 'The time will come when the Prophets and Hagiographa will be abolished, but not the Pentateuch' (p. Meg. 70d). When everybody is obedient to the commandments, there will be no further need for the prophetic exhortations which were only intended for a sinful world and not the era of perfection to be inaugurated by the Messiah.

When that happy period arrives there will be another reason why special prophets will be superfluous. Since all will be mentally and ethically perfect, they will have attained to that state where they become entitled to prophetic gifts. 'The Holy One, blessed

---

[1] Ezekiel, being less familiar with divine visions, devotes several chapters to their description (i. viii. x); but Isaiah, to whom they were a common experience, only describes them once (chap. vi).
[2] See Introduction, p. xviii.
[3] See Antiq. xx. v. 1 and viii. 6.

be He, said, In this world only individuals are endowed with prophecy, but in the World to Come all Israel will be prophets; as it is said, "It shall come to pass afterward that I will pour out My spirit upon all flesh; and your sons and your daughters shall prophesy, your old men shall dream dreams, your young men shall see visions" (Joel ii. 28)' (Num. R. xv. 25).

§ II. The Torah

It must already have become evident to the reader that the Talmud has its roots in the Hebrew Scriptures. For almost every thought and every utterance warrant is sought in the sacred text. 'As it is said' or 'as it is written' follows practically every statement. The Rabbis, whose teachings comprise the Talmud, would have denied that they were originators of Jewish thought. All they would have admitted was they were excavators in the inexhaustible mine of the divine Revelation contained in the Scriptures and brought to light treasures that lay hidden beneath the surface.

To study the inspired Writings, to meditate upon them, to extract from them all they could be made to produce was, accordingly, the chief privilege as it was the greatest duty of the Jew. Unless one appreciates the place which the Torah occupied in the life of the Rabbis and their attitude towards it, any attempt to understand and evaluate their teachings is an impossibility.

Perhaps no better approach could be made to this subject than by bringing together the references to Torah which are contained in the Mishnaic Tractate, *Pirké Aboth*, 'The Chapters of the Fathers.' The teachers whose aphorisms are there preserved lived between the second century before the common era and the end of the second century of the present era. They were the pioneers of the Talmud whose labours gave the impetus to that devoted study of the Torah which resulted in the Rabbinic literature. Some extracts have been previously cited but are included to enable the reader to appreciate the cumulative effect of the whole.

'Moses received the Torah on Sinai and handed it down to Joshua; Joshua to the Elders; the Elders to the prophets; and the prophets handed it down to the men of the Great Assembly. They said three things: Be deliberate in judgment; raise up many disciples; and make a fence round the Torah' (I. 1).[1]

'Simon the Just [2] was one of the last survivors of the Great

---

[1] On this paragraph, see Introduction, p. xix.
[2] On his identification, see Introduction, p. xx.

Assembly. He used to say, Upon three things the world is based: upon the Torah, upon divine worship, and upon acts of benevolence' (I. 2).

'Let your house be a meeting-house for the wise (in Torah); sit amidst the dust of their feet, and drink their words with thirst' (I. 4).

'Whoso engages in much gossip with women brings evil upon himself, neglects the study of the Torah, and will in the end inherit Gehinnom' (I. 5).

'Provide yourself with a teacher (of Torah), and get yourself a companion, and judge all men in the scale of merit' (I. 6).

'Be of the disciples of Aaron, loving peace and pursuing peace, loving your fellow-creatures, and drawing them near to the Torah' (I. 12).

'He who does not increase his knowledge decreases it; and he who does not study (Torah) deserves to die; and he who makes a worldly use of the crown of the Torah shall waste away' (I. 13).

'Fix a period for your study of the Torah' (I. 15).

'An excellent thing is the study of the Torah combined with some worldly occupation, for the labour demanded by them both makes sin to be forgotten. All study of the Torah without work must in the end be futile and become the cause of sin' (II. 2).

'An empty-headed man cannot be a sin-fearing man, nor can a person ignorant (of Torah) be pious, nor can a shamefaced man learn, nor a passionate man teach, nor can one who is engaged overmuch in business grow wise (in Torah)' (II. 6).

'The more Torah the more life. . . . He who has acquired for himself words of Torah has acquired for himself life in the World to Come' (II. 8).

'If you have learnt much Torah, ascribe not any merit to yourself, for thereunto were you created' (II. 9).

'Qualify yourself for the study of the Torah, since it does not come to you as an inheritance, and let all your deeds be done for the sake of Heaven' (II. 17).

'Be watchful in the study of the Torah, and know what answer to give to the unbeliever; know also before Whom you toil and Who is your Employer Who will pay you the reward of your labour' (II. 19).

'It is not your duty to complete the work, but neither are you free to desist from it. If you have studied much Torah, much reward will be given you; and faithful is your Employer to pay you the reward of your labour; and know that the grant of reward unto the righteous will be in the Hereafter' (II. 21).

'If two sit together and interchange no words of Torah, they are a meeting of scorners, concerning whom it is said, "The godly man sitteth not in the seat of the scorners" (Ps. i. 1); but if two sit together and interchange words of Torah, the *Shechinah* abides between them; as it is said, "Then they that feared the Lord spake one with the other; and the Lord hearkened and heard, and a book of remembrance was written before Him for them that feared the Lord and that thought upon His name" (Mal.i ii. 16). Now, the Scripture enables me to draw this inference in respect of two persons: Whence can it be deduced that if even one person sedulously occupies himself with the Torah, the Holy One, blessed be He, appoints unto him a reward? Because it is said, "Though he sit alone and meditate in stillness, yet he taketh it (viz. the reward) upon him" (Lament. iii. 27)' (III. 3).

'If three have eaten at a table and have spoken there no words of Torah, it is as if they had eaten of sacrifices to dead idols, of whom it is said, "For all their tables are full of vomit and filthiness; the All-present is not (in their thoughts)" (*sic* Is. xxviii. 8). But if three have eaten at a table and have spoken there words of Torah, it is as if they had eaten at the table of the All-present, to which the Scripture may be applied, "And He said unto me, This is the table that is before the Lord" (Ezek. xli. 22)' (III. 4).

'Whoso receives upon himself the yoke of the Torah, from him the yoke of the kingdom and the yoke of worldly care will be removed; but whoso breaks off from him the yoke of the Torah, upon him will be laid the yoke of the kingdom and the yoke of worldly care' (III. 6).

'When ten people sit together and occupy themselves with the Torah, the *Shechinah* abides among them; as it is said, "God standeth in the congregation of the godly" (Ps. lxxxii. 1). And whence can it be shown that the same applies to five? Because it is said, "He hath founded His band upon the earth" (Amos ix. 6). And whence can it be shown that the same applies to three? Because it is said, "He judgeth among the judges" (Ps. lxxxii. 1). And whence can it be shown that the same applies to two? Because it is said, "Then they that feared the Lord spake one with another; and the Lord hearkened and heard" (Mal. iii. 16). And whence can it be shown that the same applies even to one? Because it is said, "In every place where I cause My name to be remembered I will come unto thee and I will bless thee" (Exod. xx. 24)' (III. 7).

'He who is walking by the way and studying (Torah), and breaks off his study and says, "How fine is that tree, how fine is that fallow!" him the Scripture regards as if he had forfeited his life' (III. 9).

'Whoso forgets one word of his study, him the Scripture regards as if he had forfeited his life; as it is said, "Only take heed to thyself, and keep thy soul diligently, lest thou forget the things which thine eyes have seen" (Deut. iv. 9). Now, one might suppose that the same result follows even if a man's study has been too hard for him. To guard against such an inference it is said, "Lest they depart from thy mouth all the days of thy life" (ibid.). Thus, a person's guilt is not established until he deliberately and of set purpose removes the lessons from his heart' (III. 10).

'He in whom the fear of sin comes before wisdom (i.e. knowledge of the Torah), his wisdom shall endure; but he in whom wisdom comes before the fear of sin, his wisdom will not endure. Whose works exceed his wisdom, his wisdom shall endure; but he whose wisdom exceeds his works, his wisdom will not endure' (III. 11 f.).

'Beloved are Israel, for unto them was given the desirable instrument (viz. Torah); but it was by a special love that it was made known to them that that desirable instrument was theirs, through which the world was created; as it is said, "For I give you good doctrine, forsake ye not My Torah" (Prov. iv. 2)' (III. 18).

'Where there is no Torah, there are no manners; where there are no manners, there is no Torah. Where there is no wisdom, there is no fear of God; where there is no fear of God, there is no wisdom. Where there is no knowledge, there is no understanding; where there is no understanding, there is no knowledge. Where there is no meal, there is no Torah; where there is no Torah, there is no meal' (III. 21).

'The laws concerning the sacrifices of birds and the purification of women are ordinances of moment; astronomy and geometry are the after-courses of wisdom' (III. 23).[1]

'He who learns (Torah) in order to teach, to him the means will be vouchsafed both to learn and to teach; but he who learns in order to practise, to him the means will be vouchsafed to learn and to teach, to observe and to practise' (IV. 6).

'Make not of the Torah a crown wherewith to aggrandize yourself, nor a spade wherewith to dig. So also used Hillel to say, "He who makes a worldly use of the crown of the Torah shall waste away." Hence you may infer that whosoever derives a

---

[1] The intention of this aphorism is that the apparent trifling matters of the Torah are of first-rate importance, while the secular sciences are of secondary concern.

profit for himself from the words of the Torah is helping in his own destruction' (IV. 7).[1]

'Whoever honours the Torah will himself be honoured by mankind, but whoever dishonours the Torah will himself be dishonoured by mankind' (IV. 8).

'Whoever fulfils the Torah in the midst of poverty shall in the end fulfil it in the midst of wealth; and whoever neglects the Torah in the midst of wealth shall in the end neglect it in the midst of poverty' (IV. 11).

'Lessen your toil for worldly goods and be busy in the Torah. If you neglect the Torah, many causes for neglecting it will present themselves to you; but if you labour in the Torah, He has abundant recompense to give you' (IV. 12).

'Be cautious in study (of Torah), for an error in study may amount to presumptuous sin' (IV. 16).

'There are three crowns: the crown of Torah, the crown of priesthood, and the crown of royalty; but the crown of a good name excels them all' (IV. 17).

'Wander forth to the home of the Torah, and say not that the Torah will come after you; for there your associates will establish you in the possession of it, and lean not upon your own understanding' (IV. 18).

'There are four characters suggested by those who attend the House of Study: he who goes and does not practise secures the reward for going; he who practises but does not go secures the reward for practising; he who goes and practises is a saint; he who neither goes nor practises is a wicked man' (V. 17).

'At five years the age is reached for the study of Scripture; at ten for the study of the Mishnah and at fifteen for the study of the Talmud' (V. 24).

'Turn it (the Torah) and turn it over again, for everything is in it; and contemplate it, and wax grey and old over it; and stir not from it. You can have no better rule than this' (V. 25).

The sixth chapter is an addition to the tractate and is known as 'The Chapter on the Acquisition of the Torah.' Practically the whole of it is related to our subject.

'Whosoever labours in the Torah for its own sake merits many things; and not only so, but the whole world is indebted to him. He is called friend, beloved, a lover of the All-present, a lover of mankind. It clothes him in meekness and reverence, fits him to

---

[1] In the Talmudic age and for many centuries later the teachers, apart from professional instructors of children, were honorary and earned their livelihood by manual labour.

become just, pious, upright, and faithful; it keeps him far from sin, and brings him near to virtue. Through him the world enjoys counsel and sound knowledge, understanding and strength, as it is said, "Counsel is mine, and sound knowledge; I am understanding; I have strength" (Prov. viii. 14). It also gives him sovereignty and dominion and discerning judgment; to him the secrets of the Torah are revealed; he is made like a never-failing fountain, and like a river that flows on with ever-sustained vigour; he becomes modest, long-suffering, and forgiving of insults; and it magnifies and exalts him above all things' (VI. 1).

'Every day a *Bath Kol* goes forth from Mount Sinai proclaiming these words: Woe to mankind for contempt of the Torah, for whoever does not labour in the Torah is said to be under the divine censure. It is likewise said, "The tables were the work of God, and the writing was the writing of God, graven upon the tables" (Exod. xxxii. 16)—read not *charuth* (graven) but *cheruth* (freedom), for no man is free but he who labours in the Torah. But whosoever labours in the Torah, behold, he shall be exalted; as it is said, "From Mattanah to Nachaliel, and from Nachaliel to Bamoth"[1] (Num. xxi. 19)' (VI. 2).

'This is the way that is becoming for the study of the Torah; a morsel of bread with salt you must eat, and water by measure you must drink, you must sleep upon the ground and live a life of trouble the while you toil in the Torah. If you act thus, "Happy shalt thou be and it shall be well with thee" (Ps. cxxviii. 2)—happy shall you be in this world, and it shall be well with you in the World to Come' (VI. 4).

'The Torah is greater than the priesthood and than royalty, seeing that royalty demands thirty qualifications, the priesthood twenty-four, while the Torah is acquired by forty-eight. They are: by audible study, distinct pronunciation, understanding and discernment of the heart, awe, reverence, meekness, cheerfulness; by ministering to the Sages, attaching oneself to colleagues and discussion with disciples; by sedateness, knowledge of the Scripture and of the Mishnah; by moderation in business, intercourse with the world, sleep, conversation, laughter, long-suffering, a good heart, faith in the wise, resignation under chastisement, recognizing one's place, rejoicing in one's portion, putting a fence to one's words and claiming no merit for oneself; by being beloved,

---

[1] These place-names are given their ordinary signification as words: Mattanah means 'gift,' Nachaliel 'heritage of God,' and Bamoth 'high places.' The verse accordingly implies: 'He who accepts the gift (of Torah) acquires the heritage of God and ascends to the heights.'

loving the All-present, loving mankind, loving just courses, recti-
tude and reproof; by keeping oneself far from honour, not boasting
of one's learning, nor delighting in giving decisions; by bearing
the yoke with one's fellow, judging him favourably and leading him
to truth and peace; by being composed in one's study; by asking and
answering, hearing and adding thereto (by one's own reflection);
by learning with the object of teaching, and by learning with
the object of practising; by making one's master wiser, fixing
attention upon his discourse, and reporting a thing in the name
of him who said it' (VI. 6).

'Great is the Torah which gives life to those that practise it in
this world and in the World to Come' (VI. 7).

'R. José b. Kisma said, I was once walking by the way, when a
man met me and saluted me, and I returned the salutation. He
said to me, "Rabbi, from what place are you?" I said to him,
"I come from a great city of Sages and scribes." He said to me,
"If you are willing to dwell with us in our place, I will give you a
thousand thousand golden *denarii* and precious stones and pearls."
I said to him, "Were you to give me all the silver and gold and
precious stones and pearls in the world, I would not dwell anywhere
but in a home of the Torah; and thus it is written in the Book of
Psalms by the hand of David, King of Israel, 'The law of Thy
mouth is better unto me than thousands of gold and silver' (cxix.
72); and not only so, but in the hour of man's departure neither
silver nor gold nor precious stones nor pearls accompany him, but
only Torah and good works"' (VI. 9).

'Five possessions the Holy One, blessed be He, made especially
His own in His universe, viz. the Torah, heaven and earth, Abraham,
Israel, and the Temple. Whence know we this of the Torah?
Because it is written, "The Lord possessed me as the beginning
of His way, before His works, from of old" (Prov. viii. 22)' (VI. 10).[1]

This testimony, drawn from one tractate only, speaks eloquently
of the pre-eminent place which the Torah held in the life of the
Talmudic Jew. It was not merely the foundation upon which his
life was built up, but it was considered the only secure basis of the
entire cosmic order. Without Torah there would be moral chaos,
and for that reason Torah must have existed always, even before
the creation of the world. 'Were it not for Torah, the heavens and
earth could not endure; as it is said, "If it were not for My covenant
(i.e. the Torah), I would not have appointed day and night (*sic*)

---

[1] Two good English editions of the *Pirké Aboth* with annotations are
C. Taylor, *Sayings of the Jewish Fathers* (2nd ed., 1897), and R. T. Herford,
Pirké Aboth (1925).

and the ordinances of heaven and earth" (Jer. xxxiii. 25)' (Pes. 68b).
Another reason for the pre-existence of Torah is: 'You will find in
the ways of the All-present that He gives precedence to what is
dear to Him. On that account He created Torah first,[1] since it
is dearer to Him than all else He made; as it is said, "The Lord
possessed me as the beginning of His way, before His works, from
of old"' (Sifré Deut. § 37; 76a).

According to one opinion, 'the Torah preceded Creation by two
thousand years' (Gen. R. VIII. 2); but another view is, 'Nine hundred
and seventy-four generations before the creation of the world the
Torah was written and lay in the bosom of the Holy One, blessed
be He' (ARN XXXI).[2]

The thought that the world-order is dependent upon Torah is
conveyed in this way: 'The Holy One, blessed be He, made a condition with the works of Creation and said to them, If Israel accepts
the Torah you will endure; if not I will reduce you again to chaos'
(Shab. 88a). That only in its atmosphere can the human being
lead a wholesome, ethical existence is derived from the text, 'Thou
makest men as the fishes of the sea' (Hab. i. 14): 'Why are men
likened to fishes? To tell you that as the fishes in the sea immediately perish when they come to dry land, so do men immediately
perish when they separate themselves from the words of Torah'
(A.Z. 3b).

The same idea is applied more particularly to the people of Israel
in the famous parable of R. Akiba. 'Once the wicked government
(i.e. Rome) decreed that Israel should no longer occupy themselves
with the Torah. There came Pappos b. Judah and found R. Akiba
attracting great assemblies and studying Torah. He said to him,
"Akiba, are you not afraid of the wicked government?" He
replied, "I will tell you a parable: To what is the matter like?
To a fox who was walking along the bank of a stream and saw
some fishes gathering together from one place to another. He
said to them, 'From what are you fleeing?' They answered, 'From
nets which men are bringing against us.' He said to them, 'Let
it be your pleasure to come up on the dry land, and let us, me and
you, dwell together even as my fathers dwelt with your fathers.'
They replied, 'Are you he of whom they tell, that you are the
shrewdest of animals? You are not clever but a fool. For if we

[1] See pp. 28 f.
[2] This computation is based on the verse: 'The word (i.e. Torah) which He
commanded to a thousand generations' (Ps. cv. 8). But the Revelation
occurred in the age of Moses, which was the twenty-sixth generation from
Adam; therefore the Torah must have existed nine hundred and seventy-four
generations before the world was created (Gen. R. XXVIII. 4).

are afraid in the place which is our life-element, how much more so in a place which is our death-element!' So also is it with us —now while we sit and study Torah, in which it is written, 'For that is thy life and the length of thy days' (Deut. xxx. 20), we are in such a plight, how much more so if we go and neglect it!"' (Ber. 61b).

The vitalizing power of the Torah is a theme which is emphasized over and over again. '"This is the Torah which Moses set before the children of Israel" (Deut. iv. 44)—if one is worthy (by faithfulness to its precepts), it becomes an elixir of life;[1] if one is unworthy it becomes to him a deadly poison' (Joma 72b). It is the panacea for all ills. 'If one is on a journey and has no escort, let him occupy himself with Torah; as it is said, "For they are an ornament[2] of grace" (Prov. i. 9). If he has a pain in his head, let him occupy himself with Torah; as it is said, "unto thy head" (ibid.). If he has a pain in his throat, let him occupy himself with Torah; as it is said, "and chains about thy neck' (ibid.). If he has a pain in his bowels, let him occupy himself with Torah; as it is said, "It shall be health to thy navel" (ibid. iii. 8). If he has a pain in his bones, let him occupy himself with Torah; as it is said, "and marrow to thy bones" (ibid.). If he has a pain in all his body, let him occupy himself with Torah; as it is said, "and health to all their flesh" (ibid. iv. 22)' (Erub. 54a).

The Torah, as reflecting the divine mind, is perfect in every respect. 'What is the meaning of that which is written, "Whoso keepeth the fig-tree shall eat the fruit thereof" (Prov. xxvii. 18)? Why is the Torah compared to a fig? In all fruits there is a part which is refuse. In dates there are stones, in grapes there are pips, in pomegranates there are husks; but the whole of the fig is eatable. Similarly in the words of the Torah there is no refuse' (Salkut).

Still more vivid in its praise of the Torah and its absolute perfection is this extract: 'The words of Torah are likened to water, wine, oil, honey, and milk. To water—"Ho, every one that thirsteth, come ye to the waters" (Is. lv. 1). As water extends from one end of the world to the other, so the Torah extends from one end of the world to the other. As water is life to the world, so is Torah life to the world. As water descends from heaven, so the Torah descends from heaven. As water refreshens the soul, so the Torah refreshens the soul. As water cleanses man from defilement, so the Torah purifies the unclean (morally). As

---

[1] There is a play on the word for 'set' (sam), and the word for 'elixir' (sam).
[2] The Hebrew word levayah means both 'escort' and 'ornament.'

water makes the body clean, so the Torah makes the body clean (physically). As water descends drop by drop and becomes many streams, so with Torah—a man learns two legal dicta to-day and two to-morrow, until he becomes a flowing fountain of knowledge. As with water, which is not pleasant to the body unless a person is thirsty, similarly the Torah is not pleasant to him unless he yearns for it. As water leaves a high level and goes to a lower level, so the Torah abandons him whose mind is haughty and cleaves to him whose mind is humble. As water does not keep fresh in gold and silver vessels, but in the meanest vessels (of earthenware), so the Torah does not keep except with a person who makes himself lowly like an earthenware jug. As with water, even a great man is not ashamed to say to one inferior to himself, "Give me to drink," so with words of Torah a great man should not be ashamed to say to an inferior, "Teach me one chapter, or one verse, or even one letter." As with water, if a man does not know how to swim he may eventually be drowned, so with words of Torah, if one does not know how to swim in them and come to decisions with respect to them, he too will be overwhelmed.

'If you would argue that as water grows stagnant in a flask, so do the words of Torah stagnate, let them be compared to wine. As wine improves with keeping, so do words of Torah improve as they become older in the body. If you would argue that as water does not gladden the heart, similarly words of Torah do not, let them be compared to wine; as wine gladdens the heart, so do words of Torah gladden the heart. If you would argue that at times wine is bad for the head and body, so are words of Torah injurious, let them be compared to oil. As oil is a comfort to head and body, so do words of Torah bring them comfort. If you would argue that as oil is bitter at first and sweet in the end, so it is with words of Torah, let them be compared to honey and milk; as they are sweet so are words of Torah sweet. If you would argue that as in honey there are wax-cells (which are unpleasant), so possibly there are distasteful things in the words of Torah, let them be compared to milk. As milk is pure, so are the words of Torah pure. If you would argue that as milk is insipid, so are the words of Torah, let them be compared to a mixture of honey and milk. As they cannot together be harmful to the body, so can the words of Torah never be deleterious' (Cant. R. I. 2).

It follows from the perfection of the Torah that it can never be improved upon, and therefore God will never supersede it by another Revelation. This dogma of Judaism is deduced from the text, 'It is not in heaven' (Deut. xxx. 12), which is expounded thus: 'That you shall not say another Moses will arise and bring us another Torah from heaven, I have already made it known to you that "it is not in heaven," i.e. there is nothing left of it in heaven' (Deut. R. VIII. 6).

§ III. STUDY OF THE TORAH

Obviously, if the Torah is to become the rule and guide of life, it must first be known before it can exert such an influence. Consequently its study was the paramount duty of the Jew and was raised to the status of an important religious obligation. Indeed, it was in itself part of the service of God. The words, 'To love the Lord your God and to serve Him' (Deut. xi. 13), receive the comment: '"to serve" means the study of Torah' (Sifré Deut. § 41; 80a).

The Rabbis never tired of expatiating upon the duty of devoting oneself to its study. The passages which follow may be taken as typical of a very large number which could be extracted from the Talmud: 'These are the things to which no limit is set: the corner of the field (Lev. xxiii. 22), the first fruits (Exod. xxiii. 19), the offering brought on the three pilgrimage festivals (Deut. xvi. 16 f.), the practice of benevolence and the study of Torah. These are the things of which the fruits are enjoyed in this world while the capital remains for the World to Come: the honouring of parents, benevolence, restoring peace between a man and his fellow, and also the study of Torah which is equal to them all' (Peah I. 1).

The superiority of study, over all else, springs from the fact that knowledge of God's precepts must precede their performance. For that reason nothing must be allowed to interrupt it. During the Hadrianic persecutions, when edicts were issued forbidding Jews to observe their religious ordinances or study the Torah, a conference was held at Lydda and one of the questions debated was the relative importance of study and practice. 'R. Tarphon said, Practice is greater. R. Akiba said, Study is greater. The rest of the Rabbis agreed with him and declared, Study is more important because study leads to practice' (Kid. 40b). The same thought was read into the words, 'That ye may learn them, and observe to do them' (Deut. v. 1). Since learning is mentioned first it indicated that 'observance depends on study, not study on observance, and the punishment for the neglect of study is greater than for non-observance' (Sifré Deut. § 41; 79a).

'Greater is study of Torah than the rebuilding of the Temple' (Meg. 16*b*), said one teacher; and another exhorted: 'A person should not withhold himself from the House of Study and from words of Torah even at the hour of death' (Shab. 83*b*). The all-engrossing nature of this study is well illustrated by the following question and answer: 'A Rabbi asked, "Since I have learnt the whole of the Torah, may I study Greek philosophy?" In reply the verse was quoted, "This book of Torah shall not depart out of thy mouth, but thou shalt meditate therein day and night" (Josh. i. 8), and the remark was added, "Go and search at which hour it is neither day nor night and devote it to the study of Greek philosophy"' (Men. 99*b*).

No excuse was accepted for the neglect of study, as this extract forcibly demonstrates: 'A poor man, a rich man, and a wicked man presented themselves before the heavenly tribunal. The poor man was asked, "Why did you not occupy yourself with Torah?" If he answer that he was poverty-stricken and worried about his sustenance, then it is said to him, "Were you poorer than Hillel?" It is related of Hillel the Elder that for his daily work he only earned half a *denarius*; but he gave half of it to the doorkeeper of the House of Study for admission and spent the remainder on supporting himself and the members of his household. On one occasion he was without work and earned nothing, and the doorkeeper refused to admit him. So he climbed up and sat outside the window in order to hear the words of the living God expounded by Shemayah and Abtalion. Tradition has it that the day referred to was the eve of the Sabbath in midwinter and snow fell heavily. At break of dawn Shemayah said to Abtalion, "My colleague, usually the room is light, but to-day it is dark; perhaps it is cloudy." They looked up at the window and saw the form of a man. They went out and found him covered with three cubits of snow. They released him from his position, washed and rubbed him, and placed him before the fire, saying, "This man is deserving that the Sabbath should be desecrated for him."

'The rich man is asked, "Why did you not occupy yourself with Torah?" If he answer that he was rich and worried about his possessions, it is said to him, "Were you more wealthy than R. Eleazar b. Charsom, of whom it is related that his father bequeathed to him a thousand cities and a corresponding fleet of a thousand ships; yet every day he slung a bag of flour over his shoulder and went from city to city and from province to province in order to learn Torah?" On one occasion his servants (who did not know him personally) seized him for some forced labour. He said to them, "I implore you, let me free to go and study Torah." They answered, "By the life of R. Eleazar b. Charsom, we will not let you go." Although they were his servants he had never seen them before, but sat day and night engrossed in the study of Torah.

'The wicked man is asked, "Why did you not occupy yourself with Torah?" If he answer that he was good-looking and troubled by his passions, he is asked, "Were you more handsome than Joseph?" It is related of Joseph the righteous that Potiphar's wife tempted him every day. The dresses she put on for his sake in the morning she did not wear in the evening, and vice versa. Though she threatened him with imprisonment, with bodily disfigurement and with blinding, though she tried to bribe him with large sums of money, he refused to yield. Consequently Hillel condemns the poor, R. Eleazar b. Charsom the rich, and Joseph the wicked' (Joma 35b).

If Torah-study is to absorb all one's time and energies, what of the necessity of earning a livelihood? The question is treated in a discussion of the text, 'And thou shalt gather in thy corn' (Deut. xi. 14): 'What has this to tell us? Since it is written, "This book of the Torah shall not depart out of thy mouth, but thou shalt meditate therein day and night" (Josh. i. 8), it is possible to think that these words are to be understood in their literal sense; therefore there is a teaching to say, "Thou shalt gather in thy corn" i.e. conduct at the same time a worldly occupation. These are the words of R. Ishmael. R. Simeon b. Jochai said, Is it possible for a man to plough at the time of ploughing, sow at seed-time, reap at harvest-time, thresh at the time of threshing, and winnow at the time of wind—what is to become of Torah? But when Israel perform the will of the All-present, their work is done by others; as it is said, "Strangers shall stand and feed your flocks" (Is. lxi. 5); and at the time when Israel perform not the will of the All-present, their work has to be done by themselves; as it is said, "Thou shalt gather in thy corn." Not only that but the work of others will be done by them; as it is said, "Thou shalt serve thine enemies" (Deut. xxviii. 48). Abbai said, Many acted in accord with the teaching of R. Ishmael, and it proved efficacious; but he who acted in accord with R. Simeon b. Jochai did not find it so. Raba said to his disciples, I beg of you not to appear before me during the days of *Nisan* and *Tishri*,[1]

---

[1] The first and the seventh months of the year, corresponding with March–April and September–October, the time of the ripening of the corn and the pressing of the grapes. By devoting these two months to work, the remainder of the year could be safely given to study.

so that you may not be concerned about your maintenance the whole year' (Ber. 35*b*).

This is the generally accepted view of the Rabbis, that the claims of earning a living must not be completely ousted by study. The happy medium is advocated as the ideal to be adopted, and both extremes should be avoided. So, on the one hand, it is stated: 'Come and see that the later generations are not like the former generations. The former generations made their Torah their principal concern and their work only occasional, and both flourished in their hand; whereas the later generations made their work their principal concern and their Torah only occasional and neither flourished in their hand' (ibid.). But a second-century Rabbi declared: 'I set aside all worldly work and teach my son nothing but Torah, the fruit of which a man eats in this world and the capital remains for the World to Come. With worldly occupations it is otherwise: when a man falls ill or grows old or is suffering and is unable to carry on his work, he dies of hunger. With Torah, however, it is not so; but it guards him from all evil in his youth and gives him a hopeful fate in his old age' (Kid. IV. 14).

There were many, no doubt, who followed this latter example and neglected their livelihood for the knowledge of Torah. For that reason we find the exhortation to be generous in offering hospitality to students. This duty is inferred from several Biblical verses, of which one example may be quoted: '"And the Lord blessed Obed-Edom and all his house because of the Ark of God" (2 Sam. vi. 11 f.). Can we not employ here the *a fortiori* argument? If the Ark which neither ate nor drank, but which Obed-Edom swept and besprinkled, brought him a blessing, how much more so one who entertains a disciple of the wise, giving him to eat and drink, and allowing him to enjoy his possessions!' (Ber. 63*b*). It was also considered meritorious for a wealthy man to take a student of the Torah as his son-in-law, so that he should be freed from worldly cares and devote himself completely to the acquisition of knowledge (ibid. 34*b*).

The duty of learning must be given preference even to attention to the task of carrying on the affairs of the community. 'When a student of Torah engages in many diversions, they disturb him from his study. Who occupies himself with the needs of the community makes his learning to be forgotten' (Exod. R. VI. 2). It was also said: 'Over three types of persons the Holy One, blessed be He, weeps every day: over him who has the possibility of occupying himself with Torah but fails to do so, over him who has not the intellectual capacity for such study and yet engages upon it,

and over a president who rules the community with a high hand'
(Chag. 5b).

In the Tractate *Aboth* the advice was given that the Torah must
not be studied for the purpose of self-aggrandizement; and the idea
that the study must be *lishmah*, 'for its own sake,' from pure and
disinterested motives, is frequently met with. 'What is the meaning of the words, "On her tongue is the law (Torah) of kindness"
(Prov. xxxi. 26)? Is there, then, a Torah of kindness and a Torah
not of kindness? But Torah studied for its own sake is a Torah of
kindness, and if studied not for its own sake it is not a Torah
of kindness' (Suk. 49b). 'If one studies Torah for its own sake it
becomes to him an elixir of life; but if he studies it not for its own
sake it becomes to him a deadly poison' (Taan. 7a). Still clearer
is the teaching derived from the verse, 'That thou mayest love the
Lord thy God and that thou mayest obey His voice and cleave
unto Him' (Deut. xxx. 20): 'A man should not say, "I will study
the Scriptures that people may call me learned; I will study
Mishnah that people may call me Rabbi; I will teach that I may
be a Professor in the Academy." Study from love, and the honour
will come finally of its own accord' (Ned. 62a).

Since with many this would be a counsel of perfection, the
commonly adopted principle was: 'Always let a man occupy himself with Torah and the precepts even not for their own sake, since
from his doing it not for their own sake he will come to do it for
their own sake' (Naz. 23b). The same thought actuated a Rabbi
who used to offer this prayer daily: 'May it be Thy will, O Lord
our God, to grant peace in the heavenly household above and the
earthly household below, and among the students who occupy
themselves with Thy Torah, whether they devote themselves
thereto for its own sake or not for its own sake; and as for them
that devote themselves thereto not for its own sake, may it be
Thy will that they do devote themselves thereto for its own sake'
(Ber. 16b *et seq.*).

Great as the merit is to spend one's life in gaining knowledge of
the Torah, the merit becomes ever so much greater if one spreads
the knowledge by teaching. 'To what is a scholar like? A flask
containing aromatic ointment. When it is unstopped the fragrance
is diffused; when it is stopped up the fragrance is not diffused'
(A.Z. 35b). 'Whoever learns Torah and does not teach it is like
a myrtle in the desert' (R.H. 23a). 'Who teaches Torah to the
son of his fellow-man has it ascribed to him as though he had
begotten him' (Sanh. 19b); and the verse, 'Thou shalt teach
them diligently to thy children' (Deut. vi. 7), is applied to pupils

who are the equal of the teacher's own children (Sifré Deut. § 34; 74*a*).

The importance of the teacher's role is well indicated in this story: 'Rab came to a certain place where he ordained a fast because there was a drought. The precentor of the congregation conducted the service, and when he uttered the words, "He causes the wind to blow," the wind at once blew; and when he uttered the words, "He causes the rain to fall," at once the rain fell! Rab said to him, "What is your exceptional merit?" He answered, "I am an elementary teacher, and I instruct the children of the poor exactly the same as I teach the children of the rich. If any one is unable to pay me a fee I forgo it; also I have a fish-pond, and when I find a pupil negligent in his studies, I bribe him with some of the fish so that he comes regularly to learn"' (Taan. 24*a*).[1]

Despite the supreme value which was attached to studying and imparting instruction, they who are engaged in this great work should not be filled with undue pride. They are only labourers in God's sight, just the same as the men who are engaged on manual toil. Very beautiful is the saying attributed to the Rabbis of the famous Academy at Jabneh:[2] 'I am a creature of God and my neighbour is also His creature; my work is in the city and his in the field; I rise early to my work and he rises early to his. As he cannot excel in my work, so I cannot excel in his work. But perhaps you may say that I do great things and he small things! We have learnt that it matters not whether one does much or little, if only he direct his heart to Heaven' (Ber. 17*a*).

Most important of all was the emphasis laid on the fact that study of Torah was not an end it itself. The knowledge gained thereby furnished one with the equipment which helps him to live aright. 'The words of the Torah give light to a man when he occupies himself with them, and whosoever does not occupy himself with them and is ignorant of them stumbles. Parable of a person who is standing in darkness. When he starts out to walk he meets with a stone and stumbles over it; he meets with a drain and falls into it, striking his face against the ground. Why does he do this? Because he has no lamp in his hand. Such is the ignoramus who does not possess words of Torah. He meets with transgressions and stumbles and dies. For the reason that he is unacquainted with Torah he goes and sins; as it is said, "The way of the wicked is darkness; they know not at what they stumble' (Prov. iv. 19). They, on the other hand, who occupy

---

[1] See further on the position of the teacher, pp. 175 f.
[2] See Introduction, p. xxiv.

themselves with Torah have light everywhere. Parable of a person who is standing in darkness but has a lamp in his hand. He sees a stone but does not stumble over it. He sees a drain but does not fall into it, because he has a lamp in his hand; as it is said, "Thy word is a lamp unto my feet, and a light unto my path" (Ps. cxix. 105)' (Exod. R. xxxvi. 3).

§ IV. The Written Torah

The Revelation committed to writing consists of twenty-four books.[1] We find this enumeration in such statements as: 'Like a bride who is adorned with twenty-four ornaments, and if she lacks one of them the whole becomes of no value, so a disciple of the wise is obliged to familiarize himself with the twenty-four books of the Bible, and if he lacks one the whole becomes of no value' (Cant. R. iv. 11). 'A certain Rabbi used to rehearse his lessons twenty-four times, corresponding to the number of books in the Pentateuch, Prophets, and Hagiographa, before he went in to his teacher' (Taan. 8a).

In the last citation we have the three sections into which the Scriptures were divided: Pentateuch (often referred to specifically as Torah), Prophets, and Hagiographa. The last two are sometimes quoted under the designation of *Kabbalah* (tradition) (R.H. 7a).

The Pentateuch comprises five books. Two reasons are suggested to account for the number. 'Five times does the word "light" occur in Gen. i. 3–5, corresponding to the five divisions of the Pentateuch. "And God said, Let there be light," corresponds to Genesis in which the Holy One, blessed be He, was occupied with the creation of His Universe. "And there was light" corresponds to Exodus, in which Israel emerged from darkness to brightness. "And God saw the light that it was good" corresponds to Leviticus, which is filled with numerous laws. "And God divided the light from the darkness" corresponds to Numbers, in which He separated those who left Egypt from those who were destined to enter the land of promise. "And God called the light day" corresponds to Deuteronomy, which is filled with numerous laws' (Gen. R. iii. 5). An alternative suggestion was that the five books correspond to the five fingers of the hand (Num. R. xiv. 10).

The Five Books of Moses, as indicated above, are the original fountain of inspiration on which the later prophets drew. A tradition tells that 'the Torah (i.e. the Pentateuch) was given

[1] Josephus (c. Apion. i. 8), mentions twenty-two books, but he combined certain books which are separate in the Talmudic enumeration.

originally in separate scrolls' (Git. 6oa) and was subsequently issued
as a continuous and connected book.

As regards the Prophetical Writings, the traditional view of
their order is: 'Joshua, Judges, Samuel, Kings, Jeremiah, Ezekiel,
Isaiah, and the Twelve (Minor Prophets). Since Hosea preceded
the others in point of time, as it is written, "The beginning of the
word of the Lord (was) by Hosea" (i. 2), (he should have come first
among the later prophets). But was the beginning of the word of
the Lord by Hosea? Were there not several prophets between
Moses and him? R. Jochanan said, "The meaning is that he was
the first of four prophets who prophesied in that period, viz. Hosea,
Isaiah, Amos, and Micah." In that case Hosea should be placed
first (viz. before Jeremiah)! Because his prophecy was written
down together with Haggai, Zechariah, and Malachi, and they were
the last of the prophets, he is included among them. Let his,
then, be a book by itself and take precedence! Being small in
compass it might have been lost. Seeing that Isaiah was earlier
than Jeremiah and Ezekiel, he should come first in order! But
because the Book of Kings ends with the destruction of the Temple,
Jeremiah deals wholly with the destruction, Ezekiel begins with
the destruction and ends with a message of consolation, and Isaiah
deals wholly with consolation, we follow destruction with destruction
and consolation with consolation' (B.B. 14b).[1]

The order of the Books of the Hagiographa is: 'Ruth, Psalms,
Job, Proverbs, Ecclesiastes, Song of Songs, Lamentations, Daniel,
Esther, Ezra, and Chronicles' (ibid.).[2] It will be noticed that
the Book of Nehemiah is not mentioned in the list. It was included
with the Book of Ezra; and the reason why the honour was denied
him of having his name in the Scriptural Canon is: 'Because he
thought of his own welfare; as it is said, "Think upon me, my
God, for good" (Nehem. v. 19).' Another reason is that he
spoke disparagingly of his predecessors; as it is said, 'But the
former governors that had been before me were chargeable unto
the people and had taken of their bread and wine, beside forty
shekels of silver' (ibid. 15) (Sanh. 93b).

The authorship of the various books is given as follows: 'Moses
wrote his book and the section of Balaam (Num. xxiii. f.) and Job.
Joshua wrote his book and the last eight verses of Deuteronomy
(narrating the death of Moses). Samuel wrote his book, Judges

[1] In the Hebrew Bible this symmetrical arrangement is not followed, and
Isaiah precedes Jeremiah.
[2] This is not the order of the Hebrew Bible which is: Psalms, Proverbs,
Job, Song of Songs, Ruth, Lamentations, Ecclesiastes, Esther, Daniel, Ezra,
Nehemiah, and Chronicles.

REVELATION

143

and Ruth. David wrote the Psalms with the collaboration of ten Elders, viz. Adam (Ps. cxxxix), Melchizedek (cx), Abraham [1] (lxxxix), Moses (xc–c), Heman (lxxxviii), Jeduthun (xxxix. lxii. lxxvii), Asaph (L., lxxiii–lxxxiii), and the three sons of Korah (xlii–xlix, lxxxiv f., lxxxvii f.). Jeremiah wrote his book, Kings, and Lamentations. Hezekiah and his associates wrote [2] Isaiah, Proverbs, Song of Songs, and Ecclesiastes. The men of the Great Assembly wrote Ezekiel, the Twelve, Daniel, and Esther. Ezra wrote his book and the genealogy of Chronicles down to himself and Nehemiah completed it' (B.B. 14b et seq.).

The tradition as to the fixing of the Canon of the Scriptures is uncertain. In one place it is reported: 'At first they withdrew Proverbs, Song of Songs, and Ecclesiastes because they spoke parables [3] and did not belong to the Scriptures. They remained in this withdrawn condition until the men of the Great Assembly came and expounded them (in a spiritual sense)' (ARN 1). According to this view the Canon was fixed by the third century before the present era at latest; but there is definite evidence that for another five centuries the place of certain books in the Holy Writings was questioned.

The state of uncertainty with regard to some of the books, which existed at the end of the first century of the present era, is shown in this passage: 'All the Holy Scriptures defile the hands.[4] R. Judah said, The Song of Songs defiles the hands but with respect to Ecclesiastes there is dispute. R. José said, Ecclesiastes does not defile the hands but with respect to the Song of Songs there is dispute. R. Simeon said, Ecclesiastes is one of the lenient decisions of the School of Shammai, and one of the strict decisions of the School of Hillel.[5] R. Simeon b. Azzai said, I have it as a tradition from seventy-two Elders on the day they appointed Eleazar b. Azariah as head of the Academy that the Song of Songs and Ecclesiastes defile the hands. R. Akiba said, God forbid! No man in Israel ever argued that the Song of Songs did not defile the hands, because the whole world was not worthy of the day when it was given to Israel. All the Scriptures are holy but the Song of Songs is holy of holies. If there was any dispute it was with reference to Ecclesiastes' (Jad. III. 5).

[1] He is identified with Ethan.
[2] This must mean edited, since the last three books are ascribed to Solomon.
[3] i.e. they were secular compositions.
[4] This expression denotes that the object alluded to comes within the category of the holy. See p. 239.
[5] The Hillelites usually took the more lenient view as against the Shammaites; but it is reported that on three questions the former took the stricter side, one of them being that Ecclesiastes was non-canonical (Eduy. v. 3).

The statement of Akiba that the place of the Song of Songs in the Canon was never questioned is not borne out by the evidence. The Talmud records, 'R. Meïr said, Ecclesiastes does not defile the hands and there is dispute about the Song of Songs. R. José said, The Song of Songs does not defile the hands and there is dispute about Ecclesiastes' (Meg. 7a). The point at issue was whether these books were divinely inspired or secular compositions. With reference to the Song of Songs, the question turned on whether it was a love idyll or an allegory of the relationship between God and Israel. The latter view prevailed. 'The Song of Songs defiles the hands because it was said by the Holy Spirit. Ecclesiastes does not defile the hands, because it is the (personal) wisdom of Solomon' (Tosifta Jad. II. 14)

The difficulty with Ecclesiastes was caused by its apparent inconsistencies. 'The Sages sought to withdraw the Book of Ecclesiastes because its statements are self-contradictory. Why did they not do so? Because it begins with words of Torah and ends with words of Torah. It begins with words of Torah, since it is written, "What profit hath a man of all his labour which he taketh under the sun?" (i. 3). This was explained by the School of R. Jannai to signify: a man derives no profit from what is under the sun, but he does derive profit from what pre-existed the sun, viz. the Torah. The book ends with words of Torah, as it is written, "Let us hear the conclusion of the whole matter: Fear God and keep His commandments, for this is the whole of man" (xii. 13). What do the last words mean? That the whole world was only created for this, viz. Torah' (Shab. 30b).

Another book of the Hagiographa which remained for a time in a state of uncertainty was Proverbs. 'Also the Book of Proverbs they sought to withdraw because its statements were self-contradictory. Why did they not do so? They said, Did we not study Ecclesiastes and find reasons for not excluding it? Here, too, let us make a close investigation. How is the book contradictory? In one passage it is written, "Answer not a fool according to his folly" (xxvi. 4), and in the next verse, "Answer a fool according to his folly." There is no contradiction, one verse dealing with words of Torah and the other with secular matters' (Shab. 30b). The ultimate decision was, 'The Holy Spirit alighted on Solomon and he composed three books: Proverbs, the Song of Songs, and Ecclesiastes' (Cant. R. I. 1).

Likewise in connection with the Book of Esther there was doubt as to whether it was not an unwarranted addition to Scripture; but it was finally agreed that it 'was written by the Holy Spirit'

(*Meg.* 7*a*). It may be remarked that some Rabbis did not regard the Book of Job as a historical record; and we find the statement, 'Job never existed; the book is a parable' (B.B. 15*a*).

One more book gave rise to debate as to its inclusion in the Canon, viz. Ezekiel. There seem to have been two grounds of objection to it. First, several passages, especially with respect to the ritual of the Temple, were apparently at variance with the Pentateuch; but they were successfully harmonized. 'Remember Chananyah b. Hezekiah [1] for good, because were it not for him the Book of Ezekiel would have been withdrawn for the reason that its statements contradicted those of the Torah. What did he do? They brought him three hundred measures of oil (for midnight research), and he sat studying in his attic until he reconciled the passages' (Shab. 13*b*).

Another objection is indicated in the following citation: 'It happened that a child was reading the Book of Ezekiel in the house of his teacher and was studying the *Chashmal*.[2] Fire came forth from *Chashmal* and consumed him. In consequence they wished to withdraw the book; but Chananyah b. Hezekiah said to him, "If this child was wise, are all wise?"' (Chag. 13*a*). He meant that the boy was exceptional, and few would follow his example and investigate so abstruse a subject as *Chashmal*. We have doubtless to detect here apprehension about the unsettlement of religious faith which might ensue from study of the mystical chapters of the Book of Ezekiel.

When agreement was finally reached on the books which were to be included in the Canon, a strong warning was uttered against adding to the accepted number. 'The Holy One, blessed be He, said, "Twenty-four books have I written for you; beware and make no addition to them." For what reason? "Of making many books there is no end" (Eccles. xii. 12). He who reads a single verse which is not from the twenty-four is as though he read in "the outside books." Beware of making many books (to add to the Scriptures), for whoever does so will have no portion in the World to Come' (Num. R. xiv. 4).

It was an accepted dogma that the Torah was inspired by God. 'He who says that the Torah is not from heaven has no portion in the World to Come' (Sanh. x. 1). Especially with respect to the Pentateuch it was held that every word of it was verbally inspired. '"He hath despised the word of the Lord" (Num. xv. 31)—this

---

[1] This Rabbi lived in the earlier half of the first century of the present era.
[2] This is the word in Ezek. i. 27 translated 'amber.' The Talmud explains it as a class of fiery angels.

refers to one who says that the Torah is not from Heaven, and
even to one who admits that the Torah is from Heaven except a
single verse which the Holy One, blessed be He, did not utter but
Moses said it of his own accord' (Sanh. 99*a*). But great latitude
was allowed in the matter of interpretation, and no check was
placed on the ingenuity which read into, or out of, the text meanings
which seemed poles asunder from the literal intention. '"Is not
My word like a hammer that breaketh the rock in pieces?" (Jer.
xxiii. 29)—as the hammer causes numerous sparks to flash forth, so
is a Scriptural verse capable of many interpretations' (Sanh. 34*a*).

§ V. The Oral Torah

A fundamental issue with the Rabbis was the acceptance of a
traditional Torah, transmitted from one generation to another by
word of mouth, side by side with the written text. It was claimed
that the Oral Torah, equally with the Written Torah, goes back
to the Revelation on Sinai, if not in detail at least in principle.
Forty-two enactments, which find no record in the Pentateuch,
are described by the Talmud as 'laws given to Moses on Sinai.'
The rest of the Oral Torah was implied in the Scriptural text and
was deducible from it by certain rules of exegesis.

This claim on behalf of the Oral Torah met with strenuous
opposition from the Sadducees,[1] and naturally had the effect of
making the Rabbis lay exceptional stress on its importance and
validity. Hence we get declarations such as these: 'What means
that which is written, "And I will give thee the tables of stone,
and the law and the commandment, which I have written, that
thou mayest teach them" (Exod. xxiv. 12)? "Tables of stone,"
i.e. the Decalogue; "law," i.e. the Pentateuch; "commandment,"
i.e. the Mishnah; "which I have written," i.e. the Prophets and
Hagiographa; "that thou mayest teach them," i.e. the Gemara.
The verse teaches that all of them were given to Moses on Sinai'
(Ber. 5*a*). 'At the time when the Holy One, blessed be He, revealed
Himself on Sinai to give the Torah to Israel, He delivered it to
Moses in order—Scripture, Mishnah, Talmud, and Haggadah'
(Exod. R. xlvii. 1). The Rabbis went so far as to assert, 'The
Holy One, blessed be He, only made a covenant with Israel on
account of the Oral Torah; as it is said, "For after the tenor of
these words [2] I have made a covenant with thee and with Israel"
(Exod. xxxiv. 27)' (Git. 60*b*).

---

[1] See Introduction, p. xxi.   [2] i.e. spoken, not written, words.

The existence of this dual Revelation is mentioned in conversations about Judaism with non-Jews. For instance, it is related: 'The Roman governor Quietus asked R. Gamaliel, "How many Toroth were given to Israel?" He answered, "Two—one in writing and the other orally"' (Sifré Deut. § 351; 145a). It figures in the story about Hillel and the would-be proselyte, and incidentally dwells upon the essential purpose of tradition as a medium for interpreting the text. 'It happened with a heathen that he came before Shammai and asked him, "How many Toroth have you?" He answered, "Two—the written and the oral." He said, "With respect to the Written Torah I will believe you, but not with respect to the oral Torah. Accept me as a convert on condition that you teach me the former only." Shammai rebuked him and drove him out with contempt. He came before Hillel with the same request and he accepted him. The first day he taught him the alphabet in the correct order, but the next day he reversed it. The heathen said to him, "Yesterday you taught it me differently!" Hillel replied, "Have you not to depend upon me for the letters of the alphabet? So must you likewise depend upon me for the interpretation of the Torah"' (Shab. 31a).

Why, however, was it necessary for the Torah to be given in this twofold form? An answer suggested to the question is: 'The Holy One, blessed be He, gave Israel two Toroth, the written and the oral. He gave them the Written Torah in which are six hundred and thirteen commandments in order to fill them with precepts whereby they could earn merit. He gave them the Oral Torah whereby they could be distinguished from the other nations. This was not given in writing, so that the Ishmaelites should not fabricate it as they have done the Written Torah and say that they were Israel' (Num. R. xiv. 10). In the word 'Ishmaelites' we must detect one of the substitutions which were employed in the Middle Ages to circumvent the censor. Obviously Christians are meant. Since the Church adopted the Hebrew Scriptures, they ceased to be the peculiar possession of Jews. Therefore the Oral Torah, which was not accepted by the Church, safeguarded the distinctiveness of the Jewish people living in a Christian environment.

Another explanation is indicated in this passage: 'It is stated, "Write thou these words" (Exod. xxxiv. 27), and it is also stated, "For after the tenor of these words" [1] (ibid.). How is this to be accounted for? Words of Torah which are written must not be quoted orally, and words which are to be transmitted orally must

[1] The Hebrew is literally: 'For by the *mouth* of these words.'

not be committed to writing. The School of R. Ishmael explained, "Write thou *these* words"—that means, these words you are to write but you must not write down traditional dicta' (Git. 60*b*).

In this objection to the Oral Torah being put into writing we see one of its most important functions. The ordinances of the Written Torah were eternal and immutable; only when circumstances made them impossible of fulfilment—as with the sacrifices when the Temple was destroyed and the agrarian laws when the people went into captivity—were they temporarily suspended until the time they could be re-enacted. The Oral Torah which, being unwritten, remained in a flexible state, allowed the written ordinance to be adapted as the conditions of succeeding ages changed. In other words, the Oral Torah prevented the religious legislation of the community from being a fixed system, incapable of progress.

We see this purpose very clearly defined in the following citation: 'If the Torah had been given in a fixed form, the foot would have had no standing.[1] What is the meaning of the oft-recurring phrase, "The Lord spake unto Moses"? Moses said before Him, "Sovereign of the Universe! cause me to know what the final decision is on each matter of law." He replied, "The majority must be followed. When the majority declare a thing permitted it is permissible, when the majority declare it forbidden it is not allowed; so that the Torah may be capable of interpretation with forty-nine points *pro* and forty-nine points *contra*"' (p. Sanh. 22*a*).

Accordingly the religious leaders of each generation were empowered through the Oral Torah to legislate for their own time in the light of contemporary circumstances. This important principle is deduced by a curious piece of exegesis: 'It is stated, "The Lord sent Jerubbaal and Bedan and Jephthah" (1 Sam. xii. 11), and it is further stated, "Moses and Aaron among His priests and Samuel among them that call upon His name" (Ps. xcix. 6). The Scripture makes three of the least important men in the world equal in weight to three of the most important, in order to teach that Jerubbaal in his generation is like Moses in his, Bedan in his generation like Aaron in his, and Jephthah in his generation like Samuel in his. This indicates that when the most insignificant person is appointed leader over the community he is to be treated as the equal of the most eminent of persons. It is also said, "Thou shalt come unto the priests the Levites, and unto the judge that shall be in those days" (Deut. xvii. 9). Could it possibly enter your mind that a person would go to a judge who was not in his days? The meaning is, You are to go only to a contemporary

[1] An idiomatic phrase, meaning the position would have been intolerable.

authority; as the text declares, "Say not thou, What is the cause that the former days were better than these?" (Eccles. vii. 10)' (R.H. 25a, b).

In the light of such ideas the statement becomes intelligible: 'Even that which a distinguished disciple was destined to teach in the presence of his master was already said to Moses on Sinai' (p. Peah 17a). The doctrines of the Rabbis were the harvest from the seed which was sown at the time of the original Revelation.

§ VI. The Practice of Torah

The basic purpose of the Talmud was to provide the Jewish people with a body of teaching which should be more than a creed, but also a guide of life in every phase. It created the world in which the Jew moved and had his being. From the roots of the six hundred and thirteen precepts contained in the Pentateuch there grew a tree with numerous branches, the fruits of which provided the daily spiritual sustenance of whoever cared to avail himself of them.

The criticism is often made that the Talmud entangled the Jew in the bonds of legalism so that he was bound hand and foot, and lost all sense of freedom and spirituality. That is merely the outsider's view which receives not the slightest corroboration from the Talmud itself. Instead, it affords conclusive testimony to the spirit of joy and love which animated those who subjected themselves to 'the yoke of the Torah.'

'The Holy One, blessed be He, was pleased to make Israel acquire merit; therefore He multiplied for them Torah and commandments; as it is said, "The Lord was well pleased for His righteousness' sake to magnify the Torah and make it honourable" (Is. xlii. 21)' (Mak. III. 16). This citation, appended by the Prayer Book to the chapters of the Tractate *Aboth* when they are read in the Synagogue on certain Sabbaths, admirably summarizes the Rabbinic attitude towards the life under the Torah. Far from being considered a bondage, it was looked upon as a privilege and a mark of favour from God, to be appreciated with love and gratitude. The words of the Psalmist, 'O how I love Thy Torah' (Ps. cxix. 97), called forth the comment: 'Solomon said, "a loving hind" (Prov. v. 19)—such is the Torah, all love it; and whoever loves the Torah loves nothing but life. David professed his love for it in the words, "O how I love Thy Torah." Wherever I go it is with me; when I sleep it is with me. Never have I abandoned it in the slightest degree; and since I never abandoned it, it was not a burden upon me but a source of singing; as it is said, "Thy statutes have been my songs in the house of my pilgrimage" (Ps. cxix. 54)' (Midrash ad loc.; 249b).

These benedictions, which occur in the Talmud, have become part of the daily liturgy and reflect the true feeling towards the Torah: 'Blessed art Thou, O Lord our God, King of the Universe, Who hast sanctified us by Thy commandments and commanded us to occupy ourselves with the words of Torah. Make pleasant, therefore, we beseech Thee, O Lord our God, the words of Thy Torah in our mouth and in the mouth of Thy people, the house of Israel, so that we with our offspring and the offspring of Thy people, the house of Israel, may all know Thy name and occupy ourselves with Thy Torah. Blessed art Thou, O Lord, Who teachest Torah to Thy people Israel. Blessed art Thou, O Lord our God, King of the Universe, Who hast chosen us from all nations and given us Thy Torah. Blessed art Thou, O Lord, Who givest the Torah' (Ber. 11b).

A guiding principle of action was: 'Greater is he who performs (the commandments) from love than he who performs them from fear' (Sot. 31a). One manifestation of this love for the Torah was the erection of a 'fence' around it as a protection against its violation. It was therefore recommended that one should not carry out a religious precept with just the exactitude necessary for compliance with the law, but should add to it for the purpose of being quite certain that the duty had been fulfilled. 'To what is the matter like? To a man who is guarding an orchard. If he guards it from the outside, the whole of it is protected; if he guards it from within, what is in front of him is protected and what is behind him is unprotected' (Jeb. 21a). As an illustration there is the rule of 'adding from the non-holy to the holy' (R.H. 9a), in connection with the sacred days of the calendar; i.e. work is suspended before the actual time that the Sabbath or Festival commences so as not to encroach upon the sanctity of the day inadvertently.

This desire to safeguard the religious duties is exemplified in another way. 'The Sages made a "fence" to their words, so that a man shall not come from the field in the evening and say, "I will go home, eat a little, drink a little, and after that I will offer my prayers." Slumber may overcome him, and as a result he may sleep through all the night. Rather should a man come from the field in the evening and enter a Synagogue; if he is accustomed to read the Scriptures let him read; if he is accustomed to study more advanced branches of learning, let him study. Then let him

offer his prayers; after that he should eat his meal and say Grace.
Whosoever transgresses the words of the Sages in this matter is
worthy of death' (Ber. 4*b*).

Another rule which displays devotion to the Torah is *Hiddur
Mitzvah* (the embellishment of the commandment), i.e. carrying it
out with additional touches beyond what is required by the strict
letter of the law, in order to fulfil the command in the best manner
one's means allow. It is based on the words of Exod. xv. 2,
'He is my God and I will beautify (*sic*) Him,' which are treated
thus: 'Beautify yourself with the precepts of the Torah. Make
before Him a beautiful booth (Lev. xxiii. 42), a beautiful palm-
branch (ibid. 40), a beautiful ram's horn to be sounded on the
New Year (ibid. 24), a beautiful fringe (Num. xv. 38), a beautiful
scroll of the Torah written in His honour with the finest ink, with
the best pen, by the most competent scribe, and wrapped in the
purest silks' (Shab. 133*b*). The ordinances of Judaism must therefore not be performed in a perfunctory manner, but should be
infused with the spirit of enthusiasm and love. It was recognized,
on the other hand, that this desire to do honour to God may lead
to harmful excess. It might, for example, result in impoverish-
ment. Consequently the rule was laid down, '*Hiddur Mitzvah*
may only extend to a third of the value' (B.K. 9*b*), i.e. only a
third may be added to the average cost in order to 'embellish the
commandment.'

Such, then, was the spirit in which the obligations of the Torah
were expected to be discharged. Instead of being an oppressive
servitude, it was a joyous service of God which led to the sanctification of the individual life. Indeed, the entire purpose of the
Torah was to purify and elevate human existence. The phrase,
'The word of the Lord is tried'[1] (Ps. xviii. 30), was made the
support for the doctrine: 'The commandments were only given for
the purpose of refining human beings. What, for example, does it
matter to the Holy One, blessed be He, whether an animal's neck
is cut from the front or the rear?[2] But the ordinances He gave
have as their object the purification of human beings' (Gen. R.
XLIV. 1).

A whole series of commandments was intended to act as reminders
of the divine omnipresence and to keep the mind directed to His
will at all times. The principal of these are the *Mezuzah* affixed
to the door-post, the fringe on the garment and the phylacteries
on the arm and forehead. In connection with these we have the

[1] The Hebrew word means 'refined.'
[2] When it is slaughtered for food; see pp. 237 f.

statement: 'Beloved are Israel, seeing that the Holy One, blessed be He, has surrounded them with precepts. They have phylacteries on their heads and on their arms, a fringe on their garments and the *Mezuzah* on their doors; and concerning these, said David, "Seven times a day do I praise Thee because of Thy righteous precepts" (Ps. cxix. 164)' (Men. 43*b*). Each will be briefly treated in turn.

The *Mezuzah* is the literal fulfilment of the command: 'Thou shalt write them upon the posts (*Mezuzah*) of thy house and on thy gates' (Deut. vi. 9). In its traditional form it consists of a piece of parchment inscribed with the two passages Deut. vi. 4–8 and xi. 13–21, placed in a case and affixed to the right doorpost as one enters. On the outside the word *Shaddai* (Almighty) is visible. The original purpose, as already stated, was to provide the Jew with a continuous reminder that he lived even in the privacy of his home under the all-seeing eye of God, and was dependent upon His grace.[1] Therefore it was said, 'Whoever has phylacteries on his head and arm, the fringe on his garment and the *Mezuzah* on his door will presumably not commit a sin' (Men. 43*b*).

In the popular mind, however, the *Mezuzah* became an amulet which assured one of the Divine protection. Two anecdotes illustrate this quite distinctly. 'King Artaban (of Parthia) sent R. Judah the Holy a pearl of great value, with the request that he should return him something equally costly. He sent him a *Mezuzah*. The king said to him, "I sent you something that is priceless and you return me something worth a trifling amount!" He replied, "Your valuable object and mine are quite dissimilar. You sent me something which I have to guard, but I sent you something which will guard you when you are asleep"' (p. Peah 15*d*).

The other story concerns Onkelos (i.e. Akylas), a member of the Roman royal family, who became a convert to Judaism. On hearing of this, the emperor sent a succession of troops to arrest him, but they also were won over to Judaism by his words. Finally the emperor gave his soldiers strict instructions not to converse with him, and they effected his arrest. 'As they left the house,' the story continues, 'he looked at the *Mezuzah* which was fixed to the door-post, placed his hand upon it and said to them, "I will

---

[1] This explanation is found in Josephus: 'They are also to inscribe the principal blessings they have received from God upon their doors, and show the same on their arms; as also they are to bear inscribed on their head and arm whatever can declare the power of God and His good will towards them, that God's readiness to bless them may appear everywhere conspicuous about them' (**Antiq.** IV. viii. 13).

tell you what this is. The universal custom is for a human king to sit inside a room and his servants guard him from without. With the Holy One, blessed be He, His servants are inside a room and He guards them from without; as it is said, "The Lord shall keep thy going out and thy coming in, from this time forth and even for evermore" (Ps. cxxi. 8)' (A.Z. 11a).

Tephillin or phylacteries consist of two small leather cases with straps attached, in each of which is inserted parchment inscribed with four Biblical passages: Exod. xiii. 1–10, 11–16; Deut. vi. 4–9, xi. 13–21. That is the traditional method of fulfilling the law: 'Thou shalt bind them for a sign upon thine hand, and they shall be for frontlets between thine eyes' (Deut. vi. 8). Their purpose was to make the precepts of the Torah a controlling and guiding force in life, so that the ideals of Judaism should mould the thoughts and direct the actions of man. This may be seen from what is narrated of a Talmudic Sage named Rabbah. 'Abbai was sitting in the presence of Rabbah, and noticed that he was very merry. He said to him, "It is written, 'Rejoice with trembling'"' (Ps. ii. 11). He replied, "I have laid the phylacteries"' (Ber. 30b). He implied by his retort that having worn them during the day, they would have a sobering influence which would prevent him from exceeding due bounds. The commandment, 'Thou shalt not bear (so *lit.*) the name of the Lord thy God in vain' (Exod. xx. 7), was interpreted: 'Do not put on the phylacteries, bearing God's name, and then go and sin' (Pesikta, 111b).

The purpose of the fringe is described in the verse, 'That ye may look upon it and remember all the commandments of the Lord and do them' (Num. xv. 39), on which the Talmud remarks, 'This ordinance is equal to all the precepts, because seeing leads to remembering and remembering to performing' (Men. 43b). An instance is quoted in the context of a man who was saved from acting immorally by the reminder he received from the fringe on his garment (ibid. 44a). Hence it was taught: 'Whoever is particular with this ordinance is worthy of receiving the presence of the *Shechinah*' (ibid. 43b). 'The text does not read "Ye may look upon them," but "look upon Him," [1] thus declaring that whoever fulfils the law of the fringe is accounted as though he had received the presence of the *Shechinah*, since the colour of the blue thread resembled the colour of the sea which is like that of the firmament and in turn is like that of the Throne of Glory' [2] (Sifré Num. § 115;

[1] The suffix can mean 'it' or 'Him.' For homiletic purposes the latter is adopted.   [2] See Ezek. i. 25.

34*b*). The meaning is that the understanding use of the fringe kept a person's life pure, and so brought him into closer communion with God.

Here, too, we find a superstitious value attached to the religious rite as a protective force. The neglect of the wearing of the fringe, as well as the omission to fasten the *Mezuzah* to the doorpost, caused death among one's children (Shab. 32*b*); and conversely, 'Whoever scrupulously observed the law of the fringe was worthy that two thousand eight hundred servants should attend upon him; as it is written, "Thus saith the Lord of hosts, In those days shall ten men of all the languages of the nations take hold of the skirt of him that is a Jew, saying, We will go with you for we have heard that God is with you" (Zech. viii, 23)' (ibid.).[1]

Perhaps the most striking example that could be selected of the manner in which the Rabbis developed a Biblical ordinance is the Sabbath. Whereas Scripture merely lays down the general law that no manner of work is to be performed on that day, a whole Talmudic tractate is devoted to the study of what does or does not constitute a desecration of the Sabbath. The prohibited acts were classified under thirty-nine headings: 'Sowing, ploughing, reaping, binding sheaves, threshing, winnowing, selecting, grinding, sifting, kneading, baking; shearing the wool, bleaching, carding, dyeing, spinning, warping, making two thrums, weaving two threads, separating two threads (in the warp), knotting, unknotting, sewing two stitches, tearing for the purpose of sewing two stitches; hunting the stag, slaughtering it, flaying, salting (the flesh), preparing the hide, scraping (the hair), cutting it into pieces; writing two letters of the alphabet, erasing for the purpose of writing two letters; building, demolishing; kindling a fire, extinguishing it; striking with a hammer; transferring an object from one domain to another' (Shab. VII. 2).

Each item in this classification suggested various problems of definition, and infinite scope for discussion was afforded by questions as to whether a particular act came within one of the categories or not. To give but one illustration. The last-mentioned heading led to two lines of investigation. The first considered the point what involved an act of transference which was a violation of the holy day. That is the subject treated in the first chapter of Tractate *Shabbath*. The first clause of the Mishnah reads:

[1] The number 2,800 is obtained in this way. There are seventy nations, and since ten of each are concerned, we have 700. This number will hold each of the four corners of the garment, and therefore it must be multiplied by four.

'There are two acts of transferring objects (from one domain to another), and these are enlarged to four as affecting the inside (of the premises) and four as affecting the outside. How is this? The beggar, for example, stands outside and the householder inside, and the beggar stretches forth his hand into the interior and places something in the householder's hand or takes it from his hand and draws it outside. In that event the beggar is guilty (of an infraction of the Sabbath law) and the householder is free of guilt. If the householder stretched forth his hand and put something into the beggar's hand or drew from it and brought it into the house, then the householder is guilty and the beggar is free of guilt. If the beggar stretched forth his hand into the interior, and the householder takes something out of it or puts something into it, they are both free of guilt. If the householder stretched forth his hand outside and the beggar took something from it or put something into it which the former draws into the house, both are guilty.' It will be gathered from this specimen how complicated the question became under the treatment of the Rabbis.

The second question involved the point what constituted a burden which was forbidden to be carried on the Sabbath. For example, there was a ruling upon what part of a woman's attire was apparel and what an ornament, the latter being considered an unnecessary burden. 'A woman may go out on the Sabbath wearing plaits of hair, whether of her own hair or of another woman or of an animal; or with frontlets or other kinds of ornaments sewn to her headgear; or with a hair-net or false curl, in the courtyard (of her house); [1] or with wadding in her ear or shoe or prepared for a sanitary purpose; or with a pellet of pepper or a grain of salt or anything she is accustomed to keep in her mouth, provided she did not first insert it there on the Sabbath, and if it falls out she must not replace it. As for a tooth which has been re-inserted, or a gold tooth, R. Judah permits it while the Sages forbid it' (Shab. vi. 5).

This is typical of a large number of laws relating to the Sabbath, and it seems to justify the oft-made criticism that under the casuistry of the Rabbis the holy day was turned into a crushing incubus upon the Jews and was robbed of all its joy and spirituality. The truth, however, is that the people who experienced these laws in all their rigour not only failed to notice the supposed crippling burden, but joyfully proclaimed the Sabbath to be a day of light and beauty and godliness.

Here is a brief prayer which was composed by a Rabbi for recital on the Sabbath-eve: 'From Thy love, O Lord our God, wherewith

---

[1] i.e. a private domain; but she may not go into a public street.

Thou didst love Thy people Israel, and from the compassion,
O our King, which Thou didst feel for the children of Thy covenant,
Thou didst give us, O Lord our God, this great and holy seventh
day in love' (Tosifta Ber. III. 11). Only one to whom the Sabbath
was a boon and a delight could have uttered those words, and that
is precisely how it was considered. On the text, 'That ye may
know what I am the Lord that doth sanctify you' (Exod. xxxi. 13),
we have this statement: 'The Holy One, blessed be He, said to
Moses, I have a precious gift in My treasury, named Sabbath, and
I wish to present it to Israel; go and inform them' (Shab. 10b).

Nor was there the slightest austerity about its observance.
Public manifestations of mourning, which extended for a week
after the burial of a deceased relative, had to be suspended on the
Sabbath. A favourite text in this connection was, 'Call the
Sabbath a delight' (Is. lviii. 13), on the basis of which it was recommended that a lamp should be kindled in the home (Shab. 25b),
the best clothes worn (ibid. 113a) and three good meals provided
(ibid. 117b). To spend freely on honouring the Sabbath was held
to be a praiseworthy act, and the assurance was given that 'whoever lends to the Sabbath is well repaid' (ibid. 119a). A story is
told of a Rabbi who paid a visit to a colleague's house on the
Sabbath, and a bounteous supply of cooked dishes was set before
him. 'Did you know I was coming, that you have provided so
liberally?' the guest asked; to which the host retorted, 'Are you
more esteemed by me than the Sabbath?' (ibid.). This custom of
doing honour to the Sabbath gave rise to this application of the
words, 'I am black but comely' (Cant. i. 5); 'I (Israel) am black
on the weekdays but comely on the Sabbath' (Midrash ad loc.).

What loving devotion was displayed by two Rabbis of whom it
is related: 'R. Channina used to don his best clothes, and towards
sunset on Friday exclaim, "Come, let us go forth to meet Queen
Sabbath." R. Jannai used to don his best clothes on the Sabbath-
eve and exclaim, "Enter, O bride; enter, O bride!"' (Shab. 119a).

The Sabbath had for its object the hallowing of life. '"For it
is holy unto you" (Exod. xxxi. 14)—this teaches that the Sabbath
increases holiness for Israel' (Mech. ad loc.; 104a). As we have
seen, there was a current belief that the holy day endowed him
who honoured it with an 'additional soul.'[1]

Two variants of the same story indicate the special flavour
which the Sabbath introduced into the life of the people. 'The
emperor asked R. Joshua b. Chananya, "How is it that the Sabbath
food has so pleasant an odour?" He answered, "We possess a

[1] See p. 78.

spice, named Sabbath,[1] which we include in it and that gives it its fragrance." The emperor requested to be presented with some of the spice; but he was told, "It only avails him who observes the Sabbath"' (Shab. 119a). 'R. Judah entertained Antoninus on a Sabbath when all the dishes were served cold.[2] He ate and enjoyed the food. R. Judah entertained him on another occasion, but on a weekday, when the dishes were served hot. Antoninus said, "The dishes on the previous occasion pleased me better." His host answered, "They lack a certain spice." "Does, then, the king's treasury lack anything?" he asked. "The dishes lack the Sabbath," was the reply, "and have you the Sabbath?"' (Gen. R. XI. 4).

If the Sabbath is the most noteworthy instance of the elaboration of a Biblical ordinance by the Talmud, the chapter may be concluded by inquiry how an important piece of Scriptural legislation fared when circumstances rendered its performance impossible. The Temple and its ritual played a very prominent part in the life of the people, and much space is devoted in the Talmud to their description. For the Rabbis the sacrifices were divinely enacted. What, then, was their attitude when the Temple ceased to exist?

The answer is best indicated in the story told of R. Jochanan b. Zakkai and his disciple R. Joshua. 'On one occasion, when they were leaving Jerusalem, the latter gazed upon the destroyed Temple and cried out, "Woe to us! The place where Israel obtained atonement for sins is in ruins!" R. Jochanan said to him, "My son, be not distressed. We still have an atonement equally efficacious, and that is the practice of benevolence"' (ARN IV). God is likewise depicted as announcing. 'More beloved by Me are the justice and righteousness which you perform than sacrifices' (p. Ber. 4b). Another statement which He is represented as having made to David, 'Better to Me is one day spent in occupation with the Torah than a thousand burnt-offerings which your son Solomon will sacrifice before Me upon the altar' (Shab. 30a).

The greatest accomplishment which the teaching of the Talmud achieved for the Jewish people was to make them feel that the end of the Temple did not imply an end to their religion. Severe as the loss was, the way of approach to God was kept open. In addition to charity, justice, and Torah-study there was also prayer,

---

[1] Point is added to the two stories by the fact that the Hebrew word for 'dill' is *Shebeth* and has the same consonants as *Shabbath*, 'Sabbath.'
[2] Cooking is forbidden on the Sabbath and food has to be prepared before its advent.

which was declared to be even 'greater than sacrifices' (Ber. 32b).
On the basis of the words, 'We will render the calves of our lips'
(Hos. xiv. 2), the doctrine was taught, 'What can be a substitute
for the bulls which we used to offer before Thee? Our lips, with
the prayer which we pray unto Thee' (Pesikta 165b).

In this chapter only an outline sketch could be attempted of an
exposition of the Rabbinic theory of Torah. A whole volume would
be required to treat it with anything like adequate completeness.[1]
The wrong way to view the subject is from the standpoint of
modern religious conceptions. It can only be justly appraised
from the premises of the Rabbis themselves, and the only fair
test is the pragmatic one. By their interpretation of Torah they
enabled Judaism to continue in existence after the ritual of the
altar had stopped and the State been broken up, whereas their
opponents, the Sadducees, disappeared from history. The preservation of Israel's religion was their aim, and the fact that it was
realized was to them all the proof they required of the truth of
what they taught.

[1] The reader is recommended to study R. T. Herford, *The Pharisees* (1924),
where the subject is excellently treated.

CHAPTER V

DOMESTIC LIFE

§ I. Woman

THE basis of Jewish social life is the family, and the Talmud is ever watchful to conserve its purity and stability. Recognizing the all-important place which woman occupies in the life of the family, it accords to her a most dignified position. Especially when her lot among the other contemporary peoples is taken into account, the honour which is paid to woman by the Talmud offers a striking contrast. In no way is she looked upon as a being inferior to man. Her sphere of activity is different from man's, but of no less significance to the welfare of the community.

Too much prominence has been given by hostile critics to the dictum: 'A man is obliged to offer three benedictions daily: that He has made me an Israelite, that He has not made me a woman, that He has not made me a boor' (Men. 43b).[1] A study of the context makes it perfectly evident that the underlying motive is nothing else than gratitude for the privilege of having the duty of carrying out the precepts of the Torah. In this respect the responsibility of man was greater than of woman, because out of consideration of her domestic obligations she is released from one category of religious duties. The legal ruling is: 'Women are exempt from commands of "Thou shalt," [2] the observance of which depends upon a definite point of time' (Kid. I. 7). For instance, the command to dwell in booths during the Festival of Tabernacles or to put on the phylacteries is not obligatory upon a woman. Apart from this exception, the Talmud recognizes no distinction between the sexes so far as religious responsibility is concerned. The general principle is drawn from the text, 'These are the judgments which thou shalt set before them' (Exod. xxi. 1): 'Scripture places men and women on an equality with regard to all the laws of the Torah' (B.K. 15a).

Indeed, to woman is assigned the credit if she uses her influence

---

[1] In the Prayer Book version the benedictions read: 'Who hast not made me a heathen, a slave, a woman.' The thankfulness for not having been created a boor is explained by the saying: 'A boor cannot be a sin-fearing man' (Aboth II. 6).
[2] But not commands which have the form of 'Thou shalt not.'

so that her husband and sons apply themselves to the acquisition of the more advanced knowledge of Torah from which her fully-occupied life precluded her. 'Wherewith do women acquire merit? By sending their children to learn Torah in the Synagogue and their husbands to study in the Schools of the Rabbis' (Ber. 17a).

How decisive a woman's effect can be upon the life of her husband is emphatically pointed out in this passage: 'It is related of a pious man who was married to a pious woman that, being childless, they divorced one another. He went and married a wicked woman and she made him wicked. She went and married a wicked man and made him righteous. It follows that all depends upon the woman' (Gen. R. XVII. 7).

A story which pays a fine compliment to woman runs as follows: 'An emperor [1] said to R. Gamaliel, "Your God is a thief, because it is written, 'The Lord God caused a deep sleep to fall upon Adam, and he slept; and He took one of his ribs' (Gen. ii. 21)." The Rabbi's daughter said to her father, "Leave him to me; I will answer him." She then said to the emperor, "Give me an officer (to investigate a complaint)." "For what purpose?" he asked; and she replied, "Thieves broke into our house during the night and stole a silver ewer belonging to us, but left a gold one behind." "Would that such a thief visited me every day," he exclaimed. "Was it not, then, a splendid thing for the first man when a single rib was taken from him and a woman to attend upon him was supplied in its stead?" she retorted' (Sanh. 39a).

With respect to the formation of woman from a rib we have this reason suggested for the choice: 'God considered from which part of man to create woman. He said, I will not create her from the head that she should not hold up her head too proudly; nor from the eye that she should not be too curious; nor from the ear that she should not be an eavesdropper; nor from the mouth that she should not be too talkative; nor from the heart that she should not be too jealous; nor from the hand that she should not be too acquisitive; nor from the foot that she should not be a gadabout; but from a part of the body which is hidden that she should be modest' (Gen. R. XVIII. 2).

Apparently, however, the divine ideal was not realized, because we find Rabbis attributing to her the very faults which the Creator wanted to avoid. 'Four qualities are ascribed to women: they are gluttonous, eavesdroppers, lazy, and jealous. They are also querulous and garrulous' (ibid. XLV. 5). As regards the last-mentioned

---

[1] Some texts read 'a heretic'; but the words which occur later, 'Give me an officer,' indicate that the person addressed occupied a position of authority.

characteristic, it was rather unkindly said: 'Ten measures of speech descended to the world; women took nine and men one' (Kid. 49b). The opinion that women are lazy passed into a proverb: 'As she slumbers the basket falls' (Sanh. 7a); but we also have the opposite said of her, 'It is not a woman's way to sit at home idle' (p. Keth. 30a).

We do not have unanimity about her intellectual capacity. There is a remark, 'Women are light-minded' (Shab. 33b), and another which tells, 'It is the way of woman to remain at home, and for man to go into the market-place and learn intelligence from other men' (Gen. R. XVIII. 1). As against that view there is the explicit declaration, 'God endowed woman with more intelligence than man' (Nid. 45b). We also have the testimony of popular proverbs that she usually has her wits about her and prosecutes her schemes even when she does not appear to do so. Two proverbs to that effect are: 'A woman spins even while she talks,' and 'The goose bends its head while walking, but its eyes wander about' (Meg. 14b). Her tenderness of heart is likewise acknowledged: 'Women are compassionate' (ibid.).

Her love of finery and concern about her personal appearance are noted. 'The things for which a woman longs are adornments' (Keth. 65a); 'A woman's thought is only for her beauty. If a man wants to give his wife pleasure, let him clothe her in linen garments' (ibid. 59b). More details are supplied in this passage: 'These are the adornments of women: treating the eyes with kohl, curling the hair into ringlets, and rouging the face. The wife of R. Chisda used to adorn the face of her daughter-in-law. R. Huna b. Chinnena once sat in the presence of R. Chisda and (seeing this) said, "It is only permitted with a young woman, not an old one." He replied, "By God, it is even permitted with your mother and your grandmother, and even if she stood on the brink of the grave; for as the proverb tells, A woman of sixty, the same as a girl of six, runs to the sound of the timbrel"' (M.K. 9b).

One characteristic which is definitely charged against women is their partiality for the occult, and this is confirmed by contemporary writers of others races. In the Talmud we have the allegations, 'Women are addicted to witchcraft' (Joma 83b); 'The more women the more witchcraft' (Aboth II. 8); 'The majority of women are inclined to witchcraft' (Sanh. 67a), and for that reason the Scriptural command, 'Thou shalt not suffer a witch to live' (Exod. xxii. 18), is in the feminine gender.

§ II. Marriage and Divorce

To marry and rear a family was a religious command; indeed, the first of all the commands addressed by God to man (Gen. i. 28), and the Talmud stresses that view. 'The unmarried person lives without joy, without blessing, and without good' (Jeb. 62b); 'An unmarried man is not a man in the full sense; as it is said, "Male and female created He them, and blessed them and called their name man" (Gen. v. 2)' (ibid. 63a). A wife meant a home; hence the saying, 'A man's home is his wife' (Joma i. 1), and 'R. José said, Never have I called my wife by that word, but always "my home"' (Shab. 118b).

Early marriage is advocated. For a male the age of eighteen is recommended (Aboth v. 24). 'While your hand is still upon the neck of your sons [1]—from sixteen to twenty-two, or according to another opinion, from eighteen to twenty-four—get them married' (Kid. 30a). It is said that 'up to the age of twenty the Holy One, blessed be He, watches for a man to marry, and curses him if he fails to do so by then' (ibid. 29b). An imprudent marriage is deprecated, viz. when a man is not in a position to maintain a wife. From Deut. xx. 5-7 the Talmud derives the lesson: 'The Torah teaches the correct procedure: a man should first build a house, then plant a vineyard, and after that marry' (Sot. 44a). So important is it to take a wife that 'one may sell a Scroll of the Torah for the purpose of marriage' (Meg. 27a), the only other reason allowed for such a sale being to prosecute one's studies. To marry for money is severely denounced in the saying, 'Whoever marries a woman for her money will have disreputable children' (Kid. 70a). The absence of love in the parents will react upon the character of the offspring.

With regard to a girl it was urged that the father's duty was to secure a husband for her at an early age. The verse, 'Profane not thy daughter to make her a harlot' (Lev. xix. 29), was applied to a man 'who delays in arranging a marriage for his daughter while she is of suitable age' (Sanh. 76a). She was considered to have arrived at this stage when she was twelve and a half, although she ceased to be a minor when she passed her twelfth birthday.[2] According to Talmudic law, 'A man is forbidden to give his daughter in marriage while she is a minor, until she is grown up and says, I wish to marry so-and-so' (Kid. 41a). If he married her while

---

[1] i.e. while they are still under your control.
[2] A boy attained his majority a year later than a girl.

in her minority she could repudiate the marriage on reaching the age of twelve, and have it annulled without a divorce.

The conviction was general that not only are marriages made in heaven, but they are destined even before birth. 'Forty days before the formation of a child a *Bath Kol* announces, This person is to marry so-and-so's daughter' (Sot. 2a). A classic story which bears on this belief tells: 'A Roman lady asked a Rabbi, "In how many days did the Holy One, blessed be He, create the Universe?" "In six days," he answered. "What has He been doing since then up to the present?" "He has been arranging marriages." "Is that His occupation? I, too, could do it. I possess many male and female slaves, and in a very short while I can pair them together." He said to her, "If it is a simple thing in your eyes, it is as difficult to the Holy One, blessed be He, as dividing the Red Sea." He then took his departure. What did she do? She summoned a thousand male slaves and a thousand female slaves, set them in rows, and announced who should marry whom. In a single night she arranged marriages for them all. The next day they appeared before her, one with a cracked forehead, another with an eye knocked out, and another with a broken leg. She asked them, "What is the matter with you?" One female said, "I don't want him." Another male said, "I don't want her." She forthwith sent for the Rabbi and said to him, "There is no god like your God and your Torah is true. What you told me is quite correct"' (Gen. R. LXVIII. 4).

For all that, the Talmud offers wise counsel on the selection of a wife, which rather suggests that for practical purposes man had a free choice in the matter. Disparity in the ages, for example, was strongly deprecated. The Scriptural text from Leviticus cited above was also applied to the father 'who gives his daughter in marriage to an old man' (Sanh. 76a). It was similarly said, 'Who marries his daughter to an old man, or who takes an old woman as a wife for a young son, to him the verse refers, "To add drunkenness to thirst; the Lord will not pardon him" (Deut. xxix. 19 f.)' (ibid. 76b). In connection with the duty to marry a brother's widow if he died childless, Scripture declares, 'Then the elders of his city shall call him and speak to him' (Deut. xxv. 8); and the Talmud comments, 'This teaches that they gave him advice suitable for him. If he was young and she old, or vice versa, they would say to him, "What sense is there in your marrying one much younger than yourself?" or "What sense is there in your marrying one much older than yourself? Go, marry one who is about your own age and do not introduce strife into your house"' (Jeb. 101b).

Due precaution had therefore to be observed in making one's choice. 'Hesitate in selecting a wife' (ibid. 63a), is the recommendation of the Talmud. Unlike the custom which obtained in Eastern countries, Rabbinic law declared: 'A man is forbidden to take a woman to wife without having first seen her, lest he afterwards perceive in her something objectionable and she becomes repulsive to him' (Kid. 41a). The eugenic principle was also not overlooked, as may be seen from this advice: 'A tall man should not marry a tall woman lest their children be lanky. A short man should not marry a short woman lest their children be dwarfish. A fair man should not marry a fair woman lest their children be excessively fair. A dark man should not marry a dark woman lest their children be excessively swarthy' (Bech. 45b). Another recommendation was, 'Descend a step in choosing a wife' (Jeb. 63a), because to marry a woman of higher social status might cause him to be looked down upon by her and her relatives.

The purpose of marriage being the rearing of a family, and the ideal being the training of sons to be learned in the Torah, the belief in heredity led to a strong desire to marry the daughter of a scholar. 'A man should sell all he possesses, with the object of marrying the daughter of a learned man, for if he were to die or be exiled, he may be confident that his children will be learned; and let him not marry the daughter of an ignoramus, for if he were to die or be exiled, his children would be ignorant. A man should sell all he possesses with the object of marrying the daughter of a scholar or giving his daughter in marriage to a scholar. That is like uniting grapes of the vine to grapes of the vine, which is good and acceptable. But let him not marry the daughter of an ignoramus, because that is like uniting grapes of the vine to berries of the bush, which is something ugly and unacceptable' (Pes. 49a).

The ideal of matrimony, which is inculcated by the Talmud, is of the highest. The ordinary term for a marriage is *Kiddushin*, denoting 'sanctification.' It is so called because 'the husband prohibits his wife to the whole world like an object which is dedicated to the Sanctuary' (Kid. 2b). It implies the strictest chastity in both parties. 'Immorality in the house is like a worm on vegetables' (Sot. 3b), and it holds good of the husband as well as the wife. 'He among the full-grown pumpkins and she among the young ones' (ibid. 10a) ran a proverb, which indicates that infidelity on the husband's part conduces to unfaithfulness in the wife.

A clever saying is to this effect: 'When husband and wife are worthy, the *Shechinah* is with them; when they are not worthy

fire consumes them' (ibid. 17a). It is based on the fact that the
letters of the Hebrew words for 'husband' (ish) and 'wife' (ishah)
form an anagram of the two words denoting 'God' (Jah) and 'fire'
(esh). Other utterances advocating a lofty standard of domestic
life are: 'Who loves his wife as himself, honours her more than
himself, leads his sons and daughters in the right path, and arranges
for their marriage soon after puberty, to him the text refers, "Thou
shalt know that thy tent is in peace" (Job v. 24)' (Jeb. 62b).
'Honour your wife, for thereby you enrich yourself. A man
should be ever careful about the honour due to his wife, because
no blessing is experienced in his house except on her account'
(B.M. 59a). 'A man should spend less than his means on food
and drink for himself, up to his means on his clothes, and above
his means on honouring his wife and children, because they are
dependent upon him, while he is dependent upon Him Who spake
and the Universe came into being' (Chul. 84b).

Husband and wife were exhorted to look upon each other as
partners in life. Therefore a proverb urged: 'If your wife is short,
bend down and whisper to her' (B.M. 59a), i.e. the man should not
think himself too superior to consult his wife on his affairs. It is
true that the opposite opinion is given in the same context, 'Whoever follows his wife's advice falls into Gehinnom,' but it is deduced
from the extreme instance of Ahab, who followed the advice of
Jezebel to his hurt.

Especially in the early Talmudic period, when the Temple was
still standing, the arrangement of marriages was not unattended
by romance. There is a record which informs us: 'The Israelites
had no happier days than the fifteenth of Ab [1] and the Day of
Atonement, when the sons of Jerusalem used to go out dressed in
white garments which were borrowed, so as not to put to shame
anybody who did not possess his own. The daughters of Jerusalem would go out and dance in the vineyards, crying, "Young
man, raise your eyes and see whom you will choose for your wife.
Pay not attention to beauty, but rather to family"' (Taan. IV. 8).

A man's chief love was usually given to his first wife. Hence
the sayings: 'When a man's first wife dies during his lifetime, it
is as though the Temple had been destroyed in his lifetime. When
a man's wife dies in his lifetime the world becomes dark for him'
(Sanh. 22a). 'Should a man marry a woman after his first wife,
he remembers the deeds of the first' (Ber. 32b).

---

[1] Ab is the fifth month of the Hebrew calendar. The day mentioned is the
traditional anniversary of the reconciliation effected between the tribe of
Benjamin and the other tribes. See Judges xxi.

The Talmud, like the Bible, sanctioned polygamy but dis-countenanced it. Various opinions on the subject may be culled from its pages: 'A man may marry as many wives as he pleases' (Jeb. 65a), said one authority. 'He may not exceed four' (ibid. 44a),[1] declared another. While yet another Rabbi maintained: 'A man must give his wife a divorce if she desires it on his taking an additional wife' (ibid. 65a). There was agreement that the High Priest was not allowed to have more than one wife (Joma 13a). While there can be no doubt that among the masses polygamy was practised, there is no record of any Rabbi having resorted to it. Indeed, there is a story which shows how the practice was regarded with detestation. 'The son of R. Judah the Prince spent twelve years in study apart from his wife. By the time of his return she had become sterile. On hearing of this, the father said, "How shall we act? If she is divorced, people will say that the pious woman waited all those years in vain. If an additional wife is taken, people will say that one woman is his wife and the other his harlot!" He prayed on her behalf and she was healed' (Keth. 62b).

But despite all precautions, a couple at times found themselves ill-mated. A standing witticism on the subject has been preserved. 'In Palestine when a man took a wife to himself, people used to ask him whether it was *Matza* or *Motzé*' (Jeb. 63b). The key to the question is to be discovered in these two verses: 'Whoso hath found (*matza*) a wife hath found good' (Prov. xviii. 22), and 'I find (*motzé*) woman more bitter than death' (Eccles. vii. 26). That not all wives were perfect is evidenced by such remarks as: 'Among those who will never behold the face of Gehinnom [2] is he who has a bad wife' (Erub. 41b). 'Among those whose life is not life is the man who is ruled by his wife' (Betzah 32b). 'Among those who cry but nobody takes any notice of him is the husband who is ruled by his wife' (B.M. 75b).

Under the law of the Talmud, if husband and wife wished to separate there was no difficulty in dissolving the marriage. 'A bad wife is like leprosy to her husband. What is the remedy? Let him divorce her and be cured of his leprosy' (Jeb. 63b). It was even asserted, 'If one has a bad wife, it is a religious duty to divorce her' (ibid.).

In the first century of the present era the Schools of Shammai and Hillel took opposite views of the Biblical text, Deut. xxiv. 1,

[1] This was the view adopted by Mohammad. See Koran iv. 3.
[2] Because they expurgated their sins in this world through exceptional suffering.

which allows a man to send his wife away 'if she find no favour in his eyes, because he hath found some unseemly thing in her.' The phrase 'unseemly thing' is literally 'nakedness of a thing,' which the School of Shammai explained to mean, 'A man may not divorce his wife unless he discovered her to be unfaithful to him.' [1] The School of Hillel, on the other hand, understood the phrase in the sense of 'anything unseemly' and declared: 'He may divorce her even if she spoil his cooking.' [2] From the words, 'if she find no favour in his eyes,' R. Akiba argued, 'He may divorce her even if he found another woman more beautiful than she' (Git. IX. 10). The more lenient opinion of the Hillelites prevailed and was adopted as law.

The patriarchal system of the Bible was continued under the Rabbis, according to which the husband exercised absolute authority. This accounts for the ruling which is never disputed in the Talmud: 'A woman may be divorced with or without her consent, but a man can only be divorced with his consent' (Jeb. XIV. 1). Since the dissolution of marriage consisted in the presentation by the husband, either in person or through an accredited agent, of a bill of divorcement (called *Get*) to the wife, this meant that in actual practice the husband divorced the wife and the wife could not divorce the husband. That such a procedure necessarily placed disabilities upon the woman was recognized, and certain safeguards were devised which will be described later.

Talmudic law declared that 'a woman who had committed adultery must be divorced' (Keth. III. 5). Apart from this offence, the dissolution of marriage was not favoured, although sanctioned. There is the emphatic statement: 'Whoever divorces his first wife, even the altar sheds tears on her behalf; as it is said, "And this again ye do; ye cover the altar of the Lord with tears . . . because the Lord hath been witness between thee and the wife of thy youth, against whom thou hast dealt treacherously" (Mal. ii. 13 f.)' (Git. 90b). The words, 'He hateth putting away' (Mal. ii. 16), receives the comment from one Rabbi, 'If you hate (your wife) send her away'; but another explained them in this manner:

[1] This interpretation coincides with the statement of law in Matt. xix. 9.

[2] Some scholars think that this is a euphemistic expression and refers to indecent conduct which does not involve unchastity. The phrase certainly does occur in the Talmud in a metaphorical sense, but the Jewish commentators understand it quite literally in the present passage. The subject is discussed in R. T. Herford's *Christianity in Talmud and Midrash*, pp. 57 ff. Josephus also testifies to the freedom of divorce and supports the Hillelite standpoint: 'He that desires to be divorced from his wife for any cause whatever (and many such causes happen among men), let him in writing give assurance that he will never cohabit with her any more' (Antiq. IV. viii. 23).

'Hated is he who sends his wife away.' The two dicta are harmonized on the assumption that the latter refers to the first wife
and the former to the second (Git. 90b).

One safeguard against hasty divorce was the fact that it entailed
the payment of the *Kethubah*, or marriage settlement, to which
the wife was entitled. Consequently the verse, 'The Lord hath
delivered me into hands from which I am unable to rise up'
(Lament. i. 14), was applied to 'a man who had a bad wife with
a large sum due to her under her *Kethubah*' (Jeb. 63b). But if
her conduct gave rise to scandal the husband was entitled to
divorce her without paying the amount of the *Kethubah*. 'The
following have their marriage dissolved without receiving what is
due to them under their *Kethubah*: a woman who transgresses
Jewish law, such as going into public with uncovered head,[1]
spinning in the street or conversing with all sorts of men; a woman
who curses her husband's children in his presence; a loud-voiced
woman, which means one who talks in her house and her neighbours
can hear what she says' (Keth. VII. 6).

Since the purpose of marriage is the raising of a family, sterility
on the wife's part would defeat its object. It was therefore enacted:
'If one married a woman and waited with her ten years without
her bearing a child, he is not permitted to remain exempt (from
the duty of procreation). When he divorces her she may remarry,
and the second husband waits with her ten years. If she miscarry, the period of ten years is reckoned from the time of the
miscarriage' (Jeb. VI. 6).

Instead of insanity being made a ground for divorce, it was an
obstacle to the dissolution of marriage. 'If a wife became insane,
the husband cannot divorce her; and if the husband became insane,
he cannot give a divorce' (ibid. XIV. 1). The reason why an insane
woman was not allowed to be divorced was that, being deprived
of a protector, she would become the prey of evil-minded persons.
An insane husband could not grant a divorce because the giving
of the *Get* had to be a conscious act.

Although, as pointed out, in theory only the husband could end
a marriage, this was not so in fact. Talmudic law declares: 'The
Court may bring strong pressure to bear upon the husband until
he says, "I am willing to divorce my wife"' (Arach. v. 6). These
are the circumstances in which such compulsion was exercised:
refusal to consummate the marriage (Keth. XIII. 5), the husband's
impotence (Ned. XI. 12), and inability or unwillingness to support

[1] On marriage the bride covered her hair and it was considered immodest for
her to expose it.

her properly (Keth 77a). 'If a man vows he will not have inter-course with his wife, the School of Shammai allows him two weeks, the School of Hillel one week' (Keth v. 6), and if by the end of that period he does not annul his vow and resume cohabitation, he is compelled to divorce her. A woman could also free herself from a distasteful marriage by vowing to withhold herself from her husband. He has the right to annul the vow; and if she persists in her attitude, he divorces her without payment of her *Kethubah* (ibid. 63b).

A woman also has grounds for a divorce if her husband con-tracts a loathsome illness or engages in work which makes him repugnant to her. 'Should blemishes appear in a man, the Court does not compel him to divorce his wife. R. Simeon b. Gamaliel said, This is true of minor blemishes, but in the case of serious blemishes he is compelled to give a divorce. The following are the circumstances in which they force him to free his wife: if he is smitten with leprosy or develops a polypus; if he is a gatherer of dog's dung,[1] or a copper-smelter, or a tanner, whether these con-ditions obtained before marriage or they arose after marriage. R. Meïr declares with reference to all of them that even if the husband made an agreement with her,[2] she is entitled to plead, "I thought I could endure it, but now I see I cannot." The Sages maintain that (if an agreement had been made) she is obliged to endure it except in the case of leprosy, because intercourse would adversely affect him' (Keth. VII. 9 f.).

Desertion gave no ground for divorce, whatever the length of time that nothing was heard of the husband. Only if trustworthy testimony came that he had died was she allowed to remarry. An important concession was made in connection with this matter. The law that two witnesses are necessary to establish a fact[3] was relaxed in this case, and one reliable witness was accepted to have the death of the husband presumed (Jeb. 88a). She was also relieved in certain circumstances from migrating with her husband if she did not wish to. 'Should the husband desire to go to Palestine and she declines, they compel her to do so, and if she refuses she is divorced and does not receive her *Kethubah*. Should she wish to go to Palestine and he declines, they compel him to do so, and if he refuses he must divorce her and pay the *Kethubah*. Should she desire to leave Palestine and he does not, they compel her not to do so, and if she refuses she is divorced without receiving

[1] Which was used in the preparation of leather.
[2] At the time of marriage and she undertook to raise no objection.
[3] See p. 308.

her *Kethubah*. Should he wish to leave Palestine and she does not, they compel him not to do so, and if he refuses he must divorce her and pay the *Kethubah*' (Keth. 110*b*).

When regarded as a whole, the just conclusion appears to be that the divorce laws did not press heavily to the disadvantage of the woman. Despite the facility with which a union could be dissolved, the evidence does not suggest that it was abused. The high ideal of married life which was inculcated and practised under the Talmudic regime, aided perhaps by the knowledge that an irksome marriage could be ended without difficulty if necessity arose, tended to raise the standard of Jewish marital relationship to a lofty level.

§ III. CHILDREN

The intense longing for children, and sons in particular, which distinguished the Oriental is also mirrored in the pages of the Talmud. By a play of words the thought is expressed that children (*banim*) are builders (*bonim*); they not only build the future of the family but likewise of the community (Ber. 64*a*). 'A childless person is accounted as dead' (Gen. R. LXXI. 6), since he failed to carry out the principal duty which devolved upon him, and his name will perish with him. Intentional childlessness was denounced as a serious sin, as may be gathered from a legendary account of the interview between Isaiah and Hezekiah when the king lay seriously ill. 'Isaiah, the prophet, the son of Amoz, came to him and said, "Thus saith the Lord, 'Set thy house in order; for thou shalt die and not live' (Is. xxxviii. 1)." What means, "For thou shalt die and not live"?—"For thou shalt die" in this world, "and not live" in the World to Come. He asked, "Why this severe punishment?" He replied, "Because you have not performed the duty of begetting children." Hezekiah said to him, "The reason is that I have seen by the aid of the Holy Spirit that worthless children [1] will issue from me." Isaiah replied to him, "What have you to do with the secrets of the All-merciful? What you have been commanded you should perform, and let the Holy One, blessed be He, do whatever is pleasing to Him"' (Ber. 10*a*).

In cases where conception was likely to prove dangerous to the mother the use of a contraceptive was not only allowed but advocated. The law on the subject reads: 'There are three classes of women who should employ an absorbent: a minor, a pregnant woman, and a nursing mother; a minor lest pregnancy prove fatal,

[1] The allusion is to Manasseh, whom the Rabbis often denounce as among the most wicked of all the kings.

a pregnant woman lest abortion result, and a nursing mother lest she become pregnant and prematurely wean the child so that it dies' (Jeb. 12*b*).

The light in which children were regarded is well illustrated in the pathetic story of R. Meïr and his two sons. 'It happened that while the Rabbi was lecturing in the House of Study on the afternoon of the Sabbath, his two sons died at home. Their mother laid them upon a bed and covered them with a sheet. At the termination of the Sabbath, the Rabbi returned to his house and asked where the children were. His wife said to him, "I want to ask you a question. Some time ago a person came here and entrusted a valuable article to my care, and now he wants it back. Shall I restore it to him or not?" He answered, "Surely a pledge must be returned to its owner!" She then said, "Without asking for your consent I gave it back to him." She thereupon took him by the hand, led him into the upper room, and removed the sheet from off the bodies. When he saw them he wept bitterly; and she said to her husband, "Did you not tell me that what has been entrusted to one's keeping must be restored on demand? 'The Lord gave, and the Lord hath taken away; blessed be the name of the Lord' (Job i. 21)"' (Jalkut Prov. § 964).

The story not only displays perfect submission to the divine decree, but also shows that children were thought of as a precious loan from God to be guarded with loving and faithful care.

How sons were preferred to daughters, and for what reason, is reflected in many passages. For instance, there is the interpretation placed upon the statement, 'The Lord blessed Abraham in all things' (Gen. xxiv. 1)—'What means "in all things"? One Rabbi answered, That he had no daughter. Another Rabbi more gallantly answered, That he had a daughter' (B.B. 16*b*). 'A Rabbi's wife gave birth to a daughter and he was very upset about it. His father to cheer him said, "Increase has come into the world." But another Rabbi told him, "Your father has given you empty comfort; for there is a Rabbinical dictum, The world cannot exist without males and females, but happy is he whose children are sons and woe to him whose children are daughters"' (ibid.).

Sons were preferred because they were a support in old age and might fulfil their parents' ambition of becoming renowned scholars. The reluctance to have daughters is accounted for in a quotation from Ben Sira, which the Talmud preserved: 'It is written, A daughter is a vain treasure to her father. From anxiety about her he does not sleep at night; during her early years lest she be seduced, in her adolescence lest she go astray, in her marriageable years lest she does not find a husband, when she is married lest she be childless, and when she is old lest she practise witchcraft' (Sanh. 100b).[1] The same thought is contained in the explanation of the words of the Priestly Benediction: '"The Lord bless thee and keep thee" (Num. vi. 24)—bless thee with sons, and keep thee from daughters because they need careful guarding' (Num. R. XI. 5).

The fact that one's chief love is given to his children and they take precedence over his parents in his affections passed into a proverb: 'A father's love is for his children, and the children's love for their children' (Sot. 49a). To give proper care to the welfare of the young and especially to take charge of orphans was commended as a most praiseworthy act. '"Blessed is he that doeth righteousness at all times" (Ps. cvi. 3); this refers to one who well nourishes his children while they are young. Another Rabbi declared that it refers to one who brings up orphans in his house and gets them married' (Keth. 50a).

Several wise warnings are addressed to parents on the right and wrong method of dealing with children. The evil result of the favouritism which Jacob displayed toward Joseph gave rise to the advice, 'A man should never make distinctions between his children' (Shab. 10b). A happy medium is recommended between over-indulging a child and not correcting his faults and being too stern with him. 'If one refrains from punishing a child, he will end by becoming utterly depraved' (Exod. R. I. 1); but one should not chastise a child who is grown up (M.K. 17a). On the other hand, 'A man should not terrorize his children excessively' (Git. 6b). The proper course to adopt with children and women is 'to push away with the left hand and draw them near with the right hand' (Semachoth II. 6).

Instances are recorded where the threat of punishment resulted in a boy taking his life. For that reason it was advocated, 'A man should never threaten his child but punish him at once or say nothing' (ibid.).

Another wise recommendation, already quoted in a different connection, reads: 'A person should never tell a child that he will give him something and not keep his promise, because he thereby teaches the child to tell lies' (Suk. 46b). And since children have a tendency to repeat what they hear said at home, a proverb cautions parents to be very circumspect in what they speak before the young: 'The talk of the child in the street is that of his father or his mother' (ibid. 56b).

---

[1] The quotation is from Ecclus. xlii. 9 f. The Talmudic version differs in several respects from the Greek text, but the general sense is the same.

§ IV. Education

The principal responsibility that rested upon parents was to train their children for their life as members of the Community of Israel. The ideal aimed at was to forge them into secure links in the chain of continuity so that the religious heritage which had been bequeathed by the preceding generation may be transmitted unimpaired to the generation which would follow. The indispensable requisite for such a consummation was the instilling into them of a knowledge of Torah. The command, 'Thou shalt teach them diligently unto thy children' (Deut. vi. 7), was taken very seriously, and was included in the prayers offered every morning and evening.

Many are the utterances in the Talmud which dwell upon the importance of this duty. 'He who rears his children in the Torah is among those who enjoy the fruit in this world while the capital remains for him in the World to Come' (Shab. 127a). 'Whoever has a son labouring in the Torah is as though he never dies' (Gen. R. xlix. 4). 'Whoever teaches his son Torah, Scripture imputes it to him as though he had received it from Mount Horeb; as it is said, "Thou shalt make them known to thy children and thy children's children" (Deut. iv. 9), and it continues, "The day that thou stoodest before the Lord thy God in Horeb" (ibid. 10)' (Ber. 21b).

One reason for the extraordinary high value set upon education was love of learning for its own sake. A current proverb declared: 'If you have acquired knowledge, what do you lack? If you lack knowledge, what have you acquired?' (Lev. R. i. 6). But deeper still was the consciousness that the existence of the community depended upon the diffusion of knowledge. Language could scarcely convey in more forcible terms the importance of education than these aphorisms: '"Touch not Mine anointed and do My prophets no harm" (1 Chron. xvi. 22)—"Mine anointed" are the schoolchildren, "My prophets" are the scholars.' 'The world only exists through the breath of schoolchildren.' 'We may not suspend the instruction of children even for the rebuilding of the Temple.' 'A city in which there are no schoolchildren will suffer destruction' (Shab. 119b).

Very significant is the legend which formed part of an old homily: 'No philosophers have arisen in the world like Balaam the son of Beor and Oenomaos of Gadara. All the heathens assembled to the latter and said to him, "Tell us how we may successfully contend against the people of Israel." He answered, "Go to their Synagogues and Schools, and if you hear there the clamour of children re-hearsing their lessons, you cannot prevail against them; for so their patriarch (Isaac) assured them, saying, 'The voice is the voice of Jacob and the hands are the hands of Esau' (Gen. xxvii. 22), meaning that when Jacob's voice is heard in the Houses of Assembly, the hands of Esau are powerless"' (Gen. R. LXV. 20).

The consequence of this keen desire for the instruction of children was the establishment of schools. The first attempt at creating a school system was apparently made by Simeon b. Shetach in the earlier half of the first century before the present era; but a com-prehensive scheme was carried out by Joshua b. Gamala a few years before the destruction of the Temple. 'Remember for good the man named Joshua b. Gamala, because were it not for him the Torah would have been forgotten from Israel. At first a child was taught by his father, and as a result the orphan was left un-instructed. It was thereupon resolved that teachers of children be appointed in Jerusalem; and a father (who resided outside the city) would bring his child there and have him taught, but the orphan was again left without tuition. Then it was resolved to appoint teachers (for higher education) in each district, and boys of the age of sixteen and seventeen were placed under them; but it happened that when the master was angry with a pupil, the latter would rebel and leave. Finally Joshua b. Gamala came and instituted that teachers should be appointed in every province and in every city, and children about the age of six or seven placed in their charge' (B.B. 21a).

This is probably the earliest record of the adoption of universal education in any country. In course of time this excellent institu-tion appears to have declined, because we find a Rabbi declaring: 'Jerusalem was only destroyed for the reason that people neglected to send their children to school' (Shab. 119b). In making this declaration, he was not so much stating a historical fact as driving home to the parents of his own time the danger of not utilizing the schools for the instruction of their children. Not all parents were so neglectful, and we read of a certain Rabbi who 'never tasted his breakfast until he had taken his child to school' (Kid. 30a).

In the third century a Rabbi named Chiyya did much to revive interest in elementary education. A statement of his tells: 'I work that the Torah shall not be forgotten from Israel. What do I do? I go and spin flax, weave nets and catch stags. I feed orphans with the flesh, dress the skins into parchment, and write a copy of the Pentateuch. I go to a place and instruct five children in the Five Books of Moses and six children in the Six Orders of the

Mishnah; [1] then I tell them, "By the time of my return, teach each other the Pentateuch and the Mishnah." By this method I save the Torah from becoming forgotten from Israel' (B.M. 85*b*). Notice should be taken of the eagerness to impart instruction to all children, whatever the circumstances of the parents. The poor children were certainly not neglected. Indeed, there was a saying, 'Be careful of the children of the poor, since the Torah issues from them' (Ned. 81*a*).

Under Joshua b. Gamala's system the school age began at six or seven. In the Tractate *Aboth* the commencing age is given as five (v. 24); but we have it advocated in the Talmud: 'Under the age of six we do not receive a child as a pupil; from six upwards accept him and stuff him (with Torah) like an ox' (B.B. 21*a*). There was agreement among all authorities that education must begin early and only 'study in youth' can make a durable impression. A Rabbi expressed himself thus on the point: 'If one learns as a child, what is it like? Like ink written on clean paper. If one learns as an old man, what is it like? Like ink written on blotted paper' (Aboth IV. 25). Another statement on the subject is: 'If one learns Torah in his youth, the words of Torah are absorbed into his blood and issue clear from his mouth. If he learns Torah in his old age, the words of Torah are not absorbed into his blood and do not issue clear from his mouth. Similarly declares the proverb, "If you did not desire them in your mouth, how can you attain them in your old age?"' (ARN XXIV).

The evidence of the Talmud leads one to believe that schools were common and pupils numerous. A second-century Rabbi testifies: 'There were four hundred Synagogues in the town of Bethar,[2] in each of which were four hundred elementary teachers, and each had four hundred pupils' (Git. 58*a*); and a third-century Rabbi tells, 'There were three hundred and ninety-four Courts of Justice in Jerusalem, and a corresponding number of Synagogues, Houses of Study, and elementary schools' (Keth. 105*a*). The figures are, of course, exaggerated, but they point to the prevalence of educational institutions.

The greatest dignity attached to the profession of teacher and he was held in the highest esteem. In certain matters Jewish law gives him precedence even over a parent, 'because the parent only brings the child to the life of this world, whereas the teacher

---

[1] i.e. he taught each boy one section of the Pentateuch or of the Mishnah, so that he could teach the others what he had learnt, and in this way they all received instruction in the whole.

[2] In this town the last desperate stand was made by Bar Kochba in his unsuccessful revolt against Rome.

brings him to the life of the World to Come' (B.M. II. 11). The story is told of three Rabbis who were sent on a mission to inspect the state of education throughout Palestine. 'They came to a place where there were no teachers. They said to the inhabitants, "Bring us the protectors of the town." They brought them the military guard. The Rabbis exclaimed, 'These are not the protectors of the town but its destroyers!" "Who, then, are the protectors?" they were asked; and they answered, "The teachers"' (p. Chag. 76c). Since they were the guardians of the citadel of Judaism, the exhortation was given: 'Let the fear of your master be like the fear of Heaven' (Aboth IV. 15).

The highest moral and religious qualifications were demanded of a teacher. To him was applied the ideal standard described by the prophet, 'For the lips of the priest should keep knowledge and they should seek instruction from his mouth, for he is the messenger of the Lord of hosts' (Mal. ii. 7); and the comment was made, 'If the teacher is like a messenger of the Lord, seek Torah from his mouth; if he is not, then do not seek Torah from him' (M.K. 17a). Patience was an essential qualification because 'a hasty-tempered man cannot teach' (Aboth II. 6).

One authority gives strong preference to the elderly instructor. 'He who learns from the young, to what is he like? To one who eats unripe grapes, and drinks wine from his vat. And he who learns from the old, to what is he like? To one who eats ripe grapes, and drinks old wine' (Aboth IV. 26). But a colleague made the neat retort: 'Look not at the flask but at what it contains. There may be a new flask full of old wine, and an old flask that has not even new wine in it' (ibid. 27).

The Talmud provides us with some information about the methods of teaching which were then practised. The limitation of the size of the class was advocated if proper supervision was to be exercised over the individual child. 'The maximum number of elementary pupils that should be placed under one teacher is twenty-five; if there are fifty an additional teacher must be provided; if there are forty, a senior student should be engaged to assist the master' (B.B. 21a). Verbosity in a tutor is deprecated. 'A teacher should always employ conciseness of expression with his pupil' (Pes. 3b). Although books of reading were used and the art of writing was cultivated, materials were costly and scarce, and learning meant memorization by constant repetition. 'The teacher must keep on repeating the lesson until the pupil has learnt it' (Erub. 54b); and as for the student, 'If he learns Torah and does not go over it again and again, he is like a man who

sows without reaping' (Sanh. 99a). 'One who repeats his lesson
a hundred times is not like him who repeats it a hundred and
one times' (Chag. 9b).

As an aid to memory, studying the lesson aloud was recommended. A master is said to have told his pupil, 'Open your
mouth and learn the Scriptures; open your mouth and study
Mishnah so that it may remain with you' (Erub. 54a); and the
same context gives an account of a student who used to learn
his lessons without speaking them audibly, and the consequence
was he forgot all his studies after three years.

Very noteworthy is a Talmudic passage which informs us how
the infants were taught the Hebrew alphabet. To assist the
memory and to make the task of learning more attractive, words
were associated with the letters; but most important of all, the
alphabet was employed as a medium of religious and ethical
instruction. The lesson deserves to be given in its entirety.

'It is related that children now come into the House of Study
who recite things the like of which was not even said in the days
of Joshua the son of Nun. A and B are the initials of two words
meaning "Gain understanding"; G and D, "Be benevolent to the
poor." Why is the foot of G turned towards D? Because it is
the way of the benevolent to run after the poor. Why is the foot
of D turned towards G? To indicate that the poor person reaches
out to his helper. Why is the face of D turned away from G?
To teach that charity should be performed in secret so as not to
shame the recipient. H and V signify the name of the Holy One,
blessed be He. Z, CH, T, Y, K, L [1]—if you act in this manner
(towards the poor), the Holy One, blessed be He, will sustain you,
be gracious to you, benefit you, give you an inheritance, and bind
a crown upon you in the World to Come. There is an open M
and a closed M,[2] denoting that certain doctrines are open to the
reason and others closed. There is a curved N and a straight N,
hinting that if one is faithful to God when bent (by adversity) he
will be faithful in normal times. S and A [3] provide two words
meaning "Support the poor," or according to another version,
"Make mnemonics" when studying the Torah as an aid to retaining
it in memory.[4] There is a curved P and a straight P, pointing to

---

[1] Each of these letters appears in the keyword of each of the phrases that
follow.

[2] When a letter is mentioned as having two shapes, one refers to the form
it assumes as the final consonant of a word.

[3] This is a guttural sound which has no equivalent in English.

[4] Such mnemonics are actually found in the Talmud, consisting of a string
of keywords or letters.

an open mouth and a closed mouth. There is a curved TZ and a straight TZ, meaning that if one is righteous when bent (by adversity) he will be righteous in normal times. K is the first letter of "holy" and R of "wicked." Why does K turn its face away from R? The Holy One, blessed be He, says, "I cannot look upon the wicked." Why is the foot of K turned towards R? The Holy One, blessed be He, says, "If the wicked repent, I will place a crown upon him like My own." Why does the leg of K hang detached? If the wicked repent he can enter through the opening (and so find himself within the "Holy One"). SH is the initial of "falsehood" and TH the final letter of "truth." Why does the word for "falsehood" (shéker) consist of three consecutive letters of the alphabet, while the word for "truth" (ameth) consists of letters taken from the beginning, middle and end of the alphabet? Because falsehood is common, truth uncommon. Why does the word for falsehood rest on one point while the word for truth has a firm foundation?[1] To teach that truth stands but falsehood does not stand' (Shab. 104a).

In the elementary schools the chief aim was to give the pupils instruction in the Hebrew language and the Pentateuch. We are informed that in studying the Five Books of Moses the first that received attention was Leviticus, and the reason for this choice is thus stated: 'Why do we start the children with Leviticus and not with Genesis? The Holy One, blessed be He, said, Since the children are pure and the sacrifices are pure, let the pure come and occupy themselves with things that are pure' (Lev. R. VII. 3).

There is difference of opinion on the question whether Greek should be studied. So far as Greek thought is concerned, there is almost unanimity against it. One Rabbi declared vehemently, 'Cursed be the man who has his son taught Greek philosophy' (B.K. 82b). The reason for this attitude is the disturbing effect it had upon the minds of those who devoted themselves to it. A Rabbi informs us: 'There were a thousand pupils in my father's school, of whom five hundred studied Torah and five hundred studied Greek philosophy; and of the latter none were left but myself and my nephew' (ibid. 83a). It is admitted, however, that a distinction may be drawn between the Greek language and Greek philosophy (ibid.). The former received high commendation from some teachers. The blessing of Noah, 'May God enlarge Japhet and let him dwell in the tents of Shem' (Gen. ix. 27) was interpreted: 'Let the words of Japhet (i.e. the language of Greece) be in the tents of Shem' (Meg. 9b). On the other hand, when a

[1] The allusion is to the shape of the letters.

Rabbi was asked whether a man might teach his son Greek, he told him that he might do so if he found a time which was neither day nor night, quoting Josh. i. 8 in support; but a colleague asserted, 'A man may teach his daughter Greek because it is an accomplishment for her' (p. Peah 15c).

Students were classified into four types. 'There are four qualities in disciples: he who quickly understands and quickly forgets, his gain disappears in his loss; he who understands with difficulty and forgets with difficulty, his loss disappears in his gain; he who understands quickly and forgets with difficulty, his is a good portion; he who understands with difficulty and forgets quickly, his is an evil portion' (Aboth v. 15). Another characterization is: 'There are four qualities among those that sit before the Sages: they are like a sponge, a funnel, a strainer, and a sieve: a sponge, which sucks up everything; a funnel, which lets in at one end and out at the other; a strainer which lets the wine pass out and retains the lees; a sieve, which lets out the bran and retains the fine flour' (ibid. 18).

A question which remains for consideration is the place of girls in the educational system of the Talmud. On this matter we find diametrically opposite views taken. One teacher declared, 'A man is obliged to have his daughter taught Torah'; but this statement is immediately followed by the opposing view, 'Whoever teaches his daughter Torah is as though he taught her obscenity' (Sot. III, 4). The latter opinion, it must be admitted, was the one more generally held and practised. For instance, notice was taken of the fact that in the exhortation, 'Ye shall teach them your children' (Deut. xi. 19), the Hebrew word more literally denotes 'your sons,' and so excludes the daughters (Kid. 30a). One Rabbi asserted, 'Let the words of the Torah rather be destroyed by fire than imparted to women' (p. Sot. 19a); and we are informed that when a woman put a question to a Rabbi in connection with the Golden Calf, he told her, 'A woman has no learning except in the use of the spindle' (Joma 66b).

The probable view is that these utterances refer to what we should term higher education. As indicated above,[1] all religious obligations, with the exception of one class, devolved upon women as well as men. Consequently they would require instruction quite as much as men, if not as thorough. In the circumstances of that age, the woman's only sphere was the home; and the fear was lest her care of the household would suffer if she spent her time and energy in study.

[1] See p. 159.

But other reasons may be suggested for the reluctance to permit women to pursue advanced learning. The religious leaders of Israel knew of what happened in Greece and Rome, where the education of women brought them into close intercourse with men and resulted in laxity of morals. The apprehension of a like consequence may be detected in the saying quoted above about 'obscenity.' Furthermore, the Rabbis were doubtless aware of what was happening in Christendom, where women, carried away by religious fervour, gave themselves up to a life of celibacy. Such a procedure could only have been contemplated with horror in the Jewish Community where marriage was looked upon as the divinely ordained state. The Talmud denounces certain persons as being 'destroyers of the world,' among them being, 'the female Pharisee' (Sot. III. 4), i.e. the woman of excessive piety. It seems very probable that to counteract such tendencies as these, the Rabbis adopted so antagonistic an attitude to women delving deeply into the lore of the Torah.

§ V. Filial Piety

The duty to honour one's parents is a religious obligation to which the Talmud assigns a supremely important place. It is one of the precepts by the performance of which a man enjoys the fruits in this world and the capital remains for him in the World to Come (Peah I. 1). 'Scripture places the honouring of parents on an equality with the honouring of the Omnipresent; it is said, "Honour thy father and thy mother" (Exod. xx. 12) and also "Honour the Lord with thy substance" (Prov. iii. 9). It likewise places the fear (i.e. respect) of parents on an equality with the fear of the Omnipresent; it is said, "Ye shall fear every man his mother and his father" (Lev. xix. 3), and also "Thou shalt fear the Lord thy God" (Deut. vi. 13)' (Kid. 30b).

From the first two texts the lesson was drawn that the duty to parents is even stricter than that which is due to God. 'Great is the precept to honour parents since the Holy One, blessed be He, attached to it still greater importance than the honouring of Himself. It is written, "Honour thy father and thy mother," and also "Honour the Lord with thy substance." With what do you honour God? With that which He has bestowed upon you, as when you carry out such laws as the forgotten sheaf, the corner of the field, tithes, charity to the poor, etc. If you possess the means of fulfilling these commandments, do so; but if you are destitute, you are not under the obligation. With the honouring of parents, however, no such condition is made. Whether you have means or not, you must fulfil the commandment, even if you have to go begging from door to door' (p. Peah 15*d*).

In one respect, at least, the honouring of God exceeds that of parents, and that is when the latter would entail disobedience of a Divine command. 'It is possible to think that even if the father ordered his son to defile himself or not to restore a lost article which he had found, he is to obey him; consequently there is a text to teach, "Ye shall fear every man his mother and his father, and keep My sabbaths" (Lev. xix. 3). All of you are alike bound to honour Me' (Jeb. 6*a*).

Two different terms are employed above, viz. fear and honour. They are defined as follows: 'By fear is meant that he does not stand in his father's place, occupy his seat, contradict his statement or decide against his opinion. By honour is meant that he provides him with food, drink, clothing, and shelter, helps him in and helps him out' (Kid. 31*b*).

In the fifth commandment the father is mentioned first, but in Lev. xix. 3 the mother is mentioned first. To account for the difference a theory is advanced which is based upon the psychological attitude of a person towards each of his parents. 'It was revealed and known before Him Who spake and the Universe came into being that a son has a tendency to honour his mother more than his father because she wins him over with kindly words; for that reason the Holy One, blessed be He, gave the father precedence in the commandment concerning the honouring of parents. It was also revealed and known before Him that a son has a tendency to fear his father more than his mother because he instructs him in Torah; for that reason the Holy One, blessed be He, gave the mother precedence in the commandment concerning the fear of parents' (ibid. 30*b et seq.*).

The inference is that father and mother are on a plane of equality in the matter of filial piety. According to Talmudic law, however, should there be a clash in a son's duties to each, he must give preference to his father. A Rabbi was asked, 'If my father should say, "Give me a drink of water," and my mother make the same request, to whom must I attend first? He answered, "Leave the honouring of your mother and honour your father, because both you and your mother have the duty of honouring him"' (Kid. 31*a*).

A home where deference is paid to parents is graced with the Divine Presence. 'When a man honours his father and his mother, the Holy One, blessed be He, says, "I ascribe it as though I dwelt with them and I was honoured." And when a man distresses his parents, the Holy One, blessed be He, says, "Well have I done in not abiding with them, for had I dwelt with them I would have been distressed"' (ibid. 30b et seq.).

Even under provocation from his father a son must exercise restraint and do nothing disrespectful. A Rabbi was asked, 'To what limit must one go in honouring parents?' He replied, 'Should his father take a purse of money and throw it into the sea in his son's presence, the latter must not put him to shame' (ibid. 32a). Another contingency where consideration must be shown is mentioned: 'If a man sees his father transgressing a precept of the Torah, let him not say, "Father, you are violating the Torah," but he should say, "Father, thus is it written in the Torah." An objection was raised that if he were addressed in this manner he would feel pained, so an alternative form was recommended, viz., "Father, there is such and such a verse in the Torah"' (ibid.), leaving him to draw his own conclusion.

Not only has the honour to be shown in fact, but there must be the right spirit motivating the deed. The Talmud declares: 'There was a person who fed his father on fat poultry and yet inherited Gehinnom, whereas another person made his father grind at the mill and inherited Paradise. How could this be? With regard to the former, his father said to him, "My son, where did you get this poultry?" And he answered, "Old man, eat and be quiet, because dogs eat and are quiet!" With regard to the latter, he was grinding at the mill when an order came from the king to conscript grinders. He said to his father, "You take my place here and I will grind for the king, so that if there is to be any insult it will be better for it to fall upon me, and if there is to be any beating, it will be better that I should suffer it"' (p. Peah. 15c).

Some of the Rabbis were renowned for the remarkable respect they paid to their mothers. Of one it is told that 'when he heard his mother's footsteps he used to exclaim, "I stand up before the Shechinah"' (Kid. 31b). Several stories are narrated of R. Tarphon. It was reported of him that 'whenever his mother wanted to ascend her bed, he knelt down and she stepped on him; and she descended from the bed in the same way' (ibid.). 'His mother went down to walk in the courtyard of the house on the Sabbath and her shoe slipped off. So he placed his hands beneath her soles and she walked on them until she reached her bed. Once he was ill and the Sages came to visit him. She said to them, "Pray on behalf of my son Tarphon, who treats me with more honour than is due to me." They asked what he had done, and she related the

incident to them. They then exclaimed, "Even if he had performed a thousand thousand times as much, he would still not
have fulfilled half of what the Torah commands in connection
with the honouring of parents"' (p. Peah 15c).

The best stories on the subject are credited to a non-Jew. When
a Rabbi was questioned, 'To what limit must one go in honouring
parents?' he answered: 'Go and see what a certain Gentile in
Ascalon did, named Dama the son of Nethinah. On one occasion
the Sages wanted to purchase gems for the ephod at a profit to
him of sixty myriads—others say a profit of eighty myriads—but
the key was under the pillow and his father was asleep. The son
refused to disturb him. Next year the Holy One, blessed be He,
gave him his reward in that a red heifer [1] was born among his
herd. The Sages of Israel went to purchase it from him. He said
to them, "I know that if I were to demand all the money in the
world for it, you would be willing to pay; but I only ask for the
sum which I lost by honouring my father"' (Kid. 31a).

His mother, apparently, was mentally deficient and her conduct
towards him in public was at times very trying, but he endured
it with the utmost self-restraint. 'He was the president of the
city councillors. Once his mother smacked his face in the presence
of the whole assembly, and the slipper with which she struck him
fell from her hand. He picked it up and handed it to her, in order
that she should not be troubled to bend down for it' (p. Peah 15c).
'On another occasion he was wearing a silken robe embroidered
with gold and was sitting in the company of certain Roman
notabilities. She came and tore it from him, struck him on the
head and spat in his face, but he did not put her to shame'
(Kid. 31a).

Respect for parents must be shown also after they are dead.
'A person must honour his father in life and in death. When
dead, if he has occasion to quote him he should not say, "Thus
said my father," but "Thus said my father, my teacher, may I be
an atonement for his decease." [2] This applies during the twelve
months following his death; thereafter he should say, "His memory
be for a blessing in eternal life"' (ibid. 31b).

[1] See Num. xix. A perfectly red heifer was very rare and consequently
realized a big price.
[2] Meaning may the sufferings due to him for his sins alight upon me. The
belief was that the average person expiated his sins within twelve months
after death (see p. 378); therefore after that period the wording should be
altered, otherwise it might seem to imply that the deceased had been a very
sinful person whose expiation exceeded the normal period.

CHAPTER VI

SOCIAL LIFE

§ I. The Individual and the Community

MAN was not intended to live alone but as a member of society. He is a unit in the body of humanity, and that fact creates many duties for him with respect to his relationship with his fellow-men. His life is not his own to do with as he pleases. His conduct affects his neighbours as their conduct affects him. This truth is excellently illustrated by a parable suggested by the text, 'Shall one man sin, and wilt Thou be wroth with all the congregation?' (Num. xvi. 22): 'It is like a company of men on board a ship. One of them took a drill and began to bore a hole under him. The other passengers said to him, "What are you doing?" He replied, "What has that to do with you? Am I not making the hole under my seat?" They retorted, "But the water will enter and drown us all!"' (Lev. R. iv. 6).

The attitude which the individual should adopt towards the community was admirably summarized by Hillel in his aphorism: 'If I am not for myself, who will be for me? And being for myself, what am I?' (Aboth i. 14). In the first place, man must be self-reliant and avoid dependence upon others. While the giving of charity to those in need was highly commended, the thought of being the recipient of charity from others should be repugnant in the extreme. 'Make your Sabbath as an ordinary weekday (with respect to meals),[1] but do not have recourse to the assistance of your fellow-creatures' (Shab. 118a), it was urged; and another saying on the subject is: 'Flay a carcass [2] in the street and earn a living, and say not, "I am a great man and the work is below my dignity"' (Pes. 113a). A paragraph of the Grace After Meals, which belongs to the early Rabbinic period (Ber. 48b), includes the petition: 'We beseech Thee, O Lord our God, let us not be in need either of the gifts of flesh and blood (i.e. human beings) or of their loans, but only of Thy helping hand which is full, open,

---

[1] In honour of the Sabbath the fare should be of an exceptional character. See p. 156.
[2] Typical of a mean occupation.

holy, and ample, so that we may not be ashamed nor confounded for ever and ever.'[1]

Other utterances which reflect the same thought are: 'The world grows dark for him who has to depend upon the table of others; his life is not really life' (Betz. 32b). 'When a man partakes of his own his mind is at rest; even if he partake of what belongs to his father or mother or his children his mind is not at rest, and it is unnecessary to add if he partake of what belongs to strangers' (ARN xxxi). 'A man takes greater delight in one measure of his own than in nine belonging to his fellow-man' (B.M. 38a). '"And lo, in her (the dove's) mouth was an olive leaf plucked off" (Gen. viii. 11). The dove spake before the Holy One, blessed be He, "Let my food be bitter as the olive but dependent upon Thee, rather than sweet as honey and dependent upon flesh and blood"' (Erub. 18b). 'What means, "When vileness is exalted (kerum) among the sons of men" (Ps. xii. 8)? As soon as a man stands in need of the help of his fellow-creatures, his face changes like a kerum. What is a kerum? There is a bird in the coast-towns called kerum,[2] and when the sun shines it changes into many colours. The man who needs help from his fellow-creatures is as though he were sentenced to two penalties, viz. fire and water' (Ber. 6b).

Although this spirit of independence is a virtue, it must not be carried to the extent of believing that the individual can dissociate himself from his fellow-men. 'Being for my own self, what am I?' Since life has grown more complex, man's requirements are so many that he must realize how much of his comfort he owes to the toil of others. A Rabbi meditated as follows: 'How much labour Adam must have expended before he obtained bread to eat! He ploughed, sowed, reaped, piled up the sheaves, threshed, winnowed, selected the ears, sifted the flour, kneaded and baked and after that he ate; whereas I get up in the morning and find all this prepared for me. And how much labour must Adam have expended before he obtained a garment to wear! He sheared, washed the wool, combed, spun, wove, and after that he obtained a garment to wear; whereas I get up in the morning and find all this prepared for me. All artisans attend and come to the door of my house, and I get up and find all these things before me' (Ber. 58a).

The consciousness of the extent to which the wealthy are beholden to the men whose humble occupation contributes to their

---

[1] *Authorised Daily Prayer Book*, ed. Singer, p. 281.
[2] *Kerum* is no doubt to be connected with the Greek *chroma*, 'colour.' It has been suggested that the bird of paradise is intended.

well-being should have the effect of obliterating the sharp dividing-lines between class and class. A proverb of the time declared, 'If the body is taken away, of what use is the head?' (Gen. R. C. 9), which emphasizes the truth that all classes are interdependent. Another proverb points out that the fate of each is bound up with the whole: 'If the house has fallen, woe to the windows' (Exod. R. XXVI. 2).

If the individual, however exalted his status, were to understand that the work he performs is in the service of the community, harmful class-pride would be avoided. This idea was beautifully put into words by the Rabbis of the famous Academy at Jabneh: 'I am a creature of God and my neighbour is also His creature; my work is in the city and his in the field; I rise early to my work and he rises early to his. As he cannot excel in my work, so I cannot excel in his work. But perhaps you say, I do great things and he small things! We have learnt that it matters not whether one does much or little if only he direct his heart to Heaven' (Ber. 17a).

The following story is in the true Rabbinic spirit. It is related that a certain man, named Simeon, from the village of Sichnin, who was a well-digger, once said to R. Jochanan b. Zakkai, 'I am as great a man as you.' 'How so?' asked the Rabbi. 'Because my work is of as much consequence to the community as yours. When you tell a man or woman to use water which is ceremonially purifying, it is I who provide it for them' (Eccles. R. to iv. 17). Still more emphatic is the comment on the words, 'The Lord is my shepherd' (Ps. xxiii. 1): 'There is no more despised occupation in the world than that of the shepherd, who throughout his life walks with his staff and wallet; and yet David called the Holy One, blessed be He, a shepherd!' (Midrash ad loc.).

An isolated life would not be worth living. This important truth was discovered by Choni the Circle-drawer,[1] the Rip van Winkle of the Talmud. The story is told of him: 'Throughout his life this righteous man was worried over the verse, "When the Lord turned again the captivity of Zion, we were like them that dream" (Ps. cxxvi. 1). He asked, "Could seventy years [2] pass like a dream?" One day, while walking along the road, he saw a man planting a carob-tree and said to him, "Since a carob-tree does not

---

[1] He was a famous ascetic to whom the people appealed in time of drought to pray for rain. He thereupon drew a circle and declared he would not step outside it until God had sent rain (Taan. 23a). See p. 277. It has been suggested that the original meaning of his name is not 'circle-drawer' (which later legend gave it) but 'roof-tiler,' which was his occupation.
[2] That being the duration of the captivity.

bear fruit for seventy years, are you certain of living so long as to eat of it?" He answered, "I found the world provided with carob-trees; as my forefathers planted them for me, I likewise plant them for my descendants." Choni thereupon sat down, had his meal and fell asleep. While he slumbered, a grotto was formed around him so that he was hidden from view, and he slept for seventy years. On awaking, he saw a man gathering carobs from the same tree and eating them. He asked him, "Do you know who planted this carob-tree?" The reply came, "My grandfather." Choni exclaimed, "Surely seventy years have passed like a dream!" Then he went to his house and inquired whether the son of Choni the Circle-drawer still lived. They told him that his son was no more but his grandson was living. He said to them, "I am Choni," but they would not believe him. He went to the Academy where he heard the Rabbis say, "Our studies are now as clear as in the time of Choni the Circle-drawer; for when he entered the Academy he used to solve all the difficulties of the scholars." He said to them, "I am Choni," but they would not believe him or pay him the deference which was due to him. He thereupon prayed to God (that he should die) and he died. Hence arose the proverb, "Either companionship or death"' (Taan. 23*a*).

The desirability of comradeship is deduced from the text, 'Two are better than one' (Eccles. iv. 9). 'Hence it is declared, A man should acquire a friend for himself to read Scripture with him, to study Mishnah with him, eat with him, drink with him, and disclose his secrets to him' (Sifré Deut. § 305; 129*b*). Co-operation and mutual assistance are essential factors in life, as a proverb tells: 'If you will lift the load I will lift it too; but if you will not lift it, I will not' (B.K. 92*b*).

Another idea which is frequently touched upon in this connection is conformity to established custom. 'Separate not yourself from the community' (Aboth II. 5) was the advice of Hillel, i.e. do not be eager to be the exception. 'A man's mind should always be harmoniously attuned to that of his fellow-creatures' (Keth. 17*a*). A proverb likewise counselled, 'If you have entered a city conform to its laws' (Gen. R. XLVIII. 14); and it receives Biblical corroboration in a curious manner: 'A man should never depart from established practice; behold, when Moses ascended above he did not eat (Exod. xxxiv. 28), and when the ministering angels descended to earth they partook of food (Gen. xviii. 8)' (B.M. 86*b*).

That mankind comprises various types, some praiseworthy and others the reverse, was recognized. 'There are four characters among men. He who says, What is mine is mine and what is yours is yours, his is a neutral character; some say, this is a character like that of Sodom. He who says, What is mine is yours and what is yours is mine, is a boor. He who says, What is mine is yours and what is yours is yours, is a saint. He who says, What is yours is mine and what is mine is mine, is a wicked man' (Aboth v. 13).

The greatest treasure a man can acquire for himself is the respect of his fellow-men. 'There are three crowns: the crown of Torah, the crown of priesthood, and the crown of royalty; but the crown of a good name excels them all' (ibid. iv. 17). 'What is the right course that a man should choose for himself? That which he feels to be honourable to himself, and which also brings him honour from mankind' (ibid. ii. 1). 'Who is honoured? He who honours others' (ibid. iv. 1).

To be popular with one's fellows was deemed a characteristic which earned God's approval. 'He in whom the spirit of his fellow-creatures takes delight in him the Spirit of the Omnipresent takes delight; and he in whom the spirit of his fellow-creatures takes not delight in him the Spirit of the Omnipresent takes not delight' (ibid. iii. 13). This is a typical utterance of the Rabbis, showing that in their view religion is not merely concerned with the relationship between the human being and his Maker, but also with his relationship with his neighbours.

Other extracts which teach the same doctrine are: 'In the Torah, in the Prophets, and in the Hagiographa we find that a man must perform his duty to his fellows exactly as to the Omnipresent. Whence is it derived from the Torah? "Ye shall be guiltless before the Lord and before Israel" (Num. xxxii. 22). Whence is it derived from the Prophets? "The Lord God of gods, He knoweth, and Israel he shall know" (Josh. xxii. 22).[1] Whence is it derived from the Hagiographa? "So that thou shalt find favour and good understanding in the sight of God and man" (Prov. iii. 4)' (p. Shek. 47c).

The words of Isaiah iii. 10 were understood in this sense, 'Say ye of the righteous that he is good,' and suggested the following line of thought: 'Is there, then, a righteous man who is good and one who is not good He who is good towards God and his fellow-men is the righteous man who is good; but one who is good towards God and evil towards his fellow-men is a righteous man who is not good. Similarly with the text, "Woe unto the wicked that is

---

[1] The two and a half tribes, who were accused of having built an altar for idolatrous worship, were anxious to justify their action to their brethren as well as God.

evil" (*sic*, ibid. 11)—is there, then, a wicked man who is evil and one who is not? He who is wicked towards God and wicked towards his fellow-men is a wicked man who is evil; but he who is wicked towards God and not so towards his fellow-men is a wicked man who is not evil' (Kid. 40*a*).

The Talmud offers these general rules of conduct: 'Be submissive to a superior, affable to a suppliant, and receive all men with cheerfulness' (Aboth III. 16); and 'A man should always give the soft answer that turneth away wrath, increasing peace with his brethren and relatives and with all men, even the heathen in the street, so that he may be beloved above and popular on earth, and acceptable to his fellow-creatures' (Ber. 17*a*).

Loyalty to the State is strictly enjoined. 'Pray for the welfare of the Government, since but for the fear thereof men would swallow each other alive' (Aboth III. 2). This dictum receives elaboration in the Talmud as follows: '"Thou madest men as the fishes of the sea" (Hab. i. 14)—as with the fishes in the sea the big swallow the small, so with men; were it not for fear of the Government the big would swallow the small' (A.Z. 4*a*).

The Rabbis apparently believed that every ruler who was worthy of his office held his position with the divine approbation. One of the three things which God Himself proclaims is 'a good leader.' He also, in their view, demonstrated that the ruler must have the popular approval to his appointment. 'We must not appoint a leader over the community without first consulting them; as it is said, "See, the Lord hath called by name Bezalel, the son of Uri" (Exod. xxxv. 30). The Holy One, blessed be He, asked Moses, "Is Bezalel acceptable to you?" He replied, "Sovereign of the Universe! if he is acceptable to Thee, how much more so to me!" He said to him, "Nevertheless, go and tell the people." He went and asked Israel, "Is Bezalel acceptable to you?" They answered, "If he is acceptable to the Holy One, blessed be He, and to you, how much more so to us!"' (Ber. 55*a*).

The Talmud goes so far as to declare: 'Even the superintendent of wells is appointed by Heaven' (B.B. 91*b*). That being so, we can understand such remarks as, 'Whoever acts with effrontery towards a king is as though he acted in similar manner before the *Shechinah*' (Gen. R. xciv. 9), and 'He who rebels against the royal authority is guilty of an offence deserving of death' (Sanh. 49*a*). This doctrine is corroborated by the conduct of Biblical worthies. 'Always should the respect for royalty be upon you; as it is said, "And all these thy servants shall come down unto me" (Exod. xi. 8). Out of respect for the king Moses did not say,

"Thou (Pharaoh) shalt come down unto me." It may also be derived from the action of Elijah who girded his loins and ran before Ahab's chariot (1 Kings xviii. 46)' (Zeb. 102a).

In conformity with this principle we have the law, 'Who beholds the kings of Israel should say: "Blessed art Thou, O Lord our God, King of the Universe, Who hast imparted of Thy glory to them that fear Thee"; and on beholding the kings of other peoples he says: "Blessed . . . Who hast imparted of Thy glory to Thy creatures." A man should always bestir himself to run to meet the kings of Israel; and not only the kings of Israel, but even to meet the kings of other peoples, for if he is worthy, he will distinguish (in the age of the Messiah) between the kings of Israel and of other peoples' (Ber. 58a).

The fundamental principle of conduct for the Jew in relationship to the State is crystallized in the phrase, 'The law of the land is law' (B.K. 113a). It was intended to be the guiding rule for the Jew living in a country not his own, governed by laws different from those of his people. Even Jewish law must be made conformable to the law of the State if that can be done without violating a basic principle of the Torah. A clear expression of this rule is contained in the passage: ' "I counsel thee, Keep the king's command, and that in regard of the oath of God" (Eccles. viii. 2). The Holy One, blessed be He, said to Israel, I adjure you that if the Government decree harsh decrees, rebel not against it in any matter which it imposes upon you; but "keep the king's command." If, however, it decree that you annul the Torah and the precepts, do not obey but say to it, "I am prepared to perform the king's edict in whatever you desire; but 'in regard of the oath of God, be not hasty to go out of His presence' (ibid. 3)"; because they are not making you neglect the precepts but urging you to renounce the Holy One, blessed be He' (Tanchuma Noach § 10).

In spite of the deference which is demanded towards rulers, the Talmud recommends very strongly that one should not curry favour with them. 'Love work, hate lordship, and seek no intimacy with the ruling power' (Aboth I. 10); and the reason given is: 'Be on your guard against the ruling power; for they who exercise it draw no man near to them except for their own interests; appearing as friends when it is to their own advantage, they stand not by a man in the hour of his need' (ibid. II. 3).

Another piece of advice is: 'Be rather a tail to lions than a head to foxes' (ibid. IV. 20), which means, Be rather a humble member of an eminent company than associate with inferiors in order to stand out prominently amongst them. Indeed, we find it over and over again emphasized that the limelight should be avoided and positions involving conspicuousness declined. One of the things which, according to the Talmud, shorten a man's days is 'to give oneself an air of superiority. Why did Joseph die before his brothers?[1] Because he gave himself superior airs' (Ber. 55*a*). 'Authority,' it is said, 'buries those who assume it' (Joma 86*b*) and is, in fact, servitude (Hor. 10*a*, *b*).

The intention is not to induce a person to shirk the responsibilities of office, but to decry eagerness for it which is motived by selfish ambition. The thought is well expressed in the aphorism, 'In a place where there are no men strive to be a man' (Aboth II. 6), upon which the Talmud makes the remark: 'Infer from this that where there is a man, do not be a man' (Ber. 63*a*). The meaning is that where work has to be done for the community, do not be self-assertive and push yourself forward; but when the task is being neglected by others, undertake it yourself. Above all, such work must be accomplished with disinterested motives. 'Let all who occupy themselves with the affairs of the community do so in the name of Heaven, for then the merit of their fathers sustains them and their righteousness endures for ever. And as for you (God will then say), I account you worthy of great reward, as if you had wrought it all yourselves' (Aboth II. 2).

§ II. Labour

It is a man's duty to work, not only to earn his livelihood, but likewise to contribute his quota to the maintenance of the social order. Although, as we have seen, the study of the Torah was praised as the most estimable of occupations, the Rabbis were practical enough to appreciate that the world could not exist if all men devoted themselves always to such an idealistic pursuit. So we have the aphorism: 'An excellent thing is the study of the Torah combined with some worldly occupation, for the labour demanded by them both makes sin to be forgotten. All study of the Torah without work must in the end be futile and become the cause of sin' (Aboth II. 2).

The happy medium advocated for the ordinary person was: 'If a man learns two paragraphs of the law in the morning and two in the evening and is engaged in his work all the day, it is ascribed to him as though he had fulfilled the Torah in its entirety'

[1] This is deduced from Exod. i. 6: 'And Joseph died and (then) all his brethren.'

(Tanchuma Beshallach § 20). Perhaps we may detect in the following citation a Rabbinic protest against the life of the recluse who withdrew himself from the work of the world to give himself entirely to spiritual reflection: 'Greater is he who enjoys the fruit of his labour than the fearer of Heaven; for with regard to the fearer of Heaven it is written, "Happy is the man that feareth the Lord" (Ps. cxii. 1), but with regard to him who enjoys the fruit of his labour it is written, "When thou eatest the labour of thy hands, happy shalt thou be, and it shall be well with thee" (ibid. cxxviii. 2)—"happy shalt thou be" in this world, "and it shall be well with thee" in the World to Come. It is not written, "and it shall be well with thee," about the fearer of Heaven' (Ber. 8a).

The dignity of labour is upheld throughout the Talmudic literature. 'Great is work for it honours the workmen' (Ned. 49b) is the keynote struck on this theme. It must be so, because it is an important part of the Divine scheme for man. On the Rabbinic dictum, 'Love work' (Aboth 1. 10), there is this homily: 'Even Adam did not taste food until he had done work; as it is said, "The Lord God took the man and put him into the Garden of Eden to till it and keep it" (Gen. ii. 15), after which He said, "Of every tree of the garden thou mayest eat" (ibid. 16). Even the Holy One, blessed be He, did not cause his *Shechinah* to alight upon Israel until they had done work; as it is said, "Let them make for Me a sanctuary that I may dwell among them" (Exod. xxv. 8). If one is unemployed, what should he do? If he has a courtyard or a field in a state of decay, let him busy himself with it; as it is said, "Six days shalt thou labour and do all thy work' (ibid. xx. 9). For what purpose were the words "and do all thy work" added? [1] It is to include a person who has a courtyard or a field in a state of decay, that he should go and busy himself with them. A man only dies through idleness' (ARN xi).

A legend tells that 'at the time the Holy One, blessed be He, informed Adam, "Thorns and thistles shall it bring forth to thee" (Gen. iii. 18), his eyes ran with tears. He said before Him, "Sovereign of the Universe! am I and my ass to feed in the same manger?" When, however, He added, "In the sweat of thy face shalt thou eat bread" (ibid. 19), his mind immediately calmed down' (Pes. 118a). The moral is that by his labour man raises himself above the rest of the animal kingdom.

Indeed, work is the very foundation of man's existence.

---

[1] It is an axiom of Rabbinic exegesis of the Bible that there is no tautology; therefore 'labour' must mean the ordinary occupation for the gaining of a livelihood, and 'work' what we should describe as spare-time employment.

'"Therefore choose life" (Deut. xxx. 19), i.e. a handicraft' (p. Peah 15c), is a terse and forceful expression of the idea. 'A blessing only alights upon the work of a man's hands' (Tosifta Ber. VII. 8) is another utterance indicating that labour is the path to happiness. The law enacts that even if a man provide his wife with a hundred servants, she must do some of the housework herself, because 'idleness leads to lewdness and it also leads to mental instability' (Keth. v. 5).

The important place which work occupies in the scheme of the Universe is further pointed out in the treatment of the following passage: 'God came to Laban in a dream by night, and said to him, Take heed that thou speak not to Jacob either good or bad' (Gen. xxxi. 24): 'Hence we learn that the merit of labour holds a position which is unattainable by the merit of ancestors; as it is said, "Except the God of my father, the God of Abraham, and the Fear of Isaac, had been with me, surely thou hadst sent me away now empty" (ibid. 42). If so, the merit of his ancestors only availed for the protection of his wealth. "God hath seen mine affliction and the labour of my hands, and rebuked thee yesternight" (ibid.); this shows that He warned Laban against harming Jacob through the merit of the labour of his hands. In this way He taught that a man should not say, I will eat and drink and see prosperity without troubling myself, since Heaven will have compassion upon me. Therefore it is stated, "Thou hast blessed the work of his hands' (Job I. 10); a man should toil with both his hands and then the Holy One, blessed be He, will grant His blessing' (Tanchuma Vayétzé § 13).

A popular saying ran: 'Who hath not worked shall not eat' (Gen. R. XIV. 10). Moreover, one should not think of his personal requirements as the motive of his labour. This is finely exemplified in an anecdote. 'The Emperor Hadrian was passing along the lanes near Tiberias and saw an old man breaking up the soil to plant trees. He said to him, "Old man, if you had worked early there would have been no need for you to work so late in your life." He replied, "I have toiled both early and late, and what was pleasing to the Lord of Heaven has He done with me." Hadrian asked him how old he was, and the answer was a hundred; he thereupon exclaimed, "You a hundred years old and you stand there breaking up the soil to plant trees! Do you expect to eat of their fruit?" He replied, "If I am worthy I shall eat; but if not, as my fathers laboured for me, so I labour for my children"' (Lev. R. xxv. 5).

In thus eulogizing manual toil, the Rabbis practised what they preached.   We read of a few of them belonging to wealthy families, but the majority were humble workmen who earned a precarious livelihood.   The story of Hillel's poverty has already been told.[1] Of other Rabbis we learn that Akiba used to collect a bundle of wood daily and exist on the price he received for it (ARN VI); Joshua was a charcoal-burner and lived in a room the walls of which were begrimed by his manner of work (Ber. 28a); Meïr was a scribe (Erub. 13a); José b. Chalaphta was a worker in leather (Shab. 49b); Jochanan was a maker of sandals (Aboth IV. 14); Judah was a baker (p. Chag. 77b); and Abba Saul held a menial position as a kneader of dough (Pes. 34a), while he mentions that he had also been a grave-digger (Nid. 24b).

Writing in the first century, Josephus declared of the Jewish people: 'As for us we do not delight in merchandise, but having a fruitful country for our habitation, we take pains in cultivating that only' (c. Apion. I. 12).   This statement is perhaps too sweeping; but it is noteworthy that usually when the Talmud refers to men being at work, the allusion is to agricultural labour.   The passage about the creation of 'a fence to the Torah,' already quoted,[2] illustrates this, since it speaks of 'a man coming from the field in the evening' (Ber. 4b); so also in the saying of the Rabbis of Jabneh, 'My work is in the city and his in the field' (ibid. 17a).[3]

On the comparative merit of the agricultural life as against handiwork or commerce we see a sharp division of opinion.   On the one side we have sayings like: 'The workers of all trades will in the end come back to the soil.   A man who does not possess land is not really a man' (Jeb. 63a); and the verse, 'The Lord hath delivered me into hands from which I am not able to rise up' (Lament. i. 14), was applied in Palestine to one 'whose livelihood was dependent upon his money' (ibid. 63b) and not agriculture. Equally forcible is the view to the contrary: 'There is no lower occupation than that of tilling the soil.   A hundred zuz invested in business will provide meat and wine daily; a hundred zuz invested in land will only enable one to subsist on salt and vegetables; not only that, it makes him sleep on the ground (to guard the crops at night) and creates strife (with his neighbours)' (ibid. 63a). One Rabbi suggested a compromise by recommending: 'A man should divide his money into three parts, investing a third in land, a third in business, and retaining a third in his possession' (B.M. 42a).

Especially when the tenure of land became precarious, the security offered by a handicraft grew very attractive.   A proverb tells: 'Seven years lasted the famine, but it came not to the artisan's door' (Sanh. 29a). He is less affected by crises which fall so heavily upon the husbandman.

In connection with this subject the Rabbis taught: 'A man is obliged to teach his son a trade, and whoever does not teach his son a trade teaches him to become a robber. The person who has a trade in his hand is like a vineyard which is fenced in, so that cattle and beasts cannot get into it or passers-by eat of it or look into it; and whoever has no trade in his hand is like a vineyard with its fence broken down, so that cattle and beasts can enter it, and passers-by can eat of it and look into it' (Tosifta Kid. I. 11).

A distinction was drawn between the various occupations which a person could adopt, some being commended and others condemned. 'A man should not teach his son a trade which brings him into association with women. A man should teach his son a clean and light trade. A man should not teach his son to be an ass-driver, camel-driver, sailor, barber, shepherd, or shopkeeper, because these are thieving occupations. Another Rabbi remarked, Most ass-drivers are wicked, most camel-drivers are honest, most sailors are pious, the best of physicians is destined for Gehinnom, and the most honest of butchers is a partner of Amalek' (Kid. iv. 14). Another statement on this subject reads: 'There is no trade which will pass away from the world. Happy is he who sees his parents engaged in a superior occupation and woe to him who sees them engaged in a disagreeable occupation. The world cannot do without the perfumer and without the tanner; but happy is he who is a perfumer by trade and woe to him who is a tanner by trade' (ibid. 82b).

The Talmud ventures an explanation why men continue in work which by its nature must be unpleasant to those engaged in it. 'What means that which is written, "He hath made everything beautiful in its time" (Eccles. iii. 11)? It teaches that the Holy One, blessed be He, makes every occupation agreeable in the eyes of those who follow it' (Ber. 43b).

One method of earning a living was condemned in scathing terms by the Rabbis, viz. usury. A man who practised it was precluded from giving evidence in a court of law (Sanh. III. 3). 'Come and see the blindness of usurers. If a man call his fellow a villain, the latter proceeds against him even to the extent of depriving him of his livelihood; but usurers take witnesses, scribe, pen and ink, and write and seal a document to the effect, So-and-so (viz. the usurer) denies the God of Israel. Whoever has money and lends it without interest, of him it is written, "He that putteth not out his money to usury . . . shall never be moved" (Ps. xv. 5). Hence you can learn that if a man lends on interest his possessions will be moved' (B.M. 71a). 'Usurers are comparable to shedders of blood' (ibid. 61b). 'Whoever takes interest, Scripture imputes it to him as if he had performed all the evil deeds and trans-gressions in the world; as it is said, "Who hath given forth upon usury and hath taken increase, shall he then live? He shall not live; he hath done all these abominations" (Ezek. xviii. 13). But he who lends without interest, the Holy One, blessed be He, ascribes it to him as if he had performed all the precepts; as it is said, "He that putteth not out his money to usury," etc.' (Exod. R. XXXI. 13).

§ III. MASTER AND WORKMAN

The relationship between employer and employee is strictly defined by the Talmud, and the responsibilities of each are very clearly specified. The matter is viewed as a contract between the two parties which must be scrupulously honoured by both. For the master to withhold from the workman what is due to him, or vice versa, is denounced as fraud.

First as regards the duty of the employer. He must conform to the usages which govern labour in the place of his residence. 'He who engages workmen and orders them to start early or continue late, in a place where they have the custom not to start early or continue late, is not permitted to compel them (to exceed the usual hours of labour). Where it is the custom to feed the workmen he must feed them; where it is the custom to supply them with a dessert (after the meal), he must do so; all should be according to the practice of the district' (B.M. VII. 1).

The employer should be considerate towards the men working for him and not insist on strict justice should an accident occur. This anecdote will illustrate the point. 'The porters engaged by Rabbah bar Bar Chanah broke a cask of wine belonging to him, and as a penalty he took their coats from them. They went and complained to Rab who ordered him to restore their garments. He asked, "Is that the law?" Rab replied, "It is, for it is written, 'That thou mayest walk in the way of good men' (Prov. ii. 20)." [1] He gave them back their coats. The labourers then said, "We are poor and have toiled throughout the day and are hungry; we are destitute." Rab said to him, "Go and pay their wages." He

[1] He meant that good men do not insist upon strict justice but are lenient in their demands.

asked, "Is that the law?" He replied, "Yes, for it is written, 'And keep the paths of the righteous' (ibid.)"' (B.M. 83a).

Above all else, employers must pay the wages for the work done immediately they are due. The law on the subject prescribes: 'The labourer engaged by the day collects his wages during the night that ensues; if engaged by the night he collects them during the day that ensues; if engaged by the hour he collects them during the ensuing day or night; if engaged by the week or month or year or period of seven years, he collects his wages during the day of his discharge should his term end in the daytime or during the night should his term end in the night-time' (B.M. IX. 11).

To delay the payment after the allotted time is condemned as a heinous sin and rebuked unsparingly. 'Who defers paying the wages of a hired labourer transgresses five commandments of the Torah: "Thou shalt not oppress thy neighbour" (Lev. xix. 13); "Neither shalt thou rob him" (ibid.); "Thou shalt not oppress a hired servant that is poor and needy' (Deut. xxiv. 14); "The wages of a hired servant shall not abide with thee all night until the morning" (Lev. loc. cit.); "In his day thou shalt give him his hire" (Deut. xxiv. 15) and "Neither shall the sun go down upon it" (ibid.)' (B.M. 111a). 'Israel was exiled for withholding the wages of the hired labourer' (Lament. R. to i. 3). 'Whoever defers paying the wages of a hired servant is as though he took his life (lit. soul) from him. One Rabbi explained the last words to mean: as though he took his own life from himself, as it is said, "Rob not the poor . . . for the Lord will plead their cause and spoil the soul of those that spoiled them" (Prov. xxii. 22 f.). Another explained the words to apply to the person who is defrauded; as it is said, "So are the ways of every one that is greedy of gain; it taketh away the life of the owners thereof" (ibid. i. 19)' (B.M. 112a).

As for the employee, his time and energy have been purchased and these must be given honestly in return for his wages. Not to give his employer of the best he can do is as much deceit as for a shopkeeper to sell short measure. That is the view of the Rabbis not only in theory, but also in practice, as the following stories show. It is told of Abba Joseph the builder that his opinion was sought on a certain matter and he was found standing upon some scaffolding. The questioner said to him, 'I want to ask you something'; but his answer was, 'I cannot come down because I am hired by the day' (Exod. R. XIII. 1). He felt that he had no right to use any of the time which belonged to his employer for the solving of problems submitted to him.

Another incident of the same character is narrated. 'Once, at

a time of drought, the Rabbis sent to Abba Hilkiah, the grandson
of Choni the Circle-drawer, a deputation of two scholars with the
request that he should pray for rain. They went to his house
and did not find him there. They proceeded to the field and
found him ploughing the ground. They gave him greeting but he
took no notice of them. On his return home they asked him why
he had ignored their salutation; and he replied, "I hired myself out
for the day, so I was of the opinion that I had no right to interrupt
my work"' (Taan. 23*a*, *b*).

On the same principle there is the ruling: 'A man may not work
in his field by night and hire himself out for the day. He may
not starve himself or subject himself to privation because he
diminishes the work of his employer' (p. Dammai 26*b*). For the
same reason Talmudic law permits workmen to offer part of their
daily devotions while on the top of a tree or on scaffolding (Ber. ii. 4),
and to say a shortened form of the Grace after meals (ibid. 45*b*).
Another statement is to the effect: 'Whoever disregards the
instructions of his employer is called a robber' (B.M. 78*a*, *b*).

In addition to hired workmen there was another class of labourer
—the slaves, both Jewish and gentile. With respect to them also,
the Talmud lays down precise regulations for their proper treatment. First as regards the Hebrew slave. According to Biblical
law a Hebrew may lose his status of freeman from one of two
causes: he may become destitute and sell himself for food and
lodging, or he may be sold by a Court as punishment for theft.
For a man to deprive himself of his freedom was denounced as a
reprehensible act. The regulation in Exod. xxi. 6, 'His master
shall bore his ear through with an awl,' was given this symbolical
interpretation: 'Why is the ear singled out for this purpose from all
the organs of the body? The Holy One, blessed be He, said, The
ear heard My voice on Mount Sinai when I proclaimed, "Unto Me
the children of Israel are slaves" (Lev. xxv. 55), and not the slave
of slaves, and yet this person went and acquired a master for
himself; let it be pierced. And why is the door or the door-post
singled out for this purpose from all the furniture of the house?
The Holy One, blessed be He, said, The door and door-post were
My witnesses in Egypt when I passed by the lintel and the two
door-posts and declared that Israel was to serve Me and not to
be the slave of slaves, and I took him out of bondage into freedom,
and yet this person went and acquired a master for himself; let
his ear be pierced in their presence' (Kid. 22*b*).

Still worse was the circumstance where a Hebrew sold himself
for personal gain. On the words, 'If thy brother be waxen poor

and sell himself unto thee' (Lev. xxv. 39), the Rabbis remarked, 'Hence a man is not permitted to sell himself in order to put money into his purse, or to buy cattle or furniture or a house' (Sifra ad loc.).

Restrictions were placed on the owner as to the work he could impose upon a Hebrew slave. '"Six years he shall serve" (Exod. xxi. 2)—I might infer that he is to perform any task which falls on (a gentile) slave; therefore the text declares, "Thou shalt not compel him to serve as a bondman" (Lev. xxv. 39). Hence it is said that he is not to wash his master's feet for him, or put his sandals on for him, or carry vessels for him to the bath-house, or let his master lean on him when going up the stairs, or convey him about in a litter or chair or sedan, as slaves do for their owners' (Mech. ad loc.; 75a, b).

On the same text from Exodus we have the comment: 'I might understand this as implying that he must perform a task whether it bring him a sense of shame or not; therefore Scripture declares, "As a hired servant and as a sojourner shall he be with thee" (Lev. xxv. 40). As with a hired servant you are not allowed to change his occupation for him, so with a Hebrew slave you may not impose work on him different from his usual occupation. Hence it is said that his master must not set him a task which is for the service of the public, such as the work of a tailor, bath-attendant, barber, butcher, or baker. If his former occupation included one of these, he may perform it at the behest of his master, but his master may not make any change in his work for him. "As a hired servant and as a sojourner"—as a hired servant works by day and not by night, similarly a Hebrew slave is to work by day and not by night' (Mech. loc. cit.).

With respect to his general treatment the ruling is: '"Because he is well with thee" (Deut. xv. 16)—with thee in the matter of food and drink; that you may not eat clean bread and he eat mouldy bread, that you may not drink old wine and he new wine, that you may not sleep on soft cushions and he on straw. Hence the saying, Whoever acquires a Hebrew slave acquires a master for himself' (Kid. 20a).

The term of his service was regulated by the Biblical ordinances contained in Exod. xxi. 2 ff. and Lev. xxv. 39 ff.; but wherever possible the Talmud interprets the law in favour of the slave. '"He shall serve thee six years and in the seventh year thou shalt let him go free" (Deut. xv. 12). If he ran away and returned, whence do we know that he must complete the full number of his years of work? The text declares, "Shall serve thee six years."

If he fell ill and recovered, it is possible to think that he must compensate for the time of his indisposition; therefore the text declares, "In the seventh year he shall go out free for nothing"' (Sifré ad loc., § 118; 99a). The Talmud discusses whether this applies in an extreme case where he was ill the whole six years, and decides that if his indisposition lasted three years he serves for three, but if it exceeded three years he must serve for six (Kid. 17a). On the death of the master he continues in the service of the son until the expiration of his term, but not in that of the master's daughter or other heir (ibid. 17b).

In connection with the slave whose ear was pierced, Scripture commands, 'He shall serve him for ever' (Exod. xxi. 6); but the Rabbis took the last words to mean until the year of Jubilee when he regains his freedom. Furthermore, since the text reads 'shall serve *him*,' the deduction was drawn that the slave, after the original six years, was not to serve the master's son or daughter or other heir, and he became free on his master's death (Mech. ad loc.; 77b). When a slave finished his term of service the Bible orders that he should not be dismissed empty-handed (Deut. xv. 13 f.), and the Talmud fixed the amount to be given him at thirty shekels (Kid. 17a).

The possession of a gentile slave was regulated by the law. 'He is acquired by purchase, or by document, or by actual service' (Kid. i. 3). The average price was considered to be thirty *sela*,[1] that being the amount paid as compensation to the owner if one of his slaves, male or female, was gored to death by an ox (B.K. iv. 5) A form of the document used in acquiring a slave has been preserved in the Talmud and reads: 'This slave is lawfully enslaved; he is entirely precluded from any right to freedom, and from any claims by king or queen;[2] he bears upon his person no man's mark (other than the seller's); he is clear of all physical blemish and of any skin-eruption indicative of leprosy, either new or old' (Git. 86a). The third method has this definition: 'How is he acquired by actual service? If he took (the owner's) sandals off, or carried his vessels behind him to the bath-house, undressed him, washed him, anointed his body, combed his hair, clothed him, put his sandals on, and raised him up. By these means the owner establishes a claim upon him' (Kid. 22b), these being tasks which are normally performed by a slave.

Regarding the status of the gentile slave, the important point to grasp is that, forming part of an Israelite household, he was

---

[1] A *sela* was worth about three shillings.
[2] i.e. he is not liable to service for the Government or as a convicted criminal.

subject to several of the Biblical precepts. Although not considered a member of the community, he was in certain respects within the fold of the community. As such, the first obligation that devolved upon him was that of circumcision. The question is discussed in the Talmud whether this could be done against his will, and the generally accepted rule was: 'If a slave is bought from a Gentile and he does not wish to be circumcised, the owner bears with him for twelve months, and if he then persists in his refusal, he must be resold to Gentiles' (Jeb. 48b).

The gentile slave, when circumcised, did not hold the same status as an Israelite either civilly or religiously. He was not allowed to give evidence in a court of law (R.H. I. 8). In a claim for damages, if injured by a person other than his master, he receives no compensation 'for loss of dignity' (B.K. VIII. 3).[1] He could not own property in his own right. 'What a slave has acquired his master has acquired' (Pes. 88b), i.e. it passes into the master's possession.

From the point of view of religion he was not under the obligation to visit the Temple on the three pilgrimage-festivals (Chag. I. 1). Together with women and minors he was exempt from reciting certain parts of the daily liturgy and from donning the phylacteries (Ber. III. 3). He could not be included in the quorum of three required for the more formal recitation of the Grace after meals (ibid. VII. 2), but slaves were allowed to constitute a quorum among themselves (ibid. 45b). With regard to the ten adult males necessary for a Congregational Service the Talmud states: 'Nine free men and a slave may be reckoned together for a quorum. Against this is quoted: It happened that R. Eliezer went into a Synagogue and did not find ten there, so he freed his slave and with him completed the requisite number. Since he freed him he was included; but had he not freed him, he would not.[2] Two had been required to complete the quorum, so he freed one slave and fulfilled the obligation of having ten with the other' (ibid. 47b). We see from this extract that only in an emergency was a slave permitted to contribute to a quorum in the Synagogue; and all agree that eight freemen and two slaves would not answer the purpose.

Full burial honours were likewise not paid to slaves, apart from some exceptional instances. 'When R. Gamaliel's slave, Tabi, died, he accepted condolence on his behalf. His disciples said to him, "Our master! you taught us that one may not accept condolence on the death of slaves!" He replied, "My slave, Tabi, was

---

[1] See pp. 326 f.
[2] This proves that a slave cannot be counted into the quorum, otherwise it would not have been necessary for the Rabbi to free his slave for the purpose.

not like other slaves; he was a worthy man"' (Ber. II. 7). The Talmud has this comment on the foregoing: 'At the burial of male and female slaves, we do not stand in a row for them,[1] nor do we pronounce over them the benediction of mourners and the condolence of mourners.[2] It happened that R. Eliezer's female slave died and his disciples went in to comfort him. He went into the courtway but they followed him. He entered the guest-chamber but they entered after him. He said to them, "I imagined you would be scalded with tepid water;[3] but now you are not scalded even with hot water. Have I not taught you: On the death of male and female slaves we do not stand in a row for them, nor do we pronounce over them the benediction of mourners and the condolence of mourners? What, however, do we say over them? As we say to a man on the death of his ox or ass, 'May the Omnipresent repair your loss,' so do we say to a man on the death of his slaves, 'May the Omnipresent repair your loss.'" There is a further teaching: We do not speak a funeral oration over male and female slaves. R. José said: If he was a worthy man we say of him, "Alas, the good and faithful man who derived pleasure from his work." He was asked, In that case, what have you left to be said over worthy men who are not slaves?[4] There is a further teaching: We do not call male and female slaves, "Father so-and-so," or "Mother so-and-so." But R. Gamaliel's slaves used to be called in this manner. This is an actual fact to upset the teaching just quoted! No, it is different with them, because they were highly esteemed' (ibid. 16b).

In general, the regulation which applied to women[5] held good also of slaves, viz. that they were exempt from the commandments the performance of which depended upon a point of time.

The welfare of the slave was carefully guarded and he was not left to the mercy of his master. The law of Exod. xxi. 20, 'If a man smite his servant and he die under his hand, he shall surely be punished,' was explicitly referred to a heathen slave (Mech. ad loc.; 83a). Similarly the enactment of Exod. xxi. 26, that a slave goes free if his tooth or eye was knocked out, was applied to a heathen slave (Mech. ad loc.; 85a).

---

[1] The custom was, and still is, for the friends who attend the funeral to form themselves into two rows through which the mourners pass receiving words of condolence.

[2] The first is said after the meal on returning from the cemetery. The second is a formula: May the Omnipresent comfort you in the midst of the other mourners of Zion and Jerusalem.

[3] i.e. I gave you a plain hint that I did not wish to receive your condolence.

[4] What higher praise could be spoken of any man?

[5] See p. 159.

Generally speaking, the Israelite treated his slave with consideration. It is, for example, told that 'when R. Jochanan ate meat
he always gave some to his slave. When he drank wine he also
gave him some, and applied the text to himself, "Did not He that
made me in the womb make him?" (Job xxxi. 15)' (p. B.K. 6c).

In the ordinary way a slave remained in his master's service
until death released him; but he could gain his freedom if anybody
paid the owner the usual price or if the owner gave him a certificate
of manumission (Kid. I. 3). Several other circumstances are mentioned which secured him liberty. 'If a man bequeaths his
possession to his slave, the latter immediately becomes a freeman' (Peah III. 8), because it was the obvious intention of the
owner that he should be free, since a slave could not own property.
'A slave who marries a freewoman in the presence of his master [1]
goes forth into freedom' (Git. 39b et seq.); and 'A slave who lays
the phylacteries in the presence of his master goes forth to freedom'
(ibid. 40a). In both cases there is the implied intention to release
him, seeing that a slave could not marry a free Jewess nor was he
entitled to wear the phylacteries, that being a duty which devolved
only upon an Israelite. A very considerate regulation was: 'If
one sell his slave to a heathen or to one who resides outside the
Holy Land, he obtains his freedom' (ibid. IV. 6).[2]

Nevertheless the slave class was despised and credited with
certain faults. Slaves were generally supposed to be lazy. 'Ten
measures of sleep descended into the world; slaves took nine of
them and the rest of mankind one' (Kid. 49b); 'A slave is not worth
the food of his stomach' (B.K. 97a). They were untrustworthy:
'There is no faithfulness in slaves' (B.M. 86b). Their moral
standard was low: 'The more maidservants the more lewdness,
the more menservants the more robbery' (Aboth II. 8); and 'A slave
prefers a dissolute life with female slaves (to a regular marriage)'
(Git. 13a).

§ IV. PEACE AND JUSTICE

The stability, as well as the happiness, of a community can only
be assured when it rests upon a foundation of peace. Talmudic
aphorisms on this subject are numerous. Some examples are:
'By three things is the world preserved: by truth, by judgment,

[1] That means with his master's knowledge and consent.
[2] If the slave runs away from his heathen master and flees to an Israelite
for protection he is not surrendered. His action is taken to indicate that
he desires to continue to conform to the precepts which he observed before
he was sold.

and by peace; as it is said, "Judge ye the truth and the judgment of peace in your gates" (Zech. viii. 16)' (Aboth I. 18). '"Ye shall not cut yourselves" (Deut. xiv. 1)—do not form yourselves into sections, but be all of you one band' (Sifré ad loc., 94a).[1] '"The Lord shall be unto thee an everlasting light" (Is. lx. 19)—when you will all be a single band; as it is said, "Ye are alive every one of you this day" (Deut. iv. 4). It is the experience of the world that if a man takes a bundle of reeds he is unable to break them while they are tied together; but if they are taken singly, even a child can break them' (Tanchuma Nitzabim § 1).

In the absence of peace there can be neither prosperity nor well-being. '"The land shall yield her increase" (Lev. xxvi. 4)—lest you should say, Behold there is food and drink (what more do we want?). But if there is no peace, there is nothing; so the text continues, "I will give peace in the land" (ibid. 6). It declares that peace is equal in worth to everything' (Sifra ad loc.). 'Beloved is peace, since the benedictions only conclude with the hope of peace. Similarly the priestly benediction concludes with "and give thee peace" (Num. vi. 26), thus teaching that the blessings are of no avail unless accompanied by peace' (Num. R. XI. 7).

That God intended the world to be blessed with peace is illustrated in this manner: 'Mankind was first created as a single individual because of the various families which have issued from him, that they should not quarrel one with the other. Since now there is so much strife although he was created one, how much more so if there had been two created!' (Sanh. 38a).

Great praise is bestowed upon the peacemaker. One of the virtues of which man eats the fruit in this world and the capital remains for the World to Come is 'establishing peace between a man and his fellow' (Peah. I. 1). Strikingly beautiful is this legend: 'A Rabbi was standing in a market-place when Elijah appeared to him. The Rabbi asked him, "Is there anybody in this market-place who will have a share in the World to Come?" Elijah answered there was not. In the meanwhile there came two men, and Elijah said, "These will have a share in the World to Come." The Rabbi asked them, "What is your occupation?" They answered, "We are merrymakers; when we see men troubled in mind we cheer them, and when we see two men quarrelling we make peace between them"' (Taan. 22a).

One of Hillel's favourite maxims was, 'Be of the disciples of Aaron, loving peace and pursuing peace' (Aboth I. 12), and it was elaborated as follows: 'How is one a lover of peace? It teaches

[1] There is a play of words here: 'to cut' is *gud*, and 'band' is *agudah*.

that a man must love peace to abide in Israel among all individuals in the same way that Aaron loved peace to abide among all individuals; as it is said, "The law of truth was in his mouth; he walked with Me in peace and uprightness and did turn many away from iniquity" (Mal. ii. 6). What means "did turn many away from iniquity"? When Aaron walked along the street and met a wicked man, he gave him greeting. The next day, when that person wanted to commit a transgression, he would say to himself, "How can I, after doing such an act, lift up my eyes and look at Aaron? I should feel ashamed before him who gave me greeting." As a consequence he would refrain from doing wrong. Similarly, when two men were at enmity with each other, Aaron would visit one of them and say to him, "My son, see how your friend is behaving; he beats his breast, tears his garment, and cries, 'Woe is me, how can I look in to the face of my friend? I am ashamed before him since it was I who acted shabbily towards him!'" Aaron would continue to sit with him until he had banished all enmity from his heart. Then he went and spoke exactly the same words to the other party until he had removed all enmity from him. The result was that when the two men met they embraced and kissed one another' (ARN xii).

Another famous peacemaker was R. Meïr, of whom this story is narrated: 'He used to lecture in the Synagogue every Sabbath-eve and a certain woman attended to listen to him. On one occasion he prolonged his discourse, and when the woman arrived home she found the lamp extinguished. Her husband demanded to know where she had been, and she told him that she had been listening to the lecturer. He took an oath that he would not allow her to enter the house until she spat in the Rabbi's face. By means of the Holy Spirit R. Meïr knew what had happened, pretended that his eyes were sore, and announced, "Let any woman who is able to cure a sore eye by a spell [1] come and do so." The woman's neighbour said to her, "Now is your opportunity of getting back into your house. Pretend that you can cure him and spit in his eyes." She went to him, and he said to her, "Are you able to use a charm for the eyes?" Out of respect for him she replied that she could not; but he told her to spit seven times into his eyes (without a charm) and he would be better. When she had done so he said to her, "Go, tell your husband that he wanted you to spit only once, but you have done it seven times." His disciples exclaimed, "Is the Torah to be despised in this way! If she had informed us of what had happened, we would have brought him

[1] It usually included the use of spittle, see p. 253.

here and chastised him with straps until he became reconciled with his wife." He replied to them, "Should not the honour of Meïr be like the honour of his Maker? If Scripture allows the divine Name, written in holiness, to be blotted out by water (see Num. v. 23) for the purpose of establishing peace between husband and wife, should this not be so all the more with Meïr?"' (p. Sot. 16*d*).

The harmful consequences of quarrelling are forcibly pointed out. 'Strife is like the aperture of a leakage; as the aperture widens so the stream of water increases. Strife is like the plank of a bridge; the longer it exists the firmer it becomes' (Sanh. 7*a*). A proverb tells: 'He who gives vent to his wrath destroys his house' (ibid. 102*b*). 'There are three classes of people whose life is scarcely life: the (too sensitively) compassionate, the irritable, and the melancholic' (Pes. 113*b*).

To avoid quarrelling is highly commended. Another proverb runs: 'Happy is he who hears (an insult) and ignores it; a hundred evils pass him by' (Sanh. 7*a*). 'When two quarrel, he who keeps silence first is more praiseworthy' (Kid. 71*b*). 'There are four kinds of tempers: he whom it is easy to provoke and easy to pacify, his loss disappears in his gain; he whom it is hard to provoke and hard to pacify, his gain disappears in his loss; he whom it is hard to provoke and easy to pacify is a saint; he whom it is easy to provoke and hard to pacify is a wicked man' (Aboth v. 14).

Not content with lauding peace, the Talmud indicates what is essential for its maintenance and what is apt to destroy it. The causes are summarized in this statement: 'The sword comes into the world for the delay of justice, and for the perversion of justice, and on account of the offence of those who interpret the Torah not according to its true sense' (Aboth v. 11). Truth and justice are the prerequisite to peace and its surest safeguard. The maxim quoted above, 'By three things is the world preserved: by truth, by judgment, and by peace' (ibid. i. 18), is cited in the Talmud with this comment: 'The three are really one; if judgment is executed, truth is vindicated and peace results' (p. Taan. 68*a*). Another doctrine based upon it is: 'Do not despise justice, since it is one of the three feet of the world; and take care not to pervert justice, for by so doing you shake the world' (Deut. R. v. 1).

The supreme importance of justice is inculcated in the teaching that it is greatly superior to the offerings in the Temple. 'Sacrifices were only offered within the Sanctuary, but righteousness and justice apply both within it and without. Sacrifices only atoned for one who sinned in error, but righteousness and justice atone for him who sins either in error or intentionally. Sacrifices are

only offered by human beings, but righteousness and justice must
be practised both by human beings and the celestial creatures.
Sacrifices are only offered in this world, but righteousness and
justice must be done both in this world and the World to Come.
The Holy One, blessed be He, declares, The righteousness and
justice you perform are dearer to me than the Temple' (Deut. R.
v. 3). Among the answers to the question, Upon what does the
world stand? is this: 'Upon one pillar and its name is the Righteous,[1]
as it is said, "The righteous is the foundation of the world" (Prov.
x. 25)' (Chag. 12b).

The attitude of the Rabbis towards justice in the governing of
the State is admirably reflected in this legend: 'Alexander of
Macedon visited King Katzya,[2] who displayed to him an abundance
of gold and silver. Alexander said to him, "I have no need of
your gold and silver. My only purpose in coming is to see your
customs, how you act and administer justice." While they were
engaged in conversation, a man came before the king with a case
against his fellow from whom he had bought a field with its scrap-
heap and in it discovered a bundle of coins buried. The purchaser
contended, "I bought the heap but not the treasure hidden in it";
and the vendor asserted, "I sold the heap and all it contained."
While they were arguing together, the king turned to one of them
and asked, "Have you a son?" "Yes," he replied. He asked the
other, "Have you a daughter?" and he answered, "Yes." "Let
them marry and give them the treasure," was the king's decision.
Alexander began to laugh, and Katzya inquired, "Why do you
laugh? Did I not judge well? Suppose such a case happened
with you, how would you have dealt with it?" He replied, "I
would have put them both to death and confiscated the treasure."
"Do you, then, love gold so much?" said Katzya, and made a
feast for him at which he was served with golden cutlets and
golden poultry. "I do not eat gold," he exclaimed; and the king
retorted, "A curse alight upon you! if you do not eat gold, why
do you love it so intensely?" He continued to ask, "Does the sun
shine in your country?" "Certainly," was the reply. "Does
rain descend in your country?" "Of course." "Are there small
cattle in your country?" "Of course." "A curse alight upon you!
you only live, then, by the merit of those animals!"' (p. B.M. 8c).

The administrators of justice accordingly bear a heavy responsibility, since upon them depends the fate of the entire community.
'A judge should always imagine that a sword was pointed at his

[1] i.e. God in His aspect of righteousness.
[2] He reigned over a country behind the mysterious 'dark mountain.'

heart and Gehinnom yawned at his feet' (Sanh. 7a). 'Whence is it derived that when three sit and judge, the *Shechinah* is with them? It is said, "He judgeth among the judges" (Ps. lxxxii. 1)' (Ber. 6a). 'A judge who administers justice equitably causes the *Shechinah* to alight upon Israel; as it is said, "He judgeth among the judges." And a judge who does not administer justice equitably causes the *Shechinah* to depart from Israel; as it is said, "For the spoiling of the poor, for the sighing of the needy, now will I arise, saith the Lord" (ibid. xii. 5)' (Sanh. 7a).

How injustice ruins the happiness of the community is strongly remarked in this passage: 'If you see a generation afflicted with many troubles, go and scrutinize the judges of Israel, because all the adversities which come upon the world are only due to the judges in Israel; as it is said, "Hear this, I pray you, ye heads of the house of Jacob and rulers of the house of Israel, that abhor judgment and pervert all equity," etc. (Micah iii. 9 ff.). They are wicked and yet put their trust in Him Who spake and the world came into being. Accordingly the Holy One, blessed be He, brings upon them three punishments corresponding to the three transgressions of which they are guilty; as it is said, "Therefore shall Zion for your sake be ploughed as a field, and Jerusalem shall become heaps, and the mountain of the house as the high places of the forest" (ibid. 12). Moreover, the Holy One, blessed be He, does not cause His *Shechinah* to alight upon Israel until the evil judges and officials are exterminated from Israel; as it is said, "I will turn My hand upon thee, and thoroughly purge away thy dross, and will take away thy alloy; and I will restore thy judges as at the first, and thy counsellors as at the beginning; afterward thou shalt be called the city of righteousness, the faithful city" (Is. i. 25 f.)' (Shab. 139a).

The qualifications which should be possessed by a judge are set very high. 'He should be appointed as judge in his city who is wise, humble, sin-fearing, of good repute, and popular with his fellow-men' (Tosifta Sanh. VII. 1); and it is stated, 'Who appoints a man as judge who is unfitted is as though he had set up an idolatrous image in Israel' (Sanh. 7b).[1]

That the strictest impartiality was demanded of a judge is strikingly demonstrated in this piece of exegesis: '"Thou shalt not respect the person of the poor" (Lev. xix. 15)—you shall not say, He is poor; and since I and this rich man[2] are under the obligation to support him, I will pronounce judgment in his favour

[1] See further on this subject, pp. 305 f.
[2] The other party to the suit.

and he will then be able to maintain himself honourably' (Sifra
ad loc.).

The warning against bribery receives the most extreme interpretation. '"Thou shalt take no bribe" (Exod. xxiii. 8). What
has the text to teach? That a judge may not acquit the guilty
or condemn the innocent? Behold, it has already been stated,
"Thou shalt not wrest judgment" (ibid. 6)! But a bribe may not
be taken even to acquit the innocent or condemn the guilty'
(Keth. 105a). 'It is unnecessary to state that a judge may not
accept a bribe of money; but even a bribe of words [1] is forbidden.
For instance, a Rabbi was passing over a bridge when a man gave
him his hand to support him. He asked, "Why have you done
this?" and the reply came, "I have a lawsuit pending." "Then,"
said the Rabbi, "I am disqualified from deciding it"' (ibid. 105b).

In the face of this demand for the strictest justice it may seem
strange to find one teacher, R. Ishmael, offering the advice, 'When
an Israelite and a Gentile are the parties to a suit, if it is possible
to give the former the judgment according to the Jewish code of
law, do so and tell him that such is our law; if he can be given
judgment according to the gentile code of law, do so and tell the
non-Jew that such is his law. If neither code is of avail, use a
subterfuge. Such is the opinion of R. Ishmael; but R. Akiba
denied the admissibility of a subterfuge because of the sanctification of the Name' [2] (B.K. 113a). The view of R. Ishmael is
denounced by R. Simeon b. Gamaliel, who said: 'If the Gentile
comes to be judged by the Jewish code, then decide accordingly;
if he wishes to be judged by the gentile code, then decide accordingly' (Sifré Deut. § 16; 68b). We have to detect in the opinion
of R. Ishmael an attempt to counterbalance the disabilities and
injustices which the Jew usually suffered in non-Jewish Courts,
but it was rejected by the Rabbinic authorities.

[1] i.e. something immaterial.   [2] See p. 23.

CHAPTER VII

THE MORAL LIFE

§ I. Imitation of God

From the theory of Torah which underlies the whole of Talmudic doctrine, it inevitably follows that the way to the living of the moral life must be sought, and could only be found, in the Divine Revelation. What the Torah commands and prohibits is the sure guidance, and morality consists in compliance with its precepts.

This thought is quite explicitly expressed by the Rabbis. They make this comment on the phrase, 'These words, which I command thee this day, shall be upon thine heart' (Deut. vi. 6): 'Put these words upon your heart that thereby you may recognize the Holy One, blessed be He, and cleave to His ways' (Sifré Deut. § 33; 74a). On the verse, 'That ye may remember and do all My commandments and be holy unto your God' (Num. xv. 40), there is this significant exhortation: 'Parable of a man who had fallen into the sea. The captain of the boat threw him a rope and said, "Cling to this rope and do not let go of it; if you loosen your hold upon it you will drown!" Similarly said the Holy One, blessed be He, to Israel, "So long as you cleave to the commandments, 'you cleave unto the Lord your God and are alive every one of you this day' (Deut. iv. 4); and it is also said, 'Take fast hold of instruction, let her not go; keep her, for she is thy life' (Prov. iv. 13). 'And be holy'—so long as you fulfil the commandments you are rendered holy"' (Num. R. xvii. 6).

In addition to instituting the precepts of the Torah, God set the Israelites an example of obedience by fulfilling them Himself. 'It is the custom of a human king to make a decree, and if he desires to obey it himself he does so, but if not it is obeyed by others. With the Holy One, blessed be He, it is otherwise. When He makes a decree He performs it first; as it is written, "Thou shalt rise up before the hoary head, and honour the face of the old man, and thou shalt fear thy God: I am the Lord" (Lev. xix. 32)—I am He Who fulfilled the command of rising up before the hoary head first'[1] (Lev. R. xxxv. 3).

---

[1] This is based on the Rabbinic theory that the words 'Abraham stood yet before the Lord' (Gen. xviii. 22) were a reverential alteration of the Scribes from an original text, 'The Lord stood yet before Abraham,' since the chapter opens with 'The Lord appeared unto him (Abraham)' (Gen. R. xlix. 7).

Therefore, not only in His commandments did God provide the human being with guidance to the true way of life, but in Himself He set the example which is to be followed. The Imitation of God is, in Rabbinic literature, set forward as the ideal after which man should strive. God is the Pattern after which human life must be delineated. Conspicuous in Him are the qualities which should be prominent in human conduct.

This doctrine is taught in several places: 'What means the text, "Ye shall walk after the Lord your God" (Deut. xiii. 4)? Is it, then, possible for a man to walk after the *Shechinah* of which it is written, "The Lord thy God is a devouring fire" (ibid. iv. 24)? But the meaning is to follow the attributes of the Holy One, blessed be He: as He clothed the naked (Gen. iii. 21), so do you clothe the naked; as He visited the sick (ibid. xviii. 1), so do you visit the sick; as He comforted mourners (ibid. xxv. 11), so do you comfort those who mourn; as He buried the dead (Deut. xxxiv. 6), so do you bury the dead' (Sot. 14*a*).

'"To walk in all His ways" (Deut. xi. 22)—i.e. the characteristics of the Holy One, blessed be He; as it is said, "The Lord, the Lord, a God full of compassion and gracious, slow to anger, and plenteous in mercy and truth" (Exod. xxxiv. 6); and it is said, "Whosoever shall be called by (*sic*) the name of the Lord shall be delivered" (Joel ii. 32). But how is it possible for a man to be called by the name of the Holy One, blessed be He? As the All-present is called compassionate and gracious, so be you also compassionate and gracious, and offering free gifts to all. As the Holy One, blessed be He, is called righteous (Ps. cxlv. 17), be you also righteous; as He is called loving (ibid.), be you also loving' (Sifré Deut. § 49; 85*a*).

'"This is my God and I will adorn (*sic*) Him" (Exod. xv. 2) Is it, then, possible to adorn God? Yes, by resembling Him; as He is compassionate and gracious, be also compassionate and gracious' (Mech. ad loc.; 37*a*). 'The King has a retinue; what is its duty? To imitate the King' (Sifra to Lev. xix. 2). 'Be like Me; as I repay good for evil, so do you repay good for evil' (Exod. R. xxvi. 2). 'A man should always learn from the mind of his Maker. Behold the Holy One, blessed be He, ignored (lofty) mountains and hills and caused his *Shechinah* to alight on Mount Sinai (which is lowly), and ignored all the fine trees and caused His *Shechinah* to alight upon a bush' (Sot. 5*a*). Similarly, man should not be haughty and should associate with the humble.

The Rabbis, on the other hand, did not overlook that in the Bible qualities are attributed to God which should not be copied by man, such as jealousy and anger; and they offer a reason why in such matters the doctrine of Imitation does not apply. '"I the Lord thy God am a jealous God" (Exod. xx. 5)—I am the Master of jealousy and jealousy is not master of Me' (Mech. ad loc.; 68a). 'With a human king wrath controls him, but the Holy One, blessed be He, controls His wrath; as it is said, "The Lord avengeth and is full of wrath" ¹ (Nahum i. 2)' (Gen. R. xlix. 8).

The doctrine of the Imitation of God is, accordingly, not only the actual foundation of Talmudic ethics but its motive and inspiration. It created the feeling in man that when his life was morally right, he gained the approval of his Maker, but more important than that, established his kinship with God. It thereby provided the all-sufficient incitement to righteous conduct.

§ II. Brotherly Love

R. Akiba said of the command, 'Thou shalt love thy neighbour as thyself' (Lev. xix. 18), that it was 'a fundamental principle of the Torah.' His colleague, Ben Azzai, cited as a principle of still greater importance, 'This is the book of the generations of Adam . . · in the likeness of God made He him' (Gen. v. 1) (Sifra ad loc.). Universal love is here proclaimed not merely as the ideal advocated in the Torah but as the only true standard of human relationship. While the first Rabbi referred to the explicit commandment, the second teacher based the ideal on the doctrine that all human beings are descended from one ancestor and are therefore bound together by the kinship of a common origin, and also that they share one inestimable privilege, viz. of having been created in the divine likeness. 'With a solemn warning was the declaration made, "Thou shalt love they neighbour as thyself." I (God) created him; and if you love him, I am faithful to repay you a good reward; but if you do not love him, I am the Judge to exact a penalty' (ARN xvi).

Another expression of the same idea is the following: 'What message did the Torah bring to Israel? Take upon yourselves the yoke of the kingdom of heaven, vie one with the other in the fear of God and practise loving deeds towards one another' (Sifré Deut. § 323; 138b).

Whether the term 'neighbour' in Leviticus applies only to a fellow-Israelite, or is universal in its scope, is not a question which concerns us here.² Note must, however, be taken of the

¹ The Hebrew is literally 'master of wrath.'
² See on the subject, R. T. Herford, *Talmud and Apocrypha*, pp. 144 ff.

assertion which is often made that the law of love as expounded in the Talmud is limited to the members of the Israelite community.[1] It is true that in commenting on the word 'neighbour' in connection with Biblical legislation, the Talmud frequently specifies that the Israelite is meant to the exclusion of the Gentile; but it does so because the Scriptural text is to be understood in that way. It cannot be logically or justly deduced from this fact that the Rabbis advocated the practice of ethical principles in connection with none but co-religionists.

It may also be freely conceded that among the thousands of *obiter dicta* from hundreds of Rabbis, there are some which do not reveal feelings of brotherly love towards men not of their faith and race. Bitter experience sometimes found expression in a harsh utterance. This matter has already been touched upon;[2] but an unbiased examination of the literature can only lead to the conclusion that in general the Rabbinic outlook in the sphere of morals was universal and not national. In many ethical maxims the term employed is *beriyyoth*, which means 'creatures,' 'human beings,' and cannot possibly be given a restricted connotation. 'Be a lover of your fellow-creatures' (Aboth I. 12), was Hillel's exhortation. Some of them, indeed, make definite reference to the non-Jew, e.g. 'One may not steal the mind of (i.e. deceive) his fellow-creatures, not even a Gentile' (Chul 94a); 'More serious is stealing from a Gentile than from an Israelite, because it involves in addition profaning the Name' (Tosifta B.K. x. 15).

We perceive the same broad principle in the treatment of such a law as, 'If thou meet thine enemy's ox or his ass going astray, thou shalt surely bring it back to him again' (Exod. xxiii. 4). On this the remark is made: '"Thine enemy's ox," that refers to a Gentile who is an idolater; from here we learn that idolaters are everywhere designated enemies of Israel' (Mech. ad loc.; 90a). The intention is that although there must of necessity exist a feeling of antagonism towards idol worshippers, it must not overrule the claims of humanity. In many matters of this kind the Talmud permits the Jew to go beyond the strict letter of the law 'because of the ways of peace,' i.e. so as not to disturb harmonious relationship. An instance is the ruling with respect to the poor: 'We do not prevent the poor of the Gentiles from benefiting under the ordinances concerning gleanings, forgotten sheaves, and the corner of the field (Lev. xix. 9 f.)' (Git. v. 8); and this is expanded

---

[1] For a full and frank discussion of this question, the reader is referred to C. G. Montefiore, *Rabbinic Literature and Gospel Teachings*, pp. 59 f.

[2] See p. 66.

into: 'Our Rabbis have taught, We must support the poor of the Gentiles with the poor of Israel, visit the sick of the Gentiles with the sick of Israel, and give honourable burial to the dead of the Gentiles as to the dead of Israel, because of the ways of peace' (ibid. 61a).

The story has been told [1] how Hillel answered the request of the heathen who wished to be converted to Judaism on condition that he was taught the whole Torah while he stood on one foot. The Rabbi answered him, 'What is hateful to yourself, do not to your fellow-man' (Shab. 31a). This is the Talmudic formulation of the Golden Rule. Great stress has been laid by theologians of a certain school upon the fact that Hillel's maxim is worded in the negative, [2] whereas the Gospels have it in a positive form. Profound ethical differences are detected by them in the variation; but they who have no theological axe to grind will probably agree with the conclusion of Professor Kittel: 'In reality almost everything which has been thought to exist in delicate difference between the negative and positive form is due to modern reflection on the subject. For the consciousness of the age of Jesus the two forms were scarcely distinguishable. The proof of that is that in the oldest Christian literature the two forms are recorded promiscuously. The idea of a difference between them was quite unapparent to the men of antiquity.' [3]

Even the negative form could produce fine ethical fruit, as is evidenced by a variant to the story of Hillel. 'It is related that an ass-driver came to R. Akiba and said to him, "Rabbi, teach me the whole Torah all at once." He replied, "My son, Moses our teacher stayed on the Mount forty days and forty nights before he learned it, and you want me to teach you the whole of it all at once! Still, my son, this is the basic principle of the Torah: What is hateful to yourself, do not to your fellow-man. If you wish that nobody should harm you in connection with what belongs to you, you must not harm him in that way; if you wish that nobody should deprive you of what is yours, you must not deprive your fellow-man of what belongs to him." The man rejoined his companions and they journeyed until they came to a field full of seed-pods. His companions each took two but he took none. They continued their journey and came to a field full of cabbages.

---

[1] See p. 65.
[2] Hillel was probably quoting, because Tobit iv. 15 has, 'What you yourself hate do to no man.' An instructive article on 'The "Negative" Golden Rule' appeared in the *Journal of Religion*, viii. pp. 268–79, by G. B. King, who traces it in several pre-Christian sources.
[3] Quoted by Montefiore, op. cit., p. 151.

They each took two but he took none. They asked him why he
had not taken any, and he replied, "Thus did R. Akiba teach me:
What is hateful to yourself, do not to your fellow-man."'[1]

The rule receives many applications in the Talmud. 'A man
should always be of the pursued and not of the pursuers' (B.K.
93a); 'They who are oppressed and oppress not, who listen to
insults without retorting, who act lovingly and are happy under
trials, of them it is written, "Let them who love Him be as the
sun when it goeth forth in its might" (Judges v. 31)' (Shab. 88b);
and there is a proverb, 'Be the cursed and not the curser' (Sanh. 49a).

It becomes still clearer in the elaboration of two aphorisms: 'Let
your fellow-man's honour be as dear to you as your own' (Aboth II,
15): 'How is this? It teaches that just as a man has a regard for
his own honour, so must he have a regard for the honour of his
fellow-man; just as he desires that there should be no reflection
on his good repute, so must he be anxious not to damage the reputation of his fellow-man' (ARN xv). Similarly with the maxim:
'Let the property of your fellow-man be as dear to you as your
own' (Aboth II. 17): 'How is this? It teaches that just as a man
has a regard for his own property, so must he have a regard for the
property of his fellow-man; just as he desires that there should be
no ugly rumours about (the way he acquired) his property, so must
he be anxious that no reflection should be made with respect to
his fellow-man' (ARN xvII).

In addition to the command to love there is the command not
to hate. '"Thou shalt not hate thy brother in thy heart" (Lev.
xix. 17)—it is possible to think that (all the Torah requires is) you
should not curse him or smite him or slap his face; therefore the
text adds "in thy heart," the intention being to forbid hatred
which is in the heart' (Sifra ad loc.). 'Hatred of one's fellow-
creatures' is one of the three vices 'that put a man out of the
world' (Aboth II. 16).

A concrete illustration of the teaching is given in connection
with one of the heroines of the Talmud: 'There were some lawless
men living in the neighbourhood of R. Meïr and they used to vex
him sorely. Once R. Meïr prayed that they should die. His wife,
Beruriah, exclaimed, "What is in your mind? Is it because it is
written, 'Let sinners cease out of the earth' (Ps. civ. 35)? But
the text can be read so as to mean, 'Let sins[2] cease out of the

---

[1] This story is given in the second recension of ARN, ed. Schechter, xxvi.
p. 53.
[2] The same consonants may be vocalized to give the word for 'sins' instead
of 'sinners.' The Hebrew text in the Talmudic era had no vowels, so
Beruriah's reading reflected her magnanimity.

earth,' Glance also at the end of the verse, 'and let the wicked
be no more'—i.e. when 'sins shall cease' then 'the wicked will be
no more.' Rather should you pray that they repent and be no
more wicked!" R. Meïr offered prayer on their behalf and they
repented' (Ber. 10a).

No finer summary of the Rabbinic teaching on the subject of
brotherly love could be suggested than the pithy epigram: 'Who is
mighty? He who turns an enemy into his friend' (ARN xxiii).

§ III. Humility

Whereas one Rabbi declared 'saintliness' to be the supreme
virtue, a colleague maintained: 'Humility is the greatest of all
virtues; as it is said, "The spirit of the Lord God is upon me,
because the Lord hath anointed me to preach good tidings unto
the meek" (Is. lxi. 1). It is not stated "to the saints" but "to
the meek"; hence learn that humility is the supreme virtue'
(A.Z. 20b). Great praise is bestowed upon one who possesses this
characteristic. 'Who is a son of the World to Come? He who is
humble, of lowly disposition, enters and leaves a room with bent
form, and studies Torah constantly without claiming any credit
for himself' (Sanh. 88b). 'If one makes himself lowly, the Holy
One, blessed be He, raises him on high; and if one raises himself
on high, the Holy One, blessed be He, brings him low' (Erub. 13b);
'Whoever runs after greatness, greatness flees from him; and
whoever flees from greatness, greatness runs after him' (ibid.).

Meekness is so favoured by God that it causes the attraction of
the *Shechinah*, while pride has the reverse effect. 'The Holy One,
blessed be He, only causes His *Shechinah* to alight upon him who
is brave, rich,[1] wise, and meek' (Ned. 38a). '"And Moses drew
near unto the thick darkness" (Exod. xx. 21). His humility
induced him to do that; as it is said, "The man Moses was very
meek" (Num. xii. 3). Scripture informs us that whoever is humble
finally causes the *Shechinah* to dwell with man upon earth; and
whoever is arrogant defiles the earth and causes the *Shechinah* to
depart. He is also called an abomination; as it is said, "Every one

---

[1] Maimonides understood these words in the special sense given to them by
the Rabbis. 'By "rich" they designate the moral perfection of contentment,
for they call the contented man rich, their definition of the word "rich"
being, "Who is rich? He who is contented with his lot" (Aboth iv. 1).
Likewise "brave" stands for a moral perfection; that is, one who is brave
guides his faculties in accordance with intelligence and reason. The Rabbis
say, "Who is brave? He who subdues his passions" (ibid.)' (*The Eight
Chapters of Maimonides on Ethics*, ed. Gorfinkle, p. 80).

that is proud in heart is an abomination to the Lord" (Prov. xvi. 5)' (Mech. ad loc.; 72a). 'He who walks with an erect carriage (i.e. haughtily), even a distance of four cubits, is as though he pushed against the feet of the *Shechinah*; for it is written, "The whole earth is full of His glory" (Is. vi. 3)' (Ber. 43b).

The severest condemnation is meted out to the haughty. 'Every man who is filled with an arrogant spirit is as though he had worshipped idols, denied the basic principle of religion, and committed every kind of immorality; he deserves to be hewn down like an idolatrous image; his dust will not be moved [1] and the *Shechinah* laments over him. Not like the attribute of the Holy One, blessed be He, is the attribute of the human being. With men the exalted notice the exalted, but the exalted do not notice the lowly. With the Holy One, blessed be He, it is otherwise; He is exalted and notices the lowly. Whoever is possessed of an arrogant spirit, the Holy One, blessed be He, says, I and he cannot dwell in the world together' (Sot. 4b et seq.).

Some maxims on this subject in the Tractate *Aboth* read: 'A name made great is a name destroyed' (I. 13). 'Reflect upon three things and you will not come within the power of sin: know whence you came, and whither you are going, and before Whom you will in future have to give account and reckoning. Whence you came —from a putrefying drop; whither you are going—to a place of dust, worms, and maggots; and before Whom you will in future have to give account and reckoning—before the Supreme King of kings, the Holy One, blessed be He' (II. 1). 'Be exceedingly lowly of spirit, since the hope of man is but the worm' (IV. 4). 'Be humble of spirit before all men' (IV. 12). 'A good eye (i.e. unenvious disposition), a humble mind, and a lowly spirit are attributes of the disciples of Abraham our father' (V. 22).

One class of pride was singled out for special warning, viz. the pride of scholarship. Since the greatest value was attached to learning and the highest honours paid to those who possessed it, they were particularly liable to succumb to the vice of self-glorification. For that reason, the idea that humility must accompany knowledge finds frequent mention. Meekness is one of the forty-eight qualifications requisite in a student of the Torah.[2] 'What means that which is written, "From the wilderness to Mattanah" [3] (Num. xxi. 18)? If a man makes himself like a wilderness in which

---

[1] i.e. will not share in the Resurrection.

[2] See the passage cited on pp. 130 f.

[3] Mattanah is the name of a place; but as a Hebrew word it means 'gift' and is here taken to indicate the gift of Torah.

all may tread, his learning will endure in him, otherwise it will not' (Erub. 54a). '"It is not in heaven . . . neither is it beyond the sea" (Deut. xxx. 12 f.). You will not find Torah in those who are arrogant nor in traders whose business calls for much travelling' (Erub. 55a). 'Whoever exalts himself by means of words of Torah, to what is he like? To a carcass flung into the road from which passers-by protect their nose and keep away. If, however, a man stultifies himself with words of Torah, lives on dates and locusts, wears shabby garments, and keeps watch at the door of the learned, people may deem him a fool, but in the end you will find that he is in possession of the entire Torah' (ARN xi).

The Talmudic evidence proves that the Rabbis, taking them as a whole, were conspicuous for their humility. The supreme example is Hillel, the most famed of them all and likewise the humblest. A favourite saying of his was: 'My abasement is my exaltation and my exaltation is my abasement' (Lev. R. 1. 5). On his death, the funeral oration pronounced over him was worded: 'Alas, the humble and pious man, the disciple of Ezra' (Sot. 48b).

The following anecdote illustrates this side of his nature. 'Our Rabbis have taught: A man should always be meek like Hillel and not hasty-tempered like Shammai. It happened that two men made a wager that whoever succeeded in making Hillel lose his temper should receive four hundred *zuz*. That day chanced to be the eve of the Sabbath and Hillel was washing his head. One of the men came to the door of his house and shouted, "Is Hillel here?[1] Is Hillel here?" Hillel wrapped himself, came out to him and asked, "What do you want, my son?" "I have a question to put to you." "Ask it, my son." "Why are the Babylonians round-headed?" "You have put an important question to me. The reason is that they have no skilled midwives." The man went away, waited a brief while, and returned shouting, "Is Hillel here? Is Hillel here?" The Rabbi wrapped himself, came out to him and inquired, "What do you want, my son?" "I have a question to put to you." "Ask it, my son." "Why are the inhabitants of Palmyra blear-eyed?" "You have asked an important question. The reason is that they live in sandy districts." The man went away, waited a brief while, and returned shouting, "Is Hillel here? Is Hillel here?" The Rabbi wrapped himself, came out to him and inquired, "What do you want, my son?" "I have a question to put to you." "Ask it, my son." "Why are the Africans broad-footed?" "You have asked an important

---

[1] This was an intentionally rude way to ask for the Rabbi, the object being to ruffle his dignity.

question. The reason is that they live in marshy districts."
The man said, "I have many more questions to ask, but I am afraid
of provoking your anger." Hillel folded the wrapper round himself, sat down and said, "Ask all that you desire." "Are you
Hillel whom people call Prince in Israel?" "I am." "If so,
may there not be many like you in Israel!" "Why, my son?"
"Because I have lost four hundred *zuz* through you." The Rabbi
then told him, "Be careful, Hillel is worthy that you should lose
still another four hundred *zuz* on his account rather than you
should make him lose his temper"' (Shab. 30*b et seq.*).

§ IV. CHARITY

Conspicuous among the features which distinguish the moral life
is the eager desire to be as helpful as possible to one's fellow-
creatures who stand in need of assistance. Charity, as conceived
in the Talmud, falls into two distinct categories. The first is
almsgiving, which is designated *Tzedakah.*

The use of this word to denote monetary help to the poor is
interesting and explains the attitude taken up by the Rabbis
towards this form of charity. Its proper meaning is 'righteousness.' Some scholars detect the new connotation already in the
Bible. In the Aramaic portion of Daniel (iv. 27) there is the
statement: 'Break off thy sins by *Tzidkah* and thine iniquities by
shewing mercy to the poor.' Whether the word signifies here
'righteousness,' or is defined by the second clause as 'almsgiving,' cannot be determined with certainty; but in the Book of Ecclesiasticus,
composed in the second century before the present era, we find the
change definitely made. In iii. 14, 'For the *relieving* of thy father
shall not be forgotten,' the Hebrew text has *Tzedakah*; and in
vii. 10, 'Neglect not to give alms,' the Hebrew has 'In *Tzedakah*
be not behindhand." [1]

The alteration of the significance of the term could not have
been accidental, and is the effect of the theory that assisting the
poor is not an act of grace on the part of the donor, but a duty.
By giving alms he is merely practising righteousness, i.e. performing
a deed of justice. All man's possessions are but a loan from the
Creator of the Universe, to Whom belong the earth and the fullness
thereof, and by his charity he merely secures a more equitable
distribution of God's gifts to mankind. No better definition of the

---

[1] A similar usage is perhaps to be noted in Matt. vi. 1 f.: 'Take heed that
ye do not your *righteousness* before men. . . . When therefore thou doest
alms, sound not a trumpet before thee.'

Rabbinic idea of *Tzedakah* could be suggested than this utterance: 'Give unto Him of what is His, seeing that you and what you have are His; this is found expressed by David who said, "For all things come of Thee, and of thine own have we given Thee" (1 Chron. xxix. 14)' (Aboth III. 8). It also explains the Talmudic law: 'Even the beggar who is maintained by charity must himself practise charity' (Git. 7*b*). Nobody is exempt from the duty.

An act of charity, accordingly, not only helps the needy but confers spiritual benefit upon the giver. 'More than the householder does for the beggar, the beggar does for the householder' (Lev. R. XXXIV. 8). An interesting account has been preserved of a conversation between R. Akiba and the Roman Governor of Palestine, Tineius Rufus, on this subject. 'Tineius Rufus asked, "If your God loves the poor why does He not provide for them?" Akiba answered, "So that we may be delivered through them from the penalty of Gehinnom." [1] The Roman said, "On the contrary, it should make you liable for Gehinnom. I will give you a parable: To what is the matter like? To a human king who was angry with his slave, imprisoned him and ordered that he was not to be provided with food or drink; and then a person goes and feeds him and gives him to drink. When the king hears of it, will he not be angry with him? You are called servants, as it is said, 'Unto Me the children of Israel are servants' (Lev. xxv. 55)." Akiba replied, "I will give you a parable: To what is the matter like? To a human king who was angry with his son, imprisoned him and ordered that he was not to be provided with food or drink; and then a person goes and feeds and gives him to drink. When the king hears of it, will he not reward him? We are called children, as it is said, 'Ye are children of the Lord your God' (Deut. xiv. 1). Behold, it was He Who declared, 'Is it not to deal thy bread to the hungry, and that thou bring the poor that are cast out to thy house?' (Is. lviii. 7)"' (B.B. 10*a*).

Akiba's remark about charity being a medium of expiation is found elsewhere in the Talmud: 'Who prolongs his stay at table prolongs his life; perhaps a poor man will come and he will give him some food. So long as the Temple was in existence, the altar used to atone for Israel, but now a man's table atones for him' (Ber. 55*a*), by having the poor as his guests.

How great is the merit derived from almsgiving is the moral of this story. 'It was said of R. Tarphon that he was exceedingly rich but did not give to the poor. Once R. Akiba met him and asked, "Would you like me to buy a town or two for you?" He

---

[1] i.e. charity is a means of atonement for sin.

agreed and forthwith handed him four thousand golden *denarii*. Akiba took them and distributed them among the poor. After a while Tarphon met him and asked, "Where are the towns you bought for me?" Akiba took him by the hand and led him to the House of Study; he then brought a copy of the Psalms, placed it before the two of them, and they went on reading until they reached the verse, "He hath dispersed, he hath given to the needy; his righteousness endureth for ever" (Ps. cxii. 9). Akiba exclaimed, "This is the city I bought for you." Tarphon stood up, kissed him, and said, "My master and guide, my master in wisdom and guide in right conduct!" He handed him an additional sum of money to disperse in charity' (Kallah).

Since the help of God's afflicted children must have His approval, it follows that He shows His pleasure by rewarding the donor. This belief is already found in the Apocrypha. The Biblical verse, 'Righteousness delivereth from death' (Prov. x. 2), assumes the new form, 'Alms doth deliver from death, and shall purge away all sin. Those that exercise alms and righteousness shall be filled with life' (Tobit xii. 9). Many tales are recounted in the Talmud which illustrate by actual occurrences the truth of the saving power of charity. A few specimens follow.

'R. Akiba had a daughter about whom the astrologers foretold that she would be bitten by a snake and die on the day she entered the bridal chamber. He worried very much over the matter. On her wedding-day she took her brooch and stuck it in the wall, and it chanced to pierce through the eye of a snake. Next morning, when she pulled out the brooch, the (dead) snake was clinging to it. (On being informed of the incident) R. Akiba asked her what she had done, and she told him, "In the evening a poor man came begging at the door, and everybody was busy with the wedding festivities so that nobody heard him. I therefore got up and took the marriage gift which you presented to me and handed it to him." He said to her, "A deed of great merit have you performed." He went forth and preached, "Charity doth deliver from death—not merely from an unnatural death but from death itself"' (Shab. 156b).

'Benjamin the righteous was appointed to administer the charity fund. On one occasion, during a period of drought, a woman came begging, "Rabbi, support me." He replied, "By the Temple service, there is nothing left in the fund." She said to him, "Rabbi, if you do not help me, a mother and seven children will perish." He thereupon supported her with his own money. Later he fell ill and was at the point of death. The ministering angels spoke before the Holy One, blessed be He, "Thou hast declared that whoever saves one life is as though he had saved the whole world; now Benjamin the righteous has saved the lives of a woman and her seven children; shall he die at a young age?" His fate was at once rescinded and twenty-two years were added to his life' (B.B. 11a).

'R. Meïr visited the town of Mamla and noticed that all the inhabitants had black hair.[1] He asked them, "Are you descended from the house of Eli, of whom it was written, 'All the increase of thine house shall die in the flower of their age' (1 Sam. ii. 33)?" They replied, "Rabbi, pray on our behalf"; and he said to them, "Go, occupy yourselves with charity and you will be worthy of reaching old age"' (Gen. R. LIX. 1).

Other material benefits were popularly supposed to accrue from almsgiving. 'What should a man do to secure sons? Let him spend his money freely on the poor' (B.B. 10b). 'Whoever runs after charity (to practise it), the Holy One, blessed be He, provides him with the means wherewith to do it' (ibid. 9b), i.e. it will lead to prosperity. 'If a man sees that his means are becoming straitened, let him devote some of them to charity; how much more so if they are abundant. Whoever shears off part of his possessions and devotes it to charity is delivered from the penalty of Gehinnom. Parable of two lambs which are passing through the water, one shorn and the other unshorn. The lamb which is shorn passed over safely, but the unshorn did not' (Git. 7a).[2] A Rabbi advised his wife, 'When a beggar comes, hand him bread, so that the same may be done to your children.' She exclaimed, 'You are cursing them!'[3] He replied, 'There is a wheel which revolves in the world'[4] (Shab. 151b). She was not to reject an appeal, so that if her children should ever be in want, they should not be turned away empty-handed. Charity offers security in another respect: 'When the Temple stood, a man contributed his shekel and was atoned thereby; but now the Temple no longer exists, if they practise charity, well and good; but if not, heathen nations come and confiscate their property by force' (B.B. 9a). A proverb declared: 'The door which is not opened for charity will be opened to the physician' (Cant. R. to vi. 11).

It would, however, be wrong to conclude from the foregoing that

---

[1] The people died young there, and there were no grey-haired men and women.

[2] The wool on its body soaked in the water and weighted it so that the animal perished. This is somewhat analogous to the teaching about the difficulty of the rich in entering the kingdom of God (Matt. xix. 24).

[3] By suggesting the possibility of their being reduced to beggary.

[4] viz. the wheel of fortune, so that the rich became poor and the poor rich.

almsgiving was only prompted by interested motives. There are numerous passages which demonstrate that charity was prized for its own sake as a supreme virtue. For example, 'Charity is equal to all the other precepts put together' (B.B. 9a). 'Whoever practises charity and justice is as though he filled the whole world with loving-kindness' (Suk. 49b). 'Greater is he who practises charity than all the sacrifices' (ibid.). 'Great is charity, for it brings the Redemption (of the Messiah) near' (B.B. 10a). 'The salt of money is its diminution'[1] (Keth. 66b). 'When a beggar stands at your door, the Holy One, blessed be He, stands at his right hand' (Lev. R. xxxiv. 9). 'Whoever shuts his eye against charity is as though he worshipped idols' (B.B. 10a).

The harm which can be done by indiscriminate almsgiving was recognized and discounted. One Rabbi, at least, was unperturbed by the possibility of undeserving people receiving assistance. He said: 'We must give credit to the impostors among the poor; were it not for them, if a man were asked for alms and did not give them at once he would be incurring punishment' (p. Peah 21b). This Rabbi, Eleazar b. Pedath, was exceedingly poor and on some occasions actually had nothing to eat (Taan. 25a); yet it is recorded of him that he always gave away a trifle in charity before offering his prayers (B.B. 10a).

The idea that every little helps is taught in this way: 'What means that which is written. "He put on *Tzedakah* as a coat of mail" (Is. lix. 17)? It is to inform you that as in a coat of mail link is joined to link to constitute it, so with charity farthing is added to farthing to realize a large sum' (B.B. 9b). A scale of relief is found in the Talmud: 'To the vagrant beggar must be given not less than a loaf worth a *dupondium* when flour costs four *seah* for a *sela*. If he stays overnight, he is to be provided with sleeping accommodation; and if he stays over the Sabbath, he must receive food for three meals' (Shab. 118a), these being obligatory on the Sabbath.

Almsgiving should not consist in just handing out a dole. The circumstances of the applicant and the style of living to which he has been accustomed must be taken into consideration. '"Thou shalt surely lend him sufficient for his need" (Deut. xv. 8)—you are not commanded to enrich him, but to give him what he requires, even a horse or a slave. It is told of Hillel that he gave a poor man, who had come from a well-to-do family, the one horse with which he used to do his work and the one slave who attended upon him'

---

[1] i.e. giving part away in charity adds to the flavour of what is enjoyed by the owner. A variant of 'diminution' is 'loving-kindness.'

(Sifré Deut. § 116; 98*b*). In another version, the addition is made that when Hillel was once unable to provide him with a slave to run in front of the horse, he did so himself (Keth. 67*b*).

Nor should a man think that he has done his duty to an applicant by handing him a trifle. '"Blessed is he that considereth the poor" (Ps. xli. 1). It is not written, "Blessed is he that giveth to the poor." It refers to a man who considers how the meritorious act can best be carried out' (p. Peah 21*b*). To the same effect is the saying: 'Superior is he who lends money to the poor than the giver of alms; and best of all is he who invests money with a poor man in partnership' (Shab. 63*a*).

Consideration must be shown to the poor in another sense. 'If a man were to give his fellow all the good gifts in the world but his face is sullen, it is ascribed to him as though he had given him nothing; but who receives his fellow with a cheerful countenance, even if he give him nothing, it is ascribed to him as though he had given him all the good gifts in the world' (ARN xiii). '"If thou draw out thy soul to the hungry" (Is. lviii. 10)—if you have nothing to give him, comfort him with words. Say to him, "My soul goes out to you because I have nothing to give you"' (Lev. R. xxxiv. 15).

Most important of all, true charity is practised in secret. The best type of almsgiving is where 'a person gives a donation without knowing who receives it, and a person receives it without knowing who donated it' (B.B. 10*b*). It is reported that 'in the Temple there was a Chamber of Secret Charity. God-fearing persons used to deposit their contributions in it secretly, and the poor who were descended from well-to-do families were supported from it in secret' (Shek. v. 6). A similar institution was established in every Palestinian city (Tosifta Shek. ii. 16). 'A Rabbi saw a man give a *zuz* to a beggar publicly. He said to him, "Better had you given him nothing rather than give him and put him to shame"' (Chag. 5*a*).

So far the first aspect of charity, almsgiving, has been treated. The second, called *Gemiluth Chasadim*, 'the bestowal of loving acts,' is superior in ethical quality and of greater value to mankind. It is one of the three pillars upon which the world, i.e. the social order, rests (Aboth i. 2). The two phases of charity are thus contrasted: 'Greater is benevolence than alms in three respects —almsgiving is performed with money and benevolence with personal service or money; almsgiving is restricted to the poor, and benevolence can be displayed to poor and rich; almsgiving can only be done to the living, and benevolence both to the living and dead' (Suk. 49*b*). 'The Pentateuch begins with an act of benevolence and concludes with an act of benevolence. At the beginning it is said, "And the Lord God made for Adam and for his wife coats of skins, and clothed them" (Gen. iii. 21); and at the end it is said, "And He buried him (Moses) in the valley" (Deut. xxxiv. 6)' (Sot. 14a).

Gemiluth Chasadim, accordingly, comprehends all those kindly deeds which alleviate the burdens of the afflicted and sweeten human relationship. But certain acts receive special mention in this connection. One of them is the entertainment of wayfarers. It, together with the visitation of the sick, is specified as a virtue of which man eats the fruit in this world and the capital remains for him in the World to Come (Shab. 127a). Of hospitality to needy strangers it is said, 'Greater is the reception of wayfarers than the reception of the *Shechinah* (ibid.). The recommendation was, 'Let your house be open wide, and let the poor be the members of your household' (Aboth 1. 5). Two of the Bible heroes who are praised for this virtue are Job and Abraham. Of the former it is related that he made 'four doors to his house so that the poor should not be troubled to go round it to find the entrance' (ARN vii); and the Bible tells of the patriarch, 'Abraham planted a tamarisk-tree (*eshel*) in Beersheba' (Gen. xxi. 33). This is explained as follows: '*Eshel* means a lodging-place where Abraham used to receive passers-by, and when they had eaten and drunk,[1] he would say, "Stay the night and bless God"' (Gen. R. LIV. 6). His house also was said to have been always open for wayfarers (ibid. XLVIII. 9). Of R. Huna it was told that 'when he used to sit down to a meal, he opened the doors and exclaimed, "Let whoever is in need enter and eat"' (Taan. 20b).

The praiseworthiness of taking charge of orphans has already been referred to.[2] Another act of benevolence which was highly praised was helping a bride, especially if poor, to get married by supplying her with an outfit and with a dowry. That kindly deed was read into Micah's revelation of the Divine will: '"What doth the Lord require of thee, but to do justly and to love mercy, and to walk humbly with thy God?" (vi. 8)—"to do justly," i.e. justice; "to love mercy," i.e. benevolence; "and to walk humbly," i.e. carrying out a dead body to burial and attendance on a bride'[3] (Mak. 24a).

Visiting the sick is another feature of benevolence which receives

[1] The term *eshel* is accordingly explained as made up of the initials of three words: *achilah* 'eating,' *shethiyah* 'drinking,' and *linah* 'lodging overnight.'
[2] See p. 172.
[3] The connection is to be sought in the fact that the word for 'humbly' also gives the meaning of 'modesty.' To see that a corpse is reverently interred and not exposed to the public, and to help a poor girl to marry, are aids to morality.

commendation. It is one of God's acts which man should imitate.[1] 'Whoever visits the sick takes away a sixtieth part of his illness. If so, let sixty people visit him and set him on his feet again! The meaning is, each takes a sixtieth part of what is left by the others' (Ned. 39*b*). 'When one of R. Akiba's disciples was ill, none of the Sages went to visit him; but R. Akiba visited him, and because he swept the room and sprinkled water over the floor, the invalid said to him, "You have restored me to life." The Rabbi went out and preached, "Whoever does not visit the sick is as though he sheds blood"' (ibid. 40*a*). Another authority declared: 'Whoever visits the sick causes him to recover, and whoever does not visit the sick causes him to die' (ibid.).

Highest of all is benevolence performed to the dead, since it must be done from pure motives. Jacob said to Joseph: 'Deal kindly and truly [2] with me, bury me not in Egypt' (Gen. xlvii. 29 f.). The Rabbis ask: 'Is there, then, a kindness of falsehood? He meant by his words, If you do to me an act of kindness after my death, it is a kindness of truth' (Gen. R. xcvi. 5). An unattended corpse is called in Hebrew *meth mitzvah*, 'a dead body which is a religious obligation'; and such importance is attached to its burial that even a High Priest who is a Nazirite must personally perform its interment, if there is nobody else available, although in either capacity he is forbidden to defile himself by contact with the dead (Sifré Num. § 26; 9*a*).

To assist at a funeral is a duty of sacred importance. 'The study of the Torah may be interrupted to bear out a corpse and to help a bride to marry' (Meg. 3*b*). 'Whoever sees a body being conveyed to burial and does not accompany it, commits a transgression because of the injunction, "Whoso mocketh the poor [3] blasphemeth his Maker" ' (Prov. xvii. 5). If he accompany it, what is his reward? Of him Scripture states, "He that is gracious to the poor lendeth unto the Lord" (ibid. xix. 17) and "He that is gracious unto the needy honoureth Him" (ibid. xiv. 31)' (Ber. 18*a*). And finally, there is the duty of comforting the mourner which is also one of the deeds in which man should imitate God; but it is advised, 'Comfort not your fellow-man in the hour when his dead lies before him' (Aboth iv. 23), because he is usually not in the frame of mind to receive words of consolation. The funeral is followed by seven days of mourning during which he should be visited and cheered.

---

[1] See p. 211.
[2] The Hebrew is literally 'kindness and truth,' which could idiomatically represent 'kindness of truth.' [3] And there is none so poor as the dead.

§ V. Honesty

A virtue which should distinguish the moral life is integrity in business dealings, and the Talmud attached much importance to it. There is a statement to the effect that 'when a person is brought before the tribunal (after death) the first question put to him is, Have you been honest in your transactions?' (Shab. 31a). Equally emphatic is this passage: '"If thou wilt do that which is right in His eyes" (Exod. xv. 26)—this refers to commercial dealings, and teaches that he who acts honestly is popular with his fellow-creatures, and it is imputed to him as though he had fulfilled the whole of the Torah' (Mech. ad loc.; 46a).

The disastrous consequence of dishonesty in the life of the community is taught in the dictum: 'Jerusalem was destroyed because honest men ceased therein' (Shab. 119b).

Strict laws are laid down in the Talmud for the regulation of the business world. The following are specimens: 'The shopkeeper must wipe his measures twice a week, his weights once a week, and his scales after every weighing' (B.B. v. 10). '"Ye shall do no unrighteousness in judgment, in meteyard, in weight, or in measure" (Lev. xix. 35). "In meteyard" refers to the measurement of land, that he may not measure for one in summer and for another in winter;[1] "in weight," he may not keep his weights in salt;[2] "in measure," he may not make the liquid produce a foam' (B.M. 61b).

'Whence is it that we may not give exact measure in a place where the practice is to give a heaped measure and vice versa? The text declares, "A perfect measure" (Deut. xxv. 15). And whence is it that if the seller says, "I will give exact measure," in a place where the practice is to give a heaped measure, "and reduce the price"; or "I will give a heaped measure," in a place where the practice is to give exact measure, "and increase the price," he is not allowed to do so? The text declares, "A perfect and just measure." Whence is it that we may not give exact weight in a place where the practice is to give overweight and vice versa? The text declares, "A perfect weight." And whence is it that if the seller says, "I will give exact weight," in a place where the practice is to give overweight, "and reduce the price"; or "I will give overweight," in a place where the practice is to give exact weight, "and increase the price," he is not allowed

[1] If a field is to be divided up, the measurements must be taken at the same time, because in summer the measuring-line is dry and contracted.
[2] This makes the weights heavier.

to do so? The text declares, "A perfect and just weight"'
(B.B. 89a). Since there is the possibility of fraud in departing from
the adopted custom of the place, such deviation is not permitted.

Even practices which are now regarded as lawful are denounced
in the Talmud. 'Of them who store up the produce (to increase
the price), who practise usury, who give short measure, and who
unsettle the market,[1] Scripture declares, "The Lord hath sworn
by the excellency of Jacob, Surely I will never forget any of their
works" (Amos viii. 7)' (B.B. 90b).

Anecdotes are related which show how scrupulous the Rabbis
were in their dealings. 'It happened that Phineas b. Jaïr was
living in one of the cities of the South, and some men who visited
there left two measures of barley in his possession and forgot
about them when they departed. He sowed the barley and each
year stored the produce. After seven years had elapsed the men
returned to that town. He recognized them and told them to
receive what belonged to them. It also happened that Simeon b.
Shetach bought an ass from an Arab. His disciples found a gem
suspended round its neck and said to him, "Rabbi, it is true of
you, 'The blessing of the Lord maketh rich' (Prov. x. 22)." He
answered them, "I bought the ass and not the gem. Go, return
it to the owner." The Arab exclaimed, "Blessed be the God of
Simeon b. Shetach"' (Deut. R. III. 3).

Not merely actual fraud, but every form of deception, is for-
forbidden. 'There are seven kinds of thieves, and chief of all is
he who deceives his fellow' (Tosifta B.K. VII. 8). 'It is forbidden
to deceive a fellow-creature, even a Gentile' (Chul. 94a). 'With
the righteous their yea is yea and their nay is nay' (Ruth R. to iii.
18). 'The Holy One, blessed be He, hates a person who says one
thing with his mouth and another in his heart' (Pes. 113b).

§ VI. Forgiveness

The harmony which should reign in the community will inevitably
be disturbed occasionally by differences occurring between individuals. It should, consequently, be the desire of the good citizen
to see that such quarrels are quickly ended and peaceful relationship restored. To achieve this result two conditions are essential.
The first is that the party who is in the wrong should be eager to
admit his fault and beg the pardon of the person he has offended.

The Talmud is very firm on this point and even describes the
procedure which should be followed. 'One who has sinned against

[1] By false rumours so as to enhance the value of their goods.

his fellow-man must say to him, "I have acted wrongly against you." If he accept him, well and good; if not, he brings persons and conciliates him in their presence; as it is said, "He maketh rows (of people, *sic*) before men and saith, I have sinned and perverted that which was right, and it profited me not" (Job xxxiii. 27). If he does that, Scripture says of him, "He hath redeemed my soul from going into the pit, and my life shall behold the light" (ibid. 28). Should the offended person have died, he must conciliate him over his grave and say, "I have acted wrongly towards you"' (p. Joma 45c).

Another teacher declares: 'If one wrongly suspected another he must conciliate him; nay more, he must bless him' (Ber. 31b). A limit, however, was set to the number of times attempts at reconciliation were to be made; according to one view, not more than three times (Joma 87a). A Rabbi said of himself, 'Never did the curse of my fellow-man ascend my bed' (Meg. 28a), by which he meant that he always succeeded in pacifying any one he had offended during the day before he retired to rest.

Secondly, it was the duty of the aggrieved party to accept the apology when made to him and not nurse his grievance. The advice was given: 'A man should always be soft as a reed and not hard like a cedar' (Taan. 20b); 'Forgive an insult done to you' (ARN xli). A certain Rabbi, on going to bed, used to offer the prayer: 'Forgive whoever has caused me trouble' (Meg. 28a).

A wise recommendation, which would tend to lessen quarrels and quickly heal them when they did happen, is: 'If you have done your fellow a little wrong, let it be in your eyes great; if you have done him much good, let it be in your eyes little; if he has done you a little good, let it be in your eyes great; if he has done you a great wrong, let it be in your eyes little' (ARN xli).

The injunction of Lev. xix. 18, 'Thou shalt not take vengence nor bear a grudge,' received this definition: 'What means vengeance and what means a grudge? Vengeance is where a person says to his fellow, "Lend me your sickle," and he refuses; and the next day the latter person says, "Lend me your axe," and he replies, "I will not lend you anything, in the same way that you declined to lend me." A grudge is where a person says to his fellow, "Lend me your axe," and he refuses; and the next day the latter person says, "Lend me your garment," and he replies, "Here it is! I am not like you who declined to lend me what I wanted." They who are insulted but do not retaliate with insult, they who hear themselves reproached and make no retort, they who do (the will of God) from love, and they who are happy under affliction, of them Scripture declares, "Let them that love Him be as the sun when it goeth forth in its might" (Judges v. 31). He who forgoes retaliation, his sins are remitted; when his pardon is asked he grants it' (Joma 23a).

To refuse to repair the breach and reject the overtures when they are made is an attitude which is censured. 'Whoever is compassionate toward his fellow-creatures (and forgives wrongs done to him), compassion is shown to him from Heaven; and whoever is not compassionate toward his fellow-creatures, compassion is not shown to him from Heaven' (Shab. 151b). The favourite quotation of a first-century Rabbi was: 'Rejoice not when thine enemy falleth, and let not thine heart be glad when he stumbleth, lest the Lord see it, and it displease Him, and He turn away His wrath from him' (Prov. xxiv. 17 f.) (Aboth IV. 24). The meaning is that the man who declines to forgive, preserves the enmity and is glad when misfortune befalls the other person, becomes thereby the guilty party and God's anger is turned away from the other and directed towards himself.

§ VII. TEMPERANCE

A characteristic attitude is taken up by the Talmud towards the pleasures of life. Recognizing that what has been created by God for man's enjoyment must be essentially good, it not only counsels men to indulge in them but even condemns those who abstain from them. The Rabbis assume the standpoint that God wants His creatures to be happy, and it must therefore be sinful deliberately to shun physical happiness and material well-being. To feel oneself to be in His Presence is itself a source of light and joy 'There is no sadness in the presence of the Holy One, blessed be He, as it is said, "Strength and gladness are in His place" (1 Chron. xvi. 27)' (Chag. 5b). 'The *Shechinah* does not alight in the midst of idleness, sadness, jocularity, levity, or idle chatter, but in the midst of the joy of a religious duty' (Pes. 117a).

Throughout the Rabbinic teaching there is found advocated a wise moderation, and both extremes—of austerity and hedonism —are censured as harmful. No virtue was attached to poverty as such; rather the contrary. 'Where there is no meal, there is no Torah' (Aboth III. 21), it was remarked, by which was intended that the lack of proper sustenance hinders the acquisition of that knowledge which is essential to the fulfilment of the Divine will. 'Worse is poverty in a man's house than fifty plagues' (B.B. 116a). The Rabbis perceived value in such amenities as 'a beautiful home, a beautiful wife, and beautiful furniture as means of putting a man into a cheerful frame of mind' (Ber. 57*b*). They even declared: 'In the Hereafter a man will have to give judgment and reckoning for all that his eye saw but he did not eat' (p. Kid. 66*d*); and their definition of a rich man is: 'He who derives pleasure from his wealth' (Shab. 25*b*).

It is related that because of his criticism of the Roman administration, R. Simeon b. Jochai had to hide himself to save his life. He and his son concealed themselves in a cave for twelve years. On hearing that the king was dead and the decree rescinded, he came out of his hiding-place. He saw men ploughing and sowing, and exclaimed: 'They forsake the life of eternity and busy themselves with the life that is transitory.' Wherever he and his son turned their eyes, the land was at once consumed by fire. A *Bath Kol*[1] issued forth and said to them: 'Have you left your cave to destroy My world? Go back to it!' (Shab. 33*b*). The maintenance of the social order has God's approval; therefore man is entitled to enjoy the fruits of his labour.

But the other extreme has likewise to be avoided. To accumulate riches in order to indulge in luxury is not in accord with His will. 'When Solomon erected the Temple, he said to the Holy One, blessed be He, in his prayer, Sovereign of the Universe! if a man pray to Thee to give him wealth and Thou knowest that he will abuse it, do not grant it to him; but if Thou seest a man using his riches well, grant his request; as it is said, "Render unto every man according to all his ways, whose heart Thou knowest" (2 Chron. vi. 30)' (Exod. R. XXXI. 5).

There is a wealth of meaning in the definition: 'Who is rich? He who rejoices in his lot; as it is said, "When thou eatest the labour of thine hands, happy art thou and it shall be well with thee" (Ps. cxxviii. 2)—"happy art thou" in this world, "and it shall be well with thee" in the World to Come" (Aboth IV. 1). It crystallizes the viewpoint of the Rabbis towards the material world.

So that a man should be in a fit condition to work his best, it is his duty to see that his body is well nourished. 'Grind with the teeth and you will find it in the heels' (Shab. 152*a*), i.e. a plentiful supply of food strengthens the body. And a proverb taught, 'The stomach carries the feet' (Gen. R. LXX. 8). The following story of Hillel points the same moral: 'When he ended his lesson with his disciples, he accompanied them part of the way. They asked him, "Master, where are you going?" "To bestow an act of

[1] See pp. 46 f.

kindness upon a guest who is in my house." [1] "Have you, then, a guest always with you?" "Is not the unhappy soul a guest within the body, here to-day and gone to-morrow!"' (Lev. R. xxxiv. 3).

As with food, so also with drink. Total abstinence was not considered a virtue. We have such utterances as: 'There is no gladness without wine' (Pes. 109a). 'At the head of all medicines am I wine; where wine is lacking drugs are necessary' (B.B. 58b). 'Why is it said, "And make atonement for him (the Nazirite), for that he sinned against the soul" [2] (Num. vi. 11)? Against which soul has he sinned? But he withheld himself from wine. And we may apply the *a fortiori* argument: If a person who withholds himself from wine is called a sinner, how much more so is he a sinner who withholds himself from all enjoyments' (Taan. 11a).

For all that, the Rabbis fully appreciated the evils of excess and uttered a warning against them. Rather curious is this legend: 'When Noah came to plant a vineyard (Gen. ix. 20), Satan appeared before him and asked, "What are you planting?" "A vineyard." "What is its nature?" "Its fruits are sweet whether fresh or dry, and of them wine is made which gladdens the heart." "Come, now, let us two form a partnership in this vineyard." "Very well," said Noah. What did Satan do? He brought a sheep and slew it under the vine; then he brought in turn a lion, a pig, and a monkey, slew each of them and let their blood drip into the vineyard and drench the soil. He hinted thereby that before a man drinks wine he is simple like a sheep and quiet like a lamb in front of its shearers. When he has drunk in moderation, he is strong like a lion and declares there is none to equal him in the world. When he has drunk more than enough, he becomes like a pig wallowing in filth. When he is intoxicated he becomes like a monkey, dancing about, uttering obscenities before all, and ignorant of what he is doing' (Tanchuma Noach § 13).

Other sayings on the subject are: 'When wine enters, sense goes out; when wine enters, the secret comes out' [3] (Num. R. x. 8). 'The tree from which Adam ate was the vine, for there is nothing which brings lamentation upon man so much as wine' (Sanh. 70a, b). 'Why does the section of the Nazirite adjoin the section of the woman suspected of adultery (Num. v. f.)? To inform us that whoever sees such a woman in her disgrace should separate himself from wine' (Ber. 63a), since, 'Wine leads both man and

---

[1] He meant that he was going to satisfy his appetite.
[2] That is the literal translation of the Hebrew.
[3] The numerical value of the letters of *yayin* 'wine,' viz. seventy, equals that of *sod* 'secret.'

woman to unchastity' (Num. R. x. 4). 'Do not become intoxicated and you will not sin' (Ber. 29b). 'One cup of wine is good
for a woman, two are degrading, three make her act like an
immoral woman, and four cause her to lose all self-respect and
sense of shame' (Keth. 65a). 'Wine ends in blood' (Sanh. 70a).
'Wine at midday' is one of the things that 'put a man out of the
world' (Aboth III. 14). It has likewise a bad effect upon the
physical constitution. 'Abba Saul said, It was once my occupation to bury the dead, and I made it a practice to observe their
bones. I thus perceived that he who indulged in strong drink,
his bones appeared to be scorched; if to excess, they were without
marrow; but if in due measure, they were full of marrow' (Nid. 24b).

But in spite of the teaching that 'he who over-indulges in fasting
is called a sinner' (Taan. 11a), we hear of Rabbis who were ascetics.
Of one it is related that he used to fast throughout the year except
on certain days when it was not permitted (Pes. 68b); and of
another it is reported that he was 'satisfied with a measure of
locusts for his food from the Sabbath-eve to the next Sabbath-
eve' (Ber. 17b).

National disaster induced many to lead the ascetic life, but a
Rabbi tried to dissuade them by showing how illogical they were.
'When the Second Temple was destroyed, many in Israel took
upon themselves to abstain from meat and wine. R. Joshua
argued with them, saying, "My sons, why do you not eat meat
and drink wine?" They answered, "Shall we eat meat of which
offerings used to be brought upon the altar but have now ceased?
Shall we drink wine of which libations used to be poured upon the
altar but have now ceased?" He said to them, "In that case, let
us stop eating bread since the meal-offerings have ceased!" "Quite
right, we will exist on fruit." "But we cannot eat fruit because
the offering of the first-fruits has ceased!" "Quite right, we will
exist on the other kinds of fruit (which were not offered)." "In
that case, we ought not to drink water since the libation of water
has ceased!" They remained silent' (B.B. 60b).

Occasionally we hear of a vow to adopt the ascetic life commended
because the motive behind it was such as could be approved.
A case in point is told by a Rabbi: 'Once there came a would-be
Nazirite [1] from the South, and I noticed that he had beautiful
eyes, a goodly countenance, and his hair was arranged in orderly
curls. I said to him, "My son, what purpose have you in destroying
your lovely hair?" He answered, "I was a shepherd for my father
in my city, and I went to draw water from the well, when I gazed

[1] To Jerusalem to offer his sacrifice and cut off his hair.

at my reflection and my passions surged over me and sought to drive me from the world. So I said to myself, "You evil person, why do you pride yourself in a world which is not yours and in a being who is destined to become worms and maggots? By the Temple-service, I will cut off my hair for the sake of heaven!" (The Rabbi continued), I immediately arose and kissed him on the head, saying, "My son, would that Nazirites like you multiplied in Israel, and concerning such as you does Scripture declare, 'When either a man or woman shall clearly utter a vow, the vow of a Nazirite to consecrate himself *unto the Lord*' (Num. vi. 2)"' (Ned. 9b).

The Rabbis also uttered a warning against the feeling of over-confidence in self which comes from prosperity. '"And thou shalt eat and be full; take heed to yourselves lest your heart be deceived and ye turn aside and serve other gods" (Deut. xi. 15f.). Moses told them, Be careful that you rebel not against the Holy One, blessed be He, since a man only rebels against Him from the midst of satiety' (Sifré Deut. § 43; 80b). 'What means "And Di-Zahab" (Deut. i. 1)? Thus spoke Moses before the Holy One, blessed be He, "Lord of the Universe! It was because of the silver and gold (*zahab*) which Thou didst bounteously give to Israel until they cried, 'It is sufficient (*dai*),' that they were induced to make the calf." The School of R. Jannai said, A lion growls not in a den full of straw but in a den full of meat. R. Oshaya said, A parable: It may be likened to a man who had a lean cow but of large build. He fed it on horse-beans and it kicked him. He said to it, "What caused you to kick me but the horse-beans on which I fed you!" R. Acha said, That is what the proverb declares, "He whose stomach is full increaseth deeds of evil"' (Ber. 32a).

For the same reason excessive merrymaking was deprecated because it might lead to censurable conduct. '"Serve the Lord with fear and rejoice with trembling" (Ps. ii. 11)—that means, where there is rejoicing let there be trembling. Mar b. Rabina made a wedding feast for his son, and noticed that the Rabbis were very merry. He seized a costly goblet worth four hundred *zuz* and broke it before them, and they became more serious. R. Ashé made a wedding feast for his son, and noticed that the Rabbis were very merry. He seized a goblet of white crystal and broke it before them, and they became more serious' (Ber. 30b et seq.).

Such is the Talmudic outlook on life's allurements. It avoids excess as well as undue self-denial. It bids man enjoy his stay on earth in the physical sense and make wise use of the faculties with which God has endowed him and the pleasures He has provided for his happiness. His laws place the check upon his appetites which would lead him to immoderate indulgence. To go beyond the limits He had prescribed is to err, and this point of view is admirably expressed in this extract: 'One who imposes vows of abstinence upon himself is as though he puts an iron collar around his neck; he is like one who builds a prohibited altar; he is like one who takes a sword and plunges it into his heart. Sufficient for you is what the Torah forbids, and do not seek to add further restrictions' (p. Ned. 41*b*).

§ VIII. DUTY TO ANIMALS

One aspect of the moral life is not concerned with man's relationship with his fellow-beings but with his relationship with animals. Since even the Decalogue shows consideration for dumb creatures and commands that they too should be allowed the Sabbath rest, and several other passages in the Bible enjoin that kindness should be shown to them, one expects to find the Talmud also teaching that lesson.

Indeed, the way a man treats animals is an index to his character. 'When Moses shepherded the flocks of Jethro, he kept the old sheep back because of the young ones and let these loose first to feed on the tender grass; then he let the others loose to feed on the grass of average quality; lastly he let the strong ones loose to feed on the tough grass. The Holy One, blessed be He, said, "Let him who knows how to shepherd the flock, each according to its strength, come and lead My people." On one occasion a kid ran away and Moses pursued it until it came to a tree where there chanced to be a pool of water. The kid stood there to drink, and when Moses overtook it he said, "I did not know you ran away because you were thirsty. You must also be tired." So he set it upon his shoulder and carried it back. The Holy, blessed be He, said, "Since you are merciful to the flock of a human being, you shall be the shepherd of My flock, Israel"' (Exod. R. II. 2).

To display inconsiderateness to an animal incurs the divine displeasure, as this story shows: 'A calf was being led to the slaughter and hid its head in the garment of R. Judah and bellowed. He said to it, "Go," since you were created for that purpose!' It was decreed in Heaven, Since he had no compassion, let s ferings come upon him. His sufferings eventually ceased because of the following incident. One day the maid was sweeping the house, and in so doing was about to sweep away some young weasels.

He said to her, "Leave them alone, for it is written, 'His mercies are over all His works' (Ps. cxlv. 9)." It was decreed in Heaven, Since he has shown compassion we will show compassion to him' (B.M. 85a).

The Talmud discusses how far the laws of the Sabbath may be violated for the purpose of rescuing an animal which was in danger. 'If an animal has fallen into a pool of water, we may bring pillows and cushions to place beneath it, and if it thereby ascends to *terra firma*, well and good. Against this statement of the law the following decision is quoted: If an animal has fallen into a pool of water, we provide it with fodder where it is so that it should not die.[1] Hence it would appear that we may provide the animal with fodder but not with pillows and cushions! There is no contradiction, the latter referring to a case where it is possible to keep the animal alive with fodder, and the former where that is not possible. If we can keep the animal alive by feeding it, we should do so; otherwise we must bring pillows and cushions. But by so doing we should infringe a regulation which prohibits one from doing anything with an article which renders it unusable! That regulation is an institution of the Rabbis, whereas preventing pain to an animal is a command of the Torah, and what is instituted by the Torah sets aside what is instituted by the Rabbis' (Shab. 128b).

With regard to the proper care of animals we have these regulations: 'A person is not permitted to acquire for himself a domestic animal or a wild beast or a bird unless he has arranged for it to be properly fed' (p. Jeb. 14d). 'A man must not eat his meal before giving food to his cattle; as it is said, "I will give grass in thy fields for thy cattle" and then "thou shalt eat and be satisfied" (Deut. xi. 15)' (Ber. 40a). The same moral is taught in this legend: 'Abraham said to Melchizedek,[2] "How is it you came forth safely from the ark?" "By reason of the charity we practised there." "But what charity was there for you to practise? Were there any poor in the ark? Only Noah and his sons were there, so to whom could you have been charitable?" "To the animals, beasts, and birds. We did not sleep but gave each its food throughout the night"' (Midrash to Ps. xxxvii. 1; 126b).

Praise is bestowed upon certain creatures for their habits which are said to be models for human beings to imitate. 'Had the Torah not been given to us for our guidance, we could have learnt

---

[1] From hunger, and rescue it when the Sabbath has terminated.
[2] A Jewish tradition identifies him with Shem, the eldest son of Noah. See the Jerusalem Targum on Gen. xiv. 18.

THE MORAL LIFE 237

modesty from the cat, honesty from the ant, chastity from the
dove, and good manners from the cock' (Erub. 100b).

The prohibition against tearing a limb from a living animal was
one of the seven commandments given to the sons of Noah as a
code for the whole human race.[1] On the basis of this law any
sport which involved the mutilation of an animal while alive would
stand condemned. For that reason the arenas were shunned by
the pious. 'One who attends the stadium sits in "the seat of the
scornful" (Ps. i. 1)' (A.Z. 18b).[2]

The Talmud describes with minute care and detail how an
animal is to be slaughtered for food, and the regulations are motived
by the desire to inflict as painless a death as possible. In the first
place, three classes of persons are not permitted to slaughter: the
deaf-mute, the imbecile, and the minor (Chul. 1. 1), the first because
he is unable to pronounce the necessary benediction, and the other
two because they are not of sufficient responsibility to undertake
so delicate a task. Secondly, the knife with which the cut is made
must be sharp and smooth and without the slightest perceptible
notch. The law states: 'The knife must be tested as to its three
sides[3] upon the flesh of the finger and upon the nail' (ibid. 17b).

Finally, five causes of disqualification are enumerated (ibid. 9a):
Shehiyah 'delay'—there must be a continuous forward and backward motion of the knife without any interruption. Derasah
'pressure'—the cut must be made gently, without the exercise of
any force. Chaladah 'digging'—the knife must not be inserted
into the flesh instead of drawn across the throat. Hagramah
'slipping'—the cut must not be made except through a prescribed
section of the neck. Ikkur 'tearing'—the cut must be done without dislocating the windpipe or gullet. Any one of these acts is
sufficient to render the carcass unfit for consumption, because it
would have inflicted pain upon the animal.

[1] See p. 65.
[2] The loathing of Jews for cruel sports of this nature has the testimony
of Josephus: 'Herod also got together a great quantity of wild beasts, and of
lions in very great abundance, and of such other beasts as were either of
uncommon strength or of such a sort as were rarely seen. These were trained
either to fight one with another, or men who were condemned to death were
to fight with them. And truly foreigners were greatly surprised and delighted
at the vast expenses of the shows, and at the great danger of the spectacles,
but to the Jews it was a palpable breaking up of those customs for which
they had so great a veneration' (Antiq. xv. viii. 1).
[3] i.e. the edge and each side of it. If from any position a notch is fe
the knife must be resharpened until the fault disappears.

CHAPTER VIII

THE PHYSICAL LIFE

§ I. CARE OF THE BODY

In one of the conversations which took place between R. Judah and his friend Antoninus, the subject of the relative responsibility of body and soul in the life of the human being was discussed. 'Antoninus said to R. Judah, "Both body and soul will be able to free themselves of the judgment (in the Hereafter)." "How?" "The body may declare, 'It is the soul that sinned, because from the day it parted from me, I have been lying like a stone silent in the grave.' And the soul may declare, 'It is the body that sinned, because from the day I parted from it, I have been flying in space like a bird.'" The Rabbi answered, "I will illustrate the matter with a parable. To what is it like? To a human king who possessed a beautiful orchard in which were choice first-fruits; and he set two watchmen over it, one lame and the other blind. The lame man said to the blind man, 'I can see some choice first-fruits in the orchard; come, let me get on your back and we will secure some to eat.' The lame man mounted the back of the blind man, and they took the fruits and ate them. After a while the owner of the orchard came and asked, 'What has become of the choice first-fruits?' The lame man said to him, 'Have I legs that I could get them!' The blind man said to him, 'Have I eyes that I could see them!' What did the king do? He ordered the lame man to mount the back of the blind man and judged them as one. Similarly the Holy One, blessed be He, will (in the Hereafter) take the soul, cast it into the body and judge them as one"' (Sanh. 91a, b).

Apart from the eschatological significance of the parable and its application, as throwing light on the view which was taken of the mode of punishment that is to be meted out to wrongdoers,[1] it also indicates the opinion that the body is equally answerable with the soul for the manner in which a man conducts himself in his life-time. One reacts on the other. A vicious soul will corrupt the body, and a diseased body cannot be the effective instrument through which a pure soul can function.

[1] See pp. 376 f.

There is a Rabbinic saying, 'Physical cleanliness leads to spiritual purity' (A.Z. 20b), and the cleanliness referred to is internal, not external, and means regular purgations. We shall see below that great importance was attached to regular motions as a rule of health, because they had moral reactions. That is why it is remarked: 'Who delays answering nature's call is guilty of transgressing the command, "Ye shall not make yourselves abominable" (Lev. xx. 25)' (Mak. 16b); and 'A disciple of the Sages should not reside in a city in which there is not a privy' (Sanh. 17b). Without such purgation the mind is unable to concentrate on the devotion which should be offered to God in the morning. Therefore it was taught: 'Whoever wishes to receive upon himself the yoke of the kingdom of heaven in perfection should first have evacuation, then wash his hands, put on the phylacteries, and offer his prayers' (Ber. 15a).

Another reason why care must be taken of the body may be deduced from the story which is told of Hillel. 'When he had finished the lesson with his pupils, he accompanied them part of the way. They said to him, "Master, where are you going?" "To perform a religious duty." "Which religious duty?" "To bathe in the bath-house." "Is that a religious duty?" He answered them, "If somebody is appointed to scrape and clean the statues of the king which are set up in the theatres and circuses, is paid to do the work, and furthermore associates with the nobility, how much more so should I, who am created in the divine image and likeness, take care of my body!"' (Lev. R. xxxiv. 3).

In this anecdote, the maintenance of the body in a clean condition is described as a religious duty, because the body is God's handiwork and as such must be treated with reverence. This idea is at the root of the law which makes a corpse a defiling agent, as may be seen from the following argument: 'The Sadducees said, "We criticize you, Pharisees, for declaring that the Holy Writings defile the hands whereas the works of Homer do not." R. Jochanan b. Zakkai replied to them, "This is not the only point for criticizing the Pharisees; they likewise declare that the bones of an ass are non-defiling but the bones of the High Priest Jochanan are defiling. Proportionate to the respect one should have for these things is their capacity for defilement, so that one should not make ladles out of the bones of his father or his mother. So is it also with the Holy Writings' (Jad. iv. 6).

Quite consistent with this opinion is the statement: 'One should wash his face, hands, and feet every day out of respect for his Maker' (Shab. 50b). How seriously this rule was taken is illustrated by a story told of R. Akiba while he was imprisoned by the Romans: 'R. Joshua the grits-dealer used to attend upon him every day and bring a supply of water. One day the jailer met him and said, "You have brought too much water; perhaps your intention is to use it for digging a hole through the prison (to enable the prisoner to escape)." He poured half of it away and gave him the remainder. When R. Joshua came to R. Akiba, the latter said, "Do you not know that I am old and my life is dependent upon what you bring me?" He told him what had happened. Akiba said, "Give me the water to wash my hands." The other exclaimed, "There is not sufficient for you to drink!" He replied, "What can I do since (they who do not wash their hands) are deserving of death? Better I die of my own account (from thirst) and not transgress the views of my colleagues." It is reported that he did not drink a drop of the water until he had washed his hands' (Erub. 21b).

The aim set the human being is, accordingly, to achieve a two-fold perfection, physical as well as spiritual. A good physique was highly regarded and was even said to have the divine approval. 'The Holy One, blessed be He, takes pride in them who are tall of stature' (Bech. 45b); and among the qualifications necessary for the *Shechinah* to alight upon a person is that he should be well-built and of imposing appearance (Shab. 92a). Conversely, they who had physical defects were thought of as particularly unfortunate. The Talmud prescribes: 'Who beholds a negro, a red-spotted or white-spotted person, a hunchback, dwarfed, or dropsical person, says, "Blessed art Thou Who variest the forms of Thy creatures"; and on beholding a person with an amputated limb, or blind, or flat-footed, or lame, or smitten with boils or a leprous eruption, he says, "Blessed be the true Judge"' (Ber. 58b). The latter is the benediction to be pronounced on hearing bad news (ibid. IX. 2), thereby indicating that such disabilities are a calamity.

As God favours those who have a good physique, that qualification was also noted in the appointment of men to positions of responsibility in the community. The rule was: 'We elect to a Sanhedrin only men of tall stature' (Sanh. 17a). A commanding presence inspires respect.

In view of the importance attached to health, the physician was an indispensable person in the communal life. It was said, 'A disciple of the Sages should not reside in a city in which there is no physician' (Sanh. 17b), because in the event of illness his indisposition would be prolonged and his studies interrupted for an unnecessarily protracted time. We find the rule in a more general form: 'It is forbidden to live in a city in which there is no physician' (p. Kid. 66d).

While the profession was respected, the practitioners were not always honoured. Indeed we have the strong condemnation, 'The best of physicians is destined for Gehinnom' (Kid. 82a). The reason may perhaps be sought in the first clause of this statement: 'A physician for nothing is worth nothing, and a physician who is far away is (as much use as) a blind eye' (B.K. 85a). The inference seems to be that the doctors were grasping, and when they did not receive an adequate fee they failed to give the patient proper attention. That they were kept busily engaged in their work is apparently hinted at in the advice, 'Do not reside in a town where the chief man is a physician' (Pes. 113a), because he is likely to be so occupied with his patients that he cannot attend properly to his civic duties.

§ II. RULES OF HEALTH

Foremost among the essentials of a well-cared-for body is cleanliness. It is not merely next to godliness, but a most important part of it. To wash the hands before touching food was strictly enjoined. '"Sanctify yourselves" (Lev. xi. 44)—i.e. washing the hands before the meal; "and be ye holy" (ibid.)—i.e. washing after the meal' (Ber. 53b).[1] 'Whoever eats bread without first washing his hands is as though he had sinned with a harlot. Whoever makes light of the washing of his hands will be uprooted from the world. Whoever eats bread without scouring his hands is as though he eats unclean bread' (Sot. 4b). A class of persons, spoken of with contempt in the Talmud, is the *Am Ha-aretz*, 'the people of the earth'; and one definition of the term is, 'Whoever does not eat his non-holy food[2] in a condition of ritual purity' (Ber. 47b). 'A person who despises the washing of the hands before a meal is to be excommunicated' (ibid. 19a). There is even a benediction prescribed for the purpose, viz. 'Blessed art Thou, O Lord our God, King of the Universe, Who hast sanctified us by Thy commandments and commanded us concerning the washing of the hands' (ibid. 60b). The cleanliness applied also to vessels used during a meal. 'Rinse the cup before drinking and after drinking' (Tamid 27b); 'A man should not drink from a cup and hand it to his fellow because of the danger to life' (Der. Eretz ix).

[1] Since the food was picked from the dish and conveyed to the mouth by the fingers, these would be stained by the meal; hence the necessity for the second washing.
[2] i.e. his ordinary daily meals.

Washing the hands must likewise be performed immediately on rising from bed, and to omit doing so was held to be injurious to health. 'A hand which touches any part of the body (without having first been washed on waking in the morning) deserves to be cut off. Such an (unwashed) hand makes the eye blind, the ear deaf, and causes a polypus. The hands remain in that dangerous condition until a person washes them three times' (Shab. 108b et seq.).

On the subject of personal cleanliness there is a teaching: 'Three things do not enter the body, but it derives benefit therefrom: washing, anointing, and regular motions' (Ber. 57b). The great importance attached to the first process is seen from the declaration: 'It is forbidden to live in a city in which there is no bath-house' (p. Kid. 66d). How highly its use was esteemed may be gathered from the comment on the words: 'I forgot what was good' (Lament. iii. 17). According to one opinion this refers to the bath-house; according to another opinion it refers to washing the hands and feet in hot water (Shab. 25b). They are the 'good' things, and to be without them is a great deprivation. Similarly the phrase, 'The delights of the sons of men' (Eccles. ii. 8), is defined as 'pools and baths' (Git. 68a).

The bath-house was one which provided the vapour-bath, and the perspiration it caused was considered most wholesome. 'There are three types of perspiring which are beneficial to the body: the perspiration caused by illness, the bath, and exertion. The perspiration caused by illness is curative; and as for that caused by a bath there is nothing to equal it' (ARN XLI). To obtain the best result the use of hot water must be followed by a cold douche: 'If one bathed with hot water and did not follow it with cold water, it is like iron which is inserted into a furnace and not afterwards plunged into cold water' (Shab. 41a). In the same way that the metal will not be properly tempered, so the body will not derive the full benefit.

Cleanliness was advocated as the finest preventative of disease. 'Better is a drop of cold water (in the eyes) in the morning, and the washing of the hands and feet in the evening, than all the eye-salves in the world' (Shab. 108b). 'Uncleanliness of the head leads to blindness, uncleanliness of clothes leads to insanity, uncleanliness of the body leads to ulcers and sores; so beware of uncleanliness' (Ned. 81a).

Especially with infants is this rule to be observed. A Rabbi quotes his mother's advice: 'The proper treatment of a baby is to bathe it in hot water and rub it with oil' (Joma 78b). That it

is an effective treatment is proved by the case of R. Channina.
'It is told of him that when he was eighty years of age he could
stand on one foot while taking off his shoe and putting it on again.
He said, "The hot water and the oil with which my mother anointed
me in my childhood have stood me in good stead in my old age"'
(Chul. 24b). Another recommendation was, 'A man should teach
his child to swim' (Kid. 29a), because it was a useful accomplishment and also created a liking for water.

To experience the full benefit of the bath, washing must be
followed by anointing. 'If one bathed and did not afterwards
anoint himself, it is like rain falling on the roof of a house' (Shab.
41a), i.e. the cleansing is superficial and does not penetrate into
the flesh.

Reference has already been made to the evils of constipation
and the necessity for regular purgation. The Talmud utters the
warning: 'If the fæcal discharge is kept back it causes dropsy, and
if the fluid in the urinary duct is kept back it causes jaundice'
(Ber. 25a). It also teaches: 'Who prolongs his stay in a privy
lengthens his days and years' (ibid. 55a). The beneficial effects
are illustrated by this anecdote: 'A certain matron [1] said to a
Rabbi, "Your face is like that of pig-rearers and usurers." [2] He
replied, "On my faith, both occupations are forbidden me; but
there are twenty-four privies from my lodging-place to the House
of Study and whenever I go there I test myself in all of them"'
(ibid.).

A prayer for thanksgiving was included in the liturgy to be said
after attending to nature's call: 'Blessed art Thou, O Lord our God,
King of the Universe, Who hast formed man in wisdom and created
in him many orifices and vessels. It is revealed and known before
the Throne of Thy Glory, that if one of these be opened, or one
of those closed, it would be impossible to exist and to stand before
Thee. Blessed art Thou, O Lord, Who healest all flesh and doest
wondrously' (Ber. 60b).

Since it was believed that 'if the blood becomes abundant, skin-
disease becomes abundant' (Bech. 44b), the process of cupping
or blood-letting was advised. 'The proper time for blood-letting
is once every thirty days. After the age of forty it should be
undergone less frequently, and after sixty with still less frequency.
The proper time for blood-letting is the first, fourth, and sixth
days of the week, but not the second and fifth' (Shab. 129b).

[1] In the parallel passage (Ned. 49b) the conversation is not with a matron
but with a *Min*, i.e. Christian.
[2] He was so healthy-looking.

Prayer is to be offered before and after the operation. Before it is performed he should say: 'May it be Thy will, O Lord my God, that this operation be a cure for me, and do Thou heal me, for Thou art a faithful Healer and Thy cure is certain, since it is not the way of human beings to cure, but thus are they accustomed.' [1] After it is performed he says: 'Blessed be He Who heals without fee' (Ber. 60a).

The after-effect of the operation is a lowered vitality, and the person must be careful how he conducts himself. The first thing he requires is a nourishing meal to reinvigorate him. 'If one has undergone blood-letting and has nothing to eat, let him sell the sandals on his feet and have a satisfactory meal. What does that comprise? One Rabbi said, "Meat, since it is flesh in the place of flesh"; [2] another said, "Wine, since it is red liquor in the place of red blood"' (Shab. 129a). Certain foods, however, are harmful and should be avoided. 'If one has undergone blood-letting he should not partake of milk, cheese, cress, poultry, or salted meat' (Ned. 54b). Another rule of health is contained in this warning: 'Who undergoes blood-letting and soon afterwards has sexual intercourse forfeits his life and his blood is on his own head' (Nid. 17a).

Together with cleanliness is combined moderation of diet as a pre-requisite for a healthy constitution. 'R. Gamaliel said, For three things I admire the Persians: they are temperate with their food, modest in the privy, and modest in their marital relations' (Ber. 8b). The general rule is prescribed: 'Eat a third (of the capacity of the stomach), drink a third, and leave a third empty' (Git. 70a). Among the mass of the people the most frugal diet seems to have been usual, whether on grounds of poverty or prudence. The Talmud mentions as the evening meal of 'the poor man,' on returning home from his work, 'bread with salt' (Ber. 2b); but even for those who could afford a more elaborate meal, it is stated: 'Bread with salt in the morning and a jug of water will banish all illnesses' (B.K. 92b); 'Who eats the minimum quantity from which Challah [3] has to be offered is healthy and blessed; who eats more is a glutton, and who eats less suffers from intestinal trouble' (Erub. 83b). 'Who wishes to be spared disorder of the bowels should accustom himself to dip (his bread in vinegar or wine). Withdraw your hand from the meal from which you are

[1] viz. to perform the operation of cupping.
[2] The patient's flesh which had been reduced during the process of blood-letting.
[3] See p. 101 n. The quantity alluded to is seven quarters of a log of flour. The log was a liquid measure equal to the contents of six eggs.

deriving enjoyment [1] and do not delay answering nature's call' (Git. 70a). 'Up to forty, eating is beneficial; after that age drinking is beneficial' (Shab. 152a).

The right time to take food is when the need for it is felt. 'While you are hungry eat, while you are thirsty drink' (Ber. 62b). As a rule the mass of people partook of two meals daily, an exception being made in honour of the Sabbath, when an additional meal was to be provided. The evening meal was taken at home after the day's toil was over; but the morning meal was eaten by the labourer while at work. The Talmud gives a time-table for different classes of persons: 'The first hour [2] is breakfast-time for gladiators, the second hour for robbers, the third hour for property-owners,[3] the fourth hour for workmen, and the fifth for people generally. Another opinion is: the fourth hour is the time for people in general, the fifth for workmen, and the sixth for the disciples of the Sages. To breakfast later than that is like throwing a stone into a wine-skin; [4] that is if he has not tasted anything previously in the morning, but if he had done so it does not matter' (Shab. 10a). R. Akiba advised his son: 'Rise up early and eat, in summer on account of the heat and in winter on account of the cold. The proverb says, "Sixty runners ran but did not overtake the man who breakfasted early"' (B.K. 92b).

A meal should be taken sitting, because 'to eat or drink standing shatters the body of a man' (Git. 70a). When a person is travelling, the quantity of food consumed should be reduced. 'One who is on a journey should not eat more than the amount that is customary in years of famine, because of disorder of the bowels' (Taan. 10b).

Moderation in all things is the wise rule to adopt. 'Do not sit too much because it is bad for piles; do not stand too much because it is bad for the heart; do not walk too much because it is bad for the eyes; but spend a third of the time sitting, a third standing, and a third walking' (Keth. 111a). 'In eight things excess is harmful and moderation beneficial: travel, sexual intercourse, wealth, work, wine, sleep, hot water (for drinking and washing), and blood-letting' (Git. 70a).

The need for rest through sleep is recognized. 'Night was created for sleep' (Erub. 65a), declared a Rabbi. 'Sleeping at dawn is like a steel edge to iron' (Ber. 62b). said another, meaning

---

[1] i.e. do not eat more than you should just because you like the food.
[2] The day was reckoned as commencing at 6 a.m. The first hour would consequently be 7 a.m.
[3] Meaning the class which does not depend on manual labour for a livelihood.
[4] i.e. useless; the body does not derive benefit from the food since its vitality had been lowered too much to ensure proper digestion.

thereby that it is health-giving and invigorating. On the other hand, 'Morning sleep puts a man out of the world' (Aboth III. 14), and 'a man is forbidden to sleep during the daytime more than the sleep of a horse. How much is that? Sixty breaths' (Suk. 26b). Another statement is: 'Food induces sleep' (Joma I. 4). The Rabbis believed that it was impossible for a human being to live without sleep for three consecutive days. This is implied in the law, 'If a man says, "I will not sleep for three days," he is castigated and must sleep forthwith' (p. Ned. 37b), because he has made a vain oath which is impossible of fulfilment except with fatal consequences. It is interesting to note that 'a sleeping potion' is mentioned in the Talmud by means of which an abdominal operation was performed (B.M. 83b).

The fact is appreciated that the state of the mind has an effect upon the state of the body, and a happy and contented frame of mind should be cultivated. It is said, for example, that 'a sigh breaks half the body of a man,' and according to another opinion 'it breaks the whole body' (Ber. 58b). 'The evil eye (i.e. envy), the evil inclination, and hatred of his fellow-creatures put a man out of the world' (Aboth II. 16). 'Three things weaken the strength of a man: fear, travel, and sin' (Git. 70a).

Finally, one should live in a clean environment; and the law forbade anything to be done which would be detrimental to the health of a town. A typical regulation is: 'A permanent threshing-floor may not be erected within fifty cubits of a city. The place for depositing carcasses, a cemetery, and a tannery may not be erected within fifty cubits of a city. A tannery may only be set up to the east of a city. R. Akiba allows it in any direction except the west' (B.B. II. 8 f.). The purpose is to safeguard the inhabitants from dust and offensive smells.

§ III. DIETETICS

The importance of diet in the preservation of health was recognized by the Rabbis, and the Talmud has many passages which treat of articles of food that are wholesome or otherwise. Bread seems to have been literally the staff of life. 'Thirteen things are said concerning bread eaten in the morning: it protects from heat, cold, injurious spirits, and demons; it makes the simple wise and helps him to win a lawsuit, assists him to learn and teach Torah, causes his utterances to be listened to, his study remains with him, his flesh does not exhale a bad odour, he is attached to his wife and does not lust after another woman; it destroys tapeworms,

and some add, it drives forth envy and causes love to enter'
(B.M. 107b).

The intention is that if a man starts the day with a nourished
stomach, he will be able to think more clearly and do his work
efficiently; it will also put him into a cheerful frame of mind. The
same thought is expressed in the remark: 'Before a man eats and
drinks he has two hearts; after he has eaten and drunk he has but
one heart' (B.B. 12b). In the Hebrew system of psychology
'heart' is the seat of intelligence; and the saying indicates that an
empty stomach has a disturbing effect on the mind and interferes
with concentration of thought.

The bread should be made of fine wheaten flour. 'Barley flour
is injurious by creating tape-worms' (Ber. 36a). It should also
be eaten cold. 'There is a saying in Babylon that hot bread has
fever by its side' (p. Shab. 4b).

Great stress is laid on the advice that to derive the fullest
benefit from eating bread, salt must be added to it and water
drunk after it. Salt and water are indispensable to life. 'The
world can exist without wine but not without water. Salt is
cheap and pepper dear; the world can exist without pepper but
not without salt' (p. Hor. 48c). 'Salt sweetens meat' (Ber. 5a),
but it 'decreases the seminal fluid' (Git. 70a). Nor should too
much of it be taken. Among the things where excess is bad and
a small quantity good are leaven and salt (Ber. 34a).

The rule advocated is: 'After every food eat salt, and after every
beverage drink water, and you will not come to harm (through
illness). Who has partaken of any food without eating salt or
drunk any beverage without drinking water will be troubled during
the day with a bad odour in his mouth and at night with croup'
(Ber. 40a). One Rabbi counselled: 'He who makes his food float
in water [1] will not suffer with indigestion. How much should he
drink? A cupful to a loaf' (ibid.). Another stated: 'There are
eighty-three diseases connected with the bile which can be counteracted by eating bread with salt in the morning and drinking a
jug of water' (B.K. 92b).

In connection with a meal this warning is sounded: 'If one ate
and did not drink, his food is blood and is the beginning of indigestion. If one ate and did not walk after it a minimum of four
cubits, his food rots (in the stomach) and it is the beginning of foul
breath. If one ate while needing to relieve himself it is like a
furnace being kindled over its ashes, and it is the beginning of a
disagreeable odour from the body' (Shab. 41a).

[1] viz. by drinking a large quantity of water with his food.

Mention has been made above of the fact that bread and salt constituted the ordinary meal of the poor, both morning and evening. If there is money for additional food, the order of preference which is recommended is as follows: '"Thou mayest eat flesh after all the desire of thy soul" (Deut. xii. 20). The Torah teaches us here a rule of conduct, viz. that a man should only eat meat to satisfy his appetite. He who possesses a *mana*[1] should buy a measure of vegetables for his pot; if he possesses ten *mana* he should buy a quantity of fish for his pot; if he possesses fifty *mana* he may buy a quantity of meat for his pot; and if he possesses a hundred *mana* he may have meat cooked for him every day. As for those who possess less than a hundred *mana*, when may they have their dish of vegetables or fish? Every Friday (for the Sabbath)' (Chul. 84a).

It is evident that meat was regarded as a luxury and must have been seldom tasted by the poorer classes. There was a popular superstition in connection with the eating of meat. 'Whoever eats the flesh of a fat ox with turnips on the night of the fourteenth or fifteenth[2] and sleeps in the (light of the) moon, even at the summer solstice, his blood is on his own head' (Kallah). In a parallel passage the consequence is said to be that 'he will be seized with ague' (Git. 70a).

The bulk of the people must accordingly have lived mainly on a vegetarian diet, and the wholesomeness of vegetables is dilated upon. A passage declares: 'Woe to the body through which vegetables keep constantly passing.[3] Against this view is quoted the statement of a Rabbi to his attendant, "If you see vegetables in the market, never ask me, With what will you wrap your bread?"' The two opinions are reconciled by the suggestion that vegetables are injurious without meat; a second opinion is, without wine; and a third view is, without wood[4] (Ber. 44b).

The last-mentioned opinion, that vegetables are harmful when eaten uncooked, is supported by another passage which reads: 'A disciple of the Sages is not allowed to reside in a city where no vegetables are to be had. From this it is to be inferred that vegetables are wholesome; but there is another teaching: Three things increase fæces, reduce stature, and take away a five-hundredth part of the light of a man's eyes, viz. bread made of coarse meal, freshly-made intoxicating liquor, and vegetables!' (Erub. 55b *et*

---

[1] A hundred shekels.
[2] Of the lunar month, i.e. when the moon is full.
[3] Meaning that vegetables form its staple food.
[4] i.e. without being thoroughly cooked over a fire of wood.

seq.). In the parallel version (Pes. 42*a*) the reading is '*raw* vegetables,' and the text continues: 'Three things decrease fæces, raise
the stature, and bring light to the eyes, viz. bread made of well-
sifted flour, fat meat, and old wine.' We also have the statement: 'All raw vegetables make the complexion pale' (Ber. 44*b*).
On the advantage of cooking the vegetables it is said: 'The broth
of beet is pleasant to the heart and good for the eyes, how much
more so for the bowels. This is, however, only so when it remains
on the stove and makes the sound Tuk tuk'[1] (ibid. 39*a*).

Some vegetables are recommended as more beneficial than others.
'He who makes it a habit to eat lentils once in thirty days keeps
croup away from the house; but not every day. What is the
reason? Because it is bad for the breath of the mouth' (ibid. 40*a*).
'Horse-beans[2] are bad for the teeth but good for the bowels'
(ibid. 44*b*). 'Cabbage is good as nourishment and beet as a
remedy' (ibid.). 'Five things are said of garlic: it satisfies, warms
the body, makes the face shine, increases seminal fluid, and kills
tape-worms. Some add that it fosters love and drives away
enmity' (B.K. 82*a*) by the feeling of comfort it engenders. 'Radish
is an elixir of life' (Erub. 56*a*), but 'one should not eat onions
because of the pungent fluid they contain' (ibid. 29*b*).

The seeds of black cumin were commonly used in the Orient.
With reference to them we have the remark: 'Whoever eats black
cumin of the weight of a *denarius*, his heart will be torn out'
(Kallah). How it may be taken with advantage is discussed:
'He who makes it a habit to use black cumin will not suffer with
pain of the heart. It is quoted in objection: Black cumin is one
of the sixty deadly poisons and he who sleeps to the east of his
store of cumin, his blood is on his own head!'[3] There is no contradiction; the latter refers to its odour and the other to its taste.
The mother of R. Jeremiah used to bake bread for him and sprinkle
black cumin upon it and then scrape it off'[4] (Ber. 40*a*).

A fish diet is considered to be very healthful. 'He who makes
it a habit to eat small fish will not suffer with indigestion; more
than that, small fish make a man's whole body fruitful and strong'
(ibid.). Apparently, however, it does not hold good of fish which
had been preserved in salt; for it is said: 'A small salted fish

[1] Representing the sound when the broth is boiling. It must be thoroughly
cooked.
[2] To counteract their harmful effect on the teeth, the Talmud states that
they should be well cooked and swallowed, not chewed.
[3] The west wind will carry the odour to him with fatal result.
[4] She allowed the flavour of the cumin to penetrate into the bread, but
would not permit it to remain because the smell was injurious.

sometimes kills on the seventh, the seventeenth, and twenty-seventh day of the month, and some say the twenty-third day. This applies only to the case where it has been roasted but not roasted thoroughly; but if it has been well roasted, there is no objection. And when it has been well roasted, it only applies to the case where one does not drink beer after it; but if he drinks beer after it, there is no objection' (ibid. 44b).

For its size the most nutritious of all is the egg, if meat be excluded. 'Any food whose minimum standard is the size of an egg, the egg is superior to it as nourishment. Better is a light-roasted egg than six measures of fine flour and a hard-baked egg than four. Of a boiled egg it is said, any food whose minimum standard is the size of an egg, the egg is superior to it as nourishment with the exception of meat' (ibid.). But too many may be harmful; because it is said: 'Whoever eats forty eggs or forty nuts or a quarter of honey, his heart will be torn out' (Kallah).

To overcome the injurious consequences of eating certain vegetables the following is advised: 'To nullify the harmful effects of lettuce eat radishes; to nullify the harmful effects of radishes eat leeks; to nullify the harmful effects of leeks drink hot water; to nullify the harmful effects of all vegetables drink hot water' (Pes. 116a).

It is dangerous to leave foodstuffs exposed overnight. 'Who eats peeled garlic or peeled onion or shelled eggs or drinks diluted liquors, any of which had been exposed overnight, forfeits his life and his blood is on his own head' (Nid. 17a).

Of fruits the most satisfying is the date. 'Dates give heat to the body, satisfy, act as a laxative, strengthen, and do not weaken the heart. When eaten in the morning and evening they are beneficial, in the afternoon they are harmful, at noon there is nothing to equal them, and they then drive away moroseness, indigestion, and piles' (Keth. 10b). 'Honey and all kinds of sweet things are bad for a wound' (B.K. 85a).

§ IV. TREATMENT OF DISEASE

In the folios of the Talmud may be found advice on the cure of ailments. Some of the passages contain genuine medical prescriptions, but others show evidence of superstitious notions. As with all ancient peoples, the principle of homœopathic magic was often resorted to for the purpose of relieving pain, and 'remedies' described below may be paralleled by similar cures mentioned in works like *The Golden Bough*.

It will also be seen that incantations not infrequently formed part of the treatment, these sometimes including Biblical verses. This practice was severely condemned by the Rabbinic authorities. 'It is forbidden to cure oneself by means of Scriptural citations' (Shebuoth 15*b*), they urged. Among those who will have no share in the World to Come is the person who utters an incantation over a wound which includes the quotation: 'I will put none of the diseases upon thee which I have put upon the Egyptians, for I am the Lord that healeth thee' (Exod. xv. 26) (Sanh. x. 1). Even this strong denunciation proved ineffective, and the practice seems to have been widespread.

First as to general rules governing the treatment of an illness. We are told: 'If the patient says he wants something and the physician says he may not have it, the former is listened to. For what reason? "The heart knoweth its own bitterness" (Prov. xiv. 10)' (Joma 83*a*). It was said that 'three garlands of dyer's madder (applied to a patient) arrest the development of disease, five cure it, and seven will even avail against witchcraft. This is provided he has not seen the sun, moon, or rain, or heard the clang of iron, the crowing of a cock, or the sound of footsteps' (Shab. 66*b*). But a Rabbi adds the remark, 'This remedy has fallen into the pit,' i.e. is no longer used.

'Six things are a favourable symptom in an invalid: sneezing, perspiration, abdominal motion, seminal emission, sleep, and a dream. Six things cure an invalid from his sickness, and their remedy is an efficacious remedy: cabbage, beet, a decoction of dried poley, the maw, the womb, and the large lobe of the liver. Some add: also small fish. Ten things cause an invalid to relapse and his sickness becomes worse: to eat the flesh of the ox, fat meat, roast meat, poultry, roasted eggs; also shaving, and partaking of cress, milk, and cheese; and bathing. Others add: eating nuts and cucumbers' (Ber. 57*b*). The principle is here recognized that diet has an important effect upon the condition of the invalid.

A common complaint seems to have been fever of one kind or another, and various methods of dealing with it are prescribed. 'For a quotidian fever take a brand-new *zuz*, go to the salt deposit, procure its weight in salt, and tie it on to the neck-hole of the shirt with a white twisted cord. Or, let him sit at the cross-roads, and when he sees a large ant carrying a load, let him take it, throw it into a copper tube, stop it up with lead and seal it with sixty seals. Then let him shake it and carry it to and fro, exclaiming, "Thy load be upon me and my load (viz. the fever) be upon thee."

A Rabbi objected, "Lest a person may have previously found this same ant and cured his illness by its means,[1] he should rather say, 'My burden and thine own burden be upon thee.'" Or, let him take a new pitcher, go to the river and say to it, "River, river! lend me a pitcherful of water for the journey I have to make." He then waves it seven times around his head, throws the water behind him and exclaims, "River, river! take back the water which thou gavest me, because the journey I had to make has gone and returned the same day"' (Shab. 66b).

'For a tertian fever take seven prickles from seven palm-trees, seven chips from seven beams, seven nails from seven bridges, seven ashes from seven ovens, seven pieces of dirt from seven door-sockets, seven pieces of pitch from seven ships, seven handfuls of cumin, and seven hairs from the beard of an old dog, and tie them on to the neck-hole of the shirt with a white twisted cord' (ibid. 67a).

'For inflammatory fever take a knife which is entirely made of iron, go to a place where there is a wild rose-bush, and tie a white twisted cord on to it. On the first day let him cut a notch in it and say, "And the angel of the Lord appeared unto him in a flame of fire"[2] (Exod. iii. 2). On the morrow let him cut another notch and say, "And Moses said, I will turn aside now and see this great sight" (ibid. 3). The next day he cuts another notch and says, "And when the Lord saw that he[3] turned aside" (ibid. 4). A Rabbi remarked, He should likewise say, "And He said, Draw not nigh hither"[4] (ibid. 5). Consequently on the first day he should recite, "And the angel of the Lord appeared unto him . . . and Moses said"; on the second day, "And when the Lord saw"; and on the third day, "And he said, Draw not nigh hither." As he finishes this, let him bow low and cut it off, exclaiming, "O bush, O bush! not because thou wast loftier than all other trees did the Holy One, blessed be He, cause His *Shechinah* to alight upon thee, but because thou wast the lowliest of all the trees did He cause His *Shechinah* to alight upon thee. As thou didst see the fire of Hananiah, Mishael, and Azariah and flee from it, so see the fever of A son of B and flee from it"' (Shab. 67a).

Two regulations which have to be carefully observed are: In all cases where an invalid mentions his name in an incantation, he should describe himself as the son of his mother and not of his

---

[1] In this case the ant was already bearing the load of the first man's fever, so the second invalid would be asking for it to fall upon himself.
[2] The flame typifies the fever which is burning in the patient.
[3] In the incantation it means 'it (the fever) turned aside,' i.e. departed.
[4] viz. the fever to the patient any more.

father (Shab. 66b); and 'In cases where the incantation has to be repeated, it must be repeated in the exact terms, otherwise it must be said forty-one times' (ibid.).

Another method of treating this illness is as follows: 'For quotidian fever drink a jug of water. For tertian fever undergo bloodletting. For quartan fever eat red meat cooked on glowing coals and drink diluted wine. For chronic fever take a black hen. cut it open cross-wise, shave the crown of the patient, place the hen over his head and leave it there until it sticks. He then stands in water up to his neck until he feels faint; after that he immerses his whole body, comes out of the water and rests. Or, let him eat leeks and stand in water up to his neck until he feels faint; after that he immerses his whole body, comes out of the water and rests' (Git. 67b).

Other forms of fever are also mentioned: 'For the fever called *Gira* take the arrow of Lilith,[1] turn the sharp point downward, throw water upon it and drink. Or, take water from which a dog has drunk at night; but let him be careful it was not water left uncovered.[2] To counteract the drinking of water which had been left uncovered, take a measure equal to a fourth of a *log* of undiluted wine' (Git. 69b). 'For external fever (eruption) take three measures of date-stones, three measures of cedar-leaves, boil each separately and sit between them. Mix them into two wash basins, get a table and rest upon it. Then soak the feet in one of them and next in the other, repeating the process until perspiration ensues. After that wash the water off. When he drinks, let him drink from the water of the cedar-leaves, but not from the water of the date-stones, because it makes one sterile' (ibid.). 'For internal fever take seven handfuls of beet, gathered from seven beds, and boil them with their mould; eat it and drink a cedar-leaf with beer or the berries of the young palm with water' (ibid. 69b et seq.).

For eye-trouble spittle was commonly used,[3] but we are told 'there is a tradition that the spittle of the first-born son of a father has healing powers, but not of the first-born son of a mother' (B.B. 126b). 'For cataract take a scorpion of seven colours, dry it in a shaded place (out of the sun), and grind it into two portions of stibium and one portion. Apply three eye-brushfuls to each eye, but not more, otherwise the eye may burst' (Git.

[1] A wedge-shaped meteoric stone. The word for 'arrow' is *gira*, so there is clearly the application of homœopathic magic.
[2] Water exposed overnight was considered to be highly dangerous. See below.
[3] cf. Mark viii. 23, and see the anecdote quoted on pp. 205 f.

69a). Cataract was also treated by painting the eye with blood (Shab. 78a).

'For night-blindness take a rope of hair, tie one end to the patient's leg and the other to the leg of a dog. Then let children make a noise with a potsherd, exclaiming, "Old dog! foolish hen!" After that collect seven pieces of meat from seven houses, place them in the socket of the door, and eat them upon the ash-heaps of the town. Then untie the rope and say, "Blindness of A son of B, leave A son of B." Then the pupil of the dog is pierced.

'For day-blindness take seven milts from animals, place them in a potsherd used by a cupper; set the patient inside a room and another person outside. The latter says, "Blind man, give me to eat." The patient replies, "Where is the door? Take and eat." After he has eaten, the seeing man must break the potsherd, otherwise the disease will befall him.

'For bleeding from the nose take a *Kohen*[1] whose name is Levi, and write his name backward. As an alternative, take a non-*Kohen* and let him write backward, "I am Papi Shila, son of Sumki."[2] Or let him write, "Taam deli bemé késeph taam deli bemé pegam." Or, take grass-roots, a rope from an old couch, a piece of paper, a crocus, the red part of the palm-branch, and burn them together. Then take a ball of clipped wool of which two threads are to be woven, soaked in vinegar and rolled in ashes, and these are to be inserted in the nostrils. Or, let him look at a stream of water which flows from east to west, part his legs and set one foot on one bank and the other foot on the other bank; let him take some mud in his right hand from under his left foot and in his left hand some mud from under his right foot. He weaves two threads of wool, soaks them in the mud and inserts them in his nostrils. Or, let him sit beneath a spout, and people should fetch water, pour it through the pipe, and say, "As this water has ceased, so may the blood of A son of B cease."

'For a flowing of blood from the mouth, we examine him with a piece of wheat-straw. If it adheres (to the blood), the flux is from the lungs and there is a remedy; if it does not adhere, the flux is from the liver and there is no cure. What is the remedy when the blood issues from the lung? Take three handfuls of sliced beets, seven handfuls of sliced leeks, five handfuls of jujube berries, three handfuls of lentils, one handful of cumin, one handful of spices, and an equal quantity of the intestines of a first-born

---

[1] A descendant in the male line from Aaron the High Priest.
[2] Most of these formulas are unintelligible and cannot be translated or explained.

animal, and boil them together. He should partake of it and then drink strong beer brewed in *Tebeth*' [1] (Git. 69a).

'The remedy to stop the flow of blood from a wound is unripe dates in vinegar; and to repair the flesh the scraped root of cynodon and the paring of the bramble, or worms from a dunghill' (A.Z. 28a).

'For toothache take a plant of garlic which has only one head, rub it with oil and salt, place it upon the thumb-nail on the side where the tooth aches, and surround it with a rim of dough, taking care that the garlic does not touch the flesh lest it produce leprosy' (Git. 69a).

'R. Jochanan was troubled with his gums [2] and went to a certain matron for treatment which she applied on Thursday and Friday. How did she treat him? One Rabbi declared, "With the water of yeast, olive oil, and salt." Another said, "With yeast itself, olive oil, and salt." A third maintained that it was with the fat of a goose's wing. But Abbai said, "I tried all these remedies and was not cured until an Arab told me, 'Take olive-stones which are not a third grown, roast them over the fire on a new hoe, and apply them to the teeth.' I did so and was cured." What is the cause of this complaint? Eating hot wheaten bread or the remains of a pie of fish-hash. What is the symptom? When any food gets between the teeth blood flows' (Joma 84a).

'For pains in the jaw, pellitory leaves are better than *mamru*,[3] and the root of pellitory still more preferable. Insert them in the mouth to obtain relief.

'For quinsy take coarse bran which comes to the top of the sieve, lentils with their mould, fenugreek, and the bud of cuscuta, and insert a quantity about the size of a nut in the mouth. To burst it, let someone blow seeds of the white cress into his throat through a stalk of wheat-straw. To heal the lacerated flesh take earth from the shaded part of a privy, knead it with honey and eat it, and it will give relief' (Git. 69a).

'For catarrh take gum-ammoniac about the size of a pistachio-nut, sweet galbanum about the size of an ordinary nut, a handful of white honey, one-fourth of a *log* of white wine according to the measure used in the town of Machoza, and boil them thoroughly together. When the gum-ammoniac is boiled the whole is boiled. Or, take a quarter of a *log* of milk from a white goat, let it drip upon three cabbage-stalks, and stir the pot with a piece of the

---

[1] The tenth month, corresponding to December–January.
[2] The meaning of the word is uncertain. Some authorities explain as scurvy, but it is clear that some dental disorder is intended.
[3] The name of a plant which cannot be exactly identified.

stem of marjoram. When the marjoram is boiled the whole is boiled. Or, take the excrement of a white dog and knead it with balm; but as far as possible one should avoid eating excrement because it causes the limbs of the body to fall off' (Git. 69b).

'For an abscess take a measure equal to a fourth of a *log* of wine with purple-coloured aloe' (ibid.). There are other methods prescribed for dealing with this trouble. 'An abscess is the fore-runner of fever. What is the remedy for it? Squeeze it between the thumb and middle finger with a snapping motion sixty times (to soften it) and then lance it crosswise, provided its head has not grown white; if it has, the remedy will not be efficacious' (A.Z. 28a). 'For an abscess use this incantation, "Bazbaziah, Masmasiah, Kaskasiah, Sarlai, and Amarlai are the angels sent from the land of Sodom to cure painful abscesses. Bazach bazich bazbazich masmasich kamon kamich. Thine appearance remain in thee, thine appearance remain in thee, thy place remain in thee (and do not spread), thy seed be like a hybrid and like a mule which are sterile; so mayest thou also be sterile in the body of A son of B"' (Shab. 67a).

'For palpitation of the heart take three barley cakes, soak them in curdled milk which is not forty days old, eat them. and then drink diluted wine' (Git. 69b). 'One who suffers from weakness of the heart should take meat from the right flank of a ram and the excrement of cattle dropped during the month of *Nisan*,[1] or failing that, twigs of a willow, and roast the flesh upon a fire made of this fuel. Let him eat the meat and drink diluted wine' (Erub. 29b).

'For asthma—others say for palpitations—take three wheat cakes, soak them in honey, eat them, and then drink undiluted wine. For angina take mint to the quantity of three eggs, one of cumin and one of sesame, and eat them. For indigestion take three hundred grains of long pepper, and each day drink a hundred of them in wine. For tape-worms take a fourth of a *log* of wine with a leaf of the bay-tree. For white worms take a seed of Eruca, tie it in a piece of cloth, soak it in water and drink the liquid; but care must be taken not to swallow the seed lest it pierce the bowels' (Git. 69b).

'For worms in the bowels eat maidenhair. With what is it to be eaten? With seven white dates. What is the cause of the complaint? Eating on an empty stomach roast meat and then drinking water, or fat meat, or the flesh of the ox, or nuts, or shoots of fenugreek followed by water. As an alternative remedy swallow white dates which are half ripe; or, observe a fast, take fat meat,

[1] The first month, corresponding to March–April.

roast it on coals, drain (the marrow of) one of the bones and swallow it with vinegar. Some declare that no vinegar should be used because it is bad for the liver. Or, take parings of the bramble peeled from top to bottom, and not the reverse way lest (worms) pass into the mouth, and boil them in beer at sunset. On the morrow stop up the nose (so as not to smell it) and drink the brew; and when having evacuation, perform it on the part of a date-palm which has been stripped' (Shab. 109b).

'For diarrhœa take fresh poley in water; and for constipation take dried poley in water. For pain in the milt take seven thin fishes and dry them in a shaded place. Each day drink two or three in wine. Or, take the milt of a goat which has not had any young, squeeze it into the cracks of an oven, stand opposite it and say, "As the milt dries, so may the milt of A son of B dry." If he has no oven, let him squeeze it between the bricks of a new house and utter the same incantation. Or, search for the body of a person who died on the Sabbath, take his hand and place it over the milt, and say, "As this hand has dried, so may the milt of A son of B dry." Or, take a thin fish, roast it in a smithy, eat it with water which is used in a smithy, and then drink water from the house of a smith. A goat which had drunk water from the house of a smith, on being cut open, was found to be without a milt (since it had dried up). Or, let him drink large quantities of wine.

'For anal worms take acacia, aloes, white lead, litharge, a charm containing aromatic leaves (*Malabathrum*) and droppings of doves, and apply them wrapped in linen rags in summer and in cotton in winter; or, drink diluted beer.

'For hip disease take a pot containing fish-brine and roll it sixty times on one loin and sixty times on the other. For stone in the bladder take three drops of oil of tar, three drops of the juice of leeks, and three drops of white wine, and inject it into the genitals. Or, take the handle of a jug and hang it on the male *membrum* or on the breasts in the case of a woman' (Git. 69b).

'For lichen take seven ears of wheat of Arzania,[1] roast them on a new hoe, extract the oil therefrom and rub on the affected part' (ibid. 70a).

'For earache take the kidney of a bald buck, cut it crosswise, place it upon some embers, and apply the moisture which exudes from it to the ear; but it must be lukewarm and neither hot nor cold. Or, take the fat of a large cockchafer, cut it open and insert in the ear. Or, fill the ear with oil, make seven threads of grass

---

[1] Famous for their large size.

and take a stalk of garlic, put a white thread round one end and set it alight; insert the other end in the ear and draw the ear close to the flame. He must be careful to keep the ear out of the draught. Having finished one thread, he uses the others in turn. Or, take wool dyed violet which has not been beaten and insert it in the ear, and draw the ear close to the flame; but he must be careful to keep it out of the draught. Or, take a hollow reed which is a hundred years old, fill it with rock-salt, burn it and apply to the ear' (A.Z. 28b).

'If one is suffering from faintness due to fasting, eat honey and other sweet things because they restore light to the eyes' (Joma 83b). 'If one is smitten with jaundice, eat ass's flesh; if one is bitten by a mad dog, eat the lobe of its liver' (ibid. 84a). 'Vinegar is beneficial against scorching heat' (Shab. 113b).

Since snakes abounded in the Eastern countries where Jews resided, advice is given how the harm they do can be counteracted. 'A child of six who is stung by a scorpion on the day he completed his sixth year, cannot live.[1] What is the cure for him? The gall of a white stork in beer; rub him with it and let him drink of it. A child of one who is stung by a hornet on the day he completed his first year, cannot live. What is the cure for him? The prickles of the date-palm in water; rub him with it and him drink of it' (Keth. 50a).

'If one has drunk water exposed overnight,[2] let him drink shepherd's-flute (*Eupatorium*). Or, take five roses and five glasses of beer, boil them together until it reaches the measure of a quarter of a *log*, and drink it. The mother of a certain Rabbi treated a man (who drank such water) as follows: She prepared for him one rose and one glass of beer, boiled them and gave him to drink. She then heated the stove, raked out the embers, placed a brick inside and sat him upon it,[3] and (the poison) came from him like a green palm-leaf. Other remedies suggested are: Drink a quarter of a *log* of milk from a white goat. Take a sweet citron, scrape it out, fill it with honey, set it upon glowing embers and then eat it. Use urine which is forty days old—a thirty-second part of a *log* for a hornet's sting, a quarter for a scorpion, and an eighth for exposed water.

'If one has swallowed a snake, he should eat cuscuta with salt and run a distance of three *mil*. If one has been bitten by a snake, take the fœtus of a white she-ass, split it open and place upon the

---

[1] Unless the remedy which is prescribed is at once applied.
[2] Into which a snake may have ejected poison.
[3] So that he thoroughly perspired.

wound' (Shab. 109*b*). An alternative prescription reads: 'If one is stung by a snake, cut open a hen (and place it over the wound) and eat leeks' (Joma 83*b*).

'If one is entwined by a snake, he should descend into water, put a basket over his head, and let it down gradually (for the snake to enter). When it is completely in the basket, he should throw this into the water, come out and go away (so that the snake should not follow him). When a snake is infuriated and about to attack a man, if there be somebody with him, he should ride on his back a distance of four cubits (so that the snake loses the trail); otherwise he should jump over a dyke or cross a river; and at night, let him set his bed upon four casks and sleep in the open. Also let him take four cats, tie them to the four corners of the bed, spread chips of wood round about so that when the cats hear (the snake gliding over them) they will devour it. If a snake pursues a man, let him run among sand (where it cannot move quickly)' (Shab. 110*a*).

To counteract the effects of too much wine, the following is recommended: 'Take oil and salt and rub them into the palms of the hands and soles of the feet, exclaiming, "As this oil is clear so may the wine of A son of B be clear." [1] Or, take the sealing clay of a wine-bottle, soak it in water and say, "As this clay is clear so may the wine of A son of B be clear"' (ibid. 66*b*).

'If one has a bone stuck in his throat, he takes a similar bone, places it on his head and says, "One, one, gone down, swallowed, swallowed, gone down, one, one." There is no objection to this being done on account of "the ways of the Amorite." [2] For a fish-bone stuck in the throat say, "Thou art stuck like a needle, shut in like a shield, sink down, sink down"' (ibid. 67*a*).

A general piece of advice is: 'Do not get into the habit of drinking medicine, and do not have the teeth extracted' (Pes. 113*a*).

[1] And not fuddle the head. [2] See pp. 291 f.

CHAPTER IX

FOLK-LORE

§ I. Demonology

So firm was the belief in evil spirits, both among the educated and uneducated classes, that the Talmud legislates for it. In their legal decisions the Rabbis prescribed for circumstances which presuppose the actuality of demons. For instance, in connection with laws regulating what may or may not be done on the Sabbath, it was enacted: 'Who extinguishes a lamp through fear of (attack by) Gentiles or robbers, or through fear of an evil spirit, is free of guilt' (Shab. II. 5); and 'If one has been forcibly driven beyond the permitted distance which one may walk on a Sabbath either by Gentiles or an evil spirit, he may only move four cubits of his own accord' (Erub. IV. 1).

An important cause of sinfulness is possession by a spirit which deprives the unfortunate person of his sense of right as well as his self-mastery. 'No person commits a sin unless there enters into him a spirit of madness' (Sot. 3a). Another statement on the subject is: 'Three things cause a person to transgress against his conscience and the will of his Maker. viz. Gentiles, an evil spirit, and the pressing needs caused by poverty' (Erub. 41b).

On the question of the origin of these harmful beings there is diversity of opinion. One view was that they were part of God's creation. Among the ten objects which were declared to have been created on the eve of the first Sabbath were the *mazzikin* or harmful spirits (Aboth v. 9). On the text, 'And God said, Let the earth bring forth the living creature after its kind' (Gen. i. 24), the observation was made: 'These are the demons whose souls the Holy One, blessed be He, created, but when He came to create their bodies He hallowed the Sabbath and did not create them' (Gen. R. VII. 5). They were, accordingly, thought of as disembodied spirits.

A variant of this theory is that they are the souls of evil men transmuted by God into a malignant form as a punishment. 'The men who planned to build the tower of Babel were divided into three classes. One said, Let us ascend to heaven and dwell there;

another said, Let us ascend and practise idolatry; and the third said, Let us ascend and wage war (against God). The first class God dispersed; the third class was turned into apes, spirits, demons, and night-devils, and as for the second class He confused their language' (Sanh. 109a).

Still another variant makes God their original Creator, but their propagation was the result of intercourse between them and the first human pair. 'During the entire period of one hundred and thirty years that Adam separated himself from Eve (after the expulsion from Eden), the male spirits became impassioned through her and she bore from them; and the female spirits became impassioned through him and bore from him' (Gen. R. xx. 11). A foundation for this belief was discovered in the Biblical text. 'All the years that Adam was under the ban he begat spirits, demons, and night-devils; as it is said, "Adam lived a hundred and thirty years, and begat a son in his own likeness, after his image" (Gen. v. 3)—from which the inference is to be drawn that hitherto he had not begotten in his own likeness' (Erub. 18b).

An entirely different theory was advanced—an evolutionary hypothesis—to explain their existence, viz.: 'The male hyena after seven years becomes a bat; the bat after seven years becomes a vampire; the vampire after seven years becomes a nettle; the nettle after seven years becomes a thorn;[1] the thorn after seven years becomes a demon' (B.K. 16a).

As for their characteristics, 'In three respects they resemble the ministering angels and in three they are like human beings. Like the ministering angels they have wings, they fly from one end of the world to the other, and they know the future. Like human beings they eat and drink, propagate and die' (Chag. 16a). Some also declare: 'They have the power of altering their appearance, and can see but are invisible' (ARN xxxvii).

That they are not visible to human beings is a blessing; because 'had the human eye been given the power of seeing them, no person could endure because of the evil spirits. They outnumber us, said a Rabbi, and surround us like the ridge round a field. Every one of us, said another, has a thousand on his left hand and myriads on his right. The crush at the public discourses, said a third, is due to them;[2] the knees grow fatigued because of them; the

---

[1] The word in the text is perhaps to be emended to another meaning 'a snake.'

[2] Expositions of the Torah were delivered in the Synagogues and Houses of Study on the Sabbaths. Although the hall may not have been overcrowded, the audience would feel crushed. This was due to the evil spirits who wished to make them uncomfortable and induce them to stay away.

wearing out of the clothes of the Rabbis is the consequence of their rubbing against them; the feet are bruised by them' (Ber. 6a).

Their numerical strength is elsewhere emphasized. 'The whole world is full of evil spirits and harmful demons, said one Rabbi; while another declared, There is not an extent of a fourth of a *kab* in the space of the Universe in which there are not nine *kabs* of demons' (Tanchuma Mishpatim § 19). R. Jochanan said: 'There are three hundred species of male demons in Sichnin,[1] but as for the female demon I do not know what she is' (Git. 68a).[2]

Although they are normally invisible, yet there are means of detecting their presence and even of seeing them. 'Who wishes to perceive their footprints should take sifted ashes and sprinkle them around his bed. In the morning he will see something resembling the footprints of a cock.[3] Who wishes to see them should take the after-birth of a black she-cat,[4] the offspring of a black she-cat, the first-born of a first-born, roast it in the fire, pulverize it, then fill his eyes with it, and he will see them. He must pour the powder into an iron tube and seal it with an iron signet, lest he come to harm. A certain Rabbi did this; he saw the evil spirits and was injured. His colleagues prayed for him and he was cured' (Ber. 6a).

While they are liable to be met with anywhere, there are certain places which they particularly frequent. Notable among them are dark, unclean, and dangerous spots and water.[5] The evil spirits seem really to be the personification of danger.

A favourite haunt is ruined buildings. A discussion on the

---

[1] A town in Galilee.

[2] On the great numbers of the demons, see Mark v. 9: 'And he asked him (the evil spirit), What is thy name? And he saith unto him, My name is Legion, for we are many.' Gilbert Murray quotes a fragment from an unknown Greek poet who wrote: 'All the air is so crowded with them that there is not one empty chink into which you could push the spike of a blade of corn' (*Five Stages of Greek Religion*, p. 50).

[3] Orientals regard the cock as a power of darkness because it crows in the dark. The Talmud (Sanh. 63b) identifies 'Succoth Benoth' (2 Kings xvii. 30) with the hen, and 'Nergal' (ibid.) with the cock.

[4] Compare R. C. Thompson, *Semitic Magic*, p. 61: 'The ashes of a black cat are a popular form of magician's stock-in-trade in the modern Arabic books of sorcery.'

[5] Exactly the same beliefs are current among the Mohammedans. 'They (the *jinn*) are also believed to inhabit rivers, ruined houses, wells, baths, ovens, and even the *latrina*; hence persons, when they enter the latter place and when they let down a bucket into a well, or light a fire, and on other occasions, say, "Permission," or "Permission, ye blessed"—which words, in the case of entering the *latrina*, they sometimes preface with a prayer for God's protection against all evil spirits' (E. W. Lane, *Modern Egyptians*, Everyman ed., p. 229). Parallels to these customs are found in the Talmudic sources.

subject is held in the Talmud. 'For three reasons one should not enter ruins: on account of suspicion,[1] of falling fabric, and evil spirits. Why mention on account of suspicion, since a sufficient reason can be derived from the danger of falling fabric? They might be new ruins.[2] Then derive it from the danger of evil spirits! This would not apply when two men entered a ruin.[3] But should there be two men, there would likewise be no ground for suspicion![4] There would be in the case of two men of ill repute. Why mention on account of falling fabric, since a sufficient reason can be derived from the grounds of suspicion and evil spirits? No, not in the case of two men of good repute. Why mention on account of evil spirits. since a sufficient reason can be derived from the grounds of suspicion and falling fabric? No, not in the case of new ruins and two men of good repute. Is there no fear of evil spirits also when there are two men? In such places where evil spirits resort there is occasion for fear. Or if you will, I can say that even in the case of a person alone and new ruins situated in a wild place there is no ground for suspicion, because a woman does not frequent such a spot; but the fear of evil spirits remains' (Ber. 3a, b). The result of the argument is that ruins must be avoided principally for the reason that demons resort there.

Another favourite haunt is the latrine. 'Whoever is modest in a privy is delivered from three things: from serpents, scorpions, and evil spirits. There was a privy in Tiberias which if two people entered, even by day, they came to harm. It was told of two Rabbis that they entered it separately and no harm befell them. Their colleagues asked them, "Were you not afraid?" They answered, "We were taught a charm: a charm for the privy is modesty and silence." Another Rabbi reared a lamb to accompany him into the privy.[5] Before Raba was appointed Principal of the Academy, his wife used to rattle a nut in a flask before him;[6] but afterwards, when he presided over the Academy, she made an aperture for him in the wall and placed her hand upon his head'[7] (Ber. 62a).

---

[1] Of going there for an immoral purpose.

[2] In that case there would not be much danger of fabric falling.

[3] We shall see below that when accompanied by a second person the danger from evil spirits is minimized.

[4] Because Jewish law permits a woman to be accompanied by two men (Kid. iv. 12).

[5] As a protection against the evil spirits.

[6] To frighten away the demons. See Frazer, *Folk-lore in the Old Testament*, III, pp. 446 f.

[7] As a more effective protection, because owing to his more exalted position he was particularly liable to attack.

The Talmud offers this incantation to exorcise the demon of a privy: 'Upon the head of a lion and upon the nose of a lioness I found the demon Bar Shirika Panda; in the valley where leeks grow I beat him, with an ass's jaw-bone I strike him' (Shab. 67a).

The belief is almost universal that evil spirits specially frequent places where there is water. 'Harmful spirits are found in wells as also in fields' (p. Jeb. 15d). A Rabbi related: 'It happened in my village that Abba José of Tzaytor was sitting and studying by the opening of a well, when the spirit which resided there appeared to him and said, "You know how many years I have resided here, and yet you come out and your wives in the evening and at the new moon, but you have not been harmed. You should, however, be informed that a certain evil spirit desires to take up its abode here which will do injury to human beings." Abba José asked, "What shall we do?" He answered, "Go and warn the inhabitants of the place and say to them, Whoever has a hoe or spade or shovel should come here to-morrow at dawn and watch the surface of the water. When they notice a ripple on the water, they should beat it with their iron implements and exclaim, 'The victory is ours!' They must not depart until they see a clot of blood on the water's surface." He went and warned the people of the village of what he had been told. They acted on the advice given, and at dawn the next day they beat with their iron implements and exclaimed, "The victory is ours! The victory is ours!" Nor did they leave the spot until they saw a kind of blood-clot upon the surface of the water' (Lev. R. XXIV. 3).

Because of the partiality of demons for places where water is, particular care must be taken with liquids, especially when they are left exposed. 'An evil spirit alights upon foodstuffs and beverages which are kept beneath a bed, even though covered within an iron receptacle' (Pes. 112a). 'One should not pour into the public road water which has been exposed overnight, nor should he sprinkle the floor of a house with it, use it for making mortar, give his or a neighbour's cattle to drink of it, nor wash his hands and feet therewith' (A.Z. 30b). 'A person may not drink water on Wednesday night or Saturday night; if he does drink, then his blood is on his own head because of danger. Which danger? An evil spirit. If he is thirsty, what is the remedy? Let him recite the passage relating to the seven "voices" in Ps. xxix. Or, let him pronounce the incantation, "Lul, Shaphan, Anigron, and Anirdaphon,[1] I sit amidst the stars, I walk among lean and fat

[1] They are apparently names of demons.

men." Otherwise, he should awaken anybody who is present and say to him, "A son of B, I thirst for water," and then he may drink. Or, let him rattle the lid against the pitcher and drink. Or, let him throw something into it and drink. A person should not drink from rivers or pools at night; and if he does drink, then his blood is on his own head because of the danger. Which danger? The danger of Shabriri.[1] If he is thirsty, what is his remedy? Should there be another person present, let him say to him, "A son of B, I thirst for water." Otherwise let him say to himself, "My mother told me, Be careful of Shabriri, Briri, Riri, Iri, Ri.[2] I am thirsty in a white cup"' (Pes. 112a). The reason why Wednesday and Saturday nights are singled out is accounted for by the belief: 'One should not go out alone at night, particularly on Wednesday and Saturday nights, because Agrath daughter of Machlath is abroad with eighteen myriads of angels of destruction, each of whom has permission to work harm by himself' (ibid. 112b).

Evil spirits shun the light and prefer darkness; therefore night is a dangerous time. 'A person is forbidden to give greeting to any one in the night-time for fear that it might be a demon' (Sanh. 44a). Another passage states: 'Walking by the light of a torch is equal to two;[3] by moonlight is equal to three. To a single person an evil spirit appears and does injury; to two it appears but does no injury; to three it does not appear at all' (Ber. 43b). Therefore one should not walk abroad in the darkness unaccompanied.

To avoid the glare of the sunlight the spirits repair to shaded places, and for this reason peril lurks in shadows. 'There are five shadows (which are dangerous on account of evil spirits): the shadow of a single palm, of a lotus-tree, of a caper-tree, of a sorb-bush, and of a fig-tree.[4] Some also add, the shadow of a ship and of a willow. The general rule is, the more branches a tree has the more dangerous is its shade, and when its thorns are dangerous its shade is correspondingly dangerous, with the exception of the service-tree, which is not dangerous despite the fact that its thorns are. A female demon said to her son, "Fly from the service-tree, because it killed your father and will also kill you." The shadows of caper-trees are the resort of spirits; the shadows of sorb-bushes

---

[1] The demon of blindness.

[2] As the syllables lessen so the demon dwindles away and the danger passes.

[3] i.e. is the equivalent of another person as protection against the evil spirits in the dark.

[4] 'And of a fig-tree' is not in the printed text of the Talmud but is found in the Munich MS. It is required to complete the number five.

are the resort of demons; roofs are the resort of *Rishpé*.[1] For what purpose is this mentioned? In connection with the amulet.[2] The spirits of caper-trees are creatures without eyes. For what purpose is this mentioned? To escape from them.[3] On one occasion a Rabbinic scholar went to relieve himself by some caper-trees. He heard a female demon coming upon him, so he fled. As she followed him, she became entangled in a palm; the palm withered and she burst. The shadows of sorb-bushes are the resort of demons. A sorb-bush which is in the vicinity of a town has not less than sixty demons. For what purpose is this mentioned? For the inscription of the amulet. Once a town-watchman went and stood by a sorb-bush which was near the town; sixty demons attacked him and he was in danger. He went to one of the Rabbis who did not know that sixty demons frequented a sorb-bush, and he wrote for him an amulet against one demon. He heard them dancing around him and singing, "This person's turban is like that of a Rabbinic scholar, but we have proved that he does not know how to pronounce a benediction." Then a Rabbi came who was aware that sixty demons haunted a sorb-bush, and he wrote an amulet against sixty demons; and he heard them say to each other, "Clear out from here"' (Pes. 111*b*).

Evil spirits not only attack human beings but also animals, which, as a result, become maddened and a source of danger. Dogs are specially liable to possession by them. 'Five things are said of a mad dog: its mouth is open, its spittle drips, its ears flap, its tail hangs between its legs, and it slinks along the sides of the streets. Some declare that it also barks inaudibly. What is the cause of its madness? One Rabbi attributed it to witches playing with the dog; another maintained that an evil spirit rested upon it. What is the point at issue between them? Whether it is to be killed by means of a projectile,[4] since whoever comes in

---

[1] The word is taken from Job v. 7: 'The sons of *Résheph* fly upward.' The Talmud comments: '*Résheph* means nothing else than evil spirits; as it is said, "The wasting of hunger and the devouring of the fiery bolt (*Résheph*) and bitter destruction" (Deut. xxxii. 24)' (Ber. 5*a*). 'Bitter destruction,' in Hebrew *kéteb meriri*, was also thought to be a demon. He is abroad from 10 a.m. to 3 p.m. during the three weeks between *Tammuz* 17 and *Ab* 9, i.e. midsummer. 'He is full of eyes, scales, and hair. He has an eye over his heart which is fatal for any one to behold' (Lament. R. to i. 3).

[2] In which the proper designation must be inserted. An amulet which is a protection against the spirit of caper-trees would not guard against the demons of sorb-bushes or the *Rishpé* of roofs.

[3] Being sightless, there would be safety in flight, since they could not see to follow.

[4] If the madness was cause by an evil spirit, contact must be avoided with the dog and it should be killed by throwing a projectile at it.

contact with the dog is in danger, and whoever is bitten by it dies. If a person comes in contact with it, what is his remedy? He should divest himself of his garments and run away. If he is bitten, what is his remedy? He takes the skin of a male hyena and writes upon it, "I, A son of B, write upon the skin of a male hyena concerning thee: Kanti kanti kleros—another version is, Kandi kandi kloros—Jah, Jah, Lord of Hosts, Amen, Amen, Selah." He divests himself of his garments, buries them in a grave for twelve months, then takes them out, burns them in a furnace and scatters the ashes at the cross-roads. During those twelve months when he drinks water, he should only drink it through a copper tube, lest he see the reflection of a demon (in the water) and subject himself to peril' (Joma 83*b et seq.*).

Certain classes of person become particularly susceptible to attack by evil spirits and need special protection. 'Three require guarding (from demons): an invalid, a bridegroom, and a bride. Another version is: an invalid, a woman in confinement, a bridegroom and bride. Some say: Also a mourner; and others add: Also disciples of the Sages at night' [1] (Ber. 54*b*).

The principal female demon was Lilith, who was thought of as a creature with long hair (Erub. 100*b*). With regard to her it was said: 'It is forbidden for a man to sleep alone in a house; and whoever sleeps alone in a house will be seized by Lilith' (Shab. 151*b*). Little is told of her in the Talmud; but she figures prominently in later Jewish folk-lore as specially harmful to women in confinement and a child-snatcher.[2]

Since the human being was so exposed to the harmful activities of evil spirits, means had to be devised to circumvent their mischievous designs. Some of these have already been indicated, such as incantations and amulets. Formulas have been quoted for the purpose of banishing demons in special circumstances; but the general rule is given: 'To exorcise a demon say, "Be split, be accursed, broken, and banned, son of mud, son of an unclean one, son of clay, like Shamgaz, Merigaz, and Istemaah' [3] (Shab. 67*a*).

---

[1] The last-mentioned are tempted by evil spirits to lapses from morality. Frazer offers parallels to this passage. For women in confinement, see *Folk-lore in the Old Testament*, III, pp. 472 ff.; for bride and bridegroom, I, pp. 520 ff.; for mourners, III, pp. 236, 298 ff.

[2] The name Lilith used to be connected with *laylah* ('night') in the sense of night-spirit; but modern scholars prefer to associate it with the Sumerian *lulu* ('wantonness'), and explain her as 'the demoness who inspires lust. See R. C. Thompson, *Semitic Magic*, p. 66.

[3] The text is uncertain, and a suggested emendation is: 'son of clay, in the name of Morigo, Moriphath and his seal.'

Even numbers, as we shall see in a later section, were regarded as unlucky since they attracted the undesirable attention of evil spirits; so to overcome them it is necessary to make them believe that an odd number is involved. A Rabbi related, 'The demon Joseph informed me, If one drinks two glasses (of a beverage) we kill; with four glasses we do not kill but with four we injure. In the case of two it is immaterial whether they were taken in error or intentionally; but with four we injure if it was done wilfully, but not if it was done in error. Should a person forget himself and chance to go out (after drinking two glasses), what is his remedy? He takes his right thumb in the left hand and his left thumb in the right hand and says, "You and I are three"; but if he hears somebody declare, "You and I are four," he should say, "You and I are five"; and if he hears somebody declare, "You and I are six," he should say, "You and I are seven." It once happened so until the person reached the number of a hundred and one, and then the demon burst' (Pes. 110a).

An exceptional knowledge of such incantations for the overcoming of demons was attributed to King Solomon. 'Many spirits and demons did Solomon vanquish' (Exod. R. xxx. 16), although the power deserted him later in life because, as it is said, 'Until Solomon sinned he ruled over the demons' (Pesikta 45b). An interesting reference to the subject is found in Josephus: 'God also enabled him to learn the art which expels demons, which is useful and works cures for men. He composed charms also by which diseases are alleviated. And he left behind him forms of exorcisms, by which people drive away demons so that they never return, and this method of cure is of very great value unto this day; for I have seen a certain man of my own country, whose name was Eleazar, curing people possessed by demons in the presence of Vespasian and his sons and captains and the whole of his soldiers. The manner of the cure was as follows: he put a ring that had under its seal one of those sorts of roots mentioned by Solomon to the nostrils of the demoniac, and then drew the demon out through his nostrils as he smelt it; and when the man fell down immediately, he adjured the demon to return into him no more, still making mention of Solomon, and reciting the incantation which he had composed' (Antiq. VIII. ii. 5).

The use of a root inside a signet-ring as an amulet is mentioned in the Rabbinic sources. 'A person may not walk out on the Sabbath wearing an amulet unless it had been written by an expert' (Shab. VI. 2). 'Which is the amulet of an expert? Such as had effected a cure a second and a third time, whether it be an amulet in writing or one consisting of roots.[1] With such he may go out on the Sabbath; obviously so if he had already been attacked by a demon, but also if he had not yet been attacked; obviously so if it is in a circumstance where there is danger, but also if there is no danger. One may tie it and untie it during the Sabbath, provided he does not insert it in a necklace or signet-ring and carry it about, because of appearances' sake' (Tosifta Shab. IV. 9).

The law with regard to written amulets is: 'Even though they contain the divine Name, they may not be rescued from fire on the Sabbath, but must be allowed to burn' (Shab. 115b). Consequently no idea of sanctity attached to them. The commentator, Rashi, mentions as verses commonly included in amulets: 'I will put none of the diseases upon thee which I have put upon the Egyptians, for I am the Lord that healeth thee' (Exod. xv. 26),[2] and 'Thou shalt not be afraid for the terror by night, nor for the arrow that flieth by day' (Ps. xci. 5). Amulets were also attached to animals, since they likewise were liable to attack. The law states: 'An animal may not go out on the Sabbath wearing an amulet, even written by an expert, and on this point the law is stricter with an animal than a human being' (Tosifta Shab. IV. 5).

Besides the carrying of written amulets, the recital of certain Scriptural texts was supposed to afford protection against demons. 'Whoever reads the *Shema* [3] upon his bed is as though he holds a two-edged sword in his hand (to ward off evil spirits); as it is said, "Let the high praises of God be in their mouth, and a two-edged sword in their hand" (Ps. cxlix. 6)' (Ber. 5a). That, indeed, was the purpose for which it was instituted. 'On what ground was it ordained that the *Shema* should be recited at home in the evening? To put the harmful spirits to flight' (p. Ber. 2d). Another favourite passage is indicated in the statement: 'In Jerusalem they used to recite "the song of the evil spirits" on the Sabbath for the relief of a stricken person. Which is it? Ps. xci. 1–9' (p. Shab. 8b). It was said with reference to this Psalm that it 'was composed by Moses at the time when he ascended Mount Sinai because he was afraid of the harmful spirits' (Num. R. XII. 3).

But the most reliable safeguard is the divine protection. 'Were it not for the shadow of the Holy One, blessed be He, which protects the human being, the harmful spirits would slay him; as it is said, "Their defence is departed from them and the Lord is with

---

[1] A particular root, employed as an amulet, is described in detail by Josephus (War VII. vi. 3).

[2] See p. 251.

[3] The *Shema* is a collection of Scriptural passages (Deut. vi. 4–9; xi. 13–21; Num. xv. 37–41), which formed part of the morning and night prayers.

us; fear them not" (Num. xiv. 9). Another version is: Were it not for the word of the Holy One, blessed be He, which protects the human being, the harmful spirits would slay him; as it is said, "I create the fruit of the lips; peace, peace to him that is far off, and to him that is near, saith the Lord; and I will heal him" (Is. lvii. 19)' (Midrash to Ps. civ. 29; 224a). On the statement, 'And all the peoples of the earth shall see that thou art called by the name of the Lord, and they shall be afraid of thee' (Deut. xxviii. 10), the remark is made: 'The word "all" is to include even the spirits, even the demons' (p. Ber. 9a). Similarly the priestly benediction, 'The Lord keep thee' (Num. vi. 24), received the interpretation, 'from harmful spirits' (Sifré ad loc.; 12a).

The divine protection against these malicious beings is secured by obedience to His commandments. 'If a man perform a religious precept, one angel is assigned to him; if he perform two precepts, two angels are assigned to him; if he perform all the precepts, many angels are assigned to him; as it is said, "For He shall give His angels charge over thee, to keep thee in all thy ways" (Ps. xci. 11). Who are these angels? They are his guardians from the harmful spirits; as it is said, "A thousand shall fall at thy side and ten thousand at thy right hand" (ibid. 7)' (Tanchuma Mishpatim § 19).

§ II. The Evil Eye

The dread of the Evil Eye was universal in past ages and still persists among the uneducated. It is no matter for surprise that traces are evident in the folk-lore of the Talmud. The term 'Evil Eye' is employed there in two distinct senses, one clearly older than the other, and the comparison helps to an understanding of the superstition.

The first signification is 'envy' or 'an ungenerous disposition,' and is found in the Bible. In a description of famine conditions the statement occurs: 'The man that is tender among you, and very delicate, his eye shall be evil toward his brother, and toward the wife of his bosom, and toward the remnant of his children which he hath remaining, so that he will not give to any of them the flesh of his children whom he shall eat' (Deut. xxviii. 54 f.). Here the meaning is 'greed' as in 'He that hath an evil eye hasteth after riches' (Prov. xxviii. 22). It denotes lack of generosity in the verse, 'Eat thou not the bread of him that hath an evil eye' (ibid. xxiii. 6), and its opposite is the 'good eye' as in the verse, 'He that hath a bountiful (*lit.* good) eye shall be blessed' (ibid. xxii. 9).

Precisely the same usage is found in Talmudic literature. R. Jochanan b. Zakkai said to his five most distinguished pupils: 'Go forth
and see which is the good way to which a man should cleave.
R. Eliezer said, A good eye; R. Joshua said, A good friend; R. José
said, A good neighbour; R. Simeon said, One who foresees the
fruit of an action; R. Eleazar said, A good heart. Thereupon he
said to them, I approve the words of R. Eleazar rather than your
words, for in his words yours are included. He said to them,
Go forth and see which is the evil way that a man should shun.
R. Eliezer said, An evil eye; R. Joshua said, A bad friend; R. José
said, A bad neighbour; R. Simeon said, One who borrows and does
not repay; R. Eleazar said, A bad heart. Thereupon he said to
them, I approve the words of Eleazar rather than your words, for
in his words yours are included' (Aboth II. 13 f.). Obviously no
superstitious notions are connected with the phrases 'a good eye'
and 'an evil eye'; they refer to magnanimity and its reverse.

The same applies to the other occurrences in the Tractate *Aboth*,
viz.: 'The evil eye (i.e. envy), the evil inclination, and hatred of
his fellow-creatures put a man out of the world' (II. 16). 'As to
almsgiving there are four dispositions: he who desires to give but
that others should not give, his eye is evil towards what appertains
to others;[1] he who desires that others should give but will not
give himself, his eye is evil against what is his own; he who gives
and wishes others to give is a saint; he who will not give and does
not wish others to give is a wicked man' (v. 16). 'A good eye,
a humble mind, and a lowly spirit are the tokens of the disciples
of Abraham our father' (v. 22).

Among other Talmudic passages where the words have the same
connotation are: 'With reference to the proportion separated as an
offering to the priests, a generous person (*lit.* a good eye) gives a
fortieth—the School of Shammai says, a thirtieth; a person of
average disposition gives a fiftieth; and a niggardly person (*lit.* an
evil eye) a sixtieth' (Terumoth IV. 3). 'As it is the way of a donor
of a gift to present it with good grace (*lit.* a good eye), so should
one who dedicates property to the Sanctuary do so with good
grace' (p. B.B. 14d).

A telling illustration of the use of 'the evil eye' as the spirit
of jealousy is the embellished account of the first interview between
David and Saul. 'The king said to him, "Thou art not able to
go against this Philistine to fight with him, for thou art but a youth"
(1 Sam. xvii. 33). David replied, "Thy servant kept his father's
sheep, and when there came a lion, or a bear, and took a lamb

---

[1] He is envious, since almsgiving brings blessing to the giver.

out of the flock, I went after him and smote him . . . and this uncircumcised Philistine shall be as one of them" (ibid. 34 ff.). When Saul asked him, "Who told thee that thou canst kill him?" he answered, "The Lord that delivered me out of the paw of the lion, and out of the paw of the bear, He will deliver me out of the hand of the Philistine" (ibid. 37). Thereupon "Saul clad David with his apparel" (ibid. 38). But it is written of Saul, "From his shoulder and upward he was higher than any of the people". (ix. 2); so when he clothed David in his apparel and saw that it fitted him, at once the evil eye entered into him. David perceiving that Saul's face had gone white, said to him, "I cannot go with these, for I have not proved them; and David put them off" (xvii. 39)' (Lev. R. XXVI. 9).

Jealousy and greed create malicious feelings towards the person who excites these passions and give rise to a wish for calamity to overwhelm him. Such an unfriendly hope is usually concentrated in a glance of hatred; hence the phrase 'the evil eye.' And the fear of it comes from the belief that through the medium of the malignant look harm will befall the intended victim.

That the glance of the eye can have injurious effects is definitely asserted in the Talmud. The power was especially attributed to the Rabbis. 'Wherever the Sages directed their gaze either death or some calamity occurred' (Chag. 5b). A story has been cited which tells that every place on which the eye of R. Siméon b. Jochai rested was scorched.[1] The same is narrated of R. Eliezer (B.M. 59b). Of several Rabbis stories are told that their look turned a person who offended them into 'a heap of bones' (Shab. 34a; B.B. 75a). One of them, who exercised this power, was even sightless, viz. R. Sheshet (Ber. 58a). Another tale of the same type refers to R. Judah. 'He saw two men throwing pieces of bread at one another, and exclaimed, "One might infer from this that there is plenty in the world!" He set his eyes upon them and there was a famine' (Taan. 24b).

With such anecdotes in circulation about the teachers, it is not surprising that the masses had a firm belief in the fearful harm which might be caused by the Evil Eye. How widespread was the damage for which it was responsible may be gathered from the statement, 'Ninety-nine die from the Evil Eye as against one from natural causes' (B.M. 107b); and the words, 'The Lord will take away from thee all sickness' (Deut. vii. 15), received the comment: 'that is, the Evil Eye' (ibid.). The Rabbis had even to make allowance for it in their legislation. 'It is permitted to

[1] See p. 231.

utter a charm against the Evil Eye, or a serpent or scorpion, and avert the Evil Eye on the Sabbath' (Tosifta Shab. VII. 23).

Not only human beings, but also cattle and other possessions, may be injured by the spell. 'A horse may not go out [1] wearing a fox's tail or a scarlet band between the eyes' (Tosifta Shab. IV. 5), as a protection against the Evil Eye. 'A man is forbidden to stand in the field of his neighbour at the time when its corn is in full ear' (B.M. 107a). The reason, as given by the commentator Rashi, is lest he damage it with the Evil Eye.

The chief safeguard against this danger is to avoid arousing jealousy. Do not make a display of your possessions, otherwise the envy of your neighbour will be excited and he will look upon them with the Evil Eye. 'A blessing is not experienced except in a thing which is concealed from the eye (of a neighbour); as it is said, "The Lord shall command the blessing upon thee in thy barns" [2] (Deut. xxviii. 8). The School of R. Ishmael taught, A blessing is not experienced except in a thing over which the eye (of a neighbour) does not rule' (Taan. 8b).

The same thought prompted the observation: 'If the first-born child is a daughter, it is a good omen for the males that are born subsequently. Some explain the dictum on the ground that she rears her brothers; but others say, the Evil Eye has no power against them' (B.B. 141a). Rashi comments that the intention is not clear to him; but it would appear to mean that, since in the Orient sons were so highly valued, if the first-born was a son, childless women or mothers who only had daughters would be envious and the danger of the Evil Eye incurred. The first child being a daughter, there would not be so much envy if sons followed.

Individuals can avoid the Evil Eye by shunning publicity. 'Although Hananiah, Mishael, and Azariah escaped from the fiery furnace, they died from the Evil Eye' (Sanh. 93a). Their fame brought them into prominence and that was their undoing. When Jacob's sons went to Egypt to buy corn, he advised them: 'You are mighty men and handsome; do not enter through one gate nor stand together in one place, so that the Evil Eye may not have power over you' (Gen. R. XCI. 6). 'Good advice is to be derived from the utterance of Joshua, viz. a person must guard himself from the Evil Eye. For that reason, "Joshua spake unto the house of Joseph, even to Ephraim and to Manasseh, saying,

---

[1] On the Sabbath; the inference is that it was customary on the other days of the week.

[2] The Hebrew word for 'barns' resembles an Aramaic word for 'conceal'; so the meaning given to the verse is: 'The Lord will command the blessing with thee in thy hidden possessions.'

Thou art a great people, and hast great power; thou shalt not have one lot only; but the hill-country shall be thine" (Josh. XVII. 17 f.). He told them, Go, hide yourselves in the forests, so that the Evil Eye shall have no dominance over you' (B.B. 118a).

Occasionally in the Talmud the Evil Eye signifies the power which excites lust. 'R. Jochanan had the habit of going and sitting at the gates of the baths, saying, "When the daughters of Israel leave, let them gaze upon me, and they will have children as beautiful as I." [1] His colleagues said to him, "Are you not afraid of the Evil Eye?" He answered, "I am come from the seed of Joseph, against whom the Evil Eye has no power; for it is written, 'Joseph is a fruitful bough, a fruitful bough by a fountain' (Gen. xlix. 22); and R. Abbahu said: "Read not *alé ayin* (by a fountain) but *olé ayin* (overcoming the (Evil) Eye)." R. José b. Channina said: From the following passage did R. Jochanan derive his reason: "And let them grow (*veyidgu*) into a multitude in the midst of the earth" (ibid. xlviii. 16); i.e. as the fishes (*dagim*) in the sea are covered by the water and the Evil Eye has no power over them, in similar manner the Evil Eye has no power over the seed of Joseph. Or if you will, say that the eye which desired not to partake of what did not belong to it [2] cannot be influenced by the Evil Eye' (Ber. 20a).

A means of averting the Evil Eye in this sense is suggested: 'He who enters a town and is afraid of the Evil Eye, let him take his right thumb in his left hand and his left thumb in his right hand and say the following, "I, A son of B, come from the seed of Joseph, against whom the Evil Eye has no power." Should he, however, be afraid of his own Evil Eye, [3] let him gaze upon the wing of his left nostril' (ibid. 55b).

§ III. Magic and Divination

The Talmud reveals very clearly a conflict between the pure, rational doctrines of the Bible and the debased beliefs and superstitions which pervaded the world in which the Jews lived. The Scriptures vehemently denounced every kind of magical practice and all attempts to pierce the veil which conceals the future from human ken by means of divination. We see several Rabbis, particularly in the earlier period, waging a brave fight to stem the tide of sorcery which threatened their community, but in

---

[1] His handsome appearance is often mentioned in the Talmud.
[2] Joseph, who rejected the advances of Potiphar's wife.
[3] i.e. his lust.

vain. In the later period even Rabbis succumbed, and credulity prevailed over faith.

In Deut. xviii. 10 f. is given a list of the magical arts which were practised by the heathen nations but were forbidden to the children of Israel. The definition of the terms in Rabbinic literature is an indication of the forms which they assumed in that age. ' "One that useth divination"—i.e. a person who seizes his staff and says, "Shall I go or shall I not go?"' This refers to the rhabdomancer. ' "One that practiseth augury"—the Rabbis say, They are persons who create an optical illusion; R. Akiba said, They are persons who determine times,' viz. auspicious and inauspicious occasions for undertaking a journey or a transaction. ' "An enchanter"— e.g. one who says, "A piece of bread has fallen from my mouth; my staff has fallen from my hand; there was a serpent on my right side, or a fox on my left side and his tail barred my way"; or one who says, "Do not begin (a journey or transaction) because it is new moon, or the Sabbath-eve, or the termination of the Sabbath."' ' "Sorcerer"—i.e. the man who actually performs magic, not merely practises the illusion. He is guilty of an infraction of the Torah while the illusionist is not.' ' "Charmer"—one who charms snakes.' ' "Consulter with a familiar spirit"—viz. a ventriloquist who makes sounds issue from his arm-pits' (Sifré Deut. § 171 f.; 107a, b). ' "Wizard"—this is a person who places the bone of a certain animal in his mouth and it speaks of its own accord. "Necromancer"—one who starves himself and proceeds to spend the night in a cemetery, so that a spirit of uncleanness may alight upon him' (Sanh. 65b).

We must first examine the effort to combat the practice of divination. 'Whence is it that we may not consult Chaldeans (i.e. astrologers)? It is said, "Thou shalt be perfect with the Lord thy God" (Deut. xviii. 13)' (Pes. 113b). The example of the first patriarch is quoted to support this view. While one Rabbi asserted, 'Our father Abraham wore an astrological table over his heart and all the kings of the East and West used to attend at his house to consult it' (B.B. 16b); there is also an emphatic denial: 'The Rabbis declared that Abraham was not an astrologer but a prophet' (Gen. R. xliv. 12). It is likewise stated: 'In the days of Jeremiah the Israelites wished to make use of astrology, but the Holy One, blessed be He, did not permit them; as it is said, "Thus saith the Lord, Learn not the way of the nations, and be not dismayed at the signs of heaven" (Jer. x. 2). In the past, your father Abraham wished to make use of astrology but I did not permit him' (Gen. R. loc. cit.). The incident referred to in the last sentence is described as follows: 'It is written, "He brought him forth abroad, and said, Look now toward heaven" (Gen. xv. 5). Abraham spoke before the Holy One, blessed be He, "Lord of the Universe! one born in my house is to be mine heir" (ibid. 3). God replied, "Nay, but he that shall come forth out of thine own bowels shall be thine heir" (ibid. 4). Abraham said, "Lord of the Universe! I have consulted my horoscope and it is not fated that I should beget a son." God answered, "Away with your astrology! The planets have no influence over Israel"' (Shab. 156a).

As a strong warning against the art the Talmud has this teaching: 'A person who refrains from practising divination is assigned a place in Heaven which even the ministering angels are unable to penetrate' (Ned. 32a). Instructive in this connection is a passage concerning King Solomon. To illustrate the Biblical statement, 'Solomon's wisdom excelled the wisdom of all the children of the east, and all the wisdom of Egypt' (1 Kings iv. 30), this story is told: 'At the time when Solomon wished to build the Temple, he wrote to Pharaoh-Necho, "Send me workmen for hire, since I desire to build the Temple." What did the Egyptian king do? He gathered all his astrologers and said to them, "Foresee and select men who are destined to die this year and I will send them to him." When these workmen came to Solomon, he foresaw by means of the Holy Spirit that they were to die in the course of the year; so he provided them with shrouds and sent them back with a letter, "Since you have no shrouds in which to bury your corpses, I am forwarding you a supply"' (Pesikta 34a). The contrast is here strongly marked between the Egyptian king who consulted astrologers and the Hebrew who derived his knowledge from 'the Holy Spirit.'

To place any faith in superstitious sources of information is conduct unworthy of a member of the House of Israel, as is forcibly taught in this anecdote: 'A certain convert to Judaism was an astrologer. On one occasion he wished to set out on a journey; but he said, "Can I set out in such circumstances?" [1] On further reflection he said, "Did I not attach myself to this holy people to separate myself from these superstitions? I will venture forth in the Name of the Creator." On the way he was seized by a tax-gatherer, to whom he gave his ass and was set free. What caused him to be penalized? The fact that he thought (first of his omens). What caused him to be saved? The fact that he trusted in his Creator. It was declared, Whoever practises divination his augury will befall him in the end' (p. Shab. 8d).

[1] The auguries were inauspicious.

Other stories were related to prove how misleading is the information obtained from such a tainted source. It was the cause of Potiphar's wife lusting for Joseph. 'By means of astrology she foresaw that she was to have a son by him; but she did not know whether the child was to be born to her or her daughter' (Gen. R. LXXXV. 2). In fact he married her daughter (Gen. xli. 45). It had tragic results in one instance: 'A proselyte to Judaism, who was a barber and an astrologer, saw through his divination that the Jews would shed his blood, but was unaware that it referred to the circumcision which would take place at his conversion. So when a Jew came to him to have his hair cut, he killed him. In this way he murdered a large number of them; one authority said, Eighty, while another said, Three hundred. The Jews offered prayers concerning him, and he reverted to heathenism' (p. A.Z. 41a).

The fact that the Talmud constantly alludes to divination and sorcery as a practice of heathens is another indication of the desire to keep the community free of it. Egypt was declared to be its home. 'Ten measures of sorcery descended to the world; Egypt took nine and the rest of the world one' (Kid. 49b). When Jethro suggested to Moses a council of helpers, he advised, 'Thou shalt provide (lit. look) out of all the people' (Exod. xviii. 21), and the comment is made, 'By means of the speculum into which kings gaze (to select their counsellors)' (Mech. ad loc.; 60a). Mesha, King of Moab, consulted his astrologers who told him that he would conquer all nations with the exception of Israel (Pesikta 13a). Sennacherib's astrologers advised him when to commence a battle if he was to be victorious (Sanh. 95a).

But despite all the efforts to suppress them, the magical arts crept into the life of the Jewish people and gained the mastery over all classes. Supernatural powers were attributed to certain Rabbis of whom wonderful tales were told.[1] Some examples may be selected.

'Once Choni the Circle-drawer was asked to pray for rain, but it did not descend. He drew a circle, stood in the centre and exclaimed, "Lord of the Universe! Thy children have set their faces on me because I am like a son of the house before Thee. I swear by Thy great Name that I will not move from here until Thou hast mercy upon Thy children." The rain began to fall in gentle drops; and he said, "That is not what I asked for, but for rain that will fill cisterns, ditches, and caves." The rain fell in torrents, and he said, "That is not what I asked for, but rain of

[1] See also what is related of them on p. 272.

Thy favour, of blessing and graciousness." Thereupon the rain descended in due measure' (Taan. III. 8).

'Pinchas b. Jaïr went to a certain place, and the inhabitants informed him that mice devoured their produce. He ordered the mice to assemble, and they began to squeak. He asked the inhabitants, "Do you know what they are saying?" "No," they replied. He told them, "They declare that your produce is not properly tithed (and for that reason they devour it)." They said to him, "Assure us (that the trouble will stop if we properly tithe the produce)." He gave them the assurance and they suffered no more" (p. Dammai 22a).

'Jannai went to an inn and asked for water, which they brought him. He noticed the women muttering, so he threw some away and it turned into snakes. He said to them, "I have drunk of your water and you will drink of mine." He made one of the women drink and she turned into an ass. He mounted her and rode into the market-place. Her companion came and released her from the spell, so that he was seen riding on a woman' (Sanh. 67b).

'If the righteous so desired they could create a Universe. Raba created a man and sent him to R. Zira, who conversed with him but he could not answer; so he exclaimed, "You are created by magical arts; return to your dust." R. Channina and R. Oshaya used to sit every Friday and occupy themselves with the Séfer Jetzirah [1] and create a three-year-old calf which they ate' (Sanh. 65b).

In the following story we see the credulity of one Rabbi and the common sense of his colleague. 'Rab told R. Chiyya, "I saw an Arab take a sword and dissect his camel. He then made a clatter with a timbrel and it stood up." R. Chiyya said to him, "Was there after it any blood or dung? If not, it was merely an illusion"' (ibid. 67b).

Another power attributed to the Rabbis is indicated in this remark: 'There is a tradition that the curse of a Sage, even when undeserved, comes to pass' (Ber. 56a). Some went still further and declared: 'Even the curse of an ordinary person should not be treated lightly' (B.K. 93a).

Stories of another type occur in the Talmud which presuppose the genuineness of astrology. Some illustrations are here given. 'The Chaldeans told the mother of R. Nachman b. Isaac that her son would be a thief. She would not allow him to be bare-headed, and said to him, "Keep your head covered so that the

---

[1] 'Book of Formation,' a work of mystical knowledge which has not survived. It is not identical with the book of similar name, traditionally attributed to R. Akiba, which is the earliest source of the Kabbalistic literature.

fear of Heaven shall be upon you, and pray for mercy." He did
not know why she told him this. One day he was sitting and
studying beneath a date-palm when his head-gear fell off. He
raised his eyes, saw the date-palm, and a longing for the fruit
overcame him so that he climbed up and bit off a cluster' (Shab.
156b). Since the tree did not belong to him, he was guilty of
stealing the fruit and the prediction was verified.

'Joseph, who was renowned for the manner he honoured the
Sabbath, had as a neighbour a Gentile who was very rich. The
Chaldeans told him that his wealth would pass into the possession
of Joseph; so he sold the whole of his property, bought a pearl
with the money and placed it in his cap. While he was crossing
the ferry, the wind blew the cap off, the pearl was thrown into the
water and a fish swallowed it. The fish was caught, and on the
Friday was brought for sale. The fishermen inquired who would
buy it, and they were told to take it to Joseph, the honourer of the
Sabbath, since he was accustomed to purchase that kind of fish.
They took it to him and he bought it. When he cut it open,
he found the pearl inside, which he sold for an immense sum of
money' (Shab. 119a).

'When R. Joseph was elected Principal of the Academy, he did
not accept the position because the Chaldeans told him that he
would reign for two years and then die' (Ber. 64a).

The following story points the moral that the forecast of a
diviner, though correct, may be averted, if it is unfavourable, by
an act of charity.[1] 'Two disciples of R. Channina went out to
chop wood. An astrologer saw them and said, "These two have
gone out but will not return." While on the way, an old man
met them and said, "Give me charity, because I have not eaten
for three days." They had a loaf of bread with them which they
cut into two and gave him one half. He ate it and prayed on
their behalf, saying, "May you save your lives this day even as
you saved my life to-day." They went out in peace and returned
in peace. There happened to be there people who had heard the
prediction of the astrologer, and they asked him, "Did you not
say that these two would go out but not return?" He answered,
"There is a liar here,[2] since his forecasts are false." For all that,
they went and investigated the matter; and they found a snake
cut in two, one half in each of the disciples' loads of wood. The
people asked them, "What happened to you to-day?" They
related the incident; and the astrologer exclaimed, "What can

---

[1] Compare the story which is told of R. Akiba's daughter on p. 221.
[2] Meaning himself.

I do if the God of the Jews is appeased by half a loaf of bread?"'
(p. Shab. 8d).

Apart from such tales as these, the Talmud provides ample
evidence that all sorts of superstitions were rife. In connection
with the decline of the national life there are the statements:
'Immorality and sorcery destroyed it all' (Sot. IX. 13), and 'When
those who employed spells as protection against God's judgment
multiplied, the divine wrath came to the world and the *Shechinah*
departed from Israel' (Tosifta Sot. XIV. 3).

The prevalence of witchcraft among the women of Israel has
already been alluded to.[1] Simeon b. Shetach, who lived in the
first century before the present era, is reported to have hanged
eighty witches in Ascalon on one day (Sanh. VI. 4). R. Jochanan
declared that nobody should be appointed to a seat on the Great
Sanhedrin unless, among other qualifications, he had a knowledge
of sorcery (ibid. 17a). The commentator Rashi explains that this
knowledge was necessary to put sorcerers to death who relied on
their magical skill to escape the penalty inflicted upon them by
the Court, and also to expose them when they tried to deceive the
judges with their tricks.

The information is given: 'People practise divination by means
of the weasel, birds, and fishes' (Sanh. 66a). An instance is told
in connection with a Rabbi named Ilish. 'He was enslaved, and
once he was sitting by a man who understood the language of
birds. A raven came and croaked. The Rabbi asked, "What did
he say?" He answered, "Ilish escape! Ilish escape!" He said,
"The raven is a liar and I place no trust in it." After a while a dove
came and cooed. He asked, "What did he say?" The other replied,
"Ilish escape! Ilish escape!" He exclaimed, "The dove is likened
to Israel; hence a miracle is going to happen to me"' (Git. 45a).

A very firm hold was taken of the people by the belief in the
influence of the planets upon human life. They were said to have
no effect upon animals (Shab. 53b), but all herbage and fruits were
under their domination (Gen. R. X. 6). As for human beings,
there was a difference of opinion whether the people of Israel was
an exception to the general rule. One Rabbi asserted: 'The
planet under which a person is born determines whether he is
wise and rich, and the planets do affect the lives of Israelites;
but another Rabbi declared, The planets do not affect the lives
of Israelites' (Shab. 156a).

The first-mentioned opinion generally prevailed, as may be
gathered from what is told of two eminent Rabbis. 'Longevity,

[1] See p. 161, and below, p. 295.

offspring, and sustenance depend not upon merit but upon the planets. Consider the instance of Rabbah and R. Chisda, who were both righteous men. One used to pray for rain and it descended, whereas the prayer of the other was of no avail. R. Chisda reached the age of ninety-two and Rabbah died at the age of forty. In the house of the former sixty [1] marriages were celebrated, but in the house of the latter sixty funerals occurred. In R. Chisda's house bread of the finest flour was eaten by the dogs and nobody was concerned about it, but in Rabbah's house there was not even barley bread for the human beings there' (M.K. 28a).

The influence of the time of birth upon the character and fate of the individual is described in some detail. 'One born on a Sunday will be wholly good or wholly bad, because on that day light and darkness were created. One born on Monday will be bad-tempered, because on that day the waters were divided. One born on a Tuesday will be rich and lustful, because on that day the herbage was created. One born on Wednesday will be wise and of retentive memory, because on that day the luminaries were suspended in. the firmament. One born on Thursday will be benevolent, because on that day fish and birds were created. One born on Friday will be active, or, according to another version, zealous to perform the precepts. One born on the Sabbath will die on the Sabbath, because on his account the holy day was profaned.[2]

'Another Rabbi expressed the opinion that not the planet of the day (of birth) determines a person's destiny but the planet of the hour. One who is born under the influence of the sun will be a distinguished man; will eat and drink of his own, his secrets will be revealed, and if he should venture to steal he will not succeed.[3] One who is born under the influence of Venus will be rich and lustful, because fire was born through that constellation. One who is born under the influence of Mercury will be of retentive memory and wise, because it is the scribe of (i.e. attendant upon) the sun. One who is born under the influence of the moon will be ailing, will build and destroy and again destroy and build, will eat and drink not of his own, his secrets will be concealed, and if he should venture to steal he will succeed.[4] One who is born under

[1] In the Talmud 'sixty' is often used to express an indeterminate number.
[2] By attending to the mother during childbirth.
[3] Everything about his life will be open and clear like the light of the sun; and as the sun does not derive its light from another planet, the person will be self-dependent.
[4] He will ail because of the moon's paleness; his works will not be stable, as the moon waxes and wanes periodically; he will not be self-dependent, as the moon receives its light from the sun; and his life will be secretive as the moon shines only at night.

the influence of Saturn will be a man whose pains will fail,[1] but others declare that all designs against him will fail. One who is born under the influence of Jupiter will be righteous.[2] One who is born under the influence of Mars will be a shedder of blood.[3] Another Rabbi declared, He will be either a cupper, a butcher, or a circumciser' (Shab. 156a).

So closely is a man's destiny bound up with his constellation that 'if he experiences the sensation of fear, although he may not see the cause of it, his planet does perceive it. What is his remedy? Let him recite the *Shema*; and if he standing in an unclean place,[4] let him move away a distance of four cubits; or let him say, "The goat in the slaughter-house is plumper than I"' (Meg. 3a). Another belief was that 'the name of a person affects his career' (Ber. 7b).

Like the other peoples of antiquity, the Jews interpreted an eclipse as a manifestation of divine anger. 'The Rabbis taught: The eclipse of the sun is a bad omen for the whole world. A parable: To what is the matter like? To a human king who made a banquet for his servants and placed a lamp before them. When he became angry with them, he ordered a slave to remove the lamp and leave them in darkness. As long as the planets are in eclipse, it is a bad omen for the enemies of Israel [5] because they are inured to calamities. A parable: When a teacher enters the class-room with a strap in his hand, who becomes perturbed? The pupil who is accustomed to receive a thrashing every day! The eclipse of the sun is a bad omen for the (gentile) peoples of the world. The eclipse of the moon is a bad omen for the enemies of Israel, because Israel fixes the calendar by the moon and the Gentiles by the sun. If the eclipse occurs in the east it is a bad omen for those who dwell in the east; if it occurs in the west it is a bad omen for those who dwell in the west; if it occurs in the centre of the heaven it is a bad omen for the whole world. If its face becomes the colour of blood, the sword is about to befall the world; if it becomes the colour of a sack (i.e. grey), the arrows of famine are about to befall the world; [6] if it becomes like both, the sword and arrows of famine are about to befall the world. If the eclipse takes place at the sun's setting, the calamity delays to come; if at its rising, the calamity hastens to come; but some authorities

[1] The Hebrew name for Saturn is connected with a root meaning 'to cease.'
[2] The Hebrew name for Jupiter signifies 'righteousness.'
[3] The Hebrew name for Mars means '(the planet which) shows redness,' and so is suggestive of blood.
[4] Where it is not permissible to recite it.
[5] A common euphemism for Israel when the context deals with anything inauspicious.
[6] The faces of men and women will be grey from hunger.

reverse the interpretation. There is no nation smitten without its deities being smitten along with it; as it is said, "And against all the gods of Egypt I will execute judgments" (Exod. xii. 12). But when Israel performs the will of the Omnipresent, he has no cause to fear any of these things; as it is said, "Thus saith the Lord, Learn not the way of the nations, and be not dismayed at the signs of heaven, for the nations are dismayed at them" (Jer. x. 2) —the nations, but not Israel, are dismayed at them. On account of four reasons is the sun eclipsed: because of the President of a Court of Law who dies and a fitting funeral oration is not pronounced over him; because of a maiden who is being assaulted in an inhabited place and nobody comes to her rescue; because of pederasty, and because of two brothers whose blood is shed at the same time. On account of four things are the planets eclipsed: forgers of documents, perjurers, those who rear small animals in the land of Israel,[1] and those who cut down fine trees' (Suk. 29a).

Some of the Rabbis appreciated the fact that belief in planetary influence and astrology was incompatible with the doctrine of Free Will which is the foundation of ethics. They accordingly put forward a half-hearted compromise in the suggestion. 'There is no reality in divination, but there is in signs' (p. Shab. 8c); 'A sign is a real thing' (Ker. 6a). What they meant may be understood from these examples: 'He who sneezes during prayer should regard it as a bad omen' (Ber. 24b). 'If one errs while saying his prayer, it is a bad omen for him; and should he be acting as precentor, it is a bad omen for those who deputed him, since a man's deputy is similar to himself. They declared concerning R. Channina b. Dosa that when praying on behalf of the sick, he would say, "This one will live, that one will die." They asked him, "How do you know?" He replied, "If my prayer is fluent in my mouth, I know that he is accepted; but if not, I know that he is rejected"' (ibid. v. 5).

An instance of his powers in this direction is on record. 'It once happened that the son of R. Gamaliel was ill. He sent two disciples of the Sages to R. Channina b. Dosa to pray on his behalf. When he saw them, he ascended to an upper chamber and prayed on his behalf. On descending he said to them, "Go, the fever has left him." They said to him, "Are you a prophet?" He replied, "I am no prophet nor a prophet's son (Amos vii. 14); but so is my tradition: If my prayer is fluent in my mouth, I know that he is accepted; but if not, I know that he is rejected." They

[1] e.g. sheep which are difficult to prevent from trespassing and grazing in the fields of neighbours.

sat down and wrote and noted the time. When they came to
R. Gamaliel, he said to them, "By the Temple-service! you have
neither understated nor overstated the time. But thus it happened; at that very hour the fever left him and he asked us for
water to drink"' (Ber. 34b).

A class of omen commonly resorted to by the Rabbis and others
was bibliomancy. They would go to a class-room, ask a boy
what verse of Scripture he had just been learning, and look for a
sign in the words. Many examples of this practice occur in the
Talmud. One only need be cited by way of illustration. When
R. Meïr tried to induce the heretic Elisha b. Abuyah to recant, he
took him into a school, and Elisha said to a child, 'Repeat for me
the verse you have just been learning.' The boy read, 'There is
no peace, saith the Lord, unto the wicked' (Is. xlviii. 22). He
was taken to another school, and after the same request the boy
read: 'For though thou wash thee with lye, and take thee much
soap, yet thine iniquity is marked before me' (Jer. ii. 22). The
process was repeated in other places with the same result, all the
verses indicating that there was no hope for him (Chag. 15a).
Another form of omen is, 'If one wakes up and a verse comes
to his mouth (spontaneously), it is to be regarded as a minor
prophecy' (Ber. 55b).[1]

One more medium of divination has to be recorded, viz. necromancy. Although direct consultation of the dead, which was
expressly forbidden in the Torah, does not seem to have been
resorted to except very rarely, there was a current belief that
knowledge could be obtained by spending the night in a cemetery
on certain special occasions during the year.

Information is provided on this subject in the course of a discussion on the question whether the dead are aware of what happens
on earth. To prove that they are so cognizant, these stories
are told: 'It once happened that a pious man gave a *denarius* to
a beggar on the New Year's eve in a time of drought. His wife
upbraided him, so he went and spent the night in the cemetery.
He heard two spirits conversing. One said to the other, "Come,
friend, let us wander in the world and hear behind the curtain [2]
what visitation is to befall the world." The other spirit replied,
"I cannot, because I am buried in a matting of reeds;[3] but do you
go and report to me what you hear." She went, and having

---

[1] Other signs upon which Jews relied as prognostications will be given under
the section dealing with Superstitions, pp. 291 ff.

[2] In the celestial Court of Justice.

[3] Instead of linen shrouds in which the body ought to be enwrapped before
interment.

wandered about, returned. The other asked, "What did you hear, friend, behind the curtain?" She replied, "I heard that if one sows in the first rainfall,[1] the hail will smite it." This man thereupon went and sowed in the second rainfall. The hail destroyed everybody's crops but not his.

'The following year he again spent the New Year's night in the cemetery, and heard the same two spirits conversing. One said to the other, "Come, let us wander in the world and hear behind the curtain what visitation is to befall the world." The other spirit replied, "Have I not told you, friend, that I cannot, because I am buried in a matting of reeds? But do you go and come and tell me what you hear." She went and wandered about and returned. The other spirit asked, "What did you hear behind the curtain?" She replied, "I heard that if one sows in the second rainfall, it will be smitten by the blast." This man went and sowed in the first rainfall. What everybody else sowed was smitten by the blast, but not his. His wife asked him, "How is it that last year everybody's crop was destroyed by hail, but not yours; and this year everybody's crop was blasted except yours?" He told her the whole story.

'It is related that very soon afterwards a quarrel broke out between the wife of that pious man and the mother of the girl (who had been buried in the matting). The former said to the other, "Come, I will show you that your daughter is buried in reed-matting." The following year the same man went and spent the New Year's night in the cemetery, and he heard those spirits conversing. One said, "Come, friend, let us wander in the world and hear behind the curtain what visitation is to befall the world." The other replied, "Leave me alone, friend; what has passed between me and you has been overheard by the living"' (Ber. 18b).

Another story runs: 'Zeiri left a sum of money in charge of his landlady. During the time he went to the school of his master and returned, she died. He followed her to the cemetery and asked her, "Where is the money?" She replied, "Go and take it from beneath the door-socket in such and such a place; and tell my mother to send my comb and tube of eye-paint through so-and-so, who will arrive here to-morrow"' (ibid.).

A third story, the most elaborate of them all, tells: 'The father of Samuel [2] was entrusted with some money belonging to orphans. At the time he passed away, Samuel was not with him. People

---

[1] i.e. from the 17th to the 23rd of the eighth month; the second rainfall is from the 23rd to the end of the month.

[2] A famous teacher in Babylon at the beginning of the third century.

called after him, "Son of the consumer of the orphans' money!" He went after his father to the cemetery and said to them,[1] "I want Abba." They replied, "There are many of that name here." "I want Abba ben Abba." They answered, "There are many of that name here." He said to them, "I want Abba ben Abba, the father of Samuel; where is he?" They answered, "He has gone up to the heavenly seminary (where the Torah is studied)." In the meantime he noticed (a former colleague named) Levi, who was seated apart. He asked him, "Why do you sit apart? Why have you not gone up (to the heavenly seminary)?" He replied, "I was told, The number of years you did not attend the seminary of R. Aphes, and caused him grief on that account, we will not permit you to ascend to the heavenly seminary." In the meanwhile his father arrived and Samuel noticed that he wept and laughed. He said to him, "Why do you weep?" He answered, "Because you will soon come here." "And why do you laugh?" "Because you are very highly esteemed in this world." Samuel said to him, "If I am so esteemed, let them allow Levi to enter"; and they permitted him to enter. He asked his father, "Where is the orphans' money?" He replied, "Go, take it from the enclosure of the mill. The upper and lower sums of money belong to us, the middle sum belongs to the orphans." He asked his father, "Why did you act in this manner?" He replied, "Should thieves come to steal they would steal ours; should the earth destroy,[2] it would destroy ours"' (ibid.).

§ IV. Dreams

In view of the importance attached to dreams in the Bible, it was natural that the Jews should think of the visions which came to them in the night as having a significance. They were supposed to be a medium of communication by God. The Talmud attributes the statement to Him: 'Although I have hidden My face from Israel, I will communicate with him through dreams' (Chag. 5b). Dreams were declared to be 'a sixtieth part of prophecy' (Ber. 57b).

Not only God, but the dead also employed dreams as a means of conveying a message to the living, and several stories of this kind are related in the Talmud. 'A person died in the neighbourhood of R. Judah without leaving anybody behind him to mourn him. Throughout the week of mourning R. Judah brought ten men to sit in the dead man's house (and mourn him). After the seven

---

[1] To the disembodied spirits who appeared to him seated in conclave.
[2] Cf. Matt. vi. 19.

days had passed, he appeared to him in a dream and said, "May your mind be at rest, as you have set my mind at rest"' (Shab. 152a, b). Raba once prayed to God to send rain. 'His father appeared to him in a dream and said to him, "Is there anybody who causes so much trouble to Heaven? [1] Change your place (of sleeping because you are in danger)." The next morning he found the (first) bed marked with the scratches of knives' (Taan. 24b).

Several folios in the Tractate *Berachoth* are devoted to the subject of dreams, and give much information concerning the manner of their interpretation. The following is an abstract: 'An uninterpreted dream is like an unread letter.[2] Neither a good nor a bad dream is fulfilled in every detail. A bad dream is preferable to a good dream.[3] When a dream is bad, the pain it causes is sufficient (to prevent its fulfilment), and when a dream is good, the joy it brings is sufficient. Just as one cannot have wheat without straw, similarly it is impossible for a dream to be without something that is vain. A dream, though it be fulfilled in part, is never completely realized. Whence is this learnt? From Joseph, for it is written, "Behold, the sun and the moon and eleven stars bowed to me" (Gen. xxxvii. 9); but at that time his mother [4] was no longer living' (Ber. 55a).

'A good man is not shown a good dream and a bad man is not shown a bad dream.[5] Whoever abides seven days without a dream is called evil. The good man sees a dream but (the next morning) he does not know what he has seen.[6] He who sees a dream and his soul is depressed (because it was bad) should have it turned into good in the presence of three. He should assemble three men and say to them, "I have seen a *good* dream"; and they should say to him, "Good it is and good may it be. May the All-merciful turn it to good; seven times may it be decreed concerning thee from Heaven that it should be good, and good may it be."

'He who has seen a dream and knows not what he has seen, let him stand before the Priests at the time that they spread their hands (to pronounce the priestly benediction in the Synagogue-service) and utter the following: "Lord of the Universe! I am Thine and

[1] By his frequent petitions.
[2] It has no effect for good or evil because it depends upon the interpretation, as will be explained. This saying was doubtless intended to discourage people from having their dreams interpreted.
[3] Because it leads to searching of heart and contrition.
[4] Represented by 'the moon.'
[5] The good man has a bad dream to make him reflect on possible misdeeds; but the bad man has a good dream so that he may have pleasure in this world, since he will be debarred from the joys of the World to Come.
[6] And without interpretation it can have no effect.

my dreams are Thine; a dream have I dreamed and I know not what
it is.   Whether I dreamed concerning myself, or my fellows dreamed
concerning me, or I dreamed concerning others, if they be good
dreams, strengthen and fortify them (and may they be fulfilled)
like the dreams of Joseph; but if they require to be amended, heal
them as the waters of Marah were healed by the hands of Moses
our teacher, as Miriam was healed from her leprosy, as Hezekiah
from his illness, and like the waters of Jericho sweetened by the
hands of Elisha.   And as thou didst turn the curse of the wicked
Balaam into a blessing, so do Thou turn all my dreams for me into
good."   He should conclude his prayer simultaneously with the
Priests so that the congregation responds with "Amen."   But if
he cannot finish with them, let him say, "Thou Majestic One in
the heights, Who abidest in might, Thou art peace and Thy Name
is peace.   May it be Thy will to grant us peace."

'A Rabbi declared, There were twenty-four interpreters of dreams
in Jerusalem.   I once had a dream and went to consult them all;
but the interpretation each gave me differed from that of the others.
Nevertheless all their interpretations were realized in me; to fulfil
that which was said, All dreams follow the mouth (of the interpreter), as it is written, "And it came to pass, as he interpreted
to us, so it was" (Gen. xli. 13).

'Three types of dreams are fulfilled: a morning dream, a dream
which his friend has about him, and a dream interpreted in the
midst of a dream.   Some add: Also a dream which is repeated.
A man is only shown (in a dream what emanates) from the thoughts
of his heart.   You may infer this from the fact that a man is never
shown (in a dream) a golden date-palm or an elephant entering the
eye of a needle'[1] (Ber. 55b).

'The Roman Emperor said to a Rabbi, "You declare that you are
wise.   Tell me what I shall see in my dream."   He replied, "You
will see the Persians[2] enslaving you, despoiling you, and making
you pasture unclean animals with a golden crook."   The emperor
reflected upon it the whole day and in the night dreamt of it.   King
Shapor said to a Rabbi, "You declare that you are very wise.   Tell
me what I shall see in my dream."   He replied, "You will see the
Romans come and take you captive and make you grind date-stones
(for fodder) in a golden mill."   The king reflected upon it the whole
day and in the night dreamt of it' (ibid. 56a).

Scriptural texts were used as a means to interpret dreams.   'Who

[1] Because he never thinks of such impossibilities.
[2] Instead of 'Persians' we should probably read 'Parthians,' and we may
have here a reminiscence of the defeat of Trajan in A.D. 116.

dreams of a well will see peace; as it is said, "Isaac's servants digged in the valley, and found there a well of living [1] water" (Gen. xxvi. 19). He will find Torah; as it is said, "Whoso findeth me findeth life" (Prov. viii. 35); another Rabbi declared that it signifies life in the literal sense. There are three (types of dreams which indicate) peace—a river, bird, and pot. A river—for it is written, "Behold, I will extend peace to her like a river" (Is. lxvi. 12). A bird—for it is written, "As birds hovering, so will the Lord of hosts protect Jerusalem" (ibid. xxxi. 5). A pot—for it is written, "Lord, Thou wilt establish [2] peace for us" (ibid. xxvi. 12). R. Channina said, But it must be a pot in which there is no meat; for it is written, "They chop them in pieces, as that which is in the pot, and as flesh within the cauldron" (Micah iii. 3)' (Ber. 56b).

Since the effect of a dream is dependent upon its interpretation, it is important to think of an auspicious text before one with a less favourable meaning comes to mind. 'Who dreams of a river should on rising say, "Behold, I will extend peace to her like a river" (Is. lxvi. 12), before another verse occurs to him, viz. "For distress will come in like a river" (ibid. lix. 19). Who dreams of a bird should on rising say, "As birds hovering, so will the Lord of hosts protect Jerusalem" (ibid. xxxi. 5), before another verse occurs to him, viz. "As a bird that wandereth from her nest, so is a man that wandereth from his place" (Prov. xxvii. 8). Who dreams of a pot should on rising say, "Lord, Thou wilt establish peace for us" (Is. xxvi. 12), before another verse occurs to him, viz. "Set on the pot, set it on" (Ezek. xxiv. 3). Who dreams of grapes should on rising say, "I found Israel like grapes in the wilderness" (Hos. ix. 10), before another verse occurs to him, viz. "Their grapes are grapes of gall" (Deut. xxxii. 32)' (Ber. 56b). Many other instances are given in the context.

Seeing an animal in a dream has its peculiar significance. 'Five things are said in connection with the ox: Who dreams that he eats of its flesh will grow rich; that an ox had gored him, he will have sons who will contend with each other in Torah; that it bit him, sufferings will come upon him; that it kicked him, a long journey is destined for him; that he rode upon it, he will ascend to greatness. Who dreams of an ass may hope for salvation (cf. Zech. ix. 9). Who dreams of a cat in a place where the word for it is *shunnara*, a beautiful song (*shirah naah*) will be composed in his honour; but where the word for it is *shinnara*, a change for the

---

[1] 'Living' water is a symbol of peace.
[2] The word used here, *shaphath*, is commonly employed in the sense of setting a pot on the fire.

worse (*shinnuï ra*) is in store for him. Who dreams of a white horse, whether standing still or galloping, it is a good omen for him; if it is roan, should it be standing still, it is a good omen; should it be galloping, it is a bad omen. Who dreams of an elephant (*pil*), miracles (*pelaoth*) will be wrought for him' (Ber. 56*b*).

In like manner, to dream of wheat, barley, and fruits has a special meaning. 'Who dreams of wheat will see peace; as it is said, "He maketh thy borders peace; He giveth thee in plenty the fat of wheat" (Ps. cxlvii. 14). Who dreams of barley (*seorim*), his iniquities will depart (*sar*). Who dreams of a well-laden vine, his wife will not miscarry; as it is said, "Thy wife shall be as a fruitful vine" (Ps. cxxviii. 3). Who dreams of the fig, his knowledge of Torah will be preserved within him; as it is said, "Whoso keepeth the fig-tree [1] shall eat the fruit thereof" (Prov. xxvii. 18). Who dreams of pomegranates, if small, his business will bear fruit like the pomegranate; if large, his business will grow like the pomegranate; if split open, should he be a disciple of the Sages, he may hope for Torah; as it is said, "I would cause thee to drink of spiced wine, of the juice of my pomegranate" (Cant. viii. 2). Who dreams of olives, if small, his business will be fruitful and multiply and endure like olives. But this applies only to dreaming of the fruit; if he dreamt of olive-trees, then he will have numerous offspring; as it is said, "Thy children like olive-plants round about thy table" (Ps. cxxviii. 3). Some say that he who dreams of the olive, a good name will proceed from him; as it is said, "The Lord called thy name a green olive-tree, fair with goodly fruit" (Jer. xi. 16). Who dreams of olive-oil may hope for the light of Torah; as it is said, "That they bring unto thee pure olive-oil beaten for the light" (Exod. xxvii. 20)' (Ber. 57*a*).

Lastly we are given a list of miscellaneous dreams and their significations. 'Who dreams of a goat, the year will be blessed for him; of the myrtle, his business undertakings will prosper, and if he has no business undertakings, an inheritance will fall to his lot from some other place. Who dreams of a citron will be honoured before his Maker; of a palm-branch, has but one heart for his Father in heaven; of a goose,[2] may hope for wisdom; of a cock, may hope for a son; of cocks, may hope for sons; of hens, may hope for a beautiful rearing of his children and rejoicing. Who dreams of eggs, his petition remains in suspense; if broken, his petition has been granted. Similarly is it with nuts and cucumbers, and all glass vessels and all such breakable articles. Who dreams that

[1] The Torah is compared by the Rabbis to the fig-tree (Erub. 54*a*).
[2] Among the Romans the goose was deemed a wise creature.

he entered a town, his desires will be fulfilled for him; of shaving his head, it is a good omen for him; [1] of shaving his head and beard, it is a good omen for him and all his family. Who dreams that he is sitting in a small boat, a good name will proceed from him; if in a big boat, then from him and all his family, but that only applies when it is sailing high on the seas. Who dreams of ascending to the roof will ascend to greatness; of descending, he will descend from greatness.

'Who dreams of blood-letting, his sins will be pardoned him; [2] of a serpent, his sustenance will be provided him; if it bit him his sustenance will be doubled for him, if he killed it, his sustenance is lost. To dream of any kinds of liquids is a bad omen, with the exception of wine' (ibid. 57a).

'To dream of any species of animals is a good omen with the exception of the elephant, monkey, and long-tailed ape. But a teacher has said, "Who dreams of an elephant, miracles will be wrought for him?" There is no contradiction; the latter refers to where it is bridled and the other to where it is not bridled. To dream of any kind of metal tool is a good omen, with the exception of the hoe, the mattock, and the axe; but this applies only when he sees them with their handles. To dream of any kind of fruit is a good omen, with the exception of unripe dates. To dream of any kind of vegetables is a good omen, with the exception of turnip-heads. To dream of any kind of colour is a good omen, with the exception of blue. To dream of any kind of birds is a good omen, with the exception of the owl, the horned owl, and the bat.

'If one dreams there is a corpse in the house, there will be peace in the house; that he was eating and drinking in the house, it is an auspicious omen for the house; that he took a vessel from the house, it is an inauspicious omen for the house' (ibid. 57b).

§ V. Superstitions

Many customs are condemned by the Rabbis as being 'of the ways of the Amorite,' i.e. they are heathenish practices which the Jew should not adopt. The fact that they are specifically mentioned is perhaps evidence that they had been assimilated by members of the Jewish Community. Among these 'Amorite ways' are the following: 'A woman drags her child among the dead.[3]

[1] Because it is so mentioned of Joseph when he was released from prison (Gen. xli. 14).
[2] Sins are described as crimson (Is. i. 18).
[3] i.e. into a cemetery.

A man ties a pad on his hip or a red thread on his finger. He counts and throws pebbles into the sea or a river. He strikes his hips, claps his hands, and dances in front of a flame. A piece of bread is taken from him, and he says, "Give it me back so that my luck shall not change." He says, "Leave a lamp on the ground that the dead may be disturbed," or, "Do not leave a lamp on the ground that the dead may not be disturbed." If sparks fall from the lamp he says, "We shall have visitors to-day." When about to begin a piece of work he says, "Let so-and-so come whose hands are swift and commence it," or "Let so-and-so whose feet are swift pass in front of us." When about to broach a vat or knead dough he says, "Let so-and-so whose hands are blessed come and begin the work." He stops up the window with thorns and ties nails to the legs of the bed of a woman in childbirth, or spreads a meal in front of her;[1] but it is permitted to stop up the window with blankets or bundles of straw and place a bowl of water in front of her, and tie a hen to her in order to be company for her.[2] A man says, "Stone this cock which crowed in the evening; or, this hen which crowed like a cock. Feed this hen with a crest because it crowed like a cock." If a raven croaked, he says, "Cry"; or he says, if it croaked, "Turn round."[3] He says, "Eat this lettuce-stalk that you may remember me; or, do not eat it because you will have cataract. Kiss the coffin of a dead man that you may see him; or, do not kiss it that you may not see him in the night. Reverse your shirt that you may have dreams; or do not reverse it that you may not dream. Sit on the broom that you may have dreams; or, do not sit on it that you may not dream. Sit on the plough that you may not make the work harder; or, do not sit on it that it may not break (while being used later on)."

'A man says, "Do not twist your hands behind your back that our work may not be hampered for us." He extinguishes a brand against the wall and exclaims *Hada* (as a protection against fire); but it is permitted to do this if he says the word to warn persons to beware of the sparks. He pours water in the public way and exclaims *Hada*; but he may say the word to warn passers-by (that they should not be drenched). He throws a piece of iron because of graves (which are demon-haunted); but it is permissible to do so as a protection against sorcery. He places a stick of firewood or iron beneath his head (when in bed); but he may do so if his

---

[1] The object is to keep the harmful demons away from her. See p. 267.
[2] This was done to set her mind at rest.
[3] In Shab. 67*b* the reading is: 'Or he says, if a female raven croaked, "Cry and turn your tail towards me as a good omen."''

purpose is to guard it (from being stolen). A woman shouts at the oven that the bread (which is baking) may not fall, or puts chips of wood in the handle of a pot that the contents may not boil and overflow; but it is allowed to put a chip of the mulberry-tree or of glass into a pot that it may boil more quickly. The Rabbis, however, forbid glass being used because it is dangerous to life. A woman commands all in the room to be silent that the lentils may cook quickly, or shouts at rice that it may cook quickly, or claps her hands for the lamp to burn brightly.

'If a snake falls on a bed, a person says that the owner is poor but will become rich; if the owner is a pregnant woman, that she will give birth to a son; if a virgin, that she will marry a great man. A woman, wanting a hen to hatch chickens, says, "I will only allow a virgin to set the hen on the eggs; or, I will only set the hen when I am naked, or with the left hand, or in pairs." A man, when about to marry, says, "There must be a pair"; or a man about to send out an agent says, "There must be a pair"; or a man says, "Add food for another at the table." [1] A woman places the shells (after the chickens are hatched) and herbs in the wall, plasters them over, and counts seven and one.[2] A woman sifts the chickens in a sieve and places a piece of iron among them; but if she did this as a protection against thunder and lightning it is allowed' (Tosifta Shab. VI).

Other 'Amorite ways' which are forbidden are: 'One inquires of his staff, "Shall I go or not go?" He exclaims, "Healing" (when somebody sneezes); but some authorities disallow the exclamation only in the House of Study because it disturbs the instruction. He exclaims, "Abundance and some left over" (when mentioning his possessions); or "Drink and leave some over"; or "Lo, Lo";[3] or "Do not pass between us so as not to cause our friendship to cease"' (Tosifta Shab. VII).

In several of the instances the intention behind the act determines whether it may be done or not. If a superstitious motive prompts it, then it is forbidden. We see this principle being applied in the

---

[1] For good luck, although the extra person is only a fiction. In each case the idea is that a couple is more auspicious than one. We shall see that in other matters an even number was regarded as unlucky.

[2] Another reading is: seventy and one. The object is that the chickens should thrive and not die.

[3] This may mean, 'Not, not,' i.e. 'may it not happen to me,' on learning of a calamity. The text quotes Job xxi. 14 in connection with it, and Blau, *Das altjüdische Zauberwesen*, p. 67 n., suggests as its translation, 'They said to God, Depart from us; for we desire, Lo, the knowledge of thy ways,' instead of 'for we desire not the knowledge.' If this is correct, Lo is the name of some superstitious object of reverence.

earlier Rabbinic period. For example, 'People may go out (on the Sabbath) with a grasshopper's egg (as a cure for earache), a fox's tooth,[1] or the nail from a cross on which a person has been hanged,[2] as a remedy. These are the words of R. Meïr; but the Rabbis forbid them even on a weekday because they belong to the ways of the Amorite' (Shab. VI. 10). One authority proposed as a general rule: 'Whatever is used as a cure cannot be classed among the ways of the Amorite; but when it is not acknowledged to be for a cure, it does come within that category' (ibid. 67a).

We find a distinct aversion from even numbers on superstitious grounds. 'There is a teaching: A man should not eat or drink in a company where there is an even number, or wipe himself twice or attend to his needs twice'[3] (Pes. 109b). 'If one drinks glasses of wine in an even number, his blood is on his own head. That is true only when he does not look into the street;[4] but if he does look into the street, he may have an even number. It is also true only if he goes out after having had an even number; but if he remains in his room there is no objection. Other Rabbis taught that to sleep or visit a privy is in this matter the equivalent of going out; and one of them added that the objection to the even number does not apply to ten' (ibid. 110a).

A Rabbi reported: 'The demon Joseph told me that Asmodeus, the king of the demons, is appointed over all matters regarding even numbers, and a king is not called a doer of harm' (ibid.). It follows, therefore, that one need not worry over this matter of even numbers; but this opinion met with opposition from colleagues who declared: 'On the contrary, a king does as he wishes; he can break down a fence to make a path for himself and nobody may prevent him' (ibid.). But we are informed that 'in the West (i.e. Palestine) people do not pay attention to even numbers' (ibid. 110b). A further limitation is mentioned, viz., 'With dishes and loaves the danger of even numbers does not apply. This is the general rule: With things which are completed by the hand of man there is no danger in even numbers; but with things which are completed by the hand of Heaven[5] there is danger with articles of food in even numbers' (ibid.).

There was a superstition about passing between two persons or

---

[1] The tooth of a live fox was a cure for oversleeping and of a dead fox for insomnia.

[2] This was supposed to be a cure for inflammation and fever.

[3] That means, in rapid succession.

[4] Between the drinking of the glasses; that would constitute a break which would obviate the dangerous consequences.

[5] e.g. the ripening of fruits.

two objects. 'Three are not allowed to pass between two persons, nor should any one pass through two of them—a dog, a palm-tree, and a woman. Some add a pig and a snake. If he has done so, what is his remedy? Let him open with "God" and close with "God," open with "not" and close with "not." [1] Should a menstruous woman pass between two men, if at the beginning of the period she kills one of them, and if at the end she creates strife between them. What is the remedy? Let them open with "God" and close with "God." If two women are sitting at the cross-roads, each on one side of the pathway, with their faces turned towards one another, it is certain they are engaged in witchcraft. What is the remedy? If there is another way, let him take it; if not, and there is somebody else with him, they should hold each other's hand and pass through; but in the event of there being nobody with him, he should exclaim, "Agrath, Azlath, Usya, and Belusya [2] have already been killed by arrows"' (Pes. 111a).

Another incantation which protects from witches is given by a Rabbi who declared: 'The chief of the sorceresses told me that if a man meets witches, let him say, "Hot excrement in broken baskets for your mouths, ye women of sorceries; may your heads grow bald, may the wind carry away your crumbs, scatter your spices, and may a blast disperse the fresh saffron which you have taken.[3] O witches, so long as He was gracious to me and I was careful, I did not come into your midst; and now that I have come into your midst, become bald for me and I will be careful"' (ibid. 110a, b).

Women are also dangerous to meet after they have been in contact with the dead. 'R. Joshua b. Levi said, Three things did the Angel of Death tell me: Do not take your shirt in the morning from the hand of the attendant and put it on; do not let your hands be washed by him who has not washed his own; and do not stand before women when they return from being with a dead person, because I leap and go before them with my sword in my hand, and I have permission to destroy. But if one met such women, what is the remedy? Let him move four cubits from his place; or if there is a river let him cross it; or if there is another road let him proceed along it; or if there is a wall let him stand behind it; but if not, let him turn his face away and say, "And the Lord said unto Satan,

---

[1] The meaning is, he should quote a Biblical passage which begins and ends with that word. Num. xxiii. 22 f. is suggested for 'God,' and ibid. 19 for 'not.'

[2] Names of demons.

[3] Hair, crumbs, and spices were used by the witches for their spells. What follows in the text is of doubtful meaning.

The Lord rebuke thee, O Satan" (Zech. iii. 2), until they have passed him by' (Ber. 51a).

Superstitious omens were common, especially as indications of what fate had in store for a person. 'If one wants to know whether he will live out the year or not, let him light a lamp during the ten days between the New Year and the Day of Atonement in a room where there is no draught. Should the light continue to burn (as long as there is oil in the lamp), he will live through the year. If one is about to undertake a business transaction and wishes to know whether it will succeed or not, let him rear a cock. Should it grow fat and well-favoured, his enterprise will prosper. If one wishes to undertake a journey and wants to know whether he will safely return to his home or not, let him stand in a dark room. Should he see the shadow of a shadow, he may know that he will return home. But this is not an infallible sign! Perhaps (through not seeing the shadow) his mind will be upset and affect his luck for the worse! (Therefore he should avoid using this test)' (Hor. 12a).

Means were adopted for circumventing or influencing fate. One method was to change either the person's name or the place of residence, thereby misleading the powers which seek to harm him. 'Change of name and change of place are among the things which help to avert the divine decree' (R.H. 16b). 'He who has bad luck in a place and does not remove elsewhere will cry but will not be answered' (B.M. 75b). 'He who is ill should not disclose the fact (to the public) on the first day, so as not to cause himself bad luck; but after that he may disclose it' (Ber. 55b). 'Since it is declared that there is reality in signs, a person should eat on the New Year pumpkin, fenugreek, leeks, beet, and dates' (Hor. 12a). These are things which grow rapidly; so eating them on the New Year will, by sympathetic magic, make a man's possessions multiply in the course of the year. A person must also be careful to avoid bringing misfortune upon himself by using words which presage calamity. In the language of the Talmud, 'A man should never open his mouth to Satan' (Ber. 60a). Another omen is: 'If dogs whine, it is an indication that the Angel of Death has entered the city. If they sport, it is a sign that Elijah the prophet has entered the city, provided there is not a bitch among them' (B.K. 60b).

People bring poverty on themselves by doing things which they should avoid. 'To hang up a basket containing food causes poverty, as the proverb says: "He who suspends a food-basket in the air suspends his sustenance." This applies only to bread, and there is no objection if it contains meat or fish, since this is customary.

Bran scattered in a house causes poverty. Crumbs left about a house cause poverty, because on Saturday and Wednesday nights [1] harmful spirits alight upon them' (Pes. 111b).

The widespread fear of leaving nail-parings about is found in the Talmud. 'Who spends the night in a cemetery or cuts his nails and throws the parings into the public path forfeits his life and his blood is on his own head' (Nid. 17a). Here, it would seem that the danger is to the person who is careless in the matter; [2] but another reason is also given: 'Three things are said about finger-nails: who buries the parings is righteous; who burns them is pious; who throws them away is wicked, lest a pregnant woman step over them and miscarry' (M.K. 18a).

Since the most honoured class in the community were the scholars, a retentive memory was highly prized. That superstitions should have accumulated on the subject is therefore to be expected. 'Five things make learning to be forgotten: eating what had been nibbled by a mouse or by a cat; eating an animal's heart; regularly eating olives; drinking water in which somebody has washed; and placing one foot over the other while washing them. Five things restore learning to the memory: bread baked on coals; soft-boiled eggs without salt; frequent drinking of olive-oil and spiced wine; and drinking the water which remains from kneading dough. Some add: dipping the finger in salt and eating it. Ten things are bad for memorizing study: passing beneath the bridle of a camel; and how much more so passing beneath the camel itself; passing between two camels or two women, or being one of two men between whom a woman passes; passing under a place where there is the foul odour of a carcass; passing beneath a bridge under which water has not flowed for forty days; eating bread not sufficiently baked; eating meat from a soup-ladle; drinking water from a conduit which passes through a cemetery; gazing into the face of a corpse. Some add: reading the inscriptions on tombstones' (Hor. 13b).

[1] See p. 265.
[2] Because the parings might be used by sorcerers to do him injury. Cf. Frazer, *Folk-lore in the Old Testament*, iii, p. 264.

CHAPTER X

JURISPRUDENCE

(a) CRIMINAL LAW · CIVIL AND CRIMINAL PROCEDURE

§ I. THE COURTS

ACCORDING to the evidence of the Talmud, there existed at the time of the destruction of the Temple and State a comprehensive system of judicial Courts throughout the land of Israel to decide questions of religious practice, try offenders against the law, and settle disputed claims. It is further alleged that the system had a continuous existence from the very infancy of the national life. We thus find the statement: 'There has been a succession of Courts from the days of Moses' (R.H. II. 9). Mention is also made of Courts presided over by prominent personalities of the Biblical age, including even the founder of the Semitic group of peoples: 'The Holy Spirit shone forth upon the *Beth Din*[1] of Shem, Samuel, and Solomon' (Mak. 23*b*). 'It is said, "And the Lord sent Jerubbaal and Bedan and Jephthah" (I Sam. xii. 11), and it is said, "Moses and Aaron among His priests, and Samuel among them that call upon His name" (Ps. xcix. 6). Scripture places three individuals of minor importance among three of the great men of the world, to teach that the *Beth Din* of Jerubbaal is as important before the Omnipresent as the *Beth Din* of Moses, and the *Beth Din* of Jephthah as important before Him as the *Beth Din* of Samuel' (Tosifta R.H. II. 3).

It is a common practice in the Talmud to refer back institutions, the origin of which is lost in the mists of the past, to the days of Moses; and the extreme antiquity which is assigned to the Jewish system of tribunals is, of course, incapable of proof, although it is foreshadowed in Deut. xvi. 18. We are on surer ground when we deal with the Supreme Court, known as the Great Sanhedrin.[2] When Ezra reorganized the community and made Torah the basis of its life, the necessity must have been felt for an authoritative body which would be competent to settle the points of doubt that would inevitably arise. In the letter of

---

[1] *Lit.* 'house of judgment,' the usual Hebrew term for a Court.
[2] A hebraized form of the Greek word *sunhedrion*.

Artaxerxes, the commission included: 'And thou, Ezra, after the wisdom of thy God that is in thine hand, appoint magistrates and judges, which may judge all the people that are beyond the river, all such as know the laws of thy God; and teach ye him that knoweth them not' (Ezra vii. 25).

In all probability the *Keneseth Hagedolah*[1] was the prototype of the Supreme Council which afterwards legislated for the people and adjudicated trials of major importance. The Talmud preserves a tradition that there was a *'Beth Din* of the Hasmoneans' (Sanh. 82a; A.Z. 36b), i.e. of the Maccabean rulers of the second century before the common era.

Josephus frequently mentions the Sanhedrin in his writings, and his description of it does not tally with the account given of it in Rabbinic literature. Christian scholars, like Schürer,[2] have concluded that the Talmudic version must be unhistorical and a fanciful description of an institution which had long ceased to exist; and they maintain that the Rabbis of a subsequent age accredited the Sanhedrin with powers and duties which it really never possessed. Jewish authorities, on the other hand, have defended its historicity and contend that the discrepancies between Josephus and the Talmud can be harmonized on the theory that the latter refers to two distinct Sanhedrins which functioned side by side—one of a political and the other of a religious character.

However this may be, it only falls within the scope of this work to describe the Courts as they are depicted in the literature of the Rabbis. An important passage bearing on the subject reads: 'At first disputes in Israel were only adjudicated by the Court of seventy-one in the Chamber of Hewn Stone, and other Courts of twenty-three which were in the cities of the land of Israel, and other Courts of three. There were three Courts in Jerusalem: (one in the Chamber of Hewn Stone), one on the Temple Mount, and one in the *Chel*.[3] If a *Halachah*[4] was required, a person went to the Court in his city; if there was not one in his city, he went to the Court in the nearest city. If the judges had heard what the *Halachah* was, they declared it to him; otherwise he and the expert of the Court proceeded to the Court which was located on the Temple Mount. If they had heard what it was, they declared it to them; otherwise he and the expert proceeded to the Court which was

---

[1] See the Introduction, p. xviii.
[2] See his *History of the Jewish People* (English trans.), II. i, pp. 165 ff.
[3] 'There were three Courts there (i.e. in the Temple)—one sitting at the entrance of the Temple Mount, a second at the entrance of the enclosure (i.e. the *Chel*), and a third in the Chamber of Hewn Stone' (Sanh. XI. 2).
[4] A decision on point of law, religious or civil.

located in the *Chel*. If they had heard what it was, they declared it to them; otherwise they accompanied the two of them to the Supreme Court which was located in the Chamber of Hewn Stone' (Tosifta Sanh. VII. 1).

We gather from this account that there were three different kinds of Courts: one with three members, the second with twenty-three, and the third with seventy-one. In all the Courts they acted both as judge and jury. Their primary function was to provide information on questions of religious practice; but they also dealt with civil disputes and criminal charges.

The Great Sanhedrin

The political Sanhedrin, mentioned above, was mainly Sadducean in character, and its membership was drawn from the priestly and aristocratic families. Specific reference is made to 'the *Beth Din* of the Sadducees' (Sanh. 52*b*). Comparatively little is related in the Talmudic sources of its particular functions.

As for the religious Sanhedrin, its powers were very responsible. 'A tribe (which had lapsed into idolatry), a false prophet, and a High Priest can only be tried by a Court of seventy-one. A voluntary war[1] can only be entered upon if so decided by a Court of seventy-one. The same body decides whether any land may be added to the boundary of Jerusalem or the enclosures of the Temple; it appoints the Sanhedrin (of twenty-three) for the tribes (cf. Deut. xvi. 18); and it finds a verdict against a city which has been guilty of idolatry (ibid. xiii. 13 ff.).[2] Whence is it that the Great Sanhedrin consisted of seventy-one members? As it is said, "Gather unto me seventy men of the elders of Israel" (Num. xi. 16). With the addition of Moses there is a total of seventy-one' (Sanh. 1. 5 f.).

The following information is given of its constitution, composition, and procedure: 'The Sanhedrin was seated in the form of a semicircle so that the members could see each other. The President sat in the centre and the elders on his right and left (in order of seniority)' (Tosifta Sanh. VIII. 1). 'Two secretaries of the judges stood in front of them, one on the right and the other on the left, and recorded the words of those who were for an acquittal and of those who were for a conviction. R. Judah said that there were three: in addition to the two mentioned, a third recorded the words

---

[1] In contradistinction to the wars which are expressly commanded in the Pentateuch against the seven nations of Canaan.

[2] The Talmud declares this to be a matter of theory rather than practice. 'A case of a city lapsing into idolatry has never been and will never be. Why did the Torah mention it? Expound it and receive the reward' (Sanh. 71*a*).

of those who were for an acquittal and those who were for a conviction. Three rows of the disciples of the Sages sat in front of them, each one in his appointed place. If the necessity arose to ordain (one of them to complete the requisite number), they ordained him from the first row. Then one from the second row moved into the first, and one from the third into the second. They further selected one out of the assembly and seated him in the third row. He did not, however, take the place of the former, but in accordance with his status' (Sanh. IV. 3 f.).

'Although the Court in the Chamber of Hewn Stone consisted of seventy-one, there must not be fewer than twenty-three present. Should one of them need to go out, he must see whether there would be that number left, otherwise he may not leave. There they sat from the time of the Continual Offering of the morning until the time of the Continual Offering of the evening. On Sabbaths and Festivals they only entered the House of Study which was on the Temple Mount. Should a question be asked of them and they had heard what the *Halachah* was, they declare it; otherwise it is put to the vote. If the majority hold the view that the act is forbidden, the Court pronounces the *Halachah* in that sense, and vice versa. From this seat of authority the *Halachah* spread throughout Israel. When the disciples of Shammai and Hillel multiplied who had not sufficiently mastered the Torah, points of doubt became numerous in Israel. So from this Court they sent out to search for whoever was learned, humble, sin-fearing, of good repute, and acceptable to his fellow-men, and appointed him a judge in his city. From there he was promoted to the Court on the Temple Mount, after that to the Court in the *Chel*, and finally to the Court in the Chamber of Hewn Stone' (Tosifta Sanh. VII. 1).

An important duty which devolved upon this Sanhedrin was to investigate the pedigree of men who presented themselves for service in the Priesthood and reject those who were disqualified by impure descent (Middoth V. 4).

The authority of the Great Sanhedrin was destroyed by the Roman general Gabinius in the middle of the first century before the present era; and having divided Judea into five districts, he 'appointed five councils which governed the people; the first was in Jerusalem, the second in Gadara, the third in Amathus (Hamath), the fourth in Jericho, and the fifth in Sepphoris in Galilee' (Antiq. XIV. v. 4). The Sanhedrin at Hamath is sometimes referred to in the Talmud, but the one in Jerusalem enjoyed the greatest prestige of all in religious and civil matters. Its power began to decline about the third decade of the first century of this era. The Talmud testifies: 'Forty years before the destruction of the Temple, the Sanhedrin was banished (from the Chamber of Hewn Stone) and sat in the trading-station (on the Temple Mount)' (Shab. 15a). It survived the downfall of the State and continued, in a more or less attenuated form, down to the end of the fourth century. 'The Great Sanhedrin suffered ten removals: from the Chamber of Hewn Stone to the trading-station, from the trading-station to (the city of) Jerusalem, from Jerusalem to Jabneh, from Jabneh to Usha, from Usha back to Jabneh, then back to Usha, after that to Shaphraam, from Shaphraam to Beth Shearim, from Beth Shearim to Sepphoris, from Sepphoris to Tiberias' [1] (R.H. 31a, b)

The Criminal Courts

Their scope is thus described: 'Criminal charges are decided by a Court of twenty-three. A person who had unnatural intercourse with an animal and the animal are tried by a Court of twenty-three; as it is said, "Thou shalt kill the woman and the beast" (Lev. xx. 16), and "Ye shall slay the beast" (ibid. 15). Whether an ox which had gored a person is to be stoned is decided by a Court of twenty-three; as it is said, "The ox shall be stoned, and his owner shall be put to death" (Exod. xxi. 29)—as the death of the owner (can only be determined by a Court of twenty-three), so also with the death of the ox. Likewise with the wolf, lion, bear, leopard, hyena, and snake, their death is decided by a Court of twenty-three.[2] R. Eliezer said, Whoever takes the first opportunity of killing them (without a trial) acts meritoriously; but R. Akiba maintained that their death must be decided by a Court of twenty-three' (Sanh. 1. 4).

'Whence is it that the small Sanhedrin consisted of twenty-three? As it is said, "The congregation shall judge . . . the congregation shall deliver" (Num. xxxv. 24 f.). Since a "congregation" judges (i.e. convicts) and a "congregation" delivers (i.e. acquits), we have a total of twenty judges. But whence is it that the term "congregation" denotes ten persons? As it is said, "How long shall I bear with this evil congregation?" (ibid. xiv. 27). Here it refers to the twelve spies with the exclusion of Joshua and Caleb (and therefore indicates a body of ten persons). Whence is it that three more are to be added to the twenty? This is deduced from the text, "To be after a majority for evil" (i.e. a conviction, sic Exod.

---

[1] These are all towns in Palestine.

[2] The trial of animals was a common procedure in ancient times and persisted down to a fairly modern period. Much curious information will be found in E. P. Evans, The Criminal Prosecution and Capital Punishment of Animals.

xxiii. 2). I infer that I may follow a majority for good (i.e. for acquittal); if so, what is the purpose of the words "To be after a majority"? They teach that there is a difference in the majority required for an acquittal and a conviction. For the former a majority of one suffices; for the latter two are necessary (and so twenty-two are required); and to avoid the Court being equally divided one more is added, giving a total of twenty-three. What must the population of a town be to qualify for a Sanhedrin of its own? One hundred and twenty. R. Nehemiah said, Two hundred and thirty, so that each member (of the Sanhedrin) should be "a ruler of ten" (Exod. xviii. 21)' (Sanh. 1. 6). The decision is in favour of the smaller figure.

This Court, like the Great Sanhedrin, had its three rows of disciples (Sanh. 17b). Its powers, like those of the superior body, were also curtailed in course of time. 'Forty years before the destruction of the Temple, cases involving the death penalty were taken away, and in the days of Simeon b. Shetach[1] civil cases were also taken away' (p. Sanh. 18a). With the end of political autonomy, the authority of the criminal Courts necessarily came to an end.

The Civil Courts

In the time of the Second Temple there were probably Courts of this kind regularly constituted in most of the Palestinian towns with fixed days for the holding of sessions. It is stated, 'The local *Beth Din* sat on Monday and Thursday' (Keth. 1. 1), and this body dealt not only with religious questions but also with claims for damages. The type of case relegated to this Court is thus specified: 'Civil cases are decided by a Court of three. The following are included under its jurisdiction: larceny, bodily injuries, indemnity for the whole of the damage or for half the damage,[2] the payment of double the loss or fourfold and fivefold (cf. Exod. xxii. 1, 4), rape, seduction, and slander. This is the view of R. Meïr; but the Rabbis declare that a charge of slander must be tried by a court of twenty-three because it may involve the death penalty' [3] (Sanh. 1. 1).

[1] Since this Simeon lived in the first century before the common era, it is probable that the text should be corrected to read 'Simeon b. Jochai.' He flourished during the reign of Hadrian, at the beginning of the second century of the present era, when the Jews were subjected to bitter oppression.

[2] The damage done by a goring ox is meant. If the ox had previously gored, the owner was liable for the whole damage, otherwise only for half (cf. Exod. xxi. 35 f.).

[3] e.g. when a priest's daughter is slandered as to her moral character. If the charge were true, she suffered death by burning (Lev. xxi. 9); consequently, by Biblical law, if the accuser made a false charge, he must suffer death (cf. Deut. xix. 19).

After the fall of the State, the Court of three continued in existence but developed into a Court of Arbitration. The method of its constitution is described in these terms: 'Civil cases are decided by a Court of three. According to R. Meïr, each party selects one judge and they jointly select the third. The Rabbis assert, the two selected judges appoint the third. Each party can reject the nominee of the third, so declares R. Meïr; but the Rabbis assert, They can only do so on bringing proof that the nominees are related to the litigants or otherwise disqualified. If, however, they are fit to act as judges or are experts, they cannot be disqualified' (Sanh. III. 1).

The parties had to sign a document in which they agree to submit the case to the decision of the three selected judges, such a document being called 'compromissa' (p. M.K. 82a).

Practice did not remain uniform as to cases being tried by less than three. On the one hand, we have the emphatic statement, 'If two judges tried civil cases, all the authorities are agreed that their verdict is invalid' (Sanh. 2b); and as regards a single judge it is said, 'Judge not alone, for none may judge alone save One' (Aboth IV. 10). Yet in the course of time, when men competent to adjudicate became scarce, the law had to be relaxed, and in civil cases 'one who is acknowledged by the public as an expert may decide alone' (Sanh. 5a), provided both parties agreed to accept his decision.

There was, lastly, a special *Beth Din* which discharged a function of considerable importance for the community, viz. the regulation of the calendar. The beginning of the month was not determined by calculation but by observation; and witnesses who had seen the new moon had to attend before this Court and undergo examination as to the validity of their evidence.

'The intercalation of the month (whether a thirtieth day is to be added) or of the year (whether a thirteenth month is to be inserted) is decided by a Court of three; such is the statement of R. Meïr. R. Simeon b. Gamaliel says, The matter is begun with three, debated by five, and decided by seven, but if the decision was made by three the intercalation is valid' (Sanh. I. 2).

The opinion of R. Simeon is explained by the Gemara as follows: 'If one judge declared it necessary to hold a session (to discuss whether the year should be intercalated) and two deem it unnecessary (since they are of the view that there is no need for intercalation), the opinion of the minority fails. If two declared it necessary to hold a session and one did not, two more judges are added, and they debate the question. Should two conclude that there is necessity to intercalate the year and three come to the opposite conclusion, the opinion of the minority fails. But if three conclude that there is such necessity and two do not, two more judges are added, because the number (for taking the decision) must not be less than seven' (ibid. 10*b*).

With respect to the procedure of the *Beth Din* in the intercalation of the month, this information is given: 'There was a great court-yard in Jerusalem named Beth-Jazek where the witnesses assembled, and there the *Beth Din* examined them in the following manner: The first pair to arrive were questioned first. The more important of the two was brought in and asked, "Say, in what position did you see the moon, in front of the sun (i.e. to the east of it) or behind it? To the north of it or the south? What was its elevation (on the horizon)? To which side was its inclination? What was the width (of the disk)?" If he answers that it was in front of the sun, his evidence is worthless. Then the second is brought in and questioned similarly. If their replies tally, their testimony stands. The remaining witnesses are only examined cursorily, not because they are required, but that they should not depart disappointed (at not having been heard) and that they should form the habit of coming (to give evidence). The President of the *Beth Din* declares, "(The new moon) is consecrated," and all the people respond with "Consecrated, consecrated"' (R.H. II. 5–7).

§ II. JUDGES AND WITNESSES

Strict regulations were laid down governing the qualifications of judges, especially in the higher Courts. The general rule was: 'All Israelites are qualified to judge civil cases; but criminal cases can only be tried by Priests, Levites, and Israelites who can give their daughters in marriage into the priesthood' (Sanh. IV. 2), i.e. who were of pure Israelitish descent. With regard to the convert the law states: 'A proselyte is permitted by the Torah to judge another proselyte (in a criminal as well as civil case); and if his mother was a Jewess, he may judge even an Israelite' (Jeb. 102*a*). Another general rule is: 'Whoever is qualified to try criminal cases is qualified to try civil cases, but there are some qualified to try civil cases who are not qualified to try criminal cases. Whoever is qualified to judge is qualified to give evidence, but there are some who are qualified to give evidence who are not qualified to judge' (Nid. VI. 4). A woman could not act as judge or give evidence (p. Joma 43*b*).

As regards the more responsible office, numerous perfections —physical, moral, and intellectual—were demanded. The ideal is stated in these terms: 'We only appoint to a Sanhedrin men of stature, possessed of wisdom and imposing appearance, of mature age, masters of the magical arts [1] and acquainted with the seventy languages,[2] so that the Sanhedrin does not have to hear a case through the mouth of an interpreter' (Sanh. 17a). Since it would have been too much to expect of every member of the Sanhedrin that he should be so accomplished a linguist, it was considered sufficient if a few only possessed the ability to speak all the languages. 'Every Sanhedrin in which there are two who know how to speak (the seventy languages) and all can understand them is qualified to act as a Sanhedrin. If there are three (who know how to speak all the languages), it is an average Sanhedrin; if there are four, it is a learned Sanhedrin' (Tosifta Sanh. VIII. 1). The use of an interpreter outside their own ranks was in this way ruled out.

In order that justice may be tempered with mercy, it was required that men who were likely to be devoid of humane feeling should be excluded. Accordingly there is the dictum: 'We do not appoint to a Sanhedrin an old man, a eunuch, and a childless man. R. Judah adds, One who is hard-hearted' (Sanh. 36b). Judges were not paid officials. 'Who takes a fee to adjudicate, his verdicts are invalid' (Bech. IV. 6).

The importance and responsibility of the judicial office have already been referred to.[3] It should not be undertaken for the honour which attached thereto, and the personal unpleasantness which might result is emphasized to deter place-seekers. 'He who shuns the judicial office rids himself of hatred, robbery, and vain swearing; and he who presumptuously lays down decisions is foolish, wicked, and of an arrogant spirit' (Aboth IV. 9).

A few guiding rules for judges are given: 'Be deliberate in judgment' (Aboth I. 1). '(In the judge's office) act not the counsel's part; when the parties to a suit are standing before you, let them both be regarded by you as guilty, but when they are departed from your presence, regard them both as innocent, the verdict having been acquiesced in by them' (ibid. 8). 'Be very searching in the examination of witnesses, and be heedful of your words, lest through them they learn to falsify' (ibid. 9). 'Say not (to your judicial colleagues) "Accept my view," for the choice is theirs (to concur); and it is not for you to compel (concurrence)' (ibid. IV. 10).

The establishment of the truth depends not only on the competence

---

[1] See p. 280.
[2] This is either a hyperbolical expression for many languages, or, it has been suggested, 'seventy languages' is the equivalent of 'the language of the seventy (the Septuagint), i.e. Greek.'   [3] See pp. 207 f.

and fairness of the judges, but perhaps to an even greater degree on the reliability of the witnesses. For that reason Talmudic law is as exacting in the high standard of qualification demanded of the one as of the other. Unless the person was known to lead a reputable life and to be utterly disinterested, his testimony was not accepted.

To help the cause of justice by acting as a witness was considered to be a sacred duty, and 'he who can give evidence in connection with his fellow-man, and does not testify, is free from the judgment of man but liable to the judgment of Heaven' (B.K. 56a). 'Three persons does the Holy One, blessed be He, hate: who speaks one thing with his mouth and another thing in his heart; who knows evidence in connection with his fellow-man and does not testify for him; and who sees something unseemly in his fellow-man and testifies against him singly' (Pes. 113b). Furthermore, 'the witnesses must know against Whom[1] and before Whom they testify, and Who will exact punishment of them' (Sanh. 6b).

A list of persons who are disqualified from acting as either judge or witness is given: 'The dice-player (i.e. gambler), lender of money on interest, the flyer of doves (who wagers on the race), and they who traffic in the produce of the Sabbatical year.[2] R. Simeon said, At first they used to call them the gatherers of the produce of the Sabbatical year;[3] but when tyrannical officials grew numerous (and made heavy exactions of the people), they altered the term to traffickers in the produce of the Sabbatical year. R. Judah said, When (does the disqualification of gamblers, etc.) apply? Should they have no other occupation; but if they have other means of livelihood they are qualified' (Sanh. III. 3).

Other additions to this list are found. 'The Rabbis included herdsmen,[4] tax-collectors, and farmers of the revenue' (Sanh. 25b). 'They added robbers, herdsmen, extortioners, and all who are suspected of dishonesty in connection with money' (Tosifta Sanh. v. 5). From the text, 'Both the *men*, between whom the controversy is, shall stand' (Deut. xix. 17), the rule was deduced that 'the witnesses must be men, not women or minors' (p. Joma 43b). 'In cases involving indemnity the evidence can only be given by

[1] The perjurer testifies against God, because by means of false evidence justice is perverted and He is troubled to make reparation to the wronged party (Sanh. 8a).
[2] Scripture declares: 'The sabbath of the land shall be for food for you' (Lev. xxv. 6)—for food, not for commerce.
[3] i.e. the law was made less severe, and only persons who trafficked in the produce were disqualified.
[4] Because they dishonestly allow cattle to graze on land which belongs to others.

freemen and sons of the Covenant' (B.K. I. 3). 'If a witness accepts pay to testify, his evidence is invalid' (Bech IV. 6).

Persons who stood in a certain degree of relationship to either party were not allowed to act as judge or witness. They are thus enumerated: 'Father, brother. the brother of father or mother, sister's husband, husband of father's and mother's sister, step-father, father-in-law, husband of the wife's sister—neither they, nor their sons and sons-in-law, nor a stepson himself.[1] R. José said, This is the reading of the text of R. Akiba; but the earlier text read: Uncle, first cousin, and any one competent to become an heir.[2] Also a person (may not give evidence) who was related at the time of the incident;[3] but if he subsequently cease to be akin to him [4] he is qualified to testify. R. Judah says, Even if the daughter died, leaving children, he is still regarded as a relative' (Sanh. III. 4).

'A friend and an enemy (are disqualified). What sort of friend? (One with whom he is so intimate that he becomes) his groomsman. What sort of enemy? One who has not spoken to him for three days from a feeling of hostility. The Rabbis said, Israelites are not suspected on such a ground' (Sanh. III. 5).[5]

'What is the meaning of the text, "The fathers shall not be put to death for the children, neither shall the children be put to death for the fathers"? (Deut. xxiv. 16). If its intention is to teach that fathers should not be put to death for a sin committed by children, and vice versa, behold it is explicitly stated, "Every man shall be put to death for his own sin"! (ibid.). But the meaning is, Fathers shall not be put to death by the evidence of children, and vice versa' (Sanh. 27b).

The Bible laid down the principle that at least two witnesses are required to establish the case, and the point is stressed in Rabbinic jurisprudence. '"One witness shall not testify against any person that he die" (Num. xxxv. 30)—this is the general rule, that wherever Scripture uses the word "witness" it means two unless the text specifies one only' (Sifré ad loc. § 161; 62b). 'A single witness who is uncorroborated is not believed' (R.H. III. 1).[6]

Circumstantial evidence, however convincing, was not accepted. A witness was only allowed to testify who saw the crime actually committed. As an example of testimony which was not considered

---

[1] A stepson's sons were qualified.
[2] i.e. a relative on his father's side only; therefore his maternal uncle, etc. could give evidence.
[3] e.g. a son-in-law.
[4] Through the death of the daughter to whom he was married.
[5] That they would not give true evidence through friendship or hostility; therefore they are accepted as witnesses.
[6] For an exception to the rule, see p. 169.

admissible the following is cited: 'We saw the accused run after a
man with a sword in his hand; the man who was pursued entered
a shop on account of him and the accused entered the shop after him;
there we saw the man slain and the sword, dripping with blood,
in the hand of the murderer' (Tosifta Sanh. VIII. 3). It follows,
therefore, that no charge could be sustained unless the actual
commission of the crime was seen by two men of repute.

A perjured witness was treated with the utmost severity; and
the interpretation of the Biblical law on the subject was a matter
of controversy between the Pharisees and Sadducees. 'Witnesses
who have committed perjury are not executed until the trial of the
prisoner is ended (and sentence passed upon him). The Sadducees,
however, assert that they were not executed until the prisoner had
been put to death, since it is said, "Life shall go for life" (Deut. xix.
21). The (Pharisaic) Sages replied to them, But it has already
been stated, "Ye shall do unto him as he had *thought* to do unto his
brother" (ibid. 19), from which it is evident that "his brother"
still exists! That being so, what is the meaning of "Life shall go
for life"? It would be possible to think that the witnesses should
be executed after (the judges) had received the evidence (which
was found to be untrue); therefore the text declares, "Life shall go
for life"—i.e. they are not to be executed until the trial is ended'
(Mak. I. 6). The stricter view of the Pharisees agrees with that
taken by Josephus: 'If any one be believed to have borne false
witness, let him, if convicted, suffer the very same punishment
which he, against whom he bore witness, *would have suffered*'
(Antiq. IV. viii. 15).

§ III. The Trial

The strict injunction was laid upon judges to treat both parties
to a suit equally and not to show the slightest partiality. Some
rules bearing on the point are: 'It is the duty of both litigants to
stand during the trial. If the judges wish to permit the two of
them to be seated they may do so; but it is forbidden to permit one
only to be seated, so that one stands and the other sits. Nor is it
allowed for one to speak at length and the other to be told to be
brief' (Shebuoth 30a). 'If a scholar and an ignoramus have a suit,
the former may not attend the Court in advance of the other and
take a seat, because he might appear as though he were arranging
the case (in his favour)' (ibid. 30b). 'If one party appear in
tatters and the other wearing an expensive robe,[1] the latter is told,

---

[1] *Lit.* 'robe worth a hundred *mana*,' i.e. he went out of his way to dress
himself in an extraordinarily expensive style so as to impress the judges.

Either dress like him or clothe him in a manner similar to yourself. A judge is forbidden to listen to one party before the arrival of the other' (ibid. 31a).

The procedure at the trial differed in criminal and civil cases. The principal variations are enumerated as follows: 'Both classes of trial must be conducted by means of inquiry and cross-examination; as it is said, "Ye shall have one manner of law" (Lev. xxiv. 22). The following differences, however, apply: Civil cases are tried by a Court of three; criminal cases by a Court of twenty-three. Civil cases may open with the defence or the claim; criminal cases must only open with the defence. In civil cases a majority of one is sufficient to find for the defendant or the plaintiff; in criminal cases a majority of one acquits, but two are needed to convict. In civil cases the judges may revise the verdict in favour either of the defendant or the plaintiff; in criminal cases they may revise the verdict to acquit but not to convict. In civil cases all the judges may argue either for the defendant or the plaintiff; in criminal cases they may all argue for an acquittal but not for a conviction.[1] In civil cases a judge who argues against the defendant may (after reflection) argue for the plaintiff, and vice versa; in criminal cases a judge who argues for a conviction may subsequently argue for an acquittal, but if he has once argued for an acquittal he cannot retract and argue for a conviction. Civil cases are tried during the day and concluded that night; criminal cases may be concluded the same day if the verdict is not guilty, but the following day if the verdict is guilty. For that reason (criminal cases) are not tried on the eve of the Sabbath or Festival. In civil cases and questions of ceremonial impurity and purity, the judges express their opinion, beginning with the seniors; in criminal cases they begin from the side (i.e. the juniors)' (Sanh. iv. 1 f.). This regulation prevented the judgment of the juniors from being unduly influenced by that of the elders.

When a trial involved capital punishment, a solemn charge was addressed to the witnesses to impress them with the gravity of the issues. A form of this charge has been preserved, and reads: 'Perhaps the evidence you are about to give is based on conjecture or hearsay, or something said by another witness, or the statement made by a person in whom you have confidence. Perhaps, also, you are unaware that we shall subject you to a searching cross-examination. Take note that criminal cases are not like civil cases.

[1] There must be some to put points in favour of the accused. This is a remarkable feature of the Rabbinic procedure in view of the fact that a prisoner charged with felony in England was not entitled to be defended by counsel until modern times.

In the latter a man forfeits his money and makes atonement;[1] but in criminal cases the responsibility of his blood and the blood of his seed rests upon him until the end of the world. Thus do we find it in connection with Cain who killed his brother, of whom it is said, "The voice of thy brother's bloods[2] crieth unto Me from the ground" (Gen. iv. 10). The text does not read "thy brother's blood" but "thy brother's bloods," meaning his blood and that of his seed. For that reason was man first created a single individual, to teach the lesson that whoever destroys one life,[3] Scripture ascribes it to him as though he had destroyed a whole world; and whoever saves one life, Scripture ascribes it to him as though he had saved a whole world.[4] You may perhaps say (since your responsibility is so grievous), "Why should we take this trouble upon us?"[5] But it has been said, "He being a witness, if he do not utter it, he shall bear his iniquity" (Lev. v. 1). Or perhaps you may say, "Why should we be responsible for the blood of the accused?" But it has been said, "When the wicked perish, there is shouting" (Prov. xi. 10)' (Sanh. iv. 5).

It was recommended that the cross-examination, when life was not involved, should not be too severe, since it might have a deterrent effect on the relationship between individuals. 'The Rabbis declared that in civil cases there is no necessity for inquiry and cross-examination, so that the door should not be closed against would-be borrowers' (Sanh. 3a).

The procedure in the trial of a civil case is thus described: 'How did they examine the witnesses? These were brought into Court, solemnly charged, and then sent out with the exception of the eldest among them. The judges say to him, "Tell us, how do you know that the defendant owes money to the plaintiff?" If he answers, "He himself said to me, 'I owe him the money,' or so-and-so informed me of the indebtedness," his evidence is worthless, unless he is

---

[1] Similarly a perjured witness only forfeits money for his offence.

[2] In the Hebrew the word is plural.

[3] Some texts add 'of Israel,' but this should be deleted in accordance with the reading of the Palestinian Talmud.

[4] The text adds, by way of homiletical commentary but not as part of the charge: '(Man was first created a single individual) also for the reason of peace among human beings, that one person should not say to another, "My ancestor was greater than yours," and that heretics should not say, "There are several creative powers in Heaven"; and to declare the greatness of the Holy One, blessed be He, since a man strikes many coins from one die but they are all alike, whereas the Supreme King of kings, the Holy One, blessed be He, has moulded every human being in the stamp of the first man, but they are all dissimilar. Therefore every one is in duty bound to say, For my sake was the world created.'

And for that reason withhold the evidence.

able to testify, "The defendant admitted in *our* presence [1] that he owed him two hundred *zuz*." After that the second witness is brought in and examined similarly. If their statements tally, the judges proceed to discuss the case. Should two declare him not liable and one liable, the claim is dismissed. Should two declare him liable and one not liable, then he is held liable. If one declare him not not liable and one liable—even if two declare him not liable or liable—and one says that he does not know how to decide, the number of judges is increased. [2]

'When a verdict has been arrived at, the litigants are brought into Court, and the senior judge says, "So-and-so, you are not liable; and so-and-so, you are liable." Whence is it that one of the judges must not afterwards say to the person found liable, "I was for finding you not liable but my colleagues were for finding you liable; so what could I do, since they were in the majority?"? Of such a man it is stated, "He that goeth about as a tale-bearer revealeth secrets" (Prov. xi. 13).

'So long as the person liable can produce fresh evidence, the Court has the power of setting aside the verdict. If the judges inform him, All the proofs you have must be brought within the next thirty days, and he brought such proofs within the thirty days, the verdict is set aside; but not after thirty days. R. Simeon b. Gamaliel asked, What is the man to do who could not find the proofs within the thirty days and discovered them later? [3] If the judges said to the person held liable, "Bring witnesses," and he replied, "I have none"; or they said, "Bring a proof," and he replied, "I have none"; but after the prescribed time he brought a proof or discovered witnesses, they would not be valid. Against this also R. Simeon b. Gamaliel asked, What is he to do if he was unaware that he had witnesses and then found them, or was unaware of the existence of proof and then discovered it? If the judges said to him, "Produce witnesses," and he replied, "I have none," or "Bring a proof," and he replied, "I have none"; and then seeing that he was about to be held liable, he says, "Bring so-and-so and they will give evidence on my behalf," or he took out a proof from beneath his girdle, this would not be valid (even in the opinion of R. Simeon)' (Sanh. III. 6–8).

In a criminal charge, the witnesses were similarly tested one by one, the cross-examination centring around the questions of time and place. 'They examined the witnesses under seven

---

[1] i.e. in the presence of himself and another person.
[2] Because he was in fact being tried by only two judges.
[3] The verdict may then be reversed.

headings: In which Sabbatical period (did the incident occur)?[1] In which year? In which month? On which day of the month? On which day of the week? At which hour? In which place? Did you know this man (who is charged with the crime)? Did you warn him?[2] If the charge was of idolatry, the (additional) questions put were: Which idol did he worship? How did he worship?

'Whoever prolongs the examination acts worthily. It is related that Ben Zakkai once conducted a prolonged examination concerning the stalks of figs.[3] What is the difference between cross-examination and investigation? In the former, if one witness answers, "I do not know," their evidence is invalid. In the latter, if one says, or two say, "I do not know," their evidence is still valid. In connection with both cross-examination and investigation, should the witnesses contradict each other, their evidence is invalid.

'If one witness said that it happened on the second of the month and another that it was on the third, their evidence is valid, because one might be acquainted with the intercalation of the month and the other ignorant of it;[4] but if one said it was on the third and another that it was on the fifth, their evidence is invalid. If one said it happened in the second hour (i.e. eight a.m.) and another in the third, their evidence is valid; but if one said it was in the third hour and another in the fifth, their evidence is invalid. R. Judah would allow it.[5] If one said it was in the fifth hour and another in the seventh, their evidence is invalid; because in the fifth hour (eleven a.m.) the sun is in the east and in the seventh hour (one p.m.) it is in the west.

'The second witness is next brought into Court and examined. If the evidence of the two agree, the judges open the discussion with a plea for acquittal. If one of the witnesses says, "I have

---

[1] The years were grouped together in series of sevens.

[2] According to Talmudic law it was necessary for the offender to be warned by the witnesses that the deed he was about to commit was a crime. The purpose of the warning was 'to distinguish between one who acts in error and one who acts deliberately' (Sanh. 8b).

[3] He was not at the time a fully qualified Rabbi; but being present at a murder trial, he was able, by closely questioning a witness about the thickness of the stalks of the fig-tree under which the crime was alleged to have been committed, to prove that the evidence was false. On that account he was given the name Ben Zakkai, 'Son of the innocent one,' i.e. the person who established the innocence of the accused.

[4] The beginning of the month was announced by the Sanhedrin after witnesses attested that they had seen the new moon. Some persons, in the first few days of the month, might be uncertain which day had been declared as the first.

[5] Because, in his opinion, people are liable to err to the extent of two hours. The hours of the day were reckoned as beginning at six a.m.

something to declare in favour of the accused,"[1] or one of the disciples says, "I have something to declare in favour of a conviction," the judges silence him; but if one of the disciples says, "I have something to declare in favour of an acquittal," he is brought forward and given a seat among the judges, and he does not descend from there throughout the day. Should there be any substance in his remarks they listen to him; and even if the accused says that he has something to declare in his defence, they listen to him, provided there is substance in his words.[2]

'If the judges find him innocent, they release him; if not, they defer the verdict to the morrow. Then they adjourn in couples, take a little food, but drink no wine all that day, and discuss the matter throughout the night. The following morning they repair at an early hour to the Court (and declare their views). He who is for an acquittal says, "I was in favour of acquitting and am still of the same opinion." He who is for a conviction says, "I was in favour of convicting and am still of the same opinion." A judge who (the day before) argued for the guilt of the accused may now argue for his innocence, but not vice versa. Should they make a mistake in the opinion they express,[3] the two scribes of the judges correct them. If they find him innocent they release him; otherwise they take a vote. If twelve acquit and eleven convict, he is declared innocent. If twelve convict and eleven acquit, and even if eleven acquit and eleven convict and one is neutral, or twenty-two acquit or convict and one is neutral, further judges are added.[4] Up to which number are they added? By twos up to a total of seventy-one. If thirty-six acquit and thirty-five convict, he is declared innocent; but if thirty-six convict and thirty-five acquit, they discuss the matter until one of those who were for a conviction agrees with the opposite side' (Sanh. v. 1–5).

There is a Talmudic statement which has generally been taken to mean, 'If the Sanhedrin is unanimous for a conviction the prisoner is acquitted' (Sanh. 17a), and it is usually supposed that when there is not a single judge to argue in favour of the accused, there must be a bias against him. But what of a case where the evidence is so conclusive that it is impossible to think of an acquittal; is the prisoner to go free? Such a procedure is unthinkable. The probability is that the phrase *poterin oto*, instead

---

[1] It obviously follows that he would not be allowed at that stage to testify against the accused.
[2] The accused was not allowed to give evidence against himself. The rule was: 'A man cannot incriminate himself' (Sanh. 9b).
[3] i.e. in the morning as compared with the previous evening.
[4] Because in reality only twenty-two judges were trying him.

of being understood in the sense of 'they dismiss him,' should be translated 'they dismiss his trial (forthwith),' i.e. they do not defer the verdict to the next day.[1]

§ IV. Modes of Punishment

In the case of a trial for murder which had been proved, one of two sentences could be passed upon the condemned person: banishment to a city of refuge (cf. Num. xxxv. 10 ff.) if death had been caused by an accident not due to culpable negligence, and the capital punishment if there had been deliberate homicide or criminal neglect. The distinction is thus illustrated: 'If he was levelling (the roof) with a roller which fell upon and killed a person, or he was letting a cask down from a height and it fell upon and killed a person, or he was descending a ladder and fell upon and killed a person, he is banished. But if he was drawing up a roller (on to the roof) and it fell upon and killed a person, or he was pulling up a cask and the rope snapped so that it fell upon and killed a person, or he was ascending a ladder and fell upon and killed a person, he is not banished. This is the general rule: when death is caused in the process of descent, the penalty of banishment applies; but when death is not caused in the process of descent, the penalty does not apply.[2] If the iron (of an axe) slipped from its handle and killed a person, according to R. Judah, he is not banished, but the Rabbis declare that he is. Should, however, a log (chopped from the tree) cause death, R. Judah declares that he is banished, but the Rabbis say he is not.

'If one throws a stone into the public road and kills a person, he is banished. R. Eliezer b. Jacob said, Should the stone have left his hand at the time when the person put his head forth and was struck by it, the thrower is free of guilt. If he threw the stone inside his private premises and killed a person, he is banished in the case where the injured party had the right to enter there; otherwise he is not banished; as it is said, "As when a man goeth into the forest with his neighbour to hew wood" (Deut. xix. 5). As with a forest both the injurer and the injured had the right to enter there, so with every place where the injurer and the injured

---

[1] This explanation is given in *Otzar Yisrael*, iv, p. 50; and another instance of the phrase with this signification is quoted, viz. Shebuoth 39a, where Rashi explains it in this sense. Another explanation of the passage is that where the members of the Sanhedrin witness the guilt of the accused they may not try him.

[2] The difference is based on the idea that in letting an object down, there is more negligence if anything untoward happens. He can at least see anybody who is passing below.

have the right to enter (should death occur, the sentence of banishment applies), thus excluding a place where the injured person had no right to enter. Abba Saul said, As with the hewing of wood, which is a voluntary act, so with all acts which are voluntary (does the sentence of banishment apply), excluding a father who strikes his child, a teacher who corrects a pupil, and the agent of a *Beth Din* (who carries out its sentence of scourging).[1]

'A father is sentenced to banishment for (the accidental homicide of) his son,[2] and a son for his father. All[3] are banished for an Israelite, and an Israelite is banished for them with the exception of a *Ger Toshab*.[4] One *Ger Toshab* is banished for another. A blind man[5] is not banished, according to R. Judah, but R. Meïr says that he is. An enemy is not banished, but is executed, since he is regarded as one who has a tendency (to do harm). R. Simeon said, An enemy is sometimes banished and sometimes not. This is the general rule: Whenever it is possible to say that he killed deliberately, banishment does not apply; but where it is possible to say that he killed unintentionally, he is banished' (Mak II. 1–3).

The unintentional slayer remained in the city of refuge until the death of the High Priest (Num. xxxv. 25). 'If the High Priest died after the judgment had been delivered, the accused is not banished. If the High Priest died before the judgment was delivered, and another High Priest had been appointed, and thereafter the judgment was delivered, he returns (from the city of refuge) on the death of the latter. If the judgment was delivered at a time when there was no High Priest, or the High Priest was the victim of homicide, or the accidental slayer was the High Priest himself, then the accused may never leave the city of refuge' (Mak. II. 6 f.).

'Two disciples of the Sages were deputed to accompany him on the way (to the city of refuge), lest (the avenger) kill him during the journey; and their duty was to talk him over (and make him desist)' (ibid. II. 5).

---

[1] In these three cases, the person who caused death acted from a sense of duty.

[2] If the death was not caused while he was correcting him, but through one of the circumstances described above.

[3] e.g. a gentile servant.

[4] A Gentile who settled in Palestine and, to obtain the privilege of citizenship, abjured idolatry. He is distinguished from the *Ger Tzédek* who was a full convert to Judaism. There was no need for banishment when a *Ger Toshab* had been accidentally killed because, presumably, there was no 'redeemer of blood' to avenge his death.

[5] Scripture uses the phrase 'seeing him not' (Num. xxxv. 23), thus implying that the injurer had the capacity to see but did not notice the person he injured.

Should the Court find that the homicide was deliberate, sentence of death was passed; but there was great reluctance to resort to capital punishment and every endeavour was made to avoid it. Indeed, it was remarked: 'A Sanhedrin which executed a person once in seven years was called destructive. R. Eleazar b. Azariah said, Once in seventy years. R. Tarphon and R. Akiba said, If we were members of a Sanhedrin, never would a person be put to death. R. Simeon b. Gamaliel said, In that case they would multiply shedders of blood in Israel!' (Mak. i. 10).

A death sentence took one of four forms: 'Stoning, burning, decapitation, and strangulation' (Sanh. vii. 1). This was the method of stoning: 'The judgment having been delivered, the prisoner is taken out to be stoned. The place of stoning was outside the Court; as it is said, "Bring forth him that hath cursed [1] without the camp" (Lev. xxiv. 14). One man stood at the entrance of the Court with a flag in his hand, and another, mounted on a horse, was at a distance from him but within sight. If one of the judges said, "I have something to plead in favour of the prisoner," the man at the entrance waved the flag, and the rider hurried away and stopped (the execution). Even if the prisoner said, "I have something to plead on my behalf," he is taken back to the Court four or five times, provided there is some substance in his words. Should they find in his favour, he is set free; otherwise he goes forth to be stoned, and a herald walks in front of him, announcing, "So-and-so is going forth to be stoned for having committed such-and-such a crime; the witnesses against him were so-and-so; let whoever knows anything in his favour come and declare it for him."

'When he reached a distance of about ten cubits from the place of stoning, they say to him, "Confess, since it is the way of all who are condemned to death to confess." Whoever confesses will have a share in the World to Come, because we find it so with Achan, to whom Joshua said, "My son, give, I pray thee, glory to the Lord, the God of Israel, and made confession unto Him. And Achan answered Joshua and said, Of a truth, I have sinned against the Lord, God of Israel, and thus have I done" (Josh. vii. 19 f.). Whence is it that his confession atoned for him? Because it is stated, "And Joshua said, Why hast thou troubled us? the Lord shall trouble thee this day" (ibid. 25)—this day shall the Lord trouble thee, but He will not trouble thee in the World to Come. If he does not know how to confess, they tell him to say, "May my death be an atonement for all my sins."

[1] The name of God, and whose punishment was stoning.

'When he was four cubits away from the place of stoning, they remove his garments. In the case of a man, they leave a covering in front; in the case of a woman, both before and behind. This is the opinion of R. Judah; but the Rabbis declare that a man, but not a woman, is stoned naked.

'The place of stoning was a height equal to that of two men. One of the witnesses pushes him by the loins, and should he turn himself over on his face, the witness reverses the position. If he die through the fall, the law has been carried out; but it not, the second witness takes the stone [1] and hurls it upon his heart. If he die from it, the law has been carried out; otherwise his stoning must be done by Israelites generally, as it is said, "The hand of the witnesses shall be first upon him to put him to death, and afterward the hand of all the people" (Deut. xvii. 7). The bodies of all persons stoned are subsequently hanged, so declared R. Eliezer; but the Rabbis say, Only those convicted of blasphemy and idolatry are hanged. A man is hanged with his face towards the people, but a woman with her face towards the gallows, so declared R. Eliezer; but the Rabbis say, A man is hanged but not a woman. R. Eliezer retorted, But did not Simeon b. Shetach hang women (for witchcraft) in Ascalon? They replied, He hanged eighty women, although two persons should not be judged on one day.[2] How is the hanging done? A beam is fixed into the ground from which the gallows protrude; his hands are tied together and he is suspended (by the hands). R. José said, The beam is rested against a wall (and not fixed in the ground) and he is hanged upon it after the manner of butchers (with carcasses of animals). The corpse is immediately taken down, for if it were left hanging there would be violation of the law, "His body shall not remain all night upon the tree, but thou shalt bury him the same day; for he that is hanged is the curse of God" (Deut. xxi. 23), as though to say, Why is this person hanged? Because he cursed the Name, and consequently the Name of Heaven is profaned (when anybody sees the corpse)' (Sanh. VI. 1–4).

'The body is not buried in the cemetery of his fathers; but there were two burial-grounds reserved by the Court, one for those who were decapitated or strangled, and the other for those who were stoned or burnt. When the flesh has decomposed, the bones are collected and interred in the proper place. The relatives attend upon the judges and witnesses and greet them, as though to say,

---

[1] The stone must be of such weight as to require two men to carry it. 'It is lifted by the two of them, but one drops it so that it strikes with greater force' (Sanh. 45b).

[2] Accordingly, what Simeon b. Shetach did is not a precedent to be followed.

JURISPRUDENCE 319

"Know that we have no grievance in our heart against you, seeing that you passed a just sentence." Nor are the usual mourning rites carried out in such circumstances' (Sanh. vi. 5 f.).

Execution by stoning was inflicted for the following offences: 'Incest with one's mother or stepmother or daughter-in-law, pederasty, unnatural intercourse with an animal by a man or woman, blasphemy, idolatry, passing a child through fire in connection with Moloch-worship, necromancy, soothsaying, desecration of the Sabbath, cursing father or mother, intercourse with a betrothed girl, seduction of an individual or a city to idolatry, witchcraft, and filial rebelliousness' (ibid. vii, 4).

The other methods of execution were carried out in this manner: 'The person condemned to burning is sunk in manure up to his knees;[1] a twisted scarf of coarse material is placed within soft cloth and twined around his neck; one witness pulls it at one end and the second at the other until he opens his mouth; the executioner lights a wick[2] and throws it into the mouth so that it enters and burns his entrails. R. Judah said, But if he should die by their hand (through strangling) they would not have carried out the law of burning; therefore they force his mouth open with tongs and throw the lighted wick into it.

'Decapitation was performed by striking off the head with a sword, after the manner of the (Roman) government. R. Judah said, Such a method would be shameful; but the head should be placed on a block and chopped off with a hatchet. The Rabbis replied to him, There is no more shameful death than that! Strangulation was carried out by sinking the condemned person in manure up to his knees; a twisted scarf of coarse material is placed within soft cloth and twined around his neck; one witness pulls it at one end and the second at the other until he expires' (Sanh. vii. 2 f.).

'The following are sentenced to burning: A man who has intercourse with a woman and her daughter, and a priest's daughter who acts immorally. Under the category of a woman and her daughter are included his own daughter, granddaughter, stepdaughter and step-granddaughter, mother-in-law and the mother of his mother-in-law or father-in-law. The following are sentenced to decapitation: a murderer, and the inhabitants of a city which lapsed into idolatry' (ibid. ix. 1).

'Those who suffered strangulation are: A person who struck his

---

[1] So that he cannot move about.
[2] The Gemara (Sanh. 52a) explains the word to mean liquid lead; but that is a later tradition.

father or mother, or kidnapped an Israelite (to sell him into slavery), an elder who disregarded the decision of a higher Court, a false prophet, he who prophesied in the name of heathen deities, an adulterer, and a perjured witness against a priest's daughter and he with whom she acted immorally' (ibid. XI. 1).

'If a person has made himself liable to two of the modes of execution, the severer is inflicted upon him. Should he have committed an offence which is punishable by death under two headings,[1] he is sentenced under the severer' (ibid. IX. 4). Their order in point of severity was: stoning, burning, decapitation, and strangulation (ibid. 49b et seq.).

The agonies of the execution were alleviated for the condemned criminal by his being given a drink which produced a state of stupefaction.[2] 'He who goes forth to be executed is given a grain of frankincense in a cup of wine, that his senses should become numbed; as it is said, "Give strong drink unto him that is ready to perish, and wine unto the bitter in soul" (Prov. xxxi. 6). It has been taught that gracious women in Jerusalem used to provide this potion voluntarily; but if they failed to provide it, it was supplied from the funds of the community' (Sanh. 43a).

In the following circumstance a murderer was sentenced to imprisonment for life: 'He who killed a person when there were no witnesses is incarcerated in a prison and given "bread of adversity and water of affliction" (Is. xxx. 20)' (Sanh. IX. 5). The Gemara discusses the matter in this way: 'How, then, can it be known (that he is guilty since there are no witnesses)? Rab said, When the evidence is "disjointed";[3] Samuel said, When the witnesses had failed to warn him; and another authority answered, When there was conflict in the investigation but not on the seven main questions (of time and place)' (ibid. 81b). Sentence of imprisonment was also passed on a man 'who had been punished with lashes and repeated the offence; he is fed on barley until his stomach bursts' (ibid.).

Sentence of corporal punishment was passed by a tribunal of three, although one Rabbi demanded a Court of twenty-three (Sanh. I. 2). The general rule is that lashes are inflicted for the

---

[1] e.g. intercourse with a mother-in-law, involving burning, and as an act of adultery involving strangulation.

[2] Cf. Matt. xxvii. 34; Mark xv. 23.

[3] If, for example, one of the two witnesses was disqualified because of relationship. The law also required that the two witnesses should have seen the crime from the same place or have been visible to each other. This condition may not have been fulfilled, and yet their evidence convinced the judges that he was guilty. The Torah forbade the murderer to be executed, but the Rabbis gave the judges power to punish him.

transgression of a law which the Torah prescribes in the form of 'thou shalt not' (Sifré Deut. § 286; 125a). Among the offences which merited this punishment are those relating to incest with certain relatives, violating the sanctity of the Temple, eating forbidden foods, and transgressing various ritual laws commanded in the Torah.

The maximum number of lashes was fixed at thirty-nine. 'How many strokes were administered? Forty less one; as it is said, "By number forty strokes" (Deut. xxv. 2 f.)[1]; i.e. a number near to forty. R. Judah said, There should be forty complete' (Mak. III. 10). The latter view was not adopted. Another regulation was: 'They only estimate as the number of lashes he is capable of receiving one that is divisible by three. If they estimated that he should receive forty (i.e. thirty-nine), and after a part had been inflicted they estimate that he is incapable of receiving forty, he is remitted the remainder. If they estimated that he should receive eighteen, and after a part had been inflicted they estimate that he is capable of receiving forty, he is remitted (the number above eighteen). If he had committed an offence which involved two prohibitions (and consequently two series of lashes) and they made only one estimation of the number he was to receive, he suffers them and is remitted the remainder; otherwise he receives the first series, is given time to recover, and then receives the second' (Mak. III. 11).

The method of administering this mode of punishment is described in these terms: 'His hands are tied to a post, one on each side; the Synagogue official seizes his garments (at the neck)—if they are torn or become unstitched it does not matter—until his breast is laid bare, and a stone is placed behind him. The official stands upon it with a strap of calf's leather in his hand, doubled into two and then again into four, and two thin strips (of ass's skin) are passed up and down (the other to keep it together).

'The handle was a handbreadth long and the strap a handbreadth wide, its end extending as far as the abdomen (of the condemned person). He smites him a third in front (upon his breast) and two-thirds behind. He does not smite him while he is standing or sitting, but in a bending posture, as it is said, "The judge shall cause him to lie down" (Deut. xxv. 2); and the smiter lashes him with one hand with all his force.

'The senior judge reads (during the castigation), "If thou wilt not observe to do all the words of this law . . . the Lord thy God will

---

[1] In the Hebrew text, 'by number' and 'forty stripes' really belong to different verses.

make thy plagues [1] wonderful and the plagues of thy seed" (Deut. xxviii. 58 f.). He repeats the passage (if he finished it before the lashes are ended). According to another version he reads, "Keep therefore the words of this covenant and do them, that ye may prosper in all that ye do" (ibid. xxix. 9). concludes with "But He, being full of compassion, forgave their iniquity," etc. (Ps. lxxviii. 38), and returns to the previous passage.[2] Should the person die under the hand of the smiter, the latter is exempt from responsibility; but if he added an extra lash and the person died under it, he is banished to a city of refuge. Should the person (during the scourging) make himself unclean through fæces or urine, he is remitted the remainder. R. Judah said, A man with the former, a woman with the latter' (Mak. III. 12–14).

In connection with certain offences the Scriptures use the phrase, 'That soul shall be cut off from Israel' (cf. Exod. xii. 15). The Talmud explains it to signify death at the age of fifty (M.K. 28a); but according to the Rabbinic code, persons who are guilty may undergo lashes if they repent, and so expiate their transgression. 'They who, being liable to excision, are lashed are freed thereby from the penalty of excision' (Mak. III. 15). Other offences received the sentence of 'death by the hand of Heaven,' and that was interpreted as decease at the age of sixty (M.K. 28a).

(b) CIVIL LAW

§ V. TORTS

The laws dealing with the various classes of disputes which arise between men, over personal injury or damage to property, etc., form the subject-matter of three tractates, known respectively as *Baba Kamma*, *Baba Metzia*, and *Baba Bathra*, 'The First, Middle, and Last Gate.'

Baba Kamma treats of the law of torts. In general a person was held liable for any harm which was inflicted upon another, either through his own action or anything, e.g. an animal, which belonged to him, and he was compelled to make it good. The accidents which might occur in this way are classified under four headings and are derived from four contingencies mentioned in Scripture. 'There are four principal categories of damages, viz. Ox (Exod. xxii. 5), Pit (ibid. xxi. 33 f.), Grazing (ibid. xxii. 5), and Conflagration

---

[1] The same word in Hebrew means 'plagues' and 'lashes.'

[2] Deut. xxix. 9 (verse 8 in the Hebrew) contains thirteen words and so does Ps. lxxviii. 38. If, therefore, he is to receive thirteen strokes, the first passage only is read, one lash to each word; if he is to receive twenty-six strokes both passages are read, and if thirty-nine, the first verse is repeated.

(ibid. 6). The point they all have in common is that they normally cause damage and the responsibility of guarding against it rests upon the individual; so that if injury is done, the person who occasioned it is liable to pay compensation to the amount of the damage from the best of his property' (I. I). The general rule which governed all cases of this kind is thus stated: 'Wherever I have the obligation of guarding an object, I am responsible for the damage which it causes; and wherever I am responsible for part of the damage which it causes, I am liable to pay the full compensation' (I. 2).

Each of the four categories falls into subdivisions and is minutely discussed. The following are the leading ideas and some illustrative cases. In connection with the law of the goring ox, an important distinction is drawn by Scripture (cf. Exod. xxi. 28 ff.) between an animal which was 'wont to gore' and one which had not hitherto displayed such a tendency. The latter was known as *tam*—'simple, innocent'—and the former as *muad*—('the ox of) a warned (owner).'[1] The responsibility of the owner was rightly heavier and the penalty more severe when experience should have taught him the necessity of greater precaution.

The distinction was developed by the Rabbis to apply to all cases of tort. 'Five actions come under the heading of *tam* and five under the heading of *muad*. A domestic animal is not regarded as *muad* with respect to goring,[2] pushing with its body, biting, lying down, and kicking. With regard to (damage done by) the tooth, it is *muad* in the matter of consuming what is fit for its food;[3] with regard to (damage done by) the foot, it is *muad* in the matter of breaking an article as it walks along.[4] An ox known to have a tendency to gore is *muad*; so is the ox which does damage in the private domain of the injured party. Finally, a human being is regarded as *muad*. The difference between *tam* and *muad* is that in the case of the former, compensation to the extent of half the damage is paid from (money obtained by the sale of) the animal's body; but with a *muad* the defendant pays the full amount of the damage from the best of his possessions' (I. 4). The inclusion of the human being

---

[1] The *muad* is defined as 'an ox which has gored for three days and the owner has been warned of the fact,' and a *tam* as 'an ox which has not gored for three days.' Another authority ignores the time factor and classes as a *muad* an ox which has gored on three occasions, and as a *tam* an ox which does not gore when it is patted by a child (B.K. II. 4).

[2] i.e. until it has done so three times.

[3] 'It is *muad* when it eats fruits or vegetables, but not when it eats a garment' (B.K. II. 2).

[4] In its tread; but if, as it walked, it kicked up pebbles which broke an article, it is not *muad* (B.K. II. 1).

in the class of *muad* is to be noted, and is amplified in the statement,
'A human being is always *muad*, whether acting inadvertently or
intentionally, whether awake or asleep' (II. 6). The meaning is
that a man must pay full compensation for any injury done by him,
whatever the circumstances be.

Laws dealing with harm caused by an open excavation are:
'If one digs a pit in a private domain and makes an opening in
the public way, or vice versa, or makes an opening in the private
domain of another person, he is liable. If one digs a pit in the
public way and an ox or ass falls into it and is killed, he is liable.
It is all the same whether he digs a hole that is round, or long
and narrow, or vaulted, or trench-shaped, or wedge-shaped;[1] he
is liable. If so, why does Scripture use the word "pit"? The
purpose is to indicate that as a pit must be of the depth of ten
handbreadths to kill, so with all other excavations a depth of ten
handbreadths is necessary to kill. If the depth was less than that
and an ox or ass fell into it and was killed, (the person who dug it)
is exempt from responsibility; but should the animal sustain
injury, he is liable' (V. 5).

Claims for damage caused by grazing cattle are treated as follows:
'If one collected sheep into the fold and locked them in properly,
but they broke loose and did damage, he is not liable. Should he
not have locked them in properly, and they broke loose and did
damage, he is liable. If the fold was torn down in the night, or
robbers tore it down, and the sheep went out and did damage, he
is not liable; if the robbers let them loose, they are liable.

'If he left them in the sun[2] or delivered them into the care of a
deaf-mute or a mentally defective person or a minor, and they went
out and did damage, he is liable; but if he placed them in charge
of a shepherd, then the shepherd assumes the responsibility instead
of him. If they fell (from the public road) into a garden (which
was on a lower level), payment is made for whatever they devoured
(but not for any other damage); but if they descended in the
ordinary way (without falling), payment must be made for the
damage caused.

'If one stacked produce in the field of his fellow without his
permission and the cattle of the owner of the field devoured it,
he is not liable; and should the cattle be injured through the stack,
the man who placed it there is liable. But if he stacked it there
with permission, the owner of the field is liable' (VI. 1-3).

Under the heading of Conflagration some decisions are: 'He

---

[1] i.e. wide at the opening but sloping to narrowness at the bottom.
[2] Although within a fold, but the heat caused them to break loose.

who sends inflammable materials by the hand of a deaf-mute or mentally defective person or a minor is not liable to human penalty but liable to the penalty of Heaven.[1] If he sent them by the hand of a rational person, the latter is liable. If one person is carrying fire and behind him another carrying fuel, the carrier of the fuel is liable; but if one person was carrying fuel and behind him another carrying fire, the carrier of the fire is liable. If a third person came and caused the fuel to ignite, he is liable; but if the wind caused the fuel to ignite, all are not liable' (VI. 4).

'If a spark issued from beneath the hammer and did damage, the smith is liable. If a camel was laden with flax and passed along the public road, and some of the flax penetrated into a booth, was set alight by the lamp of the shopkeeper and burnt the building, the owner of the camel is liable; but if the shopkeeper left his lamp outside, then he is liable. R. Judah said, If it was the lamp of the Festival of Chanukkah [2] he is not liable' (VI. 6).

The second half of the Tractate *Baba Kamma* deals with cases of tort of a criminal nature, as caused by theft, assault, and robbery. In connection with the punishment of theft, Scripture draws certain distinctions, sometimes the restitution being fivefold or fourfold and sometimes double (cf. Exod. xxii. 1, 4, 7). These differences in the penalty receive suggestive explanation in the Talmud: 'The disciples of R. Jochanan b. Zakkai asked him, "Why does the Torah inflict a severer punishment on the thief (who is guilty of larceny by stealing an animal and has to repay fourfold or fivefold) than on the robber (who has to restore what was stolen or its value)?" He replied, "The robber at least made the honour of the slave (i.e. man) equal to the honour of his master (i.e. God, by doing his guilty act in secret), but the thief did not even make the honour of the slave equal to the honour of his master. He, as it were, acted as though there were no seeing Eye below and no hearing Ear below"' (B.K. 79*b*).

Two reasons are suggested why 'he shall pay five oxen for an ox and four sheep for a sheep': 'R. Meïr said, Come and see how great is the virtue of work; since in the theft of an ox the guilty person withdrew it from its labour (and deprived the owner of its service) he repays fivefold; but in the case of a lamb where there is no loss of labour entailed he repays fourfold. R. Jochanan b. Zakkai said, Come and see how important is the matter of personal dignity; since the ox walks away on its own legs the thief repays

---

[1] He is regarded as morally, but not legally, responsible.

[2] The Festival of 'Dedication' which commemorates the victories of Judas Maccabeus and the restoration of the Temple-services. It is observed by lighting lamps which the law requires to be placed in a conspicuous position.

fivefold, but inasmuch as he has to carry off the lamb (and thereby suffer loss of dignity) he only repays fourfold' (B.K. 79b).

Some clauses in connection with this law read: 'More frequent is the penalty of the restitution of double than the penalty of the restitution of fourfold or fivefold, because the former applies both to an animate and inanimate object, whereas the latter applies only to an ox or sheep (Exod. xxii. 1). One who steals from a thief does not make restitution of double, nor does one who slaughters or sells an animal stolen from a thief make restitution of fourfold or fivefold.

'If he is convicted of the theft (of an ox or sheep) by two witnesses and of having slaughtered and sold it by them or two other witnesses, he repays fourfold or fivefold. If he stole and sold it on the Sabbath, or for idolatry; or stole and slaughtered it on the Day of Atonement; or stole it from his father and slaughtered or sold it and subsequently his father died; or stole and slaughtered it and afterwards dedicated it to the Temple—in all these cases he makes restitution of fourfold or fivefold. If he stole and slaughtered it for use as a remedy or to feed dogs; or he slaughtered it and it is found unfit for eating; or he slaughtered it within the Temple precincts for secular purposes—he makes restitution of fourfold or fivefold. R. Simeon exempts him in the last two cases cited.

'If he is convicted of the theft (of an ox or sheep) by two witnesses, and of having slaughtered and sold it by the evidence of one witness or his own confession, he makes restitution of double and not fourfold or fivefold. If he stole and slaughtered it on the Sabbath or for idolatry; or stole it from his father who then died, and subsequently he slaughtered and sold it; or he stole and dedicated it to the Temple and afterwards slaughtered and sold it—in these cases he makes restitution of double and not of fourfold or fivefold' (VII. 1, 2, 4).

In a claim for damages for assault, the claim may be made under five headings. 'If one injure his fellow, he is liable to recompense him on five counts: damage, pain, healing, loss of time, and humiliation. How is it with damage? If he blinded his eye, cut off his hand, or fractured his leg, the sufferer is regarded as a slave sold in the market, and an estimate is made of his former and present value. With reference to pain, if he scorched him with a spit or (pierced him with) a nail, though it be only upon his (finger or toe) nail, a place where no bruise is produced, it is calculated how much a man of equal status would be willing to accept to undergo such pain. With regard to healing, if he wounded him, he is under the obligation to pay the cost of medical attention. Should swellings occur, if they were caused by the wound, he is liable; and if not caused by the wound, he is exempt. If the wound healed, broke open, and again healed and broke open, he is liable for the cost of healing, but if it completely healed, he is not obliged to pay for the cure (if it subsequently broke open). In connection with loss of time, he is regarded as though he were the watchman of a cucumber-field,[1] since he had already received the value of his hand or foot. As for humiliation, it depends upon the (status of the) person who causes and suffers it' (VIII. 1).

The claim under the heading of humiliation is treated in this way: 'If he struck his fellow (with his fist) he pays him a *sela*, or, according to another opinion, a *mana*.[2] If he smacked him with the palm of his hand he pays him two hundred *zuz*, and if with the back of the hand, four hundred *zuz*. If he pulled his ear, plucked his hair, spat and the spittle fell upon him, stripped him of his garment, or uncovered a woman's head in the market-place, he pays four hundred *zuz*. It all depends upon the reputation of the insulted person; but R. Akiba said, Even the poor in Israel are to be esteemed as though they were freemen who had become reduced in circumstances, since they are the descendants of Abraham, Isaac, and Jacob' (VIII. 6).

In connection with this class of tort the Gemara discusses the meaning of the *lex talionis* as ordained in Scripture. The Rabbis emphatically rejected the interpretation that a physical injury is to be inflicted upon the person who damages the limb of another, and argued that in justice monetary compensation only must be paid. '"Eye for eye" (Exod. xxi. 24)—that means a payment of money. You say that it means payment of money; but perhaps the intention is that the actual eye must be forfeited! Supposing, however, that the eye of the one was large and of the other small, how can I in that case apply the Scriptural dictum "eye for eye"? . . . Or supposing a blind man had knocked out the eye of another, or a man with an amputated arm had cut off the arm of another, or a lame man had made another lame, how can I fulfil in this case "eye for eye"? And the Torah declared, "Ye shall have one manner of law" (Lev. xxiv. 22)—that means, a law which shall be the same for all of you'[3] (B.K. 83*b* et seq.).

---

[1] Such a watchman could be one-armed or lame.

[2] The *sela* was the equivalent of one Temple shekel or two common shekels and was worth four *zuz* (the smallest silver coin). The *mana* was worth one hundred *zuz*.

[3] And since the literal interpretation of 'eye for eye,' as shown, cannot be always justly applied, the words must bear another interpretation which would be universally applicable, viz. compensation in money.

The last case of tort dealt with in the tractate is that of robbery and is thus expounded: 'If one robs another of wood and makes it into vessels, or wool and makes it into garments, he repays the value of the raw material. If he robbed another of a pregnant cow which afterwards calved, or a wool-covered lamb and he sheared it, he repays the value of a cow which is about to calve and of a lamb which is ready to be shorn.[1] If he robbed another of a cow and while in his possession it became pregnant and calved, or of a lamb which became laden with wool while in his possession and he sheared it, he repays its value at the time of the robbery. This is the general rule: all robbers repay the value which the article had at the time of the robbery.

'If he robbed another of an animal and it grew old, or of slaves and they grew old, he repays the value they had at the time of the robbery; but R. Meïr declared, In the case of slaves he merely says, Here is what belongs to you. If he robbed another of a coin and it split, of fruits and they rotted, or of wine and it became sour, he repays their value at the time of the robbery' (IX. 1 f.).

§ VI. FOUND PROPERTY

Various questions relating to the acquisition and transfer of property are treated in the Tractate *Baba Metzia*, the main principles of which are enumerated in this and subsequent sections. The first circumstance dealt with is the ownership of an article which is found when its owner does not come forward to claim it. 'Two persons (appear before a Court) holding a garment, one of them declaring, "I found it," and the other likewise declaring, "I found it"; should they both say, "It is all mine," each of them takes an oath that his right to it extends to not less than one-half,[2] and then they divide its value between them. If one says, "All is mine," and the other, "Half is mine," the former takes an oath that his right extends to not less than three-quarters and the latter swears as to not less than one-quarter; thereupon the former receives three-quarters of the value and the other one-quarter.[3]

---

[1] He does not repay the value of the calf and fleece, because he had the trouble of caring for the cow and shearing the lamb.

[2] He is not required to swear that the whole is his since he will not be awarded the whole; nor is he asked to swear that half is his because it would conflict with his original claim for all of it. The implication of the oath was: I still maintain that I am entitled to the whole; but in view of the claim of the other litigant, I swear that not less than one-half is mine.

[3] The dispute is only about one-half, since the second person only claims that amount. The half is accordingly treated in the same manner as the whole in the first clause.

'If two persons were riding upon an animal, or one was riding and the other leading it,[1] and both say, "It is mine," each of them takes an oath that his right to it extends to not less than one-half, and they divide (the value of it) between them. In the event of their admitting (that they both took possession of it simultaneously), or their having witnesses to that effect, they divide it without taking an oath.

'If a person was riding upon an animal, saw a lost article, and said to his fellow, "Give it to me," and the latter picked it up, saying, "I claim it," his claim is valid; but should he hand it over to him and then say, "I claim it," his words have no force.[2]

'If a person saw a lost article and fell upon it, but another came and took hold of it, the latter has the claim to it.[3]

'Whatever is found by a person's son or daughter who is a minor, or by his male or female slave who is a Gentile, or by his wife, belongs to him. Whatever is found by his son or daughter who is of age, or by his male or female slave who is a Hebrew, or by his divorced wife even if he had not yet paid her the sum which is her due under the marriage contract, belongs to the finder' (I. 1-5).

The principle that 'Finding is keeping' only applies when hope of discovering the original owner may be presumed to be abandoned. It was consequently the duty of the finder to advertise his discovery. But with articles bearing no distinctive mark by which the owner can be identified, or when they were found in such a spot as precluded exact description, the finder became *ipso facto* the owner.

'Some found articles become the property of the discoverer forthwith, and others he must advertise. The following become his property forthwith: scattered fruit, scattered coins, small sheaves of corn lying in the public road, cakes of pressed figs, baker's loaves, fishes strung together, pieces of meat, fleeces of wool in their natural condition, stalks of flax, and strips of wool dyed purple. All these belong to the finder, in the opinion of R. Meïr;[4] but R. Judah says, Whatever has in it something distinctive must be advertised, as, for example, if one found a cake of figs in which there is a piece of a potsherd, or a loaf of bread in which are coins.

'The following articles must be advertised: fruit in a vessel or an empty vessel, money in a purse or an empty purse, heaps of

---

[1] To establish a claim over a found article, the finder must exercise over it an act of ownership, as, in this instance, riding or leading an animal.

[2] By handing over the article, he admitted himself to have been the agent of the rider, and therefore cannot claim it for himself.

[3] Falling upon it does not constitute an act of ownership.

[4] Because they are of such a nature that they cannot be identified.

fruit, heaps of coins, three coins one on top of the other, small
sheaves lying in private property, loaves of bread which are home-
made, fleeces of wool which had been removed from the workshop,
and pitchers of wine or oil'[1] (II. 1 f.).

'If a person found something in a shop, it belongs to him;[2]
should it have been between the counter and the shopkeeper,
it belongs to the latter. If he found it in front of a money-changer,
it belongs to him; should it have been between the form (on which
the coins are displayed) and the money-changer, it belongs to
the latter. If a person purchased fruits from his fellow or the
latter sent him fruits, and he found coins among them, they belong
to him; but should they have been tied in a bundle, he must
advertise' (II. 4).

'For what length of time is the finder obliged to advertise?
Until his neighbours know about it. Such is the opinion of R.
Meïr; but R. Judah says, On the three pilgrimage-Festivals[3]
and for seven days after the last of them, to enable (any person
who hears the announcement) to spend three days returning
home,[4] three days to come back, and one day for the finder and
loser to get in touch with each other.

'If the claimant correctly states the nature of the lost article[5]
but not its distinguishing marks, the finder does not deliver it to
him; and should he be an untrustworthy person, it is not delivered
to him even if he mentions its distinguishing marks. If the thing
found is an animal which earns its keep by the work it does, the
finder works and feeds it; but if it is not of this kind, he sells it.[6]
What happens to the money? R. Tarphon says, He may utilize
it, and is consequently responsible for its loss; but R. Akiba says,
He may not utilize it, and is therefore not responsible if it is lost'
(II. 6 f.).

'In Jerusalem there was a place called "Stone of Claiming,"
and whoever lost or found an article repaired to that spot. The
finder announced what he had found and the man who lost it
mentioned its distinguishing marks and recovered it' (B.M. 28b).
'After the Temple was destroyed—may it be speedily rebuilt

[1] These all have something distinctive about them which persons claiming
them could indicate.
[2] It was presumably lost by a customer, and in so public a place as a shop
there is no hope of the owner being identified.
[3] Viz. Passover, Pentecost, and Tabernacles, when all Jews assembled at
Jerusalem.
[4] To ascertain whether he has lost the article which is advertised.
[5] i.e. the announcement is merely to the effect that something has been found
and the claimant is correct in declaring what it was.
[6] And holds the money until it is claimed.

in our days—the announcement was made in the Synagogues and
Houses of Study; but when lawless men multiplied it was instituted
that the information should be passed on to neighbours and acquain-
tances, and that sufficed' (ibid.).

§ VII. BAILMENT

The section Exod. xxii. 7–15 was interpreted by the Rabbis
as denoting four different categories of bailees. 'There are four
classes of bailees: a gratuitous bailee (verses 7–9), a borrower
(verses 14, 15a), a bailee for reward (verses 10–13), and a hirer
(verse 15b). A gratuitous bailee takes an oath in every case (where
the article entrusted to him is lost or stolen, and does not repay);
a borrower refunds the value in every case; and a bailee for reward
and a hirer take an oath with respect to an animal which is injured
or captured or dies (and are not required to pay), but refund the
value in the event of loss or theft' (B.M. VII. 8).

This general statement of the law is amplified in the Tractate
Baba Metzia, and the various contingencies are provided for.
'If one entrusts an animal or articles to his fellow (who undertakes
to look after them without payment), and they are stolen or lost;
if, further, the bailee decide to pay and does not wish to take the
oath [1]—since the dictum is "A gratuitous bailee swears and is not
liable"—and subsequently the thief is found, the latter must refund
double its value; and should he have slaughtered or sold the animal,
he must refund fourfold or fivefold. To whom does he pay the
amount? To the bailee.

'If one hires a cow from his fellow and loaned it to a third person,
and it died a natural death, the hirer takes an oath that it died in
this manner, and the borrower must pay its value to the hirer.
R. José said, How is this possible? Shall (the hirer) do business
with the cow of his fellow-man? It must therefore return to the
original owner' (III. 1 f.).[2]

'If two persons deposited money with a third party, one of them
a *mana* and the other two hundred *zuz,* and subsequently they both
claim the larger sum, the bailee pays each of them one hundred
zuz and the balance remains with him until Elijah comes.[3] R. José

[1] The oath is to the effect that he has not appropriated the charge, or
neglected to guard it properly, and that it is not in his possession.
[2] Consequently the value must go to the owner and not the hirer. The
view of R. José is the one accepted in law.
[3] In popular belief the prophet Elijah will come to solve all points of dispute.
The phrase really denotes, however, an indefinite period. In the present
instance, for example, it means that the bailee holds the balance of the money
until such time as one party admits that only a hundred *zuz* was due to him.

said, In that circumstance, what has the deceiver lost (by making his claim)? The whole amount, therefore, must remain until Elijah comes' (III. 4).[1]

'If one entrusts money to his fellow (gratuitously), and the latter tied it into a bundle and slung it over his shoulder, or handed it to his son or daughter who is a minor, or did not lock it up properly, he is liable because he did not guard it in the manner obligatory upon bailees; but if he did so guard it he is not liable.

'If one entrusts a sum of money with a money-changer (for safe-keeping), should it be tied up in a bundle,[2] the latter may not use it and is consequently not responsible should it be lost; but if it was loose cash, he may use it and is responsible should it be lost. With a private person, however, whether the money is tied up or not, he may not use it, and is therefore not responsible in case of loss' (III. 10 f.).

Some of the rules relating to the responsibility of a hirer are: 'If one hired an ass to drive on a hill and he drove it in a valley, or vice versa, even when the distance is the same, and it died, he is liable.[3] If one hires an ass and it becomes blind or is confiscated by the government, the owner may say to the hirer, "Here before you is what belongs to you";[4] should it die or be injured, the owner must provide him with another. If he hired an ass to drive on a hill and he drove it in a valley, should the animal slip he is not liable; and if it became overheated, he is liable. If he hired it to drive in a valley and he drove it on a hill, should it slip he is liable, and if it became overheated he is not liable; but if it became overheated on account of ascending the hill he is liable.

'If one hired a cow (with its equipment) to plough on a hill and he ploughed in a valley, should the coulter be broken, he is not liable. If he hired it to plough in a valley and he ploughed on a hill, should the coulter be broken, he is liable. If he hired it to thresh pulse and threshed grain, he is not liable (if the animal slipped); but if he hired it to thresh grain and he threshed pulse, then he is liable, because pulse is slippery.

'If one hired an ass to carry (a definite weight of) wheat and loaded it with (the same weight of) barley, he is liable (if the animal is injured while carrying the burden). If he hired it for carrying

---

[1] R. José's opinion was not followed.
[2] The fact that the money is tied up in this manner is an indication that the owner wished it to be kept separate and not used.
[3] Because he failed to use the animal for the purpose stipulated in the contract.
[4] i.e. he is not obliged to provide him with another.

grain and loaded it with straw, he is liable because the increased bulk makes the load more difficult to carry' (VI. 3–5).

'If one person says to another, "Keep this article for me and I will (on some future occasion) keep an article for you," the latter is a bailee for reward. If he said, "Keep this for me," and the other said, "Place it before me," the latter is a gratuitous bailee.

'If one lends another money on security of a pledge, he is a bailee for reward (with respect to that pledge). R. Judah says, If he lent him money (on pledge), he is a gratuitous bailee; but if he lent him fruit, he is a bailee for reward.[1]

'He who removes a cask from one place to another and breaks it, whether he be a gratuitous bailee or one for reward, he takes an oath (that he was not negligent and is then exempt from liability)' (VI. 6–8).[2]

A man who is engaged to carry out a piece of work in his own house is legally in the same category, if the article is lost or stolen, as a person who receives remuneration to take charge of an article. 'All workmen are bailees for reward; but all who say (to the employer when the task is finished), "Take what is yours and pay us (later)," are gratuitous bailees' (VI. 6). They are not then responsible for the safe custody of the article.

In connection with borrowing the law runs: 'If one borrows a cow, and borrows its owner along with it without payment or hires his services along with it; or if he borrows the owner without payment or hires his services and afterwards borrows the cow; should it die he is exempt from liability, for it is said, "If the owner thereof be with it, he shall not make it good" (Exod. xxii. 15). But if he borrows the cow and afterwards borrows the owner or hires him and it died, he is liable, for it is written, "The owner thereof not being with it, he shall surely make restitution" (ibid. 14).

'If one borrows a cow, borrowing it for half the day and hiring it for half the day, or he borrows it for one day and hires it the next, or he borrows one cow and hires another, and it died, should the lender say, "The borrowed cow died, or, It died on the day it was borrowed, or, It died during the time it was borrowed";[3] and the other says, "I do not know," he is liable. If, however, the hirer says, "The hired cow died, or, It died on the day it was hired, or, It died during the time it was hired," and the other says, "I do not know," he is exempt. If the lender says, "It was the borrowed

---

[1] Having been relieved of the task of looking after the fruit, he has benefited by the transaction.

[2] This law was not carried out according to the strict letter. Cf. the case cited on p. 196.

[3] In each case the borrower would be liable.

cow," and the hirer says, "It was the hired cow," the latter takes an oath that it was the hired cow that died (and is not liable). If each party says, "I do not know," the loss is equally shared between them.[1]

'If one borrows a cow and the owner sends it in charge of his son or slave or agent, or in charge of the borrower's son or slave or agent, and it dies (on the way), the borrower is not liable.[2] But if the borrower said to him, "Send it in charge of my son or slave or agent," or "Send it in charge of your son or slave or agent"; or if the lender said to him, "I will send it to you in charge of my son or slave or agent," or "I will send it to you in charge of your son or slave or agent"; and the borrower replied, "Send it," and the owner sends it, should it die (on the way), he is liable. The same law applies to the return of the animal' (VIII. 1–3).

§ VIII. TENANCY

Regulations concerning the responsibilities and rights of landlord and tenant are also treated in the Tractate *Baba Metzia*. 'Who leases a house to his fellow in the rainy season[3] cannot evict him from the Festival of Tabernacles up to the Festival of Passover;[4] if in the summer, thirty days' notice must be given; in large towns twelve months' notice is necessary, whether he leased it in the summer or winter. In the case of shops, twelve months' notice must be given, whether it be in small or large towns. R. Simeon b. Gamaliel said, In the case of bakers' or dyers' shops three years' notice is necessary.[5]

'On leasing a house the landlord is obliged to supply a door, bolt, lock, and everything else which has to be made by a skilled artisan; but things which are not necessarily made by a skilled artisan must be supplied by the tenant. The manure[6] belongs to the lessor, and the right of the tenant extends only to the ashes of the oven and cooking-range.

'If a man leases a house for a year and it was proclaimed a

---

[1] The last-mentioned statement was not accepted in law.

[2] Because the borrower's responsibility only begins from the time the animal reached him.

[3] i.e. during the winter. The lessor merely accepts a tenant at so much a month without stipulating when he is to leave.

[4] These occur in October and April respectively, and so cover the entire winter period.

[5] This opinion was adopted, and the reason for it is the long credit which men engaged in these businesses have to give.

[6] Which accumulates in the courtyard from the cattle of persons other than the tenant.

leap year,[1] the tenant has the benefit of the extra month. If he leased it by the month and a leap year was proclaimed, the lessor has the benefit of the extra month. It happened in the town of Sepphoris that a man leased a bath-house at a rental of twelve golden *denarii* a year, a golden *denarius* a month. (A leap year having been proclaimed), the case came before R. Simeon b. Gamaliel and R. José, who decided that the benefit of the extra month should be equally shared by landlord and tenant.[2]

'If he leased a house [3] to his fellow and it collapsed, he must provide him with another. If it was a small house, he must not provide him with one of larger size, or vice versa; if it was a single house, he must not provide him with a double house. Nor may he decrease or increase the number of the windows except with the consent of both parties' (VIII. 6–9).

'If one leases [4] a field from his fellow, where it is the practice to reap the grain he must reap it, to uproot it he must uproot it, to plough after (reaping in order to destroy the weeds) he must so plough it. All depends upon the local custom. In the same way that landlord and tenant share the grain, they similarly share the straw and stubble; as they share the wine so they share the vine-branches and supporting sticks, the latter having to be supplied by the two of them.

'If one leases a field from his fellow which depends upon irrigation or is planted with trees, and the source (of the irrigation) runs dry or the trees are cut down, he may not make any deduction from the agreed rental. If, however, he said to him, "Lease me this irrigated field, or, this wooded field," and thereafter the source runs dry or the trees are cut down, he may make a deduction from the agreed rental.

'If one leases a field (on the term of paying the landlord a proportion of its produce) and left it fallow, an estimate is made of the amount it is capable of producing and he must pay accordingly because a clause in the agreement normally states, "If I leave the field fallow and do not till it, I shall pay an indemnity on the highest assessment." [5]

'If one leases a field from his fellow and refuses to weed it, saying to the landlord, "What has it to do with you, since I pay you your

[1] An intercalated year has thirteen months.

[2] The decision was based on the fact that the terms stated 'for a year,' but also included the monthly rental.

[3] Without specifying which house; if the house was specified in the agreement the landlord is not required to rebuild it in the event of fire or collapse.

[4] The terms of such lease were a fixed rental in money, or an agreed amount of produce or an agreed proportion of the yield of the land.

[5] Such a condition is held to apply although not expressly stipulated.

rental?" such a plea is not accepted; because the landlord can reply, "To-morrow you will quit and I shall have the trouble of clearing the weeds which grow."

'If one leases a field from his fellow (on the term of paying a percentage of what it yields) and it fails to produce, so long as it supplies sufficient to form a heap (of two *seahs*), he is obliged to work the soil. R. Judah said, How is it possible to make such a heap the criterion?[1] But so long as it yields grain sufficient to resow the field (he must work the soil).

'If one leases a field from his fellow (on the term of paying a proportion of the produce) and the crop was devoured by locusts or blasted, should the scourge have affected the whole district, he may make a deduction from the rental; but if it did not affect the whole district he may not make any deduction. R. Judah says, If he leased it for rental in money, in neither circumstance can he deduct anything.[2]

'If one leases a field from his fellow for ten *kors* of wheat a year and the grain is of poor quality, he pays the landlord from it; but if the grain was of exceptionally good quality, he has not the right to say, "I will buy wheat from the market (of standard quality) and pay you therewith." He must pay him from what he has grown.

'If one leases a field from his fellow to sow barley he may not sow wheat, but if the agreement was to sow wheat he may sow barley.[3] R. Simeon b. Gamaliel forbids also the latter. If he leased it to sow grain he may not sow pulse; but if the agreement was to sow pulse he may grow grain. R. Simeon b. Gamaliel forbids also the latter.

'If one leases a field from his fellow for a few years,[4] he may not sow flax[5] or lop sycamore trees. If he leased it for seven years, he may in the first year sow flax and lop sycamore trees.

'If one leases a field from his fellow for a Sabbatical period[6] at a rental of seven hundred *zuz*, the Sabbatical year is included in the term. If he leased it for seven years at a rental of seven

---

[1] Since the sizes of fields vary.

[2] This view was not accepted in law.

[3] To grow wheat exhausts the soil more than to grow barley.

[4] i.e. less than seven years.

[5] To sow flax would so affect the soil that the damage would outlast the lease of seven years. Similarly the trees could not grow the branches which had been cut in that space of time.

[6] Each seventh year was proclaimed as a Sabbatical year when no sowing or reaping was allowed (Lev. xxv. 1 ff.). If the agreement was for a 'Sabbatical period,' it was understood to mean a lease of seven years including the Sabbatical year.

hundred *zuz*, the Sabbatical year is not included in the term' (IX. 1-10).

With regard to the tenancy of a house which suffers damage the regulations are: 'If the lower storey of a house and the upper storey are owned by different persons and the building collapsed, they both share the timber, bricks, and plaster,[1] and they investigate which bricks were more likely to have been broken.[2] If one of the owners identifies some of the bricks as belonging to him, he takes possession of them and they are included in the calculation.

'If the lower storey of a house and the upper storey are occupied by different persons,[3] and (the floor of) the upper storey is defective and the owner refuses to repair it, the tenant has the right to descend and dwell in the lower part of the house until the owner repairs the upper storey. R. José says, The man who lives on the ground floor supplies the beams and the man who lives above supplies the plastering.[4]

'If the lower storey of a house and the upper storey are owned by different persons and the building collapsed, and the owner of the upper storey asked the owner of the lower storey to rebuild the ground floor but he refused, then the owner of the upper storey may rebuild the ground floor and reside in it until the other party refunds the cost of reinstatement. R. Judah says, Even in such circumstances, the man, if residing in the premises of his neighbour, must pay him a rental; but the owner of the upper storey should rebuild *both* floors, put a roof on the building, and reside in the lower storey (free of rent) until his costs of reinstatement are paid'[5] (X. 1-3).

§ IX. SALE AND DELIVERY

Another branch of law which is treated in the Tractate *Baba Metzia* is what constitutes an act of transfer of property through the medium of sale or barter. In the case of buying and selling, the property passes when the purchaser receives delivery of an article, not when the purchase price is paid.

'(The handing over of) a gold coin effects the purchase of a silver coin,[6] but not vice versa; a copper coin effects the purchase

---

[1] i.e. when the debris cannot be identified as belonging to one of the storeys.

[2] If the foundation collapsed, then the bricks at the bottom would have suffered more.

[3] The case dealt with here is where the owner occupies the ground floor and a tenant the upper storey, and the floor above is the ceiling of the room below.

[4] This opinion was not adopted.

[5] This opinion was likewise rejected.

[6] The point is, who is the vendor and who the vendee in the exchange of money; and the ruling is that the coin of inferior value is the merchandise. The acceptance of the more valuable coin therefore constitutes an act of purchase.

of a silver coin, but not vice versa; non-accepted coins [1] effect the purchase of accepted coins, but not vice versa; bullion effects the purchase of coins, but not vice versa; goods effect the purchase of coins, but not vice versa. This is the general rule: (The handling over of goods) effects the barter of other goods.[2]

'How is this? If the purchaser takes possession of fruits without paying over the money, neither party can cancel the sale; but if he paid over the money without taking possession of the fruits, either party can cancel the sale. Nevertheless the Rabbis declared that He Who exacted penalties from the generation of the Flood (Gen. vi) and the generation of the Dispersion (Gen. xi) will exact penalties from any one who does not stand by his word. R. Simeon says, Whoever has possession of the money has the advantage.[3]

'By overreaching [4] is meant, for example, an overcharge of four silver *denarii* in twenty-four, which is a *sela*, and that is one-sixth of the purchase price. Within which period is the deceived party allowed to retract? He is granted sufficient time to show the article to a merchant or a relative.

'The law of overreaching applies both to the buyer and seller, and to merchant and private persons alike. R. Judah says, The law of overreaching does not apply to a merchant.[5] The person imposed upon has the advantage; if he so desire, he can say, "Return my money" or "Repay what you have overcharged me"' (IV. 1–4).

'To the following cases the law of overreaching does not apply: slaves, immovable property, notes of indebtedness, and all things connected with the Temple.[6]

'Just as there is overreaching in buying and selling, so there is overreaching in speech. One must not say to his fellow, "What is the price of this?" when he has no intention of buying' (IV. 9 f.).

[1] Coins which are not current in a country.

[2] i.e. in the exchange of goods there is no consideration of which is more marketable. Therefore, if either party accepts the goods of the other the purchase is effected.

[3] That means that if the purchaser paid the money and did not receive the article, only the vendor may cancel the deal. This opinion is rejected.

[4] Cf. Lev. xxv. 14. If the overcharge is less than a sixth, the transaction is valid; if a sixth, the sum above the true price is refunded; if more than a sixth, the deal is void.

[5] Because, being an expert, he would know the correct price; and if he sold for much less, it was presumed that he did so consciously, being in need of the money. This view is not adopted since, it was thought, he also is liable to err in fixing a price.

[6] The Talmud derives this rule from the Scriptural words 'aught unto thy neighbour' (Lev. xxv. 14)—'aught' denotes things which can be handed from one person to another. It therefore excludes fields and also slaves who are regarded as real property. The word 'neighbour' excludes dealings in connection with the Temple.

The subject of the law of sale is continued in the third of the Tractates, *Baba Bathra*. Among the points discussed are what is, or is not, included in the sale of a piece of property, and regulations concerning transactions in perishable goods.

'If one sells a house, he has not sold the annexe even though it opens into it, nor the room which is within it, nor the roof when it has a railing ten handbreadths high. R. Judah says, If the roof possesses the form of a door, even though it be not ten handbreadths high, it is not sold (as part of the house).[1]

'Nor are the well and the underground cistern included, although the vendor specified in writing the depth and height of the building; but he must purchase for himself (from the vendee) a right of way (to the well and cistern if he wishes to use them). Such is the view of R. Akiba. The Rabbis, however, declare that he need not purchase a right of way; and R. Akiba admits that if the vendor specified that they were excluded from the sale, he need not purchase a right of way.[2] If he sold the well and cistern to another person (and retained the rest of the house for himself), R. Akiba says that it is not necessary for the vendee to purchase a right of way from the vendor, but the Rabbis declare that it is necessary.

'If one sells a house, the door is included but not the key; a fixed mortar is included but not a movable one; the lower millstone (which is fixed) is included but not the basket which receives the ground flour (that being movable); neither the oven nor the cooking-range is included; but should he have stated, "The house and all its contents," then they are all included in the sale.

'If one sells a courtyard, the houses, wells, ditches, and caves are included but not movable property; but should he have stated, "The courtyard and all its contents," then everything is included. In any event he did not sell him the bathhouse or the press (for wine or oil) which may be in it. R. Eliezer says, If one sells a courtyard (without further specification), he disposes of nothing else than the ground space'[3] (B.B. iv. 1–4).

'If one sells a boat, he includes the mast, sail, anchor, and whatever is required to steer it, but not the crew, nor the packing-bags (for merchandise) and the stores. Should he, however, have stated, "The boat and all its contents," then everything is included. If one sold a wagon he did not include the mules and vice versa. If one sold the yoke he did not include the oxen and vice versa.

---

[1] This view is not accepted.
[2] R. Akiba's opinion was the one adopted both in this case and that which follows.
[3] i.e. not even the buildings upon it. This view is rejected.

R. Judah says, The purchase price indicates what was sold. How so? If one said, "Sell me your yoke for two hundred *zuz*," it is obvious that a yoke (by itself) is not sold for so large a price; but the Rabbis declare that the price is no indication.[1]

'If one sells an ass, he does not include any bags that may be attached to it;[2] Nahum of Media says that they are included. R. Judah says, Sometimes they are included and at other times they are not. How so? If the ass was before him with its bags upon it and the purchaser said, "Sell me this ass of yours," then the bags are included; but if he asked, "Is that your ass? (Sell it to me)," the bags are not included.[3]

'If one sells an ass its foal is included, but if he sold a cow its calf was not included.[4] If he sold a dung-hill, he included the manure; a cistern, he included its water; a beehive, he included the bees; a dove-cote, he included the doves. If one purchases the birds of a dove-cote from his fellow, he must leave the first brood;[5] the issue of a beehive, the purchaser takes three swarms of bees and the owner may then make the remainder sterile; honeycombs, he must leave two (for the requirements of the bees in winter); olive-trees for felling, he must leave stumps of the size of two fists (for new shoots to grow)' (v. 1–3).

'If one sells fruits to his fellow (without specifying whether they are for planting or eating) and they fail to grow, even though it be flax-seed (which is normally required for planting), the vendor is not obliged to take responsibility. R. Simeon b. Gamaliel says, (If he sold) garden seeds, which are not eaten, he must take responsibility.

'If one sells fruits to his fellow, the latter must accept a quarter of a *kab* of refuse to the *seah*;[6] in the case of figs, he must accept ten wormy in a hundred; in the case of a wine-cellar, he must accept ten barrels of sour wine in a hundred; in the case of earthen jugs made from the clay of Sharon,[7] he must accept ten defective in a hundred.

---

[1] There is the possibility of overcharging; or the purchaser deliberately fixed the price high in order to make a gift to the vendor without humiliating him.

[2] All agree that the harness is included.

[3] The former question clearly implied the ass with what was upon it; the second question may well have referred to the animal only.

[4] The Gemara explains that the case is where the vendor states: 'I sell you a milch-ass, or milch-cow.' If the former, it is obvious that the foal was intended because the milk of the ass would otherwise be useless; but a cow might be bought only for the milk it yields.

[5] For the original owner, so that the parent birds should have cause to remain attached to the cote.

[6] A *kab* is a sixth of a *seah*.

[7] This clay was not of good quality.

'If one sells wine to his fellow and it becomes sour, he is not obliged to take responsibility; but if it was known to him that his wine might turn sour, then he sold it under false pretences (and the transaction is void). If he stated, "I am selling you spiced wine," [1] it must remain in good condition until the Feast of Pentecost.[2] If he sold old wine, it must be of the last year's vintage; if he sold wine guaranteed to be very old, it must be of three years' standing' (VI. 1–3).

§ X. PRESCRIPTIVE RIGHT

Undisturbed possession of property or use of an article constitutes, in Jewish law, a claim to ownership in certain circumstances. This right which results from undisturbed possession or use is called *chazakah*, 'holding, occupancy.'

'The rule of *chazakah* applies to houses, wells, ditches, caves, dove-cotes, bath-houses, presses (for oil or wine), irrigated fields, slaves, and whatever regularly yields fruits. The term of their *chazakah* is three complete years. With regard to a non-irrigated field, the term of its *chazakah* is three years, but they need not be complete. R. Ishmael says, (If he occupied the land for) three months (at the end) of the first year, three months (at the beginning) of the third year, and the twelve months of the middle year, i.e. eighteen months (it is sufficient to establish *chazakah*).[3] R. Akiba says, (It is sufficient if he was in possession) one month in the first year, one month in the last year, and twelve months of the middle year, i.e. fourteen months. R. Ishmael said, My statement (with regard to the term of eighteen months) applies to a field producing grain; [4] but in the case of an orchard [5] where he first gathers the grapes, at another time he harvests the olives, and still later collects the figs, this is reckoned as three years (for the purpose of establishing *chazakah*).[6]

'In connection with *chazakah* there are three territories: Judea, Transjordan, and Galilee. If the owner resided in Judea and a

---

[1] Which is guaranteed to keep in good condition.

[2] Which is the beginning of the summer; after that the wine may turn sour on account of the heat and the vendor is not responsible.

[3] In the first period he would have time to sow the field and in the last period to reap it. Consequently, from the agricultural point of view, he was in possession for three years.

[4] Where the reaping is done at one time.

[5] Where there are various kinds of trees, the fruits of which are gathered at different seasons.

[6] Although the three operations occur within one year. The opinions of both R. Akiba and R. Ishmael are rejected, and the law requires possession for three complete years.

person claimed a *chazakah* on his land in Galilee, or vice versa, the right is not established until the owner and the claimant are in the same territory. R. Judah said, The term of three years was only instituted so that if the owner resided in Spain[1] and a person occupied his land (in Judea) for a year, a year would be left for him to be notified and another year for his return (to dispute the claim).

'Any *chazakah* which is not accompanied by a claim[2] is not valid. How so? If somebody said to the occupant, "What are you doing on my property?" and he replied, "Nobody has ever questioned my right to be here," that is not a *chazakah*. If, however, his reply is, "Because you sold it to me," or "Because you presented it to me," or "Your father sold it to me," or "Your father presented it to me," that is a *chazakah*. In the case of property which came to one by inheritance no claim is necessary.[3] The law of *chazakah* does not apply to skilled artisans, partners, field-labourers, and guardians.[4] A husband has no *chazakah* with respect to the possessions of his wife and vice versa, nor a father to the possessions of a son and vice versa. To what does the foregoing apply? To one who claims a *chazakah* (which is disputed by the owner); but in the case of a person making a gift (which he desires to retract), or brothers who divide an estate (and one of them has taken possession of his share), or a person who has seized the estate of a proselyte,[5] if he made a door (on the property) or fenced it or made a breach in the fencing, however small, that (evidence of ownership) establishes a *chazakah*.

'These are the things to which *chazakah* applies and does not apply: if one kept his cattle in a courtyard, or used an oven or cooking-range or mill, or reared poultry (in the courtyard) or deposited his manure there—that does not establish a *chazakah*. If, on the other hand, he erected a partition ten handbreadths high for his cattle (in the courtyard) or for the oven or cooking-range or mill, or kept poultry inside the house, or he made for himself a place for his manure either (by excavating) three handbreadths in depth or (heaping it) to a height of three handbreadths—that does establish a *chazakah*' (III. 1–3; 5).

---

[1] Mentioned as a distant land involving a year's journey.
[2] That he has bought or been given the land which he occupies.
[3] i.e. to prove that it belonged to his father who bequeathed it to him.
[4] Undisturbed possession during three years does not give them ownership.
[5] Who died without Jewish heirs; his property then becomes ownerless and anybody can take it.

§ XI. Inheritance

Questions regarding bequests and inheritance of an estate and the next of kin to inherit are dealt with in the Tractate *Baba Bathra*.

'Some relatives both inherit and transmit in legal succession; others inherit but do not transmit; and still others neither inherit nor transmit. The following inherit and transmit: a father as regards his children,[1] children as regards their father, and brothers by the same father. The following inherit but do not transmit: a man as regards his mother, a husband as regards his wife, and the children of the sisters (of the deceased). The following transmit but do not inherit: a woman as regards her children, a wife as regards her husband, and brothers by the same mother.[2] Brothers by the same mother neither inherit from nor transmit to one another.

'The order of succession is as follows: (Scripture declares), "If a man die and have no son, then ye shall cause his inheritance to pass unto his daughter" (Num. xxvii. 8). Hence a son takes precedence of a daughter and all issue of a son takes precedence of her. A daughter takes precedence of the brothers (of the deceased), and all her issue takes precedence of them. The brothers (of the deceased) take precedence of the brothers of his father, and similarly with their respective issues. This is the rule: wherever a person takes precedence, his issue takes precedence next in order; but a father takes precedence of all his descendants' (VIII. 1 f.).[3]

'Son and daughter are alike in the matter of inheriting, except that a son (if the first-born, Deut. xxi. 17) takes a double share of the father's estate but not of the mother's, and daughters are maintained from the father's estate but not from the mother's.

'If a man declared (in his will), "So-and-so is my first-born but he shall not receive a double portion," or "So-and-so is my son but shall not inherit (any part of my estate) together with his brothers," his words have no force, since he made a provision which is contrary to what is prescribed in the Torah. If, however, he made a verbal disposition of his estate among his children, allotting more to one and less to another, or equalizing the first-born with the others, his words stand; but should he have used the term "inheritance,"

---

[1] i.e. a father inherits the property of his son if the latter dies without heir and also transmits his own property to his son.

[2] An uncle's property may pass to his nephew in legal succession but not vice versa.

[3] If the deceased left no direct issue, then the father or grandfather, if living, is next of kin.

his words have no force.[1] If in the beginning, middle, or end [2] he wrote "as a gift," his words stand. If he said, "So-and-so (viz. not a son) will be my heir," when he has a daughter, or "My daughter will be my heir," when he has a son, his statement is invalid because he made a provision which is contrary to what is prescribed in the Torah. R. Jochanan b. Baroka said, If the statement referred to one who was entitled to inherit,[3] it is valid; but if it referred to one who was not entitled to inherit, the statement is invalid. If he made a will bequeathing his estate to strangers and omitted his children, his act is legal, but it has the disapproval of the Rabbis. R. Simeon b. Gamaliel says, If the children have not been behaving properly, he is to be remembered for good (for disposing of his property in this way).

'If a man says, "This person is my son," he is believed (in connection with the inheritance); but if a man says, "This person is my brother," he is not believed,[4] but he shares the inheritance with the brother who does admit the relationship.[5] Should this person die (without an heir), then the property he received reverts to the brother who shared with him; and if he possessed other estate, the brothers (who did not admit the relationship) inherit together with him who did.[6] If a person died and a will was found tied to his body, it is not a valid document; [7] but if (in the will) he made an assignment to another person, whether it be one of his heirs or not, his words stand.

'If a man wills his estate to his children,[8] he must insert the words "From to-day and after my death." [9] Such is the view of R. Judah; but R. José declares it to be unnecessary.[10] If a man willed his

[1] So long as he did not use the word 'inheritance,' his allocation is considered in the light of a gift rather than a bequest, and a man is entitled to give away his possessions as he wishes; but the law imposes restrictions upon his power to bequeath.

[2] The three forms alluded to are: 'Let this field be given to my son that he may inherit it'; 'Let him inherit it and let it be given to him that he may inherit it'; 'Let him inherit it and let it be given to him.'

[3] i.e. he specified a particular child.

[4] If the other brothers do not admit the relationship.

[5] If a man left two sons, one of whom admits the relationship of a third person but the other does not, then the one who acknowledges him may give him a half.

[6] This rule applies only when they did not definitely repudiate the relationship, but simply declared that they did not know him to be their brother.

[7] Although from its position there is no reason to suspect it was a forgery. The law requires the delivery of the testamentary document.

[8] The case is where a man is about to re-marry and wishes to secure his property for the children of the first marriage.

[9] These words make the children the legal owners of the estate, and the man enjoys the income during his lifetime.

[10] Because the date of the will shows the intention; and that opinion is adopted.

estate to his son (to take effect) after death, the former is unable to sell it because it has been bequeathed to his son; nor is the son able to sell it (during the father's lifetime) because it is under the control of his father. If the father sold it, then it is sold only up to the time of his death; and if the son sold it, the purchaser has no right to it until the father's death. The father is allowed to pick the fruit and present it to whomever he pleases, but what remains picked (at the time of his death) belongs to the heirs. If a man left several sons,[1] some of them adults and some minors, the adults are not allowed to supply themselves with clothing at the expense of the minors, and the minors are not allowed to feed at the expense of the adults,[2] but they share alike. If the adults have married (at the expense of the estate), the minors may also marry (at its expense); but should the minors (after the father's death) say, "We wish to marry (at the expense of the estate) in the same manner that you married (while he was alive)," their claim is invalid, because what the father gave them is regarded as a gift.

'These regulations hold good also of daughters; but in this respect daughters have an advantage over sons. Daughters are maintained (out of the estate) at the expense of the sons, but not at the expense of other daughters.[3]

'If a man died leaving sons and daughters, should the estate be considerable,[4] the sons inherit and the daughters are maintained by them; should the estate not be considerable, the daughters inherit and the sons can go and beg.[5] Admon[6] said, "Because I am a male, am I to suffer financially?" R. Gamaliel declared, "I agree with Admon"' (VIII. 4–8; IX. 1).

[1] Without having made a will.
[2] It is assumed that the cost of clothing an adult is greater than that of clothing a minor, and the food eaten by a minor costs more than with an adult.
[3] If the man left daughters only, they divide the estate into equal shares.
[4] Sufficient to maintain all the children and provide for the daughters until they come of age.
[5] This means in effect that the sons only receive what is left after the daughters are provided for.
[6] He was a judge who resided in Jerusalem (Keth. XIII. 1). His view is not accepted.

CHAPTER XI

THE HEREAFTER

§ I. The Messiah

WHEREAS other peoples of antiquity placed their Golden Age in the dim and remote past, the Jews relegated it to the future. The prophets of Israel repeatedly allude to 'the latter days,' still unborn, as the period when the national greatness would reach its zenith. This hope took a firm grip of the popular mind and grew not only in intensity but, as time proceeded, likewise in the marvels which its realization would bring to the world. The glorious future centred around the person of a *Mashiach*, 'an anointed one,' who would be deputed by God to inaugurate this new and wonderful era.

The Talmud has hundreds of references to the Messiah and his mission, but we find only one teacher sounding a sceptical note. A fourth-century Rabbi, Hillel, declared: 'Israel has no Messiah (yet to come) since he already enjoyed him in the days of Hezekiah' (Sanh. 98*b*). He was taken to task for his remark. There may, however, have been a section of the people who believed that the splendid reign of that king witnessed the fulfilment of Isaiah's Messianic prophecies, because the Talmud expressly repudiates the thought. 'Why has the word *lemarbeh* "the increase" (Is. ix. 7; in the Hebrew, 6) a final *m* as a middle letter?[1] The Holy One, blessed be He, wished to make Hezekiah the Messiah and Sennacherib Gog and Magog;[2] but the attribute of justice spoke before Him, "Sovereign of the Universe! David, king of Israel, who composed so many songs and praises in Thy honour, Thou hast not made the Messiah, and wilt Thou make Hezekiah the Messiah for whom Thou hast performed so many miracles and yet he did not compose one song for Thee?"' (Sanh. 94*a*). Nevertheless, in the farewell scene between Jochanan b. Zakkai and his disciples, he addressed the cryptic remark to them on his death-bed: 'Prepare a seat for Hezekiah, king of Judah, who is coming' (Ber. 28*b*). His

[1] Five letters of the Hebrew alphabet, including *m*, have a different shape when they occur at the end of a word. In *lemarbeh*, although the *m* is not a final letter, the traditional text gives it that form.

[2] The allusion to Gog and Magog as the fomentors of strife before the coming of the Messiah will be explained below, pp. 350 f.

346

words are usually understood as foreshadowing the advent of the Messiah; and if that be so, this eminent Rabbi of the first century identified him with Hezekiah. As will be seen, there was considerable variety of opinion about the identity of the future Redeemer.

The belief was general that the sending of the Messiah was part of the Creator's plan at the inception of the Universe. 'Seven things were created before the world was created: Torah, repentance, the Garden of Eden (i.e. Paradise), Gehinnom, the Throne of Glory, the Temple, and the name of the Messiah' (Pes. 54a). In a later work there is the observation: 'From the beginning of the creation of the world king Messiah was born, for he entered the mind (of God) before even the world was created' (Pesikta Rab. 152b).

Naturally speculation was rife as to who the Messiah would be, and Scriptural texts were studied for enlightenment. On one point the Rabbis were unanimous, viz. he would be just a human being divinely appointed to carry out an allotted task. The Talmud nowhere indicates a belief in a superhuman Deliverer as the Messiah.

Some authorities identified him with David. The verse, 'Afterward shall the children of Israel return and seek the Lord their God and David their king' (Hos. iii. 5), was interpreted thus: 'The Rabbis declare, That is king Messiah. If he is born from among the living, David is his name; and if he be from among the dead, David is his name' (p. Ber. 5a). This opinion was sharply challenged by the citation of another passage: ' "Great deliverance giveth He to His king, and sheweth lovingkindness to His anointed (Heb. Messiah), to David and to his seed, for evermore" (Ps. xviii. 50)—it is not written here "to David" but "to David and to his seed"' (Lament. R. I. 51). The prevailing belief was that the Messiah would be a descendant of the king, and a common designation for him in Rabbinic literature is 'the son of David.'

Biblical passages which were interpreted in a Messianic sense afforded a variety of names by which he would be called. Certain Rabbinic students even exercised their ingenuity to discover for him a name similar to that borne by their teacher. 'What is the Messiah's name? The School of R. Sheila said, "Shiloh, as it is written, 'Until Shiloh come' (Gen. xlix. 10)." The School of R. Jannai declared, "Jinnon, as it is said, 'His name shall be continued (Heb. jinnon) as long as the sun' (Ps. lxxii. 17)." The School of R. Channina declared, "Chaninah, as it is said, 'I will show you no favour' (Heb. chaninah) (Jer. xvi. 13)." Others contend that his name is Menachem son of Hezekiah, as it is said, "The comforter (Heb. menachem) that should refresh my soul is far from me" (Lament. i. 16). The Rabbis maintain that his name is "the leprous one of the School of R. Judah the Prince," as it is said, "Surely he hath borne our griefs, and carried our sorrows; yet we did esteem him stricken, smitten of God, and afflicted" [1] (Is. liii. 4). Rab declared, The Holy One, blessed be He, will hereafter raise up for Israel another David, as it is said, "They shall serve the Lord their God and David their king, whom I will raise up unto them" (Jer. xxx. 9). It is not stated "has raised" but "will raise" ' (Sanh. 98b).

Other designations suggested for him are given in these extracts: 'R. Joshua b. Levi said, His name is *Tzémach* ("the branch," cf. Zech. vi. 12). R. Judan said, It is Menachem. R. Aibu said, The two are identical since the numerical value of the letters forming their names is the same' (p. Ber. 5a). 'R. Nachman asked R. Isaac, "Have you heard when *Bar Naphlé* ('son of the fallen') will come?" He said to him, "Who is *Bar Naphlé?*" He answered, "The Messiah." The other asked, "Do you call the Messiah *Bar Naphlé?*" He replied, "I do, because it is written, 'In that day will I raise up the tabernacle of David that is fallen' (Amos ix. 11)" ' (Sanh. 96b).

Mention is once made of a rather mysterious figure called Messiah son of Joseph. The passage reads: 'Messiah son of Joseph was slain, as it is written, "They shall look unto me whom they have pierced; and they shall mourn for him as one mourneth for his only son" (Zech. xii. 10)' (Suk. 52a). 'Son of Joseph,' like 'son of David,' means a descendant of the ancestor of that name; and its origin seems to be indicated in this citation: 'Our father Jacob foresaw that the seed of Esau would only be delivered into the hand of the seed of Joseph, as it is said, "The house of Jacob shall be a fire, and the house of Joseph a flame, and the house of Esau for stubble, and they shall burn among them and devour them" (Obad. 18)' (B.B. 123b).[2]

The hope for the coming of the Messiah naturally became more fervent in the time of severe national eclipse. When the oppression of the conqueror grew intolerable, the Jews instinctively turned to the Messianic predictions contained in their Scriptures. Josephus

---

[1] The Rabbis interpreted 'stricken' in the sense of 'leprous.' The verse therefore foreshadowed a Messiah who would suffer from leprosy. It is told of R. Judah the Prince that though he was grievously smitten with illness for thirteen years, yet he used to say, 'Beloved are sufferings,' as a sign of God's mercy (B.M. 85a). Accordingly it was remarked that the Messiah, as prophesied by Isaiah, would belong to the type exemplified by this Rabbi.

[2] The conception of a Messiah son of Joseph only came into existence after the failure of Bar Kochba's revolt in A.D. 135 (see Klausner, *Jesus of Nazareth*, p. 201). He figures prominently in later Jewish legends. One of them identifies him with the child restored to life by Elijah (*Seder Elijahu Rabba*, xviii. ed. Friedmann, pp. 97 f.).

records how, in the years immediately preceding the destruction of the Temple, men came forward claiming to be the Redeemer foretold by the prophets.[1] A notable instance is afforded in the following century by Bar Kochba, or, as some named him, Bar Koziba, who led the revolt against Rome and was hailed by R. Akiba as the Messiah. We are informed: 'R. Akiba expounded, "There shall come forth a star (Heb. *kochab*) out of Jacob" (Num. xxiv. 17) in the sense, "There shall come forth Koziba from Jacob." When R. Akiba beheld Bar Koziba he exclaimed, "This is king Messiah"; but R. Jochanan b. Torta remarked, "Akiba, grass will grow in your cheeks and still the son of David will not have come" ' (p. Taan. 68*d*).

To hearten the people in their misery and encourage them to persevere in the face of the severest hardships, the Rabbis preached the doctrine that there will be 'the travail of the Messiah,' i.e. his coming will be attended by pangs of suffering in the same manner that a child is born at the cost of much pain to its mother. On the principle that the night is darkest before the dawn, they taught that the world would show signs of utter demoralization before his arrival and the conditions of life prove well-nigh unbearable.

Statements to this effect are: 'In the generation in which the son of David will come youths will insult their elders, the old will have to stand up before the young, daughter will revolt against her mother, daughter-in-law against her mother-in-law, the face of the generation will be like the face of the dog (for impudence), and a son will feel no shame in the presence of his father' (Sanh. 97*a*). 'Meeting-places for study will be turned into brothels, the learning of the scribes will decay and sin-fearing men will be contemned' (ibid.). 'The son of David will only come in a generation which is wholly innocent or wholly guilty—wholly innocent, as it is said, "Thy people also shall be all righteous, they shall inherit the land for ever" (Is. lx. 21); and wholly guilty, as it is said, "He saw that there was no man and wondered that there was no intercessor; therefore His own arm brought salvation unto him" (ibid. lix. 16), and it is written, "For Mine own sake, for Mine own sake,[2] will I do it" (ibid. xlviii. 11)' (Sanh. 98*a*).

A tradition relates: 'During the period of seven years in which the son of David will come, in the first year the verse will be fulfilled, "I caused it to rain upon one city and caused it not to rain upon another city" (Amos iv. 7). In the second year the arrows of famine will be let loose. In the third year famine will

[1] See p. 124.
[2] Not for the sake of the righteous, because there are none.

be severe, and men, women, and children, and pious and saintly men will perish, and Torah will be forgotten by its students. In the fourth year there will be plenty and not plenty.[1] In the fifth year there will be great abundance; people will eat, drink, and be merry, and Torah will return to its students. In the sixth year there will be voices (from heaven). In the seventh year wars will occur, and at the conclusion of this seven-year period the son of David will come' (Sanh. 97a).

The time of his advent will be particularly marked by political unrest, culminating in bitter warfare. 'If you see the kingdoms contending with each other, look for the foot of the Messiah. Know that it will be so, because it happened thus in the days of Abraham. When the kingdoms strove with each other (Gen. xiv), redemption came to Abraham' (Gen. R. XLII. 4).

This strife is symbolized under the term 'wars of Gog and Magog' (see Ezek. xxxviii).[2] ' "Arise, O Lord, confront him, cast him down" (Ps. xvii. 13). Five petitions to "arise" did David address to the Holy One, blessed be He, in the Book of Psalms.[3] Four of them are in connection with the four kingdoms which he foresaw by the Holy Spirit would enslave Israel, and he besought Him to arise against each of them. The fifth concerned the kingdom of Gog and Magog which he foresaw would advance against Israel in might; and he said to the Holy One, blessed be He, "Arise, O Lord; O God, lift up Thine hand" (Ps. x. 12), for we have no ruler but Thee to contend with it' (Midrash ad loc.; 66b). The four kingdoms alluded to are specified in this extract: ' "When they be in the land of their enemies, I will not reject them, neither will I abhor them, to destroy them utterly, and to break My covenant with them, for I am the Lord their God" (Lev. xxvi. 44)— "I will not reject them" in the days of the Greeks, "neither will I abhor them" in the days of Nebuchadnezzar, "to destroy them utterly" in the days of Haman (i.e. Persia), "to break My covenant with them" in the days of the Romans,[4] "for I am the Lord their God" in the days of Gog and Magog' (Meg. 11a).

An interesting reference to the subject occurs in this anecdote. 'R. Chanan b. Tachlipha sent this message to R. Joseph: I met a man holding a scroll written in the Hebrew square characters in the holy tongue. I asked him, "Where did you get this?" He answered, "I was a mercenary in the Roman army and I

[1] i.e. although there will be plenty, people will be discontented.
[2] Cf. also Ezek. xxxix. 11, and Rev. xx. 8.
[3] See also iii. 7; vii. 6; ix. 19; x. 12.
[4] The text reads 'Persians,' but the substitution was occasioned by the medieval censors who detected allusions to the Church in references to Rome.

discovered it among the Roman archives." There was written in it, "After 4,291 years from the creation of the world (i.e. A.D. 531), the world will be destroyed, partly by the wars of the sea-monsters, partly by the wars of Gog and Magog, and then will the days of the Messiah occur; and the Holy One, blessed be He, will not renew the world until after seven thousand years' (Sanh. 97b).

Other calculations of the time of his advent are found in the Talmud, most of them indicating a date about the end of the fifth century. For example, Elijah told a Rabbi, 'The world will endure for at least eight-five Jubilees (i.e. 4,250 years) and in the last Jubilee the son of David will come.' The Rabbi asked him, 'Will he come at the beginning or end of the Jubilee?' He answered, 'I do not know' (ibid.). This yields a date between 440 and 490. 'If a person, four hundred years after the destruction of the Temple (which occurred in A.D. 70), should ask you to purchase a field worth a thousand *denarii* for one *denarius*, do not buy it. There is a Rabbinic teaching: After 4,231 years from the creation of the world (i.e. A.D. 471), if a field worth a thousand *denarii* is offered for one *denarius*, do not buy it' (A.Z. 9b), because the Messiah will then come and land will cease to have value.

Attempts to calculate 'the end,' i.e. the time of the Messiah's coming, were deprecated by the majority of the Rabbis on the ground that they raised hopes which were ultimately falsified. There is the emphatic warning: 'Cursed be they who calculate "the end," because they argue that since "the end" has arrived and the Messiah has not come, he never will come; but wait for him, as it is said, "Though it (the appointed time) tarry, wait for it" (Hab. ii. 3)' (Sanh. 97b). According to one opinion, 'Israel will be redeemed in *Tishri*; [1] another opinion is, they were redeemed (from Egypt) in *Nisan* and in *Nisan* they will be redeemed' (R.H. 11a).

As against the belief that God had determined an exact date for the dawn of the Messianic era, there grew up another doctrine that the date was not fixed but would be affected by the conduct of the people. That thought was read into the words, 'I the Lord will hasten it in its time' (Is. lx. 22), which were explained in this sense: 'If you are worthy I will hasten it; if you are not worthy it will be in its time' (Sanh. 98a).

We likewise read such utterances as: 'Great is repentance because it brings the Redemption near' (Joma 86b); 'All "the ends" have passed (and the Messiah has not come); it depends only upon

---

[1] The seventh month of the Jewish calendar in which the New Year occurs. *Nisan* is the first month in which the Passover is observed.

repentance and good deeds' (Sanh. 97b); 'If Israel repented a single day, immediately would the son of David come. If Israel observed a single Sabbath properly, immediately would the son of David come' (p. Taan. 64a); 'If Israel were to keep two Sabbaths according to the law, they would be redeemed forthwith' (Shab. 118b).

Imagination ran riot in the attempt to envisage the world as it will appear under the transforming hand of the Messiah. The productivity of nature will be increased to a marvellous degree. 'Not like this world will be the World to Come.[1] In this world one has the trouble to harvest the grapes and press them; but in the World to Come a person will bring a single grape in a wagon or a ship, store it in the corner of his house, and draw ·from it enough wine to fill a large flagon, and its stalk will be used as fuel under the pot. There will not be a grape which will not yield thirty measures of wine' (Keth. 111b). 'As in this world grain is produced after six months and trees grow fruit after twelve months, in the Hereafter grain will be produced after one month and trees will grow fruit after two months. R. José said, In the Hereafter grain will be produced after fifteen days and trees will grow fruit after one month' (p. Taan. 64a). Still more extravagant are the remarks: 'In the Hereafter the land of Israel will grow loaves of the finest flour and garments of the finest wool; and the soil will produce wheat the ears of which will be the size of two kidneys of a large ox' (Keth. 111b); and 'In the Hereafter women will bear children daily and trees will produce fruit daily' (Shab. 30b).

An elaborate description of the effect which the Messianic era will have upon the state of the world is contained in this extract: 'Ten things will the Holy One, blessed be He, renew in the Hereafter: (i) He will illumine the world; as it is said, "The sun shall be no more thy light by day, neither for brightness shall the moon give light unto thee; but the Lord shall be unto thee an everlasting light" (Is. lx. 19). Is, then, man able to gaze upon the Holy One, blessed be He? But what will He do to the sun? He will illumine it with forty-nine parts of light;[2] as it is said, "The light of the moon shall be as the light of the sun, and the light of the sun shall be sevenfold the light of seven days" (ibid. xxx. 26). Even when a person is ill, the Holy One, blessed be He, will order the sun to bring him healing; as it is said, "Unto you that fear My name shall the sun

[1] Here, and often elsewhere, the phrase 'World to Come' denotes the Messianic era.
[2] i.e. make its light forty-nine times more brilliant.

of righteousness arise with healing in his wings" (Mal. iv. 2). (ii) He will cause running water to issue from Jerusalem, and whoever has an ailment will find healing there; as it is said, "Every thing shall live whithersoever the river cometh" (Ezek. xlvii. 9). (iii) He will cause trees to produce their fruit every month and all persons will eat of them and be healed; as it is said, "It shall bring forth new fruit every month ... and the fruit thereof shall be for food, and the leaf thereof for healing" (ibid. 12). (iv) All ruined cities will be rebuilt and no waste place will remain in the world. Even Sodom and Gomorrah will be rebuilt in the Hereafter; as it is said, "Thy sisters Sodom and her daughters shall return to their former estate" (ibid. xvi. 55). (v) He will rebuild Jerusalem with sapphires; as it is said, "I will lay thy foundations with sapphires" (Is. liv. 11) and "I will make thy pinnacles of rubies" (ibid. 12), and those stones will shine like the sun so that idolaters will come and look upon the glory of Israel, as it is said, "Nations shall come to thy light" (ibid. lx. 3). (vi) (Peace will reign throughout nature), as it is said, "The cow and the bear shall feed together" (ibid. xi. 7). (vii) He will assemble all beasts, birds, and reptiles, and make a covenant between them and all Israel; as it is said, "In that day will I make a covenant for them with the beasts of the field," etc. (Hos. ii. 18). (viii) Weeping and wailing will cease in the world; as it is said, "The voice of weeping shall be no more heard in her" (Is. lxv. 19). (ix) Death will cease in the world; as it is said, "He hath swallowed up death for ever" (ibid. xxv. 8). (x) There will be no more sighing, groaning, or anguish, but all will be happy; as it is said, "The ransomed of the Lord shall return and come with singing to Zion" (ibid. xxxv. 10)' (Exod. R. xv. 21).

That the Messiah will inaugurate a time of abiding peace and happiness and contentment is naturally stressed. 'Not like this world is the World to Come. In this world, on hearing good tidings one utters the benediction, "Blessed is He Who is good and doeth good," and on hearing bad tidings, "Blessed be the true Judge"; but in the World to Come one will only have occasion to say, "Blessed is He Who is good and doeth good"' (Pes. 50a). 'While in this world one man builds and another uses it out, one man plants and another eats the fruit, with regard to the Hereafter what is written? "They shall not build and another inhabit, they shall not plant and another eat ... they shall not labour in vain, nor bring forth for calamity" (Is. lxv. 22 f.)' (Lev. R. xxv. 8). 'Come and see: all whom the Holy One, blessed be He, smote in this world He will heal in the Hereafter. The blind will be cured; as it is said, "Then the eyes of the blind shall be opened" (Is. xxxv.

5). The lame will be cured; as it is said, "Then shall the lame man leap as a hart" (ibid. 6)' (Gen. R. xcv. 1). 'The Holy One, blessed be He, said, In this world through the evil impulse My creatures have split up and become divided into seventy languages; but in the World to Come they will all combine to call upon My name and serve Me; as it is said, "For then will I turn to the peoples a pure language, that they may all call upon the name of the Lord, to serve Him with one consent" (Zeph. iii. 9)' (Tanchuma Noach § 19).

Chief of all will Israel be blessed by the coming of the Messiah. His oppression by a hostile world will end and he will be restored to the position of eminence designed for him by God. ' "Thou broughtest a vine out of Egypt" (Ps. lxxx. 8). As the vine is the lowliest of trees and yet rules over all the trees, so Israel is made to appear lowly in this world but will in the Hereafter inherit the world from end to end. As the vine is at first trodden under the foot but is afterwards brought upon the table of kings, so Israel is made to appear contemptible in this world, as it is said, "I am become a derision to all my people" (Lament. iii. 14); but in the Hereafter the Lord will set him on high, as it is said, "Kings shall be thy nursing fathers" (Is. xlix. 23)' (Lev. R. xxxvi. 2). 'The Holy One, blessed be He, said to Israel, In this world I set before you blessings and curses, good fortune and disasters, but in the World to Come I will remove from you the curses and disasters and bless you, so that all who behold you will declare you to be a people of the blessed' (Tanchuma Reëh § 4).

So striking will be the change in Israel's fortune that many non-Jews will attempt to join the Community, but will have to be rejected because their motive is not disinterested. 'In the Hereafter the gentile peoples will come to be made proselytes, but we will not accept any of them; for there is a Rabbinic dictum, No proselytes are to be accepted in the days of the Messiah' (A.Z. 3b).

Another confirmed belief was that the Messiah would effect the reunion of the tribes of Israel. While we find the teaching, 'The ten tribes will have no share in the World to Come' (Tosifta Sanh. xiii. 12), the Talmud usually takes the opposite view. By appealing to such texts as Is. xxvii. 13 and Jer. iii. 12, the Rabbis enunciated the doctrine of the return of the lost ten tribes (Sanh. 110b). 'Great will be the day when the exiles of Israel will be reassembled as the day when heaven and earth were created' (Pes. 88a). A law of nature will even be miraculously suspended to assist this great reunion. 'In the present world when the wind blows in the

north it does not blow in the south, and vice versa; but in the Hereafter, with reference to the gathering together of the exiles of Israel,
the Holy One, blessed be He, said, I will bring a north-west wind
into the world which will affect both directions; as it is written,
"I will say to the north, Give up; and to the south, Keep not back;
brings My sons from afar, and My daughters from the end of the
earth" (Is. xliii, 6)' (Midrash to Esth. i. 8).

The regathering of the tribes will be preceded by another wondrous
event, viz. the restoration of the Holy City. 'If a man tells you
that the scattered exiles of Israel have been gathered together
without Jerusalem having been rebuilt, do not believe him, for
thus is it written, "The Lord doth build up Jerusalem" (Ps. cxlvii.
2), and then "He gathereth together the outcasts of Israel" (ibid.).
The Israelites spoke before the Holy One, blessed be He, "Lord
of the Universe! Was not Jerusalem previously built and then
destroyed?" He said to them, "On account of your iniquities it
was laid waste and you were exiled from it; but in the Hereafter
I will rebuild and never destroy it again" ' (Tanchuma Noach § 11).

Included in the rebuilding of Jerusalem will be the re-establishment
of the Temple. This belief was deduced from several texts: ' "The
beloved of the Lord shall dwell in safety by Him" (Deut. xxxiii. 12),
i.e. the rebuilding of the first Temple; "He covereth him all the day
long," i.e. the building of the second Temple; "and he dwelleth
between His shoulders," i.e. the Temple rebuilt and perfected in
the Hereafter' (Sifré Deut. § 352; 145b). ' "That I may tell you
that which shall befall you in the latter days" (Gen. xlix. 1). Jacob
showed his sons the rebuilding of the Temple' (Gen. R. xcviii. 2).
We likewise have the observation: 'The Holy One, blessed be He,
said, I am He that made the Temple into a heap of ruins in this
world, and I am He that will make it a thing of beauty in the World
to Come. . . . He will rebuild the Temple and cause His *Shechinah*
to abide there' (Midrash to Cant. iv. 4).

The new Temple will not play quite the same part in the life
of the people as did the previous structures, because, sin having
been abolished, there will be no need for expiatory sacrifices. The
feeling of gratitude which will fill all hearts will make at least one
class of sacrifice necessary. 'In the Hereafter all offerings will
cease except the thanksgiving offering which will never come to
an end' (Pesikta 79a).

Since the Messianic era will bring such great happiness, it is
only right that the good who have passed away should be allowed
to participate in it and the wicked excluded. Consequently the
belief grew that the coming of the Messiah would be distinguished

by the resurrection of the dead if they had been worthy of this reward. This subject will be treated in the next section. As for them who live unworthily, 'Near to the days of the Messiah a great pestilence will come upon the world in which the wicked will perish' (Cant. R. to ii. 13).

There seems, however, to have been a reaction to these imaginative dreams, and we have the view expressed that the Messiah will only produce one result, viz. the freeing of Israel from his oppressors; and for the abolition of the various ills to which man is heir he will have to wait until he departs from this life. 'There is no difference between this world and the days of the Messiah except the servitude of the heathen kingdoms alone; as it is said, "For the poor shall never cease out of the land" (Deut. xv. 11)' (Ber. 34*b*), i.e. not even in the Messianic era.

Many Rabbis believed that the period of the Messiah was to be only a transitory stage between this world and the World to Come, and opinions differed on the time of its duration. 'How long will the days of the Messiah last? R. Akiba said, Forty years, as long as the Israelites were in the wilderness. R. Eliezer (b. José) said, A hundred years. R. Berechya said in the name of R. Dosa, Six hundred years. R. Judah the Prince said, Four hundred years, as long as the Israelites were in Egypt. R. Eliezer (b. Hyrcanus) said, A thousand years. R. Abbahu said, Seven thousand years; and the Rabbis generally declared, Two thousand years' (Tanchuma Ekeb § 7). Other versions read: 'R. Eliezer said, The days of the Messiah will be forty years. R. Eleazar b. Azariah said, Seventy years. R. Judah the Prince said, Three generations' (Sanh. 99*a*). 'R. Eliezer said, The days of the Messiah will be forty years. R. Dosa said, Four hundred years. R. Judah the Prince said, Three hundred and sixty-five years. R. Abimi b. Abbahu said, Seven thousand years. R. Judah said in the name of Rab, As long as the world has already lasted. R. Nachman b. Isaac said, As long as from the days of Noah up to the present' (ibid.). 'It was taught in the School of Elijah, The world will endure six thousand years—two thousand years in chaos,[1] two thousand with Torah, and two thousand years will be the days of the Messiah' (ibid. 97*a*).

---

[1] That is, the period from the Creation to the Revelation at Sinai.

§ II. Resurrection of the Dead

No aspect of the subject of the Hereafter has so important a place in the religious teaching of the Rabbis as the doctrine of the Resurrection. It became with them an article of faith the denial of which was condemned as sinful; and they declared: 'Since a person repudiated belief in the Resurrection of the dead, he will have no share in the Resurrection' (Sanh. 90a).

The prominence which this dogma assumed was the effect of religious controversy. It was one of the differences between the Pharisees and Sadducees. The latter, as we know from other sources,[1] taught that the soul became extinct when the body died and death was the final end of the human being. This denial of a Hereafter involved the doctrine of reward and punishment to which the Pharisees attached great importance, and for that reason they fought it strenuously. They made it the theme of one of the Eighteen Benedictions which formed part of the daily service of prayer: 'Thou sustainest the living with lovingkindness, revivest the dead with great mercy, supportest the falling, healest the sick, loosest the bound, and keepest Thy faith to them that sleep in the dust. Who is like unto Thee, Lord of mighty acts, and who resembleth Thee, O king, Who killest and revivest, and causest salvation to spring forth? Yea, faithful art Thou to revive the dead. Blessed art Thou, O Lord, Who revivest the dead.'[2]

We are informed that the disputation on this matter led to an alteration in the wording of the liturgy used in the Temple. 'At the conclusion of every benediction in the Sanctuary they used to say, "For ever";[3] but when the Sadducees perverted the truth and declared that there is only one world, it was ordained that the wording should be "From everlasting to everlasting"' (Ber. ix. 5).

An apparent reason why the Sadducees rejected the doctrine was that it was not taught, so they alleged, in the Pentateuch, and was therefore part of the Oral Torah which they repudiated. This view was strongly controverted by the Rabbis. The Talmud even remarks: 'There is no section of the (written) Torah which does not imply the doctrine of Resurrection, but we have not the capacity to expound it in this sense' (Sifré Deut. § 306; 132a).

---

[1] See Josephus, Antiq. XVIII. i. 4; War, II. viii. 14; and in the New Testament, Acts xxiii. 8.

[2] *Authorised Daily Prayer Book*, ed. Singer, p. 45. This prayer is referred to in Ber. v. 2. See also the prayer to be said on waking in the morning, quoted above, p. 87.

[3] Lit. 'for *a* world.' The amended form means 'from a world to a world,' i.e. from this world to the World to Come.

Much ingenuity was therefore expended to demonstrate that the Torah does teach it. A selection of these proofs will here be given.

'Whence is the doctrine of the Resurrection derived from the Torah? As it is said, 'Ye shall give the Lord's heave-offering to Aaron the priest' (Num. xviii. 28). But did Aaron live for ever to receive the offering? Is it not true that he did not enter the land of Israel? Consequently the text teaches that he is to be restored to life (in the Hereafter) and will receive the heave-offering. Hence the Resurrection is deducible from the Torah' (Sanh. 90b).

'The Sadducees asked R. Gamaliel, "Whence is it known that the Holy One, blessed be He, revives the dead?" He answered, "From the Pentateuch, the Prophets, and Hagiographa"; but they did not accept his proofs. "From the Pentateuch, for it is written, 'Behold, thou shalt sleep with thy fathers and rise up' (sic Deut. xxxi. 16)." They replied, "The meaning is rather, 'This people will rise up and go a-whoring after the strange gods.'" "From the Prophets, for it is written, 'Thy dead shall live; my dead bodies shall arise. Awake and sing, ye that dwell in the dust, for thy dew is as the dew of herbs, and the earth shall cast forth the dead' (Is. xxvi. 19)." They replied, "Perhaps this passage refers to the revival of the dead described in Ezek. xxxvii."[1] "From the Hagiographa, for it is written, 'Thy mouth is like the best wine, that goeth down smoothly for my beloved, gliding through the lips of those that are asleep'[2] (Cant. vii. 9)." They replied, "Perhaps the reference is here to ordinary movement of the lips"; in accordance with the statement of R. Jochanan who said in the name of R. Simeon b. Jehotzedek: When a legal decision of a departed authority is quoted in this world, his lips move in the grave, as it is said, "Gliding through the lips of those that are asleep." Finally he quoted for them, "The land which the Lord sware unto your fathers to give unto them" (Deut. xi. 9). It is not stated "unto you," but "unto them"; hence the doctrine of the Resurrection is deducible from the Torah.[3] Others maintain that it can be derived from, "Ye that did cleave unto the Lord your God are alive every one of you this day" (ibid. iv. 4)— obviously "Ye are alive every one of you this day"; therefore the meaning must be, even on the day when people in general are dead you will live, and as you are all alive this day so will you all live in the World to Come' (Sanh. 90b).

[1] And consequently it would have no bearing on the question of the Resurrection of the dead in the Hereafter.
[2] He understood the sleep to refer to the sleep of death.
[3] Since the 'fathers' were dead, it was necessary for them to live again if the divine promise was to be fulfilled.

'It is written, "I kill and I make alive" (Deut. xxxii. 39). It is possible to think that death is caused by one Power and life by another, as is the usual way of the world; therefore the text continues, "I have wounded and I heal." As both wounding and healing are in the hands of the same Power, so are killing and reviving in the hands of the same Power. This is a refutation of those who declare that the Resurrection is not taught in the Torah. R. Meïr asked, Whence is the Resurrection derived from the Torah? As it is said, "Then will [1] Moses and the children of Israel sing this song unto the Lord" (Exod. xv. 1). It is not said "sang" but "will sing"; hence the Resurrection is deducible from the Torah. R. Joshua b. Levi asked, Whence is the Resurrection derived from the Torah? As it is said, "Blessed are they that dwell in Thy house, they will be still praising Thee" (Ps. lxxxiv. 4). It is not stated, "They have praised Thee" but "will be still praising Thee" (in the Hereafter); hence the Resurrection is deducible from the Torah. Raba asked, Whence is the Resurrection derived from the Torah? As it is said, "Let Reuben live and not die" (Deut. xxxiii. 6)—"let Reuben live" in this world, "and not die in the World to Come. Rabina declared that it may be deduced from, "Many of them that sleep in the dust of the earth shall awake, some to everlasting life and some to shame and everlasting contempt" (Dan. xii. 2). R. Ashé deduced it from, "Go thou thy way till the end be, for thou shalt rest, and shalt stand in thy lot at the end of the days" (ibid. 13)' (Sanh. 91*b* et seq.).

In addition to the Sadducees, another sect denied this dogma, viz. the Samaritans. A polemic against them is contained in this passage: 'R. Eliezer b. José said, In this matter I proved the books of the Samaritans [2] who declared that the Resurrection is not taught in the Torah to be false. I told them, You have falsified your recension of the Torah but it has availed you nothing in your contention that the Resurrection is not taught in the Torah, because it is there stated, "That soul shall be utterly cut off, his iniquity shall be upon him" (Num. xv. 31)—"shall be utterly cut off" must refer to this world; [3] when, then, "shall his iniquity be upon him"? Must it not be in the World to Come?' (Sanh. 90*b*).

'What means that which is written, "There are three things that are never satisfied . . . the grave and the barren womb"

[1] The verb in the Hebrew has the future form in accordance with the idiom that *az*, 'then,' is followed by the verb in the imperfect tense to denote a completed action.
[2] The Talmudic text has 'Sadducees,' but it must be corrected.
[3] The Rabbis understood the phrase to mean a premature death; see p. 322.

(Prov. xxx. 15 f.)? What is the connection between "the grave" and "the barren womb"? The intention is to tell you that as the womb receives and yields up, so the grave receives and yields up. And may we not use the *a fortiori* argument? As the womb receives the seed in silence and yields up the child with loud cries, how much more so will the grave, which receives the body with loud cries of lament, yield up with loud cries! Hence a refutation of those who assert that the Resurrection is not taught in the Torah' (Ber. 15*b*).

Other arguments, apart from Scriptural exegesis, were employed to establish the doctrine. 'Should any one tell you that the dead will not live again, cite to him the instance of Elijah' (Num. R. XIV. 1). 'A heretic said to R. Gamaliel, "You declare that the dead will live again; but they have become dust and can dust come to life?" The Rabbi's daughter said to her father, "Leave him to me and I will answer him. In our city are two potters, one who forms pots out of water, and the other out of clay; who of them is the more praiseworthy?" The heretic replied, "The one who formed them from water." She retorted, "He who formed the human being from a liquid drop, shall He not the more easily be able to form him from clay?" ' (Sanh. 90*b et seq.*).

'A Sadducee said to Gebiha b. Pesisa, "Woe to you guilty ones (the Pharisees) who declare that the dead will live; since the living die, shall the dead revive? He replied, "Woe to guilty ones (the Sadducees) who declare that the dead will not live; since those who were not in existence come to life, how much more will they who have lived come to life again!" ' (ibid. 91*a*).

'It happened that a man who resided in Sepphoris lost his son and a heretic was sitting with him. R. José b. Chalaphta went to pay him a visit; and on seeing him, he sat down and laughed. The bereaved father asked, "Why do you laugh?" He answered, "We trust in the Lord of Heaven that you will again see your son in the World to Come." The heretic said to him, "Has not this man suffered enough anguish that you come to inflict further pain upon him? Can pieces of potsherd be mended? And is it not written, 'Thou shalt dash them in pieces like a potter's vessel' [1] (Ps. ii. 9)?" He replied, "With an earthenware vessel, its creation is from water and its completion in fire; with a glass vessel, both its creation and completion are in fire. If the former is broken, can it be mended? [2] But if the latter is broken, can it not be

---

[1] This verse proves that Scripture teaches a broken vessel cannot be repaired.
[2] Because its creation and completion take place in different elements, it cannot be put together again. Broken glass, on the other hand, can be remelted and then blown into another vessel.

repaired?" The heretic answered, "Glass can be repaired because it is made by the process of blowing." The Rabbi retorted, "Let your ears take note of what your mouth utters. If something which is made by the blowing of a human being can be repaired, how much more so with that which is made by the breath of the Holy One, blessed be He!" ' (Gen. R. xiv. 7).

A question, debated by several Rabbis, was: Who will enjoy the privilege of living again after death? Their opinion will be cited more fully in the sections on the World to Come and the Last Judgment. The passages which deal more generally with the subject of Resurrection display a lack of unanimity. On the one hand we read such statements as: 'They that are born are destined to die, and the dead to be brought to life again' (Aboth iv. 29); and ' "They (i.e. the Lord's mercies) are new every morning; great is Thy faithfulness" (Lament. iii. 23)—since Thou art He that renewest us every morning, we know that "great is Thy faithfulness" for the revival of the dead' (Midrash ad loc.)—which seem to have a universal application.[1] On the other hand, there is the opposite extreme expressed, 'The Resurrection is reserved for Israel' (Gen. R. xiii. 6).

Other teachers held that the future life was a reward granted only to those who deserve it. 'More important is a day of rain than the Resurrection of the dead, since the Resurrection is for the righteous and not the wicked, whereas rain is for both the righteous and the wicked' (Taan. 7a). The analogy appears to indicate that the author of this dictum did not restrict 'the righteous' to his own people, inasmuch as the rain descends upon all, irrespective of race or creed. The following utterance excludes even Israelites who have not earned the privilege: 'They who are ignorant of Torah will not live again; as it is said, "They are dead, they shall not live" (Is. xxvi. 14). It is possible to argue that this applies to all (Israel); therefore the text continues, "They are deceased, they shall not rise." These words allude to one who relaxes [2] himself from words of Torah. Whoever makes use of the light of Torah, the light of Torah will revive (after death); and whoever does not make use of the light of Torah, the light of Torah will not revive' (Keth. 111b).

The Talmud records speculations on various matters connected with the process of Resurrection. There was a firm belief that the

---

[1] There was agreement that there was no Hereafter for animals (see Midrash to Ps. xix. 1; 81b).

[2] The word for 'relaxes' is connected in the Hebrew with the word for 'deceased.'

momentous event would take place in the Holy Land. Some Rabbis took the extreme view that only they who were interred there would share in the future life. 'Those who die outside the land of Israel will not live again; as it is said, "I will set delight in the land of the living" (Ezek. xxvi. 20)—those who die in the land of My delight will live again, but they who do not die there will not' (Keth. 111a). 'Even a Canaanite maidservant in the land of Israel is assured of inheriting the World to Come' (ibid.).

Other Rabbis, while admitting that the Resurrection will occur in the Holy Land, do not go so far as to affirm that they who are buried elsewhere are to be excluded, but their bodies will have to be transported there before they come to life again. ' "Thy dead shall live; my dead bodies shall arise" (Is. xxvi. 19). The first clause refers to those who die in the land of Israel, the second to those who die outside its borders' (Keth. 111a). This thought gave rise to a curious piece of folk-lore. ' "I will walk before the Lord in the land of the living" (Ps. cxvi. 9), i.e. the land whose dead will be revived first in the days of the Messiah. What is the reason? It is stated, "He giveth breath unto the people upon it" [1] (Is. xlii. 5). Then our Rabbis who reside in Babylon will be at a disadvantage! The Holy One, blessed be He, will burrow the earth before them, and their bodies will roll through the excavation like bottles, and when they arrive at the land of Israel their souls will be reunited to them' (p. Keth. 35b).

One of the points of dispute between the Schools of Hillel and Shammai related to the order in which the human body will be re-formed. 'The School of Shammai said, Not like the formation of the human being in this world will be his formation in the World to Come. In this world, it begins with skin and flesh and ends with sinews and bones; but in the Hereafter it will begin with sinews and bones and end with skin and flesh. For it is so stated with regard to the dead in the vision of Ezekiel, "And I beheld, and lo, there were sinews upon them, and flesh came up, and skin covered them above" (Ezek. xxxvii. 8). R. Jonathan said, We draw no inferences from the dead in the vision of Ezekiel. To what were they like? To a person who entered a bath-house; what he strips off first he afterwards puts on last. The School of Hillel said, Similar to the formation in this world will be the formation in the World to Come. In this world it begins with skin and flesh and ends with sinews and bones, and it will be the same in the Hereafter; for thus declared Job, "Wilt Thou not pour me out as milk and curdle me like cheese?" (x. 10). It is not written,

[1] viz. upon the land of Israel.

"Hast Thou not poured me out?" but "Wilt Thou not pour me out?" [1] Nor is it written "curdled me like cheese" but "wilt curdle." It is not written, "Thou hast clothed me with skin and flesh" (ibid. 11) but "Thou wilt clothe"; nor is it written, "And Thou hast knit me together with bones and sinews" but "And Thou wilt knit me together." It is like a bowl full of milk; until one places rennet therein the milk keeps fluid, but after rennet is inserted the milk curdles and sets' (Gen. R. xiv. 5).

Will the bodies arise clothed or naked? The answer is: 'As man goes (into the grave) clothed, so he will return clothed. This may be learnt from the example of Samuel whom Saul beheld. He asked the witch of Endor, "What form is he of? And she said, An old man cometh up and he is covered with a robe" (1 Sam. xxviii. 14)' (Gen. R. xcv. 1). An argument in favour of this view is given in this anecdote: 'Queen Cleopatra [2] asked R. Meïr, "I know that the dead will revive, for it is written, 'They of the city shall flourish like grass of the earth' (Ps. lxxii. 16). But when they arise (from the grave), will they stand up naked or clothed?" He replied, "An argument may be based on the analogy of wheat: [3] As wheat is buried in the soil naked and comes forth with various garbs, how much more so with the righteous who are buried in their garments!" ' (Sanh. 90b). The reference is to the custom of burying the dead enwrapped in shrouds.

Another problem is dealt with in this story: 'Hadrian asked R. Joshua b. Chananya, "From what will the Holy One, blessed be He, cause the human being to grow in the Hereafter?" [4] He said, "From a bone in the spinal column called Luz." He asked, "How do you know this?" He answered, "Have it brought to me and I will show you." When this bone was fetched, they tried to grind it in a mill but it could not be ground; they tried to burn it in fire but it could not be consumed; they put in it water but it did not dissolve; they set it upon an anvil and began to strike it with a hammer, but the anvil was split and the hammer shattered without a piece of the bone having been broken off' (Gen. R. xxviii. 3).

The last question relates to whether the defects of the living

---

[1] This is the literal rendering of the Hebrew, although the English version translates in the past tense.
[2] Since this queen lived nearly two centuries before R. Meïr, the mention of her is an anachronism. The text is doubtless corrupt and the true reading is: 'The patriarch of the Samaritans.'
[3] Cf. 1 Cor. xv. 37.
[4] Since the body crumbles to dust in the grave, what distinguishable relic is there from which the resurrected person can be reconstructed?

body will reappear in the Resurrection. ' "One generation goeth and another generation cometh" (Eccles. i. 4); as a generation goes so it will come back. He who goes lame comes back lame; he who goes blind comes back blind; so that people shall not say that He put to death persons different from those He restored to life. For it is written, "I kill and I make alive" (Deut. xxxii. 39). He Who declared His power to do the more difficult task is He Who declared the lighter. "I kill and I make alive" is the more difficult task; "I have wounded and I heal" (ibid.) is the lighter. As I (God) raise up the dead with their physical blemishes, so that people shall not say, "He put to death persons different from those He restored to life," it is I that killeth and reviveth, and I who have wounded (in this world) will restore and heal them (after they have been revived)' (Eccles. R. to i. 4).

The divinely appointed agent for the accomplishment of the Resurrection is Elijah. 'The Resurrection of the dead will come through Elijah' (Sot. ix. 15), who will likewise act as the herald to announce the advent of the Messiah (see Mal. iv. 5). The reawakened life will be of endless duration. 'The righteous whom the Holy One, blessed be He, will restore to life will never return to their dust' (Sanh. 92a).

§ III. THE WORLD TO COME

In the eschatological doctrine of the Talmud a clear divergence of opinion may be traced. The earlier generations of the Rabbis identified the Messianic era with the World to Come. The promised Redeemer would bring the existing world-order to an end and inaugurate the timeless sphere in which the righteous would lead a purely spiritual existence freed from the trammels of the flesh. Subsequent teachers regarded the Messianic period as but a transitory stage between this world and the next.

That this life is only preliminary to another and higher life was universally accepted by the Rabbis. They would have given unanimous assent to the aphorism, 'This world is like a vestibule before the World to Come; prepare yourself in the vestibule that you may enter into the hall' (Aboth iv. 21). But what is to be experienced by those who will be privileged to enter 'the hall' has not been disclosed even to the seers of Israel. 'Every prophet only prophesied for the days of the Messiah; but as for the World to Come, "No eye hath seen what God, and nobody but Thee, will work for him that waiteth for Him" (sic Is. lxiv. 4)' (Ber. 34b). 'All Israel assembled by Moses and said to Him, "Our master,

Moses, tell us what goodness the Holy One, blessed be He, will give us in the World to Come." He replied to them, "I do not know what I can tell you. Happy are ye for what is prepared for you" ' (Sifré Deut. § 356; 148b).

Despite this reticence, teachers were not deterred from creating their own picture of the Hereafter. Their reflections on the problems of life compelled them to postulate a new world where the inequalities of the present world would be redressed and the divine justice made evident. That solution to the mystery of evil coloured their whole conception of the World to Come.

According to one anecdote, their theory was corroborated by experience. 'R. Joseph, the son of R. Joshua b. Levi, was ill and fell into a state of coma. When he recovered, his father asked him, "What did you see?" He replied, "I beheld a world the reverse of this one; those who are on top here were below there, and vice versa." He said to him, "My son, you have seen a corrected world. But what is the position of us students of the Torah there?" He answered, "We are there the same as here. I heard it stated, Happy is he who comes here possessed of learning; and I further heard it said that martyrs occupy an eminence which nobody else can attain" ' (Pes. 50a).

It followed, therefore, that sufferings which were innocently incurred and privations voluntarily assumed in this world must help to gain admittance into the World to Come. 'R. Judah the Prince said, Whoever accepts the delights of this world will be deprived of the delights of the World to Come, and whoever declines the delights of this world will receive the delights of the World to Come' (ARN xxviii). It was even remarked, 'Three precious gifts did the Holy One, blessed be He, give to Israel, and all of them He gave only through the medium of suffering; they are: Torah, the land of Israel, and the World to Come' (Ber. 5a). A common saying among the people was, 'Not every one has the merit of two tables' (ibid. 5b), i.e. happiness here and bliss in the Hereafter.

The great distinguishing feature between the two worlds is the revaluation of values. Things which are estimated here so highly that they are the main pursuit of man's efforts cease to exist when the bridge is crossed into the World to Come. This thought is summarized in the aphorism of a Rabbi: 'Not like this world is the World to Come. In the World to Come there is neither eating nor drinking; nor procreation of children [1] or business transactions; no envy or hatred or rivalry; but the righteous sit enthroned, their crowns on their heads, and enjoy the lustre of the *Shechinah*' (Ber.

[1] Cf. Matt. xxii. 30.

17*a*). Life will be conducted on an entirely different plane. Physical desires will no longer obtrude, and the sway of the spiritual nature of man will be dominant. What the holy day of the week is to man on this earth as compared with the working days, such will the World to Come be on a vastly enhanced scale. 'The Sabbath is a sixtieth of the World to Come' (ibid. 57*b*).

A saying of doubtful interpretation runs: 'Better is one hour of repentance and good deeds in this world than the whole life of the World to Come; and better is one hour of blissfulness of spirit in the World to Come than the whole life of this world' (Aboth IV. 22). The most satisfactory explanation is that offered by R. T. Herford, who sees in the teaching a contrast between the changefulness of the present life and the changelessness of the future life. In this world man is able to repent and perform meritorious acts, and these bring him a joy superior even to 'an eternity of static bliss' which characterizes the World to Come. 'On the other hand, in a world where there is no change, the highest and best form of existence is that of perfect peace in the beholding of God. One hour of such bliss is better, under the conditions of such a world, than all "the changes and chances of this mortal life."' [1]

Man best qualifies himself in the vestibule for the pure, spiritual atmosphere of 'the hall' by devoting himself to the study and practice of the precepts revealed by God. 'He who has acquired for himself words of Torah has acquired for himself life in the World to Come' (Aboth II. 8). Of the Torah it was said: ' "When thou liest down it shall watch over thee" (Prov. vi. 22), i.e. at the time of death; "when thou awakest," i.e. in the days of the Messiah; "it shall talk with thee," i.e. in the World to Come' (Sifré Deut. § 34; 74*b*). More explicit still is the declaration: 'In the hour of man's departure from the world neither silver nor gold nor precious stones nor pearls accompany him, but only Torah and good works; as it is said, "When thou walkest it shall lead thee; when thou liest down it shall watch over thee; and when thou awakest it shall talk with thee"; "when thou walkest it shall lead thee" in this world; "when thou liest down it shall watch over thee" in the grave; "and when thou awakest it shall talk with thee" in the World to Come' (Aboth VI. 9).

Other utterances expressive of the same thought are, 'What means, "I shall be satisfied, when I awake, with Thy likeness" (Ps. xvii. 15)? It alludes to the disciples of the Sages who banish sleep from their eyes in this world, and the Holy One, blessed be He, will satisfy them with the lustre of the *Shechinah* in the World

[1] R. T. Herford, *Pirké Aboth*, pp. 116 f.

to Come' (B.B. 10*a*). R. Nechunya b. Hakkanah, a saintly teacher of the first century, used to offer this prayer on departing from the House of Study: 'I give thanks before Thee, O Lord my God, that Thou hast set my portion with those who sit in the House of Study and not with those who sit at street corners;[1] for I and they rise early—I to words of Torah but they to vain matters; I and they labour, but I labour to receive a reward, whereas they labour and receive no reward; I and they hasten—I to the life of the World to Come, but they to the pit of destruction' (Ber. 28*b*).

'When R. Eliezer was ill, his disciples went in to visit him. They said to him, "Master, teach us the ways of life whereby we may be worthy of the life of the World to Come." He said to them, "Be careful of the honour of your colleagues; restrain your children from recitation,[2] and seat them between the knees of the disciples of the Sages; and when you pray, know before Whom you stand; and on that account will you be worthy of the life of the World to Come' (ibid.).

Since there are ever higher degrees of spirituality to scale we find it stated: 'The disciples of the Sages have rest neither in this world nor in the World to Come; as it is said, "They go from strength to strength, every one of them appeareth before God in Zion" (Ps. lxxxiv. 7)' (Ber. 64*a*).

Much attention was devoted by the Rabbis to the question of who will be admitted to, or excluded from, the joys of the Hereafter. Many *obiter dicta* occur in the Talmud declaring that the person who performs a certain action will, or will not, have a share in the World to Come. Some instances are: 'With regard to him who enjoys the fruit of his labour it is written, "When thou eatest the labour of thy hands, happy shalt thou be and it shall be well with thee" (Ps. cxxviii. 2); "happy shalt thou be" in this world, "and it shall be well with thee" in the World to Come' (Ber. 8*a*). 'Who will inherit the World to Come? He who joins the benediction "Blessed art Thou Who hast redeemed Israel" to the Eighteen Benedictions' (ibid. 4*b*).[3] 'Whoever recites Ps. cxlv thrice daily

---

[1] The Palestinian Talmud reads instead, 'with those who frequent theatres and circuses.'

[2] An obscure phrase which has been variously explained as the parading of a superficial knowledge of the Scriptures by verbal memorization, or philosophical speculation (the word is the term in medieval Hebrew for 'logic'), or reading apocryphal literature.

[3] See *Prayer Book*, ed. Singer, p. 99. The meaning is that there must be no interruption between the two prayers. The saying was probably intended to abolish a custom which was then growing up of introducing petitions of a personal nature at this point, the practice being deprecated because it tended to destroy the congregational character of the Service.

may be assured that he is a son of the World to Come.   The reason
is that it contains the verse, "Thou openest Thy hand and satisfiest
every living thing with favour" (verse 16)' (Ber. 4b).[1] 'Whoever
says the benediction (in the Grace after meals) over a full cup of
wine will be granted a boundless inheritance and will be worthy
to inherit two worlds, this world and the World to Come' (ibid.
51a).[2]

'Among those who will inherit the World to Come are: who
resides in the land of Israel and who rears his son in the study of
the Torah' (Pes. 113a). 'Whoever walks a distance of four cubits
in the land of Israel is assured of being a son of the World to Come'
(Keth. 111a). 'He who studies the laws of Judaism is assured of
being a son of the World to Come' (Meg. 28b). 'They sent a
question from Palestine to the Rabbis in Babylon, "Who will be
a son of the World to Come?" They answered, "He who is meek
and humble, walks about with a lowly demeanour, studies the Torah
constantly, and takes no credit to himself"' (Sanh. 88b).

As for those who are to be excluded, we are told: 'Whoever
crosses a stream behind a woman will have no share in the World
to Come' (Ber. 61a). 'Who puts his fellow-man to shame in public
will have no share in the World to Come' (B.M. 59a). 'Seven
classes of persons will have no share in the World to Come: a scribe,
a teacher of children, the best of physicians, the judge of a city, an
enchanter, a synagogue beadle, and a butcher' (ARN xxxvi).[3]

It must be obvious that in these utterances we cannot have a
dogmatic verdict on the eternal fate of the persons concerned.
They are nothing more than a hyberbolical expression of approval
or disapproval.   More importance must, however, be attached to
this extract: 'All Israel has a share in the World to Come, as it is
said, "Thy people shall be all righteous, they shall inherit the land
for ever" (Is. lx. 21).   The following have no share in the World to
Come: He who says that the doctrine of the Resurrection is not
deducible from the Torah, who maintains that the Torah does not
come from Heaven, and the epicurean.[4]   R. Akiba says, Also he
who reads non-canonical books,[5] and who utters a spell over a
wound, citing, "I will put none of the diseases upon thee which I
have put upon the Egyptians, for I am the Lord that healeth thee"

---

[1] By reciting this Psalm, therefore, a man would be thrice daily acknow-
edging his dependence upon the Divine mercy.

[2] The use of a full cup would indicate a sense of gratitude for the divine
bounty which had been enjoyed during the meal.

[3] These persons were supposed to be generally unconscientious in the
discharge of their duties.

[4] See p. 3.   [5] See p. 145

(Exod. xv. 26). Abba Saul says, Also he who pronounces the Tetragrammaton as it is written'[1] (Sanh. x. 1).

It is an error to read into the first sentence of this declaration any idea of favouritism on the part of God for Israel. If construed in its historical context, the intention was probably to encourage the Jews to persevere in the struggle to maintain their identity against intense pressure. Two forces were tending to obliterate the community, oppression by gentile powers and the influence of contemporary thought, both Hellenistic and Christian. Only by a determined and conscious effort, usually at a costly sacrifice, could the Jew maintain a successful resistance; and the Rabbis helped him with the teaching that he would receive his reward in the Hereafter. The survivors of the contest, who refused to succumb, constituted a 'people all righteous,' and God would recognize them as such by granting them an inheritance in the World to Come.

On the question whether Gentiles will share in the Hereafter there was not an agreed opinion. 'R. Eliezer declared, "No Gentiles will have a share in the World to Come; as it is said, 'The wicked shall return to the nether world, even all the nations that forget God' (Ps. ix. 17)—'the wicked' refers to the evil among Israel." R. Joshua said to him, "If the verse had stated, 'The wicked shall return to the nether world and all the nations,' and had stopped there, I should have agreed with you. Since, however, the text adds, 'that forget God,' behold, there must be righteous men among the nations who will have a share in the World to Come"' (Tosifta Sanh. XIII. 2).[2]

On the assumption that righteous Gentiles will enjoy the bliss of the Hereafter and the wicked will not, a point arises as to what will be the fate of the children of the latter who were too young to be charged with moral responsibility. Here, too, a similar divergence of opinion occurs. 'The children of the wicked Gentiles will have no share in the World to Come; as it is said, "For behold, the day cometh, it burneth as a furnace; and all the proud, and all that work wickedness shall be stubble" (Mal. iv. 1). This is the statement of R. Gamaliel. R. Joshua said, They will enter the World to Come; for it is written, "The Lord preserveth the simple"[3] (Ps. cxvi. 6), and "Hew down the tree and cut off his branches[4] . . .

[1] See p. 25.
[2] This may be fairly considered to be the official Jewish doctrine. Maimonides, in his digest of Rabbinic law, declared: 'The pious of the Gentiles will have a share in the World to Come' (Hil. Teshubah III. 5).
[3] The Hebrew word, translated 'simple,' is explained in the Talmud to mean 'child' (Sanh. 110b, Gen. R. LXXXVII. 1).
[4] Typifying the wicked of the Gentiles, whereas 'the stump of his roots' represents the children.

nevertheless leave the stump of his roots in the earth" (Dan. iv. 14 f.)' (Tosifta Sanh. XIII. 1). The same discussion is held in connection with the children of the wicked of Israel and opposite sides taken on the identical texts, and the remark is added: 'With respect to the children of the wicked Gentiles all agree that they will not enter the World to Come' (Sanh. 110b). If they are excluded from the blessings of the Hereafter, they will not be held to account in the matter of punishment: 'The children of the wicked of the Gentiles will not revive (in the Resurrection) nor be judged' (Tosifta Sanh. XIII. 2).

There is likewise a discussion on the stage in its life at which an Israelite child qualifies for admission to the World to Come. 'From what point of time does a minor become entitled to the World to Come? One Rabbi answered, From the hour of birth, as it is said, "They shall declare His righteousness unto a people that is born" (Ps. xxii. 31). Another declared, From the time it can speak; as it is said, "A seed shall serve Him, it shall be told of the Lord unto the generation" (ibid. 30). Other opinions are: From the time of conception; for it is written, "A seed shall serve Him." From the time of circumcision; for it is written, "I am afflicted and ready to die from my youth up" (ibid. lxxxviii. 15). From the time that it utters Amen; as it is said, "Open ye the gates, that the righteous nation which keepeth truth may enter in" (Is. xxvi. 2)—read not "which keepeth truth" but "which uttereth Amen"'[1] (Sanh. 110b).

§ IV. THE LAST JUDGMENT

The doctrine of Retribution, we have seen, was a cardinal belief of the Rabbis.[2] Apart from the fact that it was a necessary corollary of their trust in Divine justice, it afforded the only solution to the problem which was created by the unhappy plight of their people. Gentile nations could not oppress God's elect with impunity, and a day of reckoning had to come. ' "Thou overthrowest them that rise up against Thee" (Exod. xv. 7). Who are they that rise up against Thee? They are they who rise up against Thy children. It is not written, "Thou overthrowest them that rise up against us" but "against Thee"—teaching that whoever rises up against Israel is as though he rises up against the Holy One, blessed be He' (Mechilta ad loc.; 39a). That being so, God must arraign the nations for their cruel treatment of Israel.

[1] There is a play of words here. 'Which keepeth truth' is in Hebrew *skomér emunim*, and 'which uttereth Amen' is *shé-omér amén*.
[2] See pp. 110 ff.

Accordingly, besides the Tribunal before which the individual will have to appear after death, a Day of Judgment will be appointed when the gentile peoples will be placed on trial. This will happen at the beginning of the Messianic era when righteousness will be vindicated. ' "The Lord of Hosts will be exalted in judgment" (Is. v. 16). When will the Holy One, blessed be He, be raised on high in His Universe? When He executes judgment on the gentile nations; as it is said, "The Lord standeth up to plead, and standeth to judge the peoples" (ibid. iii. 13); and also, "I beheld till thrones were placed" (Dan. vii. 9). Are there, then, many celestial thrones? Is it not written, "I saw the Lord sitting upon a throne high and lifted up" (Is. vi. 1), and also, "A king that sitteth on the throne of judgment" (Prov. xx. 8)? What, then, means "thrones"? R. José of Galilee declared, The term implies the Throne and its footstool. R. Akiba declared, It refers to the thrones of the gentile nations which He will overturn; as it is said, "I will overthrow the thrones of kingdoms" (Hag. ii. 22). The Rabbis declared, In the Hereafter the Holy One, blessed be He, will sit, and the angels will set thrones for the great men of Israel who will be seated upon them; the Holy One, blessed be He, will sit with the Elders of Israel like a President of a *Beth Din* and judge the gentile nations; as it is said, "The Lord will enter into judgment with the elders of His people" (Is. iii. 14). It is not written "against the elders" but "with the elders," which indicates that the Holy One, blessed be He, will sit with them and judge the gentile nations. What means, "The hair of His head like pure wool" (Dan. vii. 9)? The Holy One, blessed be He, clears Himself with respect to the gentile nations by giving them their reward for the minor precepts which they observed in this world so as to judge and sentence them in the World to Come, that they may have no plea to make and no merit can be found on their behalf' (Tanchuma Kedoshim § 1).

Here follows a description of the trial of the nations. 'In the Hereafter, the Holy One, blessed be He, will take a Scroll of the Torah, set it upon His lap and say, "Let him who occupied himself therewith come and receive his reward." Immediately the nations of the world gather together and come in disorder. The Holy One, blessed be He, says to them, "Do not enter before Me in disorder, but let each nation present itself together with its teachers." First comes the kingdom of Rome because it is the most important; and the Holy One, blessed be He, asks, "With what have you occupied yourself?" It answers, "Lord of the Universe! many market-places have we instituted, many baths have we erected, gold and silver in abundance have we accumulated; and we only did all this for the sake of Israel that he might devote himself to the Torah." The Holy One, blessed be He, replies, "You most foolish people in the world! All that you did was for your own benefit; you instituted market-places as a resort of harlots; you erected baths for your own enjoyment; while the silver and gold belong to Me." It at once departs in despair and is followed by the kingdom of Persia, which is next in importance. The Holy One, blessed be He, asks, "With what have you occupied yourself?" It answers, "Lord of the Universe! many bridges have we constructed, many cities have we conquered, many wars have we waged; and we only did all this for the sake of Israel that he might devote himself to the Torah." The Holy One, blessed be He, replies, "All that you did was for your own benefit. You constructed bridges to receive toll from them; you conquered cities to force the inhabitants to labour for you; and as for wars I wage them." It at once departs in despair. But since the Persian kingdom saw that it availed the Roman kingdom nothing, why did it enter? Because it said, "They destroyed the Temple, whereas we helped to restore it." [1] Similarly the other nations went in one after the other; but why did they enter when they saw that it availed their predecessors nothing? They thought, "Rome and Persia enslaved Israel but we did not." What is the difference between the first two kingdoms that they are considered of importance and the remainder are not so esteemed? Because they continue in their sovereignty until Messiah comes. They will then plead before Him, "Lord of the Universe! didst Thou give us the Torah and we rejected it?" But how can they use such a plea, seeing that the Holy One, blessed be He, offered it to every people and they declined to receive it until He came to Israel who accepted it?' (A.Z. 2a, b).[2] They put forward various other arguments in their defence which are proved to be invalid; and so the trial ends in their discomfiture and the glorification of Israel.

As for individuals, God has ordained 'the day of the Great Judgment' (Mechilta to xvi. 25; 50b), which will take place after death. Talmudic law prescribes: 'Who beholds the graves of Israelites says, "Blessed be He Who formed you in judgment, Who nourished you in judgment, sustained you in judgment, and gathered you in judgment, and will hereafter raise you in judgment" ' (Ber. 58b). Not only Israelites, however, but every human being is called to account. The following extract is quite general in its scope: 'They that are born are destined to die; and the dead

[1] At the instigation of the Persian king Cyrus (Ezra i. 1 ff.).
[2] See p. 61.

to be brought to life again; and the living to be judged, to know,
to make known, and to be made conscious that He is God, He the
Maker, He the Creator, He the discerner, He the Judge, He the
witness, He the complainant; He it is that will in the Hereafter
judge, blessed be He, with Whom there is no unrighteousness, nor
forgetfulness, nor respect of persons, nor taking of bribes. Know
also that everything is according to the reckoning. And let not
your imagination give you hope that the grave will be a place of
refuge for you; for perforce were you formed, and perforce were
you born, and perforce you live, and perforce you die, and perforce
you will in the Hereafter have to give account and reckoning before
the supreme King of kings, the Holy One, blessed be He' (Aboth
IV. 29).

In many other passages the terms used are 'righteous' and
'wicked' without restriction of creed or nationality. ' "Passing
through the valley of weeping, they make it a place of springs;
yea the early rain covereth it with blessings" (Ps. lxxxiv. 6)—
"passing," i.e. the men who transgress the will of the Holy One,
blessed be He; "valley," i.e. they make Gehinnom deep for themselves; "weeping," i.e. they cry and shed tears like the well by the
side of the Temple-altar; "yea the early rain covereth it with
blessings," i.e. they acknowledge the justice of the sentence passed
upon them, saying, "Lord of the Universe! rightly hast Thou
judged, rightly hast Thou acquitted, rightly hast Thou condemned,
rightly hast Thou instituted Gehinnom for the wicked and Gan
Eden for the righteous" ' (Erub. 19a).

'The matter may be likened to a king who arranged a banquet
and invited guests to it. The king issued a decree, saying, "Each
guest must bring that on which he will recline." Some brought
carpets; others brought mattresses or bolsters or cushions or stools,
while still others brought logs of wood or stones. The king observed
what they had done, and said, "Let each man sit on what he
brought." They who had to sit on wood or stone murmured against
the king and said, "Is that honourable to a king that we, his
guests, should be seated on wood and stone?" When the king
heard this, he said to them, "Not enough that you have disgraced
with your stone and wood the palace which was erected for me
at great cost, but you dare to invent a complaint against me!
(The lack of) respect paid to you is the consequence of your own
action." Similarly in the Hereafter the wicked will be sentenced
to Gehinnom and will murmur against the Holy One, blessed be
He, saying, "Lo, we looked for His salvation, and such a fate should
befall us!" He answers them, "When you were on earth did you

not quarrel and slander and do all kinds of evil? Were you not responsible for strife and violence? That is what is written, 'Behold, all ye that kindle a fire, that gird yourselves about with firebrands' (Is. l. 11). That being so, 'Walk ye in the flame of your fire and among the brands that ye have kindled' (ibid.). Should you say, 'This have ye of Mine hand,' it is not so; you have done it for yourselves, and hence 'ye shall lie down in sorrow' (ibid.)"' (Eccles. R. to iii. 9).

Other extracts deal specifically with the judgment of Israelites. As recipients of the Torah, their responsibility was heavier. While obedience of the precepts would bring a rich reward, disobedience would ensue in a correspondingly severe punishment. 'In the Hereafter the Holy One, blessed be He, will judge the righteous and wicked of Israel. To the righteous He will grant a permit for them to enter Gan Eden and the wicked He will send back to Gehinnom. He will subsequently take them out of Gehinnom and set them in Gan Eden with the righteous, saying to them, "Lo, this is the place of the righteous (and there is still unoccupied space amongst them, so that you should not say, Even if we had repented, there would have been no room for us in Gan Eden among the righteous)." He will then remove the righteous from Gan Eden and take them into Gehinnom, saying to them, "Lo, this is the place of the wicked, and there is still unoccupied space amongst them (so that you should not say, Even if we had sinned, there would have been no room for us in Gehinnom);[1] but the wicked inherit their and your Gehinnom." That is the meaning of the verse, "For your shame ye shall have double . . . therefore in their land they shall possess double" (Is. lxi. 7). After that He will restore the righteous to Gan Eden and the wicked to Gehinnom' (Midrash to Ps. xxxi; 120a).

The intention of the phrase, 'the wicked inherit their and your Gehinnom,' is elucidated by this citation: 'After Elisha b. Abuyah became an infidel, he asked R. Meïr, "What is the meaning of, 'God hath made the one side by side with the other' (Eccles. vii. 14)?" He replied, "Whatever the Holy One, blessed be He, created, He made an opposite to it; e.g. mountains and valleys, oceans and rivers." He said to him, "Your teacher, Akiba, did not give you that interpretation, but (so he explained it) God created the righteous and wicked, Gan Eden and Gehinnom. Each person has two portions, one in Gan Eden and the other in Gehinnom. If a person is meritorious and righteous, he takes his share and that

---

[1] The words in brackets do not occur in Buber's edition but must be added to complete the sense.

of his fellow in Gan Eden; and if he incurred guilt and is wicked, he takes his share and that of his fellow in Gehinnom" ' (Chag. 15a).

In preparation for the Day of Judgment a record is kept of all that the human being does while on earth. 'All your deeds are written in a book' (Aboth II. 1). 'At the time of a man's departure from the world, all his actions are detailed before him, and he is told, "So and so have you done in such a place on such a day." He assents and is then ordered to sign the record, which he does. Not only that, but he admits the justice of the verdict and says, "Rightly hast Thou judged me" ' (Taan. 11a). 'Even superfluous remarks that pass between husband and wife are recorded against him in the hour of death' (Chag. 5b). 'The Holy One, blessed be He, will sit in judgment with the righteous and wicked. He will judge the righteous and conduct them to Gan Eden. He will judge the wicked and condemn them to Gehinnom. The wicked say, "He has not judged us fairly; He acquits whomever He likes and convicts whomever He likes." The Holy One, blessed be He, replies, "I did not desire to expose you." So what does He do? He reads out their record and they descend to Gehinnom' (Midrash to Ps. i; 12b).

When standing his trial, man will have brought up against him many misdeeds which he at the time thought too trivial to worry about. 'What does the text mean, "When iniquity at my heels compasseth me about" (Ps. xlix. 5)? The iniquities which a man treads down with his heels [1] in this world will compass him about on the Day of Judgment' (A.Z. 18a).

Among the questions addressed to him are: 'Did you transact your business honestly? Did you fix times for the study of Torah? Did you fulfil your duty with respect to establishing a family? Did you hope for the salvation (of the Messiah)? Did you search for wisdom? Did you try to deduce one thing from another (in study)? Even should all these questions be answered affirmatively, only if "the fear of the Lord is his treasure" (Is. xxxiii. 6) [2] will it avail, otherwise it will not' (Shab. 31a).

The question whether punishment is exacted of both body and soul was the theme of a parable which has already been quoted.[3] The moral was that as body and soul are equally concerned in the commission of sin, they are alike penalized. Another parable reaches the opposite conclusion. 'A priest married two wives, one a priest's daughter and the other a lay-Israelite's daughter.

---

[1] An idiomatic expression meaning to disregard as of no importance.
[2] i.e. the fear of God had been his controlling motive in all his pursuits.
[3] See p. 238.

He handed to them flour of an offering which they defiled, and each blamed the other for it. What did the priest do? He ignored the wife who was a layman's daughter and began to chide the priest's daughter. She said to him, "My lord, why do you ignore the other and rebuke me?" He answered, "She is the daughter of a layman and was not taught in her father's house (the sanctity of the flour of an offering); but you are a priest's daughter, and you were taught this in your father's house. That is the reason why I overlook her and reprimand you." Similarly in the Hereafter, the soul and body will stand in judgment. What will the Holy One, blessed be He, do? He will overlook the body and censure the soul, and when it pleads, "Lord of the Universe! the two of us sinned alike, so why dost Thou overlook the body and censure me?" He answers, "The body comes from below where people sin; but you come from above where sin is not committed. Therefore I overlook the body and censure you"' (Lev. R. IV. 5).

The opinion generally adopted was that the soul is rejoined to the body for the purpose of judgment, and is expressed in this statement: 'Throughout twelve months (after death in Gehinnom) the body exists and the soul ascends and descends; after twelve months the body ceases to exist and the soul ascends without descending' (Shab. 152b et seq.).

What is the duration of the penalty meted out to the sinful? Does the Talmud teach eternal punishment? There is at least one passage where such a doctrine seems to be implied. 'When R. Jochanan b. Zakkai was ill his disciples went in to visit him. On beholding them he began to weep. They said to him, "O lamp of Israel, right-hand pillar, mighty hammer! wherefore do you weep?" He replied to them, "If I was being led into the presence of a human king who to-day is here and to-morrow in the grave, who if he were wrathful against me his anger would not be eternal, who if he imprisoned me the imprisonment would not be everlasting, who if he condemned me to death the death would not be for ever, and whom I can appease with words and bribe with money—even then I would weep; but now, when I am being led into the presence of the King of kings, the Holy One, blessed be He, Who lives and endures for all eternity, who if He be wrathful against me His anger is eternal, Who if He imprisoned me the imprisonment would be everlasting, Who if He condemned me to death the death would be for ever, and Whom I cannot appease with words nor bribe with money—nay more, when before me lie two ways, one of Gan Eden and the other of Gehinnom, and I know not to which I am to be led—shall I not weep?"' (Ber. 28b).

It would, however, be precarious to deduce from a rhetorical utterance like this that the Rabbi actually believed in eternal punishment. The contrast between the earthly ruler and the supreme King is merely worked out to its fullest extent. The authoritative doctrine is enunciated by R. Akiba in these terms: 'The judgment on the generation of the Flood was for twelve months, on Job for twelve months, on the Egyptians for twelve months, on Gog and Magog in the Hereafter for twelve months, and on the wicked in Gehinnom for twelve months. R. Jochanan b. Nuri said, It endures only the space of time between Passover and Pentecost' (Eduy. II. 10), viz. a period of seven weeks.

Although it is definitely stated, 'The generation of the Flood will have no share in the World to Come,' and there is difference of opinion whether it will or will not 'arise for judgment' (Sanh. x. 3), we also find the remark, 'The sentence of the generation of the Flood is for twelve months. When they have endured this term they will have a share in the World to Come' (Gen. R. xxviii. 9). This is evidence of the reluctance on the part of the Rabbis to think of an endless punishment. One authority declared: 'All who descend to Gehinnom will ascend except three: he who has intercourse with another man's wife, he who puts his fellow to shame in public, and he who calls his fellow by an opprobrious nickname' [1] (B.M. 58b). The first-mentioned offence is omitted by some teachers (ibid. 59a).

The *locus classicus* on the subject reads: 'The School of Shammai declared, There are three classes with respect to the Day of Judgment: the perfectly righteous, the completely wicked, and the average people. Those in the first class are forthwith inscribed and sealed for eternal life. Those in the second class are forthwith inscribed and sealed for Gehinnom; as it is said, "Many of them that sleep in the dust of the earth shall awake, some to everlasting life and some to shame and everlasting contempt" (Dan. xii. 2). The third class will descend to Gehinnom and cry out (from the pains endured there) and then ascend; as it is said, "I will bring the third part through fire, and will refine them as silver is refined, and will try them as gold is tried; they shall call on My name and I will hear them" (Zech. xiii. 9). Concerning them Hannah said, "The Lord killeth and maketh alive, He bringeth down to Sheol and bringeth up" (1 Sam. ii. 6). The School of Hillel quoted, "He is plenteous in mercy" (Exod. xxxiv. 6); He inclines towards mercy; and concerning them said David, "I love the Lord, because He hath heard my voice and my supplications" (Ps. cxvi. 1). The whole of that

[1] Cf. Matt. v. 22.

Psalm was composed by David about them: "I was brought low and He saved me" (ibid. 6). The sinners of Israel with their bodies and the sinners of the Gentiles with their bodies descend to Gehinnom and are judged there for twelve months. After twelve months their bodies are destroyed, and their souls burnt and scattered by a wind under the soles of the feet of the righteous; as it is said, "Ye shall tread down the wicked, for they shall be ashes under the soles of your feet" (Mal. iv. 3). But the sectaries, informers, epicureans who denied the Torah [1] and denied the Resurrection, they who separated themselves from the ways of the community, they who set their dread in the land of the living,[2] and they who, like Jeroboam the son of Nebat and his associates, sinned and caused the multitude to sin (cf. 1 Kings xiv. 16), will descend to Gehinnom and be judged there generations on generations; as it is said, "They shall go forth and look upon the carcases of the men that have transgressed against Me; for their worm shall not die, neither shall their fire be quenched" (Is. lxvi. 24). Gehinnom will cease but they will not cease (to suffer); as it is said, "Their form shall be for Sheol to consume that there be no habitation for it" (Ps. xlix. 14). Concerning them said Hannah, "They that strive with the Lord shall be broken to pieces" (1 Sam. ii. 10). R. Isaac b. Abin said, Their faces will be black like the bottom of a pot' (R.H. 16b et seq.).

We gather from this extract that in the first century one of the principal Schools, influenced by a verse from Daniel, assigned the utterly wicked to eternal punishment; but the other School found such a doctrine incompatible with Divine mercy. Sinners must be penalized. They undergo twelve months of pain and then suffer annihilation because they are unworthy of entrance into Gan Eden. They who have been exceptionally wicked stay in Gehinnom for 'generations on generations.' That this expression does not signify eternity is clear from the statement that 'Gehinnom will cease.' They will not, after their sufferings there, undergo extinction, but will continue in existence as conscious entities—how and where is not explained—in a perpetual state of remorse.

---

[1] i.e. its heavenly origin; see p. 146.
[2] The phrase is defined in the Talmud as 'a president who instilled excessive fear into the community he governed, but not for the sake of Heaven,' i.e. he did it for personal motives.

§ V. GEHINNOM

The fate of the wicked, as the reader has already learnt, is to descend into a place of punishment called Gehinnom. 'A Roman lady asked R. José b. Chalaphta, "What is the meaning of the text, 'Who knoweth the spirit of man that goeth upward' (Eccles. iii. 21)?" He answered, "It refers to the souls of the righteous which are deposited in the Divine treasury; as Abigail told David through the medium of the Holy Spirit, 'The soul of my lord shall be bound in the bundle of life with the Lord thy God' (1 Sam. xxv. 29). It is possible to think that the same destiny awaits the wicked; therefore the verse continues, 'And the souls of thine enemies, them shall He sling out as from the hollow of a sling.'" The Roman lady further asked, "What is the meaning of the text, 'And the spirit of the beast that it goeth downward to the earth'?" He answered, "It refers to the souls of the wicked which descend below to Gehinnom"' (Eccles. R. to iii. 21).

Its origin predates the creation of the Universe;[1] but according to another view the pre-existence of Gehinnom only applies to its room and not to its contents. 'The space of Gehinnom was created before the Universe but its fire on the eve of the first Sabbath. It has, however, been taught, Why does not Scripture add "God saw that it was good" to the account of the second day? Because on that day the fire of Gehinnom was created? The fact is that the space of Gehinnom was created before the Universe, its fire on the second day, and the plan of creating ordinary fire entered His thought on the eve of the Sabbath, but it was not actually created until the termination of the Sabbath' (Pes. 54a).

A number of names was discovered in Scripture for the place of punishment. 'Gehinnom is called by seven designations: Sheol (Jonah ii. 2), Abaddon or Destruction (Ps. lxxxviii. 11), Corruption (ibid. xvi. 10), Horrible Pit and Miry Clay (ibid. xl. 2), Shadow of Death (ibid. cvii. 10), and the Nether world which is a tradition.[2] Are there not other names? For instance, Gehinnom—i.e. Gé, a deep "valley" into which all descend on account of "lusts" (*Hinnom*), and Topheth (Is. xxx. 33), which is so called because every one who is led astray (*mithpatteh*) by his passions falls therein' (Erub. 19a).

While the regular use of the verb 'descend' in connection with Gehinnom points to the common belief that it lies below the earth, there is also a statement, 'Gehinnom is above the firmament; others say it lies behind the mountains of darkness' (Tamid 32b). These

---

[1] See p. 347.   [2] i.e. it is not Scriptural.

mysterious mountains were supposed to be located in the extreme
west of the world. A similar view is found in this extract: 'The
sun is red in the morning and evening—in the morning because
it passes over (and catches the reflection of) the roses of Gan Eden,
and in the evening because it passes over the entrance of Gehinnom'
(B.B. 84a). Accordingly Gan Eden is in the east and Gehinnom
in the west.

On the matter of its dimensions we are informed: 'The world
is a sixtieth part of Gan Eden and Gan Eden a sixtieth part of
Gehinnom; consequently the whole world is in comparison to Gehinnom like the lid of a pot. Some declare that Gan Eden is limitless
in extent and others say the same of Gehinnom' (Taan. 10a).

With regard to its entrances the Talmud states: 'It has three—
one in the wilderness, a second in the sea, and a third in Jerusalem.
Another tradition tells, There are two date-palms in the valley
of Ben-Hinnom from between which smoke ascends and that is
the entrance of Gehinnom' (Erub. 19a).

It is divided into seven storeys, and the more wicked the person
the lower is his place of accommodation. 'Each of the seven
classes in Gan Eden has a dwelling for itself, and correspondingly
there are seven storeys for the wicked in Gehinnom, their names
being: Sheol, Abaddon, Shadow of Death, Nether world, Land of
Forgetfulness (Ps. lxxxviii. 12), Gehinnom, and Silence (ibid. cxv.
17)' (Midrash to Ps. xi. 7; 51a). From Ps. xi. 6 the deduction was
drawn that there were seven storeys, viz. Snares,[1] Fire, Brimstone,
Wind, and Flames (Midrash ad loc.; 50b). 'At the time that
Absalom's hair was caught on the tree, Sheol was split asunder
beneath him. Why did David in his lament over him exclaim
"my son" eight times?[2] Seven for the purpose of bringing him
up from the seven storeys of Gehinnom, and the eighth to unite
his head (which had been decapitated) to his body; or, according
to others, to make him enter the World to Come' (Sot. 10b).

The principal element which exists there for the torment of the
sinful is fire, but a fire of abnormal intensity. '(Ordinary) fire is
a sixtieth of (the fire of) Gehinnom' (Ber. 57b). ' "A fiery stream
issued and came forth before Him" (Dan. vii. 10). Whence does
it originate? From the sweat of the holy Chayyoth. And where
does it empty itself? Upon the heads of the wicked in Gehinnom;
as it is said, "It shall burst upon the head of the wicked" (Jer.
xxiii. 19)' (Chag. 13b). A Rabbi relates how an Arab met him in
the desert and said, ' "Come, I will show you where Korah was

[1] The plural, as also of 'Flames,' indicates two.
[2] See 2 Sam. xviii. 33 and xix. 4.

swallowed up." I saw two cracks in the ground from which smoke issued forth. He took a ball of wool, steeped it in water, set it on the end of his spear, inserted it into the hole, and when he drew it out it was completely scorched' (B.B. 74a).

There is a teaching, 'The fire of Gehinnom will never be extinguished' (Tosifta Ber. VI. 7), but it conflicts with the doctrine of the School of Hillel that Gehinnom will cease.[1] It is also stated that 'Gehinnom is half fire and half hail' (Exod. R. LI. 7), while, according to another opinion, snow is likewise found there: 'The Holy One, blessed be He, judges the wicked in Gehinnom for twelve months. At first he afflicts them with itching; after that with fire, at which they cry out "O! O!" and then with snow, at which they cry out "Woe! Woe!"' (p. Sanh. 29b).

Another element which abounds there is brimstone. 'Why does a man's soul shrink from the odour of brimstone? Because it knows that it will be judged therein in the Hereafter' (Gen. R. LI. 3). Finally it is full of smoke. 'Gehinnom is narrow on top and wide below' (Sifré Deut. § 357; 149b). The reason why it has that shape is, 'Its mouth is narrow so that its smoke may be retained therein' (Men. 99b). Legend tells that 'smoke issued from the grave of Acher' (Chag. 15b). It is likewise a place of darkness. 'The wicked are darkness, Gehinnom is darkness, the depths are darkness. I lead the wicked to Gehinnom and cover them with the depths' (Gen. R. XXXIII. 1). 'Gehinnom is (black) like the night' (Jeb. 109b). 'They who descend to Gehinnom will be judged by nothing else than darkness; as it is said, "A land of thick darkness, as darkness itself" (Job x. 22)' (Tanchuma Noach § 1). ' "And Moses stretched forth his hand toward heaven, and there was thick darkness" (Exod. x. 22). Whence did the darkness originate? From the darkness of Gehinnom' (Tanchuma Bo § 2).

The severities of Gehinnom may be mitigated, or even altogether escaped, by various means. Prominent among them is the fact that a person has undergone circumcision, unless he had been exceptionally wicked. 'In the Hereafter Abraham will sit at the entrance of Gehinnom and will not allow any circumcised Israelite to descend into it. As for those who sinned unduly, what does he do to them? He removes the foreskin from children who had died before circumcision, places it upon them and sends them down to Gehinnom' (Gen. R. XLVIII. 8). 'Israelites who are circumcised will not descend to Gehinnom. So that heretics and the sinners in Israel shall not say, "Inasmuch as we are circumcised we will not go down to Gehinnom," what does the Holy One, blessed be

[1] See p. 378.

He, do? He sends an angel who extends the foreskin and they descend to Gehinnom' (Exod. R. XIX. 4).

The patriarch helps the release of those who had been condemned. ' "Passing through the valley of weeping" (Ps. lxxxiv. 6), i.e. they who are sentenced for a time in Gehinnom; and Abraham our father comes and takes them out and receives them, with the exception of an Israelite who had intercourse with a gentile woman or disguised his circumcision for the purpose of concealing his identity' (Erub. 19a).

The recitation of certain prayers is another means of gaining immunity. 'Whoever reads the *Shema* with distinct pronunciation of its letters, Gehinnom is cooled for him' (Ber. 15b). That is an effect which originally belonged to the altar in the Temple. 'What means the word for altar (*Mizbéach*)? M=*mechilah* "forgiveness," because the altar secures pardon for the sins of Israel. Z=*zachuth* "merit," because it secures for them merit for the World to Come. B=*berachah* "blessing," because the Holy One, blessed be He, brings a blessing upon the work of their hands. CH=*chayyim* "life," since they become worthy of the life of the World to Come. He who is helped by these four things and then goes and serves idolatry will be consumed by the great fire; as it is said, "The Lord thy God is a devouring fire, a jealous God" (Deut. iv. 24). But should he repent, the fire which burns on the altar will bring him atonement and nullify the fire of Gehinnom' (Tanchuma Tzab § 14).

The principal safeguard, however, is the study of Torah. 'The fire of Gehinnom has no power over the disciples of the Sages. This may be reasoned from the salamander. If a person is anointed with the blood of a salamander, which originates in fire, he cannot be harmed by fire; how much more immune are the disciples of the Sages whose body is fire; as it is said, "Is not My word like a fire, saith the Lord?" (Jer. xxiii. 29). The fire of Gehinnom has no power over the sinners in Israel. This may be reasoned from the golden altar. If this altar, which was only covered with a plating of gold the thickness of a gold *denarius*, endured so many years and was not overcome by the fire upon it, how much more will the Israelites resist the fire who are filled, even the most empty of them, with the precepts (of the Torah) as a pomegranate is filled with seeds!' (Chag. 27a).

A tradition existed to the effect that the sufferers in Gehinnom enjoyed a respite every Sabbath. It is mentioned in a dialogue between the Roman governor, Tineius Rufus, and R. Akiba. 'The Roman asked, "How is the Sabbath different from any other day?" The Rabbi retorted, "How are you (a Roman official) different from any other man?" Rufus said, "The Emperor was pleased to honour me"; and Akiba replied, "Similarly the Holy One, blessed be He, was pleased to honour the Sabbath." "How can you prove that to me?" "Behold the River Sabbatyon [1] carries stones as it flows [2] all the days of the week, but it rests on the Sabbath." "To a distant place you lead me!" [3] Akiba said, "Behold, a necromancer can prove it, because the dead ascend all the days of the week but not on the Sabbath. You can test my statement by your father." Later on Rufus had occasion to call up his father's spirit; it ascended every day of the week but not on the Sabbath. On Sunday he caused him to ascend and asked, "Have you become a Jew since your death? Why did you come up every day of the week but not on the Sabbath?" He replied, "Whoever does not observe the Sabbath with you (on earth) does so voluntarily, but here he is compelled to keep the Sabbath." The son asked, "Is there, then, work where you are that you toil on the weekdays and rest on the Sabbath?" He answered, "All the days of the week we are under sentence but not on the Sabbath"' (Gen. R. XI. 5).

Noteworthy is the fact that at least one Rabbi denied the objective reality of a special place reserved for the punishment of the wicked. R. Simeon b. Lakish, who lived in the third century, declared: 'There is no Gehinnom in the Hereafter; but the Holy One, blessed be He, will remove the sun from its sheath and blacken (the world with its fierce rays). The wicked will be punished and the righteous healed thereby' (A.Z. 3b).

§ VI. GAN EDEN

The place of happiness allocated to the righteous is called Gan Eden, 'the Garden of Eden.' It was usually regarded as distinct from the abode of that name which had been prepared for Adam. 'What is the meaning of "No eye hath seen what God, and nobody but Thee, will work for him that waiteth for Him" (sic Is. lxiv. 4)? It refers to Eden, upon which the eye of no creature has gazed. Perhaps you will ask, Where, then, was Adam? In the Garden. But perhaps you will say that the Garden is the same as Eden! Therefore a text teaches, "A river went out of Eden to water the garden" (Gen. ii. 10). Hence the Garden and Eden are distinct' (Ber. 34b).

---

[1] A legendary river, the name being derived from 'Sabbath.'
[2] By the force of its current.
[3] That means, your evidence is far-fetched.

Its exact site was a matter of doubt. 'If Gan Eden is located in the land of Israel its entrance is Beth-Shean; if in Arabia its entrance is Beth-Gerem; if between the rivers (Mesopotamia) its entrance is Damascus' (Erub. 19a). This evidently refers to the terrestrial Garden, the Paradise of the righteous being thought of as located in heaven.[1]

As with Gehinnom, Gan Eden was supposed to consist of seven divisions for the seven degrees into which those who merit it are capable of being classified. 'There are seven classes of righteous in Gan Eden, one higher than the other. The first class is alluded to in the text, "Surely the righteous shall give thanks unto Thy name; the upright shall dwell in Thy presence" (Ps. cxl. 13). The second is alluded to in, "Blessed is the man whom Thou choosest and causest to approach that he may dwell in Thy courts" (ibid. lxv. 4). The third is alluded to in, "Blessed are they that dwell in Thy house" (ibid. lxxxiv. 4). The fourth is alluded to in, "Lord, who shall sojourn in Thy tabernacle?" (ibid. xv. 1). The fifth is alluded to in, "Who shall dwell in Thy holy hill?" (ibid.). The sixth is alluded to in, "Who shall ascend into the hill of the Lord?" (ibid. xxiv. 3), and the seventh in, "Who shall stand in His holy place?" (ibid.)' (Sifré Deut. § 10; 67a). The seven divisions, counting downward, are therefore designated as: Presence, Courts, House, Tabernacle, Holy Hill, Hill of the Lord, and Holy Place.

Another version reads: 'Seven classes will stand before the Holy One, blessed be He, in the Hereafter. Which is the highest of them to receive the presence of the *Shechinah*? It is the class of the upright; as it is said, "The upright shall behold their[2] face" (Ps. xi. 7). It is not written "His face" but "their face," i.e. the presence of the *Shechinah* and His retinue. The first class sits in the company of the King and beholds His presence; as it is said, "The upright shall dwell in Thy presence." The second dwells in the house of the King; as it is said, "Blessed are they that dwell in Thy house." The third ascends the hill to meet the King, as it is said, "Who shall ascend into the hill of the Lord?" The fourth is in the court of the King; as it is said, "Happy is the man whom Thou choosest and causest to approach that he may dwell in Thy courts." The fifth is in the Tabernacle of the King; as it is said, "Lord, who shall sojourn in Thy tabernacle?" The sixth is in the holy hill of the King; as it is said, "Who shall dwell in Thy holy hill?" The seventh is in the place of the King; as it is said, "Who shall stand in His holy place?"' (Midrash to Ps. xi. 7; 51a).

[1] Or in the extreme east of the world; see p. 380.
[2] The suffix in the Hebrew is unusual and can be translated 'His' or 'their.'

They who are admitted into Gan Eden are adjudged so that they may be accommodated in the division to which they are entitled. 'Each righteous person will be assigned a dwelling in accordance with the honour due to him. Parable of a human king who entered a city with his servants. Although they all enter through the one gate, when they take up their quarters each is allotted a dwelling according to his rank' (Shab. 152a).

The main characteristic of this heavenly abode is that the pious, who suffered privation while on earth, will now come into their own. 'In this world the wicked are rich and enjoy comfort and rest, while the righteous are poor. But in the Hereafter, when the Holy One, blessed be He, will open for the righteous the treasures of Gan Eden, the wicked, who extorted usury, will bite their flesh with their teeth; as it is said, "The fool foldeth his hands together and eateth his own flesh" (Eccles. iv. 5); and they will exclaim, "Would that we were labourers or carriers or slaves, and our fate were like theirs!" As it is said, "Better is a handful with quietness than two handfuls with labour and striving after wind" (ibid. 6)' (Exod. R. XXXI. 5).

The happiness which is in store for those who merit Gan Eden is symbolized as a wonderful banquet. The Bible makes mention of a monster called Leviathan which God slew and gave 'as meat to the people inhabiting the wilderness' (Ps. lxxiv. 14).[1] Popular fancy seized upon this and constituted it the principal course in the banquet which was to be arranged for the worthy. 'The Holy One, blessed be He, created one (Leviathan) a male and another a female; but had they mated they would have destroyed the whole world. What did He do? He emasculated the male, killed the female and preserved its flesh in brine for the righteous in the Hereafter' (B.B. 74b). 'In the Hereafter the Holy One, blessed be He, will make a banquet for the righteous from the flesh of Leviathan, and the remainder they will divide and sell as merchandise in the streets of Jerusalem.'[2] Its skin will be made by Him into a booth for the pious (ibid. 75a). For drink they will have 'wine preserved in the grape from the six days of Creation' (Ber. 34b).

The chief joy they will experience is being in the actual presence of God. 'In the Hereafter the Holy One, blessed be He, will prepare a banquet for the righteous in Gan Eden and there will be no need

---

[1] See also Ps. civ. 26; Is. xxvii. 1; and Job xli. 1.

[2] The mention of the sale of the flesh makes it doubtful whether the Hereafter in this passage is to be understood as the period after death or the Messianic era. The term has both connotations and they are sometimes confused.

to provide balsam or perfumes, because a north wind and a south wind will sweep through and sprinkle all the aromatic plants of Gan Eden so that they yield their fragrance. The Israelites will say before the Holy One, blessed be He, "Does a host arrange a meal for wayfarers and not recline with them? Does a bridegroom prepare a banquet for guests and not sit with them? If it be Thy will, 'Let my Beloved come into His garden and eat His precious fruits' (Cant. iv. 16)." The Holy One, blessed be He, replies to them, "I will do as you desire." Then he enters Gan Eden; as it is written, "I am come into My garden, My sister, My bride" (ibid. v. 1)' (Num. R. XIII. 2).

Still bolder in expression are these extracts: 'In the Hereafter the Holy One, blessed be He, will arrange a dance for the righteous in Gan Eden, He sitting in their midst; and each one will point to Him with his finger, exclaiming, "Lo, this is our God, we have waited for Him and He will save us; this is the Lord, we have waited for Him, we will be glad and rejoice in His salvation" (Is. xxv. 9)' (Taan. 31a). ' "I will walk among you" (Lev. xxvi. 12). To what is this like? To a king who went out to walk with his tenant in his orchard; but the tenant hid himself from him. The king called to him, "Why do you hide from me? See, I am just the same as you!" Similarly the Holy One, blessed be He, will walk with the righteous in Gan Eden in the Hereafter; and the righteous, on beholding Him, will retreat in terror before Him. But He will call to them, "See, I am the same as you!" Since, however, it is possible to imagine that My fear should no longer be upon you, the text declares, "I will be your God, and ye shall be My people" (ibid.)' (Sifra ad loc.).[1]

Since the study of Torah leads to piety it opens the road to Gan Eden, and they who have devoted themselves to its acquisition will be specially welcomed there. 'R. Jochanan b. Zakkai said to R. José the Priest, In my dream I saw the two of us reclining upon Mount Sinai, and a *Bath Kol* issued from Heaven concerning us, "Ascend hither! Ascend hither! Large banqueting couches and beautiful coverlets are prepared for you. You, your disciples, and the disciples of your disciples are invited into the third class" '[2] (Chag. 14b). Their particular reward is the solution of the

---

[1] We detect here the anxiety of the Rabbis to insist that there must always be an unbridgeable gulf between man, even in his highest spiritual development, and God. The two cannot ever be absolutely identical. Even in the Hereafter, although human beings will enjoy the closest possible communion with Him, He will still be God and they will still be His 'people,' i.e. human.

[2] The third of the seven classes in Paradise was reserved for the great scholars; see p. 388.

intellectual difficulties which had beset them on earth. 'As for the disciples of the Sages who wrinkle their foreheads with study of Torah in this world, the Holy One, blessed be He, will reveal to them its mysteries in the World to Come' (ibid. 14a).

In the Talmud and older Midrashim there is no attempt, beyond what has been cited, to give an elaborate description of the interior of Gan Eden and the life there. In later works this restraint is lacking and detailed accounts occur. One very striking verbal picture is found in the *Jalkut Shimeoni* (Genesis § 20), a collection of Rabbinic material which was compiled about the thirteenth century. The authorship of the passage is ascribed to R. Joshua b. Levi, a Rabbi of the third century, who is known to have had a tendency towards mysticism. For that reason it is included here, although it must remain a matter of doubt whether he is the author.

'Gan Eden has two gates of ruby, by which stand sixty myriads of ministering angels. The lustre of the face of each of them glistens like the splendour of the firmament. When a righteous person arrives, they divest him of the garments in which he arose from the grave, clothe him in eight robes of the clouds of glory, set two crowns upon his head, one made of gems and pearls and the other of gold from Parvaïm (see 2 Chron. iii. 6), place eight myrtles in his hand, and praise him, saying, "Go, eat your food in joy." They take him into a place where are brooks of water, surrounded by eight hundred varieties of roses and myrtles. Each person has a chamber allotted to him by himself according to the honour due to him. From it issue four streams, one of milk, one of wine, one of balsam, and one of honey; and above every chamber there is a golden vine studded with thirty pearls, each of them glistening like the brilliance of the planet Venus. In every chamber there is a table of gems and pearls, and sixty angels attending upon each righteous man, saying to him, "Go, eat honey in joy, since you occupied yourself with Torah which is compared to honey; and drink wine which has been preserved in the grape from the six days of Creation, since you occupied yourself with Torah which is compared to wine." [1] The ugliest of the inhabitants of Gan Eden will be like Joseph and R. Jochanan.[2] There is no night for them, and the period (which would normally have been night) is renewed for them in three watches. In the first watch, the righteous person becomes like a child, enters the department of children and plays their games. In the second watch, he becomes

---

[1] See p. 134.
[2] Both were famed for their beauty; see pp. 137, 274.

a young man, enters the department of young men and plays their games. In the third watch, he becomes an old man, enters the department of old men and plays their games.

'In every corner of Gan Eden there are eighty myriad species of trees, the most inferior of them being finer than all the aromatic plants (of this world); and in each corner are sixty myriads of ministering angels singing in pleasant tones. In the centre is the Tree of Life, its branches covering the whole of Gan Eden, containing five hundred thousand varieties of fruit all differing in appearance and taste. Above it are the clouds of glory, and it is smitten by the four winds so that its odour is wafted from one end of the world to the other. Beneath it are the disciples of the Sages who expounded the Torah, each of them possessing two chambers, one of the stars and the other of the sun and moon. Between every chamber hangs a curtain of clouds of glory, behind which lies Eden. Inside it are three hundred and ten worlds,[1] and in it are seven classes of the righteous. The first consists of martyrs,[2] such as R. Akiba and his colleagues. The second consists of those drowned at sea.[3] In the third are R. Jochanan b. Zakkai and his disciples. Such was his might (in scholarship) that he said of himself, "If all the heaven were parchment, all human beings scribes, and all the trees of the forests pens, it would be insufficient to write what I have learnt from my teachers; and yet I only took away from them as much as a dog laps from the ocean."[4] In the fourth class are they upon whom the cloud descended as a covering.[5] In the fifth class are the penitents and where they stand not even the perfectly

[1] This is based on the Talmudic homily: 'R. Joshua b. Levi said, The Holy One, blessed be He, will give each righteous person three hundred and ten worlds as an inheritance; as it is said, 'That I may cause those that love Me to inherit substance" (Prov. viii. 21)' (Uktz. III. 12). The letters of the Hebrew word for 'substance' have the numerical value of three hundred and ten.

[2] The information that martyrs occupy a pre-eminent position in Gan Eden was communicated to R. Joshua b. Levi by his son after recovery from a state of coma. See p. 365.

[3] viz. the Jewish youths and maidens who sacrificed their lives rather than be dishonoured. See p. 45.

[4] This version of this well-known hyperbole is taken partly from Sopherim xvi. 8, and partly from Sanh. 68a.

[5] It is not certain to whom allusion is made here. Possibly the reference is to great men whom God distinguished either during their lifetime or at their death by enveloping them with the cloud of glory. When Moses ascended Sinai to receive the Torah, God protected him from the envy of the angels by spreading a cloud over him (Shab. 88b). As Moses stripped Aaron of his vestments before his death a cloud covered him (Jalkut Num. § 787). Josephus also tells: 'As he (Moses) was embracing Eleazar and Joshua and was still conversing with them, a cloud stood over him on a sudden, and he disappeared in a certain ravine' (Antiq. IV. viii. 48).

righteous stand. In the sixth class are the unmarried who never tasted sin (and remained chaste). In the seventh class are the poor who are possessed of knowledge of Scripture and Mishnah and were engaged in a worldly occupation. Concerning them it is written, "Let all those that put their trust in Thee rejoice" (Ps. v. 11). The Holy One, blessed be He, sits in their midst and expounds the Torah to them; as it is said, "Mine eyes shall be upon the faithful of the land, that they may dwell with Me" (ibid. ci. 6).'

INDEX

INDEX

AARON, 74, 126, 148, 204 f., 298, 358, 389
Abba Hilkiah, 198
Abba José, 264
Abba Joseph, 197
Abba Saul, 194, 233, 316, 369
Abbahu (R.), 356
Abbai (R.), 137, 153, 255
Ab Beth Din, xxi, 371
Abigail, 123, 379
Abimi b. Abbahu, 356
Abraham, 1 f., 16, 17, 21, 41 f., 44, 51, 52, 56, 64, 79, 80, 112 f., 115, 131, 143, 211, 217, 225, 236, 271, 275 f., 350, 381
Absalom, 111, 380
Abscess, cure for, 256
Abstinence, total, 232
Abtalion (R.), 136
Acha (R.), 234
Achan, 317
Acher (Elisha b. Abuyah), 27 f., 52 f., 117, 284, 374, 381
Adam, 5, 7, 44, 50, 58, 73, 143, 185, 192, 232, 261
Additional soul, 78
Admon, 345
Adonai, 25
Adultery, 97 f., 167, 320
Æsop, 68
Agrath (demoness), 265, 295
Agriculture, 194
Aibu (b. Naggari), 348
Akiba (b. Joseph), xxv f., 13, 21, 22, 27 f., 46, 66, 67, 81, 110, 111, 114, 132, 135, 143, 167, 194, 209, 212, 214, 220 f., 226, 240, 245, 246, 275, 302, 308, 317, 327, 330, 339, 341, 349, 356, 368, 371, 374, 377, 382 f., 388
Akylas, 152
Alexander of Macedon, 16, 34, 36, 207
Alexandria, 16
Alphabet, Hebrew, moralized, 177 f.

Altar, 382
Amathus, 301
Ambition, 70
Am Haaretz, 241
Amoraim, xxxi, xxxii
Amorite ways, 291 ff.
Amram, 44, 95
Amulet, 152, 266, 267, 268 f.
Anatomy, human, 71
Anecdotes, xxiii f., 3, 4, 7, 8 f., 9, 10, 12, 16 f., 25, 48, 55, 65, 69, 75, 81, 83, 98 f., 112, 117, 131, 136, 140, 147, 152 f., 156 f., 160, 163, 166, 171, 176, 183, 186 f., 193, 197 f., 201, 204, 205 f., 207, 209, 214 ff., 218 f., 220 ff., 223 f., 226, 228, 231 f., 233 f., 235 f., 239, 240, 243, 264, 266, 268, 272, 276 ff., 283 ff., 288, 351 f., 360 f., 363, 365, 367, 376, 379, 382 f.
Angel, 20, 30, 31, 39, 40, 47 ff., 68, 70, 73, 93, 109, 187, 221, 261, 270, 276, 387, 388
—— of death, 52, 54, 57, 58, 74, 118, 295, 296
Angina, cure for, 256 ff.
Anigron (demon), 264
Animals, 65, 90, 235 ff., 266, 269, 273, 361
——, slaughter of, 237
Anirdaphon (demon), 264
Anointing with oil, 242 f.
Ant, 237
Anthropomorphisms, 7, 19
Antigonos of Socho, xx
Antioch, 46
Antiochus III, xxx
Antiochus Epiphanes, xix
Antoninus 77, 89, 157, 238
Aphes (R.), 286
Apikoros, 3, 368, 378
Apocalypse of Abraham, 2
Araboth, 30, 31, 78
Aramaic language, 49
Archangels, 50
Aristotle, 27, 29

393